T3-BNO-476

antiques international

COLLECTORS' GUIDE TO CURRENT TRENDS

antiques

General Editor: Peter Wilson

international

COLLECTORS' GUIDE TO CURRENT TRENDS

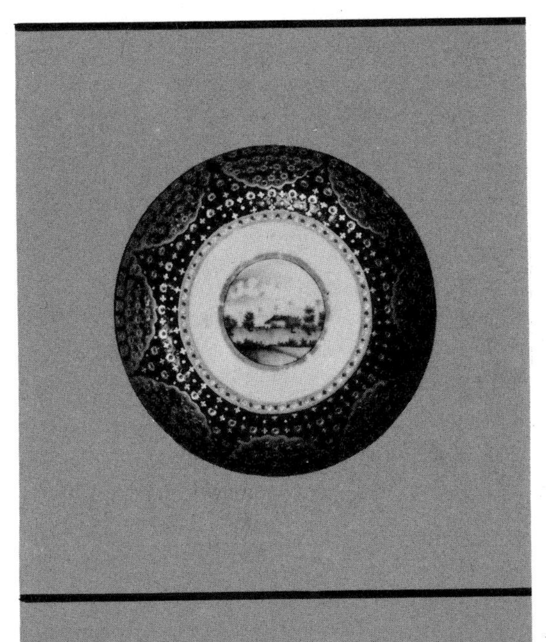

A Giniger Book
G. P. Putnam's Sons · New York

Designed and produced by
George Rainbird Ltd, London
in association with
The K. S. Giniger Company, Inc., New York
for G. P. Putnam's Sons, New York

Printed in Great Britain

First American Edition 1967

*Published simultaneously in Canada
by Longmans Canada Limited, Toronto.*
Library of Congress Catalog Card Number: 67–23637

Foreword

PETER WILSON

In recent years the layman has been made increasingly aware of the value of works of art, chiefly through the spectacular rise in price of Impressionist paintings. These, together with French furniture, which could have been acquired before the last war for a fraction of its present value, have succeeded in overshadowing such fields of collecting as Renaissance bronzes, Chinese works of art and arms and armour, which have risen proportionally faster; five years ago a collector could have acquired a good example of any of these for a sixth of their value today.

The concentration of collectors upon works of art such as these has been swelled in recent years by the collector-investor. As a result every backwater in the field of applied arts is being explored.

Taste and fashion are changing, and new fields of collecting are being opened up. Much of the pleasure of connoisseurship lies in exploring relatively unfamiliar fields, and, in financial terms, there is more fun to be had in buying inexpensively before a rise in market values than in outbidding the big buyers when the market is at its peak.

The aim of this collection of studies is to provide signposts to fields of antique collecting which are not at present fashionable, have temporarily fallen out of vogue, or have hardly yet been explored. Some of the subjects covered here are rapidly coming up in public esteem, and several of the others are likely to do so in the near future. In general, however, these are areas into which the collector can enter without overspending and with the knowledge that the intrinsic value or scarcity of what he or she is collecting is greater than present prices would suggest.

For instance, Renaissance furniture was once widely popular, but then taste turned away from its extravagance towards the more classical severity of the Georgian period. Today there is little doubt that good examples of Renaissance furniture are underestimated. Now is a good time to buy such pieces.

To take another example, the aesthetic value of the finest examples of Persian pottery is not greatly inferior to that of Chinese pottery and porcelain. Because so much of it was destroyed or buried during the Tartar invasions of the Near East, good surviving examples of Persian pottery are probably a great deal scarcer than equivalent examples of Chinese. Here, therefore, is a profitable field for the collector who wants to pursue his own course regardless of current fashion and market values.

Early American painting and furniture have been the subject of considerable study by specialists but they are still relatively unappreciated outside the United States, and will, I feel sure, continue to appreciate steadily, as English and French furniture and painting of the same periods have already done.

I anticipate the same process occurring – indeed it already is occurring – in such diverse fields as Icons, Peruvian Gold, and New Guinea Sculpture. All the time the fields of collecting are being widened. This year my own firm held its first auction sale entirely consisting of Art Nouveau – another of Vintage cars. Early prams and bicycles are being collected. I don't pretend to any knowledge myself of buttons, locks and keys, or early tobacco shop signs, but I am quite sure more and more collectors are going to turn to such curious and interesting special studies.

Those engaged, as I am, in the sale of antiques and works of art, naturally welcome keen competition, record-breaking prices and spectacular sales. But there is also interest and excitement in watching the rise into favour of hitherto underestimated artists, of collecting fields which have been neglected, and the return to favour of certain periods, such as Victoriana and Art Nouveau, which have been considered unfashionable until recently.

I hope that this book will allow the collector to deviate from the conventional with authority.

I am grateful for the immense help given to me by Howard Ricketts; it is to him that all credit is due.

Contents

Chinese Export Porcelain

page 339

MICHEL BEURDELEY
Expert national en Art d'Asie près les Tribunaux Français

Ancient Peruvian Gold

page 351

ADRIAN DIGBY
C.B.E.
Keeper of Ethnography, the British Museum, London

Early Ballooning Prints

page 361

COLONEL R. L. PRESTON
C.B.E.
The Rupert Preston Gallery

Photographic Credits and other Acknowledgements

Numerals in **bold type** indicate page numbers; numerals in *italic type* illustration numbers.

The Arts Council of Great Britain, London: 358 15

Stewart Bale Ltd, London: 335 8

The Byzantine Museum, Athens: 16 1, 18 4, 19 6, 19 7, 20 8

Connaissance des Arts, Paris: 170 8, 171 11

P. G. Coole: 323 1, 323 5, 325 6, 326 9, 326 10, 327 11, 327 12, 328 14

A. C. Cooper Ltd, London: 309 2, 309 3, 310 4, 312 7

Michael Dudley, Oxford: 75 12 a and b, 77 13

Stanley Eost, London: 194 1, 196 6, 198 8, 200 13, 201 14, 203 18, 203 19, 204 20, 205 22

Fine Art Engravers Ltd, Surrey: 122 1, 131 16

John Flower – Maps: 46, 60, 352

Anthony Forge: 331 1, 335 9

John R. Freeman & Co. Ltd, London: 16 2, 17 3, 18 5, 20 9, 22 10, 23 11, 130 14, 173 16, 173 17, 182 1, 183 2, 183 3, 183 4, 184 5, 184 6, 184 7, 185 8, 185 9, 186 10, 186 11, 187 12, 187 13, 187 14, 187 15, 189 16, 189 17, 190 18, 190 19, 191 20, 192 22, 192 23, 192 24, 194 2, 200 12, 202 16, 354 4, 354 7, 356 11, 357 12, 357 13, 359 16, 359 17, 360 19

The Heye Foundation: 352 2

Jacqueline Hyde, Paris: 74 9, 75 10, 75 11, 78 14, 78 15

Edward Leigh, Cambridge: Colour Plate 133. 123 2, 123 3, 129 12, 130 14, 130 15, 134 20, 135 21, 135 22, 136 23

Jean Pierre Leloir, Paris: 315 11, 316 12

Jean Daniel Lorieux, Paris: 191 21

Mallett at Bourdon House Ltd, London: 308 1, 310 5, 311 6

John Maltby Ltd, London: Colour Plate 253. 242 1, 242 2, 243 3, 243 4, 244 5, 244 6, 245 7, 246 8, 246 9, 247 10, 247 11, 248 12, 249 13, 250 14, 250 15, 251 16, 251 17, 252 18, 254 19, 255 20, 255 21

The Mansell Collection, London: 100 21

James Mortimer, London: 96 11, 96 12, 98 13, 98 14, 98 15, 98 16

Nickolas Muray, Washington, D.C.: 355 9

W. Keith Neal: Colour Plates 264. 257 1, 257 2, 258 3, 258 4, 258 5, 259 6, 259 7, 260 8, 260 9, 260 10, 260 11, 261 12, 261 13, 262 14, 262 15, 263 16, 263 17, 263 18, 263 19, 263 20, 265 21, 266 22

Peter Parkinson, London: 90 2, 91 4, 94 8, 95 9, 95 10, 99 19

By gracious permission of Her Majesty the Queen: Colour Plate 217. 223 17, 224 18, 225 21

Tom Scott, Edinburgh: 278 4, 286 15

Service de Documentation Photographique, Versailles: 317 13, 317 14

Courtesy Sotheby & Co., London: 124 4, 125 5, 126 6, 126 7, 127 8, 127 9, 128 10, 128 11, 129 13, 132 17, 132 18, 132 19

Charles Uht, New York: 356 10

Mabel I. Varley, Malvern: Endpapers

The Victoria and Albert Museum, London: 198 7, 199 11, 201 15, 204 21

The Victoria and Albert Museum, London (Crown Copyright): 99 17, 139 1, 140 3, 141 4, 142 7, 143 8, 143 9, 144 10, 145 12, 146 14, 146 15, 147 16, 147 17, 148 18, 150 21, 151 23, 194 1, 195 3, 195 4, 196 5, 198 9, 199 10, 202 17, 205 23, 214 2, 218 7, 222 14, 223 16, 224 20, 277 1, 279 5, 280 6, 283 10, 292 10, 292 11, 295 15, 347 25, 347 26, 349 30

Vogue Studio, London: 89 1, 91 3

Derrick Witty, London: Colour Plates 52, 76, 81, 92, 157, 168, 177, 197, 228, 273, 284, 293, 304, 313, 324, 353, 364. 47 3, 48 4, 48 5, 48 6, 49 8, 50 9, 50 10, 50 11, 51 13, 51 15, 53 16, 53 17, 53 18, 53 19, 54 20, 54 21, 54 22, 54 23, 55 24, 55 25, 55 26, 73 7, 74 8, 75 12 c, d and e, 79 16, 79 17, 85 13, 158 1, 159 2, 160 4, 160 5, 162 7, 162 8, 163 9, 164 10, 165 11, 171 10, 172 13, 172 14, 173 18, 174 1, 175 2, 176 3, 176 4, 178 5, 178 6, 178 7, 179 8, 179 9, 179 10, 180 11, 12 and 13, 181 14, 181 15, 189 17, 267 1, 268 2, 268 3, 269 4, 269 5, 270 6, 271 7, 271 8, 271 9, 272 10, 272 11, 274 12, 274 13, 275 14, 275 15, 275 16, 277 2, 281 8, 287 1, 288 2, 291 9, 298 1, 299 2, 299 3, 300 4, 300 5, 300 6, 301 7, 301 8, 302 9, 302 10, 303 11, 303 12, 303 13, 303 14, 305 15, 306 16, 306 17, 307 18, 307 19, 334 5

A. J. Wyatt, Philadelphia: 108 5

Icons

D. TALBOT RICE

Icons have always had for the devout Orthodox Christian a far profounder significance than that of their subject interest or artistic quality, for they are believed to serve as intermediaries between the material world of everyday and the spiritual world beyond, and the painter's task was to create what was virtually a receptacle for external power, to constitute a dwelling-place for the divine essence, rather than to produce a naturalistic representation in human guise. Many icons were believed to be possessed of spiritual power; all those on which divine or saintly figures were depicted had the property of acting as intermediaries between the devout human being and the divine or saintly figure portrayed, while those on which scenes from Our Lord's, the Virgin's or a saint's life were shown had an import far greater than that of merely recording an event in the Christian story. At times it was even held that the icons themselves were divine, and early in the 8th century this belief had become so intensified that in the opinion of many a state of idolatry had been reached. There was a violent reaction against it early in the second quarter of the century which we know as the 'Iconoclast' movement, and during most of the time from *circa* 730 till 843 the depiction of the divine or saintly form in art was forbidden. But the prohibition was not universally approved, there was endless argument and discussion on the subject and in the end the sacred pictures were re-admitted. Thenceforth they had a rôle of growing significance to play in the story of Orthodox thought and art throughout the whole of eastern Europe and hither Asia; that rôle was a vital one till very recent times, and indeed continues among the devout to this day. But for the average westerner it is not so much the sacred or the esoteric aspect of the icon that is of greatest interest as the artistic quality of the icons themselves and the rôle that they have to play in the story of the development of European art, and it is primarily from this point of view that this article is written. For a consideration of the problem of the icons' inner meaning the reader is referred to a book by L. Ouspensky and W. Lossky entitled "The Meaning of Icons".

The earliest icons were no doubt painted soon after the "Peace of the Church" in 313, in a style akin to the Mummy portraits of Egypt of the 3rd and 4th centuries A.D., but nothing of so early a date has come down to us. But, of the panels that survive, the earliest do come from Egypt, and elsewhere there are few that can be firmly dated before the 7th century, even if some authorities would date them to the 6th. By that time, however, two styles are to be distinguished, and two different techniques already seem to have been employed in their production. The two styles may be termed the antique or Hellenistic and the Byzantine; the two techniques are the encaustic and the tempera. The antique style still to a great extent remains faithful to the idea of representation; the figures are well

1. *The Virgin and Child between two Archangels,*
7th century
The Monastery of St Catherine, Mount Sinai

modelled and have a sculpturesque solidity, the faces are alive and natural, there is a feeling for depth and three-quarter views were often favoured; an icon of Saint Peter in the monastery of St Catherine on Mount Sinai (see colour plate facing p. 20) or a panel showing the Virgin and Child enthroned between two archangels in Sta Maria in Trastevere at Rome (especially the archangels) may be cited as examples (Ill. 1): both are probably to be dated to the 7th century.[1] Paintings of the second group are in a much more abstract, formal style; the figures are planted frontally in serried ranks, there is little search for depth, little interest in modelling, the faces are always shown full-face, and the eyes are large and profound, seeming to stare into the spiritual world beyond that of everyday; a panel of the Virgin and Child between two saints, who wear long formal robes which fall right to their feet, is typical. In depicting the saints' robes the painter was much more interested in the formal repeat patterns on the silks of which they are made than in the forms of the figures beneath them. The style is similar to that of the mosaics on the piers of St Demetrius at Salonica which must be of the first half of the 7th century and must belong to the same school. The conception is an oriental one, and if we term the group 'Byzantine' it is the oriental element in the fusion that formed Byzantine art that is to the fore here rather than the classical trend, which of course was equally, if not more, important in the formation of the new art as a whole.

The two Sinai panels were done in the encaustic technique, where the painting was accomplished by manipulating coloured waxes with hot irons; that at Rome was painted with a brush in a sort of tempera. On the whole the former method seems to have been the more popular in these early days, and our knowledge has recently been considerably augmented by the discovery of quite a number of fine examples in the monastery of St Catherine on Mount Sinai; other examples, at Kiev, which have been known since the 19th century, were in all probability taken to Russia from Sinai at the same time and in much the same way that the famous Codex Sinaiticus was taken! The encaustic technique was probably learnt in Egypt, for it was often used for Mummy portraits, but the tempera technique was known there too and some of the earliest painted panels we know are actually Coptic, so that the contribution of Egypt in early times was important, and Alexandria was no doubt a very active centre of production. But Constantinople soon outpaced it, and it is quite probable that both the Sinai icons referred to above were actually painted there. In their different ways they are characterized

[1] Many of the icons referred to here, which it is impossible to illustrate, are figured by Felecetti-Liebenfels or by Sotiriou.

2. *The Three Hebrews in the Fiery Furnace,*
3rd century
The Monastery of St Catherine Mount Sinai

3. Fragmentary icon showing *The Nativity, The Ascension and Pentecost*, 8th century
The Monastery of St Catherine, Mount Sinai

by a majesty and grandeur which is absent in a more or less contemporary panel in the Vatican – actually the cover of a reliquary and not an icon – which there is good reason to assign to Syria or Palestine; it depicts five scenes, the Maries at the sepulchre and the Ascension above, the Crucifixion in the middle, and the Nativity and the Baptism below. It was perhaps taken back to Rome by a pilgrim. The figures are rigid, the work is rather crude, yet it is expressive and forceful in the way in which the scenes are interpreted. The same rather dumpy figures characterize another panel in St Catherine's monastery on which the Three Hebrews are shown in the Fiery Furnace (Ill. 2), but the angel with them is side-face and is more Hellenistic in style. More oriental is a fragmentary icon, also at Sinai, on which parts of the Nativity, the Ascension and the Pentecost scene are shown. (Ill. 3.)

There are one or two other panels of early date in Rome or elsewhere in Italy; a famous Madonna which was disclosed below layers of overpaint in 1950 in Sta Maria Nova in Urbe (also known as Sta Francesca Romana) is the most important of them and may even have been produced in the 6th century. Its style is distinct, for it is neither as Hellenistic as the Saint Peter nor as oriental as the icon of the Virgin cited above. It probably represents a truly Roman work.[2] Several rather similar but later panels are reproduced by Wilpert in his great book on the mosaics and frescoes of Rome.

In the East the painting of such panels was precluded during the age of Iconoclasm (730–843), and though their production was resumed during the rule of the great Macedonian emperors, the so-called 'Second Golden Age of Byzantine Art', there are but few panels that survive that are to be dated before the 11th century; the most important examples are once more to be found on Sinai and include a fine quadripartite icon figuring King Abgar above and four saints below which was noted by Sotiriou; it may be as early as the 10th century. (Ill. 4.) Other icons of the 11th century that survive include fragments of a large triptych with scenes from the life of Saint Nicholas, published by Weitzmann, a panel with semicircular top illustrating the story of Christ's early life and one bearing Saints Procopios, Demetrios and Nestor (Ill. 5), both noted by Sotiriou. The first two are particularly interesting because, in contrast to all the other panels noted so far, they are narrative icons telling a connected story, the one in a series of independent scenes, each in its own frame, the other as a continuous panorama unfolding the tale on what looks like a winding road down a hill-side. Till these discoveries were made in St Catherine's monastery our knowledge of the panel-paintings of this age was virtually a blank. Now we know enough to say firstly that the encaustic technique, so popular in early times, had gone out of fashion, and secondly that the two primary manners noted as early as the 6th and 7th century were nevertheless still distinct; that associated with the East has become rather more dramatic and expressive – an icon showing the Communion of the Apostles above and the Washing of the Feet below, which is figured by Sotiriou (Plate 49), may serve to illustrate this vein, while in the other trend naturalism has disappeared in favour of a more profound spiritual approach which is intensified by the omission of detail and background so that the compositions are silhouetted in space, usually against gold; but the figures are tall and elegant and the side-face pose is not unusual. A panel showing the Deesis (Christ between the Virgin and St John), with the addition of the figure of St Nicholas behind the Virgin, which was reproduced by Sotiriou, may serve to illustrate this severe, but essentially refined and elegant art. It must surely have been executed in Constantinople. (Ill. 7.)

It so happens that quite a few panels depicting St Nicholas have survived from

[2] Ill. Pl. 33b, Felecetti-Liebenfels, W. *Geschichte der Byzantinischen Ikonenmalerei.*

4. *King Abgar and Saints*, 8th century
The Monastery of St Catherine, Mount Sinai

5. *Saints Procopios, Demetrios and Nestor*, 11th century
The Monastery of St Catherine, Mount Sinai

the next phase of Byzantine art, which may be broadly termed the Comnene (*circa* 1060–1200). Three examples in Russia are figured by Felecetti-Liebenfels (Plate 38) and another is figured by Sotiriou (Plate 81); the iconography is static and there is little to distinguish these renderings from the rather earlier depiction associated with the Deesis (Ill. 7) except that they are shown as busts. Nor was there at first much sign of any tendency to forsake the severe isolation of the figures or the rather austere poses, in any case in the work that is to be associated with the capital. In paintings done locally, however, which retain many of the features characteristic of the old oriental group, notably the dumpy figures and the expressive attitudes, there is a new interest in illustrative detail; a series of small panels with semicircular tops which are figured by Sotiriou are typical. Each bears three scenes, one set horizontally at the top and two vertically below; they depict the major feasts of the Church (Sotiriou, Plates 76–79).

Not all the icons on which scenes are depicted are, however, in this more vivid Eastern style, for it was in this age that the iconostasis began to take on the form which was later to make it so essential a part of the church equipment, and what had in early times been little more than a stone balustrade between the sanctuary and the body of the church developed into an elaborate screen, with closure slabs below and painted icons above. At first the icons were no doubt restricted to panels of Christ, the Virgin and particular saints; later they included other subjects like the Deesis, as well as a collection of scenes from Our Lord's life – the 'Feasts of the Church' as they came to be known. Quite a number of icons of this type have been discovered on Sinai, some of which may have been imports from Constantinople, while others were no doubt painted locally, though some of the men who worked in the monastery would appear to have been trained in Constantinople, notably one who painted a number of scenes from Christ's life, not each one on an individual panel as was usual, but rather a series of them on long beams. They constitute a sort of prototype for the row of individual Festival icons so usual on iconostases of later date; a section showing the Entry into Jerusalem, the Crucifixion and the Descent into Hell may serve to illustrate this (Ill. 8); the figures are tall and elegant, the compositions restrained yet impressive, and the work as a whole grand and aristocratic. Of festival icons preserved elsewhere one in the Hermitage of the Descent into Hell may be noted (Ill. 9); it is perhaps rather more restrained and severe than the rendering on the Sinai beams. It must have been taken to Russia at quite an early date, but the rather emotional character of the faces suggests that Constantinople was not the source from which it came; Salonica is a possible alternative.

Another important group of icons on Sinai is devoted to depictions of individual saints, shown in rows with often some twelve to fifteen full-length figures in each row. The individual figures are often fine and impressive, the icons as a whole somewhat monotonous from the artistic point of view, though of great interest iconographically. Sometimes the saints are shown in the act of being martyred, or on other icons there are actual scenes of martyrdom. Sotiriou describes them as 'Menologia', and they may be compared to the portraits of saints and martyrs in some of the manuscripts or those which cover the walls of the vestibules of many of the Moldavian churches of the 16th and 17th centuries; no doubt similar wall-paintings existed in earlier times, but none survives. An 11th- or 12th-century icon of similar type, though the figures are limited to three, is preserved in the Hermitage, an import no doubt from Constantinople. (Ill. 10.)

Another group of the Sinai icons which is of very special interest has recently been isolated by Professor Weitzmann; he terms it the Crusader group, and

6. *The Story of the Nativity*, 11th century
The Monastery of St Catherine, Mount Sinai

associates it with a workshop at Acre. Western elements are present, some of them French, some Italian, but the panels are basically Byzantine, the Western elements being noticeable in particular gestures and in the actual style; two typical works are a fine double-sided icon with the Crucifixion on one face and the Anastasis on the other, and a Saint George and Donor. (Ill. 11.) It is to be assigned, like most of the examples of the group, to the 13th century. Somehow the paintings seem rather more 'earthy' than does true Byzantine work; they are expressive, but emotions of a human character seem to have supplanted the essentially spiritual ones of true Byzantine art.

In Byzantine painting of the 12th century on the other hand this latter element is very much to the fore, whether in the more formal severe paintings of the Conservative style – an icon of St George in the Museum of Fine Art at Moscow of the 11th century may serve to illustrate it (Ill. 12) – or in the more progressive, humanist style which began to develop at Constantinople quite early in the century; the famous icon known as *Our Lady of Vladimir*, painted there early in the second quarter of the century, is the most important example. (Ill. 13.) Here the Child's face is pressed against that of His mother in affection and the expressions are tender and intimate, but a full realization of the rôle of the Virgin as mother above all else has not yet been reached here, for she still indicates the Child with her right hand as the future Saviour of the world and one realizes that the painting is a symbol; only later was this gesture of reverence abandoned as a mundane conception replaced the wholly spiritual one in art. A similar approach towards intimacy characterizes an icon of an angel's head – usually known as the *Golden Headed Angel* – at Leningrad, which is to be counted as a very early Russian work, though the style is still close to that which was developing in the Byzantine capital in the 12th century. It is one of the most lovely icons that have come down to us from Byzantine times. (Ill. 14.)

A panel of the Annunciation on Mount Sinai which has recently been published by Professor Weitzmann ("Festschrift von Einem", Berlin, 1960) and which is to be assigned to the last quarter of the century, in many ways contrasts with the Angel, though there are features in common, more especially the rhythmical stress of the composition. But the Annunciation icon is more mannered, more strained, and lacks the genius of the Angel. It is, however, of particular interest because of the agitated, contorted folds of the Angel's costume which we see paralleled in the wall-paintings of Kurbinovo (1191) and Kastoria (late 12th century) in Macedonia and again in Hagia Sophia at Trebizond *circa* 1260. The mannerism is better suited to wall- than to panel-paintings, though it is interesting to find it so fully developed

7. *The Deesis and St Nicholas*, 11th century
The Monastery of St Catherine, Mount Sinai

8. Painted beam; *The Entry into Jerusalem, The Crucifixion and The Anastasis*, 12th century
The Monastery of St Catherine, Mount Sinai

9. *The Descent into Hell*, 12th century
The Hermitage, Leningrad

on a panel which otherwise shows the polished, finished style which in the 12th century betokens metropolitan workmanship.

In 1204 the Latins conquered Constantinople and the rôle of the city as the chief centre of artistic development for a time came to an end. True, the Orthodox emperors were re-established there in 1261 and work of great quality was produced at Constantinople thereafter, in spite of the decline in the city's economic and political importance, but the conquest of 1204 really marks the first stage in the development of a mass of new schools of painting which were to grow to greater importance as time went on as a result of the collapse of centralized control and the creation of a number of new independent states. Yet the style of the capital exercised a very considerable influence which was intensified as the regions to the east became more and more subservient to Islam. In earlier times the dramatic art of Syria had been important and significant, and had exercised a very effective influence, but with the change of attitude towards Christian minorities in the East which grew up partly as a result of the Crusades and partly because of changes in the Islamic world itself, the Christians of the East gradually became less independent and their art more provincial, till eventually it was little more than a folk art, interesting no doubt, but wholly devoid of all the elements which make the best icons works of art of great consequence, the peers of anything that was produced in after-years elsewhere in Europe.

Before passing to a discussion of the various later schools in Greece and the Balkans a word may perhaps be said about Italy, for a good many Italian paintings of the 13th century are perhaps better to be described as icons than as paintings, even though they were done for patrons of the Latin and not the Orthodox faith. Indeed, their close relationship to icons is obvious if they are compared with a large panel from Yaroslavl in Russia, now in the Tretyakov Gallery at Moscow, or with two Sicilian icons now at Washington (Felecetti-Liebenfels, Plates 59b and 65). Felecetti-Liebenfels illustrates quite a number of the Italian ducento Madonna panels and includes also several of the painted crosses which were especially common in the Pisa region. But, however close they may be to icons, the Italian panels show certain features which are not to be found in the Orthodox world; these include in early times haloes in relief, which sometimes stand up as semicircular projections at the top of the panel, crowns on the Virgin's head and ornate details on her costume, as well as other more subtle stylistic details, notably the round, wide-open eyes in place of the almond-shaped ones so typical of the Byzantine world. At a later date, that is to say in the 16th century, haloes outlined in or adorned with dots became usual in Italy, and a large group of Madonna paintings is to be distinguished, most of which were produced in Venice or the Adriatic region, some by Greeks and others by Italians working in the Greek manner. Examples are to be found in numerous churches and galleries of the region. At first glance they appear to be very archaic and dates in the 13th or 14th

Colour Plate I. *Saint Peter*, 7th century
The Monastery of St Catherine, Mount Sinai

10. *Saints Philip, Theodore and Demetrius*,
12th century
The Hermitage, Leningrad

11. *St George and Donor*, 13th century
The Monastery of St Catherine, Mount Sinai

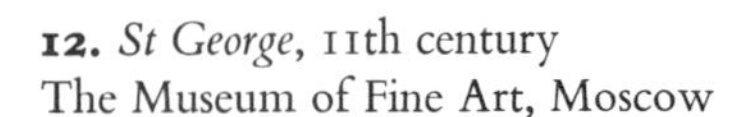

12. *St George*, 11th century
The Museum of Fine Art, Moscow

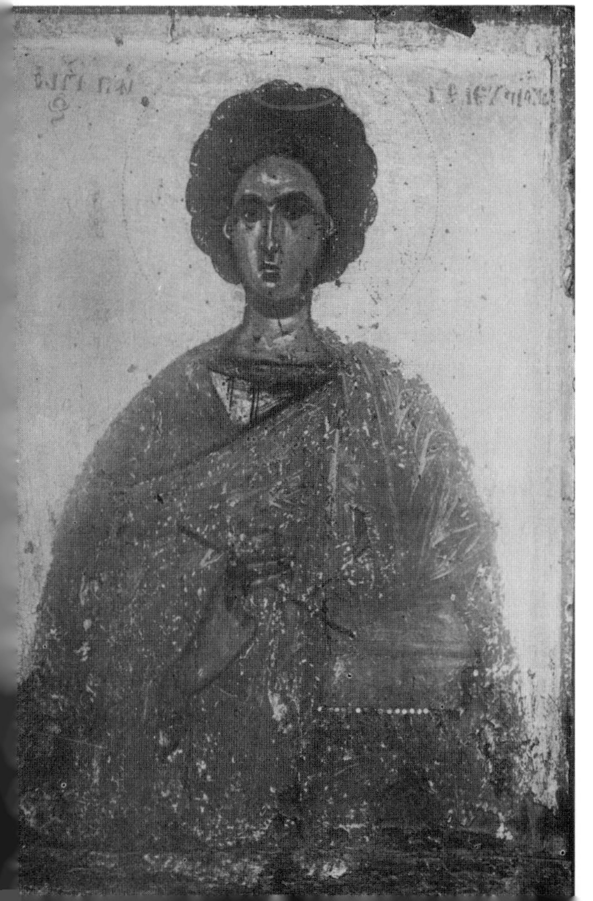

century have been suggested; in actual fact the earliest are to be dated to the 15th and the majority to the 16th century. A few panels bearing the Lamentation are to be assigned to the same school, and the early work of the Bellinis and other Venetians is often closely akin. Panels bearing the scene of the Deesis and others with groups of saints were also done, but the painters of the group do not seem to have been much concerned with other subjects.

Links between the Byzantine world and Italy seem to have been intermittent rather than continuous. In the 13th century the so-called 'Maniera Greca', to which the crucifixes and early Madonnas referred to above belong, was important; later, in the 15th and 16th centuries, the Madonnas were popular, but in the intervening centuries Greek influence was not very marked. But the school of Constantinople played a vital rôle as initiator elsewhere, and virtually all the paintings of Greece and the Balkans owe a debt to Constantinople, though from quite early in the 13th century local schools began to grow up, so that the basic Constantinopolitan style was varied to greater or lesser degree in the different regions. Perhaps the most important of these provincial schools was that of Salonica, though we can hardly distinguish it till shortly before 1300. Several schools in Yugoslavia and Bulgaria began to become distinctive with the progress of the 13th century and were fully marked by the 14th; others grew up in Greece, more especially on Mount Athos. There were also schools in Asia Minor, especially in Cappadocia and the Pontus, and important work was done in the Byzantine regions of Italy.

As yet very little research has been undertaken in the way of determining the characteristics of these various groups, though some are clear enough. It will be best, however, to begin with Constantinople, which would seem to have been important as a source of inspiration even during the Latin domination of the 13th century and which became again the main centre for the production of fine work in the 14th. A few icons may be assigned to the capital on the basis of literary or historical evidence. The most important and in many ways the most lovely is a double-sided icon from Ochrid bearing the Virgin, Saviour of Souls, on one face and the Annunciation on the other (Ills 15, 16); it was apparently given to the Archbishop of Ochrid as a present by Andronicos II Palaeologos (1282–1328) early in the 14th century. A closely similar icon from the same place, also probably Constantinopolitan, bears Christ on one face and the Crucifixion on the other; it too was no doubt presented by the Emperor, but it is far less fine, artistically speaking. The margins and backgrounds of the obverse faces of both are covered by mounts in repoussé metal, which were probably added at Ochrid soon after the panels arrived, for several other icons formerly in the Church of St Clement there, notably several of the Virgin, one of St Nicholas and two which together form an Annunciation group, are adorned in the same way, though the paintings themselves are in diverse styles. But historical records of this sort are few, and most of the icons that we know can be assigned to Constantinople only on the basis of their style. There are several such icons in Russia, which were probably ordered from Constantinople by local patrons; icons bearing the Annunciation, the bust of Saint George, the Dormition of the Virgin (Ill. 17) and the Assembly of the Apostles, all in the Museum of Fine Art at Moscow, may be noted. Though at one time there was a good deal of discussion as to the date of these panels, it would now seem that all are probably to be assigned to quite early in the 14th century, as is an enchanting little icon of the Archangel Michael in the gallery at Pisa. A number of quadripartite icons in the Sinai monastery and another of the same group which is in the British Museum were also probably produced in Constantinople in the course of the 14th century. (Ill. 18.)

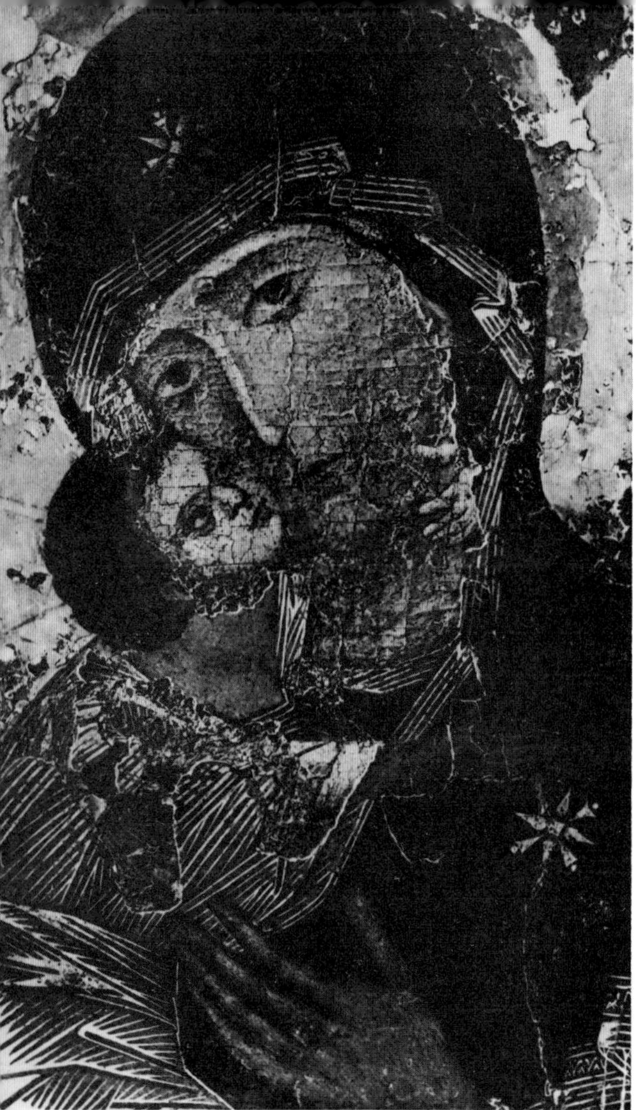

13. *The Virgin of Vladimir, circa* 1130
The Tretyakov Gallery, Moscow

14. *The Golden-Headed Angel*, 12th century
The Russian Museum, Leningrad

As the century advanced, work tended to become rather more mannered and a very characteristic use of highlights was developed; the places where the lights struck most vividly were marked by a mass of thin parallel lines, while the lights on the rest of the face or the costume were heavily over-painted in white or light tones above a dark ground. These vivid contrasts were especially prevalent in work done in Constantinople and in that of the so-called Cretan school in Greece which was developed directly from the Constantinopolitan; an icon of the *Virgin and Child, Enthroned between Archangels*, with four scenes from Christ's life above and saints below and at the side, may serve to illustrate this phase. It is to be dated to the late 15th or the early 16th century and is preserved in the Benaki Museum at Athens (Ill. 19); there is a very similar icon in the Uffizi Gallery at Florence.

Though the wall-paintings of the Macedonian school, with its centre at Salonica, are quite distinctive, it is not so easy to classify the panels. Thus a fine icon of the Pantocrator, now in the Hermitage at Leningrad, might well pass for a Constantinopolitan work were there not inscriptions on the margins, together with portraits of donors, which show that it was presented to the monastery of the Pantocrator on Athos between 1366 and 1370 by two brothers who lived not far from Salonica (Ill. 20); several closely similar icons, from various places in Greece, were shown at the Byzantine exhibition in Athens in 1964 (Nos. 200–6), and there are others in the Sinai monastery; all must have followed a Constantinopolitan model closely and it is virtually impossible to say where each was painted. Indeed, it was the duty of the painter when producing icons of such themes as the Pantocrator to show as little variation as possible, for the theme was a sacred one and was above the vagaries of human personality. It is equally hard to suggest any locality for an extremely moving, though battered, icon of the Crucifixion now in the Byzantine Museum at Athens; it came from Salonica and is usually associated with that place, but its majesty, the strangely elongated figures and the tremendously mystical, spiritual effect which it exercises are all features that characterize the work of the capital. One thing is sure – it was the work of a painter of great genius.[3]

If it is hard to find in such icons as these any features that can readily be isolated as typical of Salonica, a number of other icons where a more dramatic approach is to the fore are perhaps to be assigned there; one showing the Deposition in the Stoclet Collection at Brussels may be cited because of the stylistic resemblances to wall-paintings of the so-called Macedonian school.[4] The poses are thus forceful and angular, the painter has clearly taken great pains to render the emotion of the scene, and the painting is full of expression. A similarly dramatic approach characterizes the painting of the famous reliquary of Cardinal Bessarion at Venice, a double-sided panel mounted on a stem for carrying. The actual reliquary, perhaps to be dated to the earlier 14th century, is in silver; its outer face takes the form of a painting of the Crucifixion which is probably to be dated to the second half of the 14th century. (Ill. 21.) Another painting of the Crucifixion which is closely akin is preserved in the Cathisma of the Annunciation on the Isle of Patmos (Athens Exhibition No. 185).

Though not all the authorities would agree, it is probably safe to state that a school which was independent of Salonica grew up from the mid-13th century in Macedonia and southern Serbia; its earlier stages are represented by a large double-sided processional icon from the Church of St Clement at Ochrid, bearing the Virgin on one face and the Crucifixion on the other; we illustrate only a detail,

[3] Matthew, G. *Byzantine Aesthetics*, Pl. 25.

[4] Ill. *op. cit.*, Pl. 53.

15 and **16.** Double-sided icon: (above left) *The Virgin, Saviour of Souls*; (above right) *The Annunciation*, early 14th century
The Museum, Skopolje

the figure of St John. (Ill. 22.) It is a profoundly expressive painting, full of meaning and at the same time monumental in conception. The proportions, the modelling of the costume and even the colouring suggest a comparison with the wall-paintings of Sopoćani, done around 1265, and the icon is to be assigned to only a slightly later date. Another early Serbian work is a panel bearing the *Saint Face* or Mandelion now at Laon in France.

These lead on to the work of another school which must have flourished in Macedonia in the early 14th century, of which a large icon of the Apostle Matthew is typical; it was included in the Athens Exhibition of 1964. (Ill. 23.) It has something of the same majesty as the Crucifixion panel, but there is more movement and the figure is more dynamic and full of energy, in contrast with the more contemplative character of the Saint John of the Crucifixion group. The icon was painted for the Church of the Virgin Perebleptos at Ochrid, later known as St Clement, and is related in style to the wall-paintings there, signed by the painters Michael and Eutychios and dated shortly before 1300, and it must belong to much the same date. Only slightly later are several smaller 'Festival' icons from the iconostasis of the same church; they depict the Nativity, the Baptism, the Placing on the Cross, the Anastasis (Descent into Limbo), the Incredulity of Thomas, Pentecost, the Presentation of the Virgin in the Temple and the Dormition of the Virgin. The colouring is rather monotonous and lacks the variety and brilliance of the Constantinopolitan work, but the figures are alive and dynamic and compensate in this respect for what is absent in the way of finesse and lyricism. Some of these icons have actually been attributed to the same Michael who worked on the wall-paintings; but they are not all by the same hand, though they were all unquestionably produced in the same workshop. It has been suggested that this

17. *The Dormition of the Virgin*, 14th century
The Museum of Fine Art, Moscow

workshop was situated at Salonica, but there are very marked differences between this group of icons and some more or less contemporary paintings recently uncovered in the Church of St Nicholas Orphanos; though these are wall-paintings they are all on so intimate a scale that they may be compared with icons. If the St Nicholas paintings are to be regarded as characteristic of small-scale work in Salonica in the earlier years of the 14th century, it is tempting to assign the icons to Ochrid; we know that there was a school of wall-painters working there for King Milutin; the panels can best be described as representing King Milutin's school of icon painting.

Slightly later in date are some icons at Decani in a rather angular, uneasy style, while another distinctive school of painters was working in the Vardar region in the last quarter of the 14th and first quarter of the 15th centuries; wall-paintings and some icons done for the monastery of Zrze were perhaps their most important works, but one of these painters, Makarius, was responsible for a very remarkable panel, the Virgin Pelagonitissa. (Ill. 24.) The strange pose of the child, with head bent back in an almost impossible position, is paralleled on an icon in St Catherine's monastery on Mount Sinai (Sotiriou, Plate 235); the two must follow some lost prototype, perhaps from Macedonia; such an awkward pose could hardly have been Constantinopolitan. But though the two are akin iconographically there is something about the Zrze icon which distinguishes it as southern Slav – it is perhaps the hard outline to the faces and the stressing of their linear form. An icon of Christ from the same monastery, but of rather earlier date, is characterized by a similar severity. The paintings of another group, however, are more poetic and delicate and are more in the gentle, lyrical style which characterizes the wall-paintings of the Morava school, notably those at Kalenić and Manasija. These icons are to be distinguished as Yugoslav on stylistic grounds; in addition one type is usual there which is hardly met with elsewhere; it is made up of small double-sided icons which were hung from the coronas on which lamps were suspended. They are mostly 16th-century and represent a last burst of the elegant Constantinopolitan art of the 14th century. Subsequently finesse and elegance disappear, and the icons of the 17th, still more those of the 18th century, are usually rather crude; sometimes this is due to the influence of the monastic art of Asia Minor; sometimes it is to be attributed to mere decadence.

It is by no means easy always to distinguish icons painted in Yugoslavia from those done in Salonica or on Mount Athos; it is even harder to classify those painted in Greece. All one can say is that there were numerous schools working all over the land from the 14th century onwards. Much work was done locally in the villages, and in that case it often hardly rises above the character of peasant art, but there were schools of painting in most of the towns and monasteries, and in these painters of real ability often worked. In rendering the divine or saintly personage the set form was followed very closely, so that it is often hard to tell a work produced in the 15th century from one done in the 17th, let alone to distinguish one painted in the central part from one done in the south of Greece. And, further, the more accomplished painters seem to have travelled a good deal, and we read of men who were natives of Crete working on Mount Athos or in Venice. Nearly every one of them produced fine paintings of the Madonna. They usually show the head and shoulders only and follow the iconographic type known as Hodegetria where the Virgin holds the Child on one arm and points to Him with the other hand. Highlights on the faces are very marked; the folds of the Child's costume are often outlined in gold, and in the west of Greece and the Adriatic littoral the haloes were often adorned with intricate patterns incised

18. Quadripartite icon showing *The Annunciation, The Nativity, The Baptism* and *The Transfiguration*, 14th century
The British Museum, London

into the gesso which was laid upon the panel as a ground for the paint. Sometimes, in areas where Venetian influence was prevalent, the Virgin's costume represents a rich patterned silk. Icons of Christ Pantocrator or individual saints – Saint Nicholas was one of the most popular – adhere in the same way to the sanctity of the basic model and show equally little variation. It is only the niceties of detail in applying the highlights or rendering the costumes and the gradual penetration of Western ideas or motifs that make it possible to date these icons at all.

Panels on which scenes are depicted show rather greater variation, for scenes were not regarded with the same mystic reverence as the figures – and they were not so narrowly restricted. But even so, there was far less variation than in the Western world; though the set iconography was firmly adhered to, details could be varied, picturesque elements like flowers or trees could be added, the architectural background could become more ornate and more elaborate, and the icons could be

19. (above left) *The Virgin and Child with Four Scenes above, and Saints,* 15th or 16th century
The Benaki Museum, Athens

20. (above right) *Christ Pantocrator,* 1360–70
The Hermitage, Leningrad

enclosed in carved or painted borders, often of a wholly baroque character. (Ill. 25.) The earlier icons, like one of the Crucifixion at Monemvasea, are grand and monumental and hard to tell from ones done in the capital. In the later ones, especially those dating from after the Turkish conquests, great attention was paid to decorative details, often of Italianate character. The best of the later painters nearly all seem to have spent at least some years of their lives in Venice, where new decorative motifs came to their knowledge; or again these penetrated by way of the circulation of woodcuts, which seems to have been extensive from the 16th century onward. But however much they adopted Western motifs, the style of the work continued but little changed and, except in a few bastard works of little merit, the technique of icon painting remained a wholly distinctive one, shading, three-dimensional modelling and naturalistic representation being avoided right down to the end.

A great deal of later Greek icon painting is often described as Cretan, and the terms 'Cretan school' or 'Italo-Cretan school' are often used with little understanding of what they mean. Crete was, from the 14th century onwards, a Venetian possession, and painters there were no doubt allowed greater freedom than those on the mainland. Yet their work has little about it that is specifically Cretan, and the term would be best discarded. Nor is there very much about these later icons that can be truly termed Italian, other than the presence of superficial decorative motifs. Till more extensive researches have been undertaken and it has become possible to distinguish individual schools, it would seem best to refer to all the work done in Greece as 'Later Greek Icon Painting'.

In addition to this so-called Cretan school, most of the products of which were not produced in Crete, one or two other groups may be distinguished. In one of them pale blues, pale reds, even pink, are the dominant colours; they are perhaps to be regarded as the products of one of the islands. In another group curious pin-point eyes are usual; they are very apparent on the icon of *The Baptism.* (Ill. 26.) These icons are perhaps to be assigned to Mount Athos.

If we cannot say much as to the development of local schools, it is possible to cite the names of quite a large number of painters who worked in the centuries following the Turkish conquests. The most important of them was probably Michael Demascenos, who worked at the same time as El Greco; Theodore Poulakis painted the icon of *The Transfiguration* shown in illustration 28, and a less well-known man called Daniel the Monk was responsible for the *St John the Baptist* shown in illustration 27. The Baptist was always a favourite subject of these later

21. *The Reliquary of Cardinal Bessarion,* 14th century
The Accademia, Venice

22. *St John*, detail of an icon of *The Crucifixion*, second half of the 13th century
The Museum, Skopolje

painters and a large number of variants of the theme exist; often he has wings: a good example belongs to the Society of Antiquaries in London. His ascetic appearance was well suited to the character of the art, and the linear stylization of the Baptist's face was sometimes carried to quite surprising extremes, as on the rendering from a private collection in Britain (Ill. 28); it is probably to be dated to the early 17th century. The names of Victor, Tzane, Zamfurnari and Bizamenos may also be noted.

Though these artists worked in various places in Greece they do not seem to have ever been associated with Asia Minor, where there was of course a considerable Greek population until the exchange of populations after the First World War. In Cappadocia it would seem that an angular, expressive style was favoured, which owed a debt to the monastic school of wall-paintings in the caves of the anchorites and small monastic communities of the region. In the Pontus again a rather similar primitive, though expressive style seems to have been to the fore – an icon of the Crucifixion formerly in a private collection in Constantinople may serve as an example. (Ill. 29.) But this icon is of comparatively late date, of the 17th or 18th century, and though it is probable, it cannot be asserted that work of this character was done in Asia Minor just before or soon after the Turkish conquest.

A more clearly marked local school was that which grew up in Cyprus in the 16th and 17th centuries. The paints there tended to be rather thin in texture and monotonous in colour, the panels comparatively large, and portraits of donors, often in semi-Western costume, were frequently included; the Madonnas again often wore costumes of richly ornamented silks of the type popular in Turkey and Italy at the time. There were also local schools in Palestine and Syria, the most important of which was at Jerusalem. These icons are usually rather crude, and are characterized by very thin paint which often tends to scale off. There is a marked *horror vacui*, so that the compositions are usually crowded and the backgrounds of icons bearing single figures are adorned with an intricate engraved pattern. The figures are either expressive but primitive or show the penetration of Western influence so that they seem over-sentimentalized. The names and titles of the scenes are sometimes in Arabic. Most of the work is also comparatively late in date – of the 17th, 18th and 19th centuries – and little of it is of great artistic value.

In Bulgaria icons were perhaps rather less important than elsewhere; dark backgrounds seem to have been popular; we still have a lot to learn about the development of local styles there. In Romania there are few, if any, icons in existence

23. (right) *St Matthew*, *circa* 1300
The Museum, Skopolje

24. (extreme right) *The Virgin and Child Pelagonitissa*, 1421–22
The Museum, Skopolje

25. *The Transfiguration*, by Theodore Poulakis (1622–92)
D. Talbot Rice Collection

26. *The Baptism*, 16th century
Formerly in the possession of Stanley Casson

27. *St John the Baptist*, 17th century
Delaporte Collection

Colour Plate. *The Fight between the Suzdalians and the Novgorodians*, 15th century
The Tretyakov Gallery, Moscow

which can be dated much before the 16th century; towards the end of that century there were workshops in Bucharest, Jassy, Ciampu-Lung and Tirgoviste. The majority of the products of these schools portrayed individual figures; icons with scenes or other subjects were comparatively rare. Donor figures were often included. The colour range was limited in the earlier work; later it became richer and brighter, and Renaissance elements intruded both with regard to the style and the motifs of decoration.

More famous and on the whole also much more important from the artistic point of view than anything done in post-Byzantine times in Greece or the Balkans were the icons of Russia, for there a number of painters of real genius were at work. Some of them we know by name, many others remain anonymous, but always except at the very outset the work was different from that of the rest of the Orthodox world and the icons of Russia can be distinguished on the grounds of style and not only because the titles and names were in the Slavonic script. At the very beginning, however, this was not so: when Russia was first christianized in the later 10th century Greek was used as much as Latin is used in the Roman Catholic world of the West; Byzantine icons were imported from Constantinople and Salonica, and copied very exactly; Greek painters worked on Russian soil, and at first the work of their Russian pupils was hardly distinguishable from that of their Greek masters. This situation was, as we learn from documents, especially true of the principal city, Kiev, and of Vladimir, though practically nothing survives from there as a result of the Mongol invasion which swept over southern Russia at the middle of the 13th century and held much of the land in thrall till near the end of the 14th. Novgorod and other towns farther to the north, however, escaped, and it was there that icon painting saw its first wholly Russian developments and there that the beginnings of the Russian school can best be studied. Already in the 13th century numerous other schools had come into being, the most important of which, in addition to Kiev and Novgorod, were those of Pskov, Vladimir-Suzdal and Yaroslavl; by the 15th century that of Moscow was becoming pre-eminent, to a great extent thanks to imperial patronage. Of the more purely local schools those of Tver, Riazan, Chernigov, Polotsk, Galich and Vladimir-Volynsk were the most important, though it is not always easy to distinguish the products of one centre from those of another.

Though the Russian icons followed their Byzantine prototypes closely so far as arrangement was concerned, certain features soon came to be stressed and it is these that serve to distinguish the Russian paintings from the products of the rest of the Orthodox world. First and most distinctive perhaps was the stress laid on humanism and tenderness, especially in renderings of the Virgin and Child; again Russian work is distinguished by its love of rhythm, to be seen especially in the arrangement of the compositions or in the treatment of such details as the hair (Ill. 14).; again, especially in the later work, the figures tended to become very elongated, with long sloping shoulders and a rather effeminate appearance. At Yaroslavl numerous decorative details were included; at Novgorod a graphic approach dominated, though it did not prevent the development of a very lovely, gay and brilliant, yet poster-like colour scheme.

At first the Novgorodian work was very closely allied to the Byzantine; one of the most famous icons that are to be associated with the city, the *Golden Headed Angel*, is very close to a Byzantine original, though the smiling, tender expression of the face and the rhythmical treatment of the hair attest its Russian provenance. (Ill. 14.) It is to be dated to the 12th century. The serene character that is to the fore

28. *Head of St John the Baptist*, 17th or 18th century
A. C. Lascarides Collection

29. *The Crucifixion*, Pontic School, 18th century
Private Collection, Constantinople

here dominated in Novgorod throughout the next two centuries, but perhaps what distinguished the work of the school most was the interest in new subject-matter. The old themes, Pantocrator, Virgin, Deesis or the 'Feasts' were of course regularly depicted, but to these were added icons of saints who were wholly Russian, like Saints Boris and Gleb, or Saints Florus and Laurus, or compositions of an abstract, complicated character. Saints Boris and Gleb were quite often depicted, and a fine icon of the late 14th century now in the Russian Museum at Leningrad may be cited. It was painted in Moscow, but there is little to distinguish such early work of the Muscovite school from that done at Novgorod. Saints Florus and Laurus appear twice on a Novgorodian icon, once on either side of the Archangel Michael, and once riding amongst a troop of horses, the patron saint of which they were. (Ill. 30.) It is in icons of this type that some of the most delightful Russian work is to be found.

Stylistic developments in both Novgorod and Moscow were considerably affected by the arrival of a painter from Constantinople *circa* 1370, who is usually known as Theophanes the Greek. The highlights which had become so characteristic of Byzantine work in the 14th century had never been developed in Russia to the same extent, but Theophanes loved them, and they play an important rôle both in his frescoes and in the few panel-paintings that can be attributed to him. In Byzantium he had, so far as we can judge, worked mainly as a fresco painter. In Russia, thanks to the development of the iconostases into a structure of considerable size, icons had a more important part to play. Theophanes seems to have learnt from what he saw in Russia, so that his work assimilated something of the delicacy and charm of Russian art, yet retained the majesty of the Byzantine style; a lovely icon of the Dormition of the Virgin in the Tretyakov Gallery at Moscow has sometimes been attributed to him and sometimes to a pupil. The highlights on the faces certainly attest its closeness to a Byzantine model, though the rhythmical composition, the tall figures and the brilliant colouring are essentially Russian.

Around 1395 Theophanes moved on from Novgorod to Moscow, which was beginning to rise to importance as a result of the defeat of the Mongols at Kulikovo in 1380. There he began with work in the Cathedral of the Annunciation. He was joined by Andrew Rublev, whose fame was soon to eclipse that of his master. Little is known of Rublev's life. He was born between 1360 and 1370, became a monk in the monastery of St Sergius and the Trinity at Zagorsk, where he studied painting under the monk Prokhor, worked at Zvenigorod in 1404 and in 1405 was in Moscow. His most famous work, the Old Testament Trinity, was probably painted at Zagorsk *circa* 1411; thereafter, till his death in 1427, he was engaged in painting frescoes in the Zagorsk monastery. Thanks to the painstaking researches carried out by Soviet scholars in recent years, it is now possible to assign quite a number of icons to Rublev; one of the most lovely is an archangel at Zvenigorod (Ill. 31), which heralds in its delicate colouring and intensely spiritual feeling the rather similar figure done some seven years later as part of the Old Testament Trinity. Never were these works to be surpassed in Russian painting – or indeed elsewhere, for in sheer beauty they are the equals of the work of any other school.

While Rublev was working in and around Moscow the situation in a number of provincial schools had not been static. At Novgorod a colouring in rather bright hues, in which red and gold predominated, had been developed along very characteristic lines; at Pskov dark green backgrounds had become popular and distinctive; farther to the north severe colour contrasts and angular outlines were even more marked. Everywhere the heads tended to become large, the eyes bright and penetrating and, with the later 15th century, icons illustrating actual events

30. *Saints Florus and Laurus*, 15th century
The Tretyakov Gallery, Moscow

31. *An Archangel*, by A. Rublev; from Zvenigorod, early 15th century
The Tretyakov Gallery, Moscow

were painted, like one of the fight between the Suzdalians and the Novgorodians, which commemorates the help given to the Novgorodians by a miraculous icon, *The Virgin of the Sign*. (See colour plate facing p. 33.) Again complicated compositions associated with the rendering of scenes of an abstract character become very popular; an icon of the 16th century, probably done at Suzdal, may serve as an example; it illustrates the theme "in Thee Rejoiceth". (Ill. 32.) Here a love of detail and a hatred of open spaces is apparent, and both these factors came to be more and more developed as the 16th century went forward.

Such features are in the main absent in the work of Rublev's most important successor, Dionysius, who was born *circa* 1440 and died *circa* 1508, for his style, though somewhat mannered, was dominated by a spiritual, idealistic approach, and the tall, elongated figures and varied colouring of his work have something of the profound glory of Rublev. But the icons of the next generation tended to be small and overcharged with detail, and this tendency was carried forward both in those done in the imperial workshops and those painted at Solvychegodsk under the patronage of the Stroganov family, which have given the name 'Stroganov style' to the work of this phase. Quite a number of painters working in that style are known by name, such as Procopius Chirin, Simon Ushakov and four men of the Savin family. Their work was much admired at the end of the 19th century.

With the growth of prosperity in the 16th and 17th centuries the demand for icons increased. More churches were built and had to be supplied; private chapels were dedicated and had to be decorated and, above all, the cult of the icon as an essential in the home was developed. In consequence a very great deal of work, mostly on a small scale, was produced, and it is to this and later periods that most of the icons which have in recent years found their way to the West belong. The general standard of craftsmanship was invariably high and the necessity to adhere rigorously to a set iconographical model assured good compositions. But Western influences began to penetrate soon after 1700, and it cannot be pretended that many of the icons that were produced thereafter are great works of art; if fewer frankly bad works were produced than in the West, owing to the sanctity and quality of the handed-down models, there were also fewer works in which true artistic qualities are to be found. And with the 19th century, work often became extremely shoddy, for cheap lithographs were often mounted on wood and varnished over to look like paintings. Again, the habit of covering parts of the panel with metal frames which began in the 16th century was much developed. These were intended to do reverence to the icon, in much the same way that a figure of the Madonna is enwrapped in silks in Italy, but by the 19th century these metal coverings were often tawdry and the painters ceased to bother to complete the parts of the picture that would be covered. In fact, commercialism had entered in, and the day of the production of icons both as symbols of sincere faith and as genuine works of art had come to an end.

The story of icon painting in Russia is probably better known in the West than that of what was done in Greece or the Balkans. It is also from the artistic point of view perhaps more significant, and it has been more fully dealt with in the literature. Yet to understand it completely it is necessary to go back to the Byzantine beginnings and to treat it as part of a great phase of development which has until recently been seriously neglected in the West. The most outstanding manifestations of the art that survive in collections in Moscow, Kiev and Leningrad, on Athos, in Athens, in Skoplje and in Belgrade or in the far distant monastery of St Catherine on Mount Sinai, are not all perhaps very easy of access – but with the facility of travel in this modern age they are no longer inaccessible,

32. *In Thee Rejoiceth*, Rostov-Suzdal School, 16th century
The Tretyakov Gallery, Moscow

and the possibility of seeing at least some of the major works themselves is no longer as wholly remote as it was half a century ago. Then the study of the subject was limited in the main to the specialist; today it is within the scope of the interested amateur, and it is to him that this study is primarily dedicated.

BIBLIOGRAPHY

Only the more easily accessible books in English, French and German are noted here. There is a considerable literature in Russian, and in addition there are important articles by such writers as Xynogopoulos and Weitzmann in various learned periodicals.

BYZANTINE AND GENERAL

Wulff, O. and Alpatov, M. *Denkmäler der Ikonenmalerei*. Leipzig, 1935.
Theunissen, W. P. *Ikonen*. The Hague, 1948.
Felecetti-Liebenfels, W. *Geschichte der Byzantinischen Ikonenmalerei*. Olten and Lausanne, 1956.
Sotiriou, G. and M. *Icones du Mont Sinai* (text in Greek). Athens, 1956.
Gerhard, H. P. *Welt der Ikonen*. Recklinghausen, 1957.
Talbot Rice, D. *Byzantine Icons*. London, 1959.
Skrobucha, H. *Die Botschaft der Ikonen*. Ettall, 1961. Translated as *Icons*, London and Edinburgh, 1963.

GREEK

Chatzidakis, M. *Icones du Saint Georges des Grecs de Venise*. Venice, 1962.

BALKAN

Djuric, V. J. *Icones de Yougoslavie*. Belgrade, 1961.
Radojcic, S. *Icones de Serbie et de Macédoine*. Belgrade, 1961.

RUSSIAN

Kondakov, N. P. (translated and arranged by E. H. Minns). *The Russian Icon*. Oxford, 1927.
Muratov, P. *Les Icones Russes*. Paris, 1927.
Schweinfurth, P. *Russian Icons*. 1953.
Grabar, E., Lazareff, V., and Demus, O. *USSR: Early Russian Icons*. Unesco, 1958.
Talbot Rice, Tamara. *Icons*. London, 1958.
Onasch, K. *Icons*. London, 1961.
Talbot Rice, Tamara. *Russian Icons*. London, 1963.

Sotheby & Co. hold four to five auctions a year devoted to icons as so do Parke-Bernet, New York. They can be bought from $84 upwards depending on their country of origin, age and condition. Although the examples illustrated in this article are quite unique they should help the reader recognize the various types and characteristics pertaining to the numerous schools and countries of origin discussed. Icons can also be obtained from specialist dealers in the major art centres of the world.

Buttons

JANE FORD ADAMS

It would be as impossible to discover who invented the button as to know when and where the first wheel turned. Petrified prints dating back 200,000 years in the Neanderthal Cave, Germany, are called 'buttons'. But who is to say they were costume accessories? The German archaeologist Ernst Herzfeld did publish his belief that man wore garment buttons made of stone in Neolithic times, before 4000 B.C.

The discovery of gold buttons pre-dating the Christian era is older than scientific archaeology. For example, the excavators of Herculaneum in the 18th century found an ancient gold button they believed to be of Greek origin. Schliemann found in Mycenae some number of gold-faced buttons. Such finds continue, for in the 1950's the Italian Archaeological School of Athens was rewarded with a cache of golden jewelry comparable to Schliemann's Great Treasure of Troy, and it too contained gold buttons. W. M. Flinders Petrie recorded ivory, carnelian and glazed steatite buttons which he believed were imported from Crete to Egypt during the VI Dynasty of the Old Kingdom. Amber and bronze buttons of the early Bronze Age have been unearthed in Scandinavian areas. English digs have yielded prehistoric jet buttons. Recently wood, bone and antimony buttons from the 9th century B.C. were excavated in Iran.

Very few buttons of archaeological importance are in private collections. The same is true of buttons having a high intrinsic value, no matter what the age. Diamond buttons were worn until late in the 19th century by people of wealth. James Buchanan (Diamond Jim) Brady, flamboyant American capitalist, wore them even on his underwear. In 1927 a set of diamond trouser buttons from the possessions of Tsar Paul and the Orloff family sold at Christie's for $700.

Louis XIV holds the all-time record for diamond wearing. Saint-Simon declared that the king could not stand erect under the weight of them. In 1684 he had a 52-carat stone split to make a pair of buttons. In 1685 he bought 24 buttons, each with diamond, value 138,030 livres; 6 diamond buttons, value 30,000 livres; 75 diamond buttons, value 586,703 livres; 48 buttons and 96 diamond-trimmed button-holes, value 185,123 livres. For 'livres' read 'dollars' to arrive at approximate equivalent value: 939,856. Similar, if not quite so impressive figures could be given for other monarchs and courtiers. The Hapsburg regalia contained dozens of sets ornamented with rubies, sapphires and other gems as well as diamonds. In 1728 the Queen of Spain commissioned a Paris jeweller to make a set for her twelve-year-old son, grandson of Louis XIV and later crowned as Charles III of Spain. One hundred and eight diamonds ranging in size from three to seven carats were used.

1. Button made for Pope Clement VII by Benvenuto Cellini, from a watercolour drawing by F. Bartoli The British Museum, London

For a story of a button of tremendous intrinsic value, made the more priceless by

2. Crest livery buttons from households of English dukes: Norfolk, Somerset, Leeds, Bedford, Devonshire, Dorset, Newcastle, Wellington, Sutherland – from Firmin & Sons' pattern books

the artistic genius and masterful skill of the creator, read Benvenuto Cellini's detailed account of the cope fastening he made for Pope Clement VII in 1529–30. The materials included a large, magnificent diamond and other fine jewels; the metal, of course, was gold. God the Father accompanied by children and cherubs formed the composition. The button is thought to have been broken up as part of the indemnity paid Napoleon in 1797. Fortunately there is in the British Museum a watercolour drawing of it made by F. Bartoli. (Ill. 1.)

But what of buttons with little or no correlation between intrinsic money value and the accrued values which collectors establish on the basis of such qualities as historic interest, artistic merit, quality craftsmanship and so forth? Uniform buttons offer the perfect instance of intangible value. Buttons did not become part of the military insignia until the mid-17th century. Previously the armed forces wore regular – as distinguished from regulation – kinds. But once official designs were authorized in France and England, wearing the right buttons brought prestige, and eventually men of all ranks, from ambassadors to chimney-sweeps, wore distinctive ones with pride.

Giving some idea of the scope, pattern books maintained by Firmin & Sons, London manufacturers since 1677, built up to nearly 40,000 different designs made chiefly for British customers. Railway and steamship lines, police and fire departments, social and business organizations as well as the military were represented. By far the largest single group consisted of heraldic livery buttons bearing family crests or arms. (Ill. 2.) As Dickens told readers of "Household Words", "button-dies are among the highest objects of the die-sinkers' and medalists' art". Small sleeve buttons with words in almost microscopic print, yet legible, offer proof of this.

Excellent die-cutting is illustrated in a set of sporting buttons made for the famous bibliophile and sportsman Thomas Gosden, who tells about them in his fine press book, "Impressions of a Series of Animals, Birds, &c., Illustrative of British Field Sports: From a Set of Silver Buttons Drawn by A. Cooper, Esq., R.A. and Engraved by Mr. John Scott". Gosden states that the buttons themselves served as blocks in printing the illustrations. *Circa* 1825 he had the engraved designs copied by a die-cutter with figures as bas-relief. He then sold sets, $11.20 in silver, $2.80 in bronze. (Ill. 3.) Comparable sets were made by all of the important button-makers. Subjects might be the hunter himself, afoot or mounted.

An extraordinarily beautiful sporting set pictures the life-cycle of a stag. The button body is highly polished steel, the design is quatrecouleur gold inlay. (Ill. 4.)

"Punch" magazine greeted the opening of the 1847 shooting season with a drawing *Ye First of September*, dedicated to "bagging folly as it flies". This picture and eleven others from the pages of "Punch" between 1844 and 1849 were placed on a set of gilt buttons. The influenza epidemic of 1848, the Hungarian revolution of 1849, the opening of Parliament and the graveyard scandal are among the news topics covered. (Ill. 5.)

In the United States the decade of the 1840's produced a deluge of topical buttons, political in intent. The most colourful presidential campaign ever conducted brought victory to William Henry Harrison in 1840. A cider barrel and a log cabin were symbols placed on brass buttons worn by his supporters. Henry Clay, unsuccessful candidate in 1844, and General Zachary Taylor, "Old Rough and Ready", were pictured on campaign buttons as Harrison had been. The idea of putting a political message on clothing buttons goes back to the Andrew Jackson election of 1828; the practice is not completely abandoned to this day. (Ill. 6.)

3. Thomas Gosden's silver sporting buttons
Courtesy The Beinecke Rare Book and Manuscript Library, Yale University, New Haven, Connecticut

The most highly prized of all button Americana are ones worn to honour George Washington, not before election but at the time of his inauguration in 1789. They are hand-wrought copper or brass struck with such legends as "Long Live the President/G.W." and "Memorable Era March the Fourth 1789". (Ill. 6 and colour plate facing p. 40, Row 6, No. 3.)

Still speaking of metal buttons, the triumph of the machine over the craftsman and of popular taste over cultivated produced 'story' buttons, a type widely collected because of the simple, direct appeal. For the sophisticated, they have rather the attraction of folk art since the subjects mirror the sentimentality and whimsy of the Victorian era so delightfully. Classics such as "Aesop's Fables" are pictured; so too are such then current conversation pieces as Wagnerian opera. Pictures copied from paintings and books were popular, especially Kate Greenaway children. Heroines like Joan of Arc were portrayed in many poses. The whole animal kingdom, from ant to whale, not forgetting snakes and rats, has come down to us on buttons fashionable from *circa* 1865 to the beginning of this century. (Ills 7, 8.)

Thousands of treatments of hundreds of subjects justify calling story buttons a minor branch of the graphic arts. Books have been published in the United States describing, identifying and appraising them. Incidentally, the design may be abominable, the material cheap, the manufacture slipshod, the price sky-high. Here, as elsewhere in the collector's world, market value has a mystique of its own.

A century earlier picture buttons of quite another kind gained fame. A British cleric writing sarcastically of the French in 1715 scoffed, "Let us therefore allow them the reputation of ten thousand buttons". The country which would become incomparable for the buttons it produced as costume accessories or *bijoux de fantaisie* was already demonstrating a talent for inventiveness in design and method. The two button constructions most typical of the period were too impractical to survive in the machine age.

One was the picture button. The component parts are a glass lens which forms the top, a metal back-piece with shank attached, a metal band which binds top and back together leaving a space between for pictorial content. Thus the button is like a tiny shadow box. Albert Parent, prominent Paris manufacturer, whose book "Le Bouton à Travers les Ages" is regrettably extremely scarce, says that glass-domed picture buttons first appeared in 1775, became a sensational fad and stayed in vogue for several decades. Coloured engravings, then a new invention, were used at the beginning. Later a wide variety of media included reverse painting on glass, eglomise, miniature painting on ivory, mica, paper or satin, decoupage, habitat groupings composed of real vegetation, feathers, shells, sand, etc., carved ivory, designs made with wax, seed pearls, potter's clay – the list reads like a catalogue of 18th-century decorative skills. (Ill. 10.)

In the second distinctive construction which scarcely survived the late 18th century a facing, usually repousséd thin metal, was fitted over a mould made of wood, horn, bone or ivory. The remarkable – and impractical – feature was the shank. It consisted of cord or catgut strung through holes in the mould and held in place under the button top by mastic. (See colour plate facing p. 40, Row 5.) When the shank pulled out or wore in two, repair was impossible. Diderot's "Encyclopédie" describes the making of these buttons, with illustrations of workers, tools and finished products. Beautiful examples are quite readily available in France to this day.

Two Englishmen, Matthew Boulton and Josiah Wedgwood, developed new materials and techniques of a more substantial kind. Boulton's improved method of making steel reduced the cost while increasing the much desired brilliance of steel buttons. By pegging dozens of highly polished studs (also called points and facets) into heavy steel mounts, buttons were made that shone like diamonds in candlelight. Cut steel buttons (as they were later called) enjoyed several periods of popularity in the 19th century. The quality kept deteriorating, however, until the button was nothing more than a thin sheet of steel stamped with facets.

Boulton and Wedgwood, as close friends, joined together in various activities, among them button-making. A Boulton and Watt pattern book (*circa* 1783), held by the Birmingham (England) Central Library, contains pen-and-ink drawings of steel button mounts marked 'J. W-d camios' [*sic*] and 'W-d camio in inside' [*sic*].

Josiah Wedgwood's correspondence and the "Catalogues" indicate clearly the great importance the master potter attached to button-making. "I mean to make them [jasper-ware cameos] as fine as gems which they ought to be for buttons", he wrote. (Ill. 12.) Besides jasper-ware, he made buttons of basalt and crystalline, giving his personal attention to the whole process from potting to mounting in steel, silver, tortoiseshell, mother-of-pearl or other suitable material. It was his ambition to improve the taste of his contemporaries by putting facsimiles of Classical art at their disposal. The success of his cameo buttons is understated in the "Catalogue" of 1787, "lately been much worn by the nobility of different parts of Europe". Rival potters have copied the originals from that day to this.

Early in the 19th century Italian cameo cutters began substituting laminated shells for stone. By mid-century nearly every Victorian lady owned some shell cameo jewelry, perhaps including a set of buttons. Buttons were made from queen conch, sardonyx helmet shell, cowrie, abalone, 'smoky' oyster pearl, carved with heads, figures, scenes and flowers. Simulated cameos were made by attaching a design cut from one shell to a contrasting base. (See colour plate opposite, Row 1.)

A Birmingham trade reporter said in 1867, "The skill of the engraver, saw-piercer, and painter is called into requisition, and the inference is that a set of mantle buttons of some of the designs would cost more than the mantles upon

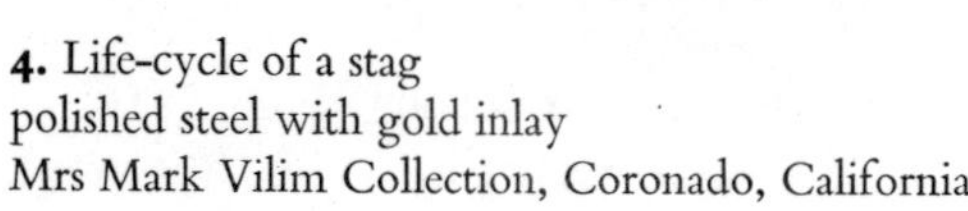

4. Life-cycle of a stag
polished steel with gold inlay
Mrs Mark Vilim Collection, Coronado, California

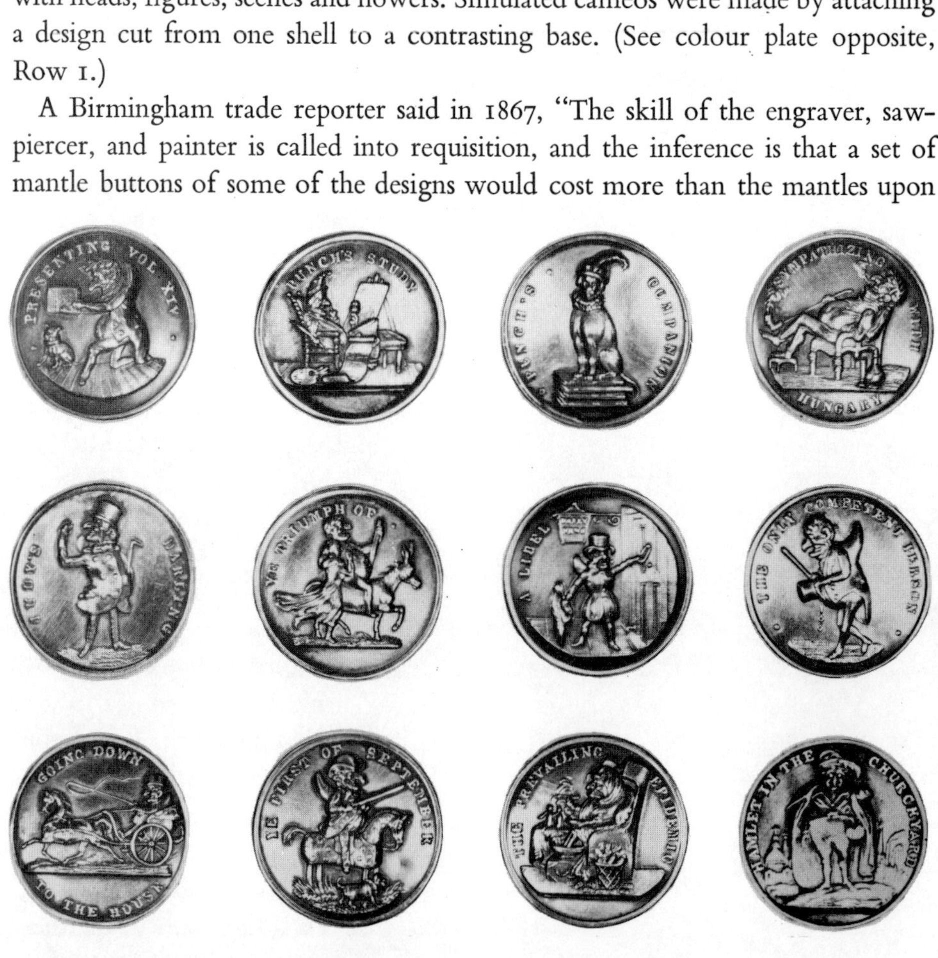

5. Buttons with pictures from "Punch", 1844–49

Colour Plate. Row 1: 19th-century cameo carved shell and narce; Row 2: 19th-century glass, chiefly from Bohemia; Row 3: Marked ceramics – Satsuma, Royal Copenhagen, Weymss, Sèvres, Chantilly; Row 4: 19th-century enamels – French, English, Japanese; Row 5: 18th-century wood- and bone-backs with cord shanks; Row 6: Commemorative buttons: honouring George III, 1789; supporting the French Revolution; celebrating the inauguration of George Washington as first President of the United States, 1789; welcoming William of Orange to England; The late Lillian Smith Albert Collection

LONG LIVE THE KING
VIVRE LIBRE OU MOURIR
LONG LIVE THE PRESIDENT
GW

6. (above) Button Americana associated with Presidents or presidential aspirants
A. H. Albert Collection, Hightstown, New Jersey

7. (centre) Saucer-shaped metal buttons with designs in part die-struck and engraved – in part mounted, 19th century

8. (below) 19th-century metal story buttons with the following subjects: Alpine Hunter; William Tell; Arrival of Lohengrin; the Madonna and Child; Meeting with Geese; Buster Brown; Fox and the Grapes; Cat and Mirror; Two Shepherdesses

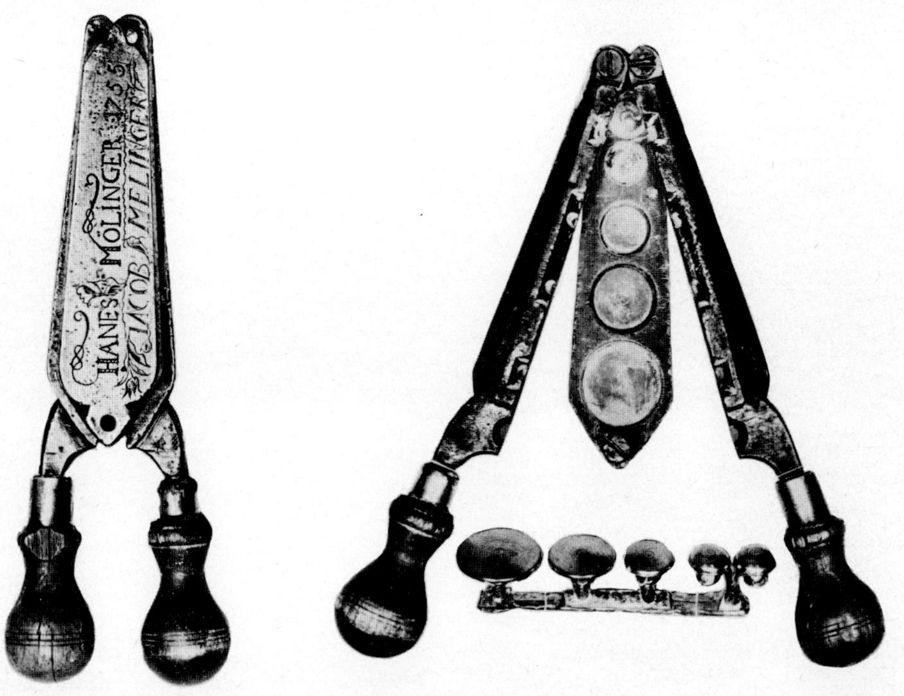

9. (right) Hand-operated brass button mould, a household tool for making pewter buttons – left: in closed position – right: in open position with casting

10. 18th-century under-glass picture buttons: *grisaille*, habitat, miniature on ivory, reverse painting on glass, rebus, gouache on paper, seed pearls with gold leaf and twisted wire

which they were to be worn." (Ill. 13.) He referred specifically to manufacturers' exhibits at the Exposition Universelle de Paris, though the same could be said of fancy pearl buttons made in England, France and Austria up until the First World War. B. Blumenthal & Co. and Bailey, Green & Elger, New York, have been fortunate in obtaining for their showrooms exhibits given gold medals, with cases and contents still as originally made up for world's fairs between 1867 and 1900.

Museums, notably the Birmingham (England) City Museum, the Carnavalet in Paris and the Cooper Union Museum for the Arts of Decoration in New York, have excellent collections of 18th- and early 19th-century mother-of-pearl buttons. They are delicate, fragile ornaments, geometrically hand carved, perhaps pierced and, in the finest examples, richly embellished with metallic foils, paste jewels, gilded bits of metal and steel 'mirrors'. Some are centred with decorative pieces as previously mentioned of Wedgwood cameos.

Conspicuous among other widely collected types are enamel, silver, ceramic, glass and horn buttons. Selection is now limited largely to 19th-century manufacture even for kinds plentiful once-upon-a-time. Enamel buttons offer an amusing instance. Bernard Palissy, writing in the middle of the 16th century, says that enamel buttons, once an expensive novelty, have become so plentiful and cheap that men of fashion are ashamed to wear what every no-account delights in. If only some would reappear elsewhere than in the Cheapside Hoard! In rare instances attributions of Limoges and Battersea have museum sanction; a few such are privately owned. The most famous name attached to 19th-century enamel buttons is Fabergé. But jewel-case treasures aside, many enamel buttons of high merit belong to the 19th century. (See colour plate facing p. 40, Row 4.)

For centuries substantial citizens in every part of the Western world made heirlooms of silver buttons. The festive dress of peasants came to be as heavily laden with silver as the courtier's with gold. It is said that Dutch navigators wore massive silver buttons as a cash reserve. Navajo Indians of the American Southwest still do the same; pawning their silver buttons is standard practice. Marking of silver sometimes gives the country of origin and in Britain silver buttons usually bear a

11. (below left) Patriotic buttons of the French Revolution. Musée Carnavalet, Paris

12. (below right) Wedgwood buttons, late 18th and early 19th century

date letter. London and Birmingham marks from around the turn of the century are most plentiful; Georgian marks are rare by comparison. (Ill. 14.)

Ceramic buttons offer great variety – bodies ranging from translucent porcelain to rugged 'chiny', from faience to plain baked clay, decorated by hand and with decalcomanias, made in places unknown and at famous potteries. (See colour plate facing p. 40, Row 3.)

The most impressive among glass buttons are paper-weights, diminutives of desk-weights, complete with pictorial canes and sulphide (cameo) enclosures. (See colour plate facing p. 40, Row 2, centre.) Small coloured glass buttons, worn in prodigious quantities in the second and third quarters of the last century, are great collectors' favourites. (See colour plate facing p. 40, Row 2.) Black glass buttons, traditionally called 'jet' and commonly mistaken for that material, are very plentiful and popular for specialized collecting. The fact that Queen Victoria established black as the most ladylike colour, always in good taste, brought about their long vogue and may still add to their prestige as desiderata.

On first encounter one is apt to be puzzled by light-weight black buttons with intricate designs remindful of die-struck metal. The material is horn/hoof and the embossing was indeed done with a die. The commonly seen backmark 'Caen' locates one centre of production. Backmarks of Cox or Wells show English manufacture and approximate date of 1830–60.

Despite the fact that cloth and thread have been among the most widely used of all button materials, few 'covered' buttons have collector appeal. Exceptions are 18th-century passementerie covers; finely embroidered specimens; covers especially woven with button-size pictures. Needlewrought covers may be as exquisite as old lace, but as with the lace, only a connoisseur can appreciate the achievement.

It is a bromide that a list of materials from which buttons have never been made would take only a fraction of the space needed to tell what materials *have* been used. So too with the kinds of collectables – the list would be all but endless. Buttons are sometimes collected as *objets d'art* for beauty and fine craftsmanship; also as coins and medals are, for their historic interest; and, like graphics, for pictorial content. Specialization may be by period, or place, or material, or even by colour, and in any number of other ways. They appeal to some as cultural artifacts; to some as a meaningful chapter in the history of costume; to others as an integral part of a larger field such as military insignia; to a few "just because". In the United States the National Button Society welcomes members with all of these diversified approaches.

13. Coachman's buttons with pictures engraved on mother-of-pearl by application of acid to specially treated stencils – some were exhibited at the Crystal Palace in 1851

14. Silver buttons from France, England, the Netherlands, Turkey, the Navajo Indian Reservation and Sweden, all 19th century

BIBLIOGRAPHY

Baily's Hunting Directory. London, annually since 1897. Currently over 300 hunt club buttons pictured and identified.

Fallou, L. *Le Bouton uniforme française (de l'Ancien-Régime à fin Juillet 1914)*. Colombes (Seine), 1915. 3,700 buttons pictured, identified and dated.

D'Allemagne, H. R. *Les Accessoires du Costume et du Mobilier depuis le treizième jusqu'au milieu du dix-neuvième siècle*. 3 vols. Paris, 1928. Historical comments and pictures of some 100 buttons.

Couse, L. E. and Maple, M. *Button Classics*. Chicago, 1941. Over 1,000 collector's buttons pictured, described and appraised.

National Button Bulletin. Official journal of the National Button Society, U.S.A. Bi-monthly since 1947.

Albert, L. S. and Kent, K. *The Complete Button Book*. New York, 1949. More than 5,700 collector's buttons illustrated, described and identified.

Perrin, O. (Ed.). *Encyclopédie de la Vénerie française*. Nearly 400 French hunt buttons pictured and identified.

Persian Pottery

ROGER BLUETT

While the title of this essay is "Persian Pottery" it should read perhaps "Persian and Islamic Pottery", for the wares which will be most discussed are those produced during the early Islamic era, from the 9th to the 14th centuries, and made over a wide area of the Middle East. The main centres of production were, however, in Persia.

At the present time it is by no means easy to write a definitive short history of the pottery of the Middle East, for while there is extensive knowledge from excavations of some of the prehistoric and very early sites, fresh excavations are constantly being made and even new cultures being discovered, as is evidenced from the finds at Amlash, which will be discussed shortly. The wares of the Islamic period are difficult to place with certainty, and in fact it would seem that we have more precise knowledge of, say, the pottery of Tepe Sialk of the fourth millennium B.C. than of some of the products of the 12th or 13th centuries A.D. This difficulty arises partly because of the similarity of wares found at different centres, and also because of the tendency to attribute pieces to the place where found rather than to the actual site of manufacture. Indeed some authorities contradict each other and the present-day attributions in Teheran seem to give nearly every piece to Gurgan, a great trading entrepôt to the south-east of the Caspian Sea, but a place where as far as we know from direct evidence only a very coarse ware was actually produced.[1] Thus there is a tendency to describe pieces rather vaguely, irritating to the museum visitor who sees a label reading 'Persian, 12th century', but nevertheless a safer description than a more precise attribution. In this essay an attempt will be made to describe the main wares made in Persia and the Islamic world, but it should be borne in mind that there may well be differences of opinion as to actual attributions.

The earliest settlement which has been excavated scientifically is at Tepe Sialk, near the site of the Islamic city of Kashan, and here at different levels, probably dating back as early as the fifth millennium B.C., have been found a series of pottery vessels, which even at this very early date were decorated with horizontal and vertical lines, probably intended to represent basket-work. By the fourth millennium animals and birds were being portrayed on pottery, painted in black on a dark red ground, and before the end of the fourth millennium it would seem that the potter's wheel had been invented. This, the greatest single step the potter ever made, opened the door to a great extension of the shapes which could be produced, while the colour of the biscuit was determined by the temperature of the kiln. Other very early sites have been discovered at Qumm, Savah, Rayy

[1] Dr Mehdi Bahrani in "Gurgan Faiences" refers to kiln wasters from Gurgan of wares similar to other factories.

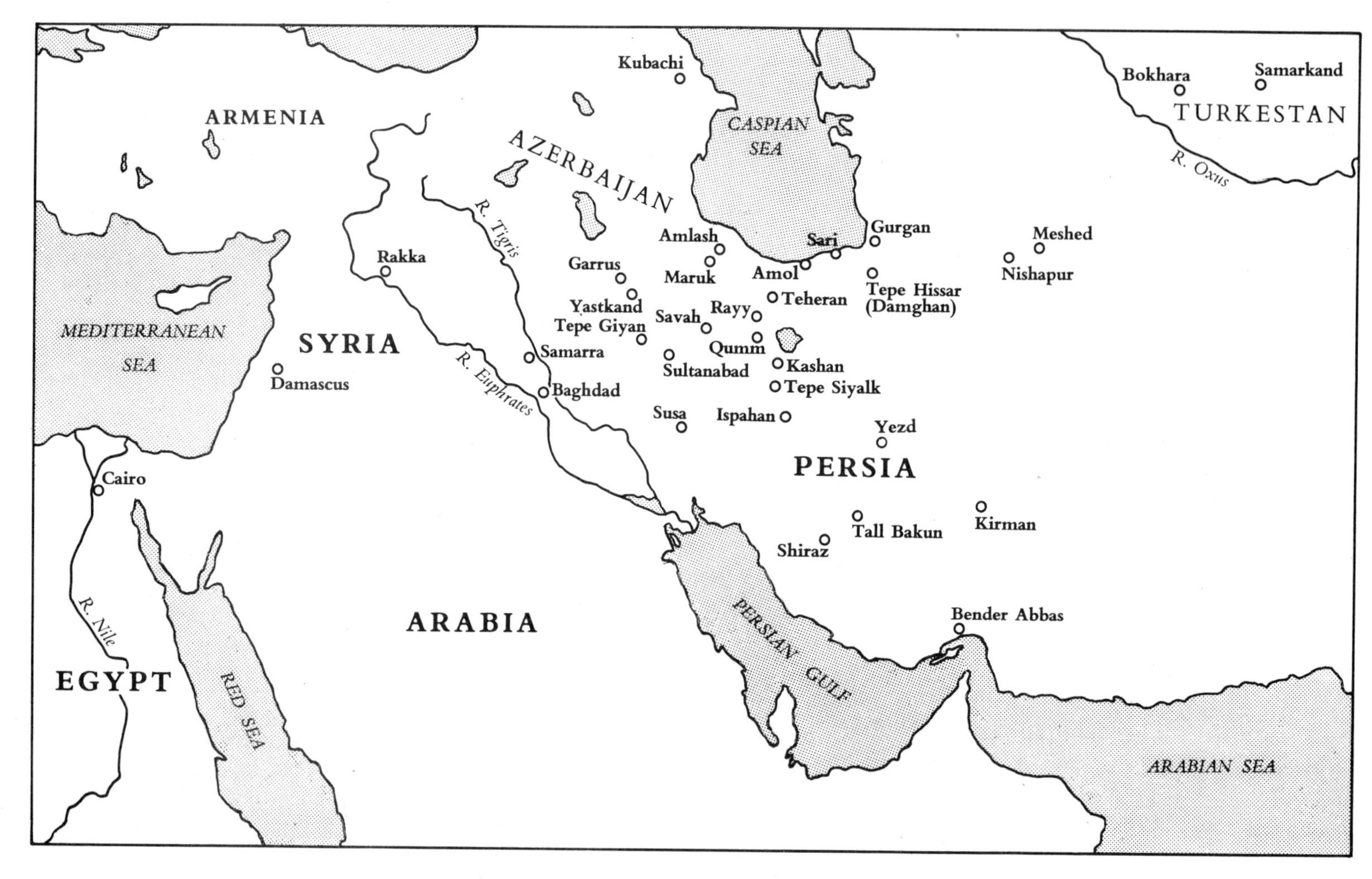

Map of Persia showing pottery-making districts

and Damghan and dating from only a little later, still in the fourth millennium, Tepe Giyan, Tall Bakun and Susa. At each of these the potters had their favourite forms; for instance, from Susa have come tall slender goblets with thin sides, and from Sialk vessels shaped like chalices.

Throughout the third millennium B.C. there seems to have been little basic difference in the work of the potter, but at Tepe Hissar (Damghan) grey-black monochrome pottery replaced the painted. During the second millennium the grey-black pottery appeared at Tepe Sialk and Tepe Giyan, but at the beginning of the first millennium an entirely new culture appeared with the arrival of invading tribes from the Caucasus and Transoxiana who within a few centuries established themselves as the ancestors of the Persians.

In the late 1940's some remarkable finds were made in the area of Amlash, an area which hitherto had been known only to the inhabitants of that remote region and perhaps to a few intrepid travellers. Some striking animals and vessels of a highly burnished red pottery started to appear on the market in Teheran and quickly attracted attention. The interest shown in these extraordinary objects, stimulated the local peasants to supply this lucrative market with further finds which soon started coming to light in considerable numbers.

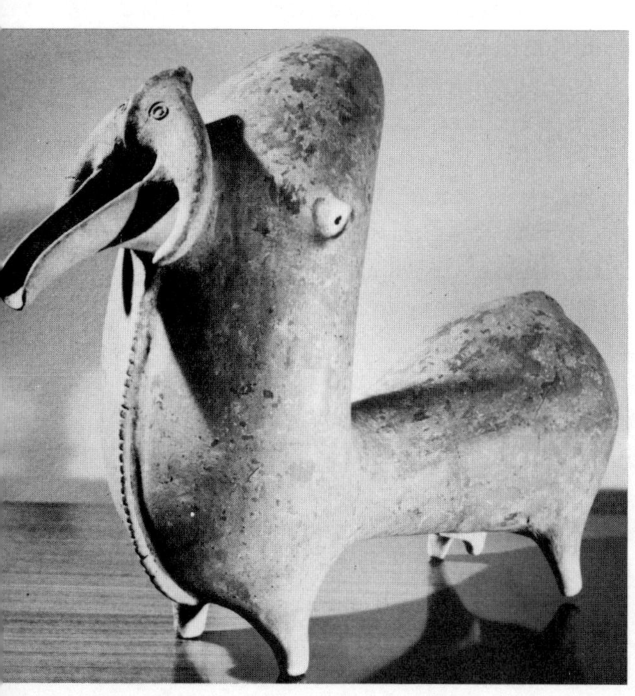

1. Amlash pottery bull, *circa* 1000 B.C. height 12½ in. (31·7 cm.)
Mr and Mrs Myron S. Falk Jr Collection, New York

How recent is the emergence of these early pottery wares from Amlash can be gauged by the fact that in the exhibition "Mostra d'Arte Iranica" held in Rome in 1956 not only were there no examples shown but no mention of Amlash is to be found in the catalogue. In the important exhibition "7,000 Ans d'Art en Iran" at Paris, 1962, however, the pottery vessels and bronze animals from Amlash found an important place, and in the interesting introduction to the exhibition "7,000 Years of Iranian Art", which toured the United States in 1964–65 and contained many of the pieces shown in the earlier French exhibition, it is pointed out that in fact the name Amlash given to this culture is a misnomer. It would

2. Jar, red pottery, 1st millennium B.C.
height 17 in. (43·1 cm.)
Dr Arthur M. Sackler Collection, New York

seem that the centre of the culture was at Marlik which has now been excavated and that Amlash itself is only a small town to the north-east of Marlik. The Marlik culture is dated approximately 1200–1000 B.C.

Of the primitive pottery to come to light there is no doubt that to many people by far the most impressive is that from Amlash or Marlik. In particular the strongly modelled bulls (Ill. 1) have caught the imagination of Western collectors not only for their power but also for the attraction of the brick-red terracotta colouring. But pottery animals and vessels from many sites in Azerbaijan and other parts of Persia are appearing in increasing numbers – strong, amusing animals and bold, magnificent pots. (Ill. 2.) One of the most characteristic shapes is a vessel with elongated spout, giving the impression of a bird beak. These will be found both plain and decorated, animal and geometric designs predominating.

There is no great volume of pottery which we can attribute to the Achaemenid (550 B.C.–330 B.C.), Parthian (250 B.C.–A.D. 226), or Sassanian (A.D. 226–651) epochs, although of course fine objects in glass and bronze, gold and silver, remain to us from those periods. Some pottery vessels are to be seen in museums, but few examples appear on the market. Noble amphora-shaped vases with vitreous blue-green or turquoise glazes and incised and applied designs are amongst the finest products of a period when the native Iranian tendencies, which had been submerged under the domination of Greek influence, were once again coming to the fore. Persia in the Parthian period was the meeting point of the Roman West and the Chinese East, and the influence of both civilizations is to be seen in Parthian art, just as indeed the influence of Persia is to be found in countries both to the east and to the west.

The great age of Persian pottery began with the start of the Islamic period, although it did not reach its full flower until the 9th century. It is generally accepted that Mohammed's flight from Mecca to Medina in A.D. 622 marked the beginning of the Islamic era and that what started as a religion expanded into a militant state which within 100 years of the death of Mohammed in 632 stretched eastward into the heart of Asia and westward from Syria and Egypt, along the whole southern shore of the Mediterranean into Spain. In fact, the armies marched faster than the religious influence permeated and centuries were to pass before the Islamic faith was adopted by a majority of the peoples in the conquered lands.

The early capital, under the Caliphate of the Umayyad family was at Damascus (A.D. 661–750), but in 750 another family, the Abbasids, seized power and removed the capital to Baghdad. The influence of the Mediterranean now weakened and Islam became primarily an Asiatic civilization with Persian influence predominating. In the 11th century the Seljuk Turks[2] came to power with the central court in no fixed place. They respected the spiritual authority of the Abbasid Caliphate which remained in Baghdad until in 1258 the Mongols sacked the city and exterminated the Caliphate.

In theory the Islamic Empire was one great state, but in practice it became a multiplicity of large and small feuding units with the centres of influence moving with the changes of political power. Thus the productions of the potter reflected the prosperity of the particular centre at which he was working, and a continuity of development was assured by this migration to the centre where he would have the best opportunities to carry on his work.

The earliest Islamic site of importance which, to some extent, has been excavated scientifically is Samarra, a city not far from Baghdad on the River Tigris which was occupied between A.D. 836 and 883, thus proving with near certainty

3. Mesopotamian lustre bowl, 9th century
diameter 10½ in. (26·6 cm.)
Jeremy Hill Collection, London

[2] The Seljuk Turks were members of a Turkish-speaking tribe from Turkestan.

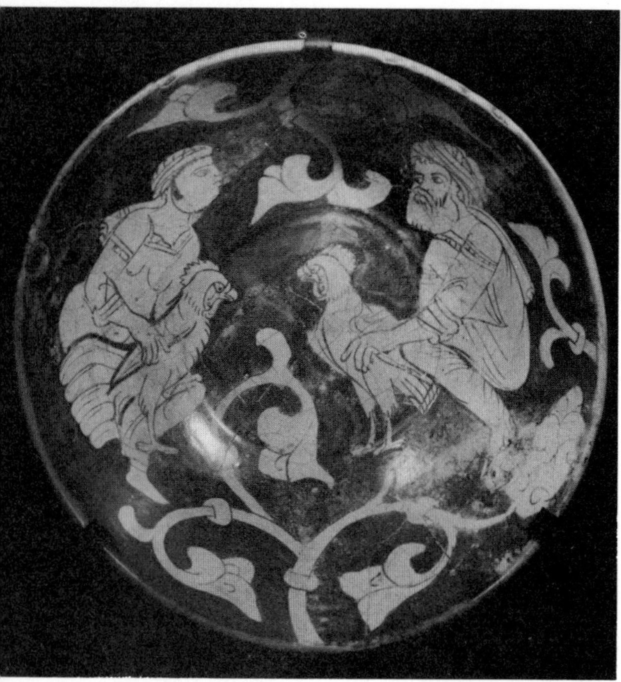

4. Egyptian (Fatimid) lustre bowl, 12th century
diameter 9½ in. (24·1 cm.)
E. de Unger Collection, Wimbledon, London

that finds from the city must be of 9th-century date. A considerable quantity of Chinese porcelain has been found in Samarra, and it would seem that, as in Europe some eight hundred years later, the local potter was stimulated to try to reproduce the hard, high-fired body of Chinese porcelain. Unable to do so, he used an opaque white glaze composed of tin oxide mixed with a modified form of lead-glaze which gave his wares a superficial resemblance. The earliest lustre wares (Ill. 3) are those made by these Mesopotamian potters who also used blue and green in their designs. It seems that the lustre technique was later carried to Egypt (Ill. 4) and thence to Persia in the migrations referred to above.

At the same time in Eastern Persia and Samarkand a largely independent dynasty, the Persian Samanids (A.D. 874–999), had become established beyond the Oxus with Bokhara as their capital and Samarkand the chief city. Very soon an entirely new school of potters was at work whose products had little in common with those of Mesopotamia. They discovered that designs which would run if painted direct on to the body remained clear and constant if a slip was first applied; and various colours were used as the ground for further decoration, principally white, tomato red, and a purplish-black sometimes approaching aubergine in colour. The decoration was then painted in similar slips under the transparent lead-glaze. The form most frequently employed was the bowl, often straight sided, the bases flat, sometimes with a slight recess. The body material is a pink or buff coloured clay.

A major centre for the production of these wares was Nishapur to the west of Samarkand, and it is by this name that they are best known today. Human figures are seldom found as motifs of decoration, while birds and animals are stylized, and by far the most common kinds of decoration are either the striking Kufik, or pseudo-Kufik script, or abstract patterns comprising flowers, half-palmettes, interlaced designs and semi-geometric forms. (Ill. 5.) It would seem that the earliest examples of these types were also the best, and for clarity of expression, simplicity and crispness of execution they were never surpassed. The use of stylization of the bird form to produce a design of extraordinary vitality is admirably shown in illustration 6, while the vigour of the Kufik script boldly but simply employed is shown to advantage in illustration 7. As time passed, the use of both script and other designs became progressively more stylized until by the 11th century the individual elements became barely recognizable. At Sari to the

5. (below left) Brown, white, red and yellowish-green Samarkand bowl, 9th–10th century
diameter 8½ in. (21·5 cm.)
Peter Harris Collection, London

6. (below right) Pale green and dark brown Nishapur bowl, 9th–10th century
diameter 9½ in. (24·1 cm.)
Peter Harris Collection, London

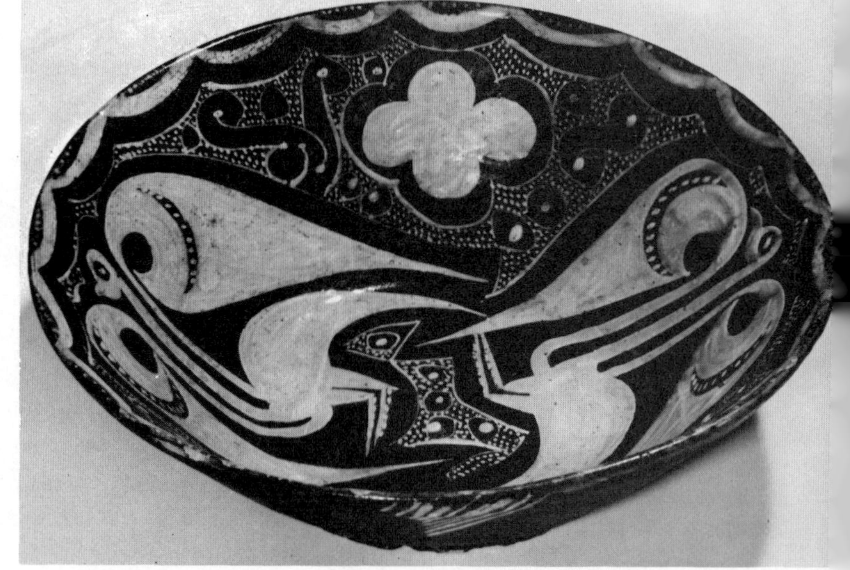

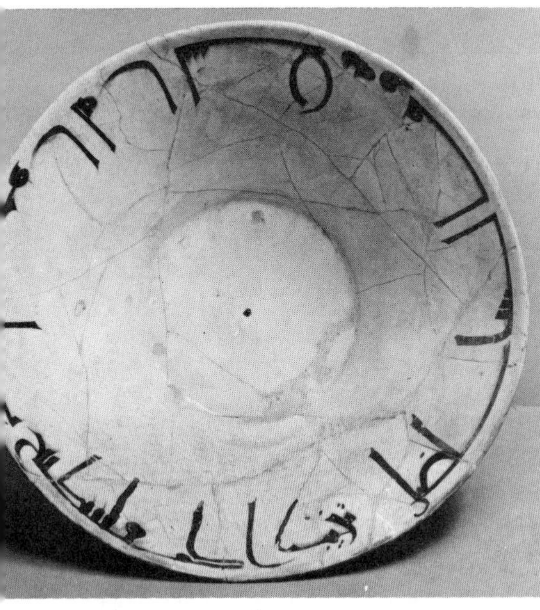

7. Dark brown script on a cream Nishapur bowl, 9th–10th century
diameter 14½ in. (36·8 cm.)
K. R. Malcolm Collection, Sunningdale, Berkshire

8. A cream Sari dish with brown and red pattern, 11th century
diameter 10 in. (25·4 cm.)
E. de Unger Collection, Wimbledon, London

south of the Caspian Sea the tradition of the East Persian styles, albeit rough and with much-simplified designs, seems to have continued after the main centres at Nishapur and Samarkand ceased production. (Ill. 8.)

Another well-known group of pottery, of which a considerable number of examples is to be found, is the so-called 'egg and spinach' glazed bowls with 'sgraffito' or etched designs under a streaky glaze of mixed green, yellow-brown and purple. (Ill. 9.) These wares, which must have been inspired by the splashed glaze wares of T'ang China, were made in quantity in East Persia, in the 9th–11th centuries, but it would seem that they were also produced in many other parts of the Middle and Near East and for all practical purposes are indistinguishable.

The 'sgraffito' technique is also to be found employed at various minor potteries, notably at Amol, to the south of the Caspian Sea where, apart from the main-stream of development, incised designs of birds, animals and geometric patterns were executed in outline on a white slip under a clear glaze. This group, though in appearance contemporary with the wares from East Persia of the 9th–11th centuries, is probably of 13th-century date. In passing mention may be made of a group of bowls formerly associated with the word 'Gabri', because when first discovered they were wrongly attributed to the pre-Islamic Zoroastrian fire-worshippers. In fact, they were probably made in the vicinity of the towns of Garrus and Yastkand. These pieces have coarse designs of birds, animals and humans, the slip having been cut away to reveal the pattern on a dark background. (Ill. 10.) A large proportion of the dishes and bowls of this group are modern fakes, and great caution must be exercised.

In the middle of the 11th century the Seljuk Turks, who had become fervent Moslems, occupied Baghdad and started the period of their ascendancy which was to last just over a century and to transform Islamic life. It took some time for the new influence to make itself felt in the field of pottery, and again it was the impact of the imported Chinese wares which stimulated the local potters; the most important change being in the actual material employed. Until the 12th century an opaque white glaze over a clay body had been used to imitate Chinese porcelain; now a translucent white body was produced with a transparent glaze which, however, is quite different from true porcelain, being softer and more brittle. The white body is an artificial paste and according to a work on the technique of the Seljuk potters, written in A.D. 1301 by Abulqasim of Kashan, himself a potter, the frit comprised powdered quartz-pebbles and potash melted together in almost equal quantities. The body material consisted of ten parts powdered quartz to one part frit and one part white plastic clay. The glaze was made of the frit to which could be added colouring agents. Body and glaze, being largely the same materials, became fused together in the firing, and the problem of glaze-flaking found in the Mesopotamian and Egyptian wares was overcome.

This lightness of body and general effect of delicacy is best seen in the Seljuk white wares, inspired in all probability by Chinese Ting ware, and made during the 12th century. Sometimes these pieces are quite plain, sometimes with carved decoration, and sometimes with pierced sides, the small holes being filled with the colourless glaze. (Ill. 11.) It is impossible to say where these pieces were made, both Rayy and Kashan producing very similar wares. The ewer (Ill. 12) shows clearly the delicacy of these white Seljuk vessels.

Perhaps some of the most striking vessels produced at this period are those decorated in monochrome or in combination with black designs with a rich turquoise glaze, of which the colouring agent is copper. The impact of this glaze is such that the collector coming fresh to Islamic pottery is generally first attracted

9. Splashed green bowl with yellow and brown, probably from eastern Persia, *circa* 10th century
diameter 12½ in. (31·7 cm.)
P. D. Krolik Collection, London

10. Garrus bowl with the design cut away to a dark background, 12th–13th century
diameter 7 in. (17·7 cm.)
E. de Unger Collection, Wimbledon, London

11. Bowl with white glaze and blue stripes, probably Rayy, 12th–13th century
diameter 7¼ in. (18·4 cm.)
P. D. Krolik Collection, London

to these wares, his appreciation of other types coming later when better acquainted with the subtle designs and colours they have to offer. Without doubt large quantities of these turquoise glazed wares, often with moulded or carved designs, were made at Rayy, but again the use of the glaze was widespread. (Ill. 13.) Other monochrome colours employed were a rich deep blue (cobalt) and an aubergine purple (manganese).

A rare type, widely regarded as being manufactured at Kashan, is the so-called 'Lakabi' ware (Lakabi=painted) in which coloured glazes were applied to a cut-out design intended to stop the glazes running. This technique seems to have met with only limited success, but the dish (Ill. 15) is a fine example of the group.

With the fall of the Fatimid dynasty in Egypt in A.D. 1171 and the destruction of the potters' quarter in Fostat (the old Cairo) it seems that, in the same way as the secret of the lustre technique had been brought to Egypt from Mesopotamia, the potters now emigrated to the Persian centres and by the late 12th and early 13th centuries were practising their craft in Rayy, Kashan and Rakka in Northern Mesopotamia. It would seem that at Rayy the designs, often of human figures, were executed in a decidedly broad and free-hand manner, frequently in alternating panels with a deep blue glaze (Ill. 16) and with the underside of bowls entirely glazed in blue. On the other hand, the gold lustre was also used as the sole means of decoration and a particularly fine example of this is shown in illustration 17.

At Kashan the introduction of lustre seems to have occurred a little later than at Rayy and more detailed, more sophisticated, designs are employed. Much more detail can be observed in the backgrounds, and delicately written inscriptions are fairly common. The bodies of bowls are usually thinner than those of other centres and a soft tone of blue or green is often used in combination with the gold lustre. The magnificent jug (see colour plate facing p. 53) is an example of this group. At Kashan too were manufactured the famous lustre-tiles which placed together formed decorative friezes in the interior of mosques and secular buildings. Many of these tiles bear dates of the 13th and early 14th centuries.

The lustre productions of Rakka, as with all types of pottery produced there, tend to be coarser and rougher than those of the other centres. The brilliance of colour is missing, and the drawing more carelessly executed. Moreover, the transparent glaze is of a greenish tone and the body of a softer material.

Towards the end of the 12th century Persian potters developed a technique for painting in polychrome enamels. These so-called 'Minai' wares were made only in Persia, and the towns of Rayy, Kashan and Sava are associated with the group, but it would seem to be impossible to distinguish between them. (Ills. 18, 19.) Two or more firings were necessary to produce the brilliant effects achieved; in the first certain colours were applied and in subsequent muffle-kiln firings the more delicate pigments which could not stand great heat were added. The range of colours found is considerable, including vivid pale blue, purple and green as ground decoration with detail added in black, white, red and with free use of gold leaf. The subjects of these 'Minai' (Minai=enamel) wares are normally human figures, often equestrian, and occasionally a story is told or an event commemorated, but generally the artist has used his motifs to produce a purely decorative design. It would seem that the larger the scale of the subject the earlier the pieces, and indeed some of the tiny and detailed drawings to be seen on pieces dating from the 13th century would seem to be the forerunners of the Persian miniature paintings of later centuries.

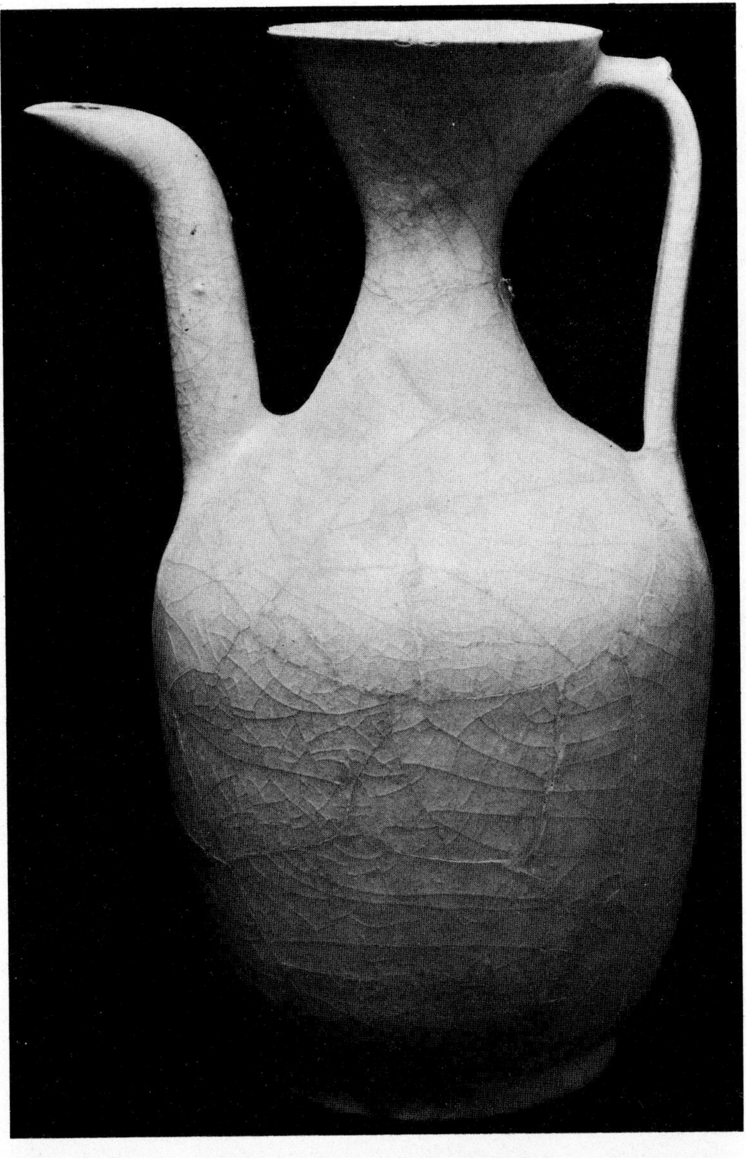

12. (above left) Ewer with white glaze, probably Kashan, 12th–13th century
height 9½ in. (24·1 cm.)
P. D. Krolik Collection, London

13. (right) Bowl with turquoise glaze, probably Rayy, 12th–13th century
diameter 9¾ in. (24·7 cm.)
P. D. Krolik Collection, London

14. (below left) Bull with turquoise glaze, probably Rayy, 12th–13th century
height 6¾ in. (17·1 cm.)
Dr E. T. Hall Collection, Oxford

15. (below right) A Lakabi dish with blue on a white ground, 13th century
diameter 14 in. (35·5 cm.)
E. de Unger Collection, Wimbledon, London

16. (above) Rayy bottle with alternating panels of lustre and blue, 12th–13th century
height 11½ in. (29·2 cm.)
The Rt Hon Malcolm MacDonald Collection

17. (below) A lustre Rayy bottle, 12th–13th century
height 12 in. (30·4 cm.)
E. de Unger Collection, Wimbledon, London

The Minai technique gradually deteriorated into a ware known as 'lajvardinia' (lajvard = deep blue), and while these pieces of *circa* A.D. 1300 still have the appeal of strong, rich colours the drawing tends to be clumsy, the designs rather dull and the body material of inferior quality. The bowl shown in illustration 20 is an unusually good example of this group; a rare form with beautiful colouring and design.

Yet another group of 12th-century wares included bowls and vessels decorated in an underglaze black slip covered with a turquoise or clear glaze. (Ills. 21, 22.) These were probably but by no means certainly made at Rayy, but it seems that pieces with other underglaze colours, notably a brilliant blue, originated at Kashan. This particular ware is finely potted, the bowls on high feet and with slightly flaring sides. The underglaze design is often most delicately painted in scrolling floral and arabesque designs, or with vivid blue stripes on a white ground. (Ill. 23.) The forms that these bowls and vessels take are amongst the most elegant produced in the Islamic world, which together with their colours and designs make them some of the most attractive wares ever made in Persia.

In the middle of the 13th century the Mongol invasion of Persia brought about a profound change in the art of the potter. At Rayy it seems that pottery production ceased in 1224 and at Rakka in 1259. Apparently Kashan continued in production under the Mongols, but new centres developed, notably at Sultanabad, where, after a period of coarse copies of the fine Kashan wares, at the beginning of the 14th century, more elaborately designed underglaze wares were produced in quantity. These reflected the taste of the Mongol invaders and Chinese motifs will be found incorporated with the native Persian designs. Mongol styles of dress, birds reminiscent of the Chinese phoenix and stylized flowers will be seen. But it should not be thought that these wares resemble in any way their contemporary Chinese counterparts. They are entirely original in concept, and show marked difference from the earlier Seljuk wares. A favourite technique is the application of thick white slip on a black or grey ground so that the design shows out in relief under the clear glaze, but straightforward underglaze decoration is also employed, the common factor being that in most instances as little white as possible is left in the background. The bowl (Ill. 24) shows the raised slip technique and the overall coloured design so typical of the class.

With the 14th century and the Mongol period came a decline in Persian pottery, which never again achieved the heights reached in the Seljuk period. This was perhaps largely because of the increasing influence of Chinese porcelain which led

18. (right) A polychrome Minai jug with a cream ground, 12th–13th century: diameter 5¼ in. (13·3 cm.)
E. de Unger Collection, Wimbledon, London

19. (far right) A polychrome Minai bowl with a turquoise ground, 13th–14th century
diameter 7½ in. (19 cm.)
Dr E. T. Hall Collection, Oxford

Colour Plate. Kashan lustre ewer, 12th century
height 14 in. (35·5 cm.)
E. de Unger Collection, Wimbledon, London

20. (above) A polychrome Lajvardinia bowl with a deep blue ground, 13th–14th century
diameter 11½ in. (29·2 cm.)
K. R. Malcolm Collection, Sunningdale, Berkshire

21. (below) A bottle with black slip under turquoise glaze, probably Rayy, 12th century
height 10 in. (25·4 cm.)
E. de Unger Collection, Wimbledon, London

to the Persian potter of the 15th–17th centuries being too engrossed with copying the original Chinese wares. This is not to deny that much attractive pottery was produced in Persia right through until the 19th century, but the main centres of Islamic ceramic wares moved elsewhere, notably to Turkey, whence the magnificent productions of Isnik continue to elicit the admiration of collectors.

Our knowledge of Persian pottery in the Mongol (A.D. 1225–1335), Timurid (A.D. 1370–1447) and Safavid (A.D. 1502–1737) periods is limited in the extreme, but one class which is known as Kubachi ware, after the small town in the Caucasus where large numbers of these pieces were found in the possession of the local inhabitants in the last century, appears to have been made over a long period, but exactly where is unknown. These pieces, although varying in decoration extensively, have in common a very soft loose-grained porous white body, a thin glaze liable to develop a wide-meshed crackle and thus give the body a brownish tone. The decoration is freely drawn and is found in blue and white, copying Chinese 15th-century originals, while turquoise and black continues as a colour scheme into the 17th century. Polychrome decoration probably dates from the middle of the 16th century, and from that date until *circa* 1630 deep blue, turquoise, dull green, opaque yellow-ochre and a thick brownish red were employed in designs often incorporating human figures.

Another group of wares is attributed to Kirman, a town in South Persia whence in all probability a class of blue and white, of polychrome and of monochrome pottery originates. The white body of these pieces is harder than those of Kubachi and comparatively the polychrome wares look fresher and more brilliant because of the harder glaze, which withstands crackle and staining, and also on account of the more brilliant colours employed. There is much blue in the polychrome pieces and the designs incorporate Persian motifs, while the blue and white is nearly always closely copied from contemporary 17th-century Ming export or transitional wares. The monochrome pottery from Kirman, with similar forms to the polychrome and blue and white, e.g. water containers for 'hubble-bubble' tobacco-pipes (Kalians), octagonal bowls, large dishes and sweetmeat trays, jars and bottles, is principally celadon, often with detail of decoration added in a thick white, blue, red or ochre slip. Deep blue was also used as a ground colour and occasionally white, but the latter was not very successful owing to the coarse texture of the glaze and its rather greenish tone.

Lustre wares were also produced in the 17th and early 18th centuries, but the places of manufacture are a closed book to us; it is clear, however, that they are quite distinct from the Kirman productions, being of a considerably harder material. Shiraz has been suggested as a possible place of manufacture on account of the large proportion of wine-bottles, but this is only conjecture.

22. (right) A bowl with black slip under clear glaze, probably Rayy, 12th century
diameter 5 in. (12·7 cm.)
E. de Unger Collection, Wimbledon, London

23. (far right) A Kashan bowl with alternating blue and white stripes, 12th century
diameter 7½ in. (19 cm.)
H. M. Langton Collection, Weybridge

24. A Sultanabad bowl with blue, grey and sepia underglaze, 14th century
diameter 8¼ in. (20·9 cm.)
H. M. Langton Collection, Weybridge

25. (above) A dish with dark blue patterning on a cream ground, 15th century
diameter 11 in. (27·9 cm.)
E. de Unger Collection, Wimbledon, London

26. (right) A Gombroon bowl with black and blue underglaze, 18th century
diameter 7½ in. (19 cm.)
Peter Harris Collection, London

While the names of other towns such as Meshed and Yezd are associated with the production of pottery little or nothing is known specifically about them, and in concluding this essay our last reproduction (Ill. 26) is an attractive bowl of so-called Gombroon[3] ware. This class is of pure white thin material, fine grained, and looks almost like glass. The decoration in black or blue is simple, and a return was made to the effective technique employed by the Seljuk potters in carving out 'patterns', and covering the 'windows' with a transparent glaze.

In this brief survey of some seven thousand years of Persian pottery it will be seen that considerably more remains to be learnt than is at present known. But however limited is our knowledge the pieces surely speak for themselves in proclaiming the neglect with which, by and large, they have been treated so far by collectors in the West.

[3] Gombroon is a name for Bender Abbas, the port on the Persian Gulf from which the wares were shipped.

BIBLIOGRAPHY

Pope, A. U. *A Survey of Persian Art.* Oxford, 1935.
Lane, A. *Early Islamic Pottery.* London, 1947.
Bahrani, M. *Gurgan Faiences.* Cairo, 1949.
Ghirshman, R. *Iran, from the Earliest Times to the Islamic Conquest.* London, 1954.
Lane, A. *Islamic Pottery, IX–XIV Centuries.* London, 1956.
Lane, A. *Later Islamic Pottery.* London, 1957.
Pinder Wilson, R. *Islamic Art.* New York, 1957.
Talbot Rice, D. *Islamic Art.* London, 1965.

Note While all the above works, and others not listed, make valuable contributions to the study of the subject it is in particular the writings of the late Mr Arthur Lane which are the standard textbooks.

Prayer Rugs

LYNNE THORNTON

The prayer rug forms a distinctive, varied and particularly interesting class of weaving throughout those Middle Eastern countries where the Islamic faith is established, and indeed forms an important part of the religious possessions of most, and certainly all well-to-do, Moslems. Five times a day the faithful are called to prayer by the words *Lā ilāh illa 'illāh* (There is no God but Allah) and the devout, facing Mecca, unrolls his rug (*Namazlik*) and prostrates himself with arms outstretched until his head touches the ground.

Knotted pile fabrics existed from early times, the earliest known being discovered near Pazirik in the Altai mountains of Siberia, dating probably from the 4th or 5th century B.C., though the technique may have been known even earlier than this. The prayer rug, however, did not develop until after A.D. 622 when Mohammed escaped from Medina to Mecca. After his death in A.D. 632 his faith spread through the Middle East, reaching the north coast of Africa and even, through the south of Europe, as far as Spain. There are no known examples of prayer rugs from this time, although it is reasonable to suppose that in a very simplified form they were made not long after the 7th century A.D. Hand-knotted rugs, woven at first principally by nomadic tribes, formed durable and transportable items of camp equipment, and the prayer rug would have originally been purely a comfort to those kneeling in prayer.

Oriental rugs are woven by knotting yarn to every pair of warp threads (which extend from end to end of the rug) and by holding these 'knots' in place by weft threads (which pass from side to side), the weft being pressed into place by a comb-like instrument. There are two kinds of knot, the Ghiordes and the Senna, which can be woven to the left or to the right. The former is nearly always found in the rugs of Asia Minor and the Caucasus, but there is no definite rule. It is the closeness of the warp threads and the number of knots which determines the fineness of the rug, the average being about 80–100 knots to the square inch and the very finest about 500–700. (Fig. 1.)

GHIORDES

SENNA

Fig. 1.

Antique rugs, particularly those of Asia Minor, were worked as though they were pieces cut from a larger repetitive pattern, the field bearing little relation to its frame, while the vertical and horizontal borders are like strips allowed to butt against each other, thus causing medallions and flowerheads to be cut in half. The Persians and Indians, however, paid more attention to the design of the corners and worked out a balanced composition. In each rug there is a band of a different shade running partially or entirely across the field (*abrash*) or a deliberate fault in the design, as it is believed that only Allah is perfect.

Wool is generally used for the pile and the sheep living in mountainous areas yield better quality wool than those living in the lowlands, the poor quality wool

Colour Plate. Ghiordes prayer rug, early 19th century
78×51 in. (198·1×129·5 cm.)
Courtesy C. John Ltd

1. (above left) Ghiordes prayer rug, early 18th century
62×50 in. (157·4×127 cm.)
Perez (London) Ltd

2. (above right) Konieh prayer rug, early 17th century
60×48 in. (152·4×121·9 cm.)
Perez (London) Ltd

3. (below left) Kulah prayer rug, late 17th century
67×52 in. (170·1×132 cm.)
Perez (London) Ltd

4. (below right) Kulah "tomb" rug, late 18th century
81×50 in. (205·7×127 cm.)
Perez (London) Ltd

tending to look dry and dull. Yak and goat hair is used, although generally in small quantities, while camel is woven in its natural state as it does not take dye easily. Cotton is sometimes used in order to pick out a design as it retains its pristine whiteness but has a hard and lustreless appearance; lately flax, hemp, jute and other cheap materials have been employed. Silk has been used for many centuries and is luxurious both to look at and to touch. Cut-silk rugs are those in which the 'cut' areas are left pileless, extra weft threads being put in the place of knots, so that the remaining areas of pile stand out in relief. Most rug-making countries of the Orient use wool for their foundation threads, but the Persians, with a few exceptions, use cotton.

Rugs used always to be dyed with colours made from insects, bark, shells, berries and plants, and although they fade a little with time, they still retain their true colour. Browns are apt to lose their lustre, however, while black, being of mineral composition, is corrosive and eats into the wool. Aniline dyes, many of which are not fast but run when wet and are of harsher colouring, were first prepared in the late 19th century. These synthetic dyes were sold in large quantities and the weavers used them in preference to the laborious task of preparing the vegetable dyes at home. These colours when faded are often drastically different from the original colour, which can be seen close to the foundation threads. There has been a practice in recent years amongst some traders to wash the rug in chloride of lime or oxalic acid in order to achieve an artificially faded effect.

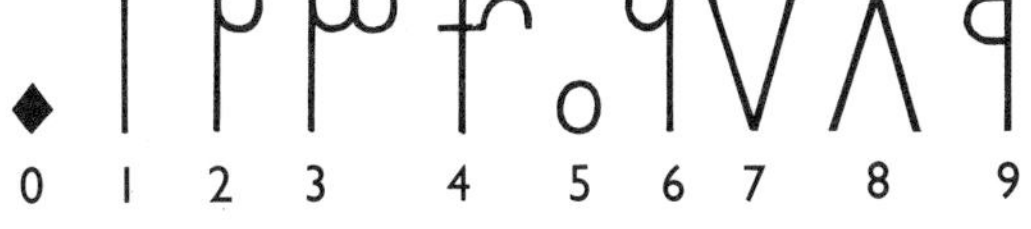

Fig. 2.

Prayer rugs are dated from A.D. 622 (the date of Mohammed's flight to Mecca) and the Arabic numerals, of which there are many modifications, are sometimes woven into the rug. (Fig. 2.)

To calculate the equivalent Christian year it is necessary to subtract from the Moslem year one thirty-third of itself and to add 622 to the remainder, *e.g.* $1253 - \frac{1253}{33} + 622 =$ A.D. 1837.

Moslems are not forbidden in the Koran to represent any form of animal or human life, and it is only later that this tradition appears. Although the Persian Sh'ia Moslems virtually disregard it, the prohibition was more closely adhered to under the stricter Sunnis.

Rugs designed specially for praying on conform to the ordinary styles of oriental weaving, but are distinctive in the shape of their field, called the *mihrab*, which is capped by a niche representing the mosque arch. This shape, either in cursive or geometric form, is common to all such rugs (although ordinary rugs without *mihrabs* are also used during prayer). According to tribal custom or differences of local usage there are also woven a large variety of symbols from the Moslem faith, including single or double columns framing the *mihrab* and sometimes showing a lamp hanging from the niche said to represent Eternal Light, hand marks at either side of the niche (the spandrels), sacred texts framing the niche or contained in panels in the borders and small motifs such as combs and ewers reminding the faithful of his religious duty of cleanliness. (Fig. 3.)

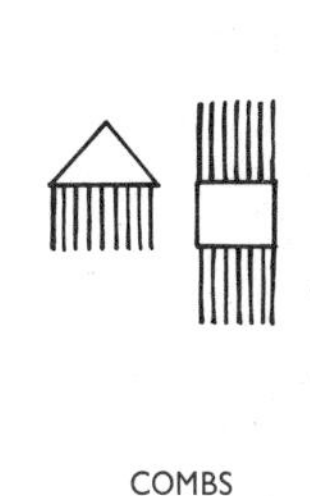

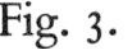

Fig. 3.

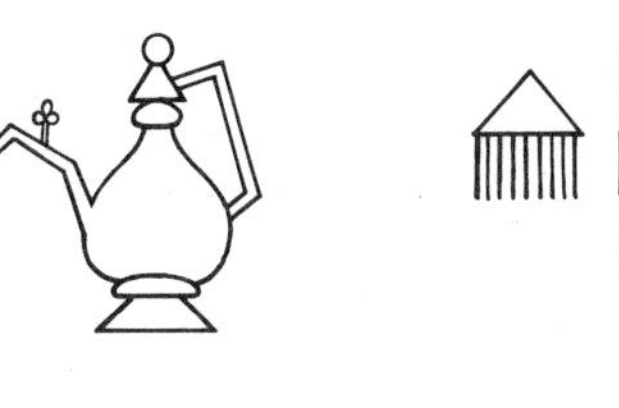

EWER COMBS

LAMP

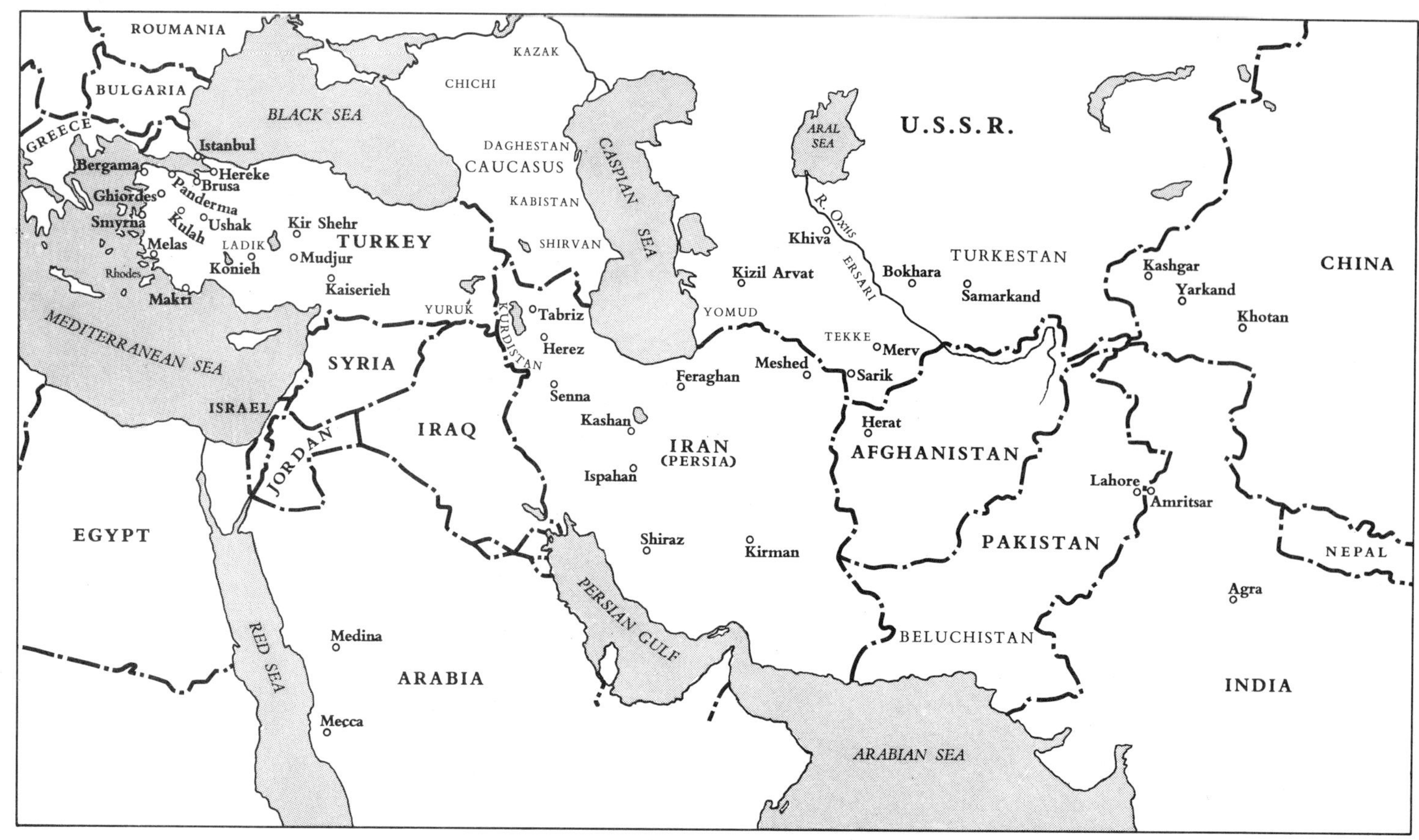

Map of carpet-making regions in the 19th century

5. Ladik prayer rug, mid-18th century
72×46 in. (182·8×116·8 cm.)
Perez (London) Ltd

ASIA MINOR

In contrast to other rug-weaving countries, the principal output of the Turks in Asia Minor has always been prayer rugs. They display a simplicity and vigour of design and colour (especially unshaded brick red, deep blue and yellow). Apart from single rugs, prayer rugs with many *mihrabs*, called *saphs*, are found; von Böde suggests that these were for floor coverings in the mosques rather than for family use.

Asia Minor had, since the mid-7th century A.D., been under Arab domination, but in the 11th century the Seljuk tribe, originally Turks who had settled in Turkestan, overran Turkey and Persia, taking over the temporal power of the Caliphs, or spiritual heads of the Moslems. It can be seen from remaining fragments that their weaving was simple and geometric in design with few colours. It was in the 13th century and again in the late 14th century that an influence from the Far East first appears. Genghis Khan swept across Asia to be followed by Tamerlane, or Timur, in conquests from Samarkand to the Mediterranean. It was through these invaders that Chinese motifs such as fret, cloud bands, lotus, pomegranates and dragons began to appear in textiles of that time, as craftsmen were transported from Asia Minor and Persia to cities in Turkestan. These craftsmen, when the Mongol power waned, scattered throughout Islam, taking Eastern traditions with them.

In the earlier Asia Minor prayer rugs the columns at either side of the *mihrab* have architectural capitals, but from the 18th century onwards these tend to become foliate or floral while the hanging lamp degenerates into a basket or clump of flowers.

In the 19th century there was a revival of traditional styles. A notable example of this are the Koun Kapu rugs which were for a long time accepted as being silk rugs woven in 17th-century Persia, with tall waisted *mihrabs* and many inscription panels. In the latter part of the last century Sultan Abdul Hamid set up the Royal Manufactories in Hereke, on the north coast of Turkey, where only the finest weavers were employed. The work was not necessarily copied from Persian designs, although it certainly shows a strong Persian influence. The rugs are

6. (above left) Makri prayer rug, late 19th century
76×40 in. (193×101·6 cm.)
Perez (London) Ltd

7. (above right) Melas prayer rug, late 19th or early 20th century
58×43 in. (147·3×109·2 cm.)
Perez (London) Ltd

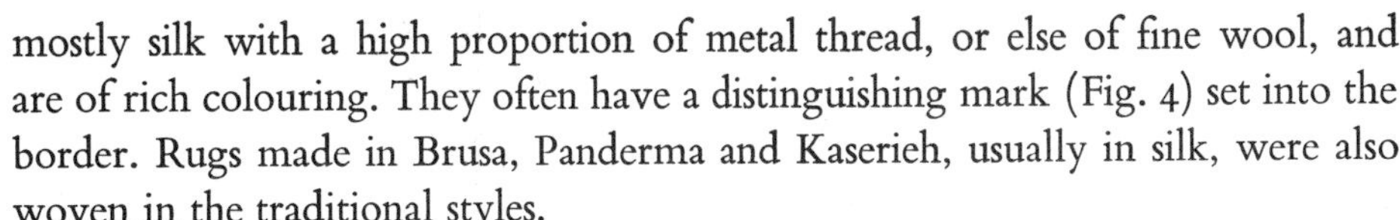

mostly silk with a high proportion of metal thread, or else of fine wool, and are of rich colouring. They often have a distinguishing mark (Fig. 4) set into the border. Rugs made in Brusa, Panderma and Kaserieh, usually in silk, were also woven in the traditional styles.

ANATOLIA

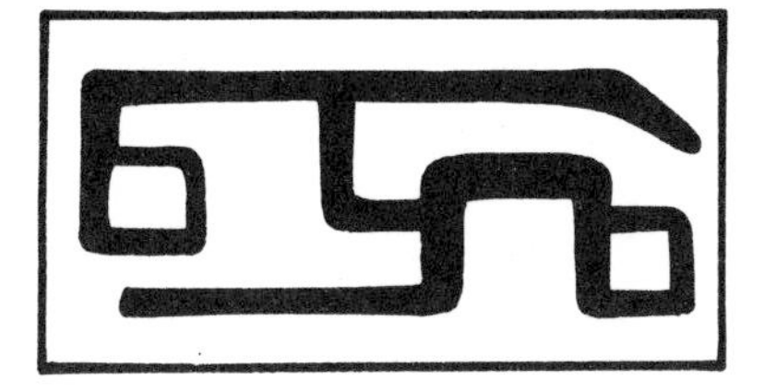

When the actual origin of an Asia Minor rug is not determined it is classified as Anatolian. The older ones have a long pile and are coarsely woven, but the late 19th- and early 20th-century ones are usually in silk of pastel colouring and the backs have a peculiarly whitish look.

Fig. 4.

BERGAMA

Named after the ancient city of Pergamos, Bergamas are one of the oldest class of rugs found in Asia Minor. They are generally of almost square shape with a geometric *mihrab*, the nap being long and the predominant colours pink, light blue and white. They have pronounced and often complex geometric spandrels and are sometimes confused with later Kazak (Caucasian) rugs, which may have been influenced by them.

8. Mudjur prayer rug, late 19th century
60×51 in. (152·4×129·5 cm.)
Perez (London) Ltd

GHIORDES

Named after the city of Ghiordes, site of ancient Gordium, they are often confused with rugs from Kulah.

In the 17th century the niche is tall and gently shaped with rounded shoulders supported by architectural columns. The spandrels are often filled with arabesques on a blue ground while the broad main border has either a giant rosette and leaf design or lozenge medallions.

In the 18th century the niche is still tall but is generally wavy, while later it is flatter with seven steps. The columns and lamp become floral and the borders more complex and better designed, the subsidiary borders growing in importance as the emphasis moves away from the main border. Besides the floral cloud band, lotus and multiple sprigged, striped borders, there is a type found which have broad zigzagging bands fringed with latch hooks. The *mihrab* is usually left plain and there are generally two cross panels compared with the one found in Kulahs. Considerable white, pale green, wine red, magenta (their most distinctive feature) and turquoise is used and they are more closely woven than Kulahs. (Ill. 1 and see colour plate facing p. 56.)

KIR-SHEHR

Named after the town south-east of Smyrna, they are very similar to Mudjur and Touzla (q.v.). They have a stepped niche with one cross panel at the bottom. Quantities of red, yellow, blue and green are used and there is often one broad cherry-red border and another in yellow.

KONIEH (KONIA)

Konieh is built on the site of ancient Iconium. The antique rugs have a pointed shaped niche with a very broad flowerhead and leaf border, but the later ones have no typical *mihrab*, although there are often latch hooks projecting from each step of the niche. Rich red, blue, yellow, green and white are used. (Ill. 2.)

KULAH (KOULA)

The rugs woven in this area south-east of Ghiordes are varied in design. The 17th-century ones have a tall shaped niche with architectural columns and a broad flowerhead and leaf border; from the early 18th century onwards the niche flattens (this is one of the ways in which it is possible to differentiate between Kulah and Ghiordes, the latter having a steeper niche), the columns become floral and there is often a stiff branch bearing floral forms running the length of the *mihrab*.

The later *mihrabs* are usually filled, with a single cross panel, which is often woven with S shapes resembling salamanders, one of the symbols of the ancient religion of Zoroaster, which included fire-worship. The borders vary, being sometimes filled with spiky Rhodian lilies, stylized plant forms or up to twenty narrow borders, alternately dark and light, with floral sprigs (*shobokli*). The earlier rugs have arabesque-filled spandrels, while the later ones have carnations, plant forms or a closely woven diaper of flecks (*sinekli*).

Illustration 4 shows a type of Kulah supposed to have been used in funeral ceremonies, called a tomb rug. The arrangement of cypress trees, with or without a small building, in the form of a ship is presumably of Greek origin, the idea that the soul is transported to future life by ship being Hellenic. Ghiordes, Kir-Shehr and Ladik also have this design. (Ills 3, 4.) The colours used are yellow, golden brown, indigo and white.

LADIK

The name is a corruption of the word Laodicea, an ancient town in the south-west of Turkey.

The 17th-century rugs have a triple *mihrab* with a pair of double columns, the spandrels are filled with giant leaves and the broad border has a giant flowerhead and leaf design or lozenge medallions.

The later ones (Ill. 5) usually have a vandyked *mihrab*, double latch hooks protruding from the apex of each niche and with a tall panel, also with vandykes, from which are woven tall-stemmed stiff tulips. A typical border of this later period has a rosette alternating with a Rhodian lily set obliquely across the border or a hooked arcaded meander design. The *mihrab* is often brick red, and turquoise, yellow, pale blue and violet are used.

MAKRI (MEGRIS)

Named after the small city opposite Rhodes on the Mediterranean coast, they date from the end of the 19th century. They have two or three narrow *mihrabs* in bright colours – red, blue, green or yellow – and a typical border is woven with diamonds joined by a single line. (Ill. 6.)

MELAS

Melas is a corruption of the name of the town Milassa, south of Smyrna, the rugs being made in the sea-coast towns near Makri.

The narrow *mihrab* has a diamond-shaped niche, the spandrels usually having a four-branch floral motif. The colours used are rich mustard yellow, red, blue and green and the foundation threads are often dyed yellow. (Ill. 7.)

9. Madjidieh prayer rug, mid-19th century
78×48 in. (198·1×121·9 cm.)
Courtesy Vigo Art Galleries, London

MUDJUR

Mudjur is in the Kir-Shehr district of the province of Konieh. They are similar in design to Touzla and Kir-Shehr (q.v.) and have a tall stepped niche with a single cross panel filled with arrowhead-like motifs. The borders are usually geometric, the inner one often being filled with diamonds or stylized flowerheads.

They are coarsely woven with a long nap and have a red woollen weft. Much green, red, blue and yellow is employed. (Ill. 8.)

MADJIDIEH

These rugs, woven in the Ghiordes district, are named after the Sultan Abd-el-Madjid (1839–61). They are strongly influenced by the European rococo style and are sometimes called 'Venetian' rugs. The *mihrab* is framed by flowers and tendrils and the ground is creamy white, magenta, yellow or pink, the designs being in buff, pink and yellow. (Ill. 9.)

TOUZLA

They are woven in the district of Touz-Cheli, in the province of Konieh and are very similar to Mudjur and Kir-Shehr (q.v.). They have a high stepped niche with a cross panel of geometric foliage, usually within a rosette border, and are woven in red, blue and green.

10. (above left) "Transylvanian" prayer rug, early 17th century
60×47 in. (152·4×119·3 cm.)
Formerly Herbert L. Bensilum Collection

11. (above right) Ushak prayer rug, mid-17th century
62×47 in. (157·4×119·3 cm.)
Perez (London) Ltd

'TRANSYLVANIAN'

It is not certain where these rugs were woven but the designs are very similar to those of antique Ladiks, Ushaks, Kulahs, Bergamas and Koniehs. They are called 'Transylvanian' because a number of them were found in churches in that area of Romania, part of the Turkish Ottoman Empire until the 17th century.

They have a tall shaped niche, slightly gathered below the shoulder, and generally have a lozenge medallion border with reciprocal trefoil guard stripes (as shown in illustration 10, where one can see clearly how the borders cut into each other). Sometimes the broad main border has a design of giant flowerheads, each with two formal leaves from which spring hyacinths (as shown in illustration 2. In later rugs from Ghiordes and Kulah this design becomes more compact and stylized.)

The colours used are red, blue, buff and yellow.

USHAK

Named after the city of Ushak near Kulah. Large *saphs* are found with two rows of *mihrabs* as well as single prayer rugs, although the district is known primarily for its antique 'Holbein' rugs and medallion carpets. They are of loose weave with a rather coarse nap and the colours are dark and light blue, brick red and yellow, with heightening in green and white.

The rug in illustration 11 shows the Chinese cloud band in the *mihrab* and Persian influence in the floral meander border.

12. Persian prayer rug, 17th century
70×46 in. (177·8×116·8 cm.)
Private Collection

YURUK

The name means 'wanderer'; they are woven by nomads, descended from the invaders from Turkestan, who live in the uplands of Anatolia.

The niche is usually stepped and the latch hook is a common feature. The borders are narrow, sometimes just a single one with a line of diamonds. They have long, coarsely woven pile, and brown, blue and pink predominate.

PERSIA

The earliest Persian weaving was extremely formal under the influence of the ruling Turkish Seljuks. By 1500, however, when the Safavid dynasty under Shah Ismael had begun, there had grown up a new form of design which was more flowing and cursive, and the rugs were woven with complex, naturalistic, floral designs, the colours being shaded and graduated; the rugs were tightly knotted and the pile closely clipped in order to gain this effect. The zenith of Persian art was in the reign of Shah Abbas I (1586–1628) who was a great patron of art and whose capital was Isfahan.

Few antique prayer rugs have survived. They have many inscriptions taken from the Koran and poetry, the *mihrab* being tall and gracefully curved and the borders closely filled with exotic flowerheads and foliate stems.

There are a great number of Persian rugs on the market today of prayer rug design which were woven purely for decorative and export purposes, but were never intended for religious purposes. These have shaped *mihrabs* and are filled with vases of flowers, animals, birds, Trees of Life and pictorial scenes, and are made in such rug-weaving centres as Kashan, Kirman, Sarouk, Meshed, Tabriz and Feraghan. Their borders are woven with floral meander and lotus or the *herati* design, which takes its name from the ancient city of Herat and consists of a central flowerhead set between four surrounding elongated leaves which curve symmetrically around the centre. (Ills 12, 13.)

CAUCASIA

The Caucasus is the isthmus connecting Europe and Asia and has at different times belonged to Russia, Turkey and Persia, now being part of the U.S.S.R. It is a land of high mountains and deep gorges and the rugs are woven by nomadic tribesmen, who use primitive, geometric forms in unshaded bright colours. Every available bit of space is filled with hooks, stars, squares and crosses and they share border designs such as barber's pole, wine glass and leaf, reciprocal trefoil, S-pattern, rosette and leaf, and tarantula and crab pattern. Another border found is the Kufic letter, named after the town of Kufah, near Baghdad. It is a corruption of the angular writing in use until the mid-12th century and can also be seen in the Ushak 'Holbein' rugs of the 16th century. (Fig. 5.)

Fig. 5.

13. Kirman rug of prayer rug design, early 20th century
80×54 in. (203·2×137·1 cm.)
Perez (London) Ltd

14. Daghestan prayer rug, dated 1869
43×53 in. (109·2×134·6 cm.)
Private Collection

CHICHI

Chichi is the name of a tribe in the north-west part of Daghestan. The niche is always geometric and the *mihrab* is filled with a diaper of hooked stars or rosettes. They have a distinctive border of rosettes separated by ribbon-like diagonal stripes.

DAGHESTAN

Daghestan means 'mountain land'. The rugs have a short nap and strongly contrasting bright colours. The niche is either square or tent shaped, but with a flattened apex, and the *mihrab* is filled with a trellis or diaper of stylized cones, plant forms or stars.

The piece illustrated has flame-like cones, which may once have been a Zoroastrian fire symbol and which are a common feature in the weaving of the Near East. The deliberate error can clearly be seen in this rug: the cones in the left-hand border face alternate ways except for the fourth and fifth cones which both face to the right. (Ill. 14.)

15. Kabistan prayer rug, early 20th century
67×41 in. (170·1×104·1 cm.)
Perez (London) Ltd

16. Kazak prayer rug, dated 1901
62×39 in. (157·4×99 cm.)
Perez (London) Ltd

KABISTAN

Made near Kuba, they are usually oblong and closely filled with jewelry, stylized lilies and hooked medallions. They have typical Caucasian borders and a small geometric niche. The piece illustrated has a bird-pattern border with reciprocal trefoil guard stripes. (Ill. 15.)

KAZAK

Kazak is a corruption of the word Cossak, the people originating from Russia who lived in the district near Mount Ararat, in order to protect the southern boundaries of Russia against invaders.

The geometric niche continues down either side of the *mihrab* and forms another niche at the lower end. They are less closely filled than other Caucasian rugs and are rather more coarsely woven. The piece illustrated has a wine glass and leaf border. (Ill. 16.)

SHIRVAN

They are woven in the district of Shirvan, south of Daghestan, extending from the Caspian Sea to the river Kur. Since almost the only approach to Daghestan was through Shirvan there was a great interchange of ideas and designs. The colours are not so sharply contrasted as in the Daghestans but are softer, blending more harmoniously.

INDIA

In the late 16th century Emperor Akbar employed expert weavers from Persia and established manufactories in Lahore where Persian designs were used. Prayer rugs are not often found; they are of heavy square knotting, similar to that of the Chinese, and wine red is used lavishly, the *mihrab* being woven with a *mille fleurs* or sunflower design.

TURKOMAN

These rugs are woven by the nomadic Turkoman tribes who wander in the district north of Persia and Afghanistan, which is bordered on the west by the Caspian Sea and on the east by the Aral Sea. Although the Turkomans are believed to have made their first appearance in this country in about the 10th century A.D., little is known until the early 18th century.

These tribes have been continually involved in internecine warfare and so have influenced each other's weavings. The whole group can be easily identified by their rich colouring: deep red, dark brown, blue, tan and some white. The modern ones are woven in Russian Turkestan and Pakistan and are of rich, bright colouring. In the best quality rugs *pashm* (the undergrowth of wool) is used, while small quantities of silk and white cotton heighten the design.

They are often called by the general name of Bokhara, which is the chief marketing town for the surrounding area. The prayer rugs (*Jai-i-namaz*) are also called Khatchli, which means a cross, because of the design of the *mihrab*. Some rugs are found which have this quartered *mihrab* of the Sarik, Tekke and Yomud prayer rugs, but do not have a single or multiple niche above; these were woven as portières for tents but were probably used for prayer as well.

17. Bokhara prayer rug, early 19th century
70×42 in. (177·8×106·6 cm.)
Private Collection

18. Sarik prayer rug, late 19th century
70×57 in. (177·8×144·7 cm.)
The Victoria and Albert Museum, London

BOKHARA

The district of Bokhara is situated on the right bank of the middle Oxus. These rugs are often called Beshir, but Hartley Clark and other experts believe they are the work of the very mixed race of people living around the city of Bokhara, which had been captured in turn by Turks, Persians and Mongols.

They show a greater Chinese influence than other Turkoman rugs, notably in the number of cloud bands and amount of yellow used. The *mihrab* is tall and bottle-shaped with a lozenge niche and the ground is woven with stylized plants or the Tree of Life. (Ill. 17.)

SARIK

The Sariks migrated to Transcaspia in *circa* 1730, together with the Salors. Both tribes were continually warring, but were finally driven out of the Merv desert by the Tekkes. They went farther south to Ulatan and Punjdeh (or Pindé), and their rugs are often known by this latter name.

They also have a quartered *mihrab*, but each panel is filled with plant forms or combs. Although there is sometimes only one niche, they can have up to nine across the top of the *mihrab*, as in the piece illustrated. The outside border often has a double bracket motif, the inner one having a stylized Tree of Life or a 'harp' border. They have dentured, 'herringbone' or diamond guard stripes with an olive-brown end panel with comb-like motifs springing from stiff branches. (Ill. 18.)

TEKKE

The Tekkes, the greatest and most powerful of the Turkoman tribes, were feared throughout the land east of the Caspian Sea, as far as Herat in Afghanistan. They now live around Merv, out of which they drove the Sariks and Salors in 1856.

The *mihrab* is quartered, each panel being filled with rows of Y's (candlebranch design), with a single niche above. The borders are filled with 'sunburst' medallions or serrated leaves and edged with double bracket motifs, all picked out in white. They generally have a diapered comb or diamond end piece. (Ill. 19.)

YOMUD

The Yomuds live between the east coast of the Caspian and the river Oxus, although there are offshoots of the main tribe. They were ousted by the Tekkes in 1718 from near Kizil-Arvat and moved to less fertile country to the north and west. The colouring is darker than the other Turkomans'; purplish red, quantities of dark brown, deep blue and green. The panels of the quartered *mihrab* are filled with lozenges or candlebranch design and there is a lower panel of large bat-like motifs. The end piece often has a diaper of diamonds and a typical border has a meandering vine fringed with latch hooks on a white ground.

CENTRAL ASIA

BALUCHI

These rugs are often confused with those of the Turkomans' because of the

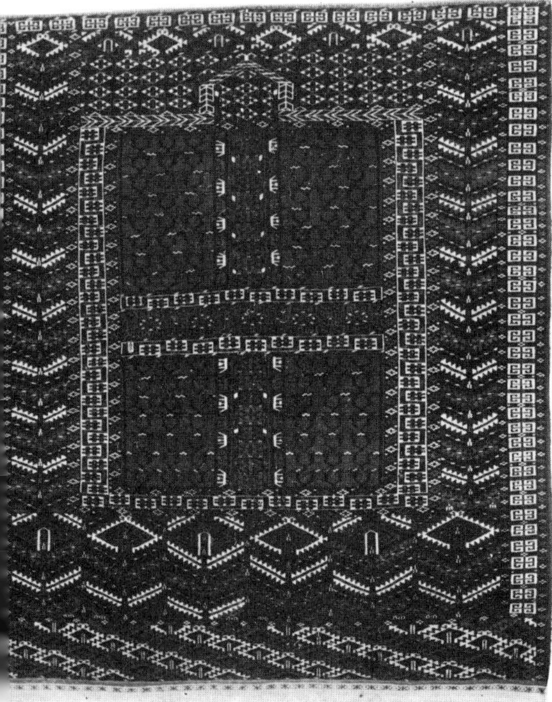

19. Tekke prayer rug, late 19th century
57×51 in. (144·7×129·5 cm.)
Perez (London) Ltd

similarity of colouring. They are, however, woven by nomadic tribes who wander along the wild and mountainous country of Baluchistan. The *mihrab* has a square or tall rectangular niche and is often woven with a stylized Tree of Life or plant forms. Tan is often used, with yellow, deep blue and red, heightened in white. (Ill. 20.)

SAMARKAND

Only *saphs*, and not single prayer rugs, are found in this district of West Turkestan. A number of them are made in Kashgar and Kotan and are marketed in Samarkand, 100 miles east of Bokhara. A typical border design is pomegranates or flowerheads growing stiffly from a central stem, the spandrels being filled with diaper or fret. The borders are woven with Chinese fret, cloud bands, foliate meander or *pao-shan-hai-shui* (a formalized design of waves).

A large amount of yellow is used, together with magenta, violet and grey. (Ill. 21.)

Fine antique and silk prayer rugs can cost several thousand dollars, but there are also a large number of good quality rugs to be bought for very much less from either auction rooms or from leading carpet dealers, many of whom are Middle Eastern in origin, and who have great knowledge of their subject.

SELECT BIBLIOGRAPHY

Hawley, W. A. *Oriental Rugs, Antique and Modern.* New York, 1913.
Hartley, C. *Bokhara, Turkoman and Afghan Rugs.* Bungay, Suffolk, 1922.
Kendrick, A. F. and Tattersall, C. E. C. *Handwoven Carpets, Oriental and European.* London, 1922 (2 vols.).
Griffin Lewis, C. *Oriental Rugs.* Philadelphia and New York, 6th revised edition, 1945.
Mostafa, Dr M. *Turkish Prayer Rugs.* Cairo, 1953.
Böde and Künel. *Antique Rugs from the Near East.* Brunswick, Berlin, 1958.
Catalogue of Temple Newsam Exhibition. *The Rug in Islamic Art.* 16 April to 28 May 1964. Leeds, 1964.

20. (above) Baluchi prayer rug, late 19th century
54×31 in. (137·1×78·7 cm.)
Private Collection

21. A Samarkand *saph*, early 20th century. 160×43 in. (406·4×109·2 cm.). Perez (London) Ltd

Locks and Keys

G. C. H. CHUBB

1. St Peter's Key, 4th century; Italian?
– said to have been given to St Gervase of Maastricht by Pope Damasus in A.D. 376
electron, an alloy of gold and silver
height 12 in. (30·4 cm.)
The Church of St Gervase, Maastricht

2. Ball padlocks found throughout Europe, 12th–17th centuries
iron
The German Lock and Metalwork Museum, Velbert

Today locks and keys are commonplace. When wealth is distributed over the population as a whole everyone needs security, and it becomes such a part of our everyday lives that few stop to think of the number of locks to be found in an average household (it runs to dozens on doors, drawers, cupboards, cases and so on), or to count the number of keys on the bunch they carry with them.

Less than one hundred and fifty years ago security was comparatively rare and only to be found in the homes of the wealthy. Then the situation was vastly different for a need for security, whether it be locks or coffers, was indicative of wealth and position, and hence something of a status symbol. Often in the Middle Ages and down into the Renaissance, locks travelled from house to house with their owners, a cost for the removal of locks from one palace and their refixing in another being a recurrent item in the Pipe Rolls of the Plantagenet and Tudor Kings of England.

The key has been a symbol of both spiritual and temporal power for centuries. Janus, the Roman god of doors and gateways, is depicted carrying a key, just as many of the sun-gods are shown carrying the key to the day. During a Roman marriage service the woman received a key to show her right to her husband's house and its contents, whilst in medieval times a woman still received a symbolic key on marriage which she could place on her husband's bier or in his tomb when he died. By doing this she discharged any liability for his debts.

Kings and nobles have constantly used the key to indicate position or favour. For instance, in feudal Europe the liege invested his liege man with a key which brought certain rights on the lord's estate in return for service, whilst later, on their appointment, keys were given to chamberlains which, although they had no function except to show authority, did give the locksmith an excuse to display his skill, many superb chamberlains' keys surviving.

Locks and keys appeal to collectors in two ways. For some the appreciation of design, decoration and highly skilled workmanship in many locks, and more often in keys, is particularly rewarding. Before the advent of industrial processes in the late 18th and early 19th centuries the locksmith created each individual lock. Modern experts have closely examined examples of the locksmiths' work of the 16th, 17th and 18th centuries and in some cases estimate that it could have taken over 3,000 manual hours to make a particular lock. These locksmiths made more than just the locks for a door, usually they made the hinges and ornamental metalwork which covered many doors as well. Their position in the community was an important one. Charles IV created the title of Master Locksmith in Germany in the 15th century and in France the publication in 1411 of the *Statuts de Serruriers* firmly established the craft with a ten-year apprenticeship before becoming a

3. Padlock with a shape common in Spain, the Netherlands and Germany in the 15th–16th centuries
iron $7 \times 4\frac{3}{4}$ in. (18 × 12 cm.)
The German Lock and Metalwork Museum, Velbert

4. English padlock, 16th century
iron $7\frac{1}{2} \times 8\frac{3}{4}$ in. (19 × 22·2 cm.)
The Victoria and Albert Museum, London

journeyman. At the end of his time an apprentice had to produce a *chef d'œuvre* as evidence of his craftsmanship, and many of these particular locks survive in collections throughout the world. In the 15th century, locksmiths formed the most powerful corporation in Paris and in 1549 the corporation had sixty members.

A lock is a metallic chameleon because it is always part of something else like a door or a chest and, as such, must assume the style and period of the article to which it is fixed. Some objects – a chalice, for example – can be fashioned and embellished without losing their basic identity, but a lock must merge its identity. Therefore, as it must not stand out, the appearance of locks has followed the main decorative trends. On the other hand, keys need not merge, and so have a much more individual character which, particularly in the 15th to the 18th centuries, becomes a portable reflection of the taste and artistry of the period.

For other collectors, the alliance of human ingenuity and mechanical prowess versus the criminal mind offers a study with an appeal all its own. In 1851 a lock-picking contest between A. C. Hobbs, the famous American locksmith, and the two leading English lock manufacturers of the time, Bramah and Chubb, gained widespread coverage in the English press. The contest developed into the "Great Lock Controversy" whose reverberations occupied many minds for a long period and which is still mentioned in articles on security even today. Hardly a week goes by without some newspaper or magazine somewhere publishing an item discussing the possibility of lock-picking or manipulation, showing that these problems still exert considerable fascination.

Door locks fall into three categories – mortice locks, rim locks and half-rim locks. A mortice lock is let into the thickness of a door from the front edge, gaining strength from being surrounded by the door and making it impossible to remove without breaking away part of the door first. A rim lock is fixed to the rear face of a door and a half-rim lock is let into the back of a door with one side of the lock flush with the rear face. Rim locks also provide excellent security, although care must be taken to see they are attached to the door in as strong a manner as possible. Door locks made by the Ancient Egyptians, Greeks and Romans were always of rim fixing because the bolt of the lock was still a bar running across the whole or most of the door from one side to the other. Although rim fixing and half-rim fixing continued to be the most popular form of fixing until the 19th century, some mortice locks were made but their proportion of the total number of door locks was small.

Locks for chests, trunks, cupboards and drawers form another group. Using the same security systems as a door lock, they are of particular interest to the collector as many antique chests and chest locks have survived. These chests were the forerunners of the modern safe which has only been made in its present form for the last one hundred and thirty years. At first ordinary door locks were used to secure safes, but as the safe itself developed to keep ahead of the 19th-century criminal there was a demand for specialist locks, which form another group.

It is difficult, if not impossible, to describe verbally the multitude of different shapes padlocks have been made in, for padlocks have been in use, particularly in the Far and Near East, for over two thousand years. Generally padlocks from the Far East resembled an animal or a god, whilst in Europe from Roman times until the 19th century four shape groups stand out. Ball padlocks, easy to distinguish because they are an iron ball with a hasp, were extremely popular, some being as small as an inch in diameter and others as large as four inches. The other groups are square, heavy padlocks for town gates; padlocks half-heart shaped when viewed end-on; and one akin to the traditional shape of today except for the bottom of

5. Padlock found in Spain, the Netherlands and Germany in the 16th–17th centuries
iron $5\frac{7}{8} \times 4\frac{3}{4}$ in. (15 × 12 cm.)
The German Lock and Metalwork Museum, Velbert

the body which was worked into a leaf pattern. All kinds of cunning devices were built into these padlocks – false keyholes, spring escutcheons, two sets of wards necessitating two different keys to open the one lock and so on.

The earliest locks were made entirely of wood except for a small number of Chinese and Indian padlocks which were in non-ferrous metals. Although metal moving parts were introduced gradually, locks were still being made with the body of wood and the wards, levers and key guides of metal as late as the 19th century. A Banbury lock has these metal moving parts set directly into a wooden body, whilst a Wood Stock lock is a complete metal lock let into a block of wood. Both of these particular locks are found frequently on church doors. Until the early 19th century iron and steel were the most common metals used in lock-making, but industrialization brought about a greater use of non-ferrous metals which took less time to work. Therefore a lock made in 1820, for example, would have a steel case and bolt with the remainder of the mechanism in brass.

Security and civilization are of an age. Primitive man dug holes in the ground, covering them with stones for his safes, and there is evidence to show he used caves or grottoes as vaults. A rope of cord tied with an intricate knot was the earliest *secure* fastening, but a cord could be easily cut, as Alexander the Great proved when he severed the Gordian Knot. Whether the Chinese were using mechanical locks before the Ancient Egyptians is open to dispute, but archaeological evidence shows the Egyptians were using locks as early as *circa* 2000 B.C.

To create an obstacle to the horizontal movement of the bar which ran across a door from side to side, the Ancient Egyptians designed a lock consisting of pins falling by gravity into holes in the bar. The key had corresponding pegs which raised the pins and allowed the bar to be moved backwards and forwards. The size of both the lock and the key varied considerably, some of the keys being so large a slave was used to carry them – "And the key of the House of David will I lay upon his shoulder", Isaiah xxii. verse 22.

6. Lock plate, 16th century; Italian
bronze gilt height 7 in. (17·7 cm.)
The Wallace Collection, London

A visitor to many parts of Africa today can still buy a wooden lock based on the Ancient Egyptian principle of four thousand years ago. The most interesting facet of this particular system is the similarity which primitive locks have to one another, although they have been found in completely different and widely separated parts of the world. For instance, collectors have found virtually identical locks in countries as far apart as Indonesia and the Faroe Islands.

Information about Egyptian locks comes mainly from carvings, as generally these locks were made entirely of wood and have long since decayed and disappeared. Some keys have been found, notably in the tombs of Luxor. These keys had iron pegs and carved ivory handles with inlays of gold and silver.

The use of springs held in tension is one of the oldest of security systems, but it is only suitable for use in padlocks. With this mechanism the shackle is separate from the body, and on its lower side carries a pair of spreading springs which enter a hole in the end of the body when the hasp and body are brought together. The springs are, in fact, flexible barbs so that when the hasp is pressed right home the springs spread out inside the body, holding the two pieces together. To unlock the lock the springs have to be compressed by pushing the key through a hole in the opposite end of the body. To increase the security the shape of the keyhole can be varied considerably, and a further development was the introduction of a thread, so that the key not only compresses the springs but screws the lock up as well and so increases the tension. This padlock, often with more than two springs, is found all over the world, but particularly in the Far East where it has been in use for many thousand years and may be man's oldest mechanical security system.

7. Rim lock complete with key and escutcheon, 17th century; French
– chiselled and engraved steel partially overlaid - note the finishing on surfaces hidden from normal view
$7\frac{1}{2} \times 5\frac{1}{2}$ in. (19×13·9 cm.)
The Victoria and Albert Museum, London

It seems strange that the Greek civilization which contributed so much to science and mechanics only employed a crude form of locking, but Greek locks were merely a bar across the door, opened from the outside by the insertion, through a hole in the door, of a long sickle or clavicle-shaped key which engaged and moved the bar. The Greek locking system has been modified, adapted and is still used in the remoter parts of Central Europe. A few Greek keys have survived and are easily distinguished because of their shape.

The Romans adopted the Egyptian system and developed it considerably. The key to the Egyptian lock was inserted through the door in a direction parallel to the movement of the bar. The Romans changed this so that the key was inserted at right angles to the bar. It is impossible to say whether it was the Egyptians or Romans who reduced the size of the bar until it became what was, in modern terms, a bolt; suffice it to say that the majority of Roman locks which have been found have had bolts and not bars. The pins in the Egyptian lock had been cylindrical, so the Romans altered them to varying geometric shapes and improved the security of the Egyptian lock further by inserting a spring above each pin. This meant the pins could not be shaken free, which had been possible with the Egyptian lock where the pins were only gravity-held.

Roman keys have been found all over Europe and the Near East. Generally they are made from bronze and iron, being distinctive in shape because this particular method of locking used a key with a flattened stem and pegs standing vertically from a spade-shaped end. Many Roman keys were worn on the finger – key rings in the true sense of the word – and these were often as small as $\frac{5}{8}$ inch in diameter. There is a tradition that the Roman himself only carried one key, his wife being responsible for the rest. The key he carried was the key to the wine cellar!

The other great contribution of the Romans to lockmaking was the development of warded locks. A ward is a piece of metal or a combination of pieces of metal fixed within a lock in the path of the key, so unless the key is notched or cut to pass over the ward it cannot either fully enter the lock or, if it does enter, it cannot turn. Simple wards are merely segments of metal, either directly under the keyhole to prevent the entry of the wrong key or somewhat to the side to prevent it turning. This form of security mechanism remained paramount from Roman times down to the 19th century and, as can be imagined over such a long period, systems of wards became highly involved and so represent the utmost in skill on the part of the locksmith. The wards were contained in a cylinder known as a box of wards which, complete with a key, could often take months of careful work. Just short of a complete circle, separate rings or segments making up the wards are bent and filed from sheet metal and joined together by brazing. Great care must be exercised to see each strip of metal forms a concentric curve for, if the curve is not exact, the key will be unable to turn easily. The cutting of keys also took a great deal of time as only a few of the cuts could be sawn or filed. The rest had to be chipped with a small chisel because of the curvature many had to describe.

If a lock is to operate from both sides the warding must be symmetrical to allow for the passage of the key. But, however complicated a ward is made, it is always possible to produce a skeleton key to operate the lock, a fact which forced the locksmith to increase the security of his locks by making the wards more intricate and forming the keyhole in different shapes. When a lock operates from one side only the key is often hollow and pivots on a pin inserted in the lock. Many locks have keyholes and pins of irregular patterned shapes as aids to security.

No locks and only a few keys have survived from the Dark Ages. Of those that have come down to us two keys from the 4th and the 7th century are outstanding.

8. Rim lock, made by Richard Bickford for Cosimo III, Grand Duke of Tuscany, 17th century; English – case of pierced brass and blue steel – left-hand dial shows the number of times the lock has been operated, right-hand dial is purely ornamental
$6\frac{5}{8} \times 10\frac{3}{4}$ in. (16·8×27·3 cm.)
The Victoria and Albert Museum, London

9. Chest lock, 15th century; French
– 'Architectural' lock showing Christ and the twelve apostles
iron
Musée de Cluny, Paris

The key of St Servais of Maastricht and the key of St Hubert, first Bishop of Liège, have basket-shaped bows whose interstices between the stakes have been richly interlaced with graceful tendrils. Before the 13th century the blacksmith paid scant attention to embellishing the locks he made, if the evidence of the many gates and grilles surviving from this period is accepted as being representative. These locks have plain, unadorned cases and, similarly, keys of the early Middle Ages possess little artistic importance, being utilitarian in design. However, they share certain basic characteristics imposed upon them by the way they were made. From the 11th to the 13th centuries keys were forged from sheet iron with a piece bent over to form the bow, a rolled stem, a fashioned extended bit and an elongated broach. Occasionally the bows were fashioned but this is unusual, the majority being shaped in crude circles or ovals. If the key was destined to be used in a monastery or church the blacksmith might make some attempt at giving it an ecclesiastical appearance, which led to the development of the lozenge- or diamond-shaped bows with a small central hole which became popular towards the end of the 13th century and continued well into the 14th century. By the 14th century a key, although still forged, was becoming increasingly the object of good workmanship, and often keys from this period have complicated bits with comb edges.

During the late 13th century and early 14th century, locks were being richly worked. A typical rim lock of the period would have a front plate decorated with scrollwork, leaves and animal heads, fleurs-de-lis and so on. As it was often difficult to find a keyhole in bad lighting conditions, a metal shield was fixed to the lock to guide a key into the keyhole. This became an increasingly important feature, particularly in German and Flemish locks, the shields being highly ornamented and often ending in leaf decoration. Of the animals the eagle, the cock's head and the dog appear most frequently. Most German locks of this and other centuries had a dog as the escutcheon representing Garm, the dog of German legend who guarded the entrance to the underworld. During the 13th century great use was made of incised lines, twisted and notched mouldings.

This trend, with only minor alterations to detail, continued into the 14th century, but the 15th century brought some fairly radical changes. Metal-working techniques changed, the forge and hammer making way for the file and saw. Gothic art and architecture was entering its last and most elaborate period, giving the blacksmith, or rather, by now, the locksmith, every chance to exploit his new techniques and exercise his artistic inventiveness.

In lockmaking the 15th century undoubtedly belongs to the French locksmith. J. Starkie Gardner comments: "In smaller objects, such as locks and knockers, an even greater degree of refinement and delicacy is reached, which is hardly surpassed by the contemporary work in gold and silver." These locks were usually square or oblong, covered with rich tracery, canopies, figures and coats of arms. Although similar Gothic decoration is found in German locks towards the end of the century it rarely occurs in England, for the English smiths were slow to experiment with the new ways of working and, disturbed as they were by civil war, they lagged behind where before they had led.

During the late 14th century and the 15th century German and French locksmiths favoured the circular key bows, which they decorated with tracery in keeping with the architecture of the period. In France these bows were pierced in imitation of the Gothic rose window, hence the popular tag of 'rose window' keys. The English locksmith still lagged behind, although there are signs in the late 15th century of his developing the bow into a trefoil shape. This graceful trefoil bow and moulded stem became typical of English keys in the 16th century.

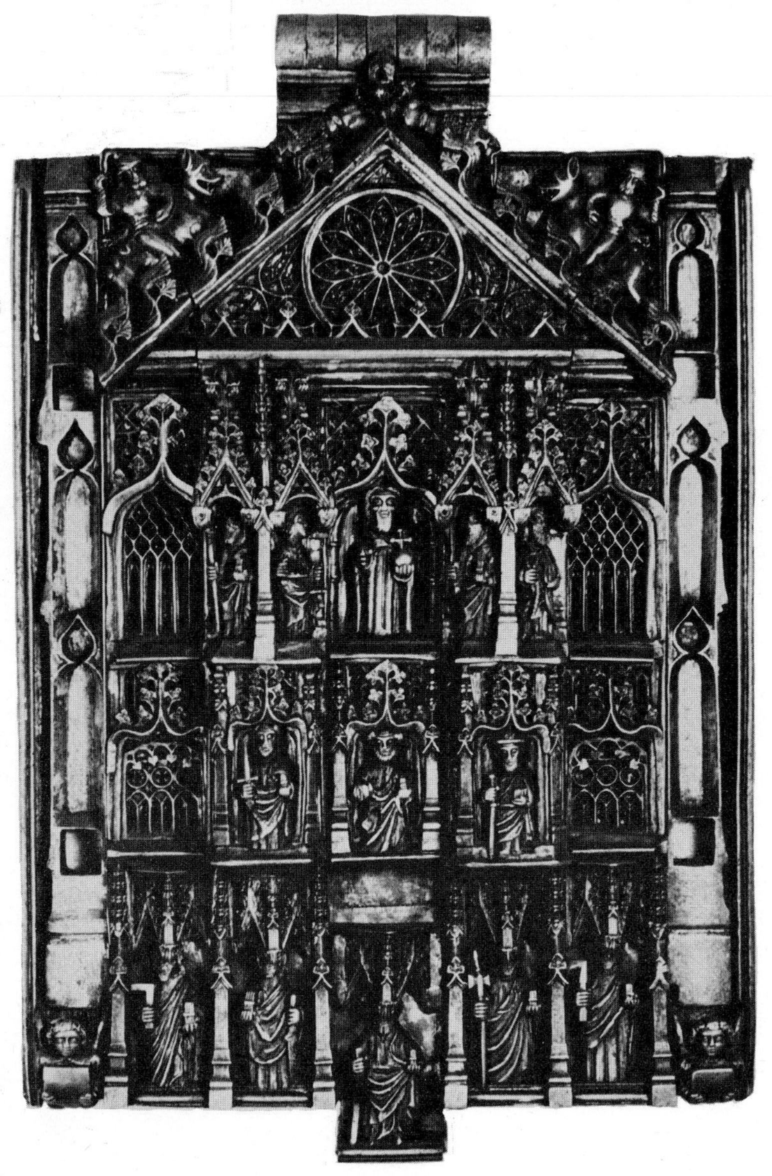

10. Chest lock, 15th century; French
– 'Architectural' lock showing Christ and the twelve apostles
iron
Musée de Cluny, Paris

11. Chest lock, 15th century; French
– detail shows apostles and saints with a central figure of Christ (or St John the Baptist)
iron
Musée de Cluny, Paris

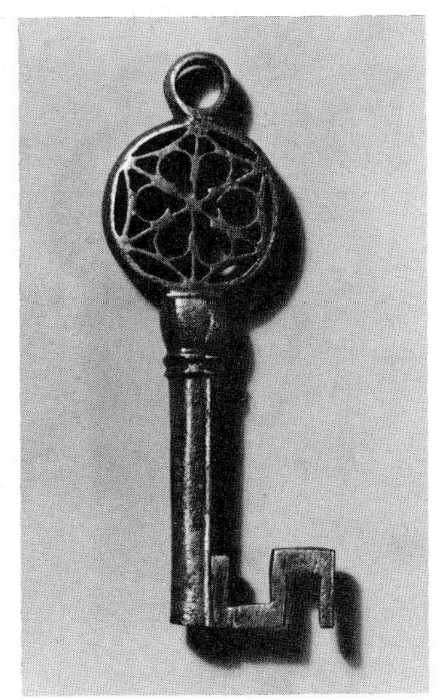

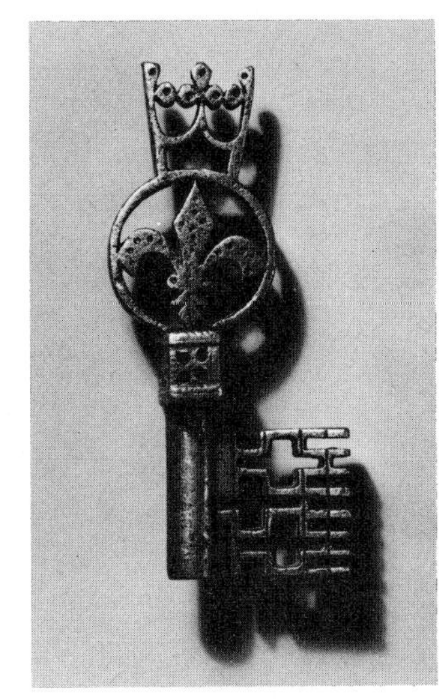

12. Development of *chef-d'œuvre* keys: (left to right) (*a*) 15th-century 'rose window' keys; (*b*) 16th-century 'rose window' key with flat turret; (*c*) 16th-century key – cushion, 'rose window' and squared turret; (*d*) another version of (*c*); (*e*) 17th-century key, the traditional shape remains but its execution reflects the period
(*a*) and (*b*) The Pitt-Rivers Museum, Oxford, (*c*), (*d*) and (*e*) The Victoria and Albert Museum

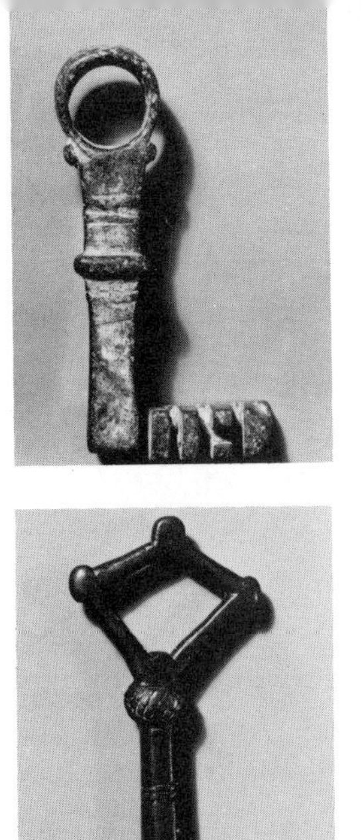

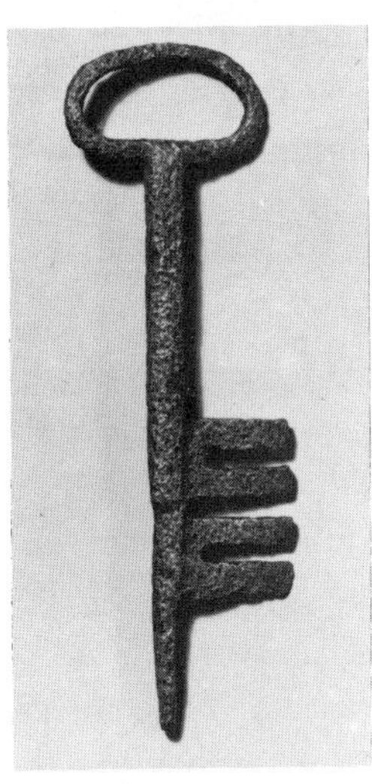

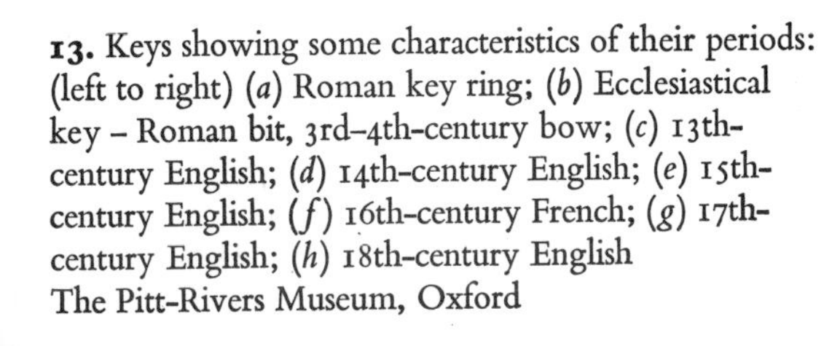

13. Keys showing some characteristics of their periods: (left to right) (*a*) Roman key ring; (*b*) Ecclesiastical key – Roman bit, 3rd–4th-century bow; (*c*) 13th-century English; (*d*) 14th-century English; (*e*) 15th-century English; (*f*) 16th-century French; (*g*) 17th-century English; (*h*) 18th-century English
The Pitt-Rivers Museum, Oxford

Colour Plate. The Aubin Lock Trophy
height 36 in. (91·5 cm.)
Courtesy Chubb & Son's Lock and Safe Co. Ltd, London

During the early 16th century, German locksmiths played down Gothic tracery in favour of a thistle pattern, so much so that the flowers, buds and leaves of the holy milk thistle will be found decorating the majority of German locks of the period. The sudden introduction of the classical style into France found French locksmiths unwilling to abandon their Gothic designs, although these had reached a perfection which could only remain stationary and so degenerate. But, in time, the solid chiselled work had to be abandoned, and lockcases made in thin repoussé iron and decorated with arabesques in the Italian fashion began to appear. Later French individuality asserted itself and lock fronts were made from sheet iron, beaten in relief and shaped to represent Corinthian porticos with garlands, caryatides, draped figures, combats, royal arms, cyphers and badges.

Towards the end of the 16th century, French locksmiths produced large numbers of keys in Renaissance style, with bows in the form of sphinxes or winged chimeras, back to back, together with masks and scrolls. Often these keys are surmounted by a ring so that the key could be suspended round the neck or from a girdle (the most famous keys of the time, such as the Strozzi key, were given by Henri III to his favourites and were worn hanging from their belts). The keys show an inventiveness of bow design that is amazing but they also have other identifiable features. The stem or pipe of the key is not only circular but angular, polygonal or trefoil in section, and the bit has a broad flat flange.

The key operating the *chef d'œuvre* locks made by apprentices in France when they finished their time followed a traditional pattern from the 15th to the 18th centuries. The key is a rose window key surmounted by a four-, six- or eight-sided turret, making this particular group easily recognizable.

Ornament in the 17th century broadly follows the 16th century, although the work is chiselled from the solid, or pierced and engraved and polished. The engraving on the lockcase and keyplate suited the location. In a palace the decoration would be royal coats of arms, in the Queen's apartments scenes from mythology, and on sea chests Neptune and mermaids! During this century two interesting movements took place. Firstly there was a move towards mortice locks which was countered by the end of the century, and secondly there was the lock *à la moderne*. This was a 17th-century, and later 18th-century, version of Gothic complete with tracery, canopies and so on. The locksmith carried his craftsmanship to the limits, decorating not only the outside of the lock but the inside as well.

On his return from exile in France, Charles II encouraged English locksmiths to produce work in the French manner. The art of the smith in England had declined during the late Middle Ages, forcing Henry VIII to invite German smiths to settle in Southwark, but under the influence of the Restoration they began to produce work in pierced and gilt brass which, by the end of the 17th century, had put them back in a position of pre-eminence.

The discovery of *fonte malléable*, the technique of making malleable metal castings, is the outstanding event of the 18th century in lockmaking on the artistic side. Discovered by Réaumur, who wrote about it in 1722, it allowed many beautiful locks to be made with bas-reliefs of Cupid and other mythological characters.

The end of the 17th century saw English keys, with flat bows of finely worked wrought iron ornamented with pierced scrolls and interlaced monograms, coveted and copied all over Europe. The bit is elaborate with many fine ward cuts but these keys became so popular they were copied extensively and the designs became sterile before declining completely. The late 18th century and the early 19th century saw a return to the unornamented elliptical bow, best seen in the early locks

14. Rim lock, 18th century; French
– repoussé brass case with a design after Watteau
$3\frac{1}{2} \times 7\frac{5}{8}$ in. (9×19·5 cm.)
Musée des Arts Décoratifs, Paris

produced by Bramah and Chubb. However, the tradition of ceremonial keys persisted into Victorian times when they were made for important occasions.

The spread of wealth is due to the growth of industry, but, unfortunately, industrialization has other effects. The concentration of population often in overcrowded conditions, the concentration of unemployed, a decline in values amongst those who have been uprooted and now live in strange surroundings and an increasing mechanical awareness – all these are factors which breed crime. Crime figures rose rapidly in Europe and America during the early decades of the Industrial Revolution just as they are rising in West Africa today. All the inventors of important security lock mechanisms (Barron, Bramah, Chubb, A. C. Hobbs and Yale) worked during the early years of the Industrial Revolution in their own countries.

In 1778 Robert Barron patented a lock which was the first major improvement in lock security for approximately a thousand years and set the trend in which security has become the dominant factor in lock design. This is not meant to imply that the 19th- and 20th-century locksmith lacks skill, rather that his skill is concentrated inside the lock to make it more secure. The Aubin Lock Trophy made in 1851 is a *tour de force* of skill and ingenuity as it traces the development of the lock over two thousand years in a trophy measuring thirty inches high. Aubin was a Wolverhampton locksmith who at the time the trophy was made worked by himself, making and repairing locks. A few attempts were made at reviving exterior decoration during the years of the Gothic Revival, some locks with embellished cases being exhibited at the Great Exhibition of 1851. The locks at Neuschwanstein must also be mentioned in this context. The 20th century seems to be achieving a balance between security and appearance by producing lockcases of simple, classic design, attractive elegant door furniture and tasteful keys.

In 1784 Joseph Bramah patented a lock which was, at that time, unorthodox, but nevertheless brilliant in conception and worthy of the inventor of so many important engineering developments. In the Bramah system the key is a hollow one – a pipe key – the end of which is provided with grooves of varying depth. These grooves are shaped to coincide with a set of corresponding spring-loaded sliders in the body of the lock. In their turn these sliders have a series of notches cut in various positions. One part of the slider is recessed in the mechanism whilst the other part rests in a fixed ring with indentations, so obstructing the movable parts of the mechanism. The insertion of the key adjusts the notches in the sliders to coincide with the slots in the fixed ring, allowing the action to release the mechanism and operate the lock. Various modifications and improvements have been made to this type of lock and it is still widely used in many countries.

In 1778 Robert Barron took out an English patent for a lock which derived its security not from wards but from spring tumblers which had to be raised to a common height by a key in order to move the bolt of the lock backwards and forwards. In 1818 Jeremiah Chubb patented his detector lock. In this lock there were a set of levers all different, which had to be raised to a common height by the insertion of the correct key before the bolt of the lock could move backwards and forwards. The insertion of the wrong key would overlift one of these levers and so set off a small mechanism known as a detector. The lock once 'detected' would be jammed and no further picking possible. The right key itself would not operate the lock, thus informing the owner of intrusion. The insertion of a setting key would re-set the lock so that it would operate normally. Later this was developed so that the correct key could re-set the lock. Vincent Eras in his book says: "Of all the patented lock constructions Chubb lever design was by far the

15. Front or face plate of chest lock, late 15th century; German
– note the typical dogs' heads, holy milk thistle motif, metal and lead-in to keyhole, shaped keyhole iron
Musée de Cluny, Paris

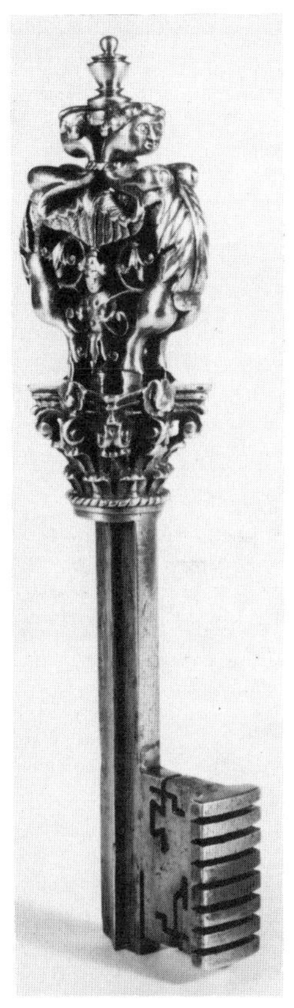

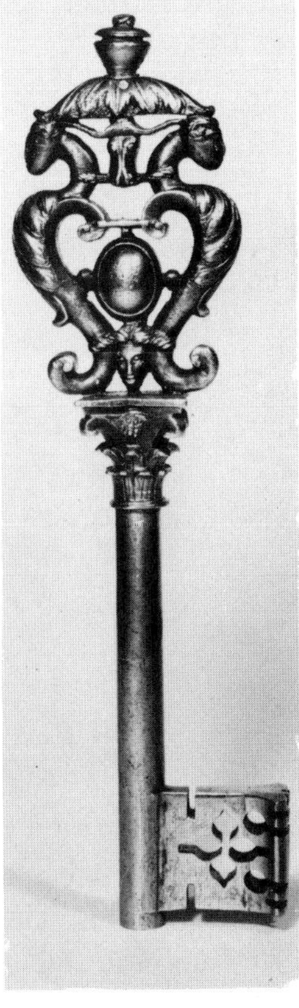

16. (left) 17th-century key with ornamental bow to fit the lock in illustration 7; French
height 5¾ in. (14·6 cm.)
(right) 17th-century key; French
height 5½ in. (13·9 cm.)
The Victoria and Albert Museum, London

17. Keys indicative of position – Chamberlain's Keys
(left) Key bearing the arms of the 1st Baron of Somerton, 18th century
gilt height 4⅝ in. (11·7 cm.)
(right) Key bearing the cypher of William III, 18th century
gilt height 5½ in. (13·9 cm.)
The Victoria and Albert Museum, London

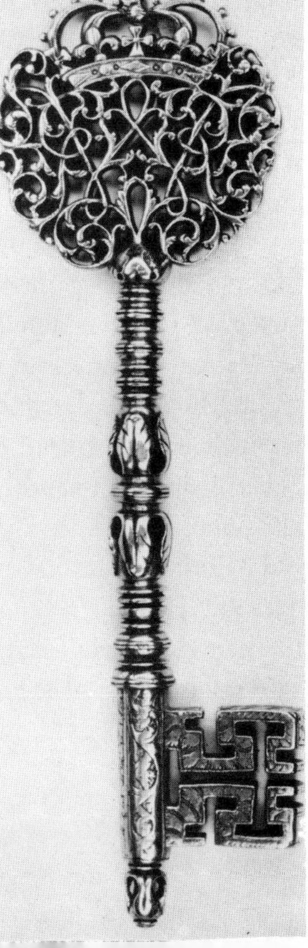

most efficient and successful so that in later years its principles have been sustained in all better class lever locks not only in England but throughout the world."

In the middle of the 19th century a famous American locksmith, Linus Yale Snr, designed a lock whose basic principle was similar to that of the Egyptian lock, although by adopting this principle he was, in fact, developing a mechanism completely different from the other mechanisms of the time. His son, Linus Yale Jnr, developed his father's ideas further and produced the pin tumbler cylinder lock which is so popular today. In a pin tumbler cylinder lock there are a series of pins and drivers which extend vertically through the cylinder and into an inner plug. Only the correct key raises the pins and drivers so that the breaks between them are lined up with the joint between the cylinder and its plug. When precisely set in this way the key can rotate the plug, activating a bolt or latch. A minute variation from the proper height of any pin prevents the key from being turned.

In Beaumont and Fletcher's play "The Noble Gentleman", written in 1615, there is a line "with a strange lock that opens on A.M.E.N." Locks operating on either letter or figure combinations have been known since the 16th century, and their invention is generally attributed to the French locksmith Cardem. His lock had a serious drawback – the combination could not be changed – but this was remedied by M. Regnier, Director of the Musée d'Artillerie in Paris. M. Regnier's lock worked on the same principle as the combination locks of today. Space does not permit a full description of keyless combination locks, which first appeared in America in the late 1850's, or time locks, invented in 1873, both of which are used extensively for securing safes and vaults. As a rule keyless combination locks have either 1,000,000 or 100,000,000 changes of code, which is not pre-set by the manufacturer and so can be altered at will.

The time lock is a clockwork mechanism, fitted inside a safe or vault door, which is pre-set by the owner to go off at a determined time in the future. The amount of time to elapse between the safe being closed and opened again is calculated and set (this can be up to a hundred and twenty hours). As soon as the lock is put on guard and the bolts of the safe or door drawn, not even the correct keys or codes will open the safe or vault until the lock has run its time and come off guard.

The lockmaker faces two difficult problems, for if a lock is to be effective it must be secure. It is easy to make a safe or chest that is so secure nobody can get in, but a totally different thing to make a chest secure against everybody except one person, the rightful owner. Equally, to make a thousand watches or a thousand cars is a matter of production because they are all the same; to make a thousand locks when each has to be different from the other is not just a matter of production but a production problem. The security of a lock was frequently ignored by locksmiths before the 19th century, so much so that in his book the famous Dutch expert Vincent Eras said: "It was the smith's strong leaning towards artistic design that proved detrimental to the security and practical size and shape of the products."

The Industrial Revolution brought with it the production line and, whilst lock manufacture did not become entirely mechanized (indeed, even today some kinds of specialist locks are still made by hand) locks lost their individuality. Utility pushed art to one side. A locksmith was expected to produce a number of locks each day, instead of creating each individual lock, as had been done since the Dark Ages. However, a consideration of the special ceremonial keys made both in the 19th and the 20th century shows that although the locksmith's ability has been curtailed by the machine and his inventiveness stifled by the demands of mass production, his skill and craft was and is by no means dead.

Bohemian Glass

LILLI GABOR

Bohemia – and Czechoslovakia of which it now forms a part – has a remarkable reputation for the excellence of its glass; indeed it has survived for some five centuries. As long ago as 1458, Pope Pius II said in his "History of Bohemia" that nowhere in Europe could there be seen "such beautiful and lofty windows, not only in towns, but even in the country". Fascinating as the early history of Bohemian glass may be, it is too well known to need repetition here. It would, however, be impossible to do justice to any account of Bohemian glass without some reference to its historical development. For the manner in which the Bohemians overcame obstacles and setbacks when their industry was threatened is not only a tribute to their national character but also to their imagination and ingenuity. It enabled them to turn apparent defeats into brilliant victories, and what is more important provides the characteristic aesthetic qualities by which Bohemian glass has come to be recognized. At its best, and even at its worst, there is always a robust, colourful character about it and an instinctive appreciation for the potentiality of the material.

In the period from the 16th century to the beginning of the 17th century, which was a decisive one in the development of European glass-making, Venetian glass was the most advanced. It influenced all European countries, including England, France, the Netherlands, Scandinavia and to some extent Germany.

Bohemia, however, followed its own rather more difficult line of development; this was largely determined by its geographical location. The glass was made according to the potash-lime formula. This was the obvious result of having readily available local raw materials: excellent quartz, good-quality limestone, abundant and cheap timber for the heating of the furnaces and the production of the ash. The combination of rich natural resources and an ever-increasing demand for glassware stimulated an intensive progress not only in the production but also in decorative techniques. In consequence a profound knowledge was gained of the material and its possibilities and this knowledge in turn gave rise to certain stylistic preferences.

From the 16th to the late 17th century Venice commanded the market for glass in Europe; its high-quality clear glass was in great demand, so much so that Venetians or Italians set up glass-houses in many European countries, including Bohemia. To satisfy the desire of the Bohemian nobility and rich burghers for the Venetian type of glassware, native glass-makers did their best to imitate the decorative techniques of enamelling, cold painting, diamond-point engraving and gilding, but with a more robust local flavour. (Ill. 1.)

1. Square Bohemian flask dated 1697
height 6½ in. (16·5 cm.)
Courtesy Sotheby & Co., London

However, in spite of their skill in imitating the Venetians, the Bohemians were forced to accept the limitations of the hard potash-lime glass-metal, which was the only kind readily available. Attempts to import the soda, indispensable for the

Colour Plate. Blue flash overlay vase and cover with enamel and gilding
height 14 in. (35·5 cm.)
Courtesy Sotheby & Co., London

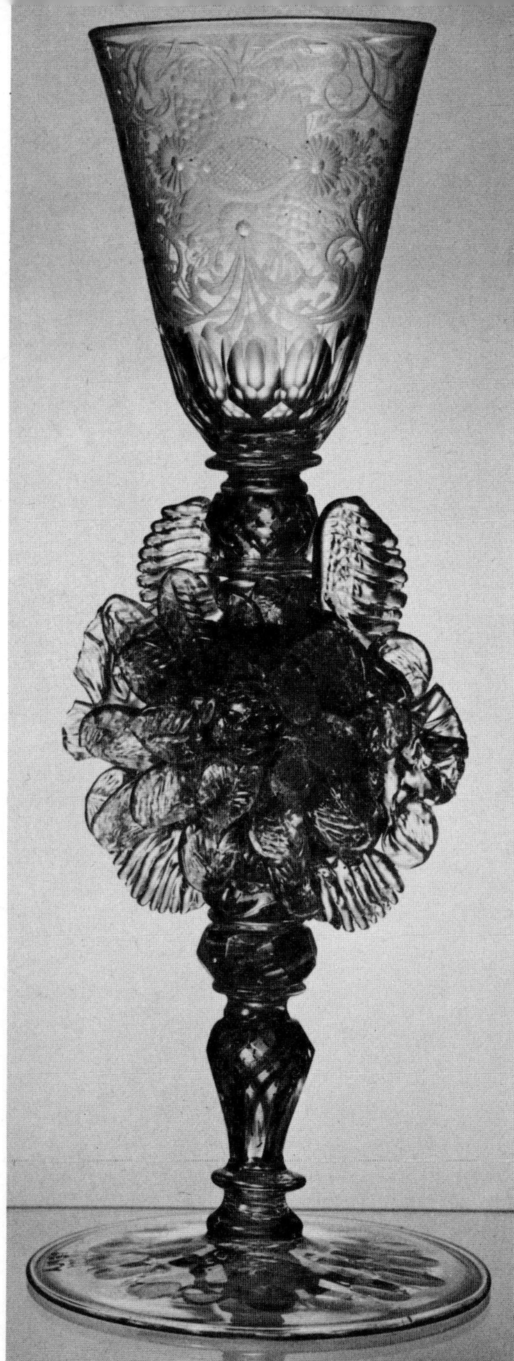

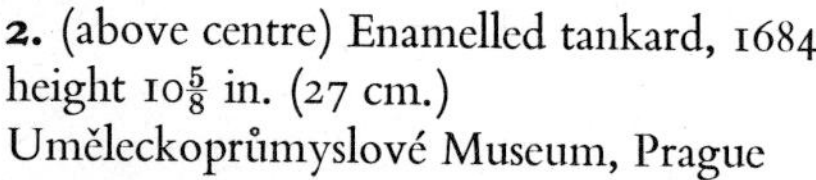
2. (above centre) Enamelled tankard, 1684
height $10\frac{5}{8}$ in. (27 cm.)
Uměleckoprůmyslové Museum, Prague

3. (above left) Goblet in Venetian style with engraved decoration, 2nd half of the 17th century
height $11\frac{3}{8}$ in. (29 cm.)
Uměleckoprůmyslové Museum, Prague

4. (above right) Beaker engraved by Caspar Lehman, 1605
height $8\frac{7}{8}$ in. (22·5 cm.)
Uměleckoprůmyslové Museum, Prague

5. (right) Engraved goblet, *circa* 1700
height $7\frac{3}{4}$ in. (19·6 cm.)
Courtesy Sotheby & Co., London

6. (far right) Goblet engraved with a portrait of Leopold I, *circa* 1700
height 8 in. (20·5 cm.)
Uměleckoprůmyslové Museum, Prague

7. Carved goblet in relief, early 18th century
height 10⅝ in. (27 cm.)
Uměleckoprůmyslové Museum, Prague

8. Silesian engraved jug, *circa* 1730
height 9½ in. (24 cm.)
Uměleckoprůmyslové Museum, Prague

manufacture of the Venetian metal, had naturally been frustrated by the Venetians; the organization of supplies from remote alternative sources was ultimately accepted as uneconomic. The indigenous basic material was not genuinely suited to the decorative styles and motifs of the Venetians, but by emphasizing the gold and enamel ornamentation the imperfections of the glass itself became relatively insignificant. A charming example of this is the enamelled tankard portraying the Virgin and Child, painted in white enamel. (Ill. 2.)

Undoubtedly the challenge from the Venetians had stimulated the Bohemians in their determination to excel at glass-making, even though their imitations were often as good as the original model. (Ill. 3.) At best the copying was a temporary solution and a new type of glass was indispensable if Bohemia was to oust the Venetians from their position as the best glass-makers in Europe, even if only in the eyes of their compatriots.

The new type of potash-lime glass which had been discovered in the 17th century was particularly suitable for making thick-walled vessels. The full exploitation of the decorative possibilities of this type of glass initiated a new and successful phase in Bohemian glass-making – it became epitomized as Bohemian crystal and was characterized by its deep engraving. The art of intaglio engraving began to flourish in the glass-making areas of Bohemia; it was consolidated by the formation of groups of glass-engravers and painters who united in guilds. They were mainly centred around Chřibská and its environs in North Bohemia.

Bohemian glass-engravers had been extremely fortunate in having as their exemplar Caspar Lehman. As early as the beginning of the 17th century Lehman, who had been gem-cutter to the court of the Emperor Rudolf, had adapted his technique to engraving glass. He had founded an engravers' school, and even though many of his pupils were subsequently forced to emigrate, the tradition and art was not lost to Bohemia. (Ill. 4.) Initially the engraving was shallow, depicting mainly stylized flower and plant motifs; later decorations were naturalistic floral and plant forms combined with birds and formalized human figures reminiscent of folk-art. (Ill. 5.) In the example illustrated, the round funnel bowl, finely engraved in a free style with two birds amongst fruiting foliage, above two engraved bands, is supported on a multi-knopped stem terminating in an upturned folded conical foot.

By the end of the 17th century the engraving was of such a high order that it could be said that glassware was the foremost expression of the Bohemian baroque style. The engraved goblet (with ruby and avanturine threads) of a portrait of Leopold I is typical of the period. (Ill. 6.) Fortunately Bohemian glass-makers were more than capable of fulfilling the contemporary desire for ostentation which characterized the taste of the late 17th and early 18th century. With its brilliant optical effects, resulting from a hitherto unachieved purity of material and superb engraving, Bohemian glass supplied exactly what was wanted. By the beginning of the 18th century it took over the leadership in glassware that Venice had enjoyed for so long. The quality of the engraving was seen to great advantage on the polygonal surfaces of decanters, crystal barrels, goblets, vases and the like. The variety and profusion of design was prodigious. The covered goblet engraved in relief shows in a cartouche a fir tree with the inscription "Aucun temps ne le change" (Ill. 7); its engraving is of such complexity that one marvels at the glass withstanding the work on it. The second is an engraved jug, with trade emblems and the inscription "Vivat Negotiae", far simpler in conception, relying more on its faceting and simplicity of design. (Ill. 8.)

Engraving was not by any means the only type of decorative technique used at

9. Double-walled goblet with gold leaf engraving, after an engraving by E. Ridinger, *circa* 1740
height 9 in. (23 cm.)
Uměleckoprůmyslové Museum, Prague

10. Bottles and a goblet with enamel decoration by Ignatius Preissler, 1725–30
height of bottle 6¼ in. (15·9 cm.), height of goblet 9¼ in. (23·5 cm.)
Uměleckoprůmyslové Museum, Prague

11. Plaque by Dominik Biman, 1834
diameter 3¾ in. (9·5 cm.)
Courtesy Sotheby & Co., London

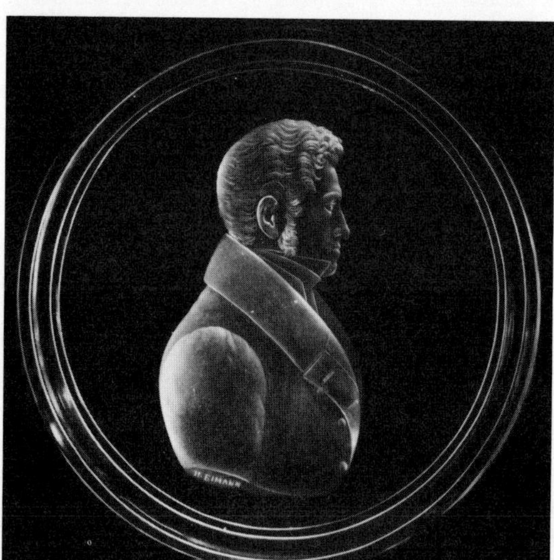

that time. Although more rare and therefore more highly prized there were the double-walled (*zwischen gold-glas*) goblets and glasses. This was an invention of *circa* 1725; it consisted of a double-walled glass vessel enclosing etched gold or silverfoil, the glass itself was frequently stained in transparent colours and engraved. The decorative themes were usually hunting scenes, coats of arms and motifs consistent with the lives and interests of those who could afford these rarities. The goblet with an equestrian theme engraved on gold leaf is an excellent example of this technique. (Ill. 9.) Gilding and enamelling were still extremely popular forms of decoration; a covered beaker, with faceted sides decorated with gilding, of an anniversary ceremony below an inscription was sold at Sotheby's in October 1965.

Among the craftsmen who contributed to the success of 18th-century Bohemian glass was Ignatius Preissler, whose paintings on glass were much sought after. The bottles and goblet with their chinoiserie decoration in black (*schwarzlot*) are typical of his work. (Ill. 10.)

Less exotic in character was the opaque white glass, often decorated with rustic scenes; it was made in cups and saucers, beakers, bowls and similar household objects, large numbers of which were sold.

By the end of the 18th century Bohemian glass was being exported all over the world. The number of glass-works and studios of artist-craftsmen had increased tremendously. The better known glass-makers in the north of Bohemia included Preissler, Kittel and Riedl; in the south there were Gerl, Müller and Hofbraedl. The most prominent of the aristocratic families who had entered into this now profitable business were the Counts Harrach and Buquoy at Nový Svět and Nový Hrady respectively. But at this point when the Bohemian glass industry was apparently set for continuing prosperity appeared a hitherto unsuspected rival.

The competitor was England; with her invention of cut lead glass she represented a powerful menace to the Bohemian glass industry. The flawlessness of English lead glass as well as its grace and simplicity of form was going to be difficult to match, let alone surpass. Bohemian glass-makers were faced with two alternatives: either to produce glassware which was equal in both quality and design to the English variety, or to invent something original and individual in harmony with their own artistic traditions.

At first an attempt was made to copy the English; the results though interesting were not successful in the same way. Bohemian cut crystal often successfully imitated English glass, particularly that produced at the glass-works of Meyer at Stříbna Hut in the Nový Hrady area, but the brilliance and luminosity were not comparable. Nevertheless by combining prismatic cutting with wheel- or diamond-point engraving a typically Bohemian article was produced.

The decorated glass of this period was marked by an interesting evolution of two simultaneous tendencies – one towards classical antiquity and the other towards a gross sentimentality. They were the stylistic precursors of the Biedermeier and the Empire periods of décor, but despite their arguable lapses into vulgarity, they had a vivacity and charm that was peculiarly Bohemian. The motifs varied from symbolic emblems of Love and similar virtues, to bouquets of flowers, landscapes, animals, religious and mythological subjects, and above all idealized portrait busts.

Many workshops were set up for the production of this sort of glass. They were often directed by famous artists, of whom the best known was Dominik Biman (1800–57). Forsaking his atelier in Prague he would spend the summer season in Marienbad, where he executed several portraits of distinguished visitors. These

12. Hyalith glass with gilt decoration, 1820–30; Buquoy glassworks. Cup height 4⅜ in. (11 cm.) Uměleckoprůmyslové Museum, Prague

13. Lithyalin bottle by Frederick Egerman height 4⅜ in. (11 cm.) The Victoria and Albert Museum, London

14. Beaker with an engraving of a horse, *circa* 1830, probably by Karl Pfohl: height 5⅛ in. (13 cm.) Uměleckoprůmyslové Museum, Prague

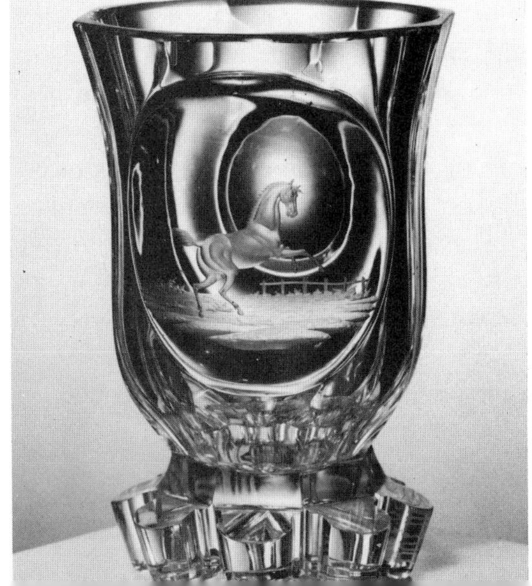

engraved portraits either on glass medallions or on ornamental vessel glass were among the best examples of 19th-century engraved Bohemian glass. (Ill. 11.) Other noteworthy portrait engravers were the Teller family, the Pfeiffer brothers, August Böhm and Anton Simm. But in spite of the skill and taste of these artists it was the coloured glass of Bohemia which was to renew its world reputation in the 19th century.

With the end of the Napoleonic wars and the increasing prosperity of the commercial and industrial *bourgeoisie*, a feeling for obvious luxury in design began to emerge. In response to this, Bohemian glass-makers, in consultation with chemical experts, began to create new varieties of glass which could satisfy the demands for novelty, in quantity as well as quality.

As early as 1820 Count George Buquoy had started to produce 'hyalith' glass; this was a jet-black glass, sometimes with fired gold chinoiserie decoration. Its composition was a closely guarded secret, but there would seem to be little doubt that the inspiration for hyalith came from Wedgwood's 'black-basalt' ware. It was a thin and fragile material, more reminiscent of quartz than of glass and mostly used for flagons, vases and above all cups and saucers. The black opaque body-colour creates a somewhat bizarre effect, and though it may not satisfy the criteria of the purist it affords a similar sort of pleasure to that provided by the contemplation of a *trompe-l'œil* painting. The pieces shown at the Victoria and Albert Museum in 1965 are splendid examples of their kind. (Ill. 12.) The peak period of hyalith production was *circa* 1835 when the passion for chinoiserie was at its height; an interesting example was sold in London recently. Its description in the catalogue gives a very good picture of the complexity of the decoration as well as contemporary taste.

> "A hyalith chinoiserie teapoy and cover of Japanese shape, with baluster body and domed foot, decorated in two-toned gold with a Chinese figure, flowering shrubs and a butterfly, the body in dense opaque-black glass and fitted in a wooden container with openwork sides and steel lock, the top with a circular medallion in blue monochrome, with a town in the background, in a style associated with Balthazar Wigand, inscribed below 'Spinnerin am Krauz'."

Some three years later Frederick Egerman (1777–1864), a distinguished and prolific inventor of glass techniques, also produced a black glass with even greater similarity to Wedgwood's black basalt. In *circa* 1820 Egerman had invented a method of producing a yellow and gold tint which gave his glass the appearance of topaz. Egerman was particularly aware of the prevailing fashion for decorating objects to look as if they were made from rare and expensive materials, while at the same time being cheap enough for a large middle-class market. His glassware, particularly with this golden-yellow stain, said to have been achieved by the addition of silver in manufacture, was immensely popular. But his most striking invention was 'lithyalin', an imitation of the colour and texture of semi-precious stones. This material could be made to resemble veined agates (Ill. 13), jaspers, etc. In harmony with the character of the glass the forms of the vases, flagons, tazzas and beakers were generally of a classic severity; with their faceted, polished sides and bold embossed ornament they recall the artifacts of ancient Greece. Unfortunately the great popularity of Egerman's finest lithyalin led to a series of imitations of a mass-produced variety, largely banal in taste and of dubious quality. Undoubtedly, Egerman's most important contribution, economically, to the Bohemian glass industry was his invention of the process whereby inexpensive imitations of gold ruby-glass were produced by replacing the gold originally used

15. Red flash engraved goblet
height $11\frac{1}{4}$ in. (28·5 cm.)
Courtesy Sotheby & Co., London

in its manufacture by copper. Until then gold ruby-glass had been rare and expensive; its relative cheapness and its obvious attraction, especially for the *nouveau riche*, encouraged production in all the important glass-works of Bohemia.

In addition to the ruby-glass there were also the cobalt, turquoise, chrysoprase and uranium coloured glasses and furthermore the new techniques of colouring allowed the glass to retain its transparency. Thus exploiting their technical and artistic abilities to the utmost, the Bohemians made a determined assault on the world market, which had been largely captured by the English in the first half of the 19th century. To this end they used their best craftsmen to engrave, cut, gild and paint their glass.

One of the most famous exponents of carved flashed glass was Karl Pfohl, who specialized in carving animals. (Ill. 14.) He was one of a group of artist-craftsmen at Kamenický Senov.

A fine example of engraved glass is the red flash goblet with cylindrical bowl, wheel-engraved with deer in a forest, supported on a faceted stem terminating in a pastry-mould foot. (Ill. 15.) The 'drawing' of the deer shows remarkable observation, in particular the foreshortened animal on the right; and the execution of the whole object is a masterpiece of virtuosity. Because of its widespread popularity ruby-glass of the 19th century can still be seen relatively frequently.

16. Pair of red overlay vases
height $10\frac{1}{4}$ in. (26 cm.)
Courtesy Sotheby & Co., London

Uranium glass, which was an invention attributed to Josef Riedel of Polubný in the Riesengebirge district, is, however, more rare. It is one of the most attractive coloured glasses of the period, its opalescent yellow or green named by Riedel for his wife: 'Anna-gelb' (Anna-yellow) and 'Anna-grün' (Anna-green).

Still more exotic than either the ruby, the uranium, or the hyalith was the overlay glass; this was said to have originated in China, but until 1841 only the glass-works at Josefinen knew the formula for its manufacture. It consisted of a core of crystal glass, in one or more layers of coloured transparent or opaque glass; the subsequent multi-layered blanks were then deeply cut in a variety of designs, revealing the lower layers and resulting in arresting ornamental designs. Among the more popular types of overlay glassware was opaque white overlay, often on a ruby or rosalin base, the top layer being cut away and the remaining surface decorated with painted and fired floral ornament. In the example illustrated the red overlay vase with cup-shaped bowl and crenellated rim is supported on a knopped spreading stem and circular foot. It is decorated in white overlay and enriched with gilding. (Ill. 16.) A more unusual example is the blue flash overlay vase and cover. (See colour plate facing p. 80.)

17. Landscape beaker, school of Samuel Mohn
height $5\frac{1}{4}$ in. (13·3 cm.)
Courtesy Sotheby & Co., London

Also fashionable in the 19th century were the enamelled glasses of the schools of Samuel Mohn and Anton Kothgasser of Vienna. (Ill. 17.) This example of the Mohn school was recently seen at Sotheby's; it shows two couples picnicking with a red-coated servant to one side, among trees, below a continuous band of green leaves, the base bearing the gilded inscription "Der Kuhstall in der Sächos Schweiz". Similar in technique are the two beakers with slightly flared sides, painted with seated girls and animals in landscapes, contained in yellow flash borders and gilt rims. (Ill. 18.)

The *Ranftbecher* painted by Anton Kothgasser are excellent specimens of his work. (Ill. 19.) This is a cylindrical beaker painted with a romantic mountain landscape with the inscription: "Brühlweg durch den Klausentahl". The second (Ill. 20) is decorated round the top with a border of birds, growing plants, an urn and an obelisk. The heavy foot is cut with diamond pattern as is the yellow-stained band just above it.

In the second half of the 19th century the introduction of mass production

18. Two beakers with painted figures and yellow flash borders: height 5¾ in. (14·6 cm.)
Courtesy Sotheby & Co., London

19. Glass beaker painted in transparent enamel colours by Anton Kothgasser, *circa* 1812
height 3⅞ in. (9·8 cm.)
The Victoria and Albert Museum, London

20. Beaker by Anton Kothgasser, *circa* 1820
height 4¼ in. (10·7 cm.)
The Victoria and Albert Museum, London

21. Wheel-engraved jug, signed and dated
A. Wohlrab; Marienbad, 1887
height 11¼ in. (28·5 cm.)
Courtesy Sotheby & Co., London

caused a considerable deterioration in glass design, and the fact that it did not decline completely into commercial banality was primarily due to the efforts of Louis Lobmeyr.

Lobmeyr was a Viennese industrialist and glass designer, founder of a studio of glass design at Kamenický Senov in the north of Bohemia; another studio was established in 1870 with a group of artist-designers at Novy Bor. Among Lobmeyr's contemporaries who shared his enthusiasm for good design was Moser at Nový Dvory near Carlsbad, Loetz at Klášterský Mlýn, Meyers at Neffe glass-works and Kralik in Vimperk. As a result of their efforts, the reputation of Bohemian glass at the end of the 19th century was once again high in world esteem.

It is doubtful whether the superbly engraved jug (Ill. 21) could have been produced without the encouragement of Lobmeyr and his followers. This jug, signed and dated "A. Wohlrab Marienbad 1887", is not only impeccable in execution but shows a quality of ornamental design, rare at that time.

A revealing indication of the English opinion of Bohemian glass is contained in George Wallis's article in the "Art Journal Illustrated Catalogue of the Great Universal Exhibition in Paris 1867". Wallis, the curator of the South Kensington Museum, wrote of the Bohemian glass exhibits, that

> "The decoration in gold of the specimens are superb, alike chemically as in their artistic effects. The raised gold is especially successful and when combined with the lighter tints of colour, so as to avoid violent contrasts, is very charming; and this is the more decided when in connection with the dead or ground-glass effects. . . . In the best examples, the Bohemian glass has that quality which the French aim at; for the gilding and colour are applied in such a manner as not to contradict the material *of* which the object itself is made, or the purpose *for* which it is made. The green glass is superb in tone and quality of colour and the contrast with the gilding is fine and artistic in effect. . . ."

Of Lobmeyr's glass he wrote:

> "The crystal glass employed by this firm in the production of candelabra, chandeliers, lustres etc.; is fine and the designs to which the material has been adapted are the most perfect of their kind in the Exhibition, with a few exceptions among the British glass."

Apart from the more conventional types of glass the closing years of the 19th century saw the invention, among innumerable others, of iridescent glass, silvered glass, coralline, 'Rose-de-Bohème', pearl-satin and tortoiseshell. There seemed to be no limit to the ingenuity and skill of the Bohemian glass-maker of that period; in fact, allowing for periods of war and foreign occupation the tradition has continued until the present day.

BIBLIOGRAPHY

Art Journal Illustrated Catalogue. The Industry of All Nations Exhibition, 1851.
Art Journal Illustrated. The Universal Exhibition, Paris, 1867.
Corning Museum of Glass. *Journal of Glass Studies*.
Czechoslovak Glass Review, 1954.
Haynes, E. B. *Glass Through the Ages*, 1964 ed.
Hettes, K. *Glass in Czechoslovakia*, 1958.
Jirik, F. X. *Ceske Sklo*, 1934.
Pazaurek, G. *Gläser Der Empire Und Biedermeierzeit*, 1923.
Poché, E. *Le Verre de Bohème*, Cahier d'Histoire Mondial. Neuchâtel, 1959.
Revi, A. C. *19th Century Glass*, 1959.
Vavra, J. *5,000 Years of Glass Making*. Prague, 1954.

Art Nouveau Jewelry

GRAHAM HUGHES

The European visual arts were in a poor state in the 1880's: imitative, unoriginal, uninspired, turgid. Turmoil always follows complacency; Impressionism, Post-Impressionism, the Modern Movement in architecture and design, all these exploded the ponderous 19th-century dogma and substituted the passionate 20th-century instincts. But in between came art nouveau. It was often much disliked at the time, and cursed as a symbol of decadence, so much so that even today eminent British octogenarians will condemn the newest 1966 design with the contemptuous words 'Nouveau art'. The fashion started suddenly *circa* 1895 and finished with the First World War which substituted squares for curves, sharpness for sensuality.

For some historians today the style represents an irresponsible shrug of the aesthetic shoulder, for others a wild and degrading craze, for others a serious universal movement like Gothic or Baroque, which lasted so short a time, not because it was trivial but because of the speed of modern communications. It is too soon finally to judge, and it does not really matter. What is certain is that the imaginative power of these artists was quite astonishing: in applied art their products have fascinating variety, spontaneity and romantic abandon.

Only some countries were affected, and only some designers in these countries. The impact was terrific in its intensity, but limited in its scope. Art nouveau was suited to the boudoir, not to the factory bench, to hand-work for wealthy individual clients, not to mass production for utility. Many prototypes were made in fabric, wallpaper, glass or silver, but with the exception of the British firm Liberty, the intended quantity production did not usually take place: industry maintained its steady progress towards efficiency of form and function, and declined the exotic fantasy which some of the leading designers' models offered them. It was the old crafts, where most of the best work was still done by hand, like silver and jewelry, that could and did adapt themselves most radically, and it was the art which has the fewest rules of all, namely jewelry, that gave the style its most splendid monument.

Applied – hence the name – means art for a particular purpose. Thus chairs need to provide a minimum degree of comfort and stability and if they fail to do so, they become sculpture or decoration. Many art nouveau chairs are indeed extremely beautiful to look at, but those modern aesthetes who enthuse about them may have used them more to rest the eye than the back. The chairs are often too uncomfortable for general use. Again, houses cannot be generally bought if their style inevitably makes them extravagant. The buildings by which art nouveau is chiefly remembered were often erected for very wealthy and exceptional clients, like Guell who commissioned Gaudí in Barcelona, Stoclet with Hoffmann in Brussels,

1. Silver pendant with blister pearls and turquoise, perhaps *circa* 1905, by C. R. Ashbee; Chipping Campden
Alan Irvine Collection

or Solvey with Horta; experiments in catering for more normal demands, like Guimard's Castel Béranger in Paris, were not financial successes. It is often said that these brilliant works carried with them the seeds of their own decay, because the style was a last *fin de siècle* gasp, so elaborate at birth that it could not be further evolved: perhaps, however, there is an altogether simpler explanation. The cheapness of the machine-made straight line, in contrast to the expense of the individual hand-made curve, provided an irresistible economic pressure against art nouveau as a universal style, and in fact killed it.

But these considerations do not apply to precious jewelry: it is always hand-made anyway, because one cannot make unique objects by machine. One wants it to be personal and unlike anyone else's, because the main purpose of jewelry is to make the wearer feel different and better, to make her feel she really has a personality distinct from anyone else's. One expects it to be expensive because value is part – although not the main part – of the precious jewelry mystique. One does not need it particularly strong or straight because jewels are inherently flimsy and sensitive, responding to individual taste, not to practical engineering requirements. Art nouveau was the ideal style for jewelry as for nothing else, and indeed of all the decorative styles in the history of art, it was the one best suited to jewels: the vocabulary of ornament in classical times was too limited and impersonal for modern femininity, romanesque was too static, gothic too regular, baroque too massive, rococo too linear, cubism too geometrical. It is not surprising that art nouveau jewels, though no longer being made today, are in great demand by wearers as well as by collectors.

Strangely little has, however, yet been recorded on the subject. Henri Vever, himself one of the two or three leading Paris designers, provides the main original source with the third volume of his "Bijouterie française du XIXe siècle", published in 1908. Since then there is nothing till the Georg Jensen monographs after 1955, describing his Danish work and origins. The author's own "Modern Jewelry 1890–1964" gives much the biggest international coverage so far. The catalogue of the 1965 Brussels exhibition "Le bijou 1900" has useful French and Belgian details. The Darmstadt Museum's excellent Jugendstil catalogue includes a substantial group of smaller pieces. But the general books on art nouveau give very small prominence to jewels: the latest and most ambitious, by Robert Schmutzler, for instance, does not even mention either Mucha or Jensen, two of the most prolific designers, and credits Louis Comfort Tiffany with no jewels, though he himself probably thought his jewels as good as his glass, and both were famous. The truth is that art historians have a strange blindness to jewelry not only of this but of every period – it is too often by unknown artists, it is so portable that it is usually divorced from its original source, its price depends upon technical gemmological factors which are outside the aesthete's field, its style depends upon the whims of women, and most important its virtue is difficult to analyse rationally: one cannot catalogue fantasy on a miniature scale so easily as, for instance, the mathematical science of architecture.

But the main problem with jewelry is the nature of the trade itself: many transactions are kept secret to avoid either the tax gatherer or the third party to a love affair, and most jewellers have a personal relationship with their clients which requires great discretion. Women do not usually want to talk freely about their jewels – there is too much money and too big a security risk involved. As for lending to exhibitions, it is like lending part of one's own anatomy. Paradoxically, although its purpose is ostentation, this is the quiet art; and there are not many people today who remember exactly what jewels were like in 1914. One has to

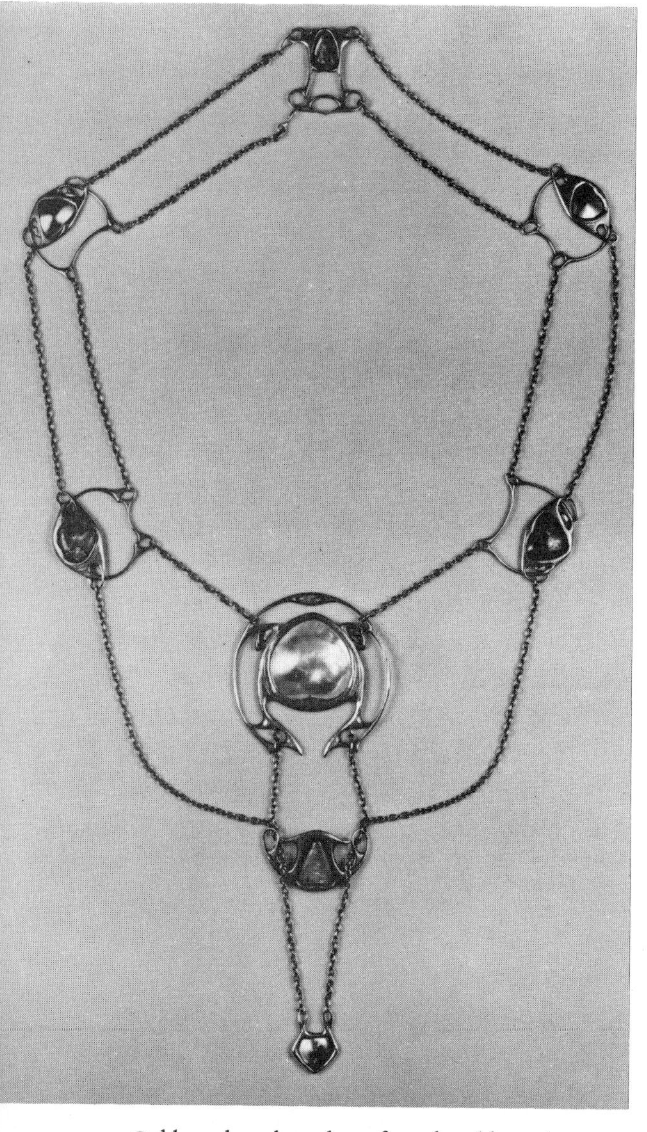

2. Gold, opals and mother-of-pearl necklace, *circa* 1903, by Arthur Lasenby Liberty; London
The Victoria and Albert Museum, London

judge from existing specimens, from the written exhibition records, dealing of course with special more than ordinary pieces, and from the books of those few firms who kept them. Alas, the present fairly common practice of photographing the finest new products or of preserving the meticulous, almost photographic original drawings, had not then started, and even if it had, it would have been of only limited use because clients' names are not usually related to the pieces. On the other hand, most jewels, unlike say pots or glass, are marked either with the designer's signature or, as in the case of British work, with the compulsory hallmark guaranteeing quality of metal.

Each country had its own particular style, often with a national name. The whole movement was so short-lived and created by such a small number of artists, each of whom remained leading influences in their own group, that national ideas remained undiluted to the end. But there were international exchanges on an inspiring scale which could only have been achieved by real idealism and romantic imagination. The international exhibitions in New Orleans 1884–85, Paris 1889 and 1900, Chicago 1893, Brussels 1897, Turin 1902, St Louis 1904, San Francisco 1915, showed the world's instinct for unity and prosperity. Ashbee of England exhibited at Vienna, Munich, Düsseldorf, Paris, and most notably designed rooms for the Prince of Hesse's castle at Darmstadt, destroyed by bomb damage in the Second World War. Mackintosh of Glasgow designed the brilliant Scottish Pavilion in the 1902 Turin Exhibition, and showed also in Vienna, Budapest, Dresden, Munich and Moscow. Joseph Hoffmann of Vienna designed and built his masterpiece not there but in Brussels, the Palais Stoclet. Van de Velde was born in Antwerp, died in Zürich, worked in Germany, Switzerland, Holland and Belgium. Tiffany studied in Paris, won a Grand Prix at Turin 1902. The St Louis 1904 exhibition represented many of Europe's leading names. Wolfers of Brussels had jewels reproduced in eighty-three art magazines all over the world 1893–1908, and the showcase he designed in 1896 for an Antwerp shop is now in the Darmstadt Museum. The different artists showed an intense interest in each other's work without ever seemingly wanting to copy it.

For Britain it may be said here as in other fields that she invented it but never quite got there. A. H. Mackmurdo (1851–1942) started the Century Guild in 1882 to drive trade out of the arts, and his 1883 book cover is the world's first recorded art nouveau design; but he abandoned the lead he had won.

C. R. Ashbee (1863–1942), another architect, and the most prolific metalworker of the time, started the Guild of Handicraft in 1888, as a craft co-operative, at Essex House in the Mile End Road, moved it in 1902 to Chipping Campden in Gloucestershire, where old houses were restored and agricultural work undertaken, retaining a London shop, and finally wound it up in 1908. Ashbee seems now to have been one of the quieter, less creative designers, but his reputation then was good: in 1912 his "Silverwork and Jewellery", privately printed, showed his interest in, but also his rather limited appreciation of craft-work. His jewels were usually clumsy and unfeminine, made of silver and one of the translucent stones, blister pearl, moonstone, turquoise or opal, but always much more metal than stone.

Next in importance probably comes the firm Liberty which was started in 1875 by Arthur Lasenby Liberty partly to popularize unsold Japanese stock remaining from the first Western showing of Japanese work, the London 1862 exhibition. William Morris managed the Farmer & Rogers oriental warehouse and inspired his friend Liberty with zeal for Japan, whose influence on art nouveau was partly due to the novelty of the country, opened to the West in 1857. Liberty in his turn

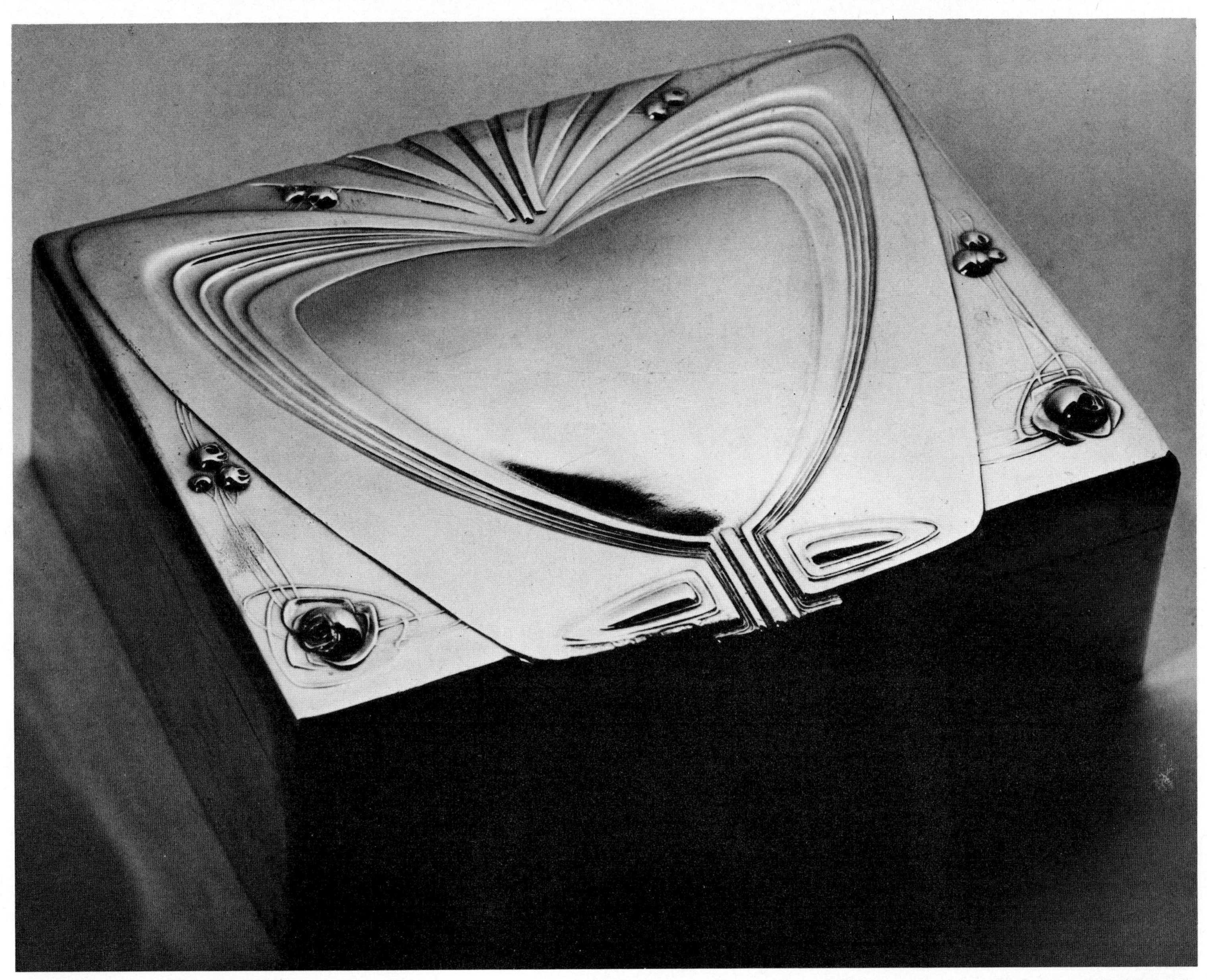

3. (above) Silver-plated jewel box in brass and pewter, *circa* 1905, perhaps by Charles Rennie Mackintosh; Glasgow: Alan Irvine Collection

4. (below) Two silver pendants (left) *circa* 1905–7, by Charles Rennie Mackintosh; Glasgow (right) 1895–97, with turquoise and amethyst, by Margaret Macdonald and Charles Rennie Mackintosh; Glasgow, Mrs Mary Newbery Sturrock Collection, Glasgow

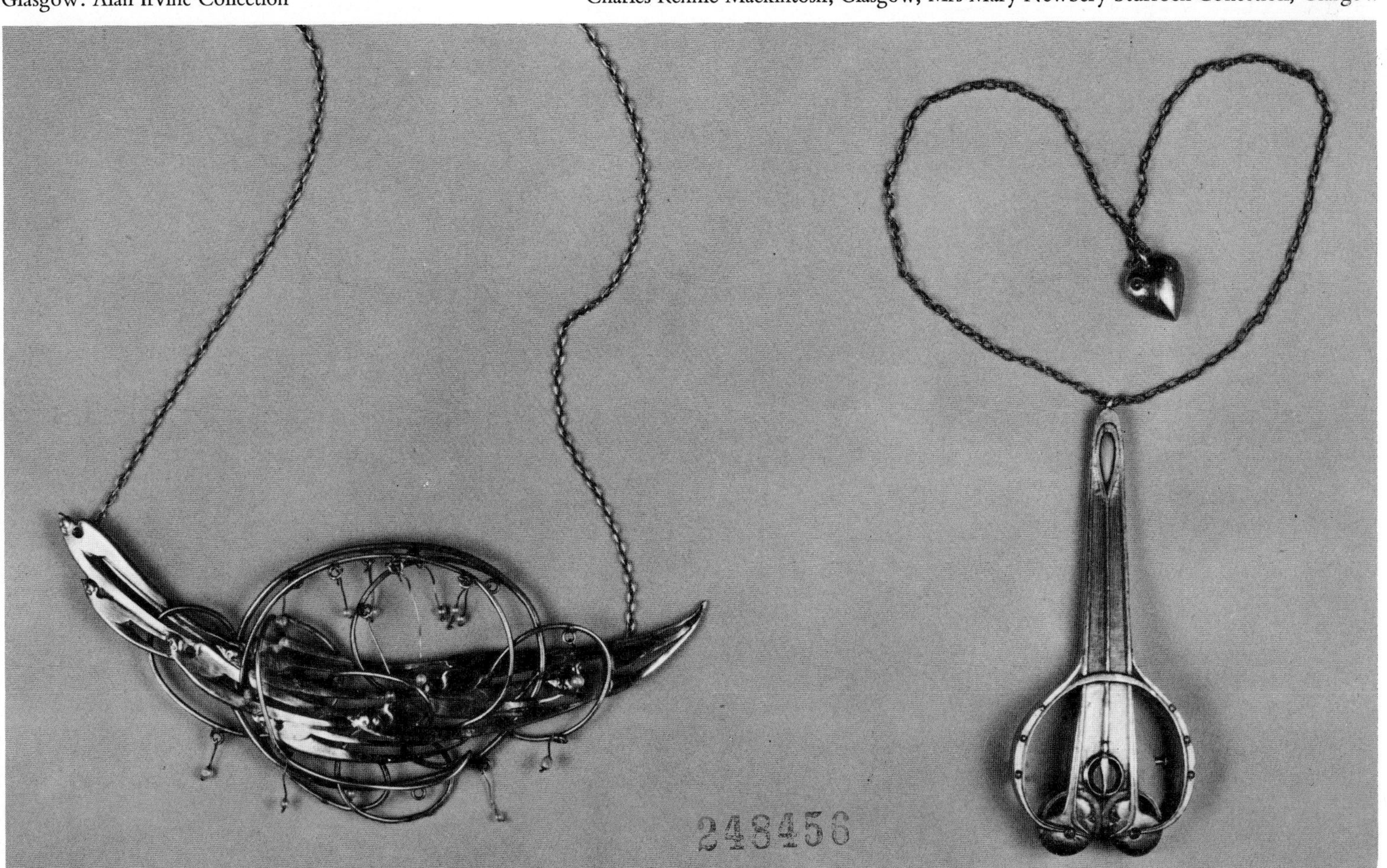

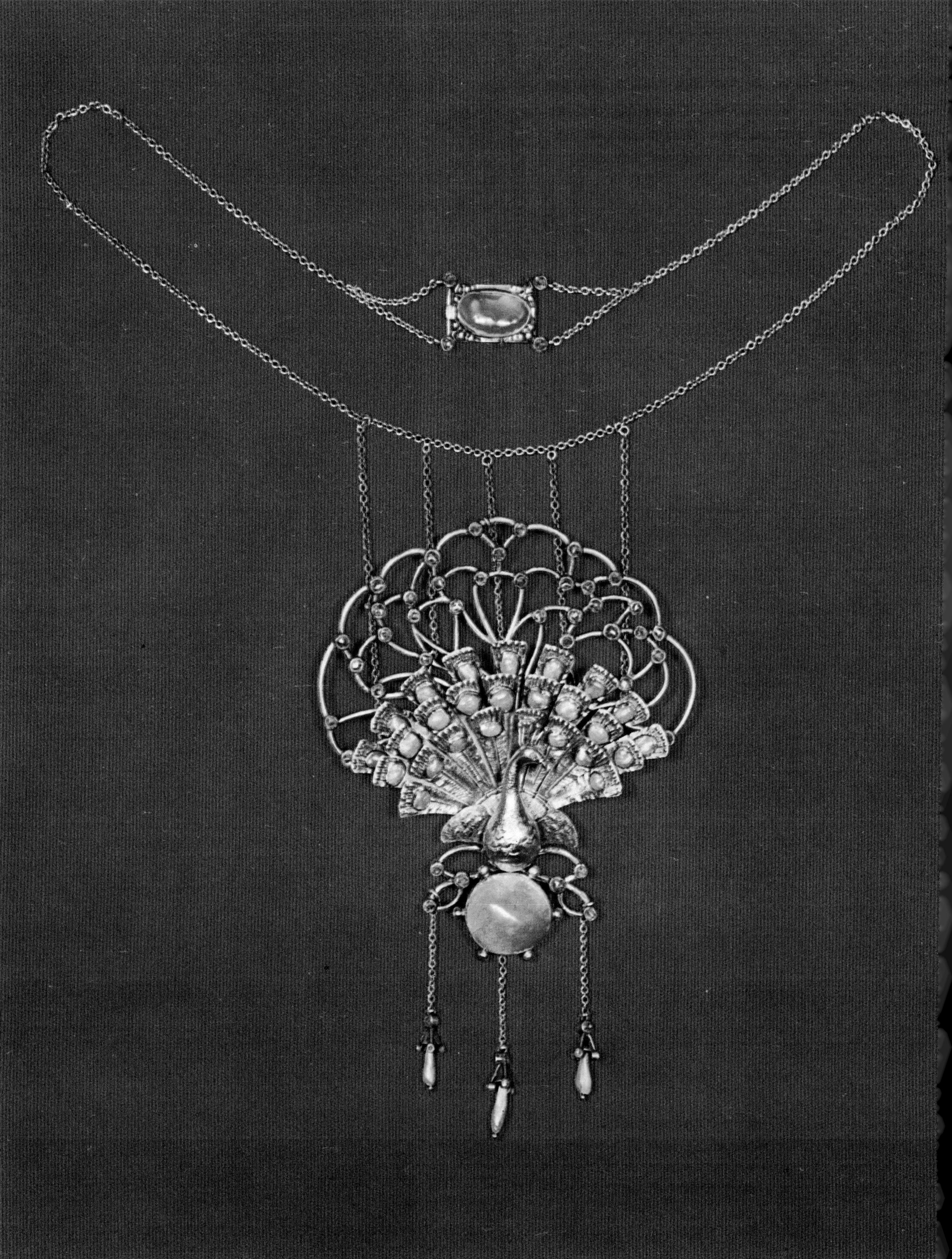

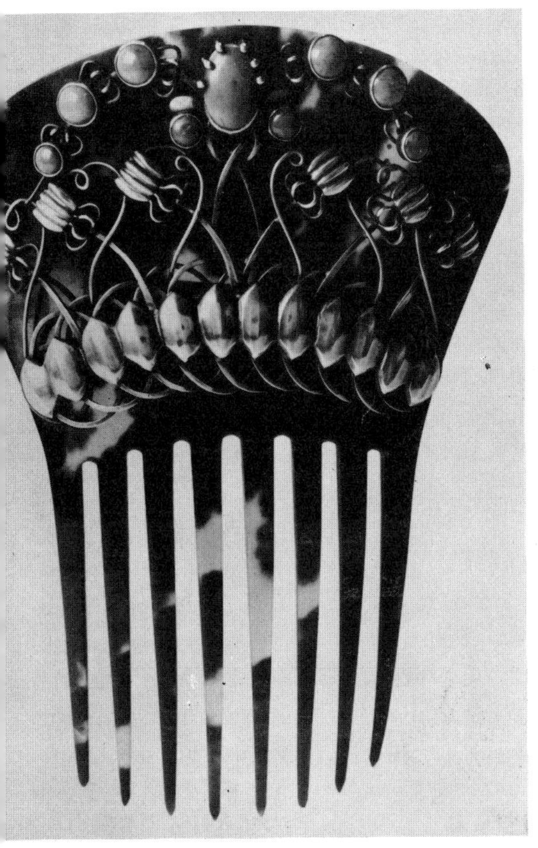

5. Back-comb, designed 1905, by Georg Jensen; Copenhagen
The Museum of Decorative Arts, Copenhagen

6. Enamelled pendant and necklace, 1905, by J. Mayer; Pforzheim
Schmuckmuseum Reuchlinhaus, Pforzheim

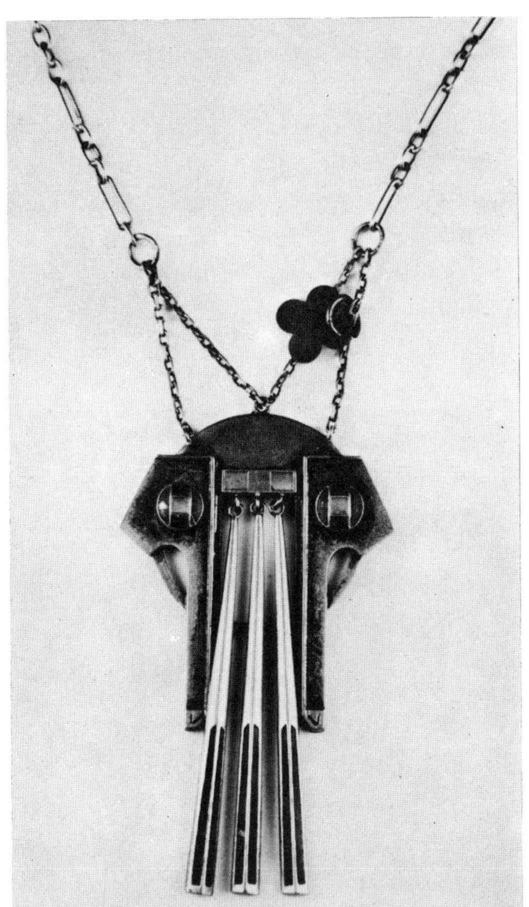

used many metalwork designers, his chief suppliers probably being William Hutton & Sons of Sheffield and W. H. Haseler & Co. of Birmingham; in 1899 he launched the 'Cymric' range of silver and jewels, still commonly seen in British antique shops, stamped with the trade name, heavily worked, soberly but not brilliantly eccentric. 'Tudric' pewter followed. Unfortunately the Liberty policy was to keep secret the names of their designers, no doubt in order to retain control over them; this means that despite splendid researches by Mrs Shirley Bury at the Victoria and Albert Museum, we do not know what proportion of the work was machine-made, or how far the firm either wanted or achieved a union of art and industry. Archibald Knox (1864–1933) was one of the more original designers, Bernard Cuzner (1877–1956) a typically devoted craftsman who looked back on his art nouveau work as a youthful irresponsibility, a whimsical betrayal of the solid materials he admired. Haseler himself conversely probably valued production for its own sake: his joint company with Liberty's was dissolved as late as 1927.

Charles Rennie Mackintosh (1868–1928) is now recognized as the world giant of the period, the one British designer whose invention never flagged, whose conviction was absolute, whose stature is comparable with van de Velde and Lalique. Only one jewel by him is known, but he designed tableware prototypes and architectural metalwork which have excited stylists everywhere, and those numerous austere art theorists who, as valid 20th-century art forms, prefer door-knobs to jewels. Mackintosh was the catalyst for a group of artists who came to be centred on the Glasgow School of Art, including his wife Margaret Macdonald (1865–1933), and her sister Frances (1874–1921), Jessie King (1876–1949), Nelson Dawson (1859–1942), Talwyn Morris (1865–1911) and others, all of whose jewels and metalwork are much commoner and less distinguished than their master's, though still dominated by his own personal idiom, as astonishing as it is logical.

If Ashbee made the most jewels, Henry Wilson (1864–1934) led in silver. Professor Pevsner surprisingly claims that Ashbee's silver is not art nouveau, in which case Wilson's with its castellated romantic medievalism is even less so: both rather homespun stylistically, Ashbee was more designer, Wilson more craftsman, though he himself might not have liked the assessment, as he was an active author and lecturer. He made great quantities of church plate and regalia, for health reasons often doing his casting at Torcello, where he made the doors for New York Anglican Cathedral; and he is a link with both the past and the future, because his style is almost so backward-looking as to be Victorian, almost progressive enough to confuse with Omar Ramsden and Alwyn Carr, the next generation of church-smiths. Wilson was a sensible serviceable bridge between the 19th and 20th centuries, with Voysey's or Dresser's austere unornamented functionalism on the one hand and the exuberant art nouveau on the other. What he carried over the bridge is not now fashionable. It is William Morris's belief in the joy of hand-work, and Morris's energies were not in vain because England is now the only country in the world where hand-made silver is still commissioned from independent artist-craftsmen.

Art nouveau in England died almost stillborn because of British reticence; as a nation they do not tend to indulge in orgies of visual fun. Walter Crane (1845–1915) called the phenomenon a "strange decorative disease". Morris himself (1834–96) was primarily a social reformer. Although his wallpapers and fabrics were commercially successful, his main artistic conviction was a sentimental one in favour of the individual as against the machine. He never reconciled the contradiction between his socialist and his artistic theories, the inability of expensive hand-work to satisfy cheap mass markets. The nearest he got was

Colour Plate I. Silver and gold pendant with chain set with pearls and diamond sparks, *circa* 1902, designed by C. R. Ashbee, made by the Guild of Handicraft; English. The Victoria and Albert Museum, London

7. Gold brooch with moonstones, opals and pearls, 1914, by Joseph Hoffmann; Vienna
length 2⅜ in. (6 cm.)
Mrs Federica Beer-Monti Collection, New York

to praise sensible designs at the expense of fantasies. As he was a very powerful and popular personality, his ideas which dominated the applied art world may have helped to undo British art nouveau, at the same time as giving a world impetus to conscientious workmanship.

In Denmark there was the work without the theory. Georg Jensen, sculptor (1866–1935), started his workshop with Mogens Bollin in 1904, and Johan Rohde, painter (1856–1935), joined him to work together from 1909, quickly growing out of the prevalent imitative and over-elaborate style, and evolving their own personal idiom which has served the Jensen name so well ever since: more bulges than curves, more bulk than line, more fleshy than sinuous, more heavy fruits than light flowers, the idea was a steady success from the beginning. The material, as in Britain, was almost always silver, often with amber, the common Polish stone; and it may be guessed that jewels formed a much bigger proportion of Jensen's output than they did of his contemporaries in England. The difference was not only that Jensen designed with more generous conviction than his British colleagues, and without the hampering influence of the Ruskin–Morris theories; it was mainly that precious jewelry and good silver hardly existed in his unaristocratic country; although silver was the foremost craft it was a small one. Jensen created a new market where almost nothing existed before; whereas in Britain there were already hundreds of factories and retail shops, there the craftsmen's task was to convert an existing taste, a task which is only now nearing success.

The year 1922 was decisive for Jensen. When art nouveau had everywhere fizzled out, he was bought up by the enlightened Pedersen family of bankers and his humble workshop was slowly transformed into the present two large factories, employing over a thousand people, including a healthy amount still of handcraftsmen with the sons of the original Pedersen as managers and with branches throughout the world. Jensen was a late starter, but he was the only one of these jewellers who can now be looked on as the source of a great national upsurge of well-organized creative energy.

In Germany the style, called 'Jugendstil' from the Munich paper, was also a commercial success, in fact it was commercial from the start, and its detail was therefore different from the start, adapted to semi-quantity production. Machine-made components were assembled in small already existing factories, mostly at Pforzheim, since the 18th century the great centre for gold and silver jewels, but also at Frankfurt, Schwäbisch Gmünd and at Hanau. The products were small, unlike French and Belgian work, light, unlike British or Danish, and anonymous,

8. Gold bracelet, 1922, by Joseph Hoffmann; Vienna
Mrs Marie Baru Collection, New York

9. (left) Silver pendant and chain with moonstones, 1907, by Henry van de Velde
Mrs Emmy Frosterus Collection, Helsinki
(right) Oxidized silver buckle with moonstones and rose diamonds, 1898–1900, by Henry van de Velde
Nordenfjeldske Kunstindustrimuseum, Trondheim

unlike any other country's: composed of tiny bars, pins, balls and angles put together in constantly varied combinations, they give the impression of only limited vocabulary. The great German pioneers of international modern architecture, Peter Behrens, Walter Gropius, Joseph Olbrich, killed the curve almost before it had appeared there, and these jiggly little jewels in silver or base metal, very often pendants of a delicate utility nature, were almost more closely related to the unique and delicate pierced floral and geometric iron jewels from Berlin of the preceding decades, than to contemporary artists' art nouveau elsewhere on the Continent. But as in Denmark, German work around 1900 led to enormous commercial expansion in the 1920's and 1930's: the new Pforzheim Reuchlinhaus Museum is the most elegant jewelry display in existence, and shows the development from the sophisticated pioneer small-scale production of 1900, to the vulgar meretricious work which today has gained for Pforzheim its undisputed place as the world's leading producer of cheap jewels.

Individual German metalwork designers like Karl Bauer (1868–1942) or Georg Kleeman (1863–1929) or Ernst Riegel (1871–1946) did not apparently have very personal styles, and the nearest the giants like Behrens or Riemerschmid, and indeed the whole artists' colony established at Darmstadt, seem to have got to jewelry was their silver tableware. The Darmstadt Museum, brilliantly rebuilt and completed in 1965, shows this German Jugendstil at its best in many media, and the fact that few native jewels are there, certainly suggests that German jewels at the time hardly rose to the art level.

Vienna was one of the first capitals to meet art nouveau, but one of the last to digest it. Of the founders of the anti-historical 'Sezession' group in 1897 which gave its name to Viennese Jugendstil, Joseph Hoffmann (1870–1956) and Koloman Moser (1868–1916) both designed jewels. Many of the leading artists, including Hoffmann and Dagobert Peche (1887–1923) supported the Wiener Werkstätte, started by Hoffmann in 1903, a society of artist-craftsmen with furnished workshops which survived till the 1930's slump and over three decades made much of the best Viennese craft-work. The style was that of 'chequerboard' Hoffmann, small squares and triangles and dots, much richer than the German, often using gold or pearls or ivory, or enamels, often producing rather big, important pieces for the wealthy classes. The great achievement is Hoffmann's Palais Stoclet in Brussels where many of the craftsmen worked 1904–11, and where some of the best of the always rare Sezession pieces are still preserved.

It was in Belgium that jewels in the 'modern style', as it was called, probably first became fashionable to wear, and it was probably Philippe Wolfers (1858–1929) who made them so, the very substantial artist whose firm Wolfers Frères

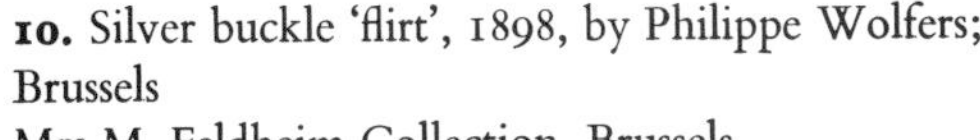

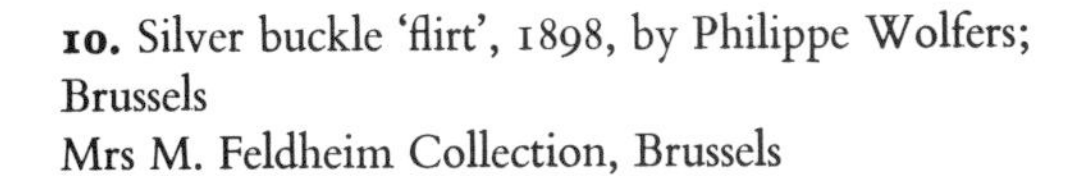

10. Silver buckle 'flirt', 1898, by Philippe Wolfers; Brussels
Mrs M. Feldheim Collection, Brussels

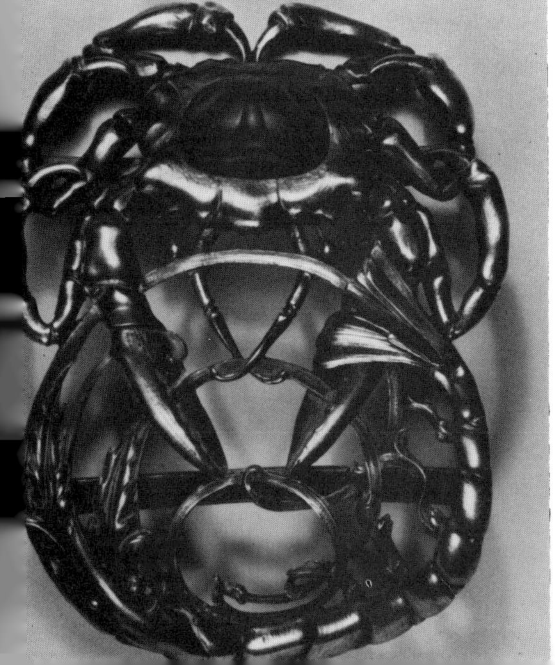

11. Pendant with two peacocks in enamelled gold with a large opal, *circa* 1903, by René Lalique; Paris width $3\frac{1}{2}$ in. (8·8 cm.)
The Gulbenkian Foundation, Lisbon

12. Gold bracelet, *circa* 1895–1900, by René Lalique; Paris
height $2\frac{1}{2}$ in. (6·3 cm.)
The Gulbenkian Foundation, Lisbon

were and still are the Belgian crown jewellers with all the power to influence opinion which that responsibility carries. It must have been this power, so seldom well exercised by its holders, that enabled Wolfers to produce a long series of very precious pieces, the finest group of which is now owned and venerated by the firm and family. He studied at the Beaux Arts in Brussels, joined the family firm which, however, had no retail shop, was much impressed with Japanese work at the Vienna International Exhibition 1873, *circa* 1890 established his own workshop in Marie Louise Square, and *circa* 1893 started using ivory from the Congo offered to artists by Leopold II. From 1905 he became increasingly interested in sculpture. In 1910 Victor Horta built the firm's present splendid workshops and showrooms. Many articles were published praising him, many of his pieces are both signed and dated and declared unique, so of all the designers he is perhaps the easiest to record: his style progressed from flowers *circa* 1890 to abstract and story themes *circa* 1905. He used more precious materials than any of his contemporaries, preferring gold to silver and metal to horn, and rubies to moonstones, and perhaps less exotic enamels than his French contemporaries. His pieces made a fine showing at Goldsmiths' Hall, London, in 1961, and must have found their spiritual home in the "Bijou 1900" exhibition held in 1965 in Horta's magnificent Hotel Solvay of 1895, now so well cherished by its owner, M. Wittamer de Camp, himself a notable Wolfers collector.

Henry van de Velde (1863–1957), born in Antwerp, worked as architectural adviser to the Grand Duke of Weimar 1899–1917, then taught at Ghent and Courtrai, working also intermittently in Holland, where he designed the superb Kröller-Müller Museum at Otterlo, and in Switzerland, where he died at Zürich. Unlike Mackintosh, with whom his strength and originality are comparable, he must have particularly enjoyed metalwork and jewels: his surviving pieces are almost all of austere silver or base metal – architect-jewellers do not seem to respond to the joys of luxury – but van de Velde's work makes up in exquisitely elaborate linear chasing for what it loses in intrinsic lustre. He strikes the perfect balance between an architect's perfectionism and a jeweller's fantasy, a rare combination of qualities which gives his jewels unique distinction.

The name "L'art nouveau" was invented by S. Bing of Hamburg for the shop he opened in Paris in 1895, from which he must have sold many of the jewels under discussion, and it is in Paris that most of these jewels were made. Always a jewel centre, it was seething with change at the turn of the century, much more so than London, its sister in wealth and politics. Impressionism in art, Proust, Victor Hugo, De Musset and symbolism in poetry, Diaghilev, Stravinsky, Debussy and Ravel in music, the Franco-Prussian War of 1870 and the Haussmann replanning on a huge scale afterwards, made women ready to try a change, and indeed even to expect it. There are far more art nouveau jewels surviving from France than from any other country, and there were far more designers of ability if not of genius.

René Lalique (1860–1945), who like Wolfers usually signed his jewels, though not with quite such full information about date and whether or not a series existed, is the most sensational figure in the field. He always wanted to draw. Son of a merchant, on his father's death in 1876 his mother apprenticed him as jeweller to Louis Aucoc, and he started courses at the École des Arts Décoratifs, abandoned for lack of time. From 1878 he studied at Sydenham, and in 1881 returned to work with various Paris firms designing wallpapers, fabrics, an industrial art journal with etchings as a guide to jewellers. By now he knew some of the customers of the firms for whom he had worked – Cartier, Boucheron, Aucoc, Destape, and in

Colour Plate II. Necklace with tiger reliefs and conventionalized tiger teeth, *circa* 1900, by René Lalique; Paris diameter closed $9\frac{1}{4}$ in. (23·4 cm.)
The Walters Art Gallery, Baltimore

13. (right) Mauve and black enamelled gold buckle face in green chrysoprase, 1899–1900, by René Lalique; Paris
length 3½ in. (8·8 cm.)
The Gulbenkian Foundation, Lisbon

14. (below) Orchid comb in ivory and horn, *circa* 1897–1900, by René Lalique; Paris
width 6¼ in. (15·8 cm.)
The Gulbenkian Foundation, Lisbon

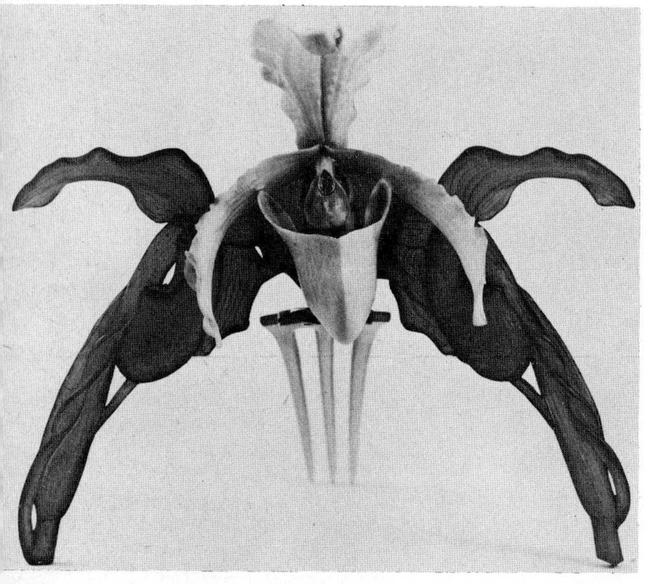

15. (centre right) Buckle in aquamarine with glass fruits and enamelled gold, *circa* 1903, by René Lalique; Paris
length 3¾ in. (9·5 cm.)
The Gulbenkian Foundation, Lisbon

16. (right) Detail of dog collar necklace of engraved glass with diamonds mounted in gold, *circa* 1906–12, by René Lalique; Paris
height 2 in. (5 cm.)
The Gulbenkian Foundation, Lisbon

17. Enamelled gold brooch with bee sucking flower, *circa* 1900, designed by Charles Desroziers, made by George Fouquet; Paris
The Victoria and Albert Museum, London

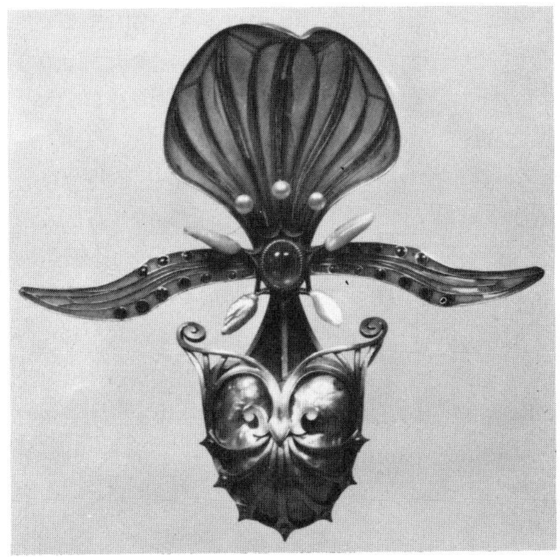

18. Orchid brooch, *circa* 1900, by George Fouquet; Paris
height 4 in. (10·1 cm.)
Courtesy Christie's, London

19. Pendant with enamelled gold, rubies, turquoise, chrysoprase showing *Omphale carrying the club of Hercules*, 1900, by Henri Vever; Paris
Musée des Arts Décoratifs, Paris

1886 he was left Destape's business. Between 1890 and 1893 he studied glass techniques in his Rue Thérèse workshop, and, equally important, attracted Sarah Bernhardt, who commissioned two groups of jewels for "Iseyl et Gismonda". In 1895 his display at the Salon for the first time made him well known – he won third prize there. The same year he opened his Place Vendôme shop and first used the feminine nude in his jewelry. In 1896 he first used horn encrusted with silver, winning a second prize. In 1897 he became Chevalier of the Légion d'Honneur. In 1903 he designed and built his shop at 40 Cours Albert I, with a great doorway in glass and pinewood, by Saint-Gobin. In 1909 he leased and in 1910 bought a glass factory at Combes-la-Ville, glass becoming more prominent in his jewels, till he finally abandoned jewelry in 1914. Eugène Feuillatre (1870–1916) worked for him, researching into the problems of enamelling on silver, and Lalique himself was a great technical innovator, using machines to reduce his large models to actual working size.

Georges Fouquet (1862–1957), the eldest son of Alphonse Fouquet, jeweller of Avenue de l'Opéra, had a stylistic affinity with Lalique, and seems to have operated on a similar scale. We know of him from his family because his son Jean is now one of the foremost Paris artist-craftsmen. Georges started work with his father in 1880, and in 1895 inherited the business and immediately modernized it, working with Tourrette, Desroziers (1905–8), Grasset and Mucha. After prizes in the universal exhibitions of 1900 and 1901, he asked Mucha to design his new shop at 6 Rue Royale, demolished 1920. He showed in Milan 1906, was president of the jewellers at the Paris 1925 and 1937 exhibitions, and member of the Union Centrale des Arts Décoratifs, thus being one of the few designers to remain in practice having outlived the epoch. His most significant connection was no doubt with Alphonse Mucha (1860–1939), the most prolific designer of the age, even if not the most original, to whose designs he made many pieces, and through whom he must have met some of the most exotic women in the world.

Henri Vever (1854–1942), author of the history of French 19th-century jewelry, inherited his firm in 1874 with his brother Paul (1851–1915) from their father Ernest, a figure of standing who had been President of the Chambre Syndicale. Henri studied at the École des Arts Décoratifs in the evenings, and by day at the ateliers of Loguet, Hallet and Dufong. In 1889, at their first exhibition, the brothers won one of the two grands prix; in 1891 at the French exhibition in Moscow they won the Croix de la Légion d'Honneur, and studied the crown jewels of the Czars there, and of the sultans in Istanbul. In 1893 Henri was Commissioner at the Chicago exhibition; in 1895 he won prizes at Bordeaux, in 1897 at Brussels, in 1900 a grand prix at Paris. Vever's work was much heavier and less spontaneous than Lalique's or Fouquet's and he probably did not pride himself as the others did on producing outstanding special masterpieces.

So much for the biggest French names: foremost among the others was Alphonse Mucha, painter, graphic designer and decorator, the best known and most prolific one of all. He started his studio with Whistler, from 1894 had a six-year contract for Sarah Bernhardt's posters and décors, published portfolios of designs which were disseminated so far that the names 'le style Mucha' and 'art nouveau' were for a time synonymous. He worked in Paris, Berlin and his native Prague, and designed rather lightweight jewels for Georges Fouquet from 1898 to 1905. He was indeed more prolific than inspired. Then there was Lucien Gaillard (born 1861), known for his interest in Japan, who exhibited at the Paris 1900 and the Glasgow 1901 exhibitions; Eugène Grasset (1841–1917), another Japanese enthusiast, who visited Egypt in 1869, studied with Viollet-le-Duc and designed for

Vever, more popularizer than creator. Victor Prouvé (1858–1943), pioneer of exotic glass made at Nancy under the inventive lead of Emile Gallé (1846–1904), Paul Liénard (1849–1900), Georges de Ribaucourt (1881–1907), L. Gautrait, Henri Dubret and others hardly established their personalities in this most personal of styles. All these artists followed the giants, but art nouveau was a medium for creators, not for followers.

The Frenchmen's chosen materials were gold or horn (first introduced in 1896 by Lalique as a change from the too-regular grain of tortoiseshell), hardly ever the less luminous metal which appealed in the northern countries, silver; and they loved enamel. *Circa* 1900 Gaillard imported several craftsmen from Japan, and both he and Lalique carried through extensive researches in glazing, becoming more and more glass minded until they eventually abandoned jewelry altogether. Smart shops for these jewels existed as nowhere else in Europe. Lalique's in the Place Vendôme where the group La Haute Joaillerie de France now mostly are, Fouquet's designed by Mucha in the Rue Royale near the present shop bearing Lalique's name but not his philosophy. Some of the Fouquet–Mucha parts preserved in the Musée Carnavalet (but not on show) give an idea of the luxuriant fittings which must have made the jewels seem quite normal.

The point is that in France, more than anywhere, art nouveau jewels were accepted by society, partly in reaction against the newly discovered South African diamonds which had swept the market in the 1880's. Sarah Bernhardt came first – she had a big collection of conventional jewels like the diamond brooch from Alfonso XII of Spain, a necklace from Franz Joseph of Austria, a fan from Umberto of Italy, a tear-shaped diamond even frôm Victor Hugo to record his weeping during her performance of Hernani. But her taste must have been for the exotic, like the huge Fouquet–Mucha snake bracelet covering most of the forearm and forefinger which caused a sensation when shown in Brussels in 1965; so keen was she on having this piece for her première in "Cleopatra" that she went in pawn for it, and Fouquet the maker had to collect payment each week from the theatre box office. It was probably Sarah who gave these jewels the impetus they missed in other countries. In 1895 Calouste Gulbenkian first admired Lalique's work in the Salon du Champ de Mars, and thereafter made the splendid collection of 146 masterpieces which he sometimes let his friends wear, like Sarah herself, but which are now in the Pombal Palace at Oeiras near Lisbon where they are Europe's most persuasive monument to art nouveau.

Elsewhere the style was sown but did not strike root. In Italy it was called the 'Stile Liberty' from the firm whence the imports came. Architecture was hardly affected, and jewels not at all, if one is to judge from such works as "Liberty a Napoli" by Renato de Fusco, "L'eta di Liberty" by Italo Cremona, the display at the Galleria Milano in 1966. The big and growing jewelry firms Calderoni, Bulgari or Buccellati retained their static dignity in the face of all temptation. In Barcelona the incredible architect Gaudí (1852–1926) made his buildings so ornamental that unlike for instance van de Velde, he seems never to have needed the diversion of jewelry designing. In the U.S.A., Louis Comfort Tiffany (1848–1943) with his original almost luminous glass technique which he called 'favrile', and very many jewels in a style somewhere between Lalique and Henry Wilson, alternating surprisingly between the very elegant and the over-thick, was a lone phenomenon. His father had founded Tiffany's in 1834 and started making jewels as well as the original glass and interior oddments, from 1848. Latterly he used Edward Moore (died 1891) as his designer, a devoted orientalist and buyer of Japanese products. So Louis had a stimulating family background. He studied in

20. Sarah Bernhardt (1845–1923), the greatest actress of her day, who probably popularized art nouveau jewelry more than anyone else, here wearing at least two pendants and two rings
Australia Hotel, Sydney

21. Caroline Otéro "La Belle Otéro" (1868–1965) in 1903 – a Spanish actress, goddess of *La Belle Epoque* between 1880 and 1914. On her skirt she wears at least four brooches

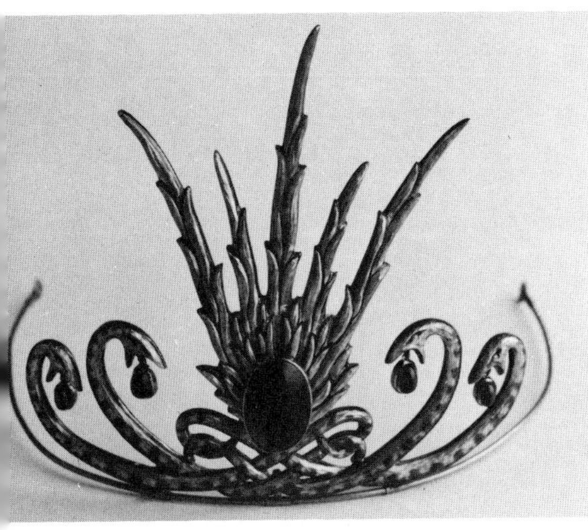

22. Diadem in enamelled gold with fire opals, probably French
Courtesy Christie's, London

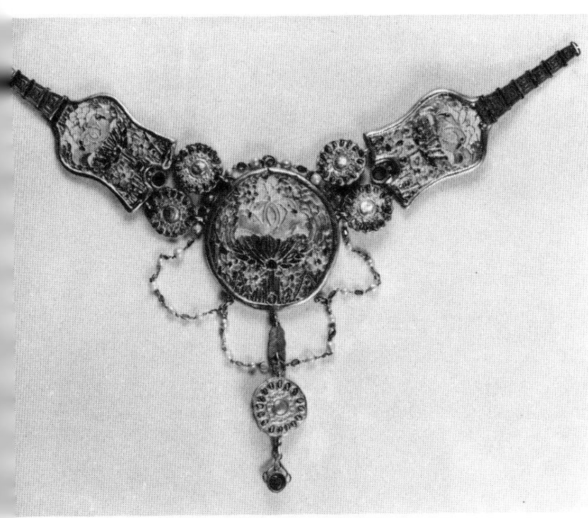

23. Necklace in enamelled gold with amethyst, sapphire, ruby and opal decoration, *circa* 1902, by Louis Comfort Tiffany; New York
Ferguson McKean Collection, Florida

London under Innes and in Paris till 1878. *Circa* 1880 he patented his new iridescent glass, in 1902 winning a grand prix at Turin. In 1879 he started Associated Artists, a decorating business which lasted till 1937. On his father's death in 1902 he became Art Director of the famous firm, from which time his 'personalized' jewels were probably as important to him as his 'favrile' glass. From 1918 he made his house at Oyster Bay, Long Island, a centre for his artist friends whose designs he sometimes made, and to whom he sometimes gave financial help. His inherited wealth and his family firm gave him the opportunity to be both original and successful, but he is alone. Louis Sullivan got the message in Paris in 1874, as a student, but alas he never designed jewels and his brilliant architecture with its lavish art nouveau details never caught on. The Americans preferred either heavy period reproductions or building based on economy of structure. This rough new society was not yet tired of artistic orthodoxy, not yet settled enough for a *belle époque* high society to establish mannerism of its own. Russia conversely was too tired. Peter Carl Fabergé (1846–1920) found sufficient novelty for his exquisite taste in the delicacies of 18th-century Dresden, and had no creative urge to unsettle him further. Art nouveau was relegated to the Moscow hotel buildings for the *nouveaux riches.*

These jewels are an exciting freak, but they are more. Idiosyncrasy in furniture or printing for instance was killed by the social revolution of 1914. Mass demand was all, the impoverished aristocracy became irrelevant, and therefore sensible objects became financially necessary. Personal fantasy went out of applied art, back to the fine arts of which it is always the essence. But jewels were changed for ever by these few designers of the 1890's, with their limited output of hand-made work. Only with jewelry are unique pieces essential, only here are the economics of mass production still irrelevant. The cage of convention was broken, and artist-jewellers everywhere today owe their market to the stimulating force of art nouveau.

The importance of the epoch is only now being recognized. But these entwined, dreamy expressions of delight are still both cheap and rare. Maurice Rheims in "L'objet 1900" investigates some present-day auction prices and finds them about one-quarter of their first retail selling price. Collectors usually aim for objects that are datable and attributable as well as beautiful and exclusive. Here is an only partly explored field, awaiting attention. As W. A. S. Benson, the British designer, says in the 1903 William Morris arts and crafts essays, "good and bad in art eludes definition: it is not an affair of reason but of perception".

BIBLIOGRAPHY

Casson, J., Langui, E. and Pevsner, N. *The Sources of Modern Art.* London, Munich, 1961.

Schmutzler, R. *Art Nouveau.* London, Stuttgart, 1962.

Rheims, M. *L'art 1900.* Paris, Vienna, 1965.

Hughes, G. *Modern Jewelry 1890–1964, an International Survey.* London (revised edition), 1964, New York, 1964, Ravensburg, 1965.

Rheims, M. *The Age of Art Nouveau.* London, 1966, Vienna, 1965, translated by Patrick Evans.

Amaya, M. *Art Nouveau.* London, 1966.

Taylor, J. R. *The Art Nouveau Book in Britain.* London, 1966.

Hughes, G. *Modern Silver, 1890–1967.* London, 1967.

Early American Painting

SABRINA LONGLAND

The title "Early American Painting" is arbitrary: in this essay it is taken in its broadest sense, and embraces the history and development of American painting from *circa* 1670 to *circa* 1840–45. The very formation and history of America was a vital factor in the growth of the art of the country, and directed its course. Artistic taste from the earliest colonial days was governed by the austere and practical way of life among the settlers struggling to establish a new nation. Housebuilding, carpentry and all the crafts necessary to living went hand in hand with being a painter; this, together with the Puritan outlook, excluded the patronage of all forms of art except portraits. The Revolution, occurring midway between these two dates, can be taken as a dividing line and a turning-point in the evolution of American painting.

Colonial portraiture was reaching an impasse when John Singleton Copley and Benjamin West emerged simultaneously on the artistic scene in 1753 and 1756 (both were born in 1738). The work of these two men is the starting-point in the significant period of American painting, which begins with the artists of the Revolutionary generation – Copley had a brilliant career in America until 1774, then left for England; from 1763 onwards West's studio in London was full of pupils and provided an art centre for a versatile group who rapidly extended in many directions the horizons of American painting, and some of whom were to be among the nation's most important artists, notably Copley, Charles Willson Peale, Rembrandt Peale, Gilbert Stuart, John Trumbull, William Dunlap (the 'American Vasari'), Washington Allston, Samuel Morse and Thomas Sully.

The revolutionary and republican spirit expressed itself in the expansion of art patronage, the growth of private collections of art, academies, and the demand for pictures other than portraits – in particular history paintings. The portrait itself, in the hands of Gilbert Stuart, underwent a transformation. Professional training had its effect on the generation following the Revolution, and Morse and Sully and their contemporaries painted highly competent portraits.

The seed of nationalism had been sown. The early and mid-19th century was an incredibly productive period in American art.

From a modest number of paintings which survive, and the few documentary references, one may gain a fairly good idea of the kind of pictures being painted in New England in the second part of the 17th century. The exhibition "XVIIth Century Painting in New England", at the Worcester Art Museum, Massachusetts,[1]

[1] "XVIIth Century Painting in New England." A catalogue of an exhibition held at the Worcester Art Museum, in collaboration with the American Antiquarian Society. July and August 1934. Compiled and edited by Louisa Dresser.

1. *Tench Francis*, 1746, by Robert Feke
oil on canvas 46×39 in. (116·8×99 cm.)
The Metropolitan Museum of Art, New York
(Purchase Maria De Witt Jesup Fund, 1934)

in July and August 1934, was the basis for a detailed study of portraiture in New England and of the rise and development of art in general in the Massachusetts Bay Colony.

Painting in the 17th-century American colonies, excluding the Spanish settlements of friars and their missions in the south-west, was almost exclusively portraiture. The pioneers were Protestants who wanted records of themselves and their families as the founders of the New World, to stand as testimony to posterity of their achievements and status in the new country. Religious painting in any form was strongly condemned. The vehemence of this doctrine is expressed in the sermons of Samuel Willard, a minister at Boston from 1678 until 1702.[2] There was no demand for still-lifes, landscapes and genre scenes which were so popular at that time in Europe. Also living conditions in 17th-century America did not offer any attraction or opportunities to such specialized painters.

Early portrait painting in New England was inevitably a provincial offshoot of that of 16th- and 17th-century England, with influence from the Netherlands. The attribution problem is almost insoluble as most of the paintings are unsigned, and although we have references to artists there are no paintings to fit the references. There are approximately two dozen American paintings that can be given with certainty to artists working in New England in the second part of the 17th century. Louisa Dresser has divided most of them into two groups, according to similarities of costumes, poses and facial types.[3]

The three portraits of the children of Robert Gibbs, a Boston merchant who died in 1674, which were seen in the exhibition "Three Centuries of American Painting", held at the Metropolitan Museum of Art, New York, from 9 April to 17 October 1965,[4] are an excellent illustration of the portraits belonging to the first group, all of which date from the years 1670 to 1679. The children are posed standing stiffly on a black-and-white tiled floor, against a plain dark background which has merely a suggestion of a draped curtain in the corner. The date 1670 is inscribed in white near the head of each child. The figures are not very sculptural or sophisticated, but the details are painted with sensitivity and delicacy. The artist was probably an undistinguished and obscure English painter who had been trained in an earlier Elizabethan tradition of miniature painting.

The interest of these three portraits is primarily archaeological and historical. They were possibly painted by the anonymous Freake limner, so called because he did the portraits of *John Freake*, an English settler who became a prosperous merchant in Boston *circa* 1660, and *Mrs Freake and Baby Mary*.[5] Both portraits have been on loan to the Worcester Art Museum since 1914.

In Louisa Dresser's second group, a good example of which is the self-portrait of *Captain Thomas Smith* (American Antiquarian Society, Worcester, Mass.), of *circa* 1690,[6] there is an attempt at boldness of facial modelling, the use of light and shade, and character portrayal which is entirely different to the soft charm and linear manner of the 1670 group. However, both groups represent long-past artistic traditions and suggest almost no awareness of contemporary European painting.

During the first three-quarters of the 18th century in America, prior to the generation of the Revolution, and before the arrival of Copley and West, painting

[2] Willard, S. "A Compleat Body of Divinity in Two Hundred and Fifty Expository Lectures on the Assembly's Shorter Catechism" (Boston, 1726). Sermons XVII and LI. The relevant extracts published in McCoubrey, pp. 3–5.

[3] Dresser, *op. cit.*, pp. 20f.

[4] Feld, Stuart P. "Loan Collection", 1965, Met. Mus. Bull., April 1965, pp. 275f.

[5] Illustr. Dresser, *op. cit.*, p. 80 and frontispiece.

[6] Illustr. Larkin, p. 20.

2. *James Badger*, the artist's grandson, 1760, by Joseph Badger
oil on canvas $42\frac{1}{2}\times33\frac{1}{8}$ in. (107×83 cm.)
The Metropolitan Museum of Art, New York (Purchase Rogers Fund, 1929)

still consisted almost entirely of portraiture. A number of painters of varied origin were active: some were emigrants with European training, others were born in the colonies and depended on imported paintings, mezzotints and the studios of the European-trained artists for their instruction. While there is nothing original about the composition or style of pre-Revolutionary portraits, many of them possess the refreshing qualities of vigour and directness or unsophisticated charm.

John Smibert (1688–1751) was a Scot. According to the notes of George Vertue he went to Italy in 1717 and spent three years in Florence, Rome and Naples, painting portraits from life and copying many old masters. In 1720 he returned to London, where portrait painting at that moment was greatly under the influence of Kneller, and remained there until 1728 when he set off for America. Vertue tells us before Kneller's death that Smibert painted and drew well, but very little of this period has so far been discovered.

In January 1729 Smibert arrived at Newport, Rhode Island, in the party of George Berkeley, whom he had met in Italy. Within a very short time he painted *Dean George Berkeley and his Family* (Yale University Art Gallery), a painting which is interesting both for its historic and artistic values.[7] The significance of Smibert's arrival in New England lies not only in the fact that he was the first important artist with a sound academic training to settle there, but also that he brought with him a great deal of studio equipment, such as plaster casts of antique sculpture, copies of old masters, mezzotints and drawings. In March 1730, three months after his arrival in Boston, Smibert held a combined exhibition of his collection of copies of old masters, and recently executed portraits of New England patrons. This was the first art exhibition ever held in America. Smibert was resourceful and ambitious, and, as Vertue wrote, preferred to be top of his profession in Boston, rather than a definitely secondary painter back home. He enjoyed a rapid success in Boston, painting portraits in the Knelleresque style, and his studio became a kind of 'academy' where younger artists could gain some idea of European painting. The verses of Mather Byles, "To Mr Smibert on the sight of his Pictures", printed in the "Daily Courant", London, 14 April 1730, give us a good idea of Boston's enthusiastic response to Smibert's exhibition.[8]

His portrait of *Nathaniel Byfield* (Metropolitan Museum of Art, New York), which was possibly painted in 1730,[9] is notable for the competence with which he has painted the sitter's flabby face and dictatorial expression, and is more realistic than his usual fashionable likenesses. Two other important pictures are the companion portraits of *Francis Brinley* and *Mrs Francis Brinley and her Infant Son* (Met. Mus.), painted probably in 1731.[10] As well as the fact that they show the artist at the summit of his power, they are of particular interest for two reasons: the portrait of *Francis Brinley* contains a view of Boston in the distance, which has been called the earliest painted view of that city, and the one of *Mrs Brinley* shows an unusual departure from contemporary practice in that the source for the baby is Italian. Her general pose probably derives from a mezzotint after Lely, but there were few English mezzotints of mothers with infants for Smibert to use as inspiration, this being a rare subject at that time in English portraiture.

The qualities of vigour and directness that I mentioned earlier are well expressed in the portrait of *Tench Francis* (Ill. 1) by Robert Feke.

Among contemporaries of Smibert and Feke were James Badger, Jeremiah Thëus, John Wollaston, John Hesselius, Joseph Blackburn and John Greenwood,

[7] Feld, Stuart P., "In the Latest London Manner", Met. Mus. Bull., May 1963, p. 301.
[8] In McCoubrey, pp. 6–8.
[9] Met. Mus. Catalogue, p. 2.
[10] Feld, Stuart P., *op. cit.*, plates 1 and 2, pp. 297f.

all of whom painted many portraits, some of eminent patrons, but with the exception of Blackburn they did not contribute anything new to colonial portraiture. Unsophisticated charm is found in some works by Joseph Badger (1708–65), born in Charlestown, Massachusetts, who was a house and sign painter and a glazier. Even if he did learn from Smibert in Boston, basically he remained a primitive painter; his portrait style is stiff and solemn, and best suited to children, to whom his archaic manner gives a certain naïve charm, as can be seen in *James Badger*. (Ill. 2.) The hands are usually wooden-looking, holding a bird, animal or flowers, and the colours sombre and olive in tone.

The companion portraits of *Gabriel Manigault* and *Anne Ashby Manigault* (Met. Mus.) painted in 1757 by the Swiss Jeremiah Thëus (*circa* 1719–74), who arrived in South Carolina *circa* 1735, are typical unoriginal colonial portraits. The solid prosperity of the affluent couple stares out at us from the canvases. Thëus avoided painting hands when possible, and made the format as simple as he could, here placing the sitters in ovals with no background. He is at his best painting the satin and lace materials of women's dresses.

John Hesselius (1728–78) was the son of the Swedish painter Gustavus Hesselius who had arrived in America in 1711. He was an itinerant portrait painter, working in Pennsylvania, Maryland, Delaware and Virginia from 1750 until 1778. His style, as seen in *Elizabeth Smith* (Brooklyn Museum, New York), followed closely that of John Wollaston, whose heavy-lidded, almond-eyed people posed stiffly against plain backgrounds are unmistakable; for example, the *Colden* and the *Reade* portraits (Met. Mus.). Hesselius could do better and less dull portraits such as *Mrs Richard Galloway* (Met. Mus.) painted in 1764, which is very close in spirit to the Quaker ladies by Badger and Thëus in the Edgar William and Bernice Chrysler Garbisch Collection, with their bonnets tied primly under the chin and austere pursed mouths.

The work of Joseph Blackburn is of a higher and different calibre. His elegant drawing-room ladies and technical competence in the painting of draperies and lace frills make it fairly certain that he was London trained, possibly as a drapery painter, and contemporary testimony tells us that he was admired for this skill.[11] Smibert had brought the Knelleresque manner with him from London; now Blackburn introduced the fashionable style of Thomas Hudson and Joseph Highmore. He was established in Boston by 1755, and worked in New England until 1763, after which time he may have settled in England. Smibert was dead (1751), Feke was dead or gone, and during these eight years the portrait field in New England was his until Copley, whom he influenced, eclipsed him completely. The group portrait *Isaac Winslow and his Family* (Museum of Fine Arts, Boston) illustrates the much-needed refinement that Blackburn brought to colonial portraiture. The shining fabric of the dresses, the delicate lace ruffles, the elegant garden in the distance, are far removed in spirit from the unflattering solidity of Badger, Thëus, Wollaston and Hesselius. But the faces are weak and the mouths affected; there is no trace of the strong modelling of Smibert's *Nathaniel Byfield* and *Francis Brinley*. *Mrs David Chesebrough* and her sister *Mary Sylvester* were both painted in 1754 and the poses derived from British mezzotints. Mary, in the mode of shepherdess, was following the latest London fashion, and, incidentally, directly influenced Copley's *Ann Tyng* of 1756. Blackburn's feeling for the various textures of rich materials was undoubtedly transmitted to the young Copley in whom it later became an outstanding skill.

The conflicting ambitions and limitations of a colonial portraitist are perfectly

[11] Met. Mus. Catalogue, pp. 12–13.

3. *The American School*, 1765, by Matthew Pratt oil on canvas 36×50¼ in. (91·4×127 cm.) The Metropolitan Museum of Art, New York (Gift Samuel P. Avery, 1897)

summed up in the *Greenwood-Lee Family*, painted *circa* 1747, by John Greenwood (1727–92).[12] Born in Boston, Greenwood was trained in heraldic decoration, japanning furniture and print-making. He set up as an independent portrait painter in 1745. This is his most ambitious work executed in America, and is aspiring, considering the date and his artisan apprenticeship. He had Smibert's Berkeley group for inspiration, which was still in the latter's studio, but a comparison of the two speaks for itself. Greenwood's handicap was his lack of European experience. He tried to paint a fashionable conversation piece, but there is no communication between the characters which stare, expressionless, at the beholder, their faces drawn with a limned sameness; the arms are lifeless, and the poses contrived. The interest and originality of the picture lies in the artist's bold attempt to do a composition beyond his scope. Greenwood for reasons unknown departed for Surinam, Dutch Guiana, in 1752, where he evidently found more opportunity for his talents, when he painted *Sea Captains Carousing in Surinam* (City Art Museum, St Louis), *circa* 1757 or 1758. It is a fascinating combination of a large group portrait and a lively genre scene, one of the earliest in American painting.

Benjamin West and Copley were born within a few months of each other. This fact makes a comparison of the development of their artistic careers most interesting, as both artists had provincial early years in America, but gained their fame on different sides of the Atlantic. West really belongs to the British school, as all his significant works were painted in England. His importance in early American painting lies in the influence that he exercised upon the crowd of young American artists who came to his studio in London.

West's *Sarah Ursula Rose* (Met. Mus.), which was painted in 1756, and Copley's *Ann Tyng* (Museum of Fine Arts, Boston), also painted in 1756,[13] illustrate the provincial painting tradition in which both artists began their careers. West was ambitious. Late in 1759, after a painting trip to New York, he departed for Italy. This was a significant moment in the history of American painting as he was the first American painter to study there. In 1763, on his way home, he decided to settle in London and achieved success as a portrait painter and teacher. Matthew Pratt's *The American School* (Ill. 3), exhibited in 1766, is now famous. Although Smibert's exhibition of 1730 and the use of his Boston studio by colonial portraitists must not be overlooked, West created the first operative American art school. His high position in the London art world enabled his protégés to make valuable contacts.

At the start of his artistic career in London he painted in an extreme neo-classical style, still absorbed by what he had learnt from the circle of Mengs in

[12] Feld, Stuart P., "Loan Collection", 1965, Met. Mus. Bull., April 1965, p. 278.

[13] Illustr. Larkin, p. 51.

Rome. This was not lasting and in 1771 he proved his innovating spirit when he painted the *Death of General Wolfe* (two versions: National Gallery of Canada, Ottawa; Kensington Palace, London), which is one of his most renowned works. As a history painting which showed the subjects in modern dress and not classical drapery, contrary to Reynolds's theories on the grand style, it caused a commotion in the art world, particularly the Indian in tribal costume in the foreground. It was rapidly engraved by Woollett, became widely known in Europe and marks a turning-point in the evolution of the modern history-piece.

In 1772 West was made historical painter to George III. The large canvas of *The Battle of La Hogue* exists in two versions: the original of 1778 is at the National Gallery of Art, Washington, D.C., the later one of *circa* 1784–85, which was chiefly the work of the assistants, in particular John Trumbull,[14] is in the Metropolitan Museum. This chaotic naval battle scene increased West's reputation as the principal painter of historical subjects in contemporary dress.

West also painted religious and literary subjects such as *Hagar and Ishmael* and *Orlando Furioso*. *Hagar and Ishmael* (Met. Mus.) was painted and exhibited at the Royal Academy in 1776. *Orlando Furioso* (Met. Mus.), undated, although another version exists of 1793, illustrates the highly dramatic style that the artist adopted in his middle years; the brushwork is broader and more painterly than before. This is even more true of *The Wise Men's Offering* (Met. Mus.). This oil sketch was done in 1794 for a stained-glass window at the west end of a private chapel at Windsor that had been ordered by George III in 1780. *The Wise Men's Offering* is an example of the best that West learnt in Italy: the colour is pure Venetian.

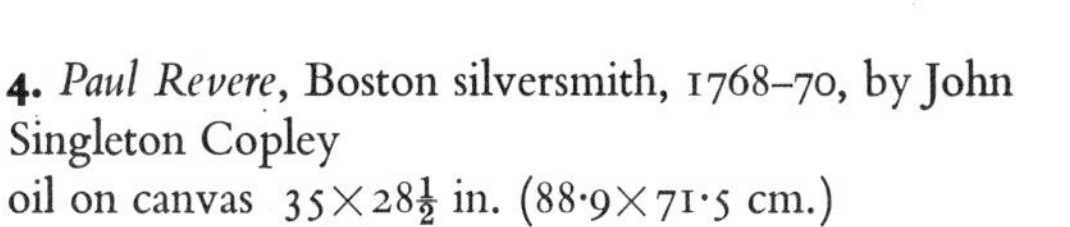

4. *Paul Revere*, Boston silversmith, 1768–70, by John Singleton Copley
oil on canvas 35×28½ in. (88·9×71·5 cm.)
The Museum of Fine Arts, Boston
(Gift of Joseph W., William B., and Edward H. R. Revere)

Benjamin West has been criticized for an inability to use eclecticism for the formation of a personal style. However true this may be, he was a pioneer in many ways; the premature 'Romantic' study for *Death on the Pale Horse* amazed the Paris art world in 1802. Seven or eight years later he painted *Omnia Vincit Amor*, or *The Power of Love in the Three Elements* (Met. Mus.), which is undated, but, according to William Dunlap, was seen by Sully in West's studio in 1809 or 1810. It has been remarked by Grose Evans[15] that West probably created the spatial confusion and merged figure-composition on purpose, to suggest the obscurity discussed by Edmund Burke.

While West studied in Italy and gained success in London, Copley developed into an artistic phenomenon in Boston. Long before he went to Europe in 1774, he was painting pictures that far surpassed any that he had ever seen, or any hitherto produced in America.

He was a phenomenon because he was largely self-taught. By 1752, when he was fourteen, there was a hiatus in colonial painting and there was no one, apart from the primitive Badger, to teach him. As a youth he was stimulated by the contents of the studio of his stepfather Peter Pelham, a mezzotint engraver, who died in 1751. The two significant points about this are firstly that he developed a keen interest in history paintings, as seen in *The Return of Neptune* (Met. Mus.) painted *circa* 1754.[16] Secondly, in 1756 he composed a book of anatomical drawings and texts, taken from European anatomy books.[17] The full-length diagram of a man, showing all the muscles (British Museum, London, sketchbook, Plate X), demonstrates how much Copley realized that there was more to painting than portraiture.

[14] Met. Mus. Catalogue, p. 30.

[15] Evans, G. *Benjamin West and the Taste of his Time*, 1959.

[16] Gardner, Albert Ten Eyck, Met. Mus. Bull., April 1962, pp. 257–63.

[17] "John Singleton Copley", exhibition held at the National Gallery of Art, Washington, D.C., the Metropolitan Museum of Art, and the Museum of Fine Arts, Boston (September 18 1965–March 1966), catalogue, p. 17, note 4.

5. *The Staircase Group*, 1795,
by Charles Willson Peale
oil on canvas 89×39½ in. (225·6×99·8 cm.)
Philadelphia Museum of Art, George W. Elkins Collection

He soon left his provincial beginnings far behind. He learnt from Blackburn, who arrived in Boston in 1755, all that he needed to unlease him on the rapid development of his own style. In *Ann Tyng* the borrowing is obvious, but in the beautiful *Mary and Elizabeth Royall* (Museum of Fine Arts, Boston), painted two years later in 1758, he had already absorbed Blackburn's fashionable elegance and sense of colour into an earthy glowing style all his own. At an early stage he accomplished what West never really managed to do all his life.

Copley's portraits of the formative period 1758–64 have several characteristics: the use of strong, bright colours, stark contrasts of light and shade, technical competence in the painting of rich fabrics, particularly satin and velvet, and a forcefulness in the modelling of the face. Already he achieved realism. Among the prosperous New Englanders whom he painted during these years, *Thaddeus Burr* of 1758–60 (City Art Museum, St Louis) is magnificent.

Copley's patrons became increasingly eminent and aristocratic and by 1765 he was at the height of his career as a portrait painter in America. The earthy colour contrasts of his earlier portraits were now tempered with a softness. The vital quality of his mature portraits (*circa* 1765 onwards) lies in the technical luxuriance, plus isolation of the sitter, which is achieved by brilliant handling of light and shadow, concentration on the head and hands, and complete harmony of colour and design between the subjects and setting. The result of this isolation of the subject is that the spectator can sense not only their personality but their exact status in life as well.

In 1765 he painted the famous *Boy with a Squirrel*, who was his sixteen-year-old half-brother Henry Pelham, in which he has caught the fresh appeal of youth. He sent the picture to London, where it was exhibited in 1766. We learn from the letters of R. G. Bruce, who conveyed it, and West,[18] that West and Reynolds both praised it highly, but found it to be "too liney", also to have, among other faults, too much attention to details and a "coldness" in the shading. West and Reynolds urged Copley to come to London, using the persuasions that only a visit to Europe was wanting to perfect him as an artist. His dilemma is expressed in his correspondence with West of 1766 and 1767, where he freely admits his depression over the desolate state of art in America. He was torn between the security of an ever-increasing income from his many patrons who only wanted portraits, and his artistic ambitions which craved history painting and Europe. His indecision can well be understood when one views the achievements of his prolific Boston years up till 1773.

Copley possessed an amazing adaptability to the nature of each of his subjects. The informal turban and dressing-gown of *Nathaniel Hurd* (Cleveland Museum of Art) was used by him in portraits of several important patrons, giving them a relaxed air. The intense directness and realism of *Paul Revere* (Ill. 4) marks a new severity and increased emphasis on the contrast of light and shade in Copley's style in the years 1770–71.

The approaching Revolution affected Copley both in his private and professional life. In *Samuel Adams* (City of Boston), of 1770–72, the gravity of the colonial situation is summed up in the accusing hand and expression. The stormy events of 1774 in Boston finally made up his mind, already full of West's and Reynolds's advice and pleas to come to Europe, and in June 1774 he left America for good. After a sojourn in Italy, he settled in London in October 1775.

It has often been said of Copley that his departure for Europe in 1774 was a great

[18] "Letters and Papers of John Singleton Copley and Peter Pelham", Collection of the Massachusetts Hist. Soc., no. 71 (1914), relevant letters published in McCoubrey, pp. 10–13.

mistake and that the individual, powerful portrait style which he evolved in New England was spoiled by direct contact and the ensuing competition with Reynolds, West and others in London. It is true that his portrait style changed distinctly, and sometimes became too concerned with fashionable elegance for his temperament, but this fact was inevitable, due to an entirely different type of patron. His London years are notable for two reasons – his portrait style became softer, with much freer brushwork, which, combined with his flair for directness, produced some remarkable portraits. The other reason is that he contributed some of the first history pictures in American painting.

The Copley Family (National Gallery, Washington, D.C.), painted in 1776–77, is enough known to need no description. It marks the final emergence of the conversation piece in American painting. The new softness and painterly brushwork of Copley's early London portraits is seen in the *Self-portrait* of 1778–80 and the unsigned *Head of a Negro*, of 1777–83 (Detroit Institute of Arts), which was perhaps a study for the Negro in *Brook Watson and the Shark*. On the strength of *Midshipman Augustus Brine* (see colour plate opposite p. 117) one can firmly say that Copley's London period was not a failure but rather a fulfilment of what his early years promised. The handling of light and shade on the face and hands is highly skilled, the brushwork fluid, and the colours, with the boy's golden hair the focal-point of the picture, rich and harmonious. Also in the early 1780's he painted another of his best London portraits, *Mrs Charles Startin, circa* 1783 (Mr and Mrs William P. Wadsworth), where the colour is laid on in large sweeping strokes, anticipating Gilbert Stuart. The artist never surpassed these four portraits, one reason being his preoccupation with large-scale history paintings, although in the 1790's he did produce the superb *Earl Howe* (National Maritime Museum, London).

The development of history painting in American art began, as has been noted, with West's *Death of General Wolfe*, followed by other subjects. Copley was not slow to explore this field and to paint events nearer in time to his generation. His earliest history paintings in London are his most successful and famous. *Brook Watson and the Shark*, shown at the Royal Academy in 1778, now known in three versions (National Gallery, Washington, D.C.; Museum of Fine Arts, Boston; Detroit Institute of Arts),[19] which portrayed a true story of 1749 in Havana harbour, is an amazing and compelling composition, in which the grisly horror of the scene is most effectively captured. In the same year that Copley painted *Brook Watson and the Shark*, William Pitt, Earl of Chatham, died as the result of an energetic outburst in the House of Lords. *The Death of the Earl of Chatham*, completed by the spring of 1781 (Tate Gallery, London), is a combination of his abilities as a portraitist and as a history painter of large group scenes in the modern tradition set by West. The preparatory portrait drawings,[20] which are final studies rather than mere working drawings, show a high standard of draughtsmanship and character portrayal.

From 1782 to 1784 Copley worked on *The Death of Major Peirson* (Tate Gallery), which was even more successful than *The Death of the Earl of Chatham*. In these three works he developed history painting further than West did. His later history pictures were not successful projects, a result of either bad choice of subject or over-ambitious composition for the scene itself, as with *The Siege of Gibraltar*, a huge undertaking which he embarked upon in 1786. The most interesting products of this vast commission are the portrait sketches, and the drawings of figures in action. The painting was not given the ovations which had greeted the respective

6. *Colonel Marinus Willett, circa* 1790–95,
by Ralph Earl
oil on canvas $91\frac{1}{4} \times 56$ in. (231×142 cm.)
The Metropolitan Museum of Art, New York
(Bequest of George Willett Van Nest, 1917)

[19] Met. Mus. Catalogue, pp. 49f.
[20] Allen, Josephine L., Met. Mus. Bull., January 1956, pp. 122–26.

7. *Self-portrait, circa* 1786, by Gilbert Stuart oil on canvas $10\frac{5}{8}\times 8\frac{7}{8}$ in. (25·4×22·5 cm.) The Metropolitan Museum of Art, New York (Purchase Fletcher Fund, 1926)

8. *George Washington*, 1796, by Gilbert Stuart oil on canvas $42\times 34\frac{1}{2}$ in. (106·6×87·6 cm.) The Museum of Fine Arts, Boston Courtesy the Boston Athenaeum

Deaths of Chatham and Peirson. Copley worked on other history paintings during the 1790's, but the public preferred pictures of events close to them in time, not remote in the 17th century.

The history paintings by West and Copley were all executed in London. Back in America, the Revolution gave sudden birth to a need for the recording on canvas of recent historical events. In 1775 Ralph Earl made sketches in Lexington and Concord, Massachusetts, of the places where the first battles had taken place. From these drawings he made four paintings, which Dunlap called "the first historical pictures, perhaps, ever attempted in America", and which were engraved before the end of the year. Earl was primarily a portrait painter, whose style in that field will be briefly discussed further on. The men whose works constituted the rise, flourishing and decline of American history painting, started by West and Copley, are: John Trumbull (1756–1860), John Vanderlyn (1775–1852), Rembrandt Peale (1778–1860), Samuel F. B. Morse (1791–1872) and Washington Allston (1779–1843), all of whom, with the exception of Vanderlyn, who went to Paris for his artistic education, studied with West.

John Trumbull believed passionately and patriotically in history painting. While working under West in 1784 the idea came to him to do a series of paintings of the important events of the Revolution, in which project he was encouraged by both West and Thomas Jefferson. As studies for this huge project he did a whole group of portrait heads of American military and political figures, now in Yale University Art Gallery, New Haven, which he used as models for the historical paintings. Trumbull's portrait studies are good, but it is indeed sad to read, in his correspondence of 1789 with Jefferson,[21] of his failure to sell engravings of the finished scenes, in particular the Battles of Bunker's Hill and Quebec. If it is sad to read of Trumbull's disillusionments over the response of the public to his history paintings, it is even sadder to trace the stormy career of John Vanderlyn, whose future seemed so assured in his early years. He attracted the attention of Aaron Burr, who paid for some instruction in portrait painting under Stuart, and sent him to study in Paris in 1796. In 1807 he painted *Marius Amid the Ruins of Carthage*[22] (M. H. de Young Memorial Museum, San Francisco), for which Napoleon gave him a gold medal in 1808, and which shows the influence of David. In 1812 Vanderlyn exhibited his *Ariadne*[23] in Paris (Pennsylvania Academy of Fine Arts, Philadelphia), bringing it to America in 1815. The heroic, grand style and subject-matter of *Marius Amid the Ruins of Carthage* and the *Ariadne* were not really suited to the forthright nature of a pioneer nation. This fact, combined with the political downfall of Aaron Burr, and the fact that the artist had been in Europe too long, contributed to the eventual failure of all his projects – in particular The Rotunda. In 1818 he built a rotunda in the north-east corner of City Hall Park, New York, with the aim that it should be a national gallery of art which would guide and influence the artistic taste of the public through its changing exhibits. About a year after the opening of The Rotunda he put on its round walls his huge panorama of *The Palace and Gardens of Versailles* (Met. Mus.), a fantastic piece of work which measures twelve by one hundred and sixty-five feet, painted between 1818 and 1819.[24] The public reception of this unique painting was not antipathetic, on the other hand not wildly enthusiastic, due probably, as Vanderlyn later realized, when writing about The Rotunda in 1824, to the nature of the subject. His grandiose

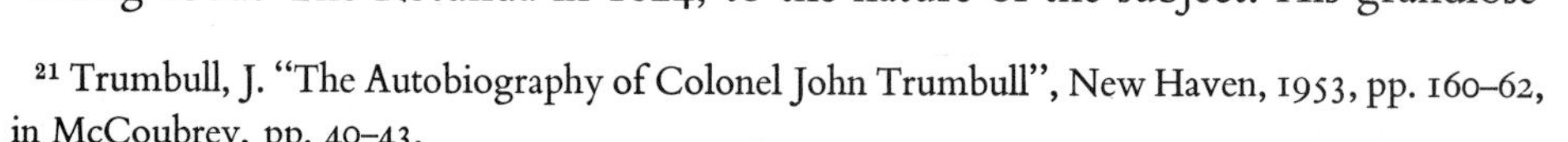

[21] Trumbull, J. "The Autobiography of Colonel John Trumbull", New Haven, 1953, pp. 160–62, in McCoubrey, pp. 40–43.

[22] Illustr. Larkin, colour section, pl. 6 (plate reversed).

[23] Illustr., *op. cit.*, p. 130.

[24] Met. Mus. Catalogue, pp. 123–25.

scheme for a popular national art gallery completely failed; in 1829, ruined by debts, he was evicted from his Rotunda by the city of New York. When in 1837 he finally managed to obtain the long-sought commission for *The Landing of Columbus* (Capitol, Washington, D.C.), for the rotunda of the Capitol in Washington (rebuilt in 1814), the picture took him eight years of procrastination in Paris to complete, and was badly received in 1845.

Samuel F. B. Morse fared a little better than Trumbull and Vanderlyn, partly on account of his preoccupation in his later years with the electric telegraph which he invented in 1832. In 1811 he had come to London, where he studied for four years with Washington Allston and West. In 1812 he exhibited the small terracotta of the *Dying Hercules*, which was a model for his forty-eight square feet of canvas of the same subject (both Yale University Art Gallery) shown in 1813. In 1815 Morse returned to America, but did not, because he could not, earn his living by history painting. However, he did paint two ambitious subjects, which are interesting in that although intended as history paintings they really turned out, unintentionally on the part of the artist, to be huge genre scenes: *The House of Representatives* (Corcoran Gallery, Washington, D.C.), painted in 1821, and *The Louvre* (Syracuse University, Syracuse, N.Y.), painted in 1832. Morse tried, and failed, to obtain commissions for four historical paintings for the Capitol; like Trumbull, he had a genuine belief in the ideal role of history painting.[25]

Washington Allston was equally doomed to failure in his efforts at history painting. Contemporary criticism suggested in 1839 that he confine himself to the beautiful, especially landscapes at which he excelled, and that he should not attempt the 'grand style'.[26] Allston is one of the most interesting figures in the history of American painting. A native of South Carolina, educated in Newport and at

[25] Samuel F. B. Morse, from a letter to James Fenimore Cooper, 20 November 1849, in "Letters and Journals of S. F. B. Morse", Boston, 1860. In McCoubrey, pp. 56–57.

[26] Ossoli, Margaret F. "A Record of the Impressions Produced by the Exhibition of Mr. Allston's Pictures in the Summer of 1839", "Works of Margaret Fuller Ossoli", Boston, 1860, vol. VI, pp. 285–92, in McCoubrey, pp. 57–60.

9. (bottom left) *Queen Victoria*, 1838, by Thomas Sully
oil on canvas 36×28⅜ in. (91·4×71·5 cm.)
The Metropolitan Museum of Art, New York
(Bequest of Francis T. S. Darley, 1914)

10 (bottom right) *Little Miss Hone*, 1824, by Samuel F. B. Morse
oil on panel 30×25 in. (76·2×63·5 cm.)
The Museum of Fine Arts (M. and M. Karolik Collection), Boston

11. *Winter Scene in Brooklyn, circa* 1817, by Francis Guy
oil on canvas $58\frac{3}{4} \times 75$ in. (149×190 cm.)
The Brooklyn Museum, New York

Harvard, he studied with West in London from 1801 to 1803, in which year he went to Paris where he visited the Louvre, a significant factor in the development of his landscape painting, as will be seen. From 1805 to 1808 he lived in Rome, and knew, among many others, Washington Irving and Coleridge. After a brief return to America in 1808, he came back to England where he lived until 1818, when emotional and financial troubles drove him back to Boston. But, like Vanderlyn, he had spent too long in Europe.

In 1817 Allston had made his first sketches for *Belshazzar's Feast*. The first sepia study for it is good, the second one less successful; he was eventually driven almost insane by the troubles he had with *Belshazzar* (unfinished, Museum of Fine Arts, Boston). He was too emotional and intensely romantic to paint the heroic.

Rembrandt Peale, best known for his 'porthole portrait' of George Washington, was as versatile as his father, Charles Willson Peale. Among numerous schemes, he managed to produce one of the rare successful history paintings in America of the early 19th century: *The Court of Death* (Detroit Institute of Arts), which was painted in 1820. Rembrandt studied under West in 1802, was one of the founders of the Pennsylvania Academy of Fine Arts in 1805 and worked in Paris in 1808. In 1814 he opened a gallery and natural history museum in Baltimore, which was not a success. However, he recovered his fortunes with *The Court of Death*, the enthusiastic reception of which caused him to abandon his museum. The letter by Rembrandt, which was published in 1845,[27] should be read, both as an explanation of the artist's aims for the moral value of the work, and as a record of contemporary public reaction to it, which was certainly lively. Its immediate success is accounted for by the fact that it is not strictly a history painting, but held a real meaning for many of the simple folks who flocked to see it, as we see from the remarks of Rembrandt's old cook, Aunt Hannah.

West had warned his pupils that history painting in America would not sell enough to earn them a living. The demands of Jefferson, who wanted Trumbull's paintings in the Capitol rotunda, to keep alive the memory of the Revolution, could not be the voice of the new republic. Trumbull, Vanderlyn, Morse and Allston did not consider carefully enough the public taste. Increasingly through the early 19th century Americans showed that the pictures they wanted and enjoyed were of ordinary everyday life – genre, landscapes, portraits.

[27] Peale, Rembrandt. Letter on his "Court of Death", published in a pamphlet, 1845, in McCoubrey, pp. 53–56.

More than any other artist Charles Willson Peale (1741–1827) represents the result of the stimulating influence that West and Copley had on American painting. He was not only versatile in a broad sense, with his many activities, but also within the portrait field. He visited Copley in 1765, went to London and West's studio in 1767, and returned to America in 1769.

He and various members of his large family, who played a vital part in the expansion of American painting, may be seen in the jolly group portrait *The Peale Family* (New York Historical Society),[28] painted in 177?. A comparison with *The Copley Family* reveals an experimental Peale, who has not quite overcome his provincial limitations. It is, however, a more relaxed scene than Copley's, and the bowl of fruit on the table is no less realistic than that in *Mrs Ezekiel Goldthwait* of 1770–77. Peale attained fame when he painted his full-length of *George Washington* (Pennsylvania Academy of Fine Arts), which was commissioned in January 1779, and of which he rapidly made many replicas, such as the version in the Metropolitan Museum, probably painted before June 1780. An excellent example of a double portrait by Peale is *Benjamin Laming and his Wife*,[29] painted in 1788. However, his masterpiece was still to come: the *Staircase Group*. (Ill. 5.) There was no precedent for this picture, which is almost a genre scene, almost photographic, so brilliantly has the artist frozen the fleeting moment at which two of his sons turn to look at the beholder as they climb a winding stair.

Peale spent more and more time with his scientific inventions and museums, although there are some superb portraits dating from the 1790's, such as *John de Peyster* (New York Historical Society) of 1798.

Ralph Earl was in England from 1778 until 1785, but unlike his compatriots was not influenced by West. After returning to America in 1785 he painted his best-known portraits, which are competent and forceful, but possess a certain primitive quality. Two fine full-lengths are *Elijah Boardman*[30] of 1789 and *Colonel Marinus Willett* (Ill. 6) which is a more distinguished example of a full-length portrait than Peale's *Washington* of twenty years earlier. *Mrs Elijah Boardman and her Son William Whiting Boardman*,[30] of *circa* 1797–98, and the group of *Mrs Noah Smith and her Children* (Met. Mus.), of 1798, illustrate Earl's ability to pose full or three-quarter figures harmoniously in the detailed setting of their homes.

Gilbert Stuart (1755–1828) was from the first interested only in portrait painting. During the years 1777 to 1782, while living and working with West, he developed a unique portrait style. He reduced background and details of dress, whenever possible, to a minimum. Using a broad technique, he painted features directly with the brush, and abhorred strong contrasts of light and shadow. He also advised that a general, pleasant expression gave a better effect than an individual

[28] Illustr. Larkin, p. 67. [29] Feld, Stuart P., *op. cit.*, p. 280. [30] Feld, Stuart P., *op. cit.*, pp. 282–83.

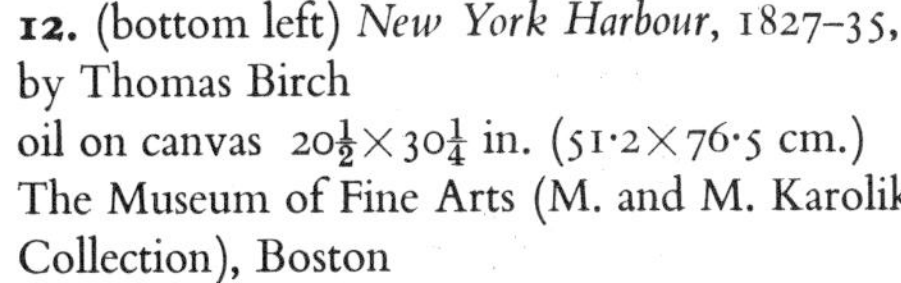

12. (bottom left) *New York Harbour*, 1827–35, by Thomas Birch
oil on canvas $20\frac{1}{8}\times30\frac{1}{8}$ in. (51·2×76·5 cm.)
The Museum of Fine Arts (M. and M. Karolik Collection), Boston

13. (bottom right) *Elijah and the Ravens*, 1818, by Washington Allston
oil on canvas 50×70 in. (127×177·8 cm.)
The Museum of Fine Arts, Boston
(Gift of Mrs Samuel and Miss Alice Hooper)

14. *Landscape – the Fountain of Vaucluse*, 1841, by Thomas Cole
oil on canvas 69×49⅛ in. (175×124·5 cm.)
The Metropolitan Museum of Art, New York
(Gift of William E. Dodge, 1903)

one.[31] Two works which show that his style was well formed by 1782 when he opened his own studio are *Man in a Green Coat* (Met. Mus.), painted probably between 1780 and 1785, and the unfinished *Self-portrait*. (Ill. 7.) *The Skater* (National Gallery, Washington, D.C.), also done in London, is a perfect illustration of his subordination of background. Stuart painted portraits in London until 1787, when debts forced him to leave for Dublin. His success may seem remarkable at first, but less so when one considers the refreshing contrast his uncluttered, flowing manner must have made with the more formal elaborate portraits by his English contemporaries.

On his return to America in 1793, he introduced the new portrait form that he had created and became the foremost American portraitist of his time. He was painting in New York in 1793 and 1794, in Philadelphia from 1794 to 1803, and in Washington from 1803 to 1805, in which year he settled in Boston. In the portraits of the Spanish envoy *Josef de Jaudenes y Nebot* and his wife *Matilda Stoughton de Jaudenes* (Met. Mus.), of 1794, despite the formal nature of the commission, he suggests rather than describes the setting; moreover, the sumptuous clothes do not swamp but enhance the faces.

Stuart's ability to capture the permanent and discard the superfluous in painting a human face is best seen in his portraits of George Washington, of which there are three types. The first portrait that he painted from life, in March 1795, at Philadelphia, shows the right side of Washington's face, and is known as the Vaughan type (original in National Gallery, Washington, D.C.). The Gibbs-Channing-Avery version (Met. Mus.) is considered to be one of the earliest and best replicas. His second portrait of Washington from life (Ill. 8) shows the left side of his face. It remained, unfinished, in the artist's studio, where he used it as a model for the later full-length Lansdowne type. At the same time, in 1796, Stuart painted his only portrait from life of *Martha Washington* (Museum of Fine Arts, Boston, lent by the Athenaeum).

Many of the portraits of his Boston period lack the vibrant quality of his early and middle years, and are smaller and simpler, often done on a wooden panel. With *Josiah Quincy* (Museum of Fine Arts, Boston), of 1824, and the unfinished *Washington Allston* (Met. Mus.), painted about the year of his death, he returned to his earlier penetrating manner. Stuart did not have pupils in any strict sense, but certain painters copied his portraits or watched him at work, notably John Trumbull and Thomas Sully.

Sully developed the free, sketchy style of Stuart, whom he visited in Boston in 1807. When in London in 1809 he was heavily influenced by Lawrence, and after his return to Philadelphia in 1810, painted portraits which possess Lawrence's chiaroscuro and fresh, unfinished look. They include: *Mrs Katherine Matthews* (Met. Mus.), of 1812–13, *Portrait of the Artist* (Met. Mus.), painted in 1821, and the oil sketch of *Mrs Huges* (Met. Mus.) which is undated, but from the fashion of the dress and hat is judged to be of *circa* 1830.

Sully's *Queen Victoria*, painted in 1838 and 1839,[32] represents the summit of the artist's career. The original oil sketch for the head (Ill. 9) shows his skill with pigment; though only a study it has a polish that Stuart never achieved. An example of Sully's still more painterly style of *circa* 1840 is seen in the *Mother and Son* (Met. Mus.).

[31] Jouett, Matthew H., "Notes on Painting from Conversations with Gilbert Stuart", in John Hill Morgan, "Gilbert Stuart and his Pupils", New York, 1939. In McCoubrey, pp. 20–25.

[32] Feld, Stuart P., *op. cit.*, p. 289; Gardner, Albert Ten Eyck, "Queen Victoria and Mr. Sully", Met. Mus. Bull., January 1947, pp. 144–48.

15. (above) *Brace's Rock, Eastern Point, Gloucester, circa* 1863, by Fitz Hugh Lane
oil on canvas 10×15 in. (25·4×38 cm.)
The Museum of Fine Arts (M. and M. Karolik Collection), Boston

16. (below) *Meditation of the Sea, circa* 1850–60, anonymous
oil on canvas 13½×19½ in. (33·5×48·6 cm.)
The Museum of Fine Arts (M. and M. Karolik Collection), Boston

Morse attained a similar sophistication and skill with light and shadow in his portraits, which vary in treatment. His imposing full-length *Lafayette* of 1824 (New York City Hall), delightful *Little Miss Hone* (Ill. 10), and the *Reverend Thomas Harvey Skinner* (Museum of Fine Arts, Karolik Collection, Boston), exhibited at the National Academy of Design in 1837, possess Stuart's painterly quality. But *The Muse – Susan Walker Morse* (Met. Mus.), painted *circa* 1835–37, has a contrasting polish and smoothness.

Interest and a growing pride in the country itself caused the gradual rise of landscape painting in America. Its beginnings as an art form were slow, and predominantly topographical. Charles Willson Peale planned landscape backgrounds as realistic surroundings for his birds and reptiles in his history museum; he also had a scheme for a panorama consisting of different views he had painted from the eight sides of a cupola. Between 1790 and 1795 four English artists – William Winstanley, William Groombridge, Thomas Beck and Francis Guy – arrived in America, who adequately satisfied the demands of literal-minded colonials wanting specific local views. Such landscapes were frequently engraved. Guy was the most independent and versatile of the four, and in the year of his death, 1820, gave a one-man show of his landscapes at the Shakespeare Gallery, near Park Theatre, New York. He was at his best painting neat-looking but delightful street scenes. His large *Winter Scene in Brooklyn* (Ill. 11) is reminiscent of 17th-century Dutch and Flemish landscape painting with its busy people and dogs in the snow.

Also in 1790 and in 1791 there arrived in New York Archibald and Alexander Robertson from Scotland, who painted delicate but conservative detailed views, such as Archibald's *View of New York City from North River* (New York Historical Society)[33] which has no attempt at middle distance. In 1825 Alexander recorded the opening of the Erie Canal with a picture of an overloaded canoe paddled by an Indian and escorted by Pan, who is embraced by Neptune leaning from a cockleshell.

Owing to the geographic and historic nature of America, the sea was an essential part of life, which fact caused seascapes and marine painting in general to be given a wide range of treatment. The versatility of American painters from necessity as well as inclination precluded any exclusive 'marine painters', although some were clearly gifted in that field. Thomas Birch (1779–1851), who arrived in Philadelphia in 1794 with his engraver father, continued but improved the topographical manner; his best works mark a departure from the vast factory of attractive but traditional landscapes reproduced through engraving. *New York Harbour* (Ill. 12) has lively waves and animation provided by the small boats in the middle foreground.

The War of 1812–15 stimulated painting with its naval victories; Birch's *The Wasp and The Frolic* (Museum of Fine Arts, Karolik Collection, Boston), painted in 1820, illustrates his ability to do salty waves, which in the *Shipwreck* of 1829 (Brooklyn Museum) and the *Seascape* of 1831 (Museum of Fine Arts, Karolik Collection, Boston) show how much broader his technique became. This, and the strong feeling of mood in both of these works, suggest that Birch may have been influenced by the harbour pictures and shipwrecks of Claude Joseph Vernet. A different and quite charming landscape is the work entitled *Skating* (Museum of Fine Arts, Karolik Collection, Boston) of *circa* 1831.

Comparable to Birch's later seascapes are those of Robert Salmon (*circa* 1780–after 1840), who arrived in Boston in 1828, having worked in England and Scotland. A comparison of his *Storm at Sea* (Museum of Fine Arts, Karolik

[33] Illustr. Larkin, p. 138.

Colour Plate. *Midshipman Augustus Brine* (detail), 1782, by John Singleton Copley
oil on canvas $49\frac{1}{2} \times 39\frac{1}{2}$ in. (125×99·5 cm.)
The Metropolitan Museum of Art, New York (Bequest Richard de Wolfe Brixey, 1943)

Collection, Boston), painted in 1840, with Birch's *Shipwreck*, reveals Salmon's sharper expression of an angry sea.

The first landscape of mood by an American artist was probably Allston's *Rising of a Thunderstorm at Sea* (Museum of Fine Arts, Boston), painted *circa* 1804 in Paris. Evident in it are the effects of the impact on him of Venetian colouring, absorbed through West and works in the Louvre, where he must also have seen Vernet's seascapes. Allston's interpretation of nature was very different from any other American landscape work of this date; mood dominates the painting. In *Landscape with a Lake* (Museum of Fine Arts, Karolik Collection, Boston), of the same year, it is one of stillness and calm, but in *Elijah and the Ravens* (Ill. 13) the dark brooding clouds of the *Rising of a Thunderstorm at Sea* have become intensified and the tiny kneeling figure is dwarfed in the desolate vastness. Allston's friendship with Coleridge in Rome had encouraged his Romantic inclinations. Until recently attributed to Allston's Paris visit of 1804 on account of its affinities with the *Rising of a Thunderstorm at Sea* and because it belonged at one time to Allston's father, is *The Deluge* (Met. Mus.) which is now accepted as the work of Joshua Shaw (*circa* 1776–1860).[34] It is one of four paintings which were exhibited by Shaw at the British Institution in 1813; the dramatic sense of doom and of man's insignificance against nature echoes Allston's imaginative landscapes, but the technique has been found to lack the glazing that he used. The two men were friends; Shaw was undoubtedly influenced by Allston in London. He painted in America and made extensive sketches which were published in 1820–21 as *Picturesque Views of American Scenery*. The English engraver John Hill, who had, incidentally, made prints in London from Turner's work, made aquatints of these and at the same time produced a *Landscape Album* of his own.

Allston's *Rising of a Thunderstorm at Sea*, *Landscape with a Lake*, and *Elijah and the Ravens* were all painted in Europe. However, their romanticism and strong response to nature anticipated the growth and flourishing of a native landscape school which burst forth in the 1820's with the scenic views of Thomas Cole (1801–48), and the other painters of the so-called Hudson River School. The evolution of a lyrical, grand landscape art out of the topographical tradition was certainly fostered by a growing interest in the scenery of the Hudson River: Dunlap painted watercolours of it, Vanderlyn had sketched Niagara Falls in 1802, Washington Irving and James Fenimore Cooper wrote about its beauty, and John Hill engraved the *Hudson River Portfolio* of William Guy Wall in 1820, who did actually finish his sketches *in situ*. Morse's landscapes painted in Cooperstown, New York, in 1827 and 1828, and his *Niagara Falls From Table Rock* (Museum of Fine Arts, Karolik Collection, Boston) of 1835, show a sensitivity to nature which had increased after painting scenery in Switzerland in the intervening years.

The principal painters of the Hudson River School include Cole, who can be called the founder, Thomas Doughty (1793–1856), Asher Brown Durand (1796–1886), Alvan Fisher (1792–1863), John Kensett (1816–72), John Casilear (1811–93) and Frederick Church (1826–1900) who was Cole's only pupil and came to his studio in 1844.

Cole's scenery sketched by the Hudson in 1825 was discovered in that year by Trumbull. He visited Europe in 1829–32, when his technique broadened and his colours became brighter, and again in 1841–42. Two emotions, expounded in his writings,[35] conflict in his ideal of mankind fused with the landscape. In the latter, his dominating themes were man's frailty, felt in *Expulsion from the Garden of Eden*

17. *Hunting Elk* (detail), 1837, by Alfred Jacob Miller watercolour $8\frac{1}{2} \times 12\frac{5}{16}$ in. (21·5×31·2 cm.) The Walters Art Gallery, Baltimore and the University of Oklahoma Press

[34] Met. Mus. Catalogue, pp. 131–33.

[35] Noble, L. L. *The Life and Works of Thomas Cole*, Cambridge, Mass., 1964.

18. *Ivory-billed woodpeckers*, by John James Audubon oil on canvas, after the watercolour of 1829 for *The Birds of America*, plate 66 39¼×26¼ in. (99·2×66 cm.)
The Metropolitan Museum of Art, New York (Purchase Rogers Fund, 1941)

(Museum of Fine Arts, Karolik Collection, Boston) of 1828, and man's impermanence amidst nature's eternal evolution, expressed in the allegorical series for which he was best known in his life-time, notably *The Course of Empire*, completed in 1836 (New York Historical Society), and *The Voyage of Life* of 1840 (Munson-Williams-Proctor Institute, Utica, N.Y.). His final mood changed to salvation through faith, as in *The Vision* (Brooklyn Museum) painted the year he died. His paintings which were inspired by nature alone now receive equal attention, such as *Landscape – the Fountain of Vaucluse*. (Ill. 14.)

A more realistic approach to nature expressed itself in the calm seascapes of Fitz Hugh Lane (1804–65), and Martin Johnson Heade (1819–1904). Lane worked as a lithographer in Boston from *circa* 1835 until 1849, when he returned to his home in Gloucester, Massachusetts, where he painted primarily sea-pieces with a growing feeling for light and atmosphere. *Maine Inlet* (Museum of Fine Arts, Karolik Collection, Boston) of 1830, *Boston Harbour, Sunset*[36] of *circa* 1850–60, his best period, and *Brace's Rock, Eastern Point, Gloucester* (Ill. 15), illustrate the point.

Heade was a native of Pennsylvania, but travelled widely; he was in Europe from *circa* 1837 to 1839, in Brazil in 1863 and 1864, and in London in 1865. Excluding his portraits, his work can be divided into three categories: landscapes, usually marine, still-lifes, and paintings of exotic tropical birds and foliage of South America. His seascapes are usually very flat, with considerable attention to detail; in the past they have been called dull and too painstaking. His romanticism, like Lane's, is combined with realism. *Approaching Storm, Beach Near Newport* (Museum of Fine Arts, Karolik Collection, Boston), painted in the 1860's, with its sultry, ominous sky, and *The Stranded Boat* (Museum of Fine Arts, Karolik Collection, Boston) of 1863, show how he depicted nature's moods through the blending of light changes. His masterpiece is considered to be *Thunderstorm – Narragansett Bay*, which was exhibited at the National Academy in 1868.[37]

A small but enchanting seascape is the anonymous *Meditation by the Sea* (Ill. 16), which from the dress of the watcher on the beach was painted *circa* 1850–60. It combines the quiet philosophical romanticism of Lane and Heade with the simple charm of a good primitive.

Penetration of the West in the 19th century by explorers, pioneer settlers and traders, and the consequent realization of a huge, mostly undiscovered continent, produced a fascination in all aspects of the West, including the Indians, who were painted avidly by George Catlin, Karl Bodmer, and, more romantically, by Alfred Jacob Miller. With the exception of the expeditions of John White and Jacques Le Moyne in the 16th century, there had never been a documentor of the Indians, although West's collection of Indian costumes and his remarks on the Mohawk braves in Rome[38] show his keen interest.

In 1829 Catlin (1796–1872) decided that his vocation was to record the appearance and ways of the Indians, which resulted, among other enterprises, in his book "Illustration of the Manners, Customs, and Conditions of the North American Indians", New York, 1841. He began his expedition at St Louis in 1830, and in 1832 went up the Missouri River, visiting various tribes, constantly making rapid sketches of every aspect of Indian life. By 1837 he had produced six hundred paintings which, when he was unsuccessful in selling them in New York, he

[36] Feld, Stuart P., *op. cit.*, p. 292.

[37] *Ibid.*

[38] Galt, J., "The Life and Studies of Benjamin West", Philadelphia, 1816, pp. 122–33. In McCoubrey, pp. 36–39.

19. *Fur-traders descending the Missouri*, 1845,
by George Caleb Bingham
oil on canvas 29×36½ in. (73·6×92 cm.)
The Metropolitan Museum of Art, New York
(Morris K. Jesup Fund, 1933)

transported, with a huge collection of Indian articles, to London, where they were exhibited at the Egyptian Hall. Two magnificent portraits painted in 1845 when fourteen Iowas came to London to take part in the *tableaux vivants* (at Egyptian Hall) are *Mu-hú-she-kaw, The White Cloud, Chief of the Iowas* and *See-nón-ty-a, Iowa Medicine Man.*[39]

Miller (1810–74) was a pupil of Sully before studying in Europe in 1833–34. In 1834 he returned to America and in 1837 travelled in the Far West where he painted Indians in romantic and beautiful landscapes. He lacked the passionate and technical interest of Catlin in their customs and the fact that they were a dying race, with the result that his Indians are often more generalized; but his use of white for highlights and the grandiose Western settings receding in blue-grey mist produce a mysterious effect, as in *Hunting Elk.* (Ill. 17.)

The surge westward and all over the land caused artists to turn to the beauties of their natural surroundings: birds, animals and flowers were exquisitely drawn and painted by John James Audubon (1785–1851) (Ill. 18) and Heade.

The mid-19th century also saw the rise of genre painting: the realism of George Caleb Bingham (1808–79) encouraged the ideal that beauty exists anywhere and everywhere (Ill. 19), but equally full of humour and perception are the genre paintings of John Quidor, W. S. Mount, J. G. Clonney and J. G. Blythe. Still-life, a rare subject in pre-revolutionary painting, flourished in the hands of the Peale family and numerous unknown Primitive painters.

Folk-art developed and flourished aside from the main stream of American painting. The most attractive was that of the Pennsylvania German communities. Also somewhat on their own independent course were the Primitives, the self-taught artisans, many of them anonymous, working from the 1790's until about the third quarter of the 19th century, when mass production finally drove them out of business. To do justice to these works of art would be a subject unto itself.

[39] Feld, Stuart P., *op. cit.*, pp. 290–91.

BIBLIOGRAPHY

MUSEUM CATALOGUES

Gardner, Albert Ten Eyck, and Feld, Stuart P., American Paintings. A catalogue of the collections of the Metropolitan Museum of Art, I. Painters born by 1815, 1965.

M. and M. Karolik Collection of American Paintings, 1815–65. Cambridge, publ. for Museum of Fine Arts, Boston, by Harvard Univ. Press, 1949 (1951).

CONTEMPORARY SOURCES

McCoubrey, John W. *American Art, 1700–1960.* Sources and Documents in the History of Art Series, New Jersey, 1965.

GENERAL

Larkin, Oliver W. *Art and Life in America.* Revised ed. April 1964.

Flexner, James T. *That Wilder Image. The Painting of America's Native School from Thomas Cole to Winslow Homer*, 1962.

Richardson, Edgar P. *American Romantic Painting*, New York, 1944.

The First Empire Style in Furniture

MALCOLM BURGESS

Political events in France after the Revolution had contributed to the adoption of a style of design which strove to recall an exemplary way of life both ancient and glorious. The destruction of the old social order during the years of the French Revolution also ensured the disappearance of all that very order's outward and visible trappings. Decorative treasures which embellished Versailles and other royal palaces symbolic of tyranny could have no place under the new régime: objects bearing the emblems of monarchy were destined to destruction. The French Revolution thus produced profound economic and social change; it was to leave an indelible imprint on style and taste; it was highly damaging to artists, cabinet-makers, silversmiths and all craftsmen engaged in luxury trades. There was no demand for fine ornaments during those years of upheaval, and many masterpieces were lost. It was often difficult to discriminate between allusions to the *ancien régime*: Gobelin tapestries depicting the arrival of Cleopatra at Cilicia, or of Louis le Grand at the Gobelin factory, were suspect, yet scenes portraying episodes such as the conflict of Romans and Sabines, or medieval battles, were preserved; fine furniture perished in a bonfire beneath the Tree of Liberty in the forecourt of the Gobelin factory. Greater still were the losses incurred through the disposal of the national treasures of France in the vast sale of royal and confiscated property belonging to the nobility held at Versailles during the Terror. It was ironical to find present the great *ébéniste* of Louis XVI's time, Riesener, appointed by the National Convention together with the painter David, to assist the Commission in deciding which works of art should be reserved. The sale lasted a year, according to Baron Davillier, in his "La Vente du Mobilier du Château de Versailles pendant la Terreur" and exceeded 17,000 lots.

Apart from the dispersal of furniture from the houses of the nobility, much property had been destroyed by the revolutionary mob, but none the less the French temperament could hardly endure for long a period devoid of decoration and barren of taste. The government managed to form a Jury of Arts Manufacturers for the encouragement of national art unsullied by monarchical ornament. When the tempers of revolution had subsided, a revival of taste occurred, and the genius inherent in the French people began to reassert itself. It is true that the French Revolution scarcely changed the organic evolution of art in France; celebrated *fondeurs-ciseleurs* of the 18th century, such as Pierre Philippe Thomire (1751–1843) who was working from the beginning of the reign of Louis XVI until almost the end of the reign of Louis Philippe, managed to maintain the high standard of workmanship which had developed under the monarchy undisturbed by social and political troubles. There was no sharp division between the tradition of Louis XVI and the new mode followed after the Revolution. Thomire and

1. One of a pair of armchairs; signed: *Jacob frères, Rue Meslée, circa* 1800
mahogany
Formerly René Fribourg Collection

other artists remained conservative and loyal to the 18th-century standards which had influenced them in their youth. Thus the strong tradition of the late 18th century may be observed in all work of the next two decades.

The style following immediately upon the cessation of the Terror is usually called *le style Messidor* or *style Directoire*. The *Directoire*, the rule by Committee of Five, lasted but four years, from October 1795 until November 1799, too short a period in which to develop an entirely original style. More exactly, the *Directoire* style embraces the end of the reign of Louis XVI, the period of the Convention (1792–95), the term of the Directorate itself, and part of the Consulate.

The return of Napoleon Bonaparte from the Italian and Egyptian campaigns, and his elevation to the title of First Consul on the 18 brumaire, an VIII (19 November 1799), which he held until the proclamation of the Empire (18 May 1804), although too late to save the dissipation of the great royal collections, nevertheless put a stop to further losses suffered by the French state.

Although there is a continuity with Louis XVI, both style and taste during the Consulate and Empire were affected not only by revolutionary philosophy, but also by the spirit of the French nation under the powerful personality of Napoleon. A feeling for modernity, a desire for fresh formulas encouraged by the military exploits of the new France now manifested themselves. Napoleon's campaigns in the East encouraged Oriental themes. The taste for the Roman and Pompeian styles was adopted at the Imperial Court, and this set the general pattern. Improved techniques in manufacture were evolved by a developing industry. The novel *style Empire* was to be the last truly great French style before the decline which came with industrialization in the later 19th century.

There was now a chance for the decorator. The stripped salons and denuded mansions required refurnishing. The spirit of the Antique, the examples set by the glorious civilizations of the ancient world as seen in perspective by an idealistic public, were in harmony with the intellectual, material and political ethos of the age of Napoleon.

The Emperor himself actively encouraged the revival of the fine arts. It was his desire to refurnish the royal residences which had suffered at the hands of the revolutionaries, to further the prestige of the dynasty and to encourage French industry. Napoleon's marriage to the Austrian Archduchess Marie Louise after his divorce from Joséphine led to an outburst of productivity from the artisans of Paris in 1809. These *fondeurs-ciseleurs-doreurs* could hardly keep up with the demands for ornaments to replenish the royal palaces and equip the fêtes and official functions which followed upon the Imperial marriage. Right from the beginning of the Empire, Napoleon had regularly subsidized the industry in addition to his own personal expenditure on the purchase of ornaments. After 1800 the subsidy was increased by five times. Napoleon set the fashion for the Empire style by acquiring the Château de Malmaison on the 2 floréal an VII (21 April 1799). Soon after, on the 18 brumaire, the First Consul ordered Charles Percier (1764–1838) and Pierre François Léonard Fontaine (1762–1853), soon to be the first architects of the Empire, to redesign the interiors and transform the house. It is the work of these two leading French designers that had such a profound influence over all furnishing styles throughout the continent of Europe and America in the early 19th century. Their designs were published in an important compendium.[1]

The most noticeable influence upon the Empire style had been the rediscovery of Greece and of Hellenic art, which had all the charms of novelty. A respect for

[1] *Recueil de Décoration Intérieur de Percier et Fontaine*, 1812 (Didot 1827 and later reproduced by Av. Guérinet, édit., 140, Faubourg St Martin, Paris, Imp. Haussedat. Châteaudun).

2. Napoleon I clock and bracket; signed: *Réhaist à Paris*, veneered in ebony and mahogany with ormolu mounts representing bee-hives and bees symbolic of Napoleon and industry and swans symbolizing the Empress Josephine
height of clock 23 in. (58·4 cm.) height of bracket 14½ in. (36·8 cm.)
Malcolm Burgess Collection

3. Empire firescreen, *circa* 1810
mahogany and ormolu *appliqués* with hinged side frames enclosing original ivory silk panels on both back and front
height 47½ in. (115·7 cm.) width 30 in. (76·2 cm.)
Malcolm Burgess Collection

antiquity was certainly no new movement in the history of art, but this time designers followed a more scholarly attitude to the reproduction of Greek and Roman art. Greece was an essential place of pilgrimage for the aristocracy, and after 1750 a visit to Greece more often than not formed the last stage of the Grand Tour. Books were produced on Greek subjects. Winckelmann had published his "Reflections on Painting and Sculpture of the Greeks" in 1755, an English translation being provided by Henry Fuseli in 1765, the Comte de Caylus produced his "Recueil d'Antiquités égyptiennes, étrusques, grecques et romaines" in 1752–57, David Le Roy brought out his "Ruines des Plus Beaux Monuments de la Grèce" six years later, and in England, Stuart and Revett brought out their work on "Athens" in 1794, and continued the first full delineations of Greek Doric architecture. Charles Pierre Joseph Normand (1765–1840) had devoted his time during the French Revolution to engraving architectural subjects, and was an assiduous worker. He had studied in Italy after winning the Premier Grand Prix de Rome in Architecture. He is famous for his publication of the "Nouveau Parallèle des ordres d'Architecture", 1819.

The inspiration of the Greek revival movement was rather less one of technique than of mood. It can be interpreted, perhaps, as a reactionary style rather than part of the oncoming wave of Romanticism; it was nevertheless considered as *avant-garde* in its own time. Ancient Greece was held to be the idol and ideal for which men yearned; thus Classicism came in handy for the propagandist efforts made by the supporters of the French Revolution, and by Napoleon himself.

The most famous name in the history of *ébénistes* and *ménuisiers* of this period is that of Jacob. The history of the dynasty of cabinet-makers and designers which formed the Jacob family is unique, because their workmanship extended over a long period and was outstanding not only for the quality of their products, but also for the diversity of design. It began with Georges Jacob in 1765 in the last years of the Louis XV style and continued on for eighty years to 1847, when the grandson, Georges Alphonse Jacob Desmalter, disgusted by the industrialization of his trade, sold up to the Jeanselme family. The founder of the dynasty, Georges Jacob, dominates the history of French furniture from 1765 to the end of the century. Not only was he a superb cabinet-maker, but he was an innovator as well, employing for the first time mahogany in the fabrication of chairs, in the English fashion. He had been a pupil of Louis Delanois, and had made chairs after the pure style of Louis XV, notable for the elegance and harmonious simplicity of their shapes. But very soon he was to adopt the new taste for geometrical line and decorative motifs inspired by antiquity. It is to him that is attributed the invention of *accotoirs rampants* (sloping arm-rests), *dossiers ajouré en lyre* (chair-backs in the shape of a lyre), *gerbes au carquois* (sheaves of quiver form) all carved out of his favourite mahogany. The Court soon came to notice the excellent workmanship, and his premises on the Rue Meslée turned out much furniture for the Queen's apartments at Versailles and the palaces of the royal family. He also executed orders for the Court of Sweden. He was able happily to adapt to his furniture motifs borrowed from Greece and Rome, which his clientèle now demanded. He created, amongst other things, for the painter David, a style of furniture drawn from prototypes depicted on Etruscan and Greek vases carved from a dark mahogany intended to resemble the patina of bronze. His friendship with David ensured a commission for him to decorate the Salle de Séances of the Convention at the Tuileries; it was a very important suite, and he entrusted the design of certain pieces to Percier and Fontaine. It may truly be said that the Empire style was elaborated by the collaboration of these four men. Although disturbed by the Comité de Salut publique, Jacob was able to go on creating, enlarging his field and making all kinds of furniture of mahogany, maple, satinwood and amaranth.

This great *ménuisier-ébéniste* Georges Jacob stamped his products "G+IACOB". Examples of his work survive in the great public collections of France, the Musée du Louvre, the Musée des Arts Décoratifs, and amongst others Fontainebleau and Malmaison. In 1796 he conceded the direction of his workshop in the Rue Meslée to his two sons, Georges and François Honoré Georges. The younger one was the remarkable designer, and succeeded in maintaining the quality which had made the reputation of his father in works which, until the death of the elder in 1803, bear the mark "Jacob frères, Rue Meslée". (Ill. 1.) Demand was very great, and the workshop expanded, making furniture for the most important personalities of the day, for Napoleon, Mademoiselle Mars and Madame Récamier. Madame Récamier's furniture has become famous, and the bed upon which she rested, one of the best pieces of design by the brothers Jacob, may be seen in the famous portrait by David.

4. Napoleon I commode; signed: *Jacob D., P. Meslée*, *circa* 1815–25
mahogany veneer and ebonized base
height 39 in. (99 cm.) width 32 in. (81·2 cm.)
Formerly René Fribourg Collection

In 1803 François Honoré Georges Jacob, called Jacob Desmalter, became sole proprietor of the workshop, and until 1815 signed his furniture "Jacob D. r. Meslée" and then with the stamp "+Jacob" until 1825. He also excelled in making all bronzes for embellishing his furniture designs. Although mahogany continued to be his favourite wood, he was also accustomed to use native woods, sometimes adding a patina in *vert antique* with inset designs of mother-of-pearl, steel, ebony and porcelain or faience plaques. He was the most representative artist of the Empire style, executing furniture after his own designs or those of Percier and Fontaine, David, Prudhon, and several others. He was the foremost supplier of the *mobilier impérial*. Examples of his work remain in the Imperial residences of Compiègne and Fontainebleau. The career of his son, Georges Alphonse Jacob Desmalter, was shorter and less distinguished. From 1825 to 1847 he furnished the royal residences Neuilly, Rambouillet, Saint-Cloud, a salon for the Duchesse de Berry at Rosny-sur-Seine, where he brought in *bois clairs*, apart from mahogany, rosewood and the light woods which were then in fashion inset with amaranth. His stamp was "A. Jacob F. et Cie+Jacob". He was a good designer, and produced his own models. Amongst other well-known *ébénistes* of the Empire period may be mentioned the names of Bernard Molitor, who was celebrated for the supreme quality of his furniture, and Claude Chapus. This latter's work is sometimes confused with that of the Belgian J. J. Chapuis (1767–1827) whose workshop was established at Brussels.

Napoleon had sponsored the work of the Jacob brothers, and had paid out of his privy purse for redecoration and furniture for the Tuileries and Saint-Cloud. In 1800 he spent 914,975.57 francs on the Tuileries, the following year 173,149 francs and in 1802 the bill was for 94,475.29 francs. The Consul's state rooms on the first floor were particularly grand – "The Consul regards luxurious décor and grandeur as a necessity; and the furniture of his apartments is rich and magnificent." This fine suite of rooms was almost completely furnished with antique pieces. The smaller rooms contained the newly created furnishings. The most famous room was Napoleon's *Cabinet de Travail*, the Jacob brothers providing most of the furniture.[2]

In the spring of 1802 Napoleon moved to the Château of Saint-Cloud, and in 1804 he ordered the Palace of Fontainebleau to be put in order and refurnished for

[2] Cf. Ledoux-Lebard, D., "The Re-furnishing of the Tuileries under the Consulate", *Apollo*, September 1964, vol. LXXX, no. 31, pp. 199–205.

5. *Secrétaire à Abattant, circa* 1800–10
mahogany, 'plum-pudding' or *acajou marqueté*, ormolu mounts, and a fall front enclosing an arched cupboard and nest of small drawers
height 49 in. (124·4 cm.) width 27 in. (68·5 cm.)
Formerly René Fribourg Collection

Pope Pius VII. A few years later he was restoring Compiègne, the Elysée, Rambouillet, Versailles, St-Germain and Meudon; outside France, residences at Turin, Florence and Rome in Italy; Laeken, Antwerp, Amsterdam, Utrecht and Haarlem in the Low Countries. Napoleon had gathered round him men of high calibre to put the policy into effect – it was a kind of artistic General Staff: the painter David; Denon, who was similar to a Minister of Fine Arts; and the architects Percier and Fontaine. First-rate craftsmen trained in the 18th century included Jacob Desmalter for furniture, Thomire and Ravrio for bronzes, Biennais and Odiot for work in precious metals, Pernon and Grand for silks. The glory of the Empire was reflected in the visible trappings of the Imperial residences. The Imperial apartments naturally took on a uniform appearance – the furniture supplied by the *grands ébénistes* matched the walls and the décor to perfection, the bronzes and the fittings echoed the ornamental repertory of military emblems in the antique taste and others representative of the times: the bee, the Imperial 'N', the swan, the eagle, the caduceus and the thyrsus. The inspirer of all this decoration was, of course, the Emperor himself.[3]

A sense of line and symmetry dominates the Empire style; it is primarily an architectural taste. Eighteenth-century artisans had taken care to soften angles, to make curves, but the art of the Imperial period sought, on the contrary, to create the very opposite effect. It was a rigid style, angular and grand. Carved ornament disappeared, marquetry became rare. The craftsmen of the First Empire replaced carved decoration with sculptured bronze, gilded matt and burnished where necessary. The bronzes of this period are distinguished by their quality of delicate chasing with a forceful design which brings to the rectilinear shapes of furnishing pieces both gravity and nobility. Thomire and Ravrio are the *maîtres-ciseleurs* of the Imperial era; their work is outstanding, the contrast between matt and burnished gilt-bronze mounts and the rich dark grained mahogany, in itself selected with care, *acajou flammé*, or *marqueté*, created an effect both of luxury and sobriety.

The use of caryatids, which had been introduced in furniture design towards the end of the 18th century, was widespread, but with a more scholarly application of antique design. Attached to each side of the façade of chests or tables, they supported the pediments and entablatures; sometimes the figures would have their hair styled with the *pshent* or the *klafft* in the manner of Egyptian head-dresses. Often bare or sandalled feet would form the base resting on a plinth inspired by Egyptian funerary monuments. The motifs executed in bronze employed during the First Empire were infinite. There were the crown of oak leaves entwined with small fluttering ribbons, garlands of vine or ivy leaves, stylized branches of laurel, palms, pine-cones, myrtle, clover, poppies and Tudor-style roses. Predominant decoration was taken from Greco-Roman motifs: the palmette, lotus, amphorae, tripods, cornucopiae, paterae (antique bronze door studs), and honeysuckle, interspersed with mythological harpies and sirens with scrolled tails, gryphons, seahorses, tritons, Medusa or Gorgon heads. Animal figures also played their part, such as eagles, swans (alluding to the Empress Joséphine), bees (alluding to the Emperor Napoleon I, possibly after the Barberini bee), butterflies, storks, serpents and lions' heads. Human figures also appear in bronze, as Victories bearing palms or wreaths and playing trumpets, dancers, goddesses in floating draperies, winged ladies emblematic of Liberty, Bacchic masks, helmeted warrior and Hermes heads. Other ornamental motifs were also introduced: stars arranged as a chaplet, winged

[3] Jarry, M., "Napoleon and the Decoration of the Imperial Residences", *Apollo*, September 1964, vol. LXXX, no. 31, pp. 212–19.

6. *Secrétaire de Compiègne, circa* 1810
black fossil marble top with a fall front enclosing numerous drawers and a shelf
height 51 in. (129·5 cm.) width 33 in. (83·8 cm.)
Formerly René Fribourg Collection

flambeaux, lyres, winged thunderbolts of Jupiter, trophies of lances surmounted by the Phrygian cap of Liberty, lictors' fasces enclosing an axe, the thyrsus of the Bacchantes and Hermes' caduceus. (Ills 2, 3.) All these gilt-bronze ornaments were applied to the mahogany, which was in general use until 1810, when an Imperial Decree forbade its importation and employment in the *mobilier impérial.* Such ornaments were often applied to yew, walnut, oak, beech, satinwood, olive wood, maple and burr-elm and burr-ash. Cuban or Nicaraguan mahogany was the most generally used wood before restrictions. It was wax-polished and varnished. Quality was not always maintained, however, and certain cabinet-makers fell into the practice of using inferior quality woods but with a selected quality veneer to disguise a poorly constructed carcass. The abolition of proper control was the cause of some of these malpractices. There was little to complain of in the joinery of preceding periods. The carefully selected wood for the exterior would be combined with an expertly made carcass.

Furniture of the First Empire includes such common pieces as:

THE COMMODE

This period produced several novel pieces of furniture, although most examples are more or less Imperial adaptations of former furnishing pieces. Commodes, as in the 18th century, contained various drawers, but under the Empire a model was devised with two doors, which became very popular. The doors concealed completely the interior drawers; such an example was called the *bas d'armoire.* Locks were usually masked by bronze escutcheons; they may have been designed as a caduceus, or flambeaux. Such pieces were known as *à serrures perdues.* Very often the sides would have engaged pilasters, caryatids or sphinx balusters. (Ill. 4.)

THE CHIFFONNIER

As in the 18th century, the chiffonnier was really a further development of the commode. There was usually a series of drawers one above the other, most often seven in number; this was sometimes called a *semainier.* There would be no doors, but the handles of the drawers would most often be lions' masks with rings, gilt-bronze knobs with Tudor-style roses of embossed or cast design; engaged columns, caryatids or sphinx balusters would on either side support an architectural

7. (right) Napoleon I *bureau plat, circa* 1810
mahogany with ormolu mounts, the knee-hole frieze with four drawers, the right-hand top drawer simulating two drawers – carved wood and gilt gesso sphinx monopodia supports
depth 32 in. (81·2 cm.) width 64 in. (162·5 cm.)
Formerly René Fribourg Collection

8. One of a pair of Napoleon I *guéridons, circa* 1810
mahogany with top inset with a panel of Carrara marble – ormolu mounts – star-shaped stretchers inlaid in mahogany and satinwood
height 28 in. (71·1 cm.) diameter 16 in. (40·6 cm.)
Formerly René Fribourg Collection

entablature. The top, as in the commode, would most often be made of marble. (See colour plate facing p. 132.)

THE SECRETAIRE A ABATTANT

A very popular form during the First Empire. Such pieces bore a severity of outline and a certain grandeur, befitting their function as a bureau. The interior arrangement resembled the Renaissance cabinet, with small drawers, niches, sometimes with columns supporting an arch, and various small compartments fitted with drawers. Mirrors were sometimes added. The front could be let down to form a desk flap when required. Beneath there would be drawers. The customary flanking caryatids supporting a frieze would complete the piece. The effect was angular and controlled. (Ill. 5.)

SECRETAIRE DE COMPIEGNE

Called after an example in the Palace of Compiègne. This fall-front desk was similar to the *secrétaire à abattant* in its upper proportions; it differed in that there were no drawers below. Instead there was a console support consisting of four columns or balusters set on a base. The back wall would be either open or would have a mirror inset. Such an arrangement added considerably to the architectural proportions and classic authority of the piece. The usual bronze mounts were applied to balusters, frieze and a formal fall-front flap. (Ill. 6.)

THE BUREAU

The First Empire continued to favour the *bureau à cylindre* which had been popular in the preceding century. As for the so-called type of bureau or *bonheur-du-jour*, the Empire required these to be more square and of a higher elevational proportion than in the 18th century. Usually a more formal style of desk was required – a pedestal writing desk of large dimensions; these were often designed to appear very grand indeed. (Ill. 7.) Such *bureaux plats* were far more massive than those in

9. (right) Napoleon I *table de milieu*, in the style of Jacob Desmalter, *circa* 1805
mahogany with rectangular green and white marble top and ormolu mounts
depth 32 in. (81·2 cm.) width 59 in. (149·8 cm.)
Viscount Mersey Collection

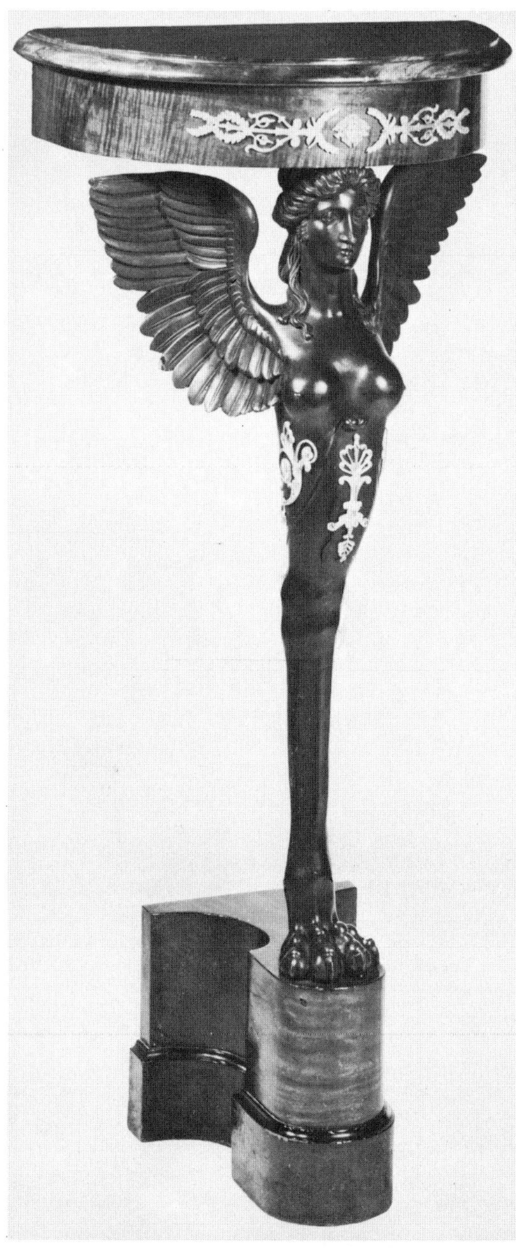

10. One of a pair of Napoleon I sphinx monopodion console tables, *circa* 1810
mahogany with bronze and ormolu mounts
height 38 in. (96·5 cm.) width 18 in. (45·7 cm.)
Formerly René Fribourg Collection

use in the 18th century. The top might rest upon a console formed of winged animal legs terminating in claw feet, or sometimes on elegant 'x'-patterned supports terminating in paws in the style of ancient Greco-Roman marble tables. Occasionally rather more delicate pieces for supports were fashioned from steel, heightened with gilt-bronze cracker ornament at the conjunction of claw and capital with gilt-bronze boss at the centre of the 'x'.

TABLES

These are more strictly copied from antique furniture than other pieces designed during this period. Many examples of antique tables in marble which were depicted in sculptural reliefs provide the patterns copied by the designers under the Empire; they were usually circular with their tops resting on a central pillar and three columns springing from a triangular concave-sided base. There were many variations of the Empire circular table; the top might be of marble, or set with porcelain plaques or different coloured woods. The support could be in the shape of winged gryphons, sphinxes, lion monopodia, and there could be a variation of column design, sometimes a baluster stem was employed, or sometimes columns combining the customary orders of architecture, Doric, Ionic or Persic columns. Such columns were mounted in gilt-bronze or dark patinated bronze to resemble the antique, studded with stars or bound with appliqué vine leaves and ribbons. A favourite design was for a circular top resting upon three monopodia – either gryphons, lions or sphinxes, while in the centre would be placed a gilt-bronze vase in the antique fashion. The round frieze could be adorned with gilt-bronze stars, wreaths, torches, honeysuckle or other classical ornament. As a variation the central vase or urn could be used as a cassolette or perfume burner. These tables are undoubtedly handsome, solidly constructed and well executed. There were often variations in the diameter of Empire tables; the smallest design often formed a work-table or *table à fleurs*, now called a *jardinière*. The top of this consisted of *tôle* painted and varnished to contain the flowers. The circular form

11. (right) Napoleon I console table, *circa* 1810
mahogany with a black fossil marble top, drawer in the frieze and a mirror back
height 35 in. (88·8 cm.) width 38 in. (96·5 cm.)
Formerly René Fribourg Collection

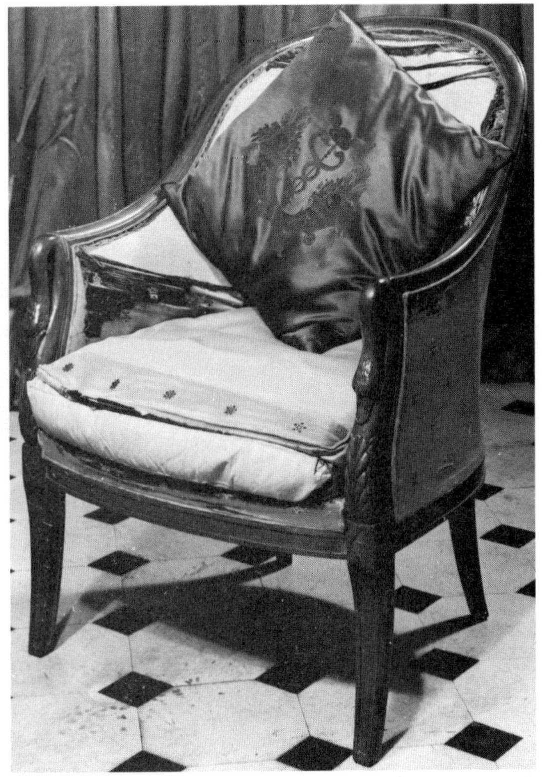

12. Directoire *fauteuil de cabinet*, *circa* 1795–9
mahogany and fruitwood with original silk cover spangled with turquoise-blue stars
Malcolm Burgess Collection

13. One of a pair of Directoire *bergères*, in the manner of Georges Jacob, *circa* 1795, mahogany
Formerly Doucet Collection

was far more numerous than the square; *guéridons* or small round tables of varying heights were much in demand. These were used to support candelabra or vases and were often made in Paris. Their proportions being slender, they could be placed anywhere in a room. (Ill. 8.) Rectangular tables for the grander rooms were also made during the Empire. They were an imitation of the Porch of the Caryatids in the Erechtheion on the Acropolis at Athens; four caryatids supported an architectural treatment at the top, perhaps with central square trestle supports at either end joined by a rectangular stretcher down the middle; this could, in its own turn, be centred by winged gryphons flanking a classical vase. (Ill. 9.)

ATHENIENNES

These small and elegant pieces were designed in the form of tripods inspired by the bronze tripods of antiquity. They were adapted to resemble a work-table, a jardinière or a basket. The *ébéniste* Weisweiler had invented a form during the end of the reign of Louis XVI in the *genre Herculanum*. These were used as a pedestal for candelabra, perfume burners or vases of flowers. They could also be employed to hold a bowl. They were usually made in pairs and were light enough to be transported from room to room, or to any place where a set of lights was needed. They were executed in mahogany, gilded wood or in bronze with a green patina relieved with gold, or even in iron and lacquered *tôle*. They could also be constructed in cast iron, or even occasionally in oxidized steel. Perhaps the most attractive of these tripods were those designed in the form of a hexagon.

CONSOLES AND SIDE TABLES

These were placed against the walls and sometimes as pier tables beneath a looking-glass. They could be oblong with caryatid supports and frieze, topped with a slab of marble, or they could resemble a semicircular half-moon or *lunette* table, often with single lion monopodion support. (Ill. 10.) They could also be backed with a glass. They were distinctive pieces of furniture made from the best quality materials and embellished with *ormolu appliqué* mounts. The console was one of the most essential pieces of furniture during the Empire period; no suite would be complete without one or more matching sets of console tables. (Ill. 11.)

CHAIRS AND SOFAS

Under the *Directoire* chairs still retained the delicate shapes usual during the reign of Louis XVI, but these shapes were modified to fit more closely to those models depicted in bas-reliefs and vase-paintings of the Greco-Roman period. (Ills 12, 13.) But with a more scholarly understanding of the ancient world the form of the chair came more closely to resemble the Greek *Klismos* or grander forms of throne as existed in the front row of seats in Greek theatres and monumental buildings of antiquity. Sabre legs in mahogany, or front legs of animal form terminating in hooves or lions' claws or, according to the Persian style, in Persic lotus and ball, became the more accepted designs. The backs might be formed to include a lyre design, or even a multiple 'x'-pattern or trellis with central boss in the style of a Roman senator's chair, while the back splat and top rail might assume a decisive curve projecting round the sides of the seat. A gondola shape was also popular. The arms would rest upon either winged gryphons, winged sphinxes or winged lions. The arm ends might terminate in lions' heads or rams' heads. In a chair of the Consulate period a frequent design included rams' heads in carved wood or gilt-bronze appliqué on either side of the curved top rail, the front legs would then probably be carved to resemble hocked animal-leg feet and hooves. (Ill. 14.) A

14. *Bergère* consulat, 1799–1804
mahogany, mounted with gilt-bronze *appliqué* rams' heads terminating each end of toprail – the front sabre legs ending in gilt-bronze animal hooves
Malcolm Burgess Collection

15. Napoleon I armchair, *circa* 1805–10
mahogany
Malcolm Burgess Collection

tendency of the later Empire was to create a heavier, more massive form of seat. There were an infinite number of variations of the Empire chair, but all these borrowed motifs from Greek, Roman, Egyptian or Persian styles of ornament. An angularity and crispness in architectural detail distinguishes the earlier forms of seat furniture. During the *Restauration*, *Charles X* and *Louis-Philippe* periods there is a noticeable softening of line, and arms, legs and back of chairs have a more curvilinear formation. (Ills 15, 16.)

Stools, *tabourets*, and 'x'-patterned seats also came into the height of fashion. These were direct imitations of the Ancient Greek folding stool with lions' heads and claw feet, rams' heads and hoof legs or the Roman *curule* chair. The more sophisticated variety would be executed in oxidized steel of slender proportions a direct representation of the folding seats used on military campaigns by Roman generals. (Ills 17, 18.)

The sofa was really an elongated extension of the chair. The same motifs applied; the arm-rests were designed in the form of winged sphinxes, caryatids or monopodia, the legs were sabre-shaped or tapering with carved enrichments, or decorated with gilt-bronze appliqué reliefs. An architectural rigidity endowed such pieces with a sense of importance. A form of sofa much in vogue was the *Méridienne* or tête-à-tête couch. One end was usually more elevated than the other, and both sides and the back were high to give a sense of enclosure to any couple seated upon it.

BEDS

The Empire bed was perhaps the most magnificent article of furniture and occupied the foremost position in the bedroom ensemble. The form was devised as a boat (*en bateau*). A feeling of solidity and assurance governed the concept of this design. The bed would often rest on a heavy square base and the sides and head-boards were embellished with a profusion of gilt-bronze enrichments. Such beds would be set under a dome or tent-shaped canopy with suspended drapes gathered over projecting gilt-bronze bosses. (Ill. 19.)

The *chaise-longue* was a modification of the Empire bed. These were inspired by the Roman dining couches and were fashionable pieces of furniture. They were often known as *Récamiers*, since the famous painting by David depicts Madame Récamier reclining on one.

MIRRORS

The *Grand Miroir à la Psyché* was one of the most original inventions of the Empire. It is really a large looking-glass fixed between two uprights in the style of a cheval glass. The glass could be set in an oval or square rim. The uprights were usually in the form of pillars or caryatids supporting an entablature and pediment. The uprights were adorned with the customary gilt-bronze fixtures and might include projecting candlesticks on a swivel; stars and allegorical reliefs were used to emblazon the architectural spaces on pediment, frieze, uprights and supports.

DRESSING-TABLES, COIFFEUSES

Dressing-tables resembled the console or the square table with the usual architectural features predominant under the Empire, and might contain a drawer in the frieze. Lyre supports were popular and the marble top made an effective ground for the articles of the toilet. A swivel looking-glass was fixed between two upright supports in the form of a miniature *psyché* above. These would similarly be equipped with projecting candle sconces. The shape of the glass frame might be rectangular, oval, octagonal or round.

16. Napoleon I *fauteuil de cabinet*, fruitwood, mounted with ormolu *appliqués*, with a swivel seat and the original green leather cover Cambacérès Collection

THE WASHSTAND

This resembled the *athénienne*, designed in imitation of an ancient tripod, *trépied-lavabo*, with columnar monopodion or console supports, with a recess at the top to contain the wash-basin, while the centre of the triangular pedestal was designed to fit the antique styled water jug. These light and portable pieces were usually known as *guéridons*. In company with these bedroom appurtenances may be noted the small *tables de nuit*, bedside tables or *somno* containing a cupboard or recess for necessary utensils.

BOOKCASES, VITRINES-BIBLIOTHEQUES

During the 18th century bookcases were comparatively rare, but with the advent of the Empire such articles of furniture assumed a greater importance. As a rule they rested directly upon a strong plinth without feet. They could be of varying sizes, both massive and of moderate proportions. They would usually be enclosed with doors and protected with well-devised locks. Such bookcases naturally lent themselves to an imposing architectural treatment, and occupied a position of authority in any *cabinet* or library. (Ill. 20.)

The grandiose, scholarly architectural quality of the early Empire style was gradually to give way to a less rigid form of design. Romanticism was soon to produce a more eclectic, more exotic conception of furniture design. Under the *Restauration* of Louis XVIII (1815–24) a return was made to the forms created in 18th-century France. During the reign of Charles X (1824–30) a strong predilection for the medieval was felt; chivalry rather than the Classic world was regarded as the perfect ideal to follow. Furniture and *objets d'art* now represented the 'Gothic' style, sometimes called the *style à la cathédrale* or *style troubadour*. There was a change in the use of wood; *bois clair* or light woods replaced the once fashionable mahogany; oak, maple, cherry, satinwood, burr-ash, burr-elm, sycamore and box were widely used. The Duchesse de Berry helped to promote the vogue for *bois clair*. The chief exponents of *bois clair* were J. J. Werner and Felix Rémond, both excellent designers and cabinet-makers, while the wood surfaces were embellished with gilt-bronze mounts by the *ciseleurs* Desnière and Matelin. It was now often the mode to inlay the wood with metal or ivory. This practice of inlaying metal on a ground of ebony or dyed wood, or rosewood on satinwood or vice versa, was peculiarly adapted to the nature of the furniture so much in use at that period, which was enlivened without the use of raised ornament that collected dust and dirt. This style of ornament was carried to a remarkable degree of perfection, the metal or wood ornament, and the wood ground in which it was inserted being stamped and cut out at the same time and expertly made to fit together.

It was not surprising that other countries in Europe should have followed the fashion of France in introducing the Antique style into furniture design. Italy had already taken up Egyptian and Etruscan motifs before the French Revolution. It was natural that those States which had inherited the arts of the Ancient Romans should adopt a style of ornament and assimilate antique patterns from the Ancient World. The ground was ripe, therefore, for the introduction of the new French Empire style through the direct influence of Napoleon and his puppet Regents, such as Gioacchino Murat, King of Naples, and his wife Caroline, and Napoleon's sister, Elisa Baciocchi, on whom had been conferred the title of Princess of Lucca. Elisa Baciocchi embarked upon grandiose schemes of decoration first in Lucca and then in Florence. Like other patrons, she relied upon French artists and craftsmen;

17. One of a pair of stools with 'x'-shaped frames; signed: *Jacob frères, Rue Meslée, circa* 1796–1803, carved mahogany with gilt wood tiger heads and paw feet
width 25 in. (63·5 cm.)
Formerly René Fribourg Collection

she also sought the advice of Percier and Fontaine. She imported silver by Biennais and furniture from a Parisian *ébéniste* named Youff. These foreign *ébénistes* set up workshops with Italian assistants. In this way a gifted Italian cabinet-maker was discovered, Giovanni Socchi, who in craftsmanship and ability for design was scarcely distinguishable from the *ébénistes* of Paris. Several works by this craftsman still remain, and include a writing-desk and chair which can be transformed into an oval table by simply winding a handle. Two of these pieces of furniture were made for the Palazzo Pitti, a third may be seen at Malmaison. This craftsman also made some little drum-shaped commodes. Besides the employment of cabinet-makers and other decorators for her various palaces and mansions, Elisa re-formed the old *Opificio delle Pietre Dure* in Florence, which began making table tops and decorative trifles in a decidedly Empire manner.

It was not long before Gioacchino and Caroline Murat carried the Empire style to Naples. Much of the finest French furniture, including pieces by Jacob, was brought from France. Examples may be seen in the Palazzo Reale, Naples, and the Palazzo Reale, Caserta. Nevertheless, they were happy to employ local craftsmen to make pieces of furniture whose opulent decorations, but less precise workmanship, indicate their Italian origin. Another famous Italian *ébéniste* working in the Neo-Classical style was Giuseppe Maggiolini of Naples. Soon the Empire style was generally accepted throughout the country. Most examples of the Italian Empire furniture date from 1815. Even as late as the 1840's furniture continued to be made in this style, the only difference being that it was slightly richer and a little more vulgar. It is not easy to give accurate dates of Italian examples seemingly

18. (above) Empire window seat with 'U'-shaped classic design, *circa* 1810, mahogany
width 30 in. (76·2 cm.)
Formerly René Fribourg Collection

19. (right) The marriage-bed of Napoleon I and the Empress Marie Louise, probably made for the Palais de Compiègne by Jacob Desmalter, mounts perhaps executed by P. P. Thomire, *circa* 1810
mahogany mounted with ormolu – in the centre of the foot a bas-relief shows the Emperor and Empress standing at either side of an altar of Love inscribed *1. Avril, 1811*
length 74 in. (187·9 cm.) width 56 in. (142·2 cm.)
width of foot and head 63 in. (160 cm.)
Formerly René Fribourg Collection

Colour Plate. Chiffonnier, *circa* 1810
walnut, black fossil marble top, drawer in frieze, gilt-bronze mounts and handles
Malcolm Burgess Collection

КРЫЛОВ
DUDEN
TURGENEV'S Literary Reminiscences
East-West Passage
PETER THE GREAT
A HISTORY OF RUSSIA
M·B·ЛОМОНОСОВ
РОКОТОВ
GARCIA LORCA
PASTERNAK

21 and **22.** Dutch Empire cabinet, *circa* 1810 oak inlaid with ebony parquetry with marquetry top and panels, gilt-bronze mounts and a drawer in the frieze
height 32½ in. (82·5 cm.) width 73 in. (33 cm.)
depth 17¼ in. (43·8 cm.)
Malcolm Burgess Collection

20. *Vitrine-bibliothèque, circa* 1810, flame mahogany (*acajou flammé*) with ormolu *appliqué* mounts in the style of P.P. Thomire, and a drawer in the plinth
height 76 in. (193 cm.) width 51½ in. (130·8 cm.)
depth 13½ in. (34·3 cm.)
Malcolm Burgess Collection

in the Empire mode, though they could have been executed as early as 1780 or just before 1850.[4]

Other countries which came under the sway of France also produced their own interpretations of the Empire style. As Paris monopolized taste, craftsmen produced versions of the *Style à l'Antique* in Austria, Germany, Poland, Spain, for Miklós Esterházy in Hungary[5] and for patrons in Holland. The Dutch Empire style still retained traditional elements from the 18th century: mahogany and oak inlaid with an elaborate marquetry in various selected woods. The effect was a lightening of the rather heavy architectural form for furniture by inlaying friezes, doors, pedestals, pediments and columns with a chevron design in ebony and satinwood, or decorating the top of commodes and tables with a Pompeian scroll and vase design. Gilt-bronze mounts could also be used in addition to marquetry. (Ills 21, 22.) Hortense, Queen of Holland, set the fashion for introducing fine French Empire furniture into her residences.

The Scandinavian countries also copied the lead of France, and Swedish Empire furniture closely follows the prevalent style; the execution was of high quality, and Swedish marble would often be employed for the tops of commodes and tables. Even the Septinsular Republic of the Ionian Islands and Corfu produced an effective style of First Empire furniture; examples may be found made by Greek craftsmen in boxwood, yew wood and walnut with gilt-bronze appliqué decoration.

As *le Style Empire* had been promoted to reflect the Imperial glory of Napoleon, often its most extravagant displays would be found outside France. Since also it had become the architectural idiom of the period of reconstruction following the destruction wrought by French troops, the style had become widespread over the major part of Europe. The other great empire, however, which seemed well suited to accept the new style, was Russia. It was now the fashion in Russia to regard the Ancient World as a respectable pattern to imitate. France had long influenced Russian culture, and through France the resurrection of the Greco-Roman world appealed to an eclectic Russian temperament. The new reign of Tsar Alexander I suggested that the dawn of a Parnassian Age was at hand. Style in furniture and in interior decoration underwent a complete change at the beginning of the 19th century; the Russian diarist, F. F. Wiegel, writing during the first decade of the 19th century remarked:

> "Consular rule in France decisively established the society and its attendant diversions: even taste was reborn then, it was more refined, less bourgeois, this was echoed in the furnishing of rooms. Everything was done *à l'antique* (the discovery of Pompeii and Herculaneum had helped this to a great extent). The Parisians had taken little trouble about Lyons and other manufacturies, but it was imperative for the government of France to save them, materials of silk again made their appearance, but they were no longer stretched upon the walls as before, but elegantly draped round the pillars, sometimes taking their place altogether. Everywhere alabaster urns appeared with mythological scenes carved on them, lamps and occasional tables, long Grecian day-beds, where the ends rested upon eagles, gryphons or sphinxes. Gilded or painted and lacquered wood was already long dismissed, smooth bronze was also cast aside; mahogany now entering into general use, began to be adorned with gilt-bronze figures of fine workmanship, lyres, small heads: Medusas, lions and even ram's heads. All this

[4] See Honour, H., "The Italian Empire Style", *Apollo*, September 1964, vol. LXXX, no. 31, pp. 226–36, and Dr G. Morazzoni, *Mobilio Neoclassico Italiano*. Milan, 1955.

[5] See Szabolcsi, H. *French Furniture in Hungary*. Budapest, 1964, pp. 32–34, pls. 43–48.

came to us no earlier than 1805, and, in my opinion, it would be impossible to devise anything better of this kind. Could the inhabitants of the surroundings near Vesuvius have imagined that within fifteen hundred years their entire way of life would be extracted from their tombs and suddenly transferred to the Hyperborean lands?"[6]

It was strange indeed, Wiegel declared, that the habits of the ancient world

"whose memory alone had been preserved in sculptures on the shores of the Aegean Sea, and of the Tiber, should now be renewed along the quays of the Seine and transported to the banks of the Neva".[7]

After 1800 much planning and rebuilding took place in St Petersburg, including the erection of many private houses. The Empire style has thus left a strong impression. Count Stroganov ordered Percier and Fontaine to produce designs of furniture to equip the Stroganov Palace. The reconstruction of Moscow after the fire of 1812 necessitated a complete refurnishing of all buildings, both public and private, throughout the city. The Russian Empire style, or, as it is called, the Alexandrine Empire style, was to last for about fifty years. The best period was from 1820 to 1826. The interpretation of French Classicism remained distinctively Russian: simplicity of design and the scorn of unnecessary trimmings. There is no doubt that the Alexandrine Empire style encouraged furniture of the greatest excellence. A distinctive note was sounded by the introduction of local woods, such as a dark Karelian birch, or a lighter kind of speckled birch. On the whole carved gilt-wood appliqué or *lepka* was preferred to adorn such pieces rather than chased gilt-bronze mounts, although sometimes both forms were used together. The customary antique motifs would be employed, but Russia particularly favoured the swan; in chairs the raised swans' feathers were carved to form the arm-rests. A vivid green malachite from the Urals was very popular in Russia at this date. The effect of the golden-coloured birch wood and gilt enrichment surrounded by the emerald malachite is glamorous, yet graceful. Later on Russia evolved her own version of the *Louis-Philippe* and *Biedermeier* styles. The furniture in most country houses and fashionable city mansions was according to this taste. Chekhov country house settings always contained such furniture.[8] Of all examples of the Empire style throughout Europe, it is the Russian version that seems the least pompous and stern. The Russianization of the Greek style was easily adopted and comfortably domesticated. Madame Vigée-Lebrun recollected the cosiness of the warm Russian houses with their small yet elegant rooms with symmetrically placed furniture and rows of family portraits on the walls. *Ebénistes* in Russia include the names of Ch. Meier, who executed many orders for the Empress Maria Feodorovna; he worked in St Petersburg. Between 1803 and 1810 he created the furniture for the private apartments of Yekaterina Pavlovna at Pavlovsk. A more prolific cabinet-maker was Heinrich Gambs, who made a splendid desk for Alexander I. His stamp is "Heinrich Gambs, St. Petersburg". In the Exhibition of 1829 at St Petersburg his work was reviewed thus:

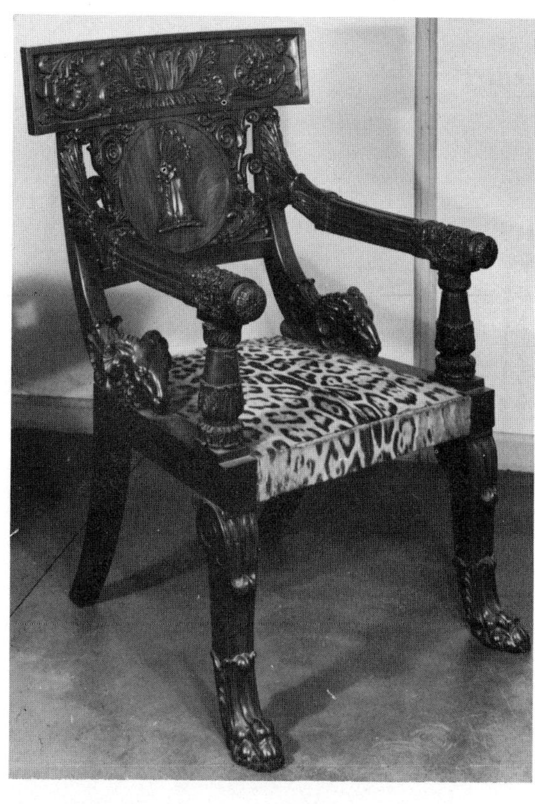

23. 'English Empire' armchair-throne showing how much the *style à l'antique* owes to the French Empire influence; signed on underside of seat rail 1811, carved Cuban mahogany with the original leopard-skin seat covering
Malcolm Burgess Collection

"his creative mind is inexhaustible in inventiveness: beautiful designs, convenience in use, pure finish, the choicest selection of woods and suitability are the everlasting unalterable qualities of his works, but what distinguishes his productions the more, and makes them inimitable is that rare talent for combining architectural art with a skill in cabinet making: all his wares are fine examples

[6] Wiegel, F. F. "Zapiski pod. red. S. Ya. Shtraikha. Artel' pisatelei", *Krug*, Moscow, 1928, tom I, pp. 179–80.

[7] *Op. cit.*, p. 177.

[8] Cf. "The Russian Empire Style", *Country Life*, 12 December 1947, pp. 1208–9.

of architecture; compositions, proportions, symmetry and even all the ornaments are according to the rules. In this art right from the very first glance you can see the skilful production of a cultivated mind. Truly Mr Gamps is a genius of his kind."[9]

Other masters were Bowman, K. I. Rossi and A. Tour. In Moscow the most important workshop was that of A. K. Pique. Pieces from Russian collections may still be found in London and other European capitals.[10]

The *Directoire* and Empire styles also reached America, where emphasis was on classical ideals of republican government. Ornamental motifs drew attention to patriotism – the Greek key or fret design, the laurel wreath, the acanthus and the lyre. The eagle was apparent everywhere, cornucopiae and sheaves of wheat represented abundance, tobacco plants and ears of corn pointed to the New World. All the furniture was of a high quality and supreme elegance. *Émigrés* from Revolutionary France were responsible for many of the pieces. The names of these include Charles Honoré Lannuier (working 1803–19), Joseph Brauwers, Anthony G. Quervelle (1789–1856) who made small articles of elegant furniture for the White House, and Michel Bouvier, who was patronized by Joseph Bonaparte and the first American merchant millionaire, Stephen Girard. The most famous cabinet-maker was the Scotsman Duncan Phyfe. It is sometimes hard to distinguish his work from English cabinet-work of the same period.[11]

It was in England, too, that French taste deeply affected the style of interior decoration, but the style which developed in England is sometimes called *English Empire*. (Ill. 23.) This comes into a category of its own and has been studied by many historians under the title of "the English Regency Style", and lack of space must necessarily preclude any further discussion of this period.

It may be recognized that the French Empire style of the early 19th century was thus far-reaching in its influence on the history of design and taste throughout Europe, Russia and America. It was the flowering of a last and truly great original style, and, like all original period styles, it has often been revived and copied.

[9] *Opisanie pervoi publichnoi vystavki Rossiiskikh manufakturnykh izdelii, byvshei v S. Peterburge*, 1829, p. 277.

[10] *The Connoisseur*, January 1965, pp. 68–69.

[11] Cf. "Classical America 1815–45", *Apollo*, November 1963, vol. LXXVIII, no. 21, pp. 410–13.

BIBLIOGRAPHY

Brunhammer, Y. *Restauration et Louis-Philippe*. Meubles et Ensembles. Librairie Centrale des Beaux-Arts. Éditions Charles Massin, Paris, 2, Rue de l'Échelle.

Bytovaya Mebel' russkogo Klassitsizma. Kontsa XVIII – nachala XIX vv. Gosudarstvennoe Izdatel'stvo Literatury po stroitel'stvu i arkhitekture. Moskva, 1954.

Grandjean, S. *Empire Furniture*. London, 1966.

Janneau, G. *Les Meubles, III: Fin Louis XVI – Directoire – Empire*. Les Arts Décoratifs. Flammarion, 26, Rue Racine, Paris, 1944.

Janneau, G. *L'Empire*. Arts et Artisans de France. Vincent, Fréal et Cie, 4, Rue des Beaux-Arts, Paris, 1965.

Jarry, M. *Le Siège Français de Louis XIII à Napoléon III*. Éditions Charles Massin, Paris.

Ledoux-Lebard, D. *Les Ébénistes Parisiens (1795–1830)*. Leurs œuvres et leurs marques. Librairie Grund, 1951.

Le Dix-neuvième Siècle Français. Collection Connaissance des Arts. Hachette, 15th February 1960. Mobilier. pp. 35–69.

Le Style Empire. La grammaire des Styles publiée sous la direction de Henri Martin. Flammarion, 26, Rue Racine, Paris, 1945.

Morazzoni, Dr G. *Mobilio Neoclassico Italiano*. Milan, 1955.

Mottheau, J. *Directoire-Empire*. Meubles et Ensembles. Librairie Centrale des Beaux-Arts. Éditions Charles Massin, Paris, 2, Rue de l'Échelle.

Renaissance Furniture

ROSS WATSON

The furniture of the Renaissance, which is very roughly the period 1450 to 1600 in Italy and 1500 to 1600 in the rest of Europe, has suffered considerable fluctuations in appreciation and popularity among collectors and the discerning public. Today it has ceded place in esteem to furniture of the 18th and even the 19th centuries, yet in the last century it was widely collected and pieces changed hands for substantial sums. Elizabethan and early Jacobean furniture (the two periods tended to be lumped together) was much admired in Victorian England and was paid the doubtful compliment of frequent copying, no doubt satisfying the desire of those who could not afford genuine examples, and put in the multitude of houses built in what they fondly hoped was the Tudor style.[1] In Italy, the heroic period of the Renaissance, the last time the Italian states were independent until the Unification, would naturally appeal to the Risorgimento. Similarly, the Germans, who achieved final unity under the heel of Prussia in 1870, had awakened to an appreciation of medieval and 16th-century art. Romanticism, which affected the whole of Europe, was by no means confined to an admiration for the Middle Ages, and the 16th century, in nearly every country an heroic age appealing to national pride, came in for its share of appreciation. This was especially so in France after the débâcle of 1870 when considerable prices were paid for Renaissance pieces, perhaps to drown a sense of humiliation and relive the glorious days of Henri II. Then there were individual collectors such as the Russians Soltykoff and Demidoff who were keen buyers of Italian furniture and paid high prices.[2] The Hamilton Palace sale of 1882 was responsible for the dispersal of a number of important pieces for four figures, including the Milanese table in the Victoria and Albert Museum. (Ill. 1.) A few years later it was bought by the Museum for about a third of the price, an indication of the turning away from Renaissance to 18th-century furniture, the Hamilton Palace sale being an important direction point in the change of taste. Thereafter, Renaissance furniture steadily declined in popularity, and interest has only revived in the last few years, partly because of the increasing scarcity of good 18th-century furniture. The moving of taste forward into the 19th century has not, however, been matched by quite the same enthusiasm for early furniture. This may be because of the size, so clearly made for larger and more magnificent rooms than the exigencies of modern life make allowance for, and perhaps too a suspicion that what is earlier must also be cruder and less sophisticated. While this is partly true, especially in England, it would be hard to condemn an Italian *cassone*, a French *dressoir* or a German cabinet on aesthetic or

[1] John Nash's *Memoirs of England in Olden Time* (1839–49) did much to make the Elizabethan period fashionable as a source for buildings and decoration.

[2] See Gerald Reitlinger, *The Economics of Taste*, 1963.

1. Table; Milanese, mid-16th century
steel gilded and inlaid with lapis lazuli
$30\frac{1}{2}$ in. (77·4 cm.)×$27\frac{1}{2}$ in. (69·8 cm.) square
The Victoria and Albert Museum, London

even practical grounds, and this article may help to plead their cause to be considered on an equal level with contemporary majolica and metalwork.

It is doubtful if the term Renaissance will ever be defined to general satisfaction. For the purposes of this article Renaissance can be taken to mean the application, however debased or misunderstood, of classical motifs derived from architecture and sculpture to ordinary household furniture. In Italy there would undoubtedly have been a time-lag before the new stylistic ideas percolated to the carpenters and woodworkers, and production of chairs and tables in the older style must have been continued to satisfy conservative taste for an even longer period. The same pattern is repeated as Renaissance art penetrated to countries outside Italy, first reaching France, then Spain, Germany and the Netherlands, arriving a little later in England. In spite of the proliferation of renaissances which used to be fashionable, there is much to be said for confining the Renaissance to Italy, for in the case of furniture it was Italian influence which revolutionized style, first in the decoration only, and later changing the whole form, so that the chair or cupboard, while functionally similar, is stylistically separated from its Gothic ancestor. It would be fascinating to know why the new motifs were so popular. The courts, notably in France and England, were clearly influential in the importation of Renaissance works, artists and craftsmen, but the importance of the prosperous middle classes was for the first time recognized politically and socially, and the new men, especially in England, were able to build and furnish houses as grand as those of the aristocracy. In the Italian city-states such a position, with the *bourgeoisie* in political control, and so the patrons and leaders of taste, had existed from the

2. Cassapanca; Italian, *circa* 1500
walnut $33\frac{1}{2}\times95$ in. ($85\times241{\cdot}3$ cm.)
The Rijksmuseum, Amsterdam

14th century, if not earlier. It is not too fanciful to imagine the new fashion in furniture, as in the other branches of art, travelling along the trade routes of Europe, which were in fact the only lines of communication, and the merchant of Antwerp, Lyons or London being among the first to adopt them. Humanism found its greatest welcome in such middle-class households as that of Sir Thomas More, while the great banker Fugger was one of the first to employ Renaissance artists in Germany, as was the financier Bohier who began Chenonceau. The new rich would be more likely to adopt the most advanced style for the furnishing of their new houses, uncluttered with the accumulated paraphernalia of those with longer pedigrees. There were other less agreeable ties which bound Italy to France, Spain and Germany and would account for the transference of Renaissance influence. From 1494, with the invasion by Charles VIII, until the defeat of Francis I at Pavia in 1525, French armies attempted with mixed success to dominate northern Italy and to capture Naples. It was just that highly decorative art epitomized in the Certosa of Pavia that the French most admired and copied. In the same way the Spaniards, already in possession of Sicily, conquered Naples under the noses of the French and eventually drove them out of Italy, establishing themselves as virtual overlords. Under Charles V the Spanish dominions and the Empire were united and the family link established a close relationship across the Alps. Again it was the more provincial styles of North and South that influenced the Spaniards, as they were more akin to the flamboyant late Gothic than the purity of Florence or the grandeur of Rome. North of the Alps, Gothic forms were mingled at first with misunderstood and ill-digested classical motifs. Indeed, it might be argued that it was the post-Raphaelite generation after 1520 who created the style that was so widely adopted throughout Europe for interior decoration, silver, pottery and furniture, and that most Renaissance furniture is in fact Mannerist. Such distinctions, although providing the art historian with ample material for discussion, need not concern us here. Mannerism, whether as a reaction to the Renaissance or a logical development, draws on the same sources, and even if many of the motifs, such as the ubiquitous strapwork first used for the Fontainebleau school and the grotesques of the Antwerp school are now called Mannerist, the term is a modern one and we shall continue to regard them as products of the Renaissance.

There is a paradox in late 15th- and 16th-century life which is reflected in its

3. Virginal; Italian, *circa* 1570
cypress $8\frac{1}{2}\times65$ in. ($21{\cdot}5\times165{\cdot}1$ cm.)
The Victoria and Albert Museum, London

4. Pandurina; French, *circa* 1570
pearwood $16\frac{1}{2} \times 4\frac{1}{2}$ in. (41·9×11·4 cm.)
The Victoria and Albert Museum, London

furniture. On the one hand, for the first time attention was paid to comfort, to the introduction of small, more intimate rooms, and on the other, the households of princes and nobles became ever grander, with the introduction in the courts of etiquette and ceremonial. The Middle Ages must have been deplorably draughty and cold, and well into the 17th century (or even 19th-century Balmoral) complaints were to be heard against insufficient heating. Large unglazed rooms certainly presented an almost insuperable problem, but the introduction of glazing, and wooden panelling for the walls in the 15th century, went some way to making life tolerable, while greater desire for privacy led to a gradual withdrawal from the Great Hall to more private apartments for dining and sitting, as well as an increase in bedrooms. It may well be that the women of the household were making their influence felt for the first time. All this meant the introduction of new types of furniture suited to more intimate and comfortable surroundings: cupboards and dressers, occasional and dining tables, and a greater variety and number of chairs. In contrast to this move in the country house, court life, and to a lesser extent that of the great nobles, became increasingly more magnificent; indeed perhaps it is possible to talk about court life only from the 16th century onwards. While some of this may be the result of the spectacular Burgundian court, the last flowering of the Middle Ages, the d'Este, Gonzaga and Medici had established brilliant courts as the centres of literary and artistic life. Through marriage, embassies, such as that which brought Raphael's *St George* to Henry VII, and above all by the writers, the refinements and glories of the Italian courts were made known throughout Europe. Castiglione's *Il Cortegiano*, immortalizing the court of Urbino, was the European handbook for those who wished to be considered gentlemen. While the courts of Francis I and Henry VIII were undoubtedly magnificent in their lavish entertainment and feasting, they were somewhat barbarous and gross in comparison with the extreme sophistication of their

5. Cassone; Florentine, 1472
83×76 in. (211×193 cm.)
The Courtauld Institute Galleries, London

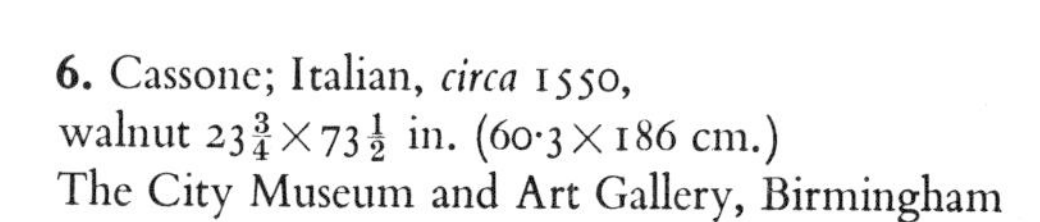

6. Cassone; Italian, *circa* 1550, walnut $23\frac{3}{4} \times 73\frac{1}{2}$ in. (60·3×186 cm.) The City Museum and Art Gallery, Birmingham

Italian counterparts. The latter half of the century saw much greater refinement and cultivation, and Elizabeth's court, with the Queen a fluent Italian speaker, and widely read in contemporary literature, attained a very high cultural level. The cult of Gloriana was itself in origin Italian and it was during this century that the praise of princes, descending at times to sycophancy, became general. Their elevation above the nobility, contrary to the medieval idea of *primus inter pares*, required a spectacular setting for the ceremonial of their daily lives and expenditure on court furnishings rose enormously. Ceremonial required suites of State Rooms for processions and receptions, a nicely graded series of ante-chambers, each more exclusive than the last until the Presence was reached. Again Italy led the way. Rome after the Sack was no longer the artistic centre, and the Counter-Reformation Popes turned away from the tradition of their art-loving predecessors. It was the new autocratic rulers such as the della Rovere and the Medici who wished by a splendid court life to emphasize their power and conceal its recent origin. The older European dynasties found it equally convenient to enhance the prestige of the monarchy in a similar way, and one of the most obvious was by building large palaces: Nonsuch, the Escorial and Fontainebleau are only the most spectacular among many. Such new ideas of grandeur were quickly adopted in France and England by the aristocracy, who were no longer contented to live in medieval discomfort and required a more dignified existence, combining some degree of privacy with, at the same time, outward display of their rank. It may be that the older families were spurred into rebuilding, altering or refurnishing their houses by the example of the upstart middle classes who, as we have seen, were among the most active admirers of Renaissance art. With birth no longer the only prerequisite of social and political eminence, much greater importance was given to the externals of living. There was certainly more emphasis on show than on comfort. The galleries of *châteaux* or *gran saloni* of *palazzi* would have richly carved tables often with marble tops, but they were for display not use. So too were many of the *cassapanche* (Ill. 2) and chairs, and there was a rigid etiquette about seating arrangements and what chairs could, and could not, be sat in and who had the right to them, which in France at least survived until the Revolution. Court life must have been most exhausting as so much time was spent standing at receptions; even in private houses most people, as at modern cocktail parties, were not expected to sit. The production of candles on a larger and more economical scale meant that there was much more artificial light which would enhance the effects of the velvet, stamped and gilded leather hangings, or tapestries on the walls. Tapestry-making now assumed the proportions of an industry and called on the greatest artists to supply designs, while books of engravings transmitted

7. Table top; Italian, *circa* 1600 marble inlay $62 \times 43\frac{1}{2}$ in. (157·4×110 cm.) The Victoria and Albert Museum, London

8. Cabinet; Italian, early 16th century
walnut
The Victoria and Albert Museum, London

9. Mirror frame; Italian, early 16th century
walnut diameter 19 in. (48·2 cm.)
The Victoria and Albert Museum, London

new styles to more provincial centres. Outside Italy and the Low Countries pictures were almost entirely confined to churches until the late 15th century, but with the spread of Renaissance art it became the fashion elsewhere to have galleries of real or supposed ancestors and to hang pictures of allegorical or mythological subjects. Painted decoration was rare in northern Europe, but there was a wealth of plasterwork. From all this it will be apparent that 16th-century houses were generally planned with more thought to aesthetic considerations, were often more splendid than before, but not necessarily always more comfortable, although this was being seriously considered for the first time. Grandeur and comfort cannot be readily reconciled and we know the inconvenience of life in the time of Louis XIV at Versailles and the nastiness of the courtiers' private habits. Diminishing degrees of outward display are found in proportion as one goes down the social scale, and in more conservative areas the more modest households probably continued to live much as their fathers and grandfathers before them. Much of Renaissance furniture remained unupholstered, so that it was as well that men and women's clothes were so padded that they carried their upholstery with them to relieve the hardness of chair, stool and bench. Cushions were known, but as often as not covered in rich brocade for display. It may seem obvious to say that furniture, and indeed all the decorative arts, are intimately bound up with social history, and yet it needs emphasizing for it is too often forgotten. How different were the customs of 400 years ago from those of today: no tea or coffee to provide the excuse for frequent sitting down, and only the very greatest lady was not busily employed supervising her household. Entertaining as we know it hardly existed outside the Court and the nobility, except for exceptional events such as weddings and christenings. Another phenomenon peculiar to the 16th century that should be stressed, as it is relevant to what would be found in houses, was the widespread

10. (right) Chairs and a stool; Venetian, mid-16th century
walnut $41\frac{1}{2} \times 21$ in. ($105{\cdot}4 \times 53{\cdot}3$ cm.) and $20\frac{5}{8} \times 19\frac{1}{2}$ in. ($52{\cdot}7 \times 49{\cdot}5$ cm.)
The Victoria and Albert Museum, London

11. (below) Dresser; French, *circa* 1600
walnut 94×43 in. ($238{\cdot}7 \times 109{\cdot}2$ cm.)
The Wallace Collection, London

interest in music, and it was in this period under Tasso, Joaquin des Près, Palestrina and Byrd that the foundations of modern music were laid down. It is no accident that musical instruments or parties appear frequently in Renaissance pictures, as family music was a favourite pastime and everyone was expected to take part in these informal concerts. Italy produced some of the finest instruments, already establishing her primacy in that field, above all lutes and virginals of which there is a beautiful example in the Victoria and Albert Museum, made *circa* 1570 and belonging to Queen Elizabeth. (Ill. 3.) Of almost the same date, 1568, is another pair in the same collection, which was made in the Netherlands for Duke William of Cleves. The underside of the lid has strapwork in relief in gold on blue with Latin texts, and the decoration of the whole case is of the highest quality. Viols and lutes also provided opportunities for highly finished work, as in the French *pandurina* of *circa* 1570 where the central panel has a carving of the Three Goddesses at the Judgment of Paris, very close in style to that attenuated elegance of mid-16th-century French sculpture of which the most famous example is the Diana of Anet. (Ill. 4.)

One of the greatest distinctions between the Renaissance and the period that went before was in the attitude towards the furniture of their houses, no longer looking on it as mere necessary equipment haphazardly acquired and kept regardless of their aesthetic qualities, but treating furniture as of importance in its own right and having a part to play in the decorative scheme. This change in attitude first appears in Italy, but how meagre were the furnishings of even the prosperous Italian middle class at the beginning of the period can be seen in the inventory of the possessions of Francesco de Marco Datini, "the merchant of Prato", drawn up in 1407.[3] The bedroom contained a bed with a low footboard acting as a bench and chest, coffers and chests for clothes, linen and jewels, a hat-stand, a cupboard, a chair and a painted *desco da parto*. There was no looking-glass, but Datini had one in his office, probably like that in the Arnolfini portrait in the National Gallery. The other main bedroom, for visitors, had two beds with head-boards, a bed for a servant or a child, a walnut trestle table, a *cassapanca*, a commode and two inlaid walnut tables. In the rest of the house there was a large permanent

[3] See Iris Origo, *The Merchant of Prato*, 1957.

12. (right) Cupboard; English, late 16th century
walnut 45×50 in. (114·3×127 cm.)
The Victoria and Albert Museum, London

13. (below) Cupboard; French, late 16th century
walnut 87×41 in. (220×104·1 cm.)
The Wallace Collection, London

dining table, a walnut trestle table, two small round tables, two chairs and a bench in the hall, and some tables and chairs in the upstairs loggia where the family sat in hot weather. Thus a prosperous and unpretentious Tuscan merchant would keep only the bare minimum of furniture. The change by the end of the century is so great as to be almost revolutionary. Now furniture was designed to harmonize with the interiors of the new *palazzi*, and it would certainly have seemed incongruous to build a house on strict classical principles and leave the details unchanged. We have no record of any great master designing furniture,[4] but it is difficult to imagine the school of Raphael not turning their attention to it, especially when we know they provided designs for silver. In the absence of classical furniture, the language of architecture and sculpture, pilasters, capitals and consoles had to be adopted. Sculpture was particularly relevant, as the scales were similar, and a Desiderio da Settignano or a Rossellino could well have turned from marble to wood. What would have been one of the earliest as well as the most elegant pieces of Renaissance furniture, had it been executed in the third dimension, is the chair in Donatello's *Annunciation* in S. Croce, Florence, dating from *circa* 1435. In fact, the closeness between *cassoni* or dowry chests and Renaissance tombs is not accidental, for both derive from Roman sarcophagi. These *cassoni* have come to be regarded as the most typical example of Italian 15th- and 16th-century furniture, but they go back to the 14th century or earlier. They must have been produced in great numbers, as every newly married woman would have had one to store the clothes, linen and jewels that made up her dowry. Naturally they varied from strictly utilitarian chests to works of art. Those made in the 15th century were the most elaborate, the wood not only being carved, but also decorated with raised gesso work, gilded and painted, the panels sometimes surviving alone. The scenes depicted were usually from classical history or mythology, but contemporary

[4] There is a tradition that Piero della Francesca designed the intarsia work in the choir stalls of Modena Cathedral.

history also appears, especially if it commemorated some member of the family. In the Courtauld Galleries, London, are perhaps the finest pair of *cassoni* that have come down to us, complete with their *spalliere* or backboards. (Ill. 5.) These *cassoni* were made for the wedding in 1472 of Lorenzo di Matteo di Morello, 'il Grande', and Donna Vaggia di Tanai di Francesco di Nerli. The very high quality of the decoration is an indication of the symbolical importance of these marriage chests commemorating the alliance of two rich and powerful families. The panels on the front of the chests and in the middle of the *spalliere* contain scenes from Roman history, while on the sides are the four cardinal virtues, with simulated brocade on the underside of the lids and on the rest of the *spalliere*. How close is the carved decoration to contemporary sculpture can be seen by comparing it to Verrocchio's Medici tomb in S. Lorenzo. Later *cassoni* were less elaborate and generally decorated in raised gesso work or deeply carved with masks, swags, strapwork and other Mannerist ornament. (Ill. 6.) They were also lower on the ground and were presumably not intended to take such a conspicuous place in the room, but were clearly very popular as quantities still exist. Other characteristic pieces of Italian furniture of this period, found in state rooms, were the richly carved tables with tops of marble and *pietre dure*. (Ill. 7.) Italy is particularly rich in a great variety of marbles and could afford to use it lavishly in architecture. *Pietre dure*, which were small pieces of marble, agate, lapis lazuli, onyx and the like arranged in a geometrical or figurative design, became a speciality of Florence well before the Grand Duke set up a factory in 1580. They were incorporated into cabinets, also a Florentine speciality, but were copied elsewhere, even in Spain and Germany. These cabinets could be very elaborate and costly and in their form made use of architectural elements, notably the triumphal arch. Such cabinets for coins and medals or natural specimens were very much part of the Renaissance ethos of the collector, which had not of course existed since classical antiquity. The Victoria and Albert Museum has a writing cabinet that almost certainly belonged to the Emperor Charles V and was perhaps made for his entertainment by the Marquis of Mantua in 1532. (Ill. 8.) The fine inlay on the drawers includes the Emperor's device and motto among the arabesques, and on the two doors is picture marquetry which was popular at the time. Although not strictly furniture, it would be an injustice to the Italian carver not to mention the mass of ecclesiastical woodwork, carved and inlaid choir stalls and sacristy panelling as well as *intarsia* work in private houses, the most notable being that of the Duke's study in Urbino and Isabella d'Este's private apartments in Mantua. Such high-quality work suggests not only master craftsmen, but also artists to provide the designs and even a man of letters to provide the programme for the humanist symbolism. An

14. Chair; French, second half of the 16th century
walnut $43\frac{1}{2} \times 22\frac{1}{2}$ in. ($110 \times 57{\cdot}1$ cm.)
The Victoria and Albert Museum, London

15. (right) Chest; French, second half of the 16th century
walnut 38×49 in. ($96{\cdot}5 \times 124{\cdot}4$ cm.)
The Victoria and Albert Museum, London

16. (above left) Cabinet; Spanish, mid-16th century
walnut 54×48 in. (137·1×121·9 cm.)
The Victoria and Albert Museum, London

17. (above right) Cabinet; Spanish, mid-16th century
inlaid with various woods 60¼×40¾ in. (153×106 cm.)
The Victoria and Albert Museum, London

important innovation which made a great difference to the somewhat sombre interiors of Italian houses was the discovery of the technique of manufacturing large looking-glasses which had hitherto been small and convex, and a German speciality. (Ill. 9.) They became a Venetian monopoly and the glass-houses of Murano sent them throughout Europe. Paradoxically it was in the merchant oligarchy of Venice, still very flourishing in spite of the new trade routes, that the most sumptuous living of the 16th century was developed. Carpaccio's *Dream of Saint Ursula* gives a good idea of the simplicity combined with elegance of a late 15th-century bedroom; but by the time of Veronese, Palladio and others had built splendid palaces on the Grand Canal for the merchant patricians, and summer *ville* on the Brenta, all furnished in the richest manner. Many of them have retained their original furniture, and some the red velvet hangings forming such an essential background to the public ceremonies and private entertainments for which Venice was even then famous. Seventeenth- and 18th-century Venetian furniture was to be especially sumptuous with gilding and rich carving, and the chairs and stool in illustration 10 show that in the Renaissance there was already that emphasis on the elaboration of detail, apart from the excellent design which is always so characteristic of Venetian art. Passing reference should also be made to the beautiful ironwork of the Renaissance, the cressets and grilles that still adorn the outside of many Italian palaces, and the candleholders, braziers and basins for indoor use. In Carpaccio's *Saint Augustine in his Study* the table has a most elegant metal support, and it was not unusual to find the whole piece made of iron. A splendid example of Milanese damascene work, enriched with lapis lazuli, is shown in illustration 1. Milan was a centre of armour-making in the 16th century when fortunes were spent on gold inlaid suits and the technique could equally well be used in furniture.

Outside Italy the most sophisticated and elegant furniture of the Renaissance came from France. It was there that the Renaissance, especially in the decorative arts, had been most quickly assimilated to produce a new and original style: that branch of Mannerism stemming from the school of Fontainebleau. Essentially a courtly style, it has the elegance, grace and emphasis on finish of detail associated with Court art, and from the beginning the Crown was much more closely concerned with the design and production of furnishings for the Royal Palaces than in England, Spain or Germany, presaging the setting up of the Gobelins in the next century. Undoubtedly, some of the best furniture, especially for the Royal Palaces, was designed by artists and architects. We know, for example, that Ducerceau provided designs for furniture, and a table at Hardwick is close in style to his work. The grotesques, strapwork and other decorative motifs of the Fontainebleau school were easily transferred to furniture, which, as with painting

18. Cabinet; German, first half of the 16th century
walnut and boxwood 55×37½ in. (139·7×95·2 cm.)
The Victoria and Albert Museum, London

19. Cupboard; German (Cologne), 1583
oak 61×50½ in. (154·9×128·2 cm.)
The Rijksmuseum, Amsterdam

20. Chair; German (Augsburg), 1574
steel 56×27 in. (142·2×68·5 cm.)
The Earl of Radnor Collection, Longford Castle

and sculpture, assumed an originality that distinguishes it from the jejune provincialism of other non-Italian woodwork. An example of the richness of detail can be seen in a dresser in the Wallace Collection where the carving is deeper and more plastic than is usual in French furniture of the period. (Ill. 11.) It is interesting to compare this with an English buffet, also from the second half of the century. (Ill. 12.) By contrast the English piece is clumsy and lumpish. More typical and of even greater delicacy is a cupboard in the same collection, of about the same period. (Ill. 13.) Here the decoration is in low relief and confined to certain areas, thus making use of the contrast with the plain surfaces. These have been embellished with plaques of marble which, together with ivory, was a popular way of enriching the decoration. Closely related to contemporary French sculpture are the three figures on the top and the graceful Venus and Diana carved on the lower doors. Female nudes and figure decoration appear much more frequently on French than on Italian furniture. All the details are of very high quality and the elegance of the general design suggests careful thought rather than haphazard carpentry.[5] The *pandurina* mentioned earlier is another example of superlative technical quality. (Ill. 4.) This attention to detail which is so characteristic of French furniture can also be seen in such an everyday object as a chair (Ill. 14), which makes much English furniture seem crude by comparison. The assurance and wit of French carvers appear strikingly in the illustrated chest. (Ill. 15.) The grinning satyr in the centre, the swags, and bold and original strapwork are typical of that sure sense of design one likes to think is peculiarly French, while the quality of execution is equally part of a tradition that was to culminate in the great *menuisiers* and *ébénistes* of the 18th century.

The 16th century was Spain's 'Golden Century', both politically and culturally. It was the great age of sculpture in wood, of Berruguete, Juni and the school of Valladolid, when such masterpieces as the Toledo choir stalls were carved. The wealth of the Indies, even with the inflation it brought, created great prosperity, especially in the trading towns. New standards of comfort, as a result of the prolonged connection with Italy, together with the apparently inexhaustible supply of bullion, were responsible for the luxurious furnishing of the houses of the rich and noble. Renaissance influence is evident in the chest or cabinet on a stand (of later date) with antique heads in roundels set against an inlaid geometrical design of Arab origin (Ill. 16), an interesting mixture of styles, and a reminder that the indigenous Moorish tradition was still very much alive in the 16th century and was not smothered by the imported classical style. Cabinets, called *vargueños*, were popular in Spain and often decorated with ironwork, for which she had long been renowned. Some were enriched with silver, which was very cheap in this period, and clearly quantities of metal must have been used, for an edict of 1594 forbade the decoration of "cabinets, desks, coffers, tables or other articles decorated with stamped, raised, carved or plain silver". Marquetry of ivory and exotic woods was also popular as a decoration and owed as much to the Moorish tradition as to the Italian Renaissance. A particularly fine example is shown in illustration 17, dating from the mid-16th century. As Italian and German cabinets were imported and copied by native craftsmen, certain identification is sometimes a problem. There was more variety of woods used in Spanish furniture than that of other countries: in addition to the usual oak and walnut, Spanish chestnut, cedar, cypress and pine are found, as well as box, yew and the other marquetry woods.

Woodcarving, both secular and ecclesiastical, had perhaps a more continuous flourishing existence in Germany than elsewhere from the Middle Ages down to

[5] The arms of Isabella II of Spain on the upper doors are of course 19th-century additions.

21. (above) Caquetoire chair; English, *circa* 1535
48×24 in. (121·9×60·9 cm.)
The Victoria and Albert Museum, London

22. (right) Table; English, *circa* 1575
oak with walnut top 34×81½ in. (86·3×206·7 cm.)
(extended 134 in. (340·3 cm.))
Aston Hall, Birmingham (annex of the City Museum and Art Gallery)

the end of the 18th century. There was, consequently, a tradition of high quality and a tendency to concentrate on the expertise of decorative carving for its own sake. As with the Flemish artists, Renaissance motifs were adapted to existing forms and, continuing the very elaborate late Gothic style, furniture is crowded with detail often bearing no relation to the form of the object, but existing at the whim of the carver. Germany in the 16th century was a place of considerable prosperity and the merchants of Cologne, Augsburg and Nuremberg were among the richest of their day, while the aristocracy were ceasing to be beer-swilling freebooters and settling down to a more civilized existence, building and furnishing new castles, such as the Archduke Ferdinand of the Tyrol at Schloss Ambras. There appears to have been a particular fondness for amber and tortoiseshell for they are frequently employed in decoration; the effect can be monotonous and overpowering when seen in quantity. The most elaborate pieces of German furniture in this manner are cabinets, which seem to have assumed a social importance outside their strictly functional purpose. They could also be decorated with marquetry or carving such as on a cabinet once at Fonthill,[6] which is severely classical in its use of Corinthian half columns and entablature to mark the divisions (Ill. 18), a reminder that it would be a mistake to regard all German furniture as overdecorated. The strapwork and other intarsia of the cupboard in illustration 19 is unmistakably German in the way it covers the whole surface, whereas French or Italian decoration would have been arranged in a more imaginative and exciting way. One of the most historic pieces, now at Longford Castle, is the steel chair made at Augsburg by Thomas Ruker in 1574 and presented by the city to the Emperor Rudolph II in 1577. (Ill. 20.) It must be one of the finest and least known examples of Renaissance furniture. The arms, back supports and seat are covered with scenes from the history of the four great Empires – Babylonian, Persian, Greek and Roman – as a delicate compliment to the Emperor, and the allegorical programme is one of great complexity. All the details are of the highest quality, and the technique must be similar to that used on helmets, shields and weapons for which Augsburg was famous.

[6] The stand may have been made for Beckford.

23. (right) Box chair; English, *circa* 1525
oak 43×27½ in. (109·2×69·8 cm.)
The Victoria and Albert Museum, London

24. (far right) Chair; English, late 16th century
oak 42½×27 in. (107·9×68·5 cm.)
Aston Hall, Birmingham (annex of the City Museum and Art Gallery)

25. Bed; English, last quarter of the 16th century
oak 86×96 in. (218·4×243·8 cm.)
Aston Hall, Birmingham (annex of the City Museum and Art Gallery)

26. Chairs; Italian with English Turkeywork, *circa* 1600
walnut 40½×21 in. (102·8×53·3 cm.)
Aston Hall, Birmingham (annex of the City Museum and Art Gallery)

Renaissance furniture arrived later in England than elsewhere as there was no political or geographical link with Italy. In spite of this there were those who knew what was happening in Italy, and if this knowledge was at first confined to literary humanism, Torrigiano worked on Henry VII's tomb and da Majano and Rovezzano were both employed at Hampton Court, which was Italianate in conception if not in style. The perfect assimilation of the Renaissance is first seen in the screen and choir stalls of King's College Chapel dating from 1530 to 1535, which from their purity of detail would seem to be the work of Italians rather than Flemings, as is sometimes suggested. Both Wolsey and the King employed teams of foreign craftsmen, but after the Cardinal's fall the flow of Italians ceased and German and Flemish artists only were employed. This would account for the watering down of Italian influences and the decidedly provincial character of later 16th-century furniture. Antwerp was closely tied economically to England and was one of the northern centres of Mannerist design; from it were imported considerable quantities of the more expensive furniture. The links with France were also close, especially under Henry VIII, and the arm-chair or *caquetoire* is similar to French examples of *circa* 1535. (Ill. 21.) Standards of comfort rose continuously and the newly built house would have a wainscoted dining parlour, one or more sitting-rooms, as well as a long gallery for exercise in wet weather, where some of the best furniture was kept. The old hall was less and less used outside ceremonial occasions, but the master's chair at the high table was still there as a symbol of lordship. Chairs were rare articles in early 16th-century houses, even the family had to sit on stools. Trestle tables which could be removed came to be replaced by permanent framed tables. An additional refinement was the draw table which allowed a large board to take up less space. (Ill. 22.) Very typical are the bulbous legs and the robust anthemion decoration. Given the coarse eating habits of the time, which the fastidious Erasmus so deplored, a private dining-room must have been an improvement, the rest of the household eating in the servants' hall. Cupboards with open shelves for the display of plate, or closed to keep food and drink left over from the meal, were found in both the Hall and the dining parlour.

Colour Plate. Table; English with Florentine top, *circa* 1600
chestnut and *pietre dure* 36 in. (91·4 cm.)×48 in. (121·9 cm.) square
Aston Hall, Birmingham (annex of the City Museum and Art Gallery)

27. Chairs; English, first quarter of the 17th century
softwood 43½×24 in. (110·4×60·9 cm.)
Aston Hall, Birmingham (annex of the City Museum and Art Gallery)

(Ill. 12.) The Elizabethans had a good deal of plate which was put out when there was company, and then locked away. It would not be on permanent display. Contemporary accounts tell us of the magnificent gold and silver displayed for Court banquets. The luxury of Henry VIII's Court is well known and even Elizabeth, in spite of her parsimony, at least encouraged others to spend fortunes on clothes, entertainments and furnishings, and the Royal Palaces were kept up as a suitable background for the ceremonial of a Court which was the political and social centre of England. With the gradual relaxing of the social taboos about chairs, the number and variety increased, and there was the evolution from the unupholstered box chair made all in one piece (Ill. 23), to a more complex form where at least the seat was padded; and the joined chair (Ill. 24) made some attempt to follow the shape of the body it contained. Beds played an important rôle in the 16th-century household, again for social reasons, and could be elaborately carved and inlaid. The baluster supports provided a great opportunity for carving, and the backboard was also decorated. (Ill. 25.) Apart from dining tables, smaller tables, often with gate-legs and flaps, became more common. Marble-topped tables are almost always of mixed parentage, with the frames made up in England and the tops imported from Italy. A fine example is at Aston Hall, Birmingham (see colour plate facing p. 153), where the local carpenter has done his best to repeat the design of the top on the edge and legs. These tables were not uncommon: the Lumley Inventory of 1590 mentions fourteen of them.[7] An interesting reversal of the traffic is a pair of chairs, also at Aston, where the frames are Italian but the upholstery is English turkeywork. (Ill. 26.) None of these examples of 16th-century English furniture shows a proper understanding of Renaissance motifs, and it was not until *circa* 1625 that from the workshop of Francis Cleyn appeared the first examples of truly Renaissance furniture in England (Ill. 27) at the same time as Inigo Jones was putting up the first strictly classical building.

[7] See *Walpole Society*, vol. VI (1917–18), pp. 15ff.

BIBLIOGRAPHY

Litchfield, F. *Illustrated History of Furniture*, 1899.
Odom, W. M. *A History of Italian Furniture*, vol. I, 1919.
Macquoid, P. *A History of English Furniture – The Age of Oak*, 1938.

Early American Furniture

IAN McCALLUM

Mrs Trollope, on returning from America in the 1830's, was asked if she found American cities at all reminiscent of English ones. "Yes," she replied, "in a way they are: like ours, they are made up of squares, but where our squares are hollow, theirs are solid." It is much the same with the majority of American antiques; they are strongly reminiscent of English ones (or Spanish or French according to provenance) but frequently with marked characteristics and significant differences. I shall attempt to indicate a few of these differences – differences between the New World and the Old, as well as differences between one region of the New World and another.

Let us start with some generalizations to which, of course, there are exceptions, but ones which serve more than usual to prove the rule. In the furniture of the American colonies you will find a noticeable absence of the carved human form. The broken, and usually scrolled, pediment generally culminates in the cartouche rather than the bust, though Shakespeare, Madame de Pompadour, "Justice" and a symbolical "Liberty" make rare appearances. The female head or head and torso, so often carved on English furniture of the 18th century, seldom appears in American furniture. Animal forms, also, are extremely rare, with the exception of some of Aesop's Fables which are illustrated on streamer drawers with carving. The hairy paw foot is only found very occasionally and then on furniture made in relatively sophisticated metropolitan centres like Philadelphia and Boston. The type of foot most widely favoured in the colonies was the claw and ball and this continued to be employed, like a number of other motifs, long after it had been discarded in England. Following the Revolution, and for obvious reasons, the eagle is the all-pervading exception to the rule, for it appears everywhere.

Richly modelled forms are uncharacteristic of colonial furniture, and though you may find evidence of the rococo as applied ornament, its spirit will seldom invest the whole body of a piece. Nor did the extremes of the 'Gothick' and Chinese tastes find favour, though here again the more sophisticated centres of furniture manufacture might incorporate motifs from them on their grander products.

The absence of elaborate marquetry and few examples of overall lacquering is probably due more to scarcity of time, materials and craftsmen versed in the techniques than to taste, because both are found occasionally and marquetry painted to 'deceive the eye' is not at all uncommon. The same observation is probably true of other forms of inlay. The Henry Ford Museum and other collections possess examples of 'false ivory' inlay, the 'ivory' in fact being composed of a hard white putty.

There is an almost entire absence of direct French influence on colonial and early

Federal furniture, with the exception of the extreme South.[1] This is unexpected, particularly in the period just before and after the American Revolution when France was in such high regard, when the political links between the two countries were so strong and when a number of distinguished Frenchmen crossed the Atlantic, one of them, L'Enfant, to become the author of the plan for the new nation's capital.

The colonies, however, were not alone in eyeing French styles askance. In the words of Mr Ralph Fastnedge "French antiques were not congenial to our taste". Horace Walpole, while finding himself "wonderfully disposed to like France and the French", was struck the most by "the total difference of manners between them and us, from the greatest object to the least". Even so, a modified French manner appears as a recurring influence on English furniture. To take two examples, the *bombé* form is frequently found in English furniture, though it is scarce in colonial, and then deriving from the Dutch or English model rather than the French.[2] Few upholstered oval-backed chairs are found in the 18th century, though the form became popular in the Victorian era. Based on a Louis XVI model, in modified form it became very popular in England, and though the more elegant version, gilded over-all and sometimes embellished with the female form, would not have found favour in the sterner atmosphere of New England and the mid-Atlantic region, simpler versions were considerably less elaborate than many types of chair being made by craftsmen in the colonies in the later 18th and 19th centuries. One can only assume that the absence of French influence in the America of the period was due to an exaggeration of the English tendency to consider French styles "too foreign".

That you will not find grand colonial furniture in the Kentian manner is hardly a matter for surprise. It was, after all, rare in England and acted more as an extension of architecture than as furniture in the usual sense. American furniture designed especially for an architectural, or decorative, setting is unusual. A particularly elegant table was exhibited recently with a curved back intended to fit into a niche, but part of the interest it aroused was due to its rarity. Most American furniture adapts itself easily to different environments, due possibly to the mobility that was, for many, inseparable from the process of colonization and the founding of a nation.

In moving from the negative side of the story – from the styles, forms and motifs which were rejected, whether consciously or unconsciously, by the independent, pioneering and sometimes Puritan spirit of the New World – to the positive side, we find the same spirit could also produce individuality and character in furniture so marked as to make its study not only a matter of interest to the connoisseur, but a reflection, for all who can read the signs, of the history of a new country.

Seventeenth-century furniture in the American colonies differed little more from the furniture of England than the furniture of one region of England did from another: Yorkshire and Derbyshire, for instance, produced types of chairs not found elsewhere in England. A detailed study of English 16th- and 17th-century country furniture would, I suspect, uncover regional differences as distinct as in

[1] A distinguished exception in the North is the work of Charles Honoré Lannuier, a cabinet-maker who emigrated to New York from France at the beginning of the 19th century, and whose furniture is described by F. Lewis Hinckley as "combining American structural techniques with an alien design".

[2] A smaller motif conspicuous for its absence in American furniture of the 18th century (apart from an occasional appearance) in Philadelphia is the scroll foot which English furniture-makers borrowed from the French.

Colour Plate. New Orleans bedroom of about 1850–60. The great bed was made by Prudent Mallard and the small upholstered love-seat by John Henry Belter of New York – the wallpaper is a reproduction of a mid-19th-century American design. The American Museum in Britain, Bath

1. Oak chest with hinged top and two drawers below, *circa* 1670–90 from Hartford County, Connecticut and a maple and hickory elbow chair with 'mushroom arms' and a four-flat back with lemon-shaped finials The American Museum in Britain, Bath

2. Red painted, slipper-foot, country-made highboy of cherry wood from Connecticut, *circa* 1730–40
The American Museum in Britain, Bath

3. A maple high chest of drawers, New Hampshire, 1775–90, probably by Samuel Dunlap II
The Henry Francis du Pont Winterthur Museum, Delaware

vernacular architecture, as colourful as in local dialect and as varied as in farm-house cooking.

The kind of minor differences to be observed in colonial furniture of the earlier periods are concentrated in such small details as exaggerated 'mushroom' tops to the front posts of turned chairs, the slanting towards the diagonal of 'turtle-back' bosses on chests, and 'butterfly' brackets in place of 'gate' legs on folding tables. All through the history of American furniture from this period onwards, the use of woods is often a clue to 'Americanness'. In particular hickory, maple and cherry were used on a wide scale and often for quite fine pieces of furniture.[3]

From the time of the Pilgrims until late into the 18th century, nearly all pottery, glass, cutlery and metalware; all china, and a large proportion of textiles were imported from Europe, the major part from the British Isles. Later, especially in the period following the Revolution, silk, porcelain and painted papers were introduced from the Orient.

A late 17th-century New England hall or parlour would have presented a picture not unlike the interior of the house the colonists had left behind in England. Because of the value of glass, and the need to conserve heat in the cold winters, windows would be smaller and fireplaces would often be larger; but, with the many imported accessories, it would be in the differences of detail in the furniture that the beginning of an 'American accent' would begin to make itself evident.

In the early 18th-century colonial interior a piece of furniture appears, deriving from the Queen Anne chest-on-stand, that was to develop a life of its own in America and to culminate in what later came to be known as the highboy; this later type of highboy had no exact parallel in England. There has been considerable confusion over terminology. The chest-on-stand (or chest-on-stand with drawers) was, in America, termed the 'highboy' long after the type made its appearance. The chest-on-chest which was also made in the colonies, though not nearly so often as in England where it almost entirely replaced the chest-on-stand, came to be known in England as the 'tallboy'; here again the 'nickname' was not adopted until late in its history.

Characteristics of the early American highboy are extreme simplicity, with gracefully curved and slender cabriole legs, often terminating in slipper, trifid or pad feet. As the 18th century progressed the form and decoration of these pieces acquired greater importance and the character varied considerably from region to region.

The fan, or shell form, was a popular embellishment, and so was fretting, rococo carving, the flame finial and the broken pediment framing an elaborate cartouche with central cabochon form (the last known in Pennsylvania as the 'Philadelphia peanut'). New Hampshire characteristics, as might be expected from its relative remoteness, show a fanciful individuality of great charm of which the highboy illustrated is an example. Besides the flat top, the pediment was a popular form for highboys and the scrolled and broken type was a favoured design. When these scrolls are taken from front to back as a solid 'roof' the form is known as a 'bonnet-top'.

As might be expected, regional similarities follow lines of communication and, in the 18th century, the rivers were among the most important. In New England the furniture of the Connecticut river valley, therefore, shows a family resemblance, with variations becoming more markedly provincial, though not necessarily

[3] A small and interesting difference in the use of woods is often found in 17th-century American chests where the oak top of the English variety is, in America, presumably for reasons of economy, often replaced by pine.

4. (above left) Cherry highboy with a bonnet top, three flame finials, cabriole legs and pad feet, *circa* 1750–70, Connecticut
The American Museum in Britain, Bath

5. (above right) Mahogany high chest with a bonnet top with elaborate central finial in the form of a pierced cartouche, side finials in the form of flames arising from urns on fluted bases – the sides of the drawers are of tulipwood and the bottoms white cedar, *circa* 1760–75, of Philadelphia origin
The American Museum in Britain, Bath

any less charming or well made, as the distance from the main lines of communication increase. In centres like Salem, Massachusetts; Newport, Rhode Island; New York and Philadelphia there is much greater sophistication in design and craftsmanship. In the history of the highboy, however, it is the New England country regions and the city of Philadelphia which figure most prominently. In Philadelphia, the type reached its culmination during the third quarter of the 18th century in chests by cabinet-makers such as Affleck, Randolph and Savery, with elaborate scroll-pediments, sometimes frontal scroll or pediment only, and sometimes full bonnet-topped. The scroll was often enhanced with flame finials and terminated in elaborately carved rosettes. In the more elaborate versions, a rococo cartouche was used as a central ornament. The scroll board below the broken pediment and the skirt above the apron was also often embellished with leafage and pierced rococo shells. A variation was the intaglio shell flanked by applied leafage on upper and lower drawer fronts. The carved motifs were derived from European designs, but assembled in a completely original manner.

New England pieces, as a rule, omit any further embellishment within these scroll boards and skirts, other than the shell or fan: they also continued to exhibit pad feet as well as the claw and ball, where in Philadelphia, in the more elaborate examples, the claw and ball foot was *de rigueur*. Additional embellishments found on Philadelphia highboys but not, as a rule, on those of other origins are shells carved on the aprons and acanthus leaf motifs on the knees of the cabriole legs. Fluted quarter columns decorating the outer corners of chest and stand are seldom absent from Philadelphia pieces, but were also employed elsewhere – in particular, on fine Connecticut pieces by such distinguished craftsmen as Aaron Chapin whose work, though he was trained in Philadelphia, has the characteristic simplicity of New England, while incorporating decorative features, such as the pierced fret within the pediment to be found on Philadelphia examples.

En suite with the highboy there was often a matching lowboy. Developing from the Queen Anne dressing, or side table, the exaggerated overhang of the top, in the colonial examples, is one means of distinguishing it from its English prototype; this feature is less prevalent as time goes on and as the decoration and characteristics of the lowboy came to resemble its companion piece, the highboy.

In the first half of the 18th century, the secretary-bookcase and the desk developed along much the same lines in America as in England, though, until 1785, the bookcase doors were only very rarely glazed in American examples. The claw and ball foot is found more, and bracket foot less frequently in America than in England; the differences in the use of woods referred to before apply in this type of furniture as in others. Shell motifs are common on bookcases, so are scroll pediments, often of the bonnet-top type.

6. Mahogany chest or chest-on-chest, 1765–80, Newport – the ten-lobed shells are cut from the solid drawer fronts, which are hollowed on the reverse side The Henry Francis du Pont Winterthur Museum, Delaware

Between the years 1750 and 1780 there were made in Newport, R.I., by the Townsend and Goddard families, secretary-bookcases, kneehole commodes and chests of drawers which were given the term 'blockfront', a reference to the vertical blocks, sometimes applied, but more usually cut from the solid, which, flanking a central 'reverse block' or niche, formed the front of the drawers. On the Townsend–Goddard pieces the tops of the blocks are carved with elaborate shell motifs, and these also appear at times on Connecticut blockfronts. However, blockfronts from other regions – and the form crops up from New Hampshire to Virginia – usually display plain blocks. There is only one example of a blockfront highboy (in the Henry Francis du Pont Winterthur Museum); indeed, the monumental effect produced by blocking does not look well perched up in the air on high legs.

There has been vigorous controversy over the origin of the blockfront form. It is certainly found 'in embryo' on some English Queen Anne furniture, as it also is on certain pieces of Boulle. Expert opinion, however, now favours the "native designs produced in southern and central German states through the second quarter of the eighteenth century, and later in states as far North as Mecklenburg and Holstein".[4]

American tables follow English design fairly closely. Early tables of the refectory kind may show Scandinavian or German influence as do later tables of the same type from regions where these immigrants settled. The butterfly-wing folding table is, until the later 'trick-leg' tables of Duncan Phyfe, rare in being a feature of purely American origin.[5] Tea tables, pedestal tables, card, side and dining tables show certain differences in the use of mahogany, walnut and local woods, alongside an American simplicity and a tendency to 'ring the changes' of style less often; otherwise they exhibit a close family relationship to their English models.

There is a greater variety among American chair types and there is one feature which, though it appears on other kinds of furniture, on chairs can provide an easily observed indicator of regional origin – the claw and ball foot. In Massachusetts the ends of the claws bend back and appear to be grasping the ball tightly;

[4] Hinckley, F. L. *A Directory of Antique Furniture*. New York, 1953.

[5] In Macquoid's *Dictionary of English Furniture* there is a precedent for the idea of the butterfly-wing bracket in an English folding table of 1610, where the drop-leaf is supported by an open-frame bracket very much less elegant, however, than the butterfly-wing bracket.

the ball is high and the shape tends towards the oval. In the finest Newport pieces only the nails of the claw join to the ball, the rest of the claw being undercut. The New York claw and ball is blocky and the back claw is often a continuation of the back of the leg. In much Philadelphia furniture the ball is flattened so the claw sits lower on the ground, giving an air of solidity without sacrifice of elegance. However, these pointers should be taken as a general guide only because, as may be expected, there is considerable variation within regions in these as in other details.

In English furniture pieces which are transitional between one period and another are quite often encountered; as a rule, however, this reflects provincial conservatism. In American furniture, transitional pieces were made in important centres and by the finest craftsmen. The chair illustrated was made in New Jersey by a Philadelphia craftsman and could be nothing but American, with the prominent ears terminating a sinuous top rail and with elegantly carved shells on the front rail and knees so characteristic of the Philadelphia style. But most striking of all is the use of the solid 'Queen Anne' splat back in combination with features usually associated with the later Chippendale manner. If you found such a combination in England it would be on a rough, if charming, country piece. This chair, however, is of a high standard of craftsmanship, and when you find transitional features on a piece of furniture of this quality you may be sure of its American origin.

7. Mahogany side chair with bowed top-rail with a central shell, solid carved splat, central shell on the seat skirting, carved knees, claw and ball feet and slip-in seats, *circa* 1700–76, from Philadelphia or Maddonfield, New Jersey, attributed to Samuel Mickle
The American Museum in Britain, Bath

8. Mahogany ladder-back side chair with slip-in seat, *circa* 1785, attributed to Daniel Trotter of Philadelphia – horizontal splats of back are curved and are each divided horizontally into three elements, with a circular ornament in the centre
The American Museum in Britain, Bath

The Philadelphia ladder-back chair by Daniel Trotter, *circa* 1785, illustrates some other interesting differences between English and American chairs. The English ladder-back of about ten years earlier, placed beside it, shows clear rococo influence in form, if not in detail: whereas Philadelphia chairs are more likely to show the influence in detail than in form. The Trotter chair reflects little influence of the rococo at all; instead, it has a crisp simplicity of outline that seems firmly to reject the over-fanciful and combines this with evidence of a highly assured technique. It also features an archaism – a carved fret design on the front rail which harks back a quarter of a century.

The best-known name in American furniture of the Federal period is, of course, Duncan Phyfe, who drew on a variety of sources for his inspiration – Robert Adam and Chippendale, Sheraton and Hepplewhite – to produce a style which is often very much his own. The settee illustrated is a particularly elegant product of his workshops, revealing a strong influence of the Empire while retaining lively originality.

In Philadelphia at about the same time, two cabinet-makers, Ephraim Haines and Henry Connelly, were making chairs owing something to Sheraton, but which also recall the banister-backs of the 17th century, replacing the naïve 'architecture' of the earlier chair with split, fluted columns embellished with acanthus leaf decoration. Later on, painted chairs grew in popularity in America as in England, the best known being the 'Hitchcock' chair, mass-produced between 1820 and 1850 in Hitchcocksville, Connecticut, with stencil designs and gold lining on a black or green ground. The rocker, a chair many consider originated in America, is sometimes found painted in the Hitchcock manner.

The mid-19th century saw the development of various new techniques in the manufacture of furniture. Perhaps the most celebrated is the special laminating process devised by John Henry Belter, the New York cabinet-maker, by which he was able to provide elaborately carved wafer-thin sections to his rosewood furniture which, at the same time, was immensely strong. The secret of his own technique of lamination died with him. In style his furniture is often described as

9. Empire style mahogany sofa, *circa* 1815–25, attributed to Duncan Phyfe
– the seat, three-panel back and curved arms are caned – the crest rails of the back and arms are carved
The American Museum in Britain, Bath

being in the French manner and indeed, at several removes, many of the motifs can be traced back to that source. The same may be said of Southern Victorian furniture of the type represented in the colour illustration. The cabinet-maker was Prudent Mallard; of Scots-French parentage, he worked in New York for Duncan Phyfe before moving South to become the leading cabinet-maker in New Orleans in the period preceding the Civil War. Victorian furniture of this kind is not untypical of many Southern interiors today. Before the Civil War the Southern States were both prosperous and fashionable, and interiors would often be redecorated and refurnished according to the taste of the time; the furniture illustrated here represents the last period of ante-bellum prosperity.

There is a dearth of fine 18th-century Southern furniture due, no doubt, to attrition and disposal at times of refurnishing, though the Civil War, too, must have taken its toll. Characteristically Southern pieces are tall hunting tables and wine coolers, the latter being much more often found in the South than in New England. Slave labour often created Southern pieces and the use of Southern woods like cypress can give them a very special character of their own.

A description of the American chair, however brief, cannot omit the Windsor. From 1730 to 1870 Windsor chairs were made in greater volume and variety than any other type of chair in America, and many of them achieved an elegance and grace of line that made them, as Thomas Ormsbee has said, "not out of place in handsome colonial homes".[6] In America the first examples were called Philadelphia chairs because that is where they made their début. Characteristic of American Windsors is a tendency towards greater splay in the legs by comparison with English examples, and an absence of the typically English ornamental back splats and spindles. There was a larger number of variant types of Windsors in America than in England – nine in all – two of which are original to America: the writing-arm Windsor, with an arm forming a cantilevered writing ledge, and the arrow back, which first appeared in 1810, though presumably inspired by earlier memories.

The two qualities, economy of material and elegance achieved through simplicity of form, are both signally evident in the furniture of the only religious sect in America ever to achieve a completely consistent 'aesthetic' in most branches of their activities – The Shakers. For this reason no consideration of the history of American furniture can ignore them. "Hands to work and hearts to God" was one

[6] Ormsbee, T. H. *The Windsor Chair*, 1962.

of their mottoes, and in all their artifacts, but particularly in their furniture, you see reflected a purity of intention that abhors pretence and even the most simple decoration, stressing instead economy and fitness for purpose, producing a strong 'family' resemblance to some modern furniture: in fact, many Shaker sayings about design principles presage, uncannily, the prophets of 20th-century functionalism.

In considering early American furniture from a distance, there is a tendency to place exclusive emphasis on the furniture of New England and what are now the mid-Atlantic States, forgetting the fact that other cultures also made an important contribution to the development of America. This imbalance of attitude may partly be due to the many splendid museums along the eastern seaboard where early American furniture, primarily of English ancestry, can easily be studied and enjoyed.[7]

However true it is that furniture showing the influence of Spanish, French, Scandinavian and German (aside from the Pennsylvania German) colonists and immigrants is small in quantity, it does exist and examples are found in a number of places, of which I mention just a few – Spanish in New Mexico, French along the Canadian border,[8] Scandinavian in the Pacific North-West and German in Wisconsin. A study of the contribution of these other cultures reveals the same complex cross-currents we have observed in English-derived furniture resulting, in the same way, from their transplantation to a new continent alongside one another, and to other subtle reasons connected with the beginnings of a specifically American culture. To take one minor example, in some Spanish Colonial furniture of New Mexico can be seen the influence of Regency design from the eastern seaboard – perhaps of Duncan Phyfe – which is not really surprising since this furniture travelled west along the Santa Fe trail, and would certainly have made a lively impression on a New Mexican Spanish craftsman.

10. One of a pair of matching mahogany side chairs in the Sheraton style, attributed to Ephraim Haines of Philadelphia
– straight reeded crest curved to back terminating in button-topped blocks carved with rosettes, round fluted side posts and three flat reeded columnar splats carved with rosettes and acanthus leaves
The American Museum in Britain, Bath

Pennsylvania German furniture and crafts deserve special mention because the Rhineland Germans and Swiss who settled in Penn's 'Colony' produced between 1750 and 1850, in their self-contained communities, a large quantity of painted furniture, of pottery, of chalkware (painted 'plaster of Paris' ornaments), of needlework and of *Frakturschriften* (elaborately decorated baptismal and marriage certificates inscribed with Gothic lettering known as *Fraktur*).

In contrast to the plain Shaker furniture illustrated here, Pennsylvania German furniture is painted, grained, stippled and often decorated with spongework as well; among the most popular painted motifs were tulips, birds and hearts.[9]

Early American furniture, then, is a guide-line to early American culture. Much of it is rare and expensive, but the great public collections are displayed with exemplary skill and clarity for all to see. Here it has only been possible to give the

[7] To name only a few of the larger and more accessible ones, there are Sturbridge Village and Deerfield in Massachusetts and Cooperstown in New York State. At the Van Cortlandt Mansion on the Hudson you can see the home environment of a 18th-century Dutch *patroon*. At the Museum of Fine Arts in Boston there is a magnificent collection of American furniture collected by the late Maxim Karolik, at New York's Metropolitan Museum there is a separate American wing and in a superb setting near Wilmington, Delaware, is the Henry Francis du Pont Winterthur Museum which covers the field of the American decorative arts and where particularly fine examples of 18th-century Southern furniture can be studied. A fine collection is also to be seen in Williamsburg.

[8] French influence on furniture in North America is seen at its most powerful in Canada and an exceptionally fine collection of French-Canadian furniture is exhibited at the Detroit Museum of Fine Arts.

[9] Especially fine Pennsylvania German collections are to be seen at the Henry Francis du Pont Winterthur Museum, the Philadelphia Museum of Fine Arts and the Metropolitan Museum, New York.

11. Shaker Room. Brother's armed cherrywood rocking chair, *circa* 1820, from Hancock, Massachusetts – four slats – mushrooms on the top of the front posts are part of the post turning and not applied pieces as in the late 19th-century Shaker chairs; drop-leaf cherrywood table, *circa* 1815, from New Lebanon, New York; candle stand from the Second Family, New Lebanon, New York – legs in the form of intersecting crescents, and a disc replaces the usual cross base under the top; one-slat pine dining chair from Hancock, Massachusetts, *circa* 1810–20 – the one slat proved insufficient support for the back and was discarded in favour of the double slat – after meals when the floor was being cleaned the chairs were hung on the pegboard; stove with stove board, from New Lebanon, New York, *circa* 1810–20 – wood-burning 'box' stoves were made in various styles and referred to by the world as 'stoves of the Shaker improvement'. The American Museum in Britain, Bath

barest outline of characteristics and to point out some of the many differences between American and English 18th-century furniture designs. That there are more than one might suspect is, perhaps, due to one of the following factors: (1) the multiple migrations and settlements of western Europeans, other than English, in America; (2) the physical distance from London, the centre where furniture design theoretically originated; (3) the psychic removal of America from English empathy for two decades 1765 to 1785. During this period the unique rococo Philadelphia highboy and lowboy developed, and in New England the unique blockfront pieces came into their full maturity.

I have not intended to suggest that American furniture was not based on European design books, for it definitely was; but instead to draw attention to the fact that some of the combinations of these designs produced forms that can be called unique. I do, however, suggest that the study of furniture design and recording of large numbers of regional interpretations has progressed very far in America. Perhaps farther than in most countries of Western Europe, where further research into regional characteristics would, I am sure, provide much interesting information on precedents and prototypes for early American furniture.

BIBLIOGRAPHY

Best concise summary is Schwartz, M. D., "Furniture 1640–1840" in *The Concise Encyclopedia of American Antiques*, ed. Helen Comstock. New York, 1955.

BEST STANDARD WORKS ARE:

Andrews, E. D. *Shaker Furniture*. New York, 1950.

Metropolitan Museum of Art. *Handbook of the American Wing*. New York, 2nd ed., 1942.

Comstock, H. *American Furniture*. Viking, 1962.

Downs, J. *American Furniture in the Henry Francis du Pont Winterthur Museum*. New York, 1952.

Lockwood, L. V. *Colonial Furniture in America*. New York, 1926, 2 vols. Reissued 1951.

McClelland, N. *Duncan Phyfe and the English Regency*. New York, 1939.

Miller, E. G. *American Antique Furniture*. Baltimore, 1937, 2 vols. Reissued 1948.

Nutting, W. *Furniture of the Pilgrim Century*. Framingham, Mass., 1924.

Nutting, W. *Furniture Treasury*. Vols. 1 and 2, Cambridge, Mass., 1928; vol. 3, Framingham, Mass., 1933. Vols. 1–2 reissued in one vol. 1954.

Sack, A. *Fine Points of Furniture: Early American*. New York, 1950.

Later Ormolu Clock Cases

HOWARD RICKETTS

The French ormolu mantle clock, whose popularity was to last for well over a century, emerged as a result of the newly formed partnership between sculpture and clock-making which took place in the mid-18th century. This in itself was a revival of the sculpturally-cased clock which had achieved a certain success in Germany and Italy in the previous century, and in turn had evolved from the 16th-century table clock; this had been the first easily portable domestic clock. The movement was contained in a drum-shaped case which in the better-quality pieces was in gilt-bronze with a narrative relief. (Ill. 1.) In this the ornament was essentially restrained, unmonumental and quite definitely subservient to the more functional aspects of the piece. From this emerged, sixty years later, the first sculptural clock in which the movement took second place to the animal or human form which supported it.

The new baroque style which swept Europe in the 17th century forced the portable sculptural clock into decline, and the royal patronage of Louis XIV which brought about a renaissance of the clock industry instead produced a spate of heavy pedestal clocks, ponderously constructed out of tortoiseshell enriched with intricate ormolu mounts. Such grand pieces cannot be easily accommodated in a present-day interior, and it is fortunate for the modern collector that this style was soon to be stripped of its pomposity with the advent of the rococo – a feather-light construction of scrolls, asymmetrically arranged to reduce the overall weight of the design – and later by the rocaille which, as its name implies, introduced wave and shell motifs into the restless rococo scheme. The heavy pedestal, popular under Louis XIV, gave way to the wall-bracket as a means of support, but the free-standing clock not dependent on either of these accessories for its existence finally emerged free from previous encumbrances, to be placed on a table or mantelpiece according to the whim of the owner (Ill. 2), as an indirect result of chinoiserie, which ran a parallel course with rococo and the rocaille.

1. Table clock, *circa* 1580, possibly Italian and one of six decorated with the identical frieze of Orpheus Courtesy Sotheby & Co., London

Chinoiserie was the expression of the European vision of Cathay. Travellers returning from the East elaborated on the civilized life which existed in China and which the artist then attempted to convey on canvas. It was pictures by Watteau which really ignited the craze in France. Pattern books of engravings freely adapted from his, and later Pillement's representations of Chinese life were soon adapted for use in the decoration of furniture, snuff-boxes and porcelain, and affected nearly every backwater in the applied arts. In clock-case making the symmetrical proportions of the face hardly fitted into a rococo theme and under the influence of chinoiserie it now assumed a less important place in the overall design. The supporting figures either of Chinamen or of an elephant (Ill. 3) cast in the round were contrived to catch the eye. It was because of the popularity of this

2. (right) Louis XV mantle clock by Gille l'Aîné of Paris
the squat bracket shows the last trace of the wall bracket support
height 25 in. (63·5 cm.)
Courtesy Sotheby & Co., London

3. (below) Louis XV 'Elephant clock', *circa* 1755
height 20 in. (50·8 cm.)
Courtesy Sotheby & Co., London

4. (far right) Louis XV cartel clock, the movement by Julien le Roy, mid-18th century
height 31 in. (78·7 cm.)
Courtesy Sotheby & Co., London

5. (right) Louis XVI ormolu clock, the figure of a nymph adapted from Falconet's *The Three Graces*
height 18 in. (45·5 cm.)
Courtesy Sotheby & Co., London

6. The Avignon clock designed by Louis Simon Boizot and executed by Philippe Gouthière
height 26¾ in. (67·9 cm.)
The Wallace Collection, London

7. Louis XVI clock, the figure of a putto is taken from a Sèvres bisquit model by Boizot, executed in 1779
– adapted from *Enfanta la Cage* sculpted by Jean Baptiste Pigalle two years earlier
height 18½ in. (46 cm.)
Courtesy Sotheby & Co., London

Colour Plate. Ormolu clock with a figure of Paris, early 19th century, by D'Epine; Paris
height 24½ in. (62·2 cm.)
The Victoria and Albert Museum, London

marriage of sculpture to clock-making that the so-called 'mantle clock' emerged. The wall bracket which in the past had faithfully reflected in its own decoration the form of the clock above became obsolete simply because no feasible form of ornament could be convincingly adopted to support the new-style clock. Last traces of the bracket can be found in the Cartel clock in which the two elements were amalgamated and contrived to fit flat against the wall. (Ill. 4.)

Under the *ancien régime* in France the Court at Versailles dictated the taste of the period. The most eminent craftsmen gathered under the patronage of the Crown or the leading families, who for the most part emulated their royal mentors. It was a period in which the extravagant task of refurbishing suites at Versailles was in the hands of few, and the leading mount-makers of the period were to be found working not only for the royal *ébénistes*, but also mounting porcelain and bronze statuettes and helping in the production of clocks. It was a two-class society. The artisans worked almost exclusively for the ruling class; the rich *bourgeoisie* which was to emerge in the following century hardly existed. This resulted in ormolu-mounted clocks being made exclusively for the nobility because the two components, the movement and the case, combined to form too expensive an entity for any but the very rich. As yet no cheap substitute for either of these could be found to make production of less good quality clocks economically viable.

The name 'ormolu' was given to gilt-bronze in the 18th century, but it was not simply invented then. It really emerged in its earliest form in the Middle Ages, when craftsmen applied gilding on a copper base to imitate their Byzantine counterparts who used solid gold. The method employed to produce a piece of gilt-bronze remained basically unchanged from the 16th to the late 18th century. It would be done in two stages: the casting of the metal and the gilding. The most common method of bronze casting was the *cire-perdue* or lost wax technique. In this the bronze figures emerge hollow, so that little metal is wasted as in solid casting. However, only one cast could be obtained from the one wax model, as it was destroyed in the process. The second stage would entirely depend on the function of the bronze. If it was cast as a decorative statuette it would then be artificially patinated and lacquered, but if it was designed as a mount or a figure for a clock it would more probably be placed in the hands of the gilder. In mercury-gilding an amalgam of gold and mercury – the former granulated before the two ingredients were mixed into a paste – would be applied to the bronze and the mercury would be vaporized with heat to leave the solidified gold. This would then be 'fixed' or stabilized by verdigris.

On the surface this would appear to be an economical method of gilding if it had not been for the fact that the fumes emitted in the vaporizing stage were extremely bad for the craftsmen whose life expectancy was radically cut by doing this work. Quite naturally few volunteered for this occupation, and those who did were attracted solely by the high wages which had to be eventually borne by the customer.

The application of sculpture in a dominant position in the clock case during the reign of Louis XV brought about the emergence of a new group of sculptors who almost usurped the authoritative position of the designer, or at least supplied him with the most important motifs. There was an overlap period from *circa* 1750 until the sculptor's eminence was crystallized with the advent of Neo-classicism.

The rise of Neo-classicism occurred in England, in the form of the severe wood-cased bracket clock, rather earlier than it did in France. The return to the purest styles in Greek antique sculpture, then known only through Italian copies, was itself a rejection not only of the baroque, but also of the Age of Reason and

8. Directoire clock with the negro boy 'Paul' height 13 in. (33 cm.)
Private Collection, France

9. Empire clock with negro lovers, the figures probably inspired by a bust of negroes by Houdon height 19 in. (48·2 cm.)
Private Collection, France

rococo. The propagators of Neo-classicism advocated only the purest form, but paradoxically this was a romantic ideal in itself, and in the Neo-classical movement can be seen the origins of the Empire style and the Romantic movement. The clocks produced during these three periods are certainly allied.

The prevalent motifs, taken from classical origins, included Corinthian columns, the laurel wreath and Greek key-frets. Incorporated into this architectural form were figures, mostly draped in classical robes, which were not allowed to interfere with the basic outline of the nude body. This fashion placed sculpture high above any other art form during the two decades immediately before the Revolution, and was directly reflected in the design of the clock case.

To meet this universal demand for sculptural clock cases, the designers turned for inspiration towards the Sèvres porcelain factory which had been for some time producing statuettes in biscuit porcelain. Although the factory did not employ the most famous and fashionable portrait sculptors of the period, such as Lemoyne or Houdon, it did nevertheless have two key sculptors as directors of the sculpture department which was responsible for the original maquette in terracotta or plaster from which the porcelain moulds were made.

The first of these was Etienne Maurice Falconet who was director from 1758 until 1766. His work at the factory pre-dated the rise of Neo-classicism, and as a result many of his works were copied by ormolu-workers at a later date after he had gone to Russia where he executed various marble figures, including *The Three Graces* for the Empress Catherine. This model (Ill. 5) appears on later clock cases adapted in many forms which continued for some time after his death. By the time Neo-classicism had 'taken over' in the field of the applied arts, Louis Simon Boizot was director of the sculpture department. An example of the influence of the Sèvres factory on clock-making can be found in an Avignon clock (Ill. 6) in the Wallace Collection, London, which was specially commissioned from this sculptor and was executed in ormolu by Gouthière, the most celebrated ormolu-craftsman of the period. This piece exemplifies the close link which existed in the production of excellent quality clocks, but further down the scale copies were made in ormolu of biscuit originals, and it is possible that the porcelain factory was unaware of the plagiarization of their models. They had every opportunity of employing the services of the best modellers in France. Young men were tempted to work under the patronage of the Crown, or else were 'discovered' at the factory, since many amateur modellers took their clay maquettes to be baked in the manufactory's ovens.

The Sèvres factory did in fact produce clock cases in biscuit as well as detached figures, but comparatively few have survived – either because of the fragility of the material or because their models were thought during this period to look more attractive in ormolu and marble.

During the decade immediately before the downfall of the monarchy in 1793, the form of the clock gives an impression that France was a timeless state. The euphoric atmosphere generated by the Queen's dilettante excursions into bucolic pursuits at Versailles was reflected in case designs. The main feature – the dial – almost disappeared; the vertical chapter ring was replaced by a horizontal band carrying the chapters; and in many cases it is found as either a table-top around which sit classical figures, or as a globe discreetly calibrated around its circumference with the time of day nonchalantly indicated by a Cupid's arrow.

The Revolution rather naturally halted this great 'sculptural' period in clock-making, but it was only temporary. A new rich *bourgeoisie* emerged to take the place of the old nobility, and until a new style appeared during the First Empire,

10. (above left) First Empire ormolu clock
height 16½ in. (42 cm.)
Norman Hartnell Collection

11. (above centre) A politically inspired clock in the Empire style commemorating the 'July Days'
Private Collection, France

12. (far right) Ormolu clock case with parts interchangeable with other clock cases, *circa* 1820; French
Formerly Lady Juliet Duff Collection

the clock case discreetly borrowed all that was permitted from pre-Revolution prototypes.

One of the few examples of Directory clock-case making which anticipated the Empire period was the Negro mantle clock (Ill. 8), one of the earliest examples of which shows a young Negro carrying the movement on his back. The subject was taken from the popular novel "Paul and Virginie", by Bernardin of Saint-Pierre in the French Caribbean colonies. The sculptor successfully attempted to reproduce the colour of the negroid skin in brown patinated bronze as opposed to gilded bronze.

During the early days of the Empire the clock was not only a timepiece but also a vehicle for patriotic demonstrations. The Emperor appears in many guises, and in the piece shown in illustration 10 is seen meditating by a fireside whilst a widow, allegorical of the Spirit of France, is anxious to demonstrate her willingness even to destroy letters – possibly from her husband killed at the front – for the furtherance of the Napoleonic cause. Most of the clocks reflect in some way the various events of the time. The Nile campaign is symbolized by the Sphinx and the anthemion motif, and the amatory ideals of the previous century gave way to a patriotic ardour in which even Cupid had to work for his living, either driving a triumphal chariot or on sentry duty at the Emperor's tent.

Not only was the style of the clock changed but also the mounts and types of metal employed were modified. The juxtaposition of matt and polished ormolu was appreciated for the first time. This certainly succeeded in lightening the visual effect. The somewhat heavy marble bases were overlaid with vignettes of acanthus or anthemion in matt ormolu, and the combined use of patinated bronze and ormolu was exploited to the full. Without these contrasting effects the Empire clock might well have looked as heavy as the Victorian black marble clock which was popular in England half a century later.

For the first time clocks are produced in varying qualities. Under the *ancien régime* comparatively few low-grade pieces were produced, but as the *bourgeoisie* became more affluent, so the clock-maker had to satisfy the needs of both ends of the scale in a so-called 'one-class' society. Expensive methods of casting were reserved only for the finest clock cases and from now on the process of sectional casting which had been done before was revived on a wider front, so that more than one cast could be taken from the mould. For example, a figure of a Muse

13. Romantic clock with a hunter in medieval costume
height 15$\frac{3}{4}$ in. (40 cm.)
Howard Ricketts Collection

14. Ormolu and silvered-metal clock
height 16 in. (40·6 cm.): Howard Ricketts Collection

15. A 'Cathedral' clock: height 9$\frac{7}{8}$ in. (25 cm.)
Musée des Arts Décoratifs, Paris

might well have the arms screwed into the sleeves, but it was not until the Second Empire in 1870 that the cheaper quality pieces were crudely moulded in half and pieced together. Another economy was to eliminate 'undercutting' in the model, so that an unlimited amount of casts could be taken from the original model, almost like a jelly from a mould. But perhaps the most important step towards producing a good-quality but economical clock came with the marketing of Frédéric Japys movements. From 1810 onwards he manufactured at his workshop at Badeval a type of movement in which the parts were interchangeable and the attachments to the case adjustable to meet the requirements of almost any mantle clock. It was indeed a prolific period in clock-making and most pieces dating from this time are of quite good quality; the few pieces which are not were nearly all made in the Empire style in other parts of Europe. Above all, the case makers were adventurous not only in the use of materials, but also in the elaborate designs which in some cases strove for a patriotic effect which to the modern eye is amusingly naïve. One hesitates to imagine how much farther the clock case could have been from reality in the classical sense if Napoleon had not been defeated in 1815. The restoration of the monarchy called for a revival of 18th-century motifs, but this tangle of styles was firmly ironed out with the advent of the Romantic era which swept Europe in the 1820's. In England Sir Walter Scott's novels inspired an interest in medieval architecture and objects and similarly in France the works of Victor Hugo, whose first historical novel was published in 1822, sparked off a return to the age of chivalry. Consequently clock cases made during the reign of Charles X and Louis-Philippe reflect this fashion.

The form adopted for the 'Romantic' clock is a somewhat more monumental version of the Louis XVI clock except that such predominating figures as knights in armour or romantic huntsmen (Ill. 13) replace the figures taken from classical mythology. The various firms who specialized in these clock cases successfully exported a large proportion of their pieces. Many clocks were sent to England and the rest of Europe, and to simplify warehousing the various components were marked with ink, probably so that the warehouse employees could make up an order working simply from a numbered list. Packaging was also made easier as the clocks were constructed with five main component parts, divided between the rockwork superstructure which contained the movement and supported the figure, and the simple oblong base which slotted into an elaborate stand. By conforming to a standard size many of these pieces were interchangeable; figures could be rearranged, and rockwork superstructures remounted on bases which could be fitted with any type of stand. This is really the first time that the Industrial Revolution had made its presence felt on clock-case designs. Japys's influence had revolutionized the movement, and the only refinement in these clocks is that the two supporting bars were elongated and cut with a long screw for attachment to either a deep or shallow case. This technique of manufacturing produced a good-quality and economical clock which could satisfy the demands of a broader stratum of society.

Two other variations in style changed the form of the clock case during the Romantic era. The first was a reflection of the popularity of sculpture in animal form. The 'Animalier' school of sculptors whose bronze statuettes of animals were popular from the middle of the 1830's until the end of the century almost certainly inspired the clock (Ill. 14) in which a stallion is attempting to rescue a mare from drowning in a fast-moving river. It represents the most dramatic period of the Romantic movement in clock-making and succeeded in livening up the somewhat static form of the sculptural clock case. The 'cathedral' clock marks the end of the

16. Design for a mid-19th century pastiche of a Louis XV mantle clock

17. A 'proto-art nouveau' design for a sculptural clock case probably inspired by the English sculptor Monti

18. Art nouveau clock, 1889, signed by the Belgian sculptor Van de Voorde
height 16¼ in. (41·2 cm.)
Courtesy Sotheby & Co., London

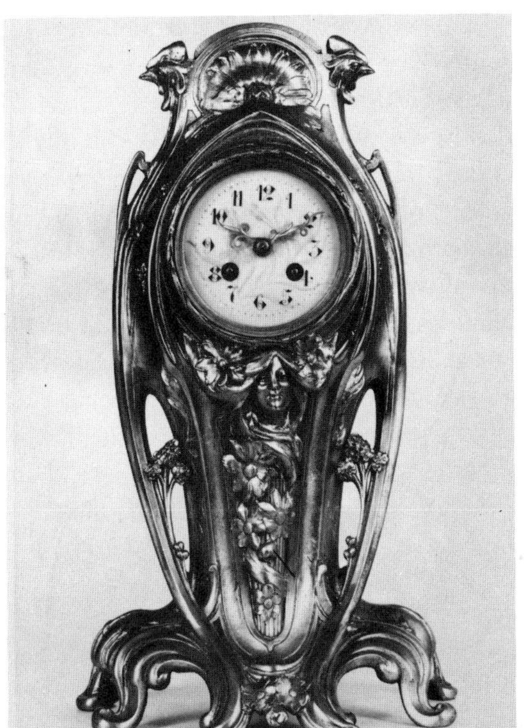

Romantic era. (Ill. 15.) It appeared first of all in the Paris 1839 Exhibition, and after that was produced in all sizes and qualities.

The invention of electro-gilding shortly after 1840 made ormolu a little cheaper, but gradually the cost of the base metal rose, and experiments were made with alternative metals. In the very low-grade case, stamped brass columns substituted ormolu ones, and were 'gilded' with a clear golden lacquer which was not very durable. This marked the decline in clock-case making; the machine gradually replaced the craftsman, and in the penultimate period of ormolu clock-making every economy was pursued to bring the timepiece within the means of even the working classes.

Paradoxically during the Second Empire designers reverted to 18th-century originals for inspiration. The opening of the Musée Rétrospectif in 1865 displayed to the French nation the magnificent 18th-century works of art and furniture which were mainly loaned by Lord Hertford. Among these objects were twelve fine Louis XV and Louis XVI clocks, and as the fashion for 18th-century pieces became more prevalent so the clock-makers produced copies of 18th-century originals, and cheaper editions for less rich customers. (Ill. 16.) Eighteenth-century pieces had become a status symbol with the new-rich industrial class and the maintenance of a supply of fine original pieces was helped by a constant flow of forgeries.

This revival soon broadened itself to embrace the baroque and the rococo, and after a time a hybrid emerged quite devoid of any original form. Whole cases were stamped out of brass or made out of spelter, a tin-coloured soft metal, and in these cheaper-quality clocks clock-making can be seen at its lowest ebb. The ponderous effect of this revival is reflected in the Garniture de Cheminée in which the clock is flanked by candelabra *en suite*.

This stylistic quagmire was drained by the advent of art nouveau, which began to make itself felt *circa* 1885. It was in itself an important transitional style which coupled the revivals and spiritualism of the 19th century to the modern forms of the present century. (Ill. 17.) Its origins are extremely diversified; inspiration was derived from Romanesque scrollwork, Gothic ornament and foliate designs from the rococo period, but the simplicity of line which really instigated the modern style in architecture in the 1920's was taken from Japanese furniture and prints.

Foremost amongst the originators of this style was William Morris, whose arts and crafts movement was aimed against mass production in favour of a closer relationship between the designer and the craftsman.

Art nouveau evokes a picture of swirling strapwork and languid beauties terminating in foliage (Ill. 18), and although this can be described as 'classical' in its approach it was the break-away from 19th-century conventions which made possible the clinically formal 'line' of the 1920's. Clock-case makers who worked in the art nouveau style experimented with different materials such as pewter, hardstones and glass; these proved to be more economical and consequently the ormolu case could not survive.

Book-illustration; the Art of Arthur Rackham

BERTRAM ROTA

Few artists in book-illustration can have given as much pleasure to as many people through as long a creative life as did Arthur Rackham. From his first published vignette in 1884 to the triumph which he completed on his death-bed in 1939 his work ranged over surprisingly wide fields. One thinks most readily of his fairies, gnomes and grotesque trees, but the terrifying interpretation of horror shown in his illustrations for Poe's "Tales of Mystery and Imagination", the strength of his drawings for Wagner's "Ring", the grace of many of his figures and the sheer fun of so much else demonstrate his breadth of vision and his power to evoke images which seem to be truly in accord with the author's conception.

This accord between author and artist is the essence of the art of illustration. In recent times Ernest Shepard achieved it for A. A. Milne; so did Ilbery Lynch for Ernest Bramah ("The Transmutation of Ling" is sheer delight). The veteran American illustrator Maxfield Parrish caught the spirit of Kenneth Grahame's "Dream Days" and "The Golden Age" enchantingly; but these are examples of one subject or one theme. Rackham's work encompassed so many and such diverse subjects that his success with them marks out his extraordinary ability to lose himself in the writer's imagination and to transmute it by his craftsmanship into a visual realization acceptable to almost everybody.

There is a degree of danger in illustrating works of imagination at all, since one reader's conception of what the author intended may be so different from another's. It is Rackham's achievement that we all feel we know just what Toad and Badger or the Rhine Maidens looked like. Most of his interpretations have proved so universally acceptable that we sense a collaboration rather than two separate approaches to a theme, even with writers of earlier centuries. Malory, Andersen, Grimm, Ibsen, Poe, Goldsmith, Barham and many more waited long but not in vain for their most convincing visual interpreter.

1. Self-caricature from *The Arthur Rackham Fairy Tale Book* published by Harrap, 1933
approximate size 4×2¾ in. (10·1×6·9 cm.)

Arthur Rackham was born in London in 1867, the fourth of twelve children of a middle-class family. He displayed an early talent for drawing and a natural bent for fantastic themes. In youth he decided to become a professional artist and he applied himself with vigour to his craft, both at art school and in practice. He was never without a sketch-book and a box of watercolour paints, and from an early voyage to Australia to his later wanderings on the Continent he would busily sketch landscapes and buildings, people and animals, and the trees which always so much attracted him. On his pen or pencil sketches he would note meticulously the shade of colour of a roof or a stream, a garment or a tree-trunk, for subsequent colouring.

It is to this acute observation that we owe the verisimilitude of the buildings which provide the background for some of the drawings for "The Pied Piper of

2. Design for the spine of *Grimm's Fairy Tales* published by Constable, 1909
approximate size 10×2 in. (25·4×5 cm.)

Hamelin" and the glinting ripple of sunlit rivers in "The Compleat Angler". Conscientiousness was his watchword, in observation, creation and eventually in reproduction. Proof after proof of a colour plate would be rejected, until the mechanical processes came as near as could be to realizing his intention. He was often at war with his publishers, and when one of them produced a cheaper edition of "Peter Pan in Kensington Gardens", cut down in size and sacrificing the proportions of the original drawings, Rackham castigated them by decorating the title-page of a copy of that edition with a pen-drawing of himself hanging from a gallows, and by changing their designation as "Publishers" to "Hangmen: drawing and quartering a speciality".

Success did not come early or easily. The young Rackham worked in an insurance office and began his commercial career in art by occasional contributions to the cheaper illustrated papers. The first work for which he received a fee (of $3) was a decorative initial letter, representing a Frenchman swallowing a frog, in the popular journal "Scraps" in 1884. This began a long series of drawings for periodicals, as it became known that this accomplished young artist was ready to turn his hand to the needs of editors. "The Pall Mall Budget", "The Westminster Gazette", Cassell's Magazine, "Little Folks", "Punch" and many other magazines gave him work. The boys' paper "Chums" provided him with the hardest task of all, when he was required to produce a weekly drawing of a dramatic subject, without any text on which to base it. The supporting text would be written afterwards, inspired by the situation the artist devised. Rackham admitted that with the whole field of imagination open to him, but with no prompting from a text, he could think of nothing more original than an express train thundering down its track towards a victim bound hand and foot across the rails.

Trifling as this is, it perhaps shows the natural inclination of the born illustrator. Provide the motivating thought and he will respond, even multiplying the force of the author's words by his interpretation. Rackham achieved this by his thorough familiarity with his texts and by his capacity to sink himself into the minds of the creators of the characters he drew, with such an understanding sympathy that the result appeared to be one work in two mediums.

Coincident with his work for periodicals the artist was accepting commissions for occasional illustrations as diverse as landscapes for travel guides (a Norddeutscher Lloyd brochure, "To the Other Side", was the first, in 1893) and illustrations for such books as Anthony Hope's "Dolly Dialogues", 1894, and Stanley Weyman's "The Castle Inn", 1898. Decreasingly but throughout his career he provided one or more drawings or decorations for some seventy-five books which he did not wholly illustrate, while seventy-eight books were illustrated entirely by him and fifty-seven periodicals printed his drawings, in varying numbers.

The core of any collection of Arthur Rackham's illustrated books must be the long series of 'classics' which began with "Rip Van Winkle" in 1905 and ended with "The Wind in the Willows" in 1940. All but two of these (published for the American Limited Editions Club alone) exist in two forms: an 'ordinary', 'regular' or 'trade' edition and a limited de-luxe edition, usually signed by the artist and sometimes by the author as well. Most are quarto volumes, the regular editions being bound in cloths of various colours with lettering and decorative designs in gilt. The de-luxe editions were usually bound in full or half vellum or parchment, printed on superior paper, numbered and signed. The limitation varied from 250 to 1,130 copies, but the average number was around 500. The regular editions were printed in quantities increasing as the years went by up to several thousand.

3. From *Goblin Market* published by Harrap, 1933
approximate size 3×3 in. (7·6×7·6 cm.)

4. From *Goblin Market* published by Harrap, 1933
approximate size 4¼×3 in. (10·7×7·6 cm.)

Many were reprinted but only a few remain available in current editions today. They must be sought in the antiquarian bookshops.

A set of these books makes a noble array and offers a remarkable demonstration of the achievement of an artist in a field which is still insufficiently appreciated, for the extra pleasure and understanding it has given to readers of the words alone. For those who might wish to acquire them all, either in their limited or regular forms, or merely to possess one or two of their favourites, a list of Arthur Rackham's major illustrated works is appended.

Irving, Washington. *Rip Van Winkle.* 1905.
Barrie, J. M. *Peter Pan in Kensington Gardens.* 1906.
Carroll, Lewis. *Alice's Adventures in Wonderland.* 1907.
Barham, R. H. *The Ingoldsby Legends.* 1907.
Shakespeare, William. *A Midsummer Night's Dream.* 1908.
Swift, Jonathan. *Gulliver's Travels.* 1909.
Lamb, Charles and Mary. *Tales from Shakespeare.* 1909.
Grimm, The Brothers. *Fairy Tales.* 1909.
Fouqué, de la Motte. *Undine.* 1909.
Wagner, Richard. *The Rhinegold and the Valkyrie.* 1910.
Wagner, Richard. *Siegfried and The Twilight of the Gods.* 1911.
Aesop. *Aesop's Fables.* 1912.
Mother Goose. *The Old Nursery Rhymes.* 1913.
Rackham, Arthur. *Arthur Rackham's Book of Pictures.* 1913.
Dickens, Charles. *A Christmas Carol.* 1915.
The Allies' Fairy Book. 1916.
Grimm, The Brothers. *Little Brother and Little Sister.* 1917.
Malory, Sir Thomas. *The Romance of King Arthur.* 1917.
Steel, Flora Annie. *English Fairy Tales.* 1918.
Swinburne, Algernon Charles. *The Springtide of Life.* 1918.
Cinderella. 1919.
Some British Ballads. 1919.
The Sleeping Beauty. 1920.
Stephens, James. *Irish Fairy Tales.* 1920.
Phillpotts, Eden. *A Dish of Apples.* 1921.
Milton, John. *Comus.* 1921.
Hawthorne, Nathaniel. *A Wonder Book.* 1922.
Morley, Christopher. *Where the Blue Begins.* 1925.
Shakespeare, William. *The Tempest.* 1926.
Irving, Washington. *The Legend of Sleepy Hollow.* 1928.
Goldsmith, Oliver. *The Vicar of Wakefield.* 1929.
Walton, Izaak. *The Compleat Angler.* 1931.
Moore, Clement C. *The Night Before Christmas.* 1931.
Dickens, Charles. *The Chimes.* New York, 1931.
Ruskin, John. *The King of the Golden River.* 1932.
Andersen, Hans. *Fairy Tales.* 1932.
Rossetti, Christina. *Goblin Market.* 1933.
Rackham, Arthur. *The Arthur Rackham Fairy Book.* 1933.
Browning, Robert. *The Pied Piper of Hamelin.* 1934.
Poe, Edgar Allan. *Tales of Mystery and Imagination.* 1935.
Ibsen, Henrik. *Peer Gynt.* 1936.
Shakespeare, William. *A Midsummer Night's Dream.* (New illustrations. New York, 1939.)
Grahame, Kenneth. *The Wind in the Willows.* New York, 1940.

For the converted there is much more pleasure to be had. Gathering as large a collection as is possible of Arthur Rackham's printed work is a continuing delight. A few collectors were earlier in the field. Frederick C. Coykendall, an American enthusiast, published a catalogue of books illustrated by Rackham in the United States in 1922. George L. Lazarus spent some thirty years in assembling in England

Colour Plate. Rat and Mole loading the boat, from *The Wind in the Willows* published by the Limited Editions Club of New York, 1940 and Methuen, 1950
Mrs Barbara Edwards Collection, Basingstoke, Hampshire

Arthur Rackham

5. (above left) The Pied Piper from *The Pied Piper of Hamelin* published by Harrap, 1934
approximate size 4×5¼ in. (10·1×13·3 cm.)

6. (above right) *Peter Pan in Kensington Gardens* published by Hodder & Stoughton, 1906
10×7½ in. (25·4×19 cm.)

7. *Undine* published by Heinemann, 1909
10×7½ in. (25·4×19 cm.)

8. Robinson Crusoe from *Mother Goose* published by Heinemann, 1913
approximate size $4\frac{1}{2}\times3$ in. (10·1×7·6 cm.)

9. Imp from *A Wonder Book* published by Hodder & Stoughton, 1922
approximate size $1\frac{1}{2}\times1\frac{1}{2}$ in. (3·8×3·8 cm.)

10. Santa Claus from *The Night before Christmas* published by Harrap, 1931
approximate size 3×2 in. (7·6×5 cm.)

the largest collection yet recorded. Sarah Briggs Latimore and Grace Clark Haskell gathered important collections and described them in their Bibliography, published in Los Angeles in 1936. These two ladies, who lived a few miles apart in California, and collected independently, were brought together and persuaded to collaborate in the bibliography of which they both felt the need, by Ellen Shaffer, then of Dawson's Bookshop in Los Angeles and now the Rare Book Librarian of the Free Library of Philadelphia. They lived to see their collections transported 3,000 miles across the continent and housed 90 miles apart, in New York and Philadelphia, where they can be enjoyed by countless visitors.

The Lazarus Collection is now in the Humanities Research Center of the University of Texas, the Latimore Collection is at Columbia University in New York, and the Haskell Collection is at the Free Library of Philadelphia. All have been augmented since their acquisition. Other notable gatherings exist, and the well has not yet run dry, though patience may be needed to extract the treasure. Unrecorded printings may yet be found and bring a sense of discovery.

The expense is not great, by modern standards. Even the best – the limited signed editions – range nowadays (in 1965) from about $14 for the slightest and commonest to $140 or so for the rarest. The regular editions, in their original printings, may still be bought for between three and thirty dollars. The lesser works can be picked up for nominal sums. "Mr. Gladstone in the evening of his days" or "The Homes and Haunts of Thomas Carlyle" may well be found marked at a few dollars on the shelves of a bookshop where it is not known that each contains a single drawing by Rackham. But time is running out. The excitement, and indeed the importance, of preserving these examples of an insufficiently appreciated art of our time are ours for perhaps a few more years.

No collector of Arthur Rackham's printed work could fail to desire an original. Here the going gets harder. The demand is increasing while the supply diminishes. Through the generosity of benefactors Columbia University, of New York, acquired in 1958 most of the original drawings which Rackham left in his portfolios at his death – some three hundred originals and a long series of sketch-books in which his publications were planned; but the sketches and watercolours which he released during his life, mainly through the long series of exhibitions at the Leicester Galleries in London and elsewhere, occasionally appear in the market again. Though a good watercolour may now command $280–$840, that is a ludicrously small price in comparison with the current values of works of art in more popular but not more significant fields.

Rackham's acknowledged eminence in his art substantially began in 1905, with the publication of "Rip Van Winkle". In the United States appreciation grew notably in and after 1919, when his work was exhibited in New York. His reputation has since progressed in both countries and has widened across the world. His books have been published in America, France, Germany and other countries. Original drawings have been acquired for the Tate Gallery, the Victoria and Albert Museum, the Fitzwilliam Museum at Cambridge and other provincial galleries in the United Kingdom; by the Melbourne National Gallery in Australia and by institutions in the United States, Paris, Vienna and Barcelona. An early watercolour was accepted for the Royal Academy exhibition in 1888, and gold medals were awarded to him in Milan in 1906 and Barcelona in 1912.

The chorus of praise from his fellow-artists swelled generously and his lasting fame was assured before the century was two decades old. In the collecting world E. A. Osborne led the way by his researches, published in "The Book-Trade Journal" in London in 1936. Miss Latimore and Mrs Haskell produced the first

11, 12 and **13.** Rip Van Winkle from *Rip Van Winkle* published by Heinemann, 1903
11 and 12. approximate size $4\frac{3}{4} \times 3\frac{1}{2}$ in. ($12 \times 8{\cdot}8$ cm.)
13. $4\frac{1}{4} \times 2\frac{1}{4}$ in. ($10{\cdot}7 \times 5{\cdot}7$ cm.)

full-scale bibliography in Los Angeles in the same year and a check-list by Bertram Rota, appended to Derek Hudson's "Arthur Rackham; his life and work" in 1960, extended the record.

While gaining adult recognition of his craftsmanship Rackham continued to touch the hearts of children. His correspondence included scores of letters from young people, who were always answered graciously, often in illustrated letters signed with a self-caricature. In many of the artist's drawings his own likeness can be discovered. A bird with folded wings may display his bespectacled long nose, or he may be identified amongst the characters of a group. He proved to be the ideal link between the authors whose writings he enlarged and the audience for which they were intended.

Rackham was sometimes told by visitors that he had convinced them that he really believed in fairies. To one of them he replied, "But of course. Haven't you seen them in Cornwall?" At this meeting he professed his ignorance of business affairs, explaining that he left such matters to his agents; but he named precisely the obtainable price for the drawings which his guest purchased. Throughout his life he had a lively sense of the marketable value of his work, neither over-estimating it nor falling behind. The drawings offered in early exhibition catalogues at a few guineas look startlingly cheap now. They will look even more so as the years go by.

While working professionally Rackham demonstrated his sheer delight in drawing for pleasure. He designed such things as a delicious wedding testimonial for Maggie Brown (a companion on a walking-tour in Europe, whose "Surprising adventures of Tuppy and Tue" he illustrated in 1897 and 1904); invitation cards, menus and programmes for meetings of the Langham Sketching Club, the Titmarsh Club and the St John's Wood Art Club; and the long series of his personal Christmas greeting cards from 1900 until 1934. Examples of these joyous *jeux d'esprit* can still sometimes be found.

Accepting the commercial inducement, the artist produced a few designs for advertising. One was the centre of a colossal window-display fitment for Colgate's Cashmere Bouquet Soap. (Surely only Bruce Rogers's diamond-lozenge design of initials for the side of a railway wagon can equal it as an un-collectable piece, yet that vast hunk of wood is let into the wall of the library of a collector of the works of the great American typographer.) In "Punch" in 1928 Rackham graced an advertisement for Eno's Fruit Salts, and he did the same for boxes of Cadbury's chocolates in 1933. He designed a very few bookplates; for his own collection of his own books, for his daughter, for G. L. Lazarus and for Robert Partridge, and he illustrated a few catalogues of books. Simpkin Marshall's "Best Books of the Season" for 1933–34 and 1935–36 bear cover-designs potent enough to convert the illiterate to book-buying, and the delightful cover-design for the sheet music of Walter Carroll's pianoforte suite "River and Rainbow" must have encouraged many a young pianist to choose that work for practice.

Rackham made one venture into theatrical design. He provided the décor and the costume-designs for a production of "Hansel and Gretel" at the Cambridge Theatre in London in 1933. The drop-scene, showing the two main characters playing under a tree, on the branches of which sit birds and gnomes, while witches fly around on brooms, catches the gay spirit of Grimm's fantasy to a nicety. The costumes were equally successful, but the labour involved discouraged the artist from repeating the effort.

This bare recital of some of Arthur Rackham's achievements must end with a tribute to his last and perhaps his most successful work. When Kenneth Grahame's

14. Two grotesque trees from *A Wonder Book* published by Hodder & Stoughton, 1922 approximate size $2\frac{1}{2} \times 3\frac{1}{2}$ in. (6·3×8·8 cm.)

"The Wind in the Willows" was about to be published in 1908 the author hoped that Rackham would illustrate it. Regretfully the artist had to decline, his other commitments at that time being too heavy. The book appeared with only an undistinguished frontispiece by another hand, and it was many years before Ernest H. Shepard furnished the text with drawings sympathetic enough to gain considerable success.

Rackham remained attracted by the subject so particularly suited to his talents, but forbore to compete with his friend Shepard. Then, in 1936, George Macy, the publisher of the long series of illustrated classics issued by the Limited Editions Club of New York, invited him to provide sixteen illustrations for an edition designed by Bruce Rogers, for American publication only. Rackham leapt at the chance and commenced lovingly upon his inspiring theme; but his health was failing and it was not until 1939 that the last drawing was done.

Lying ill in bed, and exhausted, he asked for the set of illustrations to be brought to him. It was then that he noticed that in the last drawing, which shows Rat and Mole loading their boat for a picnic, there were no oars in the boat. (See colour plate facing p. 176). A perfectionist to the last, he called for his brushes and with great difficulty painted in a pair of shipped oars. Then he sank back, saying "Thank goodness, that is the last one". Alas, that it was indeed the last of all.

Arthur Rackham did not live to see the lovely book he had helped to make, and another ten years went by before a new edition published by Methuen in 1950 made his final masterpiece available in Britain. In 1951 the hundredth printing of "The Wind in the Willows" was celebrated by the publication in London of a limited de-luxe edition, with Rackham's illustrations, which fittingly crowned his outstanding career in a gentle art.

For information incorporated in this essay the writer is indebted particularly to Mrs Barbara Edwards, the artist's daughter; to Mr Derek Hudson, author of "Arthur Rackham; his life and work" (1960); to Miss Ellen Shaffer, rare book librarian of the Free Library of Philadelphia; and to the several bibliographers and collectors who have helped to record and preserve the works of Arthur Rackham.

15. Group of goblins and old folk from *Andersen's Fairy Tales* published by Harrap, 1922 approximate size $4 \times 8\frac{1}{2}$ in. (10·1×21·5 cm.)

The Glass of Emile Gallé

RICHARD DENNIS

Emile Gallé was a designer of glass, furniture and pottery, besides being a chemist, botanist, successful businessman and an author. It is in his rôle as a designer that he led and encouraged the 'Ecole de Nancy', the foremost centre of the art nouveau movement in France. His most successful and prolific medium was glass, to which he devoted most of his energy and talents and for which he is best known today.

1. Emile Gallé painted by Victor Prouvé in 1892
oil on canvas
Musée de l'Ecole de Nancy

He was born in Nancy in 1846 to Charles Gallé, a dealer in glassware and faience. The father had a shop in Nancy where he sold glass that had been made at Miesenthal in the Saar valley and pottery from the long-established works at St-Clément. The majority of these articles, decorated with his own designs, were for everyday use, especially the table. The faience bore the Gallé signature added to the stencilled St-Clément mark, and some pieces were signed 'G.R.' for Gallé-Reinemer (his wife's family name).

In 1865 Emile left the Lycée in Nancy, where he had excelled in philosophy, and for the next four years he studied, first at the art school in Weimar and then, under his father's guidance, the techniques of glass-making at Miesenthal and of pottery manufacture and decoration at St-Clément and Raon-l'Etape. Here he first met Victor Prouvé, the artist, with whom he was to be closely associated. He was a keen student of the chemistry of glass and an enthusiastic botanist. However, his studies were interrupted by the Franco-Prussian War. In 1871 he returned to civilian life. His father, a successful businessman, was able to continue financing his studies and experiments, although at the same time Emile designed for him. In the same year Emile visited London with his father, who was showing at the 'Arts of France' exhibition. He also spent some time in Paris and later travelled in Italy and Switzerland. In 1873 his father built a large house in Nancy called 'La Garenne', which was conventional in style and surrounded by a large garden, densely cultivated with flowers and shrubs. Here Emile built a workshop and studio. In the following year Charles Gallé turned his business affairs over to his son, and from 1874 onwards we can distinguish the works of Emile. In 1875 Emile married Henrietta Grimm, the daughter of a country pastor, and they moved into part of 'La Garenne'. His wife inherited a shop specializing in the sale of mirrors, which they immediately sold. Emile had no association with it.

Gallé's early glass designs of the 1870's can be divided into three groups: the largest, enamelled with designs based on historic sources; the second, enamelled with floral and animal motifs; and the third, pieces of a more experimental and personal nature, where enamelling may not be the major medium of decoration. In the first group old techniques as well as designs were used; for example, there is an ice pail in the Musée de l'Ecole de Nancy, made in 1874, in the German 18th-century *zwischen gold-glas* technique and enamelled in colours between the layers of

2. Enamelled casket after a Sicalo-Arabic model of the 13th century, 1878
Musée de l'Ecole de Nancy

3. Vase enamelled with Monsieur Dumollet, *circa* 1878
height $5\frac{7}{8}$ in. (15 cm.)
Cazalis Collection, Paris

4. Acid-etched and enamelled jug, 1878
Musée de l'Ecole de Nancy

glass with an 18th-century vineyard scene. During Gallé's studies in Paris he had encountered the work of the glass enameller Joseph Brocard, and many pieces were made under his influence, some following closely Syrian designs of the 14th century and Isnik pottery design. The casket shown in illustration 2 dates from 1878 and is after a Sicalo-Arabic ivory model of the 13th century. The thick clear-glass walls are finely enamelled with translucent and opaque colours; the background is cut away and frosted with black and brown particles which have the appearance of iron filings. In his writings Gallé refers to the difficulties of producing strong enamels with a glassy texture that are not affected by the temperature when fired. He continued to experiment with enamels and later was able to produce a tremendous variety of translucent and opaque colours.

'Clair de Lune' was the name Gallé gave to a coloured glass he perfected, possibly inspired by the Chinese 18th-century porcelain glaze of that name. It has a pale blue tint which alters as the light is directed on to it, made by adding potassium and cobalt oxide to the metal, producing a fine shade of sapphire. Pieces of this period in this technique are inspired by earlier forms; an example is a large candlestick in the Musée des Arts Décoratifs in the French style of the late 17th century, which is dated 1875. The small vase (Ill. 3) from the collection of M. Cazalis, Paris, is enamelled on swirled clear glass with an amusing representation of M. Dumollet, an early 19th-century traveller about whom popular songs were written. The colours are yellow, blue and red, and the style is immediately reminiscent of a type of simple enamelled glass made in various Central European countries, especially Germany, during the second half of the 18th century.

There are not many recorded pieces belonging to the second group, although several were bought for the Musée des Arts Décoratifs at Nancy (now in the Musée de l'Ecole) from Emile Gallé early in 1904.[1] The pieces included a casket enamelled with fleurs-de-lis, an object with daisy petals and grasshoppers, a vase with a cross of Lorraine and thistles, a vase enamelled with myosotis, and a jug of Japanese inspiration (Ill. 4) dating from 1878, with a fish amongst seaweed on a translucent green ground. This piece and several others were reproduced for the 1900 International Exhibition and marked '*Réédité*'.

The last group comprises very individualistic pieces; each is an original design and probably experimental. Their influence can be seen in pieces made ten or fifteen years later. In the Musée de l'Ecole de Nancy there is a clear glass bowl deeply cut and engraved in the form of the head of a Japanese monster, in rock

[1] These pieces are discussed in *La Lorraine*, the magazine of the Ecole de Nancy, nos. 3–4, 1–15 fevrier 1904, p. 34.

5. Wheel-cut and enamelled bowl of obscure symbolism, *circa* 1878
height 4 in. (10·1 cm.)
Private Collection, London

6. Blown and moulded sweetmeat and cover with enamelling, 1880
Musée des Arts Décoratifs, Paris

7. Cut, enamelled and acid-etched liqueur glasses, *circa* 1885
Madame Perdrizet Collection, Nancy

crystal style, and a bowl dating from 1876 enamelled with symmetrical angular patterns and very stylized foliate medallions.

The bowl shown in illustration 5, probably dating from the late 1870's, is of obscure symbolism, and is cut and engraved with a large winged helmet over a sphere with spears and Egyptian fan motifs. It has been suggested that it has political significance. The enamelling on the base is Syrian in style and appears on several early pieces.

Gallé's early work culminated in the Paris *Union Centrale* exhibition of 1878, where he had a measure of success. His 'Clair de Lune' was very popular and was soon copied in other European countries, in Germany under the name of *Mondschein* and in England under the name of moonlight glass. In the same year Gallé built new furnaces and decorating workshops in Nancy, only a few hundred yards from 'La Garenne'. This was to be the permanent site of all his enterprises. Although continuing to borrow from historical sources, he developed new techniques and designs and by 1884 was able to show a wide range of decorative glass at the Exposition des Beaux-Arts. Many of Gallé's pieces are documented or inscribed, but most of the dating of new designs and the introduction of new techniques can be established from his notices of the Paris expositions,[2] in conjunction with pieces acquired by museums at these expositions. The covered glass shown in illustration 6 is in the Musée des Arts Décoratifs and is of the finest quality, dated 1880, although the shape is inspired by Renaissance rock crystal and Silesian 18th-century sweetmeat glasses. The blown moulded bowl is finely enamelled with foliate designs. Other pieces of the early 1880's had naturalistic enamelled wild flowers, plants and insects, often on an amber-tinted or smoky glass. Quasi-heraldic designs too are found. Few of these pieces would have been unique, as illustration 6 probably was, and the designs were first painted with an outline as a guide to the enameller. Another technique introduced at this time was that of inserting coloured glass fragments into the clear glass which diffused to a certain degree, depending on the heat. This technique had previously been used by Eugène Rousseau, whose glass Gallé had undoubtedly seen in Paris.

Gallé was now employing numerous artists and craftsmen, and through the 1880's designed several sets of table glass which obviously had to be produced on a commercial scale. The simplest were of writhen or dimpled clear glass, enriched with gilding; there were also elegant drinking glasses with coloured glass bowls supported on tall slender stems, and more expensive ones acid-etched or enamelled as shown in illustration 7. The table glass is of a new conception; the shapes are original, the designs simpler or more naturalistic than those used by his contemporaries. This glass strongly influenced later designers. A more elaborate decanter shown at the 1884 exhibition (Ill. 8) was one of the first *verrières parlantes*, enamelled in relief with the figure of the Queen from the *Ballade des Dames du Temps Jadis*, by François Villon. The quotation in Gothic script has an acid-eaten background, producing a parchment effect. Several liqueur sets exist with variations of this theme.

All Gallé glass is signed, with the exception of some table glass, but the wording varies considerably. At this period the signature is sometimes simply 'Emile Gallé' or 'E. Gallé', possibly with 'Nancy' or a Lorraine cross. Sometimes the full inscription '*Cristallerie d'Emile Gallé, modèle et décor déposé*' appears, or '*E. Gallé fecit*', as in illustration 5, which has yet another signature, the rarely found '*E. Gallé Comp.*'. The signatures are painted in script or incised in diamond point, either discreetly concealed on the base or under an enamelled motif, but always in sympathy with

[2] These notices are published in Emile Gallé's *Écrits pour l'Art*, Paris, 1908.

8. Acid-etched and enamelled decanter with the Queen from the *Ballade des Dames du Temps Jadis*, by François Villon, 1884
Musée de l'Ecole de Nancy

9. Enamelled vase with bronze mount showing Chinese influence, *circa* 1889
height 6¾ in. (17 cm.)
Cazalis Collection, Paris

the object and, as his style changes, the signatures change accordingly. In 1885 Gallé established a depot in Paris for the sale of his glass, located at 12 Rue Richer, but many pieces were sold to the public in shops in Paris or Nancy. There is an early enamelled bowl in the writer's collection on which the Gallé signature has been erased and the engraved shop name, *l'Escalier de Cristal*, added.

There are few pieces dated between 1884 and the Paris exhibition of 1889. Perhaps Gallé held back new designs for the exhibition, at which he launched a succession of new ideas, at last finding his own style, inspired by Japanese and Chinese art, but interpreted in his own way. He continued to use enamels but to a different effect, rarely turning to historical models and relying upon the wild flowers and insects of Lorraine. Illustration 9, from the Cazalis Collection, shows a rectangular vase decorated in the Chinese taste with translucent and opaque enamels. The bronze mount featuring snails at the four corners was cast at Gallé's own foundry. The signature of this vase is delicately incorporated in a painted flowerhead. 'Clair de Lune' glass was used very successfully at this time with enamelled flowers and insects in Gallé's new style. The original drawings, dated 1889, for the piece shown in illustration 10 are still in existence.[3] This wonderful shape, an arum lily, was used in various ways such as for vases, flacons and dishes, and can be seen on the right of illustration 7 used as a liqueur glass. This example is enamelled on both sides with fruiting branches and insects on a swirling amber-tinted glass.

For the 1889 exhibition Gallé created a very interesting group of *verre-double* glasses with a very dark brown or black overlay and a carved design, revealing in parts the clear glass base. He referred to them in his notice as 'Noir (Hyalite)'. The most famous of this group is the Orpheus vase.[4] It is in the Musée des Arts Décoratifs and was made in 1888 for the exposition. The figures were designed by Victor Prouvé, who drew all Gallé's human subjects. The Orpheus vase is unique as may be others in this group, but some were repeated, such as *l'Amour chassant les papillons noirs* of which there are at least three versions, one in the Musée des Arts Décoratifs. Not all the vases of this group have mythological subjects. For instance illustration 11 shows a small *Noir* vase from a private London collection. The overlay of thistles was a motif dear to Gallé: they are often found with a Lorraine cross and occasionally with the words '*Qui frotte qui pique*', alluding to the German occupation of Alsace and Lorraine. Allied to this group and of the same period are a number of vases with a black overlay and a section or overlay of brilliant blue glass like that of the central collar of a vase in the Musée de l'École de Nancy. (See colour plate facing p. 189.) The bamboo shape, which had previously been used by E. Rousseau,[5] is reminiscent of a Chinese archaic bronze form; the central blue collar is a separate piece of glass inserted between the overlaid moths.

It must be mentioned that there were exceptions to this new style, such as a glass shown in the 1889 exhibition painted in sepia in the manner of Preissler, the German 18th-century *Hausmaler*.

Following the Paris exhibition of 1889, which had been a tremendous success for Gallé, he opened a shop in Frankfurt and was soon to exhibit in numerous foreign capitals. He enlarged his workshops and surrounded them with beds of

[3] These drawings appear in *Les Artistes de tous les Temps, Série D, le XXe siècle*. "Emile Gallé" by Louis de Fourcaud, Paris, 1903, opp. p. 8, "vases en forme de fleurs", and in T. Charpentier, "l'École de Nancy", *Jardin des Arts*, November 1960, p. 25.

[4] This vase is illustrated in Rosenthal, L., *La Verrerie Française depuis cinquante ans*, ed. G. Vanoest, 1927, pl. VIIIA.

[5] This is illustrated in Polak, A. D. A., *Modern Glass*, 1962, pl. 3.

10. Enamelled vase in the form of an arum lily, *circa* 1889
Private Collection, London

11. 'Noir' vase with carved overlay of thistles, *circa* 1889
Private Collection, London

flowers. Little remains today, except a wooden door designed by Vallin, a furniture-maker of the École de Nancy, carved with a stylized tree and incorporating a saying of Gallé, "*Ma racine est au fond des bois*".

In Gallé's notice of the 1889 exhibition he devoted a chapter to "Applications industrielles; Vulgarisation artistique", and explained at length how he produced glass on a commercial scale in order to reach a far wider public. The production of individual pieces in a glass-works is extremely costly; the sort of glassware made by Gallé is very expensive unless it is produced in series, using quantities of a particular colour, a repeated shape, or acid. But in his industrial production Gallé set and kept a very high standard, unlike the Bohemians who at this time painted glass to simulate flashing or colouring in the mass, thus making the colours impermanent.

Enamelling could never be an industrial process, but in the 1890's Gallé produced several series of vases, each having similar enamelled decoration on a common ground but having shapes which varied considerably, several pieces being made in each shape. There is one series with enamelled shells and seaweed being swept by the movement of the sea, represented by swirling vaseline-coloured glass; there are other series with underwater themes such as fish nets and aquatic plants; there is also a large series with a translucent green ground, acid-etched with a design of ferns and enamelled with fungi and orchids.

From 1889 Gallé marketed the vases for which he is better known, those coloured in the mass, usually cased, *verre-double* or *-triplé* and carved with designs from nature. Their counterparts, which must have had some influence on Gallé, were the Chinese cased vases of the 18th and 19th centuries, carved with animal and floral designs, and the 19th-century moulded French opalines, yet these related pieces cannot be compared with Gallé's sympathetic rendering of nature. These cased 'Nature' vases, made continuously until his death in 1904, fall into three groups: the unique, often presentation pieces inscribed and dated; finely carved vases produced in very limited numbers; and a large quantity of commercial pieces made in series with a similar design adapted to different shapes, each shape repeated several times. The piece shown in illustration 12 (in the Musée des Arts Décoratifs) is almost certainly unique;[6] made in 1892, it is superbly carved on the underside with the husks of a fir-cone and above with branches bearing cones and spines. It is one of the *vases de tristesse* which were made to be buried with the dead. The practice was not authorized by the Church on the grounds of paganism and for fear that the coffins would be violated by archaeologists. The lip is inscribed with the sentimental lines from Sully Prudhomme, "*A des forêts qui ne sont plus*", and the base is carved in wood with further pine husks. Another interesting base is found on a vase, "*les Anémones de Pâques*", inscribed to Henri Hirsch[7] in 1892; the glass base is one with the vase, and shaped like a Chinese hardwood stand. In the same museum is another unique cased vase carved with fir-cones and pine-needles, known as the '*Vase Prouvé*'; it was presented in 1896 when he was awarded the *Légion d'honneur*.

Pond and marine life were among Gallé's favourite subjects. There is an interesting cased vase of 1889, in the Musée de l'École de Nancy, carved with newts in various stages of growth on a ground flecked with green and blue pondweed. It is inscribed with a quotation from Gautier referring to the duckweed spreading its dark curtain over the pond. Gallé often found inspiration in poetry for his glass, ranging from Victor Hugo to his contemporary Lorraine poets. Another *verrière*

[6] This vase is illustrated in Louis de Fourcaud, "Emile Gallé", *op. cit.*, opp. p. 12.

[7] M. Hirsch, a magistrate, was a friend and patron of Gallé whose collection is now in the Musée de l'Ecole de Nancy.

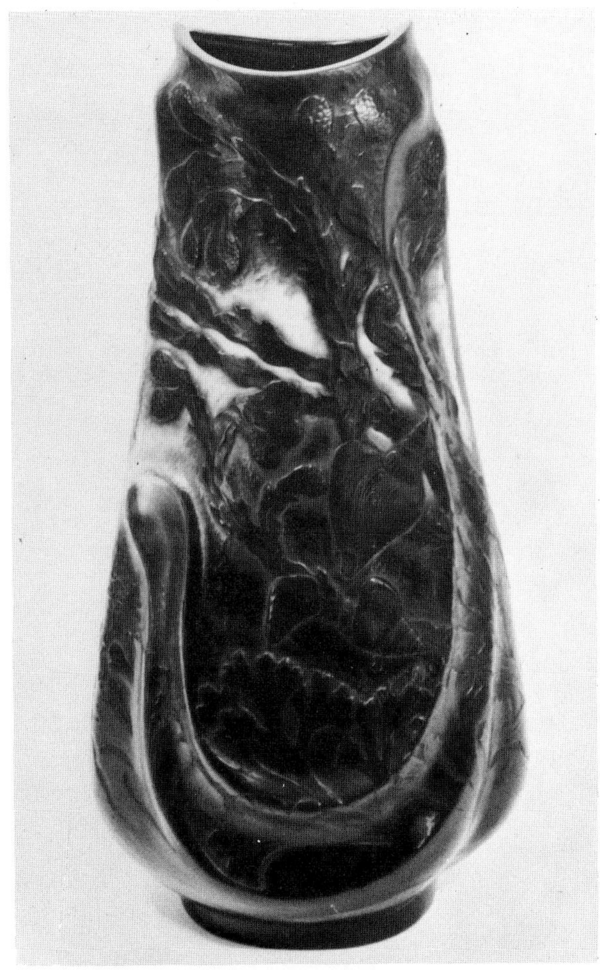

12. (above left) 'Vase de Tristesse' in carved brown glass on wood stand, 1892
Musée des Arts Décoratifs, Paris

14. (below left) 'Paysage de verre', carved yellow glass shading to red, *circa* 1899
Musée de l'Ecole de Nancy

13. (above right) Carved vase in metallic grey on an amber base, *circa* 1895
height 11¼ in. (28·5 cm.)
Private Collection, London

15. (below right) Cased vase, carved in red and clear glass, *circa* 1895
Musée de l'Ecole de Nancy

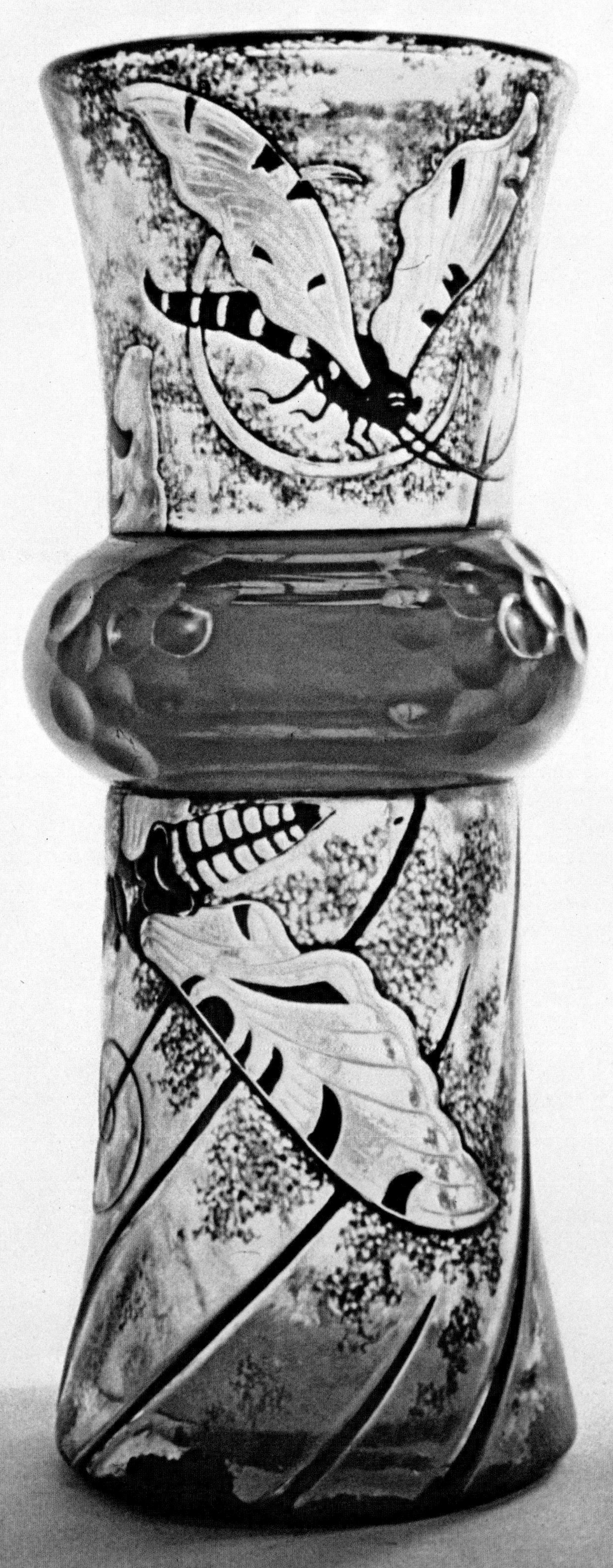

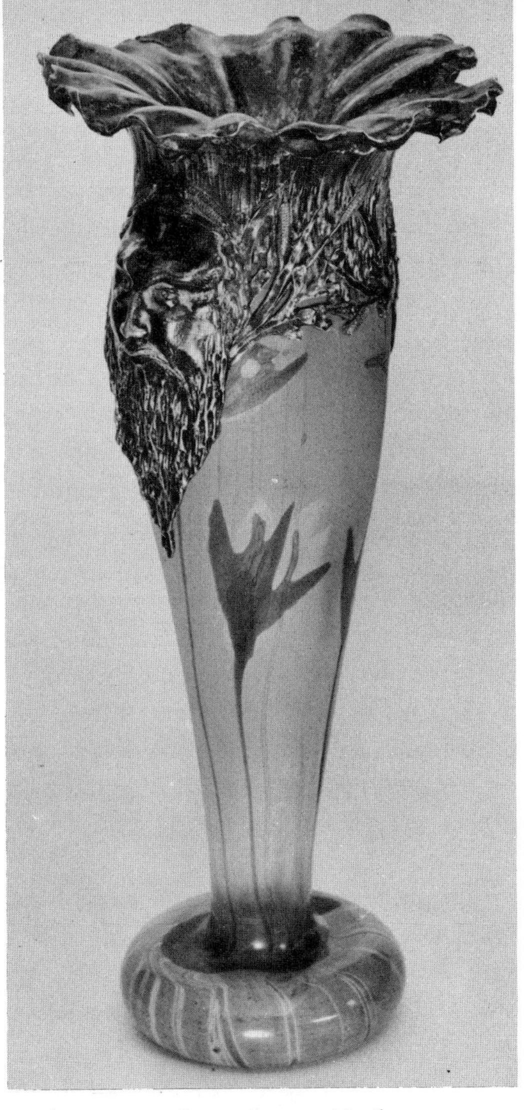

16. 'Marqueterie de verre' vase with silver mount by a Paris *métier*, *circa* 1900: height 9 in. (22·8 cm.) Private Collection, London

17. Moulded vase with floral marquetry on a jade-like ground, *circa* 1897: height 8½ in. (21·5 cm.) Private Collection, London

Colour Plate. 'Noir' vase of Chinese form, *circa* 1889 Musée de l'Ecole de Nancy

parlante in the same museum is carved with aquatic plants and an octopus with a quotation from Baudelaire: "the sea, the green sea, comforts our toil". Gallé's version of the art nouveau movement in glass lies in these cased 'Nature' vases. The form and decoration of the piece shown in illustration 13 are very evocative of the movement; the seaweed and shells appear to be carved from a metallic opaque grey layer on an amber ground, but as with many of Gallé's cased glasses, the colours change, depending on the direction from which they are lit. The signatures on cased vases are quite different from those on the enamelled pieces; more usually 'Gallé' is found without the Christian name or initial, carved in relief or incised into a smooth surface, the 'G' often with a long tail, sometimes written vertically and simulating Oriental script. Important pieces may have presentation inscriptions and some are dated, but most of the dated pieces refer to the Paris exhibitions.

In the 1890's Gallé designed a group of cased vases which he called *paysages de verre*, carved with wooded landscapes. (Ill. 14.) A very similar vase was presented to his friend and admirer Sarah Bernhardt in 1899.[8] There is also a series of vases, *circa* 1894, carved with black fishing boats and gulls against a brilliant orange sunset.

There are numerous other series of cased 'Nature' vases, carved with fruiting branches, wild flowers, orchids, dragonflies, grasses, moths and even seahorses, in which no industrial processes have been used, except for the repetition of the object, which then differs from its companions to the extent that accidents in glass production produced a slightly different colour or shape. Every conceivable colour of glass is found, produced by different metal oxides as rare as iridium and thallium. Other effects were produced by inserting gold and silver leaf, enamel, clouds of glass particles, cabochons of glass, 'latticinio techniques', polishing, etc. Shapes are as diverse as Oriental, classical, or pure art nouveau, symbolic of growth and nature. Dating within this period is sometimes difficult but is gradually being ascertained; there is a large series carved with opaque pink insects and flowers on a mottled green and blue ground, in various shapes, of which one bowl is dated 1890 and an almost identical bowl 1903.

Illustration 15 shows an example of a large series of pieces with carved sealing-wax-red casings dating from the 1890's. The influence of Chinese and Japanese art on this piece is unmistakable, although the shape is highly original; the red overlays, carved with poppies, have the same colouring and texture as cinnabar lacquer. Other objects simulate Japanese *Guri* lacquer: the overlay is cut through with scrolls which, unlike the Japanese, are asymmetrical; the appearance of great depth is effected by a clear glass layer in the middle which appears red until inspected closer. Many in this series are signed with an impressed stamp on the base.

In 1897, Gallé launched a new technique called *marqueterie de verre*. The design was not carved in cameo but made up of pieces of semi-molten glass pressed into the surface before it was cooled and then carved if necessary for further effect. The process was very difficult and many vases cracked in the making. The result was similar to marquetry furniture. Illustration 16 illustrates a piece in which crocuses have been inlaid by this technique, the ground has been frosted, and the stems formed when the vase was blown. Several of this type have been recorded, but they differ considerably in size and in the arrangement of the flowers.[9] This one has been mounted in oxidized silver by a *métier* in Paris. Many of Gallé's vases were mounted by the best silversmiths of the day, including Froment-Meurice and

[8] Another appears in *La Lorraine*, *op. cit.*, frontispiece.

[9] Another larger and unmounted is illustrated in *La Lorraine*, Sommaire de janvier 1905, opp. p. 21.

18. Vase of simulated stone, *circa* 1900
Musée de l'Ecole de Nancy

19. 'The Hand' in iridescent marbled greens, blues and browns, *circa* 1900
Musée de l'Ecole de Nancy

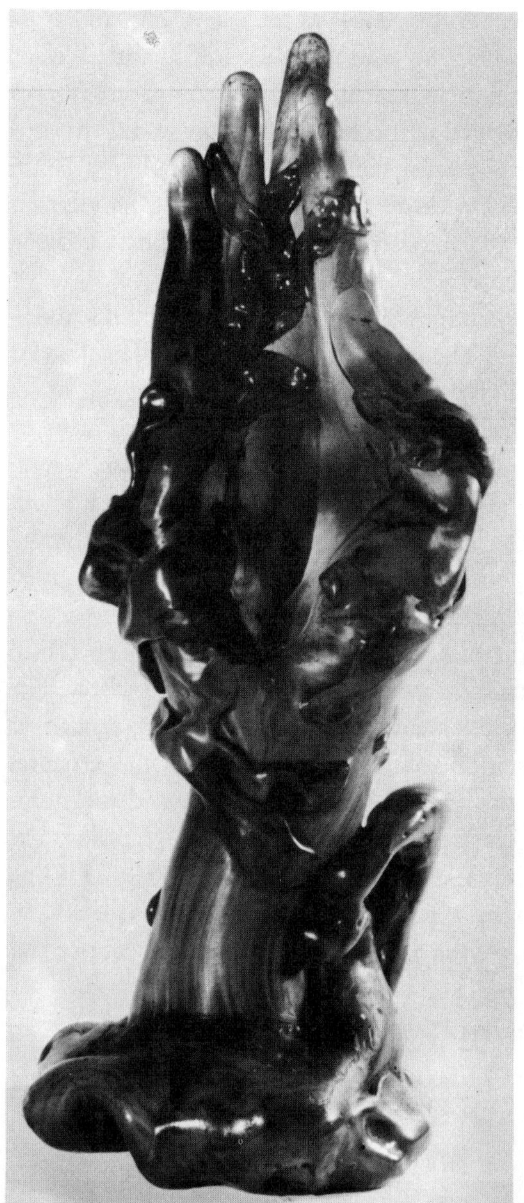

Falize. At the 1889 exhibition Gallé introduced his imitations of hardstones in glass, and explained them at length in his notice for the exhibition.[10] He mentions a smoky quartz and amethyst bowl, inscribed with the legend which literally translated reads, "Sweet amethyst comforts dark grief", now in the Musée des Arts Décoratifs. Another of the same type was presented to the President of the Republic. Gallé also discusses imitations of amber, jade, alabaster, agates, onyx, etc. Illustration 17 shows a marquetry vase, *circa* 1897, with a floral design on a ground resembling jade. The vase is made from a two-piece mould and presumably was repeated. Another series, launched in 1897, was carved with orchids on an imitation alabaster ground.[11]

Prior to the 1900 exhibition Gallé designed a group of highly original pieces, simple but sophisticated in style yet complex in production. In form they are either abstract or simply expressive of the rhythm of growth. Some are monochromes and others simulate stone, as the little vase in illustration 18 from the Musée de l'École de Nancy, where there is another with marquetry fossils on a small simulated-stone cylinder. Another group of this date with smooth surfaces on glass coloured in the mass consists of vases and flacons modelled in the form of fruits, vegetables and gourds.

The extravagance of some of Gallé's designs is illustrated in the fantastic hand (Ill. 19), *circa* 1900. It has an iridescent finish, as found on other pieces of this period; it is life-sized, superbly modelled, and rises, Dali-like, from the sea with deflated fronds of seaweed wrapped round and clinging to the fingers, a fascinating conception in glass.

The 1900 International Exhibition in Paris was Gallé's greatest hour. The display was sensational, centred by a working glass-furnace,[12] with all the implements of manufacture, antique models and pieces of his vases broken in the making. The furnace was surrounded by vitrines containing art nouveau glass: unique pieces, like *l'Amphore aux algues*, an enormous green glass amphora, inscribed and encrusted with shells, mounted in iron; marquetry vases, including a *tour de force* with lines from Victor Hugo and silver mounts by Cardeilhac, now in the Musée des Arts Décoratifs; *paysages de verre*, *porcelaine de verre* and rare carved 'Nature' vases. Gallé's industrial production was also well represented, for by 1900 he was employing some 300 craftsmen and the larger part of his production must have been acid-worked vases with floral designs. He condoned the use of hydrofluoric acid for eating away desired parts of the overlay only where it did not affect the finished result and could be used to hasten the process or produce an effect an engraving tool could not. Illustration 20 shows a typical example of the innumerable series produced at this time. Its mauve overlay round the iris has been removed by acid to different depths, giving the flower a three-dimensional effect, the surface is polished, and it is signed on the base "*Gallé déposé*". There may possibly have been a hundred of this model made and yet others were made with similar overlay on different shapes. Many of these series are in only two colours, some have been finished with an emery wheel on the reliefs or on the background, and the signatures are usually moulded in relief. Other popular motifs besides flowers were grape vines, oak branches, seaweed and honeycombs.

With the advent of electric light, new shapes and designs had to be created to replace the gas lamps, brackets and shades. Gallé was not a person to ignore an

[10] This notice is published in *Écrits pour l'Art*, *op. cit.*, p. 335.

[11] An example is illustrated in Pazaurek, G. E., and Nachfolger, H. S., *Moderne Gläser*, 1911, frontispiece, right.

[12] A photograph of the furnace is published in *Moderne Gläser*, *op. cit.*, fig. 71.

20. 'Verre-double' vase with acid-etched mauve design on a clear ground, *circa* 1900 height 12 in. (30·4 cm.). Private Collection, London

21. 'Les Coprins', 1904 height 32½ in. (82·5 cm.) Robert Walker Collection, Paris

opportunity like this; he produced many table and hanging lamps between 1900 and 1904. Illustration 21 shows a remarkable lamp from the collection of Mr Robert Walker, Paris. The mushroom shades are wheel-cut *verre-triplé*, the writhen stalks have silver insertions and the base is forged iron. It is over two and a half feet high and was made in 1904 for the Salon of 1905.[13] But as electric lamps lend themselves more readily to commercial production, the majority were of the acid-cut, cased type with flower and insect motifs and bronze mounts. The chandelier shown in illustration 22, *circa* 1904, is from the collection of Mme Perdrizet, one of Gallé's daughters, and hangs in 'La Garenne' amongst art nouveau marquetry panelling, and furniture from the Gallé factory. It is acid-etched and supported by brass dragonflies, the glass container at the base being used for its original purpose.

Till the last year of his life Gallé was designing important pieces. In 1904 he presented the magnificent piece of glass sculpture shown in illustration 23 to his close friend, the writer Louis de Fourcaud. Called simply *le Lys*, it is inscribed "*Louis de Bousés de Fourcaud en toute affection d'esprit et de cœur. E. Gallé. 1904*". Two other versions of *le Lys* exist, one in the Conservatoire des Arts et Métiers and another in a private collection.

Emile Gallé died of leukaemia in September 1904 when he was fifty-six. The business had been thriving, there was a tremendous demand for vases in his 'Nature' style, and his heirs, Mme Gallé and four daughters, saw no reason why the factory should close down. With two sons-in-law to run the business, Victor Prouvé as the family adviser and Emile Lang as manager, they continued to produce 'Art Glass' in Gallé's style until the factory finally closed in 1935. However, without the inspiration of Emile Gallé they could not hope to continue or compete with what had gone before. All the glass made in this long 'post Gallé' period was cased and acid-cut with naturalistic decoration, nearly always on an unpolished ground still frosted as a result of the acid. There is never any sign of wheel-work; they are usually *verre-double* as opposed to *-triplé* with somewhat sickly colours and insipid designs. The signatures are very similar and consist simply of 'Gallé' in cursive script, acid-etched in relief. A star was used part of the time, in conjunction with the signature, supposedly between 1904 and 1914.

There is conjecture concerning the distinction between some pre-1904 commercial vases and 'post Gallé' glass. Several pre-1904 photographs have been studied and only a very few show acid-etched vases that may have a frosted background, such as the three standard or 'post Gallé' vases illustrated in illustration 24. The vast majority of acid-etched, frosted background vases were certainly made after 1904. It is unfortunate that the signature was retained, as this has obviously confused people and led many to misunderstand Gallé's work.

Emile Gallé holds an important position in the history of decorative glass as the leading innovator and designer of a new style which influenced glass production throughout Europe and America, a creative movement that gave a new status to glass as an artistic medium. He rebelled against the unimaginative engraved and cut glass from Bohemia and England and against the mechanically applied traditional designs of the French opalines which were in vogue when Gallé was first experimenting with glass. Gallé was an eclectic, who searched among numerous historical sources and eventually found his own style by the time of the 1889 exhibition. Influenced by Japanese and Chinese art, by Eugène Rousseau, and by

[13] This lamp is illustrated in *La Lorraine*, Sommaire de janvier 1905, opp. p. 8. Another version of the lamp is in the Musée de l'École de Nancy.

his deep love and understanding of nature, he developed his own 'Nature' style, his version of the art nouveau in glass. Gallé, like many painters, turned to nature for inspiration, desiring to express the essence of growth. His motifs were the wild flowers, orchids, trees and insects of his beloved Lorraine, not the conventional compositions of the 19th century. Because he was a chemist and a practising botanist fascinated with glass as a medium, it was inevitable that his 'Nature' style in glass should predominate over all his productions.

As an original glass artist of the art nouveau movement he found rich and influential patrons such as Proust, the Count of Montesquieu, Princess Bibesco and Sarah Bernhardt. These associations led to commissions destined for great figures of the day such as Pasteur, the President of the Republic, the Tsar of Russia and the Queen of Italy.

Gallé reconciled himself successfully with industrial production: he set a high standard, was a good employer of labour, was able to reach a wide public who were unable to afford his luxury glass, and thus attained greater commercial success. As the firm expanded, his numerous activities prevented his personal touch in many places but he still found time to write authoritative articles on botany.[14]

In 1889 he referred without malice to his imitators who made 'genre Gallé' and expressed the hope that they would produce good designs, but in many cases it was not so, although several firms, notably the Daum brothers, marketed some very beautiful vases.

Gallé was one of the first designers to sign his glass; previously it had only been the enamellers or engravers who had added their signatures. But for Gallé's followers it was the accepted practice. It was partly due to the new status Gallé had given glass as an artistic medium that there emerged exciting new glass-makers such as Tiffany and Marinot, and the *pâte de verre* exponents Dammouse and Décorchement.

Gallé was a pioneer and inventor, but what gives his innovations and inventions so much significance is the fact that he was primarily an artist who expressed with sincerity and sensitivity the vision of his day.

[14] Gallé's publications are listed in *Écrits pour l'Art, op. cit.*, p. 373.

22. (above) Chandelier in acid-etched, cased glass with brass mounts, *circa* 1904
Madame Perdrizet Collection, Nancy

23. (below left) 'Le Lys' carved in multi-coloured glass and inscribed to Louis de Fourcaud, 1904
Musée de l'École de Nancy

24. (below right) 'Post-Gallé' vases, cased and acid-etched, *circa* 1920
height 6 to 7½ in. (15·2 to 19 cm.)
Private Collection, London

SELECTED BIBLIOGRAPHY

Demoriane, H. "Le Cas Etrange de Monsieur Gallé", *Connaissance des Arts*. August, 1960.
Fourcaud, L. de. *Les Artistes de tous les Temps, Série D, le XXe Siècle*, "Emile Gallé". Paris, 1903.
Gallé, E. *Écrits pour l'Art*. Paris, 1908.
Pazaurek, G. E. *Moderne Gläser*. Leipzig, 1901.
Polak, A. D. A. *Modern Glass*. London, 1962.
Rosenthal, L. *La Verrerie Française depuis Cinquante Ans*. Paris and Brussels, 1927.

Fans

PETER THORNTON

BAROQUE FANS (1660–1735)

Very few European fans made before 1700 now survive, and only a handful exist which can be dated earlier then *circa* 1660. The collector need not therefore pay much attention to the early history of the fan – about which the specialists are anyway extremely vague – and he can concentrate his attention on the fans of the Baroque period and later.

While comparatively few Baroque fans have come down to us, it is worth keeping an eye open for them because they are generally of a high quality. The age of the mass-produced fan had not yet dawned and users of the fan were still confined to a small, rich and – for the most part – discriminating group of people in each country.

By the middle of the 17th century, the folding fan with a pleated leaf had become dominant. The rigid type, shaped more like a ping-pong bat and derived in the misty past from the simple palm-leaf fans of primitive peoples, had finally been superseded by the more practical folding type which seems to have appeared on the European scene during the 15th century, perhaps imported by Portuguese mariners and anyway coming from the Far East where both the rigid and the folding types had long been in use. Portraits of the Elizabethan period (say, *circa* 1590) show ladies carrying both the rigid form, which by this time usually had its leaf composed of feathers, and the folding form. By the time of Charles II (*circa* 1665) few rigid fans seem to have been in use. A late and very rare specimen is shown in illustration 1. This is made with brightly coloured feathers sewn on to a net ground stretched on a wire frame that is fixed to a turned wooden handle. Charming as this fan is, however, it is unlikely that it represents the highest quality available at the period. Fans with ivory and jewelled handles were certainly obtainable by those who could afford them. Several engraved designs of the period exist for such handles, and a beautiful specimen, which has long since lost its ostrich-feather leaf, is shown in illustration 1.

As far as one can judge from illustrations and the few surviving examples, the earlier European folding fans were decorated in quite a simple manner with geometric patterns, scrollwork and other formal ornament. But, by the middle of the 17th century, when the period which interests us here opens, more ambitious painted scenes were beginning to appear on fan-leaves. There was usually one large, single scene. Indeed, the earliest pictorial fan-leaves seem to have been painted first as a rectangular picture, after which the fan-shaped leaf was then cut out. There was no border on such leaves and parts of the design were sometimes lost when the leaf was cut out of the rectangle. (Ill. 2.) As the century progressed, however, the scene becomes more specially suited to the fan's shape (colour plate I).

1. (right) Feather fan, late 17th century
The Countess of Rosse and Messel Collection
(far right) Ivory fan-handle, late 16th or early 17th century
The Victoria and Albert Museum, London

Borders still remained very simple and there was little filling-in with ornament in the corners.

Baroque fan-leaves were made of thick white paper, or of brown leather, or of thin white kid (which the collectors often call 'chicken skin', for reasons best known to themselves). A specimen in the Leonard Messel Collection even has a leaf composed of pieces of mica alternating with paper, so as to present a largely transparent surface when the fan is open.

In the third quarter of the 17th century Paris was already becoming the principal centre for the production of fashionable luxury goods – especially those intended for feminine use. From the surviving examples, it would seem that French fans of the period mostly had paper leaves and were painted with topical subjects. (Ill. 2.) A fine group of fans exists, mostly decorated with mythological subjects and with charming naturalistic flowers on the back – again often, although not always, on a dark ground. (Ill. 3.) This group is often thought to be Flemish, although it is quite possible that such fans are in fact Parisian. (The fan shown in colour plate facing p. 196 [above] has such flowers on the back.) It is at any rate probably fair to say that most French or North European fans of the High Baroque period had scenes painted on rather dark grounds.

Italian fans, on the other hand, often seem to have light-coloured grounds and therefore appear brighter than their French counterparts. Again, the painting usually consists of an overall scene and often depicts a mythological subject. (Ill. 4.) But Italy, and particularly Rome, was already the principal goal of aristocratic young men making their Grand Tour, and Italian fan-makers were quick to see that considerable profits might be made from providing fans decorated with scenes that would appeal to these rich young tourists, and which they would be tempted to buy and take home as souvenirs of their journey. Favourite subjects were scenes of Roman buildings and small copies of the famous frescoes in the great Roman palaces – frescoes by Guido Reni, the Carracci, and the other post-Renaissance painters then so particularly admired. (Ill. 6.) This tourist trade was clearly a lucrative one, for fans of this class continued to be produced in large quantities throughout the 18th century. (Ill. 18.)

Certain fans that are probably Italian have white kid leaves which are delicately cut (*découpé*) with pierced, lace-like ornament. (Ill. 7.) Possibly such kid fans were originally scented. We know that scented leather fans were produced at this period in Italy.

The decoration of another kind of Italian Baroque fan-leaf is executed in pen

2. French fan-leaf showing the Marriage of Louis XIV to Marie-Thérèse in 1660
The British Museum, London

and ink. Both black and red ink is used, sometimes in combination. The drawing is usually excellent (Ill. 5) and is often confined to the reverse face.

The sticks and guards (the two extended outer sticks which protect the fan when closed) of Baroque fans are often superbly decorated. The sticks are most frequently of ivory, sometimes carved and sometimes studded with silver *piqué* ornament. Mother-of-pearl was beginning to come into use by *circa* 1700 for fans. The marvellous fan shown in illustrations 4 and 5 has pierced and carved sticks, set with mother-of-pearl ornaments; the guards have *piqué* decoration as well. Later on, complete sticks were made of this material.

Apart from the pleated form of folding fan, there is the so-called *brisé* type which does not have a leaf at all. Instead, the sticks are made broad enough to overlap all the way up and thus form a surface "for agitating the air". Since the *brisé* fan has no leaf to hold the sticks evenly spaced when open, the sticks are fitted with a ribbon threaded through slots at the broad end – that is, at the opposite end from the rivet or pin from which the sticks radiate. (Ills 8, 9, 19.)

The *brisé* form is also of Oriental origin. I know of no early European examples, although the form may have reached Europe along with the pleated kind. But this type does not seem to have been imitated in Europe until somewhere around 1700 – long after the pleated form had gained the ascendancy over the cumbersome rigid type. By the end of the 17th century, the various East India companies of Europe were importing huge quantities of Oriental fans, mass-produced with an astute commercial eye on the European market. Among these were *brisé* fans of the type shown in illustration 8; indeed, a high proportion of them may have been of this sort. This is brightly coloured (predominantly red) and has considerable charm. Fans of this kind must have had great appeal for the Europeans of the day, and it is hardly surprising that the importers found a ready market for such wares. It will be noted that, although the decoration is mainly Oriental, the central figures are intended to represent Europeans. It should perhaps be said that fans of this type are sometimes stated to be European, but this is not the case.

The European imitations of this *brisé* type begin to appear around 1700. They must have constituted a small but important proportion of European fan-production by *circa* 1720. The vogue for this type then faded away and *brisé* fans do not seem to have been made in Europe during the middle decades of the 18th century at all. Early imitations of the kind of fan shown in illustration 19 then started to come in during the 1780's.

The European *brisé* fans of the first third of the 18th century are usually known as '*Vernis Martin* fans' among collectors, because the painted decoration is varnished

3. (below left) Back of a French or Flemish fan, late 17th century
The Victoria and Albert Museum, London

4. (below right) Italian fan, early 18th century
The Victoria and Albert Museum, London

5. Reverse of the fan shown in illustration 4

and it was recalled, probably by some acute dealer in the last century, that the most famous executors of varnished and painted decoration during the 18th century had been the brothers Martin who had had important workshops in Paris during the second quarter of the century. The Martin establishment produced painted (or japanned, as it is called in England) work of the highest quality, and supplied panels for the decoration of rooms, furniture and carriages. Their work was distinguished by the fine varnish they used and for the use of which they were granted letters patent in 1730 – the '*Vernis Martin*'. Whether they made fans at all, I do not know, but it is worth noting that most of the so-called '*Vernis Martin* fans' seem to have been made rather before 1730 (the one shown in illustration 9 must have been made somewhere between 1710 and 1725), and most of them, although not the one illustrated here, are of nothing like sufficiently high quality to have come from the famous Martin workshops. No, these small japanned *brisé* fans must have been made in a number of workshops in Paris (and perhaps also in Holland). Their quality varies considerably and many are of atrociously poor workmanship. The best, on the other hand, are superb. They have been much sought by the richer collector, however, and many spurious examples were consequently produced during the last century to satisfy this demand. The ivory used for these reproductions is often of rather thicker section than the originals; the brushwork also tends to lack the precision of the 18th-century fan-painter's creations.

A few of these small ivory *brisé* fans have pierced sticks, cut to produce Baroque scrollwork with a central medallion that is painted – all visible when the fan is open. Such variants are rare and seem to belong to the early phase of the vogue for these little fans, for it should be noted that they are much smaller than the contemporary pleated fans. None of these *brisé* fans are decorated with Rococo scrollwork, which suggests that they were all made before *circa* 1735, when Rococo embellishment began to assume an important place in the European repertoire of decoration.

ROCOCO FANS (1735–65)

Works of art of the Rococo period have on the whole been despised until quite recently in this country. The fans of this period must have done much to encourage this viewpoint, for most Rococo fans are indeed frivolous confections, of no consequence at all, poorly painted with insipid scenes in mostly rather pale colours, and with sticks carved with weak scrolls and *rocaille* work. But, again, it is a question of quality. The finest Rococo fans are marvellous and possess all the best qualities of the idiom; their decoration has that tautness and vigour about it which pervades the best work of the period in other fields, and there is a precision about the painting that is very different from the childish brushwork of the average fan-painter of the day. (See colour plate opposite [below]; Ill. 14.)

6. Italian fan with a representation of Guido Reni's *Aurora* fresco in the Casino Rospigliosi-Pallavicini in Rome, *circa* 1720
The Victoria and Albert Museum, London

As Europe became richer during the 18th century, so the demand for luxury wares like fans increased. Mass production was now introduced, with sticks being subcontracted to cottage industries in the provinces, and even being imported from China, after which they were provided with leaves in Europe. The printing of fan-leaves (discussed later) was also an innovation which enabled large quantities of cheap fans to be produced at no great cost and primarily for a mass market. But high-quality fans were of course still required by the discriminating minority, and these are quite worthy of the attention of the discriminating collector today.

An astonishing amount of nonsense has been written about fans and many authorities have failed to apply even the most rudimentary art history to their studies in this field. Thus many fans decorated with asymmetrical Rococo

Colour Plates. (above) Baroque fan, probably French, late 17th century. The British Museum, London
(below) French Rococo fan, about 1740
The Victoria and Albert Museum, London

7. Italian fan with *découpé* leaf, early 18th century
The Countess of Rosse and Messel Collection

8. Ivory *brisé* fan made in the Far East for export to Europe, early 18th century
The Victoria and Albert Museum, London

9. French ivory *brisé* fan of exceptionally high quality, *circa* 1720
The Victoria and Albert Museum, London

10. (above left) English fan, second quarter of the 18th century
The Victoria and Albert Museum, London

11. (above right) English printed fan, dated 1740
The Countess of Rosse and Messel Collection

scrollwork have been labelled 'Early 18th century', or even '17th century', whereas they cannot possibly be earlier than *circa* 1730 – when the Rococo idiom first makes its appearance – and few of them are likely to have been made much before 1740. But, after that date, Rococo scrollwork is to be found in profusion on fans, especially on the sticks. Such ornament still remained in use until well into the 1770's.

The fans of the 1740's were often rather larger than those of earlier periods. (See colour plate facing p. 196.) The colours were lighter and brighter, and fan-painters were no longer afraid to leave substantial areas of their fans undecorated. (Ill. 10.) The scenes were now confined to the centre of the leaves, and the decoration in the corners now assumed greater importance and began to cover a larger area. This corner-decoration normally consisted of flowers and scrollwork, also of a Rococo character. And whereas the sticks of the Baroque period usually had rounded shoulders, those of the Rococo are mostly squared. The carving is often intricate and a scene – either carved or painted – usually appears on the central portion of the sticks when the fan is opened.

At this point it is perhaps worth issuing a warning about signatures on fans. The 18th-century fan-painter very rarely signed his work, and the collector should be extremely suspicious if he is offered a signed fan unless it is printed (in which case the printer's name is often given) or made after *circa* 1840, because in the 19th century it became a common practice for artists of all calibres to paint and sign fans. But the 18th-century fan-painters were artisans and members of a trade guild. They were without doubt jealous of their trade monopoly and would have been quick to attack any outsider who tried to infringe it by decorating fan-leaves. It is therefore unlikely that the painters of easel pictures undertook to paint fans, as is sometimes suggested, and it is even more unlikely that any great European painter ever bothered to decorate a fan. A possible exception is Watteau, who was after all a composer of ornament and did in fact design a composition for a fan which was engraved and published. But one should mistrust any attribution to any of the great masters of the day. Certainly Boucher influenced the fan-painters of his time (see colour plate facing p. 196 [below]), but I doubt very much if he was responsible for any of this work himself.

Paris was now the principal centre of fan-production in Europe and enjoyed a considerable export trade. The French style was of course imitated everywhere. A flourishing industry was also established in London, and the best English fans of the period are very good. English fans often have a good deal of white ground exposed; the French equivalent sometimes has a coloured ground or is decorated over much of its surface. However, there must have been plenty of exceptions to such generalizations.

The size of fans decreased somewhat after *circa* 1755. The sticks then also became more slender and no longer overlapped; they resembled the spokes of a wheel and

12. (above left) English printed fan dated 1741 and signed 'F. Chassereau'
The British Museum, London

13. (above right) Portuguese fan showing an English vessel in Lisbon harbour, dated 1739
The Victoria and Albert Museum, London

so no longer presented an uninterrupted surface for an expansive scheme of decoration. The sticks of fans made during the later decades of the century therefore tended to be decorated individually, without relation to each other. Sometimes they were now carved to produce a curious effect when closed. For instance, one form (the so-called 'Pagoda stick' type) had guards composed, as it were, of a bunch of rods, linked by several collars up their length. These sticks looked, when closed, somewhat like the legs of furniture in Chippendale's 'Chinese Taste'; indeed, it was to meet the demand for fancy goods in this vein that such fans were made. They were naturally also furnished with leaves painted with chinoiserie subjects to suit. The carving of the sticks to produce ornament that could only be seen when the fan was closed seems to have been a favourite form of embellishment with Spanish and Portuguese fan-makers in the middle of the 18th century. The Portuguese fan shown in illustration 13 has a spiralling garland of flowers running round its closed sticks. The effect can only be partly appreciated when the fan is open, as in the photograph.

Something should perhaps be said about the "Myth of The Spanish Fan". I have come across no evidence that Spain was an important centre of fan-production during the 18th century, in spite of the general belief that many of the best fans come from Spain. A Spanish economist, writing towards the end of the century, quite definitely states that the finest fans used in Spain at that period came from France and that many also were imported from England. Of course fans were made in Spain, but they are likely to have been of inferior quality to the best French productions; this is borne out by the very few documented Spanish fans of the period which have come to my attention. A well-known type of fan which is frequently labelled 'Spanish' is the so-called *battoir* fan which has very wide pleats and thus only a few sticks, widely spaced. It is possible that some of these are in fact Spanish, but I believe that most of them are French, possibly made specially for export to Spain. Their decoration is rich and colourful; as with other types of fan, the quality varies. It should be added that splendid fans were made in Spain during the 19th century, and it is perhaps this fact which has given rise to the myth. To be fair, however, it is just possible that the 'myth' springs from the early history of the fan in Europe. As we have already noted, it seems probable that it was in Portugal that folding fans first came into use. The fashion will then have spread to Spain – where rigid fans had no doubt been in use since time immemorial. During the 16th century, when Spain was a great power and, in consequence, produced luxury goods on a large scale, it is perfectly conceivable that the finest fans were produced in Spain. But this still does not mean that the best 18th-century fans are Spanish – which is what has often been claimed.

On the other hand, Italy continued to produce beautiful fans right through the 18th century, many of them still for the tourist trade. It is uncertain whether the superb fan shown in illustration 14 is French or Italian. This is one of a group, all decorated with mythological scenes (usually from the lives of the gods) exquisitely painted on the front, but with Chinese subjects on the back and Chinese-type flowers in the corners on the front. These Chinese passages are no mere essays in chinoiserie; they are close imitations of the Chinese style of painting – so much so that it has even been debated whether this is the work of a Chinese or a European artist. My own view is that these fans are in fact among the finest products of the Parisian workshops, that they represent the high-point of fan-painting under Louis XV, but we do not yet know. It should be added that numerous inferior fans decorated with chinoiseries – that is, with completely fanciful renderings of Oriental subjects – were made at this period. Most of these are of no great quality. Chinoiserie fans then seem to disappear from the European scene during the Louis XVI period, roughly from 1770 onwards.

LOUIS XVI AND NEO-CLASSICAL FANS (1765–1800)

During the 1760's the shape and decorations of European fans began to take on a different character. In both their shape and their ornamentation a certain stiffness now appears, and this grows more marked as the century draws to a close. The guards assume a spade-like shape, broad and rectangular alongside the leaf, and narrow near the rivet. Urns and the other beloved motifs of Neo-classicism are often carved on the guards, mostly within oval medallions. The leaf is now mostly painted with three separate scenes, again often confined within rigid oval framings. Towards the end of the period, the leaf is often of silk instead of paper; to the silk, sequins of brass and trimmings of gilt thread were frequently stitched. (Ill. 17.) At the same time, highly coloured metal foil was occasionally pasted behind the openwork carving of the guards. The total effect is gaudy and bordering on the vulgar. But, again, it has to be recognized that high-quality fans were still being made at this stage – like the one shown in illustration 17. Shortly before 1800, sequins of polished steel instead of brass were often used. Indeed, there is a group of fans dating from *circa* 1810 which have leaves of coloured net decorated solely with steel sequins or with small pressed brass ornaments.

Few French fans of the period are of much interest; even those of high quality seem somewhat mechanical in execution when compared with the finest products of the preceding three or four generations. The Italian fans, on the other hand, tend to retain some of the charm of their predecessors. The kind of 'tourist fan' on which a famous painting was reproduced continued to be made, and the scene still occupied the whole front surface of the leaf until quite late in the century, following the old Baroque tradition of fan-painting (cf. Ill. 6). It is only the sticks which give an indication of the real date of such fans, for these are usually up to date in their decoration. Tourist fans with scenes of famous Italian sights (Ill. 18; views of Vesuvius were particularly popular) were also much produced and some of these are well painted. Their subsidiary ornament is often 'Pompeian' towards the end of the century, echoing the current interest in the archaeological discoveries then being made in Italy.

An interesting and rare fan is reproduced in illustration 15. This is not only dated 1771 but is signed on the back, as if part of an inscription on a drawing. Note

14. (below left) French or Italian fan, mid-18th century
The Victoria and Albert Museum, London

15. (below right) Italian fan signed 'Francesco Stagni' and dated 1771
The Countess of Rosse and Messel Collection

16. Italian fan printed in red, *circa* 1770
The British Museum, London

the widely spaced sticks with urns and quivers of arrows on the guards, and the rigid oval compartments on the leaf, all typical features of the period, as we have noted. Untypical, however, is the real charm of the painting.

PRINTED FANS

It was the English who first began to produce fans with printed leaves towards the end of the 1720's. Once the engraved plate had been made, there was virtually no limit to the number of leaves that could be produced quickly and cheaply from it. The scenes on early English printed fans are badly drawn and the colours are crudely daubed on in a fairly random manner. The sticks are simple, to match. Such fans were ephemeral objects; they would not have been regarded as in any way precious at the time and most of them have therefore been thrown away. Early English printed fans are thus rare. A specimen of somewhat above average quality is shown in illustration 11.

The ephemeral character of such fans is also demonstrated by the subjects printed on them. These are mostly topical – scenes from current plays and operas, political happenings, etc. In about 1740, however, printed fans of better quality began to become available. The English specimen shown in illustration 12 has a leaf which is considerably better drawn than that of the fan illustrated in illustration 11, while the Italian fan reproduced in illustration 16 is in quite a different class. It is finely printed in red and must date – judging from the decoration of the sticks – from around 1770.

Later in the century, fans were printed with all kinds of things – advertisements (for watering-places, coach time-tables, etc.), political cartoons, plans of the seating in some theatre, etc. But these again are rather poor specimens of the fan-maker's art and have no aesthetic interest whatsoever. Only occasionally do they attain a certain charm; the fan from the 1790's shown in illustration 20 is an unusually pleasing example.

Many late 18th-century printed fans are to be found in the Schreiber Collection, now in the Print Room of the British Museum; a two-volume catalogue of this collection was published in 1893 and is useful for those interested in this facet of fan history.

Printed fan-leaves were also much used in the 19th century. A particularly charming tinted specimen of *circa* 1825 is shown in illustration 21. This is Parisian.

Later, it became the practice for the less competent fan-painters to apply their colours rather thickly over a faintly printed scene. Lithographed fan-leaves became common in the 1840's; these again were coloured over, and a particular kind of brassy gilding distinguishes many fans of this variety. This gilding is quite different from the much less brilliant gold paint of the 18th century. Many fans of this class are apparently Spanish.

17. French fan, *circa* 1785
The Victoria and Albert Museum, London

18. Italian fan-leaf with a scene of St Peter's, Rome, late 18th century
The Victoria and Albert Museum, London

NINETEENTH-CENTURY FANS

Towards the end of the 18th century a type of *brisé* fan with intricate pierced decoration began to be imported in large quantities from China. They came in various qualities and sizes; most of them are small, but it is possible that the smaller versions are of later date – probably after 1800 – when the hooped skirt had gone out and women's dresses were comparatively narrow (for it can be taken as a general rule that the size of the fans at any given period increases or decreases in conformity with the ground area covered by women's skirts). The larger versions of these fans may then mostly belong to the end of the 18th century, when the full skirt was still in fashion. (Ill. 19.)

At first glance these fans seem extraordinarily delicate in execution but they are in fact rather repetitive (they must have been mass-produced in China) and, to my mind, they are curious rather than beautiful. Most of them are made of ivory, but they were also produced in tortoiseshell, wood and silver filigree. Such fans were also imitated in Europe in ivory or wood, but also in horn or mother-of-pearl. The later European versions, those dating from around 1820, often have pointed tips, an echo of the neo-Gothic taste then raging in Europe.

19. Chinese export fan with the monogram of Lord Macartney, who visited China in 1792–94
The Victoria and Albert Museum, London

When women's skirts began to increase in size again, towards 1830, the fans increased in size to correspond. (Ill. 21.) It was during the second quarter of the century that the brassy gilding already referred to became particularly popular. *Brisé* fans again came into fashion in the 1860's, after having again yielded pride of place to the pleated form for a while. The common form of mid-century pleated fan had wide overlapping sticks with rounded shoulders and a comparatively narrow leaf which gave the whole thing a somewhat stumpy appearance that went well with the crinoline, then also attaining its greatest circumference. *Circa* 1870 the typical High Victorian fan appeared. This was large and elongated and again echoed the form of women's dresses which were slim in front and trailed away voluminously behind. The shoulderless guards of these long fans are often made of unadorned mother-of-pearl that is of a milky white kind, very different from the silvery substance used during the 18th century. The leaves are often of gauze or silk, with a painted scene that is frequently signed by the artist. (Ill. 22.)

All kinds of fancy fans were made during the 19th century. In the Victoria and Albert Museum's excellent collection of fans is one late 19th-century specimen which has guards shaped like a bulrush, the head being made of brown velvet. Feather fans were also popular; the ostrich-feather fan becoming the accepted fan for Court use where it was retained until well into the 1920's. The cigarette finally killed the fan, for it was of course difficult to manage both at the same time – they just do not go together! Possibly, when it is no longer smart to smoke cigarettes, the fan will come back, because people like to have something for their hands to play with – to soothe their nerves or to cover up their shyness – and the fan offers plenty of scope for that. But perhaps the whole tempo of modern life precludes the fan's revival.

20. English printed fan, dated 1792
The Victoria and Albert Museum, London

ORIENTAL FANS

Something has already been said about fans made in the Far East for the European market. Another type of export fan not mentioned so far is the Cantonese fan, which has a pleated leaf of silk, gaudily painted (blue predominating) with scenes in which small figures appear, each furnished with a small applied oval of ivory that forms the face. It is said that the cost of such a fan was determined by the number of faces on it. Most of these Cantonese fans date from the middle decades of the last century, when they were very popular (many survive), but the type seems to have begun to appear on the European scene already in the late 18th century.

The export fans, however, were for the most part cheap mass-produced articles, intended to dazzle the Occidental consumer either with their colourfulness or with the intricacy of their workmanship. The best are charming; most of them are curious; and hardly any have pretensions to being regarded as works of art. In China and Japan, on the other hand, the fan has long been regarded as a symbol of rank. Superb fans were therefore made for home consumption. These were both of the pleated and the rigid kind, while *brisé* fans were also used for certain purposes, notably in the theatre. The painting of fan-leaves, moreover, has long been regarded as a facet of the Fine Arts in the Far East, and as a genre that was in no way beneath the dignity of the greatest painters to practise. Fan-leaves (often unused because they were so precious) by the great masters from the Sung Dynasty onwards were keenly sought by collectors and assembled in albums – just as easel-paintings have been collected by European princes ever since the Renaissance. What is more, the essays of the earlier Chinese masters have since been copied and paraphrased over and over again. I must refer the reader to works on Chinese painting and Chinese art generally for more information on this subject. The same applies to Japanese fans, since much the same tradition prevailed in Japan.

A curious point that the collector of European fans will note about the fans made in the Far East is that the Oriental fan-painter, when he sets out to paint a leaf for a folding fan, almost always makes the horizon curve with the arc of the fan-leaf. A European fan-painter, on the other hand, regards his fan-leaf merely as an awkward shape cut out of a rectangular picture with a *horizontal* horizon. It is rather as if the European were always hoping to be mistaken for a great artist whose work happened to have been cut up and pasted on a fan, whereas the Oriental artists regarded the painting of fan-leaves as an entirely worthy undertaking with its own special rules which they were perfectly happy to observe.

One might continue this line of thought and say that it was *because* the painting of fans was not regarded as anything more than a trade in Europe (at least, until well into the 19th century), that most European fans are such poor things. For any painter of fans who was capable of better things would have moved on into the higher ranks of the artistic hierarchy. But throughout the period which concerns us here, there has been a demand for fans of high quality, and there was at each

21. French printed fan signed 'Bosselmann sculp.', *circa* 1825
The Countess of Rosse and Messel Collection

22. (above left) French fan made for the Princesse Marie d'Orléans, *circa* 1885
The Victoria and Albert Museum, London

23. (above right) Chinese fan-leaf painted by Chou Ch'en, active *circa* 1500–35
The Victoria and Albert Museum, London

stage a handful of fan-makers who produced fans that are worthy of the discriminating collector today. These are no mere 'pieces of nonsense', like the run-of-the-mill fans, but are charming and frequently exquisite little works of art.

REPRODUCTIONS AND FAKES

A large number of fans were made during the 19th century which had 18th-century subjects depicted on their leaves. Usually the scenes consisted of ladies and gentlemen in more or less convincing renderings of 18th-century dress, placed in Watteauesque poses. Few discerning collectors will be misled by these fans. The sticks will usually indicate their true date. But sometimes a fan-leaf of this type will have been pasted, as a replacement, on to a set of genuine 18th-century sticks. It is advisable to inspect the faces and hair-styles on fans of this type. Even when depicting an 18th-century woman, the 19th-century artist tends to draw the face in a 19th-century manner, and he will almost certainly fail to make the hair-style look right. Indeed, it is useful to have a working knowledge of 19th-century illustration and about 19th-century hair-styles before one embarks on fan-collecting. The 19th-century painter will often show the 18th-century *coiffure* as white, whereas the powdered wigs were really greyish and were rendered as such at the time.

Outright fakes, intended to deceive, are, of course, also not unknown in this field. It is especially the richer kind of fan that receives the faker's attention, since it is these which are likely to bring the greater rewards. The faker's brushwork is often too free and lacks the crispness of the 18th-century painting. Landscapes tend to be too romantic and are not the mere vignette or background that is all the 18th-century fan-painter ever ventured. What is more, the sticks are often too thick in section. One should also suspect any fan with a double fan-leaf – that is, with a second leaf pasted on the back of the sticks. This was a 19th-century practice. It was sometimes adopted when an old fan was being restored – for, of course, these delicate objects were frequently in need of repair. Indeed, many old fans have been repaired, and the collector has to consider the degree and manner of the restoration in order to determine whether a fan is still worth acquiring or not. The possibilities and permutations are endless, and only experience will teach the collector to recognize them all for what they really are.

BIBLIOGRAPHY

Perceval, M. J. *The Fanbook.* London, 1920.
Rhead, G. W. *History of the Fan.* London, 1910.
von Boehn, M. *Das Beiwerk der Mode.* Munich, 1928.
Madrid, Arte Español, Exhibition *El abanico en Espana*, 1920.
Leningrad, The Hermitage Museum.
Encyclopaedia Britannica, article on "Fans".
Thornton, P. K. "Une des plus belles collections d'éventails du monde" (The Messel Collection), *Connaissance des Arts.* April, 1963.
Exhibition "Viften – The Fan", Copenhagen, May 1957. Organized by Count Weddel in collaboration with the Musée des Arts Décoratifs, Paris.
Catalogue of the Schreiber Collection, British Museum Print Room, compiled by L. Cust, 1893.

Tobacco Figures as Shop Signs

GEORGE HARTMAN

Many years ago when shopkeepers and merchants restricted themselves to a particular trade and medicines and cures were only sold by the chemist, stockings by the hosier and tobacco and snuff by the tobacconist or snuff merchant, such shops were identified for the benefit of many of the population who could neither read nor write by the sign of their trade. It was also an appealing form of visual advertisement to catch the curiosity of the passer-by and encourage him to step inside. The sign of the hosier was a carved human leg, while the grocer displayed a sugar-loaf and the chemist a carboy; outside the premises of the musical instrument maker hung a hautboy.

Of these many distinctive signs few survive in this day when household needs are mostly catered for in one brightly lit and soulless store whose sign should properly be a cash-register wired for sound. One of these, surely an anachronism in a welfare state, is the sign of the pawnbroker, the three golden pills of the Lombardy bankers who were formerly chemists; the other the neon-lit pole outside the barber's shop.

All these signs, which included the painted signboards outside the wine shop, usually of the god Bacchus, and the signboards of the coffee shop, were of inanimate objects with one exception, that of the snuff and tobacco merchants who advertised their trade by a carved human effigy.

To seek the reason for this it is necessary to recall briefly the early history of tobacco, and how it came to be introduced into Europe. Historians are agreed that tobacco was first introduced from the Americas in the middle of the 16th century, although Columbus records seeing the natives smoking on his first voyage to the Bahamas and the West Indies in 1492. On the Continent it was at first primarily used on medicinal grounds in the form of snuff taking, but in England tobacco was used essentially for smoking, the fashion for snuff taking coming later, in imitation of the French.

Although there is evidence that tobacco was imported into England as early as 1555 by Sir John Hawkins, it is generally agreed that it was through Sir Walter Raleigh that it became popular in England for smoking and the blame for what he termed "this abuse" and "that vile barbarous custom" was certainly laid squarely on Raleigh by James I in his treatise "Counterblaste to Tobacco" published in 1603.

At about the same time as the habit of smoking was becoming generally popular and the import and sale of tobacco a commercial business, London was full of the arrival of the Princess Pocahontas, daughter of a Red Indian chieftain and an early convert to Christianity, who arrived in England in 1616 in company with her husband, Captain John Rolfe. Since America was to the greater part of the population a land of legend and its natives inhabitants of another world, it was a

1. (right) Princess Pocahontas, *circa* 1620
height 40 in. (101·6 cm.)
Rattray Collection

2. (far right) The Black Boy, mid-17th century
height 28 in. (71·1 cm.)
The Castle Museum, York

3. (right) The Black Boy, early 18th century
height 48 in. (121·9 cm.)
Rattray Collection

4. (far right) The Turk, early 18th century
height 54 in. (137·1 cm.)
Rattray Collection

5. The Saracen, early 18th century
height 60 in. (152·4 cm.)
Rattray Collection

6. The Turk, 19th century
height 28 in. (71·1 cm.)
Pinto Collection

stroke of genius on the part of an enterprising tobacco merchant to adopt as a sign for his shop an effigy of a native of that legendary land, a native of whom many had heard but few had seen. The success of this sign caused other merchants to follow suit, and *La Belle Sauvage* as she came to be known, a pipe of peace in her hand, soon adorned the premises of other fashionable merchants. (Ill. 1.) Although the tobacco figure was to appear in many other guises in the succeeding centuries, that of Princess Pocahontas is the rarest and the most appealing.

Since England in the 17th century was a predominantly masculine society and smoking a man's prerogative, it is understandable that once the initial excitement over Princess Pocahontas had died away, her effigy should be replaced by that of a male figure, and she was superseded by the Blackamoor (Ill. 2), *At The Sign of The Black Boy* soon becoming a popular address for tobacco merchants. It is surely not entirely coincidence that this was also a popular sobriquet for Charles II, and to this day many inns called The Black Boy carry his portrait as a sign. It is curious that this figure, whilst retaining the essential note of exoticism of the earlier figure, represented a native of Guinea rather than of America, where tobacco was grown; it was probably inspired by the then current vogue for 'Blackamoor' slaves who were captured by slave-traders on the Guinea Coast and brought to England to serve as pages at Court and in the houses of the nobility.

The Black Boy was dressed in a crown and skirt of tobacco leaves painted alternately red, green and gold, and usually carried a plug of tobacco or a bundle of tobacco leaves under his left arm and in his right hand a clay pipe.

The Castle Museum at York possesses an unusual example as he does not carry the customary pipe but is shown instead with a curious bell-shaped bundle in his left hand, possibly intended to represent a leather water-carrier. In the 17th century the modelling of some of these figures appears to be curiously out of proportion, with long torsos and short legs more in keeping with the actual stature of these natives, but in the succeeding century the effigy had become more European in appearance and those which have survived have something of the air of a blackened comedian. (Ill. 3.) The quality of the carving of the later examples and the greater refinement of detail resulted in a more majestic stance but in the process they lost much of the simplicity of their predecessors which was a great part of their appeal. As a tobacco sign the Blackamoor was not peculiar to any country and was equally popular as a shop sign for snuff sellers and tobacco merchants everywhere.

In time the appealing but scantily dressed Blackamoor came to offend puritanical tastes, and his effigy was replaced by others more fully clothed, some of which, while retaining the sense of the exotic thought essential to the trade, had but little in common with tobacco and its land of origin, and the 18th century saw the appearance of the Turk or Saracen – who were quite interchangeable in the public imagination – and the Indian Prince (Ills 4, 5), the inspiration coming rather from the Orient than from the New World. Although the carving of these figures was of a higher order than the appealing naïvety of the Blackamoors, through the loss of association with the land where tobacco was grown they can hardly have touched the public imagination as strongly, since no tobacco was imported at that time from the Moslem world, though this was in some way compensated by the wider knowledge of the Orient; it was not in fact until the middle of the 19th century, as a result of the Crimean War, that enthusiastic smokers acquired a taste for Turkish tobacco, and some of the later effigies of Turks reflect this demand (Ill. 6) which was to endure until the Great War when the only tobacco available was Virginian and the taste for smoking Turkish was

Colour Plate. The Red Indian Chieftain, 19th century: height 92 in. (233·6 cm.)
The Henry Ford Museum, Dearborn, Michigan

7. Saracen's head, 19th century
height 24 in. (60·9 cm.)
Rattray Collection

consequently largely superseded. The Eastern figures were shown in long flowing robes with baggy trousers, their heads sometimes surmounted by a crescent, the long-stemmed pipe of the earlier figures being replaced in the 19th century by a cigar.

The popularity of tobacco figures as a means of attracting trade led to a demand among less prosperous merchants for a cheaper sign of which the Saracen's head (Ill. 7) is an example, although these often lack the quality of their larger prototypes.

At the end of the 18th century there appeared the Sailor, a figure found chiefly in seaports such as Bristol where tobacco shipments were unloaded. He was mostly depicted with a long clay pipe and a tobacco pouch, some of the finer examples with bulging cheek to hint at the quid or 'chew' of tobacco favoured by seafaring men. (Ill. 8.) His appeal was not only through direct association as the carrier of tobacco but also as a teller of tall stories of an exciting world of unfamiliar lands beyond the experience of his less-travelled countrymen. Such figures have gained an added fascination today in that they depict contemporary dress, for like the Highlander which the craftsman carved in the likeness of his own countrymen, these figures were shown dressed in the costume of the time and are therefore easier to date accurately than those of the Orient: thus the black scarf worn by British sailors as a mark of perpetual mourning after the death of Nelson at Trafalgar.

At the same time there were other rarer figures which retained the appeal of a more direct association with the land of tobacco. A magnificent example is the Virginian Planter (Ill. 9) from the Rattray Collection in Perth, which contains the finest collection of tobacco figures in England. This is one of the few figures which is directly related to tobacco growing as opposed to those which represent the carrier or the indulger.

Almost as popular in America as the Highlander was in Britain was the Red Indian which stood guard over many a cigar store. A more-than-life-size example is the figure carved by Arnold and Peter Ruef of Tiffin, Ohio, *circa* 1880. (See colour plate facing p. 209.) This figure is now in the Henry Ford Museum at Dearborn, Michigan.

8. (right) The Sailor, 19th century
height 54 in. (137·1 cm.)
Rattray Collection

9. (far right) The Virginian Planter, 19th century
height 42 in. (106·6 cm.)
Rattray Collection

10. The Highlander, early 18th century
height 24 in. (60·9 cm.)
Rattray Collection

11. The Highlander, early 18th century
height 75 in. (190·5 cm.)
Rattray Collection

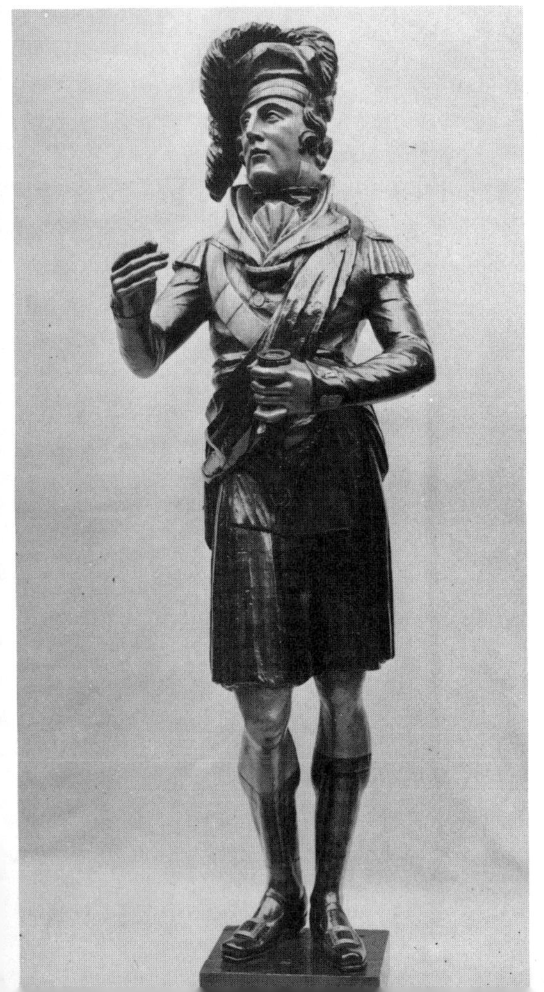

By far the most popular figure and one which exists today in greatest numbers is that of the Highlander, a splendid figure in full regalia. At the outset the Highlander was more of political than commercial significance, and although it was found outside the shops of tobacco merchants, it indicated to those who sympathized with the Stuart cause that the owner of the shop was himself a Jacobite and that those of similar persuasion could be assured of a friendly reception there. Behind many of these shops was a smoking parlour where Jacobites could safely meet to discuss the affairs of the day.

The first of these effigies was placed outside the Haymarket premises of an enterprising Scot from Edinburgh, David Wishart, in 1720, shortly after the second abortive rising of 1719. Such figures were depicted either in flat cap and doublet and trews or in bonnet and kilt, and carried either a Highland targe or shield or alternatively a sword. A rare contemporary example is the Caricature Highlander (Ill. 10) whose significance was entirely political.

In time all these figures came to be dressed in the kilt, and the sword and targe disappeared, the Highlander being shown in the act of taking a pinch of snuff. The Rattray Collection contains one of the finest examples of the Highlander (Ill. 11), a magnificent life-size figure of an Officer of a Highland Regiment, of commanding presence and strongly drawn features, shown in the act of conveying a pinch of snuff to his august nose. The Castle Museum at York contains a similar figure in a particularly resplendent bonnet (Ill. 12); this figure stood until recently outside a tobacconist's shop in Hull, and has always been known as Phineas, a name also given to another effigy of a Highlander, which was presented some years ago to University College, London, although no one has so far been able to suggest the reason for the choice of this particular name.

Such figures were placed outside the premises of tobacco merchants specializing in the sale of snuff, and it is interesting to note that whereas other figures are shown with the attributes of smoking, the Highlander is purely representative of snuff taking and no other figures are recorded with the snuff mull of the Highlander. Apart from the early political significance of the Highlander it is reasonable to suppose that he came to be associated exclusively with the sale of snuff, not only because snuff taking was more fashionable in Scotland, but also on account of the strong sympathy that has always existed between Scotland and France, the country which had given refuge to the exiled James Stuart and his Court at St-Germain, and where tobacco was used more extensively for snuff than for smoking.

Following the '45 and the final eclipse of the Stuart hopes, the wearing of the kilt and tartan were suppressed by order of the Duke of Cumberland. A printed appeal was circulated in London, supposedly from the Tobacco Highlanders, proclaiming their loyalty to the legitimate Crown and hoping that they would not be put to the expense of buying new clothes:

> "We hear that the dapper Wooden Highlanders who so heroically guard the doors of snuff shops intend to petition the Legislature in order that they may be excused from complying with the Act of Parliament with respect to the change of dress, alleging that they have ever been faithful subjects of His Majesty, having constantly supplied his Guards with a pinch out of their mulls when they marched by; and, so far from engaging in any rebellion, that they have never entered a rebellious thought: Whence they humbly hope that they shall not be put to the expense of buying new clothes."

Due to the proscription of the wearing of the kilt, the tobacco figures of Highlanders were mostly destroyed owing to their size, and the consequent difficulty

12. The Highlander, early 19th century
height 82 in. (208·2 cm.)
The Castle Museum, York

13. The Highlander, early 19th century
height 39 in. (99 cm.)
Rattray Collection

in concealing them, and those which exist today date from after 1786 when the prohibition was lifted. When popular demand led to their reintroduction, they were shown in the costume of the day and many of them are consequently dressed as Officers in Highland Regiments at the time of the Peninsular War in which those Regiments played so active a part.

The more impressive tobacco figures were life-size and stood guard in the doorway of the shop, but many were made on a smaller scale, measuring between two and four feet, and these were placed either over the window or over the door, while some probably stood on the shop counter.

Nearly all tobacco figures were brightly coloured, not only to attract the eye of the passer-by but also to give some protection against the inclemency of the British climate. An exception is the majestic Highlander (Ill. 13) which shows no traces of colouring and is one of the few figures recorded in this state. For this reason it is likely that as with some of the other smaller figures it stood inside rather than outside the shop.

A curious item and in itself a rarity, although not strictly a tobacco figure in the accepted sense, is the snuff pedlar's staff, lately in the Pinto Collection. Just under six feet in height and cut from a single tree fork (Ill. 14), it shows an old woman seated taking a pinch of snuff, an open snuff-box on her knee. The style of the costume would appear to date this staff to the early 19th century and although it is probably the only surviving example, it is not unlikely that such staffs were in fact carried by itinerant pedlars as a mark of their trade.

Who carved these magnificent and appealing relics? It seems probable that they were made by the same craftsmen who carved the strongly modelled figureheads which graced the prows of so many merchantmen and men-of-war of the time, but with the coming of the Industrial Revolution and the gradual replacement of the Wooden Walls of England, there was no longer any call for such effigies; perhaps the same craftsmen who made the nursery rocking-horses and the merry-go-round figures of the Victorian age had a hand in some of the later examples.

Very few tobacco figures are still in use today for the purpose for which they were originally intended, and like the carved ships' figureheads they are mostly in museums or in the hands of private collectors. They are rarely offered for sale on the open market, but when this happens they are eagerly sought after; a recent example of a snuff-taking Highlander from the early 19th century was sold at Sotheby's for $336, and at this price it would be folly indeed for such figures to be left outside a shop-front whence they can be so easily removed.

BIBLIOGRAPHY

Pinto, E. H. *Wooden Bygones of Smoking and Snuff Taking*. Hutchinson, 1961.

I am especially grateful to Mr Charles Rattray of Perth for his help and generosity over the loan of photographs of Tobacco Figures from the Rattray Collection; also for the loan of the notes of a lecture on "Tobacco Trade Figures" given by his father the late Mr Charles Rattray of Perth at Stationers' Hall, London, on 3 March 1937.

My thanks are also due to Mr and Mrs Edward H. Pinto for their interest and encouragement.

14. (right) Snuff Pedlar's Staff, early 19th century
height 70 in. (177·8 cm.)
Pinto Collection

Small-Swords and Military Swords

A. V. B. NORMAN

The classic small-sword hilt of the 18th century has a long and somewhat complicated pedigree. Among its ancestors are the rather light French rapiers of the types illustrated in the engravings of Abraham Bosse (1602–76). For instance, in *The Fan* he illustrates a hilt very similar to that on a sword in the Wallace Collection[1] which has the elongated pommel typical of the period and big functional arms of the hilt supporting on their ends large shells inclined towards the hand, in a manner clearly deriving from the 'Pappenheimer' hilt. This sword has vertically recurved quillons, the front one forming a partial knuckle-guard. A hilt of similar form, but with only one shell, at Rosenborg, bears the initials of Ulrich, youngest son of Christian IV of Denmark, who died in 1633.[2]

1. Rapier with steel hilt; French, *circa* 1630
The Wallace Collection, London

Another ancestor is a long rapier also in the Wallace Collection[3] with blade of triangular section, two large lattice-filled shells, long straight quillons and rather small arms. (Ill. 1.) It resembles very closely a sword illustrated in No. 7 of Bosse's "Le Jardin de la Noblesse Françoise" of 1629, although in this case the arms are absent.

The latest ideas in France on fencing technique, in which speed was the essence of both defence and attack, required a lighter and more manageable sword than these, and another ancestor of the small-sword must therefore be the very light civilian rapier with no other guards except a pair of short, stout quillons (Ill. 2), such as is worn by Frederik III of Denmark in his portrait of 1652 at Frederiksborg Castle.[4] The Waffensammlung at Vienna has a sword of this type with a hilt of crystal, dated on the blade 1647, and another with onyx and enamel hilt, dated on the blade 1664. The majority, however, are less rich, like that of Frederik III of Denmark which is of steel partially overlaid with silver.[5] Today these weapons are usually called 'pillow swords', but the contemporary term was probably 'scarf-sword', presumably because they were often worn on a waist or shoulder sash as in the *Portrait of Claes Hendriksz. de Mett* by Jacob Frans van der Merck (*circa* 1658–64).[6] For instance, James Howell in his "Lexicon Tetraglotton", 1660, XLIV, refers to "A short, or scarf-sword: Spada corta, ó spada da banda".

A heavier version of this hilt was occasionally used in the field, longer in the grip to balance the longer blade and with a side-ring on the outer side of the

[1] *Wallace Collection Catalogues, European Arms and Armour*, 1962, no. A548.

[2] Hoff, A., Schepelern, H. D., and Boesen, G. *Royal Arms at Rosenborg*, I. Copenhagen, 1956, no. 19. Hereafter cited as *Rosenborg*.

[3] Catalogue no. A507.

[4] Schepelern, H. D. "Portræter som Vaabenhistorisk Kilde, II", *Vaabenhistorisk Aarbøger*, VI, 1949–51, pp. 51–73, fig. 2.

[5] Respectively nos. A1591; A1592; and *Rosenborg*, I, no. 26.

[6] Leiden, Stedelijk Museum de Lakenhal, 1949. Catalogue no. 298.

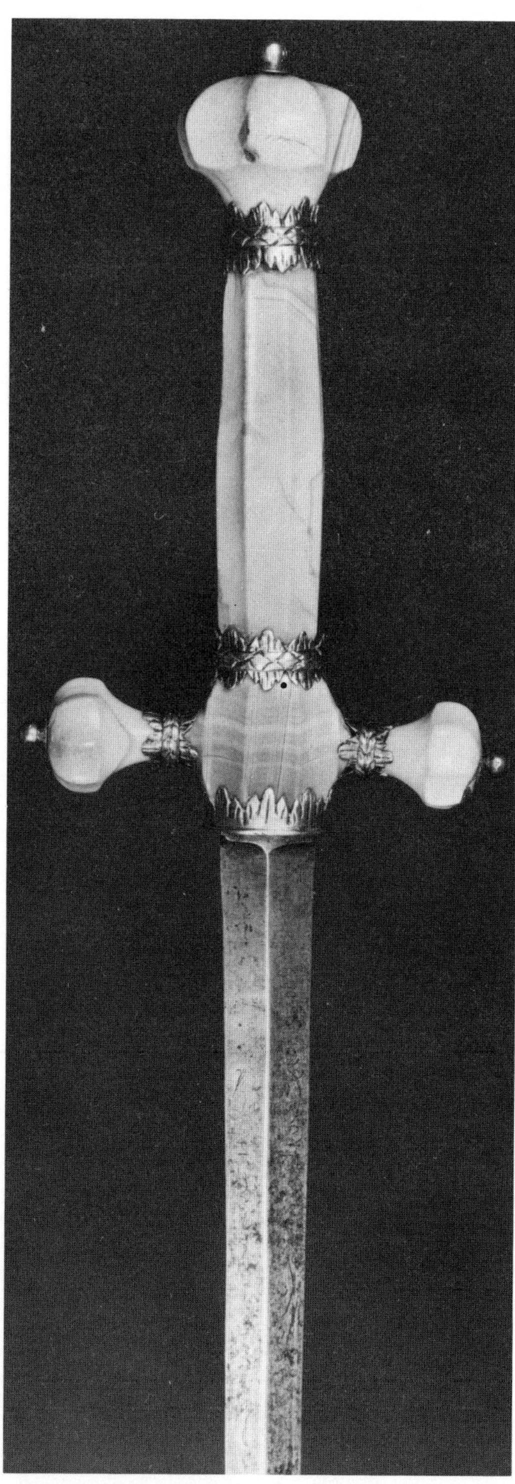

2. Light rapier with hilt of pink, white and cream agate with silver mounts, *circa* 1650 The Victoria and Albert Museum, London

quillons. The portrait of Colonel Russell at Ham House, signed by Michael Wright and dated 1659, shows such a sword almost identical to one made in Denmark in 1648 for Frederik III.[7] The Wallace Collection sword No. A680 with an idealized princely head as a pommel is a parade version in which the quillons are replaced by busts of Mars and Venus and the side-ring by a female bust supported by Cupid.

When Charles X Gustav of Sweden was crowned in 1654 a sword of the very latest fashion was bought for him in Paris.[8] On each side of the blade is a shell only slightly inclined towards the hand, and there are a pair of short quillons and very small arms. The grip is longer than later examples and the pommel heavier to balance the long blade. The hilt is decorated all over with small, equestrian figures in vigorous motion in high relief. A very similar sword at Windsor is said to have been presented to John, 1st Duke of Marlborough.[9] A plain version of this hilt is shown in Philip de Champaigne's portrait of the young Charles II of Great Britain in the Museum of Art, Cleveland, Ohio, which is dated 1653.

Although Sir William Hope of Balcombie writing in 1687 is the first to tell us that the fingers were no longer passed through the arms of the hilt,[10] the portrait of Charles II at Cleveland already has arms too small to accommodate a finger. Since they were no longer necessary a number of swords similar to that of Charles X were made without arms, although the quillons were still well clear of the shells as on a sword in the Wallace Collection[11] and on Prince Rupert's sword in his portrait by Sir Peter Lely of *circa* 1665–66, now at Windsor Castle.

Although none of these swords has a knuckle-guard and Sir William Hope both illustrates and describes a small-sword without this guard in 1687, the completely developed hilt is already illustrated in *The Listening Housewife* by N. Maes in the Wallace Collection which is dated 1656.[12] Once the knuckle-guard became *de rigueur* towards the end of the century it was sometimes added to an old hilt, as on a sword in the Victoria and Albert Museum.[13]

The small-sword hilt once formed, only developed very slowly over the next century, and hilts are datable more easily by their decoration than by their shape. Seventeenth-century swords are usually rather long in the grip, have a knuckle-guard with a rather square profile, and large arms. The shells usually have very pronounced rims. Very early examples have pommels of ovoid or horizontally flattened spherical form, while a little later spherical pommels were popular. Until well into the 18th century the knuckle-guard and the edges of the shells often had twin drop-shaped swellings as on the sword in illustration 4, although these have already disappeared on a sword in the Metropolitan Museum of Art, New York, with a London silver hilt of 1689–90.[14]

In the first half of the 18th century the curve of the knuckle-guard became more flowing, the arms became smaller, the rims to the shells less pronounced, and inverted pear-shaped or egg-shaped pommels were adopted. By the 1750's the arms had in many cases atrophied into little more than tiny claws, as on a silver hilt by John Fayle of Fleet Street with the London date-letter for 1759–60.[15] At

[7] *Rosenborg*, I, no. 24.

[8] Ossbahr, C. A. *Kongl. Lifrustkammaren*, I. Stockholm, 1897, pl. XXVI, 2; Inv. no. 3440.

[9] Laking, G. *The Armoury of Windsor Castle.* London, 1904, no. 59, pl. 8.

[10] *The Scots Fencing-Master.* Edinburgh, 1687, pp. 11–12.

[11] Catalogue no. A685.

[12] *Wallace Collection Catalogues, Pictures and Drawings*, 1928, no. 224.

[13] Registration no. M170–1951.

[14] Dean, B. *Metropolitan Museum of Art, Catalogue of Court Swords and Hunting Swords.* New York, 1929, no. 5, pl. V.

[15] Aylward, J. D. *The Small-Sword in England.* London, 1960, fig. 41.

the same time the front quillon sometimes reappears as on a silver hilt, probably by Joseph Clare, with the London date-letter for 1758–59.[16] This sword also illustrates the beginning of a new fashion; the inlets between the two shells are filled with cockleshell ornament, thus foreshadowing the single oval shell which became popular in the late 1760's. A silver hilt by Stevens of Temple Gate, with the date-letter for 1768–69, has an almost oval shell.[17] This form of shell also appeared in France about this time as on a gold and diamond hilt bought for the coronation of Christian VII of Denmark in 1766,[18] but did not become popular until the 1770's.

3. A Walking sword with chiselled and gilt steel hilt; French, *circa* 1655
The Wallace Collection, London

From the 1760's hilts are usually slimmer in all their parts, often with olive-shaped pommels and very thin guards and grips; there is a tendency for the turn of the knuckle-guard to be slightly sharper above the hand than near the pommel. In England urn-shaped pommels became popular in the 1780's under the influence of Neo-classical taste, but only very slowly ousted the olive shape. In late swords by London makers the place of the arms of the hilt is taken by small badges or laurel wreaths which support the knuckle-bow and quillon or quillons, as on the gold-hilted sword presented by the States of Jersey to General George Don, made in 1809–10 by John Ray and James Montague.[19]

The urn pommel and oval shell were to become standard for English small-swords of the 19th century. In France, however, although hilts continued to be made in traditional form during the first decade of the 19th century, as on the sword of Jérome Bonaparte as King of Westphalia (1807–13) formerly in the Dreger Collection,[20] a new style was also developed. The new taste demanded a single shell, often of pelta shape turned sharply towards the blade and covering the top of the scabbard. The knuckle-guard was frequently stirrup-shaped. Nicolas Noël Boutet, who made Jérome Bonaparte's sword, also made one in the new fashion *circa* 1809 for Joseph Fouché, duc d'Otrante, which is still in the possession of his family.[21] (Ill. 22.)

This style became the most fashionable in Europe for the whole 19th century and was also adopted to a limited extent in Great Britain; for instance, in the full dress sword of the Royal Company of Archers, and in a presentation hilt of 1822 given to Lieutenant-General Sir Samuel Whittingham by the planters of Dominica.[22]

It was probably the rococo desire for asymmetry which led to the increasing popularity in the middle of the 18th century of a previously rare form of shell, heart-shaped and pierced near the upturned point by the fore quillon. It became widespread outside France and a very simple gilt brass version was adopted for the British heavy cavalry, probably in 1796, for wear on certain dismounted duties.[23] It was fitted with a very long spadroon-blade. This sword was also adopted by General Officers and is shown in James Northcote's portrait of Sir John Moore in

16 Tower Armouries, Inventory no. IX, 798.

17 Aylward, *op. cit.*, fig. 43.

18 *Rosenborg*, I, no. 48.

19 Scottish United Services Museum, Acquisition no. 1939–62.

20 Dreger, E. H. M. *Waffensammlung Dreger*. Berlin, 1926, no. 112, pl. 60.

21 Seitz, H. "Quelques armes exquises de la Manufacture de Versailles", *Armes Anciennes*, no. 10, 1958, pp. 65–73, pl. XIII.

22 Sold Sotheby's, London, 30 November 1962, Lot 51, illustrated in catalogue.

23 Sumner, P. "Uniform and Equipment of the Royal Scots Greys", *Journal of the Society for Army Historical Research*, XVI, 1937, p. 49. Major-General Lord Cathcart's Orders, 25 September 1797, quoted by Sir George Arthur in *The Story of the Household Cavalry*, II. London, 1909, pp. 449–501.

Colour Plate I. (right) Gold boat-shell hilt set with diamonds; probably French, *circa* 1750 – it has been remounted, since the blade is decorated in a style typical of the early 19th century and bears the national badges of the Union of 1801
The Royal Collection, Windsor Castle

4. Silver military hilt by Thomas Vicaridge; London, 1705–6
J. M. Wallace Collection

5. Chiselled and gilt steel military hilt; German, *circa* 1750 – the guards open out to form a basket-hilt
The Wallace Collection, London

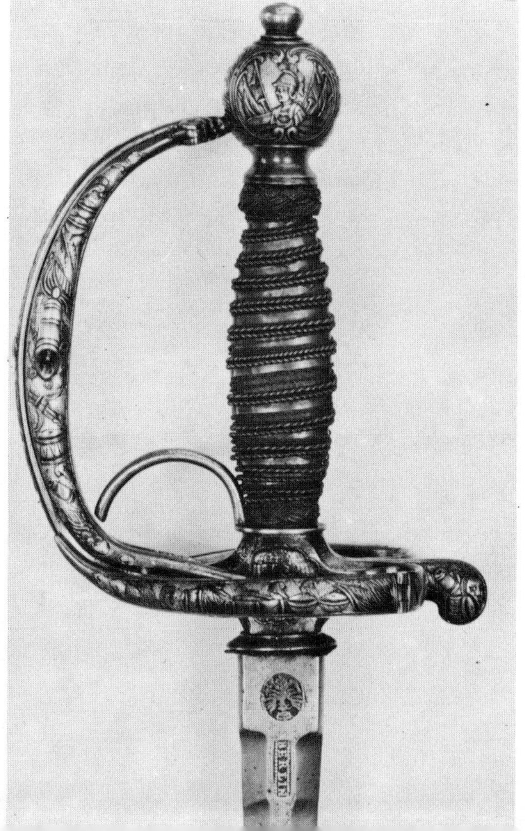

the Scottish National Portrait Gallery, painted *circa* 1801 or 1802. Few have any regimental device, but those of the 2nd Life Guards have blades etched with their initials and badge. The "Dress Regulations" of 1822 describe this sword for all heavy cavalry for full dress, that is, Court dress, as the 1834 Regulations make clear: "gilt guard, pommel and boat shell".

Military swords of the mid-17th century often have hilts with two pierced shells and a knuckle-bow, but no arms or fore quillon, as in Lely's portrait of Charles I and the Duke of York at Syon House, painted in 1647. The hilt continued to be used by military men throughout the 18th century and is illustrated for instance in *A Representation of the Cloathing of his Majesty's Household and of all the Forces upon the Establishments of Great Britain and Ireland*, 1742, while a version of it already in use in the 2nd (or the Queen's Royal) Regiment of Foot, among others, was ordered for all infantry officers in 1796.[24] It had either a spadroon-blade or a two-edged blade of diamond section. The 1st Royal Regiment of Foot had a broad two-edged blade of a special pattern and had their badge on the shells in relief.[25] This sword was replaced in the British Service with a sabre by the "Dress Regulations" of 1822, but elsewhere it still remained popular, for instance the Danish infantry officers' sword of 1837 and the United States non-commissioned officers' sword of 1840.

This form of hilt developed in two ways. Scroll guards were used to link the knuckle-guard and the outer edge of each shell, giving protection to the thumb and knuckles as in Michael Wright's portrait of General Monk dated 1668, at Longleat, and as on a sword with the mark of Thomas Vicaridge with the London date-letter for 1705–6. (Ill. 4.) Alternatively, the knuckle-guard was linked to the outer edge of each shell by a short loop-guard which gave a heart-shape to the hilt when viewed from the point of the blade, as on a finely chiselled and engraved London hilt of 1676–77 in the Victoria and Albert Museum.[26] Sir George Chalmers's portrait of Cornet James Dalrymple in the uniform of 2nd (or Royal North British) Dragoons in which he served from 1749 to 1753 shows a gilt hilt heart-shaped before the hand.[27] About the middle of the 18th century a number of these heart-shaped hilts were made with knuckle-guards which opened up to form a basket-hilt. Steel hilts of this type chiselled with military trophies, bright against a gilt ground, are in the Berne Historical Museum and in the Wallace Collection.[28] (Ill. 5.)

Wootton's portrait of the Duke of Cumberland at the Battle of Laffeldt, at Inveraray, painted in 1747, illustrates a hilt which combines the heart-shaped guard with scroll guards to protect the knuckles. In many swords of this type the place of the shells is taken by small S-shaped bars within the outline of the heart. Illustration 6 shows an example in a private collection, with a silver hilt, decorated in the writhen style of contemporary English small-swords. It bears the London date-letter for 1763–64. Variants of this hilt were used by many British cavalry regiments perhaps as a result of the Duke of Cumberland's order of *circa* 1755: "Neither does His Royal Highness approve of a whole Basket hilt to the Officers and Mens' swords, which deprives them of the use of their right hand in case their Bridles

[24] ffoulkes, C., and Hopkinson, E. C. "Swords of the British Army", *Journal of the Society for Army Historical Research*, XIII, 1934, p. 67.

[25] Norman, A. V. B. "Notes on some Scottish Infantry Swords in the Scottish United Services Museum", *Journal of the Arms and Armour Society*, V, 1965, pp. 4 and 11–12, pl. IV.

[26] Registration no. M153–1937.

[27] Prestonfield House, Midlothian.

[28] Respectively Catalogue nos. 568 and A693.

Colour Plate II. (far right) Small-sword with gold and enamel hilt by James Morisset; London, 1781–2 – presented to Lieutenant-Colonel James Hartley by the Honourable East India Company
The Victoria and Albert Museum, London

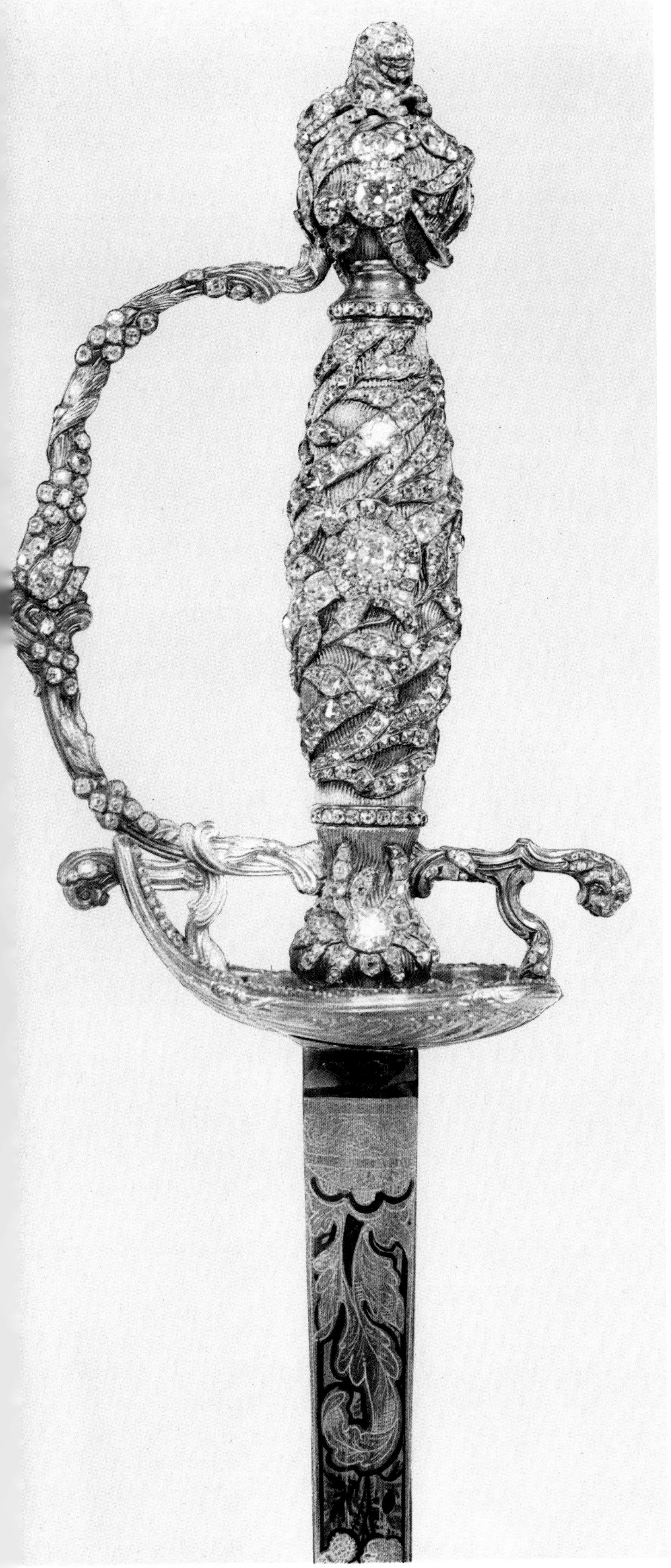

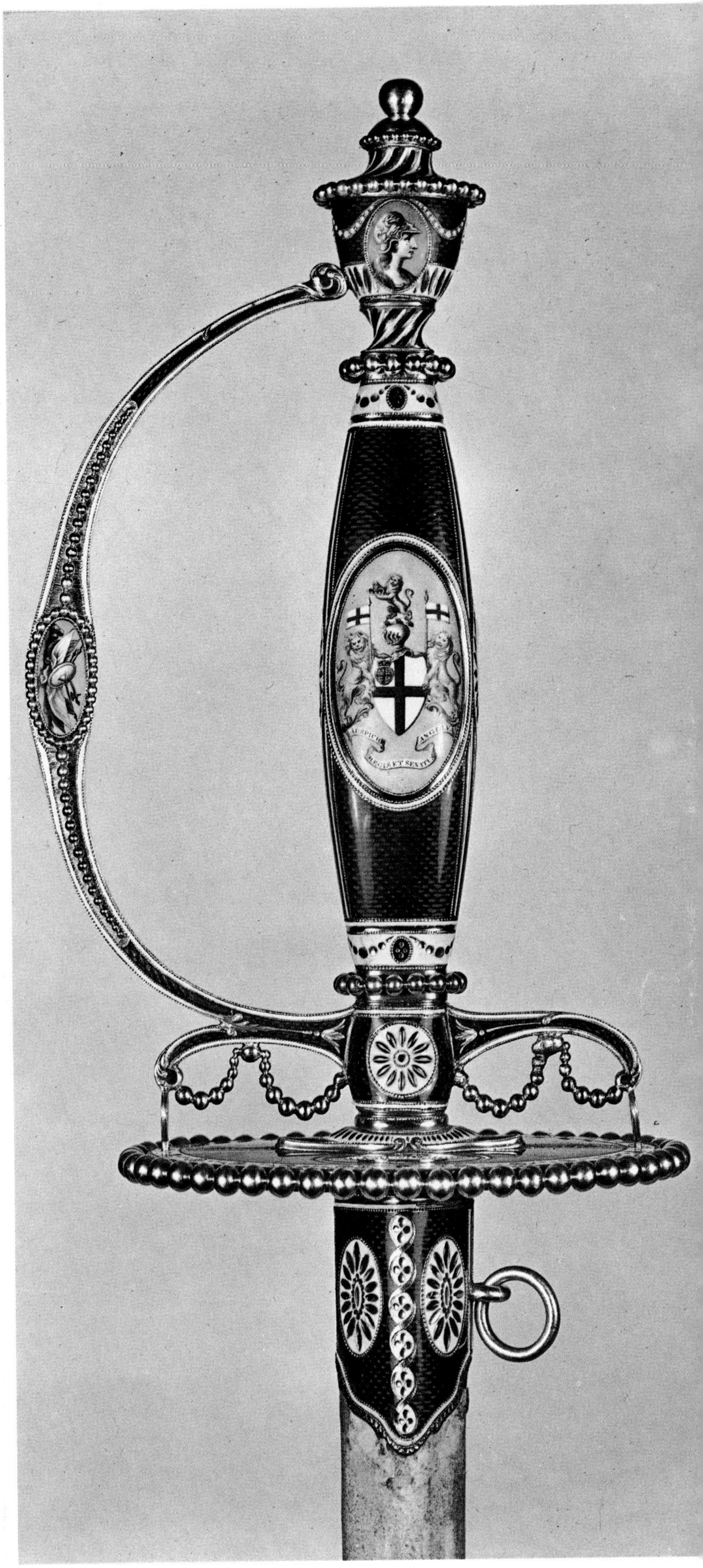

6. Spadroon with silver hilt by James Perry; haftmaker, London 1763–4
Courtesy Sotheby & Co.

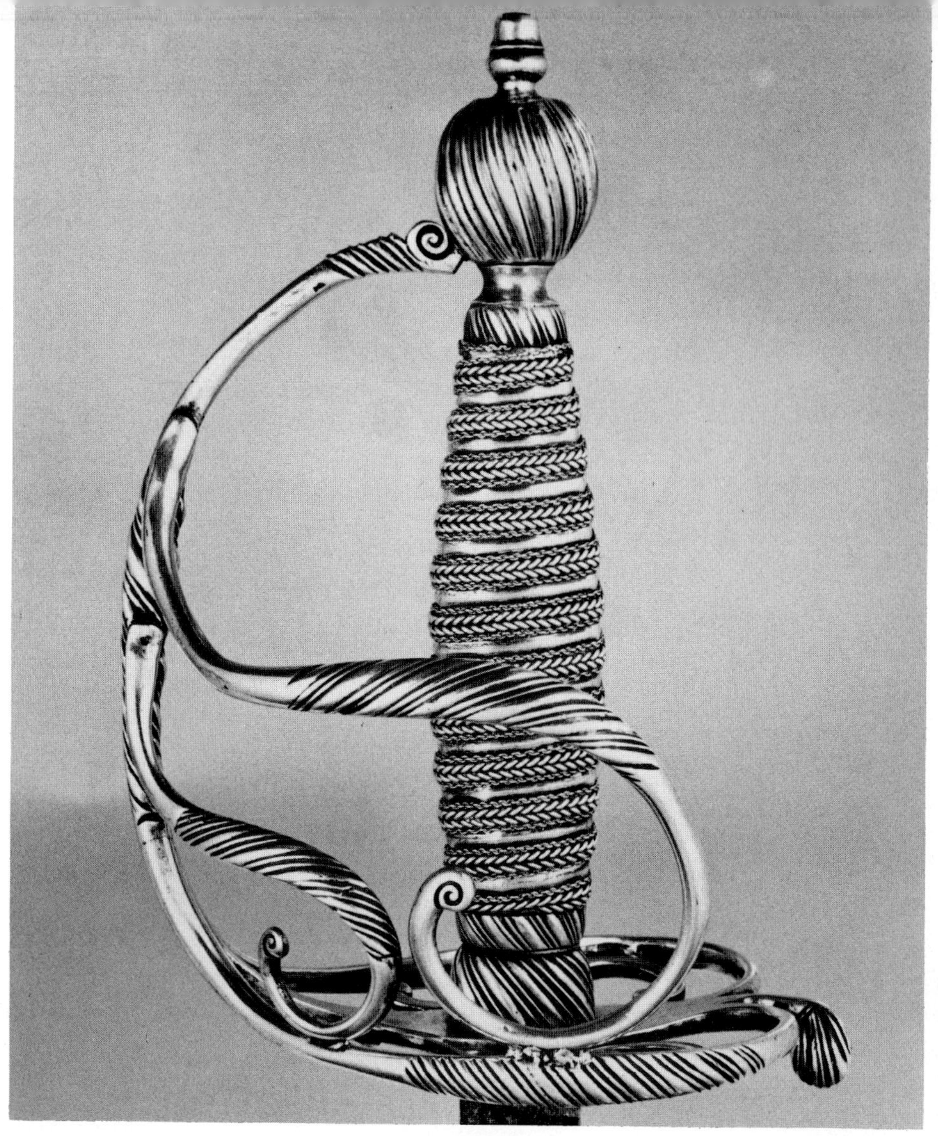

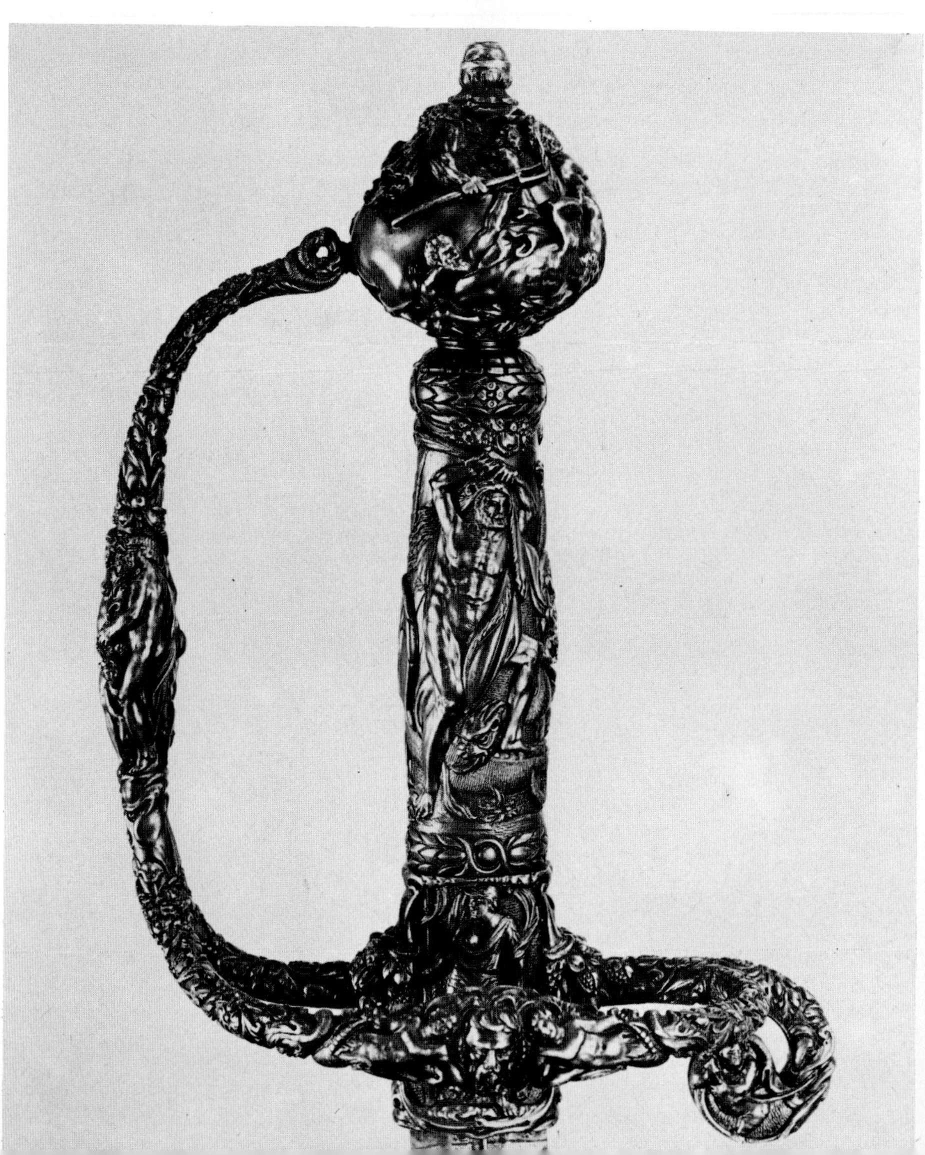

7. Loop-guard hilt of steel chiselled with the Labours of Hercules; possibly French, *circa* 1670
The Victoria and Albert Museum, London

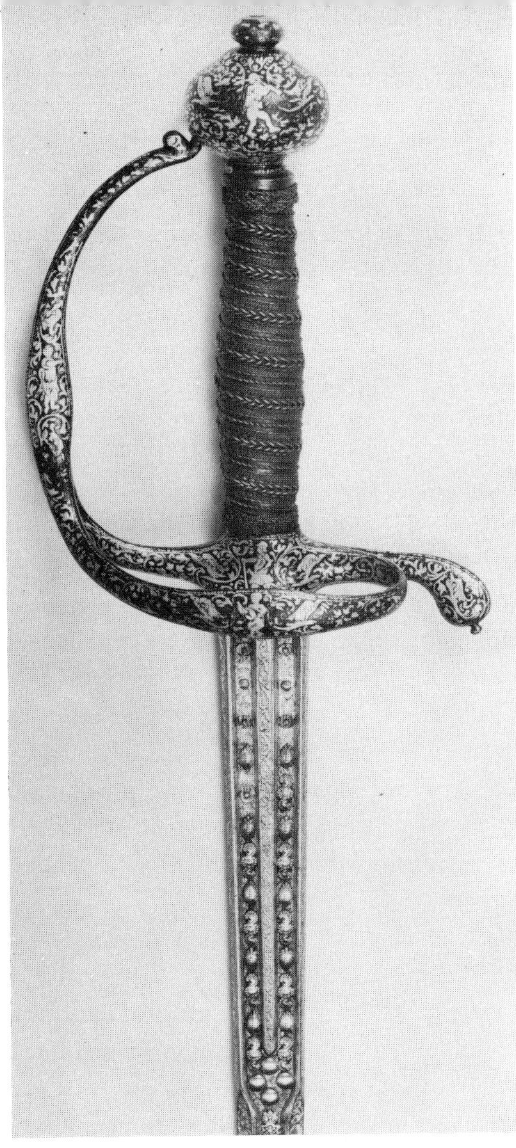

8. Loop-guard hilt of steel counterfeit-damascened with gold; signed "*Au duc d'Orléans*"; French, *circa* 1660
The Wallace Collection, London

are Cut, or broke, and no Officer can possibly Salute well with them."[29] They were used both by cavalry and infantry officers as in Reynolds's portraits of Cornet N. Winter, 11th Dragoons, 1759, and Captain R. Orme, 2nd Regiment of Foot Guards, 1756,[30] and on both straight and curved blades.

As an alternative to the conventional small-sword many people, and British officers in particular, preferred a hilt without arms or shells, but with a single bar branching off the centre of the knuckle-guard and curving round to join the base of the quillon, thus forming a loop in front of the hand on the outside of the hilt. The type is illustrated in a painting by Ter Borch of *circa* 1643 formerly in a Berlin private collection.[31] The pommel is rather pointed and the single quillon long and curled. A sword in the Victoria and Albert Museum illustrates the type, while similar hilts apparently by the same hand are at Windsor and in Roskilde Cathedral.[32] (Ill. 7.) The last came from the grave of Ove Skade of Kærbygaard, who died in 1664. Some early examples have the loop partly guarded by a small shell on the centre of the quillons curving towards the blade, as on a sword in the Wallace Collection.[33] In other cases the loop is entirely filled with a plate, usually decoratively pierced as on the sword of Field-Marshal Carl Gustav Wrangel at Skokloster.[34]

This style of hilt passed through all the decorative phases of the small-sword. One of the swords of Charles X at Stockholm is incised and gilt with classical figures under canopies in the style of Jean Bérain.[35] The portrait of Jacob de Graeff of *circa* 1674 by Ter Borch shows the typical globular pommel and swellings at the centre of the guards as well as the curving, atrophying quillon, typical of the small-sword of the period.[36] A sword in the Wallace Collection of about the third quarter of the century is decorated with gold counterfeit-damascening on a russet ground with small figures amid foliage.[37] (Ill. 8.) Although this hilt is signed "Au duc d'Orléans" the type appears to be rare in France, but common in areas of German influence. For instance, it is illustrated alongside the normal small-sword hilt in J. G. Krünitz, "Oekonomisch-Technologische Encyklopäedie", Berlin, 1777, figs. 458 and 459. The Victoria and Albert Museum have an ormolu hilt of this form with grip of German enamel, and another hilt of chiselled and gilt steel, possibly made at Tula in Russia.[38] The Swedish Royal Collection includes a gold hilt decorated with blue enamel in the most flamboyant rococo taste.[39] Except in England many of the mid-18th-century examples have the centre of the loop flattened out and expanded to form a decorative feature. The sword presented by the young Prince William Henry to Lieutenant Walter Locke, R.N., in 1786 is a restrained silver-gilt version of this hilt in which the loop-guard forms a complete ring.[40] Whereas the majority of loop-guard hilts are fitted with the two-edged

[29] Sumner, P. "Standing Orders for the Dragoons, *circa* 1755", *Journal of the Society for Army Historical Research*, XXIII, 1945, p. 99.

[30] Respectively in Southampton Art Gallery and in the National Gallery, London.

[31] Gudlaugson, S. J. *Gerard Ter Borch*, I. The Hague, 1959, pl. 25.

[32] Respectively Registration no. M659–1910; Laking, *op. cit.*, no. 69; Ada Bruhn, "Sværd og Kaarder i Roskilde Domkirke", *Vaabenhistorisk Aarboger*, VI, 1949–51, fig. 11*a–b*.

[33] Catalogue no. A673.

[34] Seitz, H. *Svärdet och Värjen som Armévapen*. Stockholm, 1955, fig. 94.

[35] Ossbahr, *op. cit.*, I, pl. XXIV, 2.

[36] Gudlaugson, *op. cit.*, pl. 265.

[37] Catalogue no. A671.

[38] Respectively Registration nos. 142–1889 and 1731–1888.

[39] Ossbahr, *op. cit.*, I, pl. XXVI, 6.

[40] Bosanquet, H. T. A. *The Naval Officer's Sword*. London, 1955, no. 61.

blades which contemporary writers advocate for service, Locke's sword has the light back-edged spadroon-blade which was becoming very popular for naval and military officers.

The adoption in *circa* 1773 of a stirrup hilt of East European origin by the British light cavalry, then the *élite* arm of the service, had a profound effect on the military small-sword. Some regiments adopted the true stirrup hilt with a back-plate on the grip curving over the end to replace the pommel. If the loop-guard is present it is parallel to the "Foot of the Stirrup Iron" and flows smoothly into it at each end instead of curling inwards at the rear end. Most examples have faceted steel guards and backplates, but a silver-hilted example with the London date-letter for 1792–93 is in the Tower Armouries.[41] They appear to have been particularly popular among the Irish Volunteer Regiments raised for the French Revolutionary Wars and are also illustrated by Edward Dayes in his prints of the 5th (Northumberland) and 9th (or East Norfolk) Regiments of Foot and probably in that of the 6th (or 1st Warwickshire) Regiment, all of 1792. The Tower Armouries have recently acquired a steel-hilted example with additional scroll guards outside the hand supporting between them as a badge a bugle-horn stringed. The spadroon-blade is etched with the arms and motto of the United States of America.

A more elegant form of the stirrup hilt developed under the new Classical taste. (Ill. 9.) These have horizontally reeded grips, usually of ivory, occasionally of cow-horn or ebony, often encircled by a metal band bearing an oval cartouche engraved with a device or initials. The pommel is usually cushion-shaped but is occasionally urn-shaped. The loop-guard which is almost always present flows into the foot of the stirrup at each end and is usually supported at the centre by a pierced diamond or a badge. The centres of the guards are often decorated with five graduated balls. The majority are mounted in gilt brass, but silver and steel examples are also found.[42]

The earliest recorded example was presented by the Duke of Clarence to L. Hobbs in 1789, while silver hilts with date-letter for 1792–93 and 1793–94 are known. Although best known as the Naval Officers' sword of *circa* 1790 to 1805, they were also carried by the officers of many regular and auxiliary infantry regiments, including the 7th (or Royal Fusiliers), 8th (or King's), 57th (or the West Middlesex), 71st (Highland), 95th (probably the untitled corps of 1794–96), the Buckinghamshire Militia, St James Loyal Volunteers, Oxford University Volunteers, 1st Tower Hamlets Volunteers, Loyal Greenwich Volunteers and all three Regiments of the Royal Edinburgh Volunteers. Sergeant-Major Gould of the Royal Edinburgh Volunteers was painted *circa* 1807 with this sword and the Regiment probably did not change their equipment before their disbandment in 1814. Steel examples occasionally have one or more scroll guards outside the hand.[43] The sword of the St James Volunteers had an ebony grip, gilt brass mounts, and no outer guard.[44]

This sword was adopted by the Navy and some regiments in France and called *à l'Anglais*; it was also used by the Austrian Navy, and the Bavarian forces.[45] One in the Norwegian Army Museum is believed to have been given by King

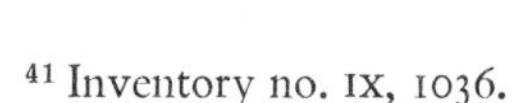

[41] Inventory no. IX, 1036.

[42] May, W. E., "The 5-Ball type of Sword Hilt", *Journal of the Arms and Armour Society*, IV, 1963, pp. 153–56, pl. XLVI; Norman, A. V. B., *loc. cit.*, pp. 1–2, 4 and 6–7.

[43] e.g. a sword sold at Sotheby's, London, 22 March, 1965, Lot 51.

[44] *The Wilkinson Sword Exhibition of Arms & Militaria*. London, 1965, no. 367, illustrated.

[45] e.g. Berne, Historical Museum, Catalogue no. 666.

9. Spadroon with gilt-brass stirrup-hilt and ivory grip, carried by the Royal Edinburgh Volunteers – made by R. Johnston; London, between 1798 and 1814
Sir Ian Forbes-Leith, Bart. Collection, Aberdeenshire

10. Stirrup-hilted spadroon with silver hilt marked CLARK – a swordsmith of this name is recorded at Philadelphia, U.S.A., *circa* 1800
J. M. Wallace Collection

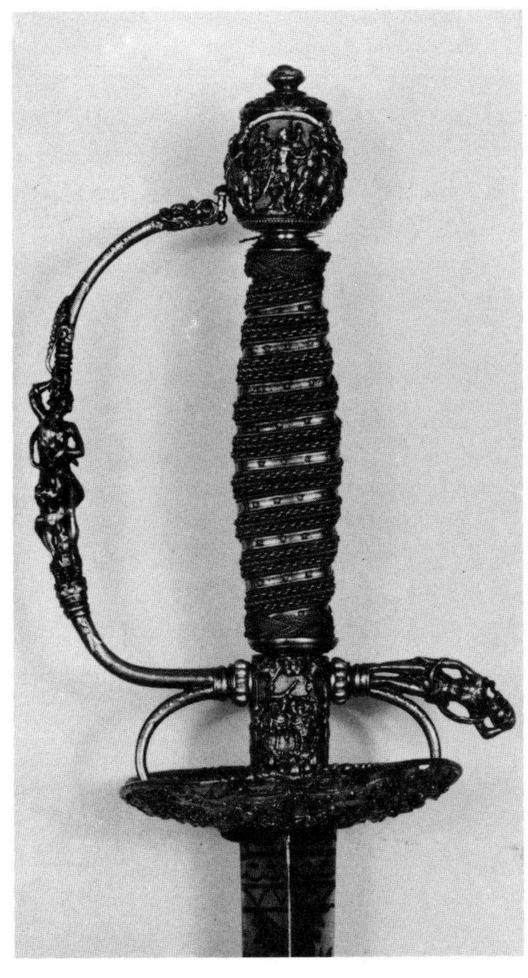

11. Small-sword with chiselled and gilt steel hilt decorated with scenes from the history of Alexander the Great – the hilt French, *circa* 1670; scabbard mounts *circa* 1750; the blade redecorated *circa* 1800
The Wallace Collection, London

12. Drawing for small-sword shells attributed to C. Eisen; French, *circa* 1760
Sven Gahlin Collection

Christian Frederik to his equerry Major Brock in 1814.[46] In the United States of America this hilt, very often with a pommel in the form of an eagle's head, was popular during the years between 1790 and 1840, both for infantry and artillery officers. (Ill. 10.) They are usually of brass or gilt but a silver example was made by Geer Terry of Enfield and Worcester, Mass., *circa* 1800.[47] The reeded grip, cartouche and urn pommel are also found with a curved knuckle-guard and a single scroll guard as on the walking-out swords of the 78th (Highland) Regiment of Foot before 1796.

Since the sword formed an essential part both of uniform and of fashionable dress, its decoration followed the changing dictates of contemporary taste. Probably the very finest were specially designed and were the work of medallists, like the sword in the Wallace Collection illustrating the history of Alexander with minute figures in such high relief that on the pommel they are almost free-standing.[48] (Ill. 11.) The gold hilts made as presents for the wedding of Louis XV in 1725 were designed by Juste Aurèle Meissonnier (1693–1750), and two original drawings for shells decorated with military scenes, attributed to C. Eisen (1720–78), are in the collection of Mr Sven Gahlin. (Ill. 12.) For more ordinary hilts ornament was probably taken from the design book of gunsmiths and jewellers. The motifs of the former could be adopted to cover the shells and pommels, while the latter often included one or two drawings of complete hilts among other objects.[49] In fact, no hilts are so far recorded which exactly copy any of the published designs, but the decoration of busts amid fine strapwork and foliage published early in the 18th century by Johann Jacob Baumgartner of Augsburg is closely paralleled by a silver hilt in the Metropolitan Museum of Art, New York.[50] (Ill. 13.)

Mid-17th-century hilts are either severely plain or, like the coronation sword of Charles X, are covered with cavalry battles in high relief framed by baroque strapwork and foliage. Others are chiselled with medal-like portraits, as on the early hilt in the Tower Armouries with the head of a young prince and on another at Windsor with portraits of members of the house of Brandenburg.[51] The quillons are often chiselled in the round with human figures or hermes. When the knuckle-guard is present the central swelling is in the form of fighting figures.

Later 17th-century hilts are sometimes chiselled all over with lush, baroque acanthus foliage occasionally inhabited by tiny figures.[52] (Ill. 14.) The similarity to the chiselling of northern Italian gun mounts shows that these hilts must have been made in the same area if not by the same craftsmen. Northern European hilts tend to be less ornate; the acanthus foliage is usually confined to the knob of the knuckle-guard, the quillon block, the end of the quillon, the top and bottom of the pommel, and parts of the shell, as on an elegant gold and enamel hilt made by Joannes Kalkoen of Amsterdam *circa* 1670.[53]

Hilts of the last quarter of the 17th century and the first half of the 18th century

[46] Holm, T. "Hærmuseet 1860–1960", *Hærmuseet Akershus, Årbok*. Oslo, 1960, pp. 9–84, illustrated on p. 63.

[47] Peterson, H. *The American Sword, 1774–1945*. New Hope, Pennsylvania, 1954, p. 220, no. 180.

[48] Catalogue no. A687.

[49] Hayward, J. F. "The Origin of Small-sword Ornament", *Apollo*, XLVIII, 1948, pp. 33–35, 86–88, 103–4 and 107; XLIX, 1949, pp. 76–78 and 80.

[50] Dean, B., *op. cit.*, no. 43, pl. XXXIII.

[51] Respectively Inventory no. IX.1012, and Laking, *op. cit.*, no. 58.

[52] An example of each of these styles can be seen in the Victoria and Albert Museum, respectively Registration nos. M17–1956 and M71–1947.

[53] Victoria and Albert Museum, Registration no. M60–1947.

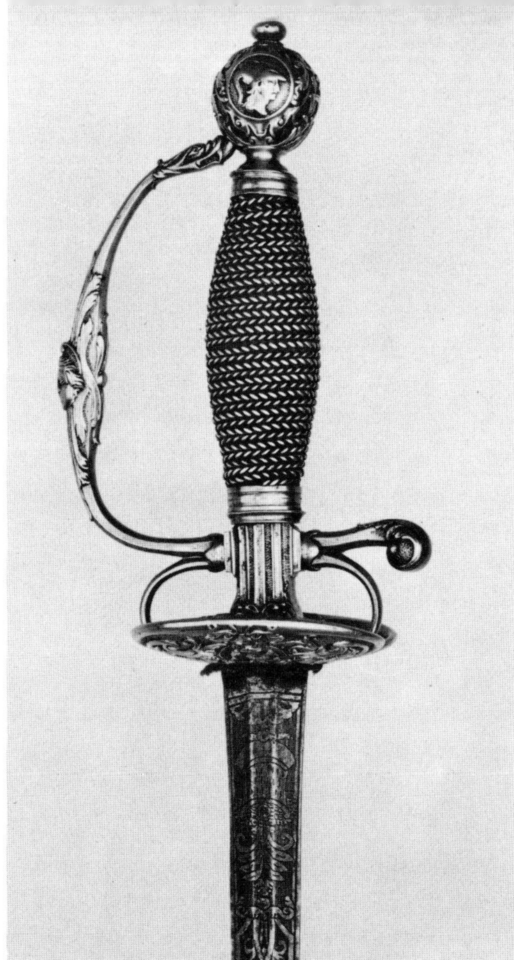

13. Small-sword with silver hilt probably based on the designs of Johann Jacob Baumgartner of Augsburg; first quarter of the 18th century
The Metropolitan Museum of Art, New York (Gift of Jean Jacques Renbell, 1926)

14. Small-sword with chiselled steel hilt; North Italian, late 17th century
The Victoria and Albert Museum, London

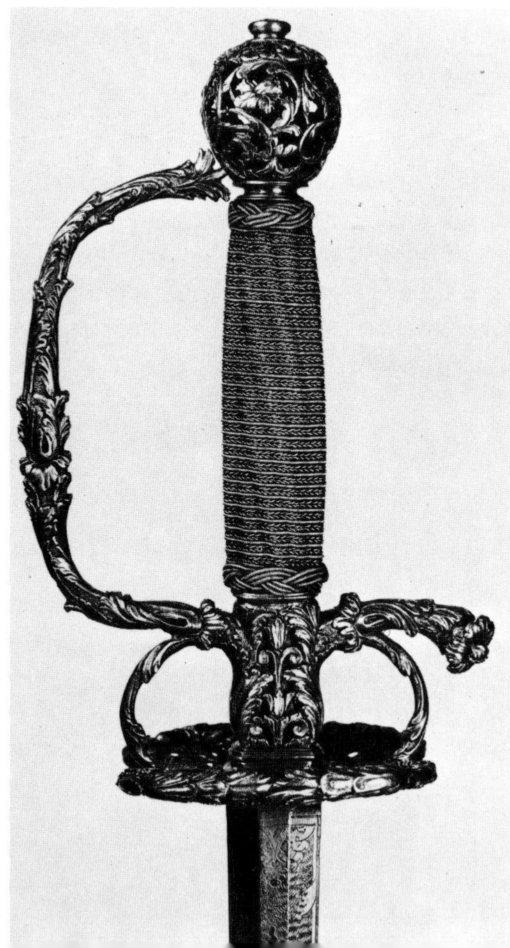

are often encrusted with gold on a black or russet ground with small figures amid strapwork and foliage. The inspiration for the figures, often in Classical dress and under canopies, is clearly the work of Jean Bérain. His influence is still seen clearly on a miniature sword of *circa* 1730 in the Wallace Collection on which figures symbolic of the Arts and Sciences are surrounded by Bérainesque strapwork, swags and canopies which mingle with rococo shells and an unusual wave-like motif.[54] (Ill. 15.)

The earliest record of the application of rococo decoration to sword hilts is the two pages of designs by Meissonnier for the wedding of Louis XV.[55] The metal grips are surrounded with spirals of flutes and flowers or clouds. Only the decoration of the quillon blocks shows any marked tendency to asymmetry. None of these swords has apparently survived, but a hilt decorated with diamonds in the Residenz at Munich is in much the same style.[56] The Metropolitan Museum of Art has a hilt with the Paris date-letter for 1736–37, with high rococo decoration of shells, animals, foliage and, on the grip, a waterfall.[57] On the other hand a hilt of the first quality chiselled with heads based on medals, amid purely symmetrical strapwork and showing no trace of the rococo was made between 1737 and 1745.[58]

The most flamboyant rococo designs are those published by Jeremias Wachsmuth of Augsburg about the middle of the century. In these the whole hilt is made up of completely abstract shell-like flutings, the shells have become almost a single square plate and the knuckle-guard and arms are completely asymmetrical in shape. A solid gold hilt of this type but with decoration including figures in Classical dress is in the Metropolitan Museum of Art, while a diamond-studded sword, later used by George IV and now at Windsor, is of related design.[59] (See colour plate facing p. 216.) Judging by the garnitures surviving at Dresden these jewelled hilts formed part of a set of costume jewelry all with matching stones. In some cases the whole hilt is made of semi-precious stone set with jewels.

The search for colour contrast also led to the use of grips of painted enamel or porcelain, a fashion apparently particularly popular in the German lands; blued steel was encrusted with flamboyant sprays of flowers in silver and golds of various colours, and in one extreme case the hilt was mounted with tortoiseshell *piquée* with gold.[60]

The more usual rococo hilts are of conventional form but decorated with foliage, scrolls, hunting scenes and trophies of war, music, love and the chase. The source of much of this decoration has still to be traced, but among those used equally by gunmakers and hilt-makers were the designs which Giles de Marteau added to the *Nouveaux dessins d'Arquebuseries* of de Lacollombe between 1730 and 1749, C. Huet's *Trofées de Chasse*, before 1741, the *Divers sujets de Chasse* of Viriclix, *Ier Cayer de Trophées*, by J. Juillet, 1768, and de Marteau's engravings of animals after the drawings of Charles Dagommer. Most important of all were the groups of animals by J. B. Oudry, including the *Recueil de divers animaux de chasse* and the series he himself engraved in 1725, which were both freely plagiarized by the makers of later designs and were still used on gun mounts in the 19th century

[54] Catalogue no. A688.

[55] *Oeuvre de Juste Aurèle Meissonnier*. Paris, n.d. 8me livre, pls. 51 and 52.

[56] Brunner, H. "Die Waffen in der Schatzkammer der Residenz München, Fortsetzung", *Waffen- und Kostümkunde*, 1960, pp. 101–10, fig. 2.

[57] Dean, B., *op. cit.*, no. 51, pl. XL.

[58] Buttin, C. "Epée à garde d'acier ciselée de medaillons sur fond d'or", *Arethuse*. April 1925.

[59] Respectively Dean, B., *op. cit.*, no. 70, pl. LIII, and Laking, *op. cit.*, no. 27.

[60] Dean, B., *op. cit.*, no. 47, pl. XXXVII.

15. Small-sword with chiselled and gilt steel hilt decorated in the style of Jean Bérain; French, *circa* 1730
The Wallace Collection, London

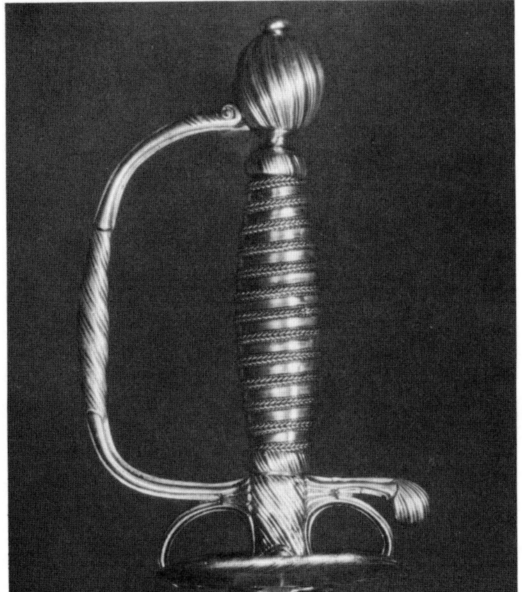

16. Small-sword with silver hilt; London, 1750–1
The Victoria and Albert Museum, London

17. Small-sword with gold hilt decorated with blue and grisaille enamels; Paris, between 1783 and 1789
The Royal Collection, Windsor Castle

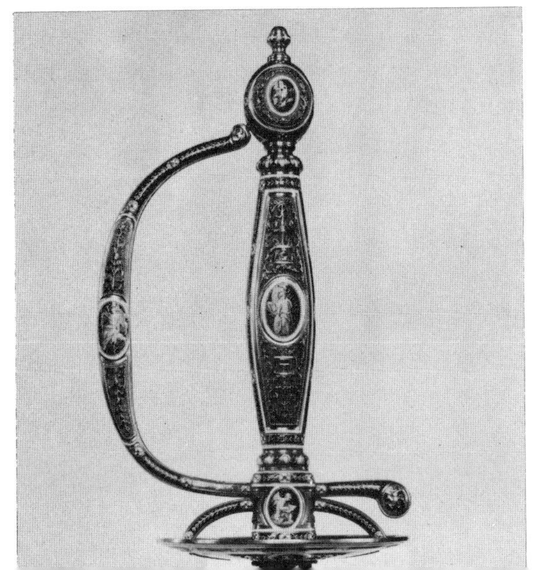

A pleasant, restrained rococo hilt with pommel, guards and the rims of the shells writhen was particularly popular in England. Identical silver hilts are found by different makers and with date-letters in the 1750's and early 1760's. (Ill. 16.) A sword with hilt of this type, with the London date-letter for 1753–54, is preserved at Mount Vernon, Virginia, as the weapon carried by Colonel Washington when A.D.C. to Major General Braddock in 1755.

Rococo decoration remained fashionable in some circles until *circa* 1770, and two silver hilts with Paris date-letters for 1768–69 in the Metropolitan Museum are still in this style.[61]

The decoration of French hilts in the 1770's and 1780's consists usually of low-relief chiselling or encrusting with silver and gold with a variety of trophies suspended by bows of ribbons often in cartouches, rows of husks and laurel or palm sprays. (Ill. 17.) The background is very often a pierced trellis with a small flower at each intersection. Figures, when present, tend to be small and delicate and usually single. A hilt in the new taste, with the Paris date-letter for 1769–70, has the guards and rims of the shells chiselled with closely overlapping laurel leaves, the centre of each side of the pommel, of the shells of the knuckle-guard and of the quillon block decorated with an Apollo head on a sunburst, and the remainder of the hilt pierced with a delicate floral trellis.[62]

One group, perhaps designed by the same man but clearly executed by different craftsmen, has small military figures – heavy cavalry, hussars, light dragoons, grenadiers, musicians and battalion privates – all carefully distinguished and probably based on drawings by Charles Parrocel (1688–1752). (Ill. 18.) There is still a slight hint of the rococo in the floral sprays on the guards of these hilts, but they can be dated by a silver-gilt example with Paris marks of 1786–89. The majority are of steel with the decoration bright or blue on a gilded ground. One in the Wallace Collection is picked out in gold of different colours (Ill. 19), while another, possibly a sword of Louis XVI, is entirely of ivory.[63]

English hilts of the second half of the 18th century were usually rather differently decorated. Many are of steel finely chiselled and pierced with lace-like scrolls, sometimes almost resembling filigree. These can be dated by nearly identical hilts in silver such as one in the Victoria and Albert Museum with the London date-letter for 1752–53.[64] General Washington is shown wearing a sword of this type with his uniform as Commander-in-Chief painted by Charles Willson Peale in 1780 and now in the Metropolitan Museum of Art. A silver hilted sword by Feesey of Pall Mall, London, believed to have belonged to Washington, and now preserved at Mount Vernon, is probably the very weapon shown in this portrait. The decoration of this type of hilt occasionally includes rows of small pyramids probably in imitation of diamond or paste jewels, as for example the hilt of 1758–59 in the Tower, mentioned above, and on a hilt by John Fayle with the London date-letter for 1759–60.[65] The fashion was seized upon by the versatile Matthew Boulton of Soho, Birmingham, who produced hilts of cut steel of very hard temper faceted all over and highly burnished. Two pages of his pattern drawings of hilts survive. The first showing hilts with oval pommels is dated 1775, which is confirmed by a very similar silver-hilted sword in the

[61] Respectively Dean, B., *op. cit.*, nos. 65 and 74, pls. L and LVI.

[62] Dean, B., *op. cit.*, no. 75, pl. LVII.

[63] Respectively Dean, B., *op. cit.*, no. 87, pl. LXV; Catalogue no. A691; Dean, B., *op. cit.*, no. 93, frontispiece and pl. LXX.

[64] Registration no. 1734–1888.

[65] Aylward, *op. cit.*, fig. 41.

18. Small-sword with gold hilt chiselled with military figures – one of three similar hilts in the Royal Collection – mounted by Lecourt, Fourbisseur du Roy, Paris, *circa* 1785
The Royal Collection, Windsor Castle

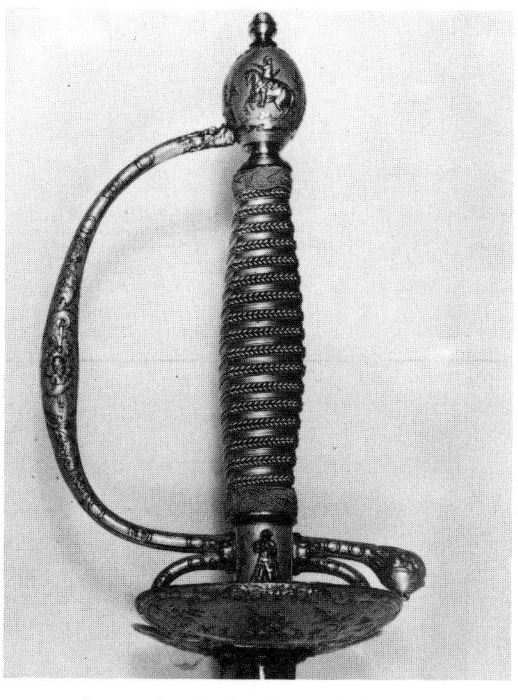

19. Small-sword with chiselled and gilt steel hilt decorated with small military figures; French, *circa* 1785
The Wallace Collection, London

20. Small-sword with silver hilt; London, 1776–7
The Victoria and Albert Museum, London

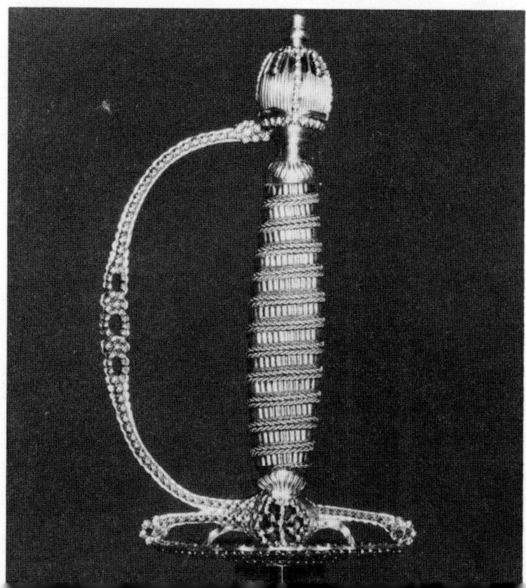

Victoria and Albert Museum with the London date-letter of 1776–77.[66] (Ill. 20.) The second sheet consists entirely of urn pommel hilts with oval shells faceted and fluted all over in Neo-classical taste. This became the standard type of small-sword for civilian Court wear in Great Britain thereafter. Occasionally small Wedgwood cameos were set in the metal, as in another sword in the Victoria and Albert Museum.[67]

Hilts, either totally enamelled or inset with enamelled cartouches, were particularly popular for presentation swords in England at the end of the century. The best-known groups are those made by James Morisset, and John Ray and James Montague. The underside of the oval shell is usually undecorated and engraved with an inscription. Morisset certainly made presentation swords for the Honourable East India Company (see colour plate facing p. 216), and it seems likely that either he or Ray and Montague made the very rich enamelled Katars at Windsor and in the Wallace Collection, presumably for presentation by the Company to Indian princes.[68]

A number of hilts are known made of blued steel decorated by Indian craftsmen with gold inlay of flowers or Oriental palaces set in gardens in a style found on North Indian weapons. Conventional hilts as well as those with oval and boat-shell guards occur. Scabbard mounts occur so blades must have been exported to India for mounting, but as some bear English cutlers' names they were presumably re-exported for sale in England.[69]

At a later date a magnificent small-sword with gold hilt brilliantly enamelled in white, green and red, was made at Jeypore, and presented to the future Edward VII during his visit to India in 1875–76. It is of the type with a single shell overlapping the top of the locket.[70]

Japanese craftsmen were also employed to make hilts for the European market; these were made of the black alloy of copper and gold called *shakudo*, and partly gilded. The decoration usually consists of small flowers or plants in purely Japanese taste. The form of some hilts and the presence of mouldings encircling the centre of the knuckle-bow and the roots of the guards at the quillon block suggest that they are early 18th century. The Victoria and Albert Museum, however, has a hilt of the most advanced rococo taste with boat-shell and asymmetrical knuckle-bow.[71] The fact that it was mounted by Jan Hosse of Amsterdam tends to confirm that this group of hilts was made for the Dutch East India Company, possibly in their factory at Deshima in Japan. Several of these hilts have the archaic feature of the knuckle-bow screwed to the pommel. That this is not a sign of early date is shown by its appearance on the rococo hilt just mentioned.

Sword knots to prevent the weapon being lost in action are occasionally illustrated in the late 16th century, but by the second half of the 17th century the hilt of walking swords was very often decorated with a large ribbon wound round the knuckle-guard with the heavily fringed ends hanging well below the hilt, as in the engravings of A. Trouvaine (1656–1708). The ends were sometimes knotted up into a great bow. Sword knots were worn or discarded at different periods throughout the 18th century according to the whims of fashion. In the second half of the century almost all regimental swords had knots, usually of silver or gold

[66] Registration no. 1724–1888.

[67] Registration no. 1735–1888.

[68] Respectively Inventory no. 2237 and Catalogue no. O1423.

[69] e.g. Aylward, *op. cit.*, fig. 18.

[70] Clarke, C. P. *Catalogue of the Collection of Indian Arms at Marlborough House.* London, 1891, no. 118, colour plate.

[71] Registration no. 1736–1888.

21. Small-sword with cut steel hilt mounted by Thomas Gray of Sackville Street, London, *circa* 1800
The Royal Collection, Windsor Castle

22. Small-sword with gold and lapis lazuli hilt by Nicholas Noël Boutet – made for the Duc d'Otrante, *circa* 1809
Castle of Elghammar, Sweden

lace, and there is almost always a ring at the pommel end of the knuckle-bow to attach the knot. Some English cut-steel hilts have sword knots made of strings of cut-steel beads *en suite* with the hilt. (Ill. 21.) Two French hilts even reproduced in steel the great bow on the front end of the grip, a fashion which M. Moreau le jeune illustrates in "La Grande Toilette" in "Monuments du Costume", Neuwied sur le Rhin, 1789.[72]

Sir William Hope, who uses the names small-sword or rapier indiscriminately, describes three kinds of blades for thrusting – "the *Rapier*, *Königsberg*, and Narrow *Three-Cornered Blade*, which is the most proper Walking Sword of all Three, being by far the lightest". However, he advocates a light two-edged shearing-sword for practical use since it can also be used for cutting.[73] Most of the early hilts discussed are fitted with long narrow blades of diamond section with a long fuller on each side often marked with the maker's name. The long grip and rather large pommel of early hilts were required to balance this type of blade. The hollow-ground triangular section blade was known from the early 16th century at least, but only came into general use gradually. Its stiffness and lightness make it an ideal blade for swift thrusting, and yet it is strong enough to use for a firm parry.

The plates of the article "Fourbisseur" in Diderot's "Encyclopédie" illustrate the kind of blades used *circa* 1755; two are of flattened diamond section, two of flattened hexagonal section; four are two-edged with fullers, and four are triangular. Two of these last are heavily reinforced near the hilt. The article on fencing advised the flat blade for use in the army both for horse and foot. Many small-swords are fitted with two-edged blades sometimes reinforced near the hilt, but those of triangular section are the most common. Henry Blackwell, writing in 1705, recommends German blades as the best and gives the length as thirty-six inches, which is longer than most blades of the period. John McArthur, writing in 1780, advises a blade length of thirty-one inches, and there is a general tendency for blades to be lighter as time goes by. The poor quality of military blades is perhaps explained by the Duke of Cumberland's orders mentioned above which continue "no Officer is supposed ever to Fight himself, anymore than to defend his Head, his business is to see the Men fight and do well; that's sufficient".

Blades are usually etched and gilt on the forte with strapwork, scrolls, foliage sprays, coats of arms and figures of heroes or figures symbolic of virtues. German blades, which were by far the most popular, are often signed by their maker. One group of double-edged blades is etched all over and has the fuller set with small silver studs (Ill. 8), and in one case with pearls and corals. In the second half of the century the gilding was often set off against a ground of rich blue oxide. About 1800 line etching gave way to the removal of broad areas by acid, leaving the design in low relief, and the accentuating of the design by contrasting frosted and bright steel, and blue and gold. (See colour plate facing p. 216.) The full effect of this work is seen not on small-sword blades but on the sabres of light dragoon type which now became popular for presentation swords.

[72] Respectively Dean, B., *op. cit.*, no. 96, pl. LXXIII; *Hallwylska Sammlingen; Beskrivande Förteckning. Grupperna XXXIV och XXXV.* Stockholm, 1926, Group XXXIV, v. b. 25.
[73] *A New Short and Easy Method of Fencing.* Edinburgh, 1707, p. 200.

The author would like to thank Mr A. Grimwade for identifying the maker of the hilt in illustration 6, and Mr H. L. Peterson for his suggestion as to the maker of the hilt in illustration 10. The author is especially grateful to Mr C. Blair for his invaluable help and advice.

The Minor Pre-Raphaelites

RICHARD ORMOND

The Pre-Raphaelites have always aroused interest, and the major figures of the movement, Hunt, Millais and Rossetti, have been the subject of much critical and biographical study. The story of the founding of the Pre-Raphaelite Brotherhood in 1848 and of its subsequent development is well known, but many of the lesser Pre-Raphaelite figures have remained in relative obscurity, not always deserved. In fact, extensive research into the lives and works of most of the Pre-Raphaelite associates and followers is long overdue. This essay cannot pretend to be anything more than a general survey, within arbitrary limits, and is intended to give some idea of Pre-Raphaelite influence in its broadest context.

Although the Pre-Raphaelite Brotherhood was founded in a spirit of revolt against established values in art, it was not trying to emulate the archaisms of early Italian art, as its name might imply. The early Pre-Raphaelites were primarily reacting against a debased, 18th-century academic tradition and the triviality of the popular genre school. They had vague, and often confused ideas of founding a new art, where a direct study of nature would enhance the reality of their poetic subjects. Their early works, inspired by the Bible, literary sources like Dante, Shakespeare and Keats, and the contemporary world, were characterized by brilliant, jewelled colours, and the minute rendering of observed detail. This fusion of poetic sentiment with such an astonishingly realistic technique produced a few works of genuine intensity, where the setting for the figures, often in a landscape, both echoes and complements the emotion of the subject. Such works as Millais's *Christ in the House of his Parents*, 1850 (Tate Gallery, London), Hunt's *Early Britons Sheltering a Missionary from the Druids*, 1850 (Ashmolean Museum, Oxford) or Rossetti's *The Girlhood of Mary Virgin*, 1849 (Tate Gallery), have an uncompromising adherence to actuality, within the terms of their subject, and a stark, even awkward, simplicity which is entirely effective. It was because the Victorians were used to idealized renderings of such subjects that contemporary critics attacked the early works of the Pre-Raphaelites with such extraordinary virulence from 1850 onwards. The discovery too that these young painters had joined together in a mysterious and sinister Brotherhood (they signed their early pictures, 'P.R.B.') gave weight to the belief that there was a conspiracy to undermine true artistic values.

The Brotherhood itself was really formed through the enthusiasm of Rossetti, who, though a less technically proficient painter than Hunt or Millais, was more intelligent and imaginative. It was he who invited his brother, William Michael Rossetti, Thomas Woolner and James Collinson to join the Brotherhood (Hunt invited Frederic Stephens) in order to enlarge its scope and importance. Sir John Everett Millais (1829–96) was sceptical of the value of these new recruits

1. (above) *Mother and Child, circa* 1848, by Frederic Stephens
oil on canvas 18½×25¼ in. (46·9×64·1 cm.)
The Tate Gallery, London

2. (below) *The Italian Image Boys at a Roadside Alehouse*, 1849, by James Collinson
oil on panel 44×31 in. (117·6×78·7 cm.)
Brooks Collection

3. Study for the oil painting *The Renunciation of Queen Elizabeth of Hungary*, 1850, by James Collinson
pen and ink 12×17¾ in. (30·4×45 cm.)
The City Museum and Art Gallery, Birmingham

although their work gave promise of future excellence, and they were enthusiastically admitted. The Brotherhood itself was not unlike an undergraduate society, meeting once a week, but lacking any of the communal sense of purpose that its name might imply. While the members criticized and commented on each other's paintings, and discussed artistic theories in general, they were equally ready to discuss any other topic, or merely to give vent to their high spirits. Their only collective effort was the publication in 1850 of four numbers of their magazine, "The Germ", an expression of the literary preoccupations of the group. It must be remembered that the influence of Pre-Raphaelitism was never confined to pictorial art, but had wide repercussions on the whole aesthetic and cultural climate of the later 19th century. By 1852 the Brotherhood as such had broken up, and would probably not have been heard of again if three of its members had not been highly gifted painters.

The lesser members of the Pre-Raphaelite Brotherhood did not, in the event, live up to their early promise. William Rossetti (1829–1919) soon gave up any pretence of artistic activity, and settled down as the secretary of the group. He later became an influential literary and art critic, and after his brother's death in 1882 edited and wrote several important books about him and Pre-Raphaelitism in general. Frederic Stephens (1828–1907) also became an art critic, as well as an art historian, but he did produce a few early paintings. While most of those that survive are rather crude and immature, his *Mother and Child* (Ill. 1) has a typical Pre-Raphaelite quality of detached observation, and an almost hypnotic rendering of detail, which give the painting a frozen quality of truth. Stephens, suffering like Charles Collins from an over-critical attitude to his own work, ceased to paint after 1850, and destroyed many of his early pictures.

The influence of Pre-Raphaelitism on a minor talent is well illustrated in the case of James Collinson (1825–81). A somewhat somnolent character, and the butt for several Pre-Raphaelite practical jokes, he was engaged for a short time to Christina Rossetti. His *Italian Image Boys* (Ill. 2),[1] which has only recently come to light, and is one of the few Pre-Raphaelite works actually signed 'P.R.B.', was probably begun in the early part of 1848, before Collinson had felt the full influence of his colleagues. Essentially a genre work in the manner of Wilkie, with its dark interior

[1] I must express my thanks to the previous owner of this picture, Mr Taylor, who not only provided me with a photograph, but allowed me to publish it.

Colour Plate. *February in the Isle of Wight*, 1866, by John Brett
watercolour and body colour 15⅝×13½ in. (40×34·2 cm.)
The City Museum and Art Gallery, Birmingham

and absence of any dramatic action or poignant emotion, the only evidence of Pre-Raphaelite influence is in the wealth of detail displayed throughout the work. Much more Pre-Raphaelite in spirit is Collinson's *Queen Elizabeth of Hungary* (Johannesburg Art Gallery), started the following year, where the saint is shown kneeling at the foot of a cross, renouncing her earthly honours and possessions. The subject has just that quality of dramatic intensity so dear to the Pre-Raphaelite pictorial imagination, but which in the hands of a weaker talent like Collinson's has a slightly strained and artificial character. The treatment of the subject and its execution are a little wooden, like the study for the finished painting (Ill. 3), with its almost mechanical outlines and stiff gestures. In 1850 Collinson returned to the Roman Catholic Church, and severed his connection with his Pre-Raphaelite colleagues soon afterwards. In later years he produced a number of charming but uninspired genre pieces, like *The Empty Purse*, *circa* 1856 (Tate Gallery), and *Childhood*, 1855 (National Gallery of Canada, Ottawa).

4. *Alfred, Lord Tennyson*, 1856, by Thomas Woolner
plaster medallion diameter 10 in. (25·4 cm.)
The National Portrait Gallery, London

The last member of the original Pre-Raphaelite Brotherhood was Thomas Woolner (1825–92), the only sculptor of the group. It is difficult to trace anything specifically Pre-Raphaelite in his work, which during his early years was largely concerned with portrait medallions in the absence of more important commissions. After a romantic but fruitless journey to Australia in search of gold (1852–54), Woolner returned to England, and became in time a respected and established member of the Royal Academy. His later relations with his Pre-Raphaelite colleagues were not generally cordial. It is chiefly as a personality, rather than as an artist, that Woolner is important in the history of Pre-Raphaelitism, though his poetry, originally inspired by Rossetti, stems from a romantic and narrative intention similar to that of many early Pre-Raphaelite paintings. It was through Woolner that the Pre-Raphaelites became acquainted with the poet Coventry Patmore, who stimulated Ruskin to write in their defence in 1851, and who also introduced them to one of their heroes, Tennyson, whose poems they later illustrated with such success (Moxon Edition, 1857). Woolner's medallion of Tennyson (Ill. 4) is sympathetic, but in a conventional and straightforward style.

Revolving around the original Brotherhood of seven members there were inevitably many followers and peripheral figures. The link between them was chiefly artistic, but it was complicated by friendships that had few artistic aims in common. It must be remembered too that the various members of the Brotherhood soon began to develop in very different directions. Millais's work, after his election to the Royal Academy in 1853, became increasingly sentimental and debased, while Hunt turned almost exclusively to Biblical and religious works as a result of his first visit to the Holy Land in 1854. Rossetti, after his two early paintings of 1849 and 1850, *The Girlhood of Mary Virgin* and *Ecce Ancilla Domini* (both in the Tate Gallery), gave up any attempt to follow the Pre-Raphaelite precept of truth to nature, developing his own highly original and imaginative style. Thus, while his work continued to be regarded as typically Pre-Raphaelite, it bears little relation to that of Hunt or Millais. In fact, there is no set formula with which one may easily describe the essential characteristics of Pre-Raphaelitism, because of the many cross-currents and divergences within the movement itself. Even the Pre-Raphaelite concern with detail is no touchstone, for artists like J. F. Lewis, with his scenes of Eastern life, and J. P. Frith, with his scenes of contemporary life, were independently employing a similar technique. The same is true of William Dyce (1806–64), who is often regarded as a precursor of the Pre-Raphaelite movement. His early religious works, inspired by the achievements of the German Nazarene school in Rome, are much more in the spirit of early

. *Gethsemane*, *circa* 1850, by William Dyce
il on canvas $16\frac{1}{2} \times 12\frac{3}{8}$ in. (41·9×33·9 cm.)
'he Walker Art Gallery, Liverpool

Italian art than any Pre-Raphaelite picture, but Dyce began increasingly to employ minutely rendered landscapes as a setting for his figures. This is clear in his mysterious, but beautiful *Gethsemane* (Ill. 5), which may owe something to Pre-Raphaelite example, as well as to the visionary landscapes of Samuel Palmer. Dyce's treatment tends to be harder than that of the Pre-Raphaelites, and his colour more restrained and limited, but he produced a number of successful *plein-air* landscapes and subject pictures like *Pegwell Bay*, 1859 (Tate Gallery), *A Scene in Arran*, 1859 (Aberdeen Art Gallery) and *George Herbert at Bemerton*, *circa* 1860 (Guildhall Art Gallery, London).

Undoubtedly the most important painter connected with the Pre-Raphaelite Brotherhood was Ford Madox Brown (1821–93). In many ways one of the major figures of the movement, he is only included in this essay because in the past his great talent has never been fully appreciated. Most of his early years were spent in Europe, and his early paintings are in a Continental, historical tradition. Although his *Chaucer at the Court of Edward III*, 1845–51 (Art Gallery of New South Wales, Sydney), is essentially a large academic composition, inspired by the German Nazarenes, its concern with detail and the realistic effects of sunlight foreshadows the preoccupations of the Pre-Raphaelites. In 1848 Rossetti introduced himself to Brown, becoming his pupil for a short time, and his close friend for life. By 1850 Brown's work was Pre-Raphaelite in every sense of the word, and during the following decade he produced a few of the masterpieces of the movement.

Perhaps his most interesting painting is *Work* (Ill. 6), which reflects a profound concern with the contemporary scene. Painted in Heath Street, Hampstead, the composition is dominated by the English navvies, "the outward and visible type

6. *Work*, 1852–65, by Ford Madox Brown
oil on canvas $54\frac{1}{2} \times 77\frac{1}{8}$ in. (138·4×195·8 cm.)
The City Art Gallery, Manchester

7. *Pretty Baa-Lambs* (detail), 1851–59, by Ford Madox Brown
oil on panel 24×30 in. (60·9×76·2 cm.)
The City Museum and Art Gallery, Birmingham

of *Work*",[2] around whom are grouped all those who do not work, the idle and superfluous rich, the unemployed, the brain-workers (in fact, Carlyle and the Rev. F. D. Maurice, the two figures on the right of the picture), and so forth. The painting abounds in every kind of contrast, detail and incident. It is a composite and compressed statement about the nature of the Victorian world, seen through entirely honest and dispassionate eyes. This quality of intelligent and truthful observation unites the visual and symbolic elements of the picture, and makes the actual scene extremely real and convincing. It is, however, impossible to separate the subject from its treatment. The meticulous and impersonal rendering of detail, the strong and direct sunlight, the sharp outlines, the brilliant and strident colours, are all a necessary expression of the absolute detachment and truth of Brown's vision. *Work* is an example of a contemporary theme ideally suited to Pre-Raphaelite treatment and technique, like Brown's other great masterpiece, *The Last of England*, 1855 (City Museum and Art Gallery, Birmingham). This haunting image of an emigrant couple leaving England for ever has a more direct visual impact than *Work*, and a more personal and emotional message, though it was partly inspired by the great emigration movement of the early 1850's. Collinson's *Answering the Emigrant's Letter*, 1850 (Collection of William King), seems very insipid in comparison.

Unfortunately such subjects are rare among Pre-Raphaelite works. It is true that the Pre-Raphaelites did paint contemporary subjects, but they were concerned with those pathetic human dilemmas which so obsessed the Victorians, such as the theme of the fallen woman as in Hunt's *The Awakening Conscience*, 1854 (collection Sir Colin Anderson), or the theme of frustrated love as in Hughes's *Long Engagement*. (Ill. 9.) Such subjects were inspired by a romantic and literary imagination, and reflect little of the social consciousness implicit in *Work*. Brown was not, however, wholly exceptional. Paintings like Deverell's *Irish Vagrants, circa* 1850 (Johannesburg Art Gallery), or Wallis's *Stone-Breaker* (Ill. 16) have something of the same social awareness and seriousness of purpose, but they are isolated examples and not part of a flourishing tradition. The depiction of the contemporary world remained in the hands of trivial genre painters and popular illustrators, who, even if they were as talented as Frith, lacked any ethical or profound motive.

Brown also painted a number of landscapes, which reflect his delight in painting the natural world more simply and effectively than his narrative works. *Pretty Baa Lambs* (Ill. 7), which, despite its title, is not in the least sentimental, has a rather stark composition – the unrelieved vertical of the woman and child seen abruptly

[2] See *The Exhibition of* Work *and Other Paintings*, by F. M. Brown, a descriptive catalogue of pictures which he exhibited in 1865.

8. *The Eve of Saint Agnes*, 1856, by Arthur Hughes
oil on paper centre 25¾×22½ in. (65·4×57·1 cm.)
sides 23¼×11¾ in. (59×29·8 cm.)
The Tate Gallery, London

9. *The Long Engagement*, 1859, by Arthur Hughes
oil on canvas 41½×20½ in. (105·4×52 cm.)
The City Museum and Art Gallery, Birmingham

against a distant panorama – which is softened by the brilliant colours of the foreground, and the almost impressionist rendering of space and sunlight in the landscape beyond. Other landscapes, like *An English Autumn Afternoon*, 1852–54 (City Museum and Art Gallery, Birmingham), or *The Hayfield*, 1855 (collection John Gillum), reflect his profound sensitivity to the English countryside, where the mass of observed detail is unified by the strong, warm colours, and a real sense of light and atmosphere. Unfortunately in his later works Brown returned to the generalized and historical themes of his youth, his style coarsened, and his later pictures, particularly his wall-paintings for the Manchester Town Hall, tend to be rather exaggerated and melodramatic.

Another important figure connected with the early history of the Pre-Raphaelites is Arthur Hughes (1830–1915), who remains undeservedly obscure. Remote and unworldly, his personality lacked those definite qualities which still make Rossetti, for instance, so alive. Hughes's first exhibited work at the Royal Academy, *Musidora*, 1849 (City Museum and Art Gallery, Birmingham), is in a conventional, academic style, but by the early 1850's he was a complete convert to Pre-Raphaelite principles, as evidenced by his tender and poignant *Ophelia*, 1852 (City Art Gallery, Manchester). Hughes became very friendly with the members of the Brotherhood, sharing a studio with the sculptor Alexander Munro, and in 1857 collaborating with Rossetti and others in the painting of the Oxford Union murals. In the following year, however, he retired to the suburbs to escape from a London existence and society in general, passing his long life quietly and happily with his family.

A good example of his delicate and poetic talent is *The Eve of St Agnes* (Ill. 8), taken from Keats's poem, where the velvet quality of his brushwork is admirably suited to depicting the mysterious colours and shadows of the night, the secret meeting and escape of the lovers. Keats, still relatively neglected at this period, was enthusiastically admired by the Pre-Raphaelites, who, if they did not appreciate his intellectual control over his medium, were overwhelmed by the force of his imagination, and his sensuous enjoyment of the visible world. He provided themes and images with which they could give expression to their romantic and idealistic vision of the world.

If, in *The Eve of St Agnes*, the Victorian obsession with romantic love, itself the outcome of a rigid restraint between the sexes, is sublimated in a poetic analogy, it is poignantly expressed in *The Long Engagement*. (Ill. 9.) This story of an ageing couple who are still unmarried is simply told, in the acute anxiety of the clergyman, and the tender solicitude of his fiancée, her name, Amy, carved long ago on the tree and now covered by ivy to suggest the passing of time. What gives the picture its peculiar power is its startling and prismatic colour (even by Pre-Raphaelite standards), its obsessive rendering of every leaf and tendril of the forest scene, and its quality of claustrophobic space, which convey an overwhelming sense of sexual frustration far more directly than the story itself. *The Long Engagement* seems to sum up the whole Victorian ethos, and to express that sexual tension which was such a feature of the age, and of which Pre-Raphaelite art is such an accurate reflection. Hughes's *April Love*, 1856 (Tate Gallery), is less agonized, revealing as it does the freshness and tenderness of adolescent love, while *Home from Sea*, 1863 (Ashmolean Museum, Oxford), possibly his masterpiece, deals with a more straightforward emotion – grief over the loss of a mother. Although Hughes continued to paint and exhibit regularly, his later works lack the tense and imaginative quality which had saved his art from sentimentality and weakness. This degeneracy is not true of his delightful book-illustrations, particularly those for George Macdonald's fairy tales, Tennyson's "Enoch Arden" (1864) and Christina Rossetti's "Sing-Song" (1872), where his wistful and poetic fancy is given free rein.

The last of the important artists associated with the Pre-Raphaelite Brotherhood is Walter Deverell (1827–54). Good-looking, high-spirited and popular, he died young in tragic and poverty-stricken circumstances. Inevitably his *œuvre* is very small, but those paintings which do survive reveal a gifted, though immature talent. His best-known work is *The Pet* (Tate Gallery), a delightful and broadly painted study of a young woman feeding her pet bird. Three of his other pictures were inspired by Shakespeare, the scene of his *As You Like It* (Ill. 10) probably being the mock marriage between Rosalind and Orlando, with Celia as the priest (Act IV, sc. I). While the figures themselves are a little stilted and awkward, they are set in a woodland scene of extraordinary beauty and freshness.

10. *A Scene from "As You Like It"*, *circa* 1850,
by Walter Deverell
oil on canvas $25\frac{3}{8}\times30\frac{1}{8}$ in. (64·2×77 cm.)
The City Museum and Art Gallery, Birmingham

Holman Hunt did not excite the same hero-worship as Rossetti, but there are two interesting artists who owe a direct debt to him. Thomas Seddon (1821–56) travelled with Hunt in the Holy Land on the latter's first visit there in 1854, and his *View of Jerusalem* (Ill. 11), with its hot colouring and precise topographical detail, is closely related to Hunt's landscapes of the same period. Seddon painted a number of Eastern scenes which were well received when he exhibited them on his return home. He did not live to fulfil his early promise, however, dying in Alexandria on his second visit to the East in 1856. Robert Martineau (1826–69) spent some time in Hunt's studio in the early 1850's, but little is known about his life. Although most of his paintings have the same laboured and intensive quality as those by Hunt, they lack Hunt's seriousness of purpose and power of emotion. Martineau's *The Last Day in the Old Home*, 1862 (Tate Gallery), on which he spent

11. *Jerusalem and the Valley of Jehosophat from the Hill of Evil Counsel*, 1854, by Thomas Seddon
oil on canvas 25×32 in. (63·5×81·2 cm.)
The Tate Gallery, London

12. *The Last Chapter*, 1863, by Robert Martineau
oil on canvas 27¾×16⅛ in. (70·4×41 cm.)
The City Museum and Art Gallery, Birmingham

13. *Convent Thoughts*, 1851, by Charles Collins
oil on canvas 33⅛×23¼ in. (84×59 cm.)
The Ashmolean Museum, Oxford

several years, is too diffuse as a scene, and too obvious as a study of contrasted emotion between the various members of the departing family, to rank as anything more than an elaborate genre piece. The same triviality and rather mannered quality is apparent in *Kit's Writing Lesson*, 1852 (Tate Gallery), and *Katherine and Petruchio*, 1855 (Ashmolean Museum, Oxford). Much more Pre-Raphaelite in feeling is Martineau's *The Last Chapter* (Ill. 12), where the simplicity of design, recalling the effect of many of the best woodcuts of the period, and the restraint and delicacy of the treatment produce a romantic and evocative image.

Before considering the influence of Ruskin and Rossetti, it would be worth while to consider some of those artists who were temporarily or indirectly affected by Pre-Raphaelitism. Charles Collins (1828–73), brother of Wilkie Collins the novelist, painted one minor Pre-Raphaelite masterpiece, *Convent Thoughts* (Ill. 13), which suffered from the same abusive criticism as other Pre-Raphaelite pictures when exhibited at the Royal Academy in 1851. Despite what Hunt called its "puerile leading idea"[3] – the young nun, with an illuminated missal in her hand, studying the significance of a passion flower – the painting of the flowers and gardens has a hallucinatory clarity and brilliance. Collins, who was very friendly with Hunt and Millais, did paint other works of considerable merit, but in later years he turned almost exclusively to literature. Henry Bowler (1824–1903), unlike Collins, is not known to have had any personal connection with the Pre-Raphaelites, but his picture, *The Doubt. Can these Dry Bones Live?* (Ill. 14), on the theme of Tennyson's "In Memoriam", was clearly influenced by their example. So too was *Broken Vows*, 1856 (Tate Gallery), by Philip Calderon (1833–98), for whom this was no more than a youthful experiment in a career devoted to profitable but unimportant history paintings. More interesting than Bowler or Calderon is William Windus (1822–1907), a Liverpool artist who was largely responsible for the success of the Pre-Raphaelites at the annual exhibitions of the Liverpool Academy, and who also introduced them to Liverpool patrons, at a time when their work was denigrated elsewhere. Windus's *Burd Helen*, 1856 (Walker Art Gallery, Liverpool), taken like Elizabeth Siddal's *Clerk Saunders* (Ill. 19) from a medieval ballad, has the romantic intensity and highly worked technique of Pre-Raphaelite art, but lacks the robust simplicity of the original ballad. *Too Late* (Ill. 15) is concerned with a contemporary tragedy, the agonized meeting of the returning lover and his loved one who is dying of consumption, presumably because of his desertion. Here, as in many Pre-Raphaelite works, the figures are posed against the landscape, rather than in it, which creates the impression of a highly keyed backcloth, flattening the space behind the figures and heightening the emotional tension between them. Windus was a rather melancholy and neurotic personality, who painted little of importance besides the two works mentioned. He is an excellent example of Pre-Raphaelite influence on a provincial talent.

Henry Wallis (1830–1916), like Collins and Bowler, is really only known for one work, *The Death of Chatterton*, 1856 (Tate Gallery), actually painted in the attic in Gray's Inn where the young poet had committed suicide, with George Meredith as the model. *The Stone-Breaker* (Ill. 16), also called *Thou Wert our Conscript*, has never attracted the attention it deserves. Exhibited at the Royal Academy in 1858, with a quotation from Carlyle about the deformity, captivity and defacement of labour, it represents a stone-breaker who is dead, not asleep. The figure recalls Courbet's work in its direct and simple realism, but the landscape, with its unearthly colours, has something almost mystical about it. To turn

[3] *Pre-Raphaelitism and the Pre-Raphaelite Brotherhood*, by Holman Hunt (1905–06), vol. II, p. 314. There are also useful references to Collinson, Deverell, Brown, Hughes and others.

14. (above left) *The Doubt. Can These Dry Bones Live? circa* 1855, by Henry Bowler
oil on canvas 24×20 in. (60·9×50·8 cm.)
The Tate Gallery, London

15. (above right) *Too Late*, 1858, by William Windus
oil on canvas 38×30 in. (96·5×76·2 cm.)
The Tate Gallery, London

from Wallis's harsh statement about the lot of the working man to that most delightful of Victorian paintings, *The Travelling Companions* (Ill. 17), by Augustus Egg (1816–63) is an abrupt jump, and it is debatable whether Egg's work should be illustrated here at all. Already well known for his romantic, historical works, before the founding of the Pre-Raphaelite Brotherhood in 1848, his *Past and Present*, 1858 (Tate Gallery), depicting the tragedy caused by a wife's infidelity in a series of three paintings, reveals a kinship with Pre-Raphaelite themes and treatment. So does *The Travelling Companions*, a study in symmetry, with its contrast between the cool interior of the railway carriage and the hot Mediterranean landscape outside, its delight in the rendering of textures, and its charming still-life motifs. Egg was friendly with Hunt, and sympathetic to the aims of the Pre-Raphaelites, but he remained independent of the movement.

The position of Ruskin (1819–1900) in the history of Pre-Raphaelitism has always been difficult to assess. His two famous letters to *The Times* (1851) in defence of the Pre-Raphaelites, his further support of their efforts, and his friendship with Millais and Rossetti, have led to the idea that he was the prophet of the movement. Although in his writings, particularly in his influential "Modern Painters" (1843–46), he had already argued in favour of a detailed truth to nature, he only partially appreciated the intentions of the Pre-Raphaelites, and had little direct influence on their work. His popularization of the movement, while beneficial to the painters, has helped to obscure its essential characteristics, and has led to several misunderstandings. Ruskin was himself a talented amateur watercolourist, ceaselessly recording details of architecture, street scenes, Old Master paintings, rocks and natural phenomena of all kinds, or mountain scenes. Sometimes his style is broad and atmospheric, like the work of his beloved Turner, at other times tight and finicky. His *Coast Scene Near Dunbar* (Ill. 18) strikes a balance between the sensitive observation of the seaweed, rocks and water, and the strong and effective patterns of light and shade. The Pre-Raphaelite artist on whom Ruskin had most direct influence was John Brett (1830–1902), famous chiefly for *The Stone-Breaker*, 1857–58 (Walker Art Gallery, Liverpool), and *The Val d'Aosta*, 1858 (collection Sir William Cooper), which was commissioned and supervised by Ruskin. With its amazing detail, it is a display of incredible virtuosity, but even Ruskin admitted that the mirror Brett had held up to nature was "Mirror's work, not Man's".[4] Brett's later works are not wholly worthless, as most critics suggest, though he never again achieved the same intensity of vision. His watercolours have a real freshness and delicacy of colour, like *February in the Isle of Wight* (colour plate facing p. 229), while even his repetitive sea-pieces often have considerable quality.

Brett's work represents the realist strain in Pre-Raphaelite art at its purest, a realism which Rossetti had abandoned because it fettered his imagination. Rossetti fused his mystical and romantic obsession with Love into a highly original and imaginative style, which was to have wide influence on his contemporaries. It can be seen, though in weakened form, in the work of his wife, Elizabeth Siddal (1834–62). The intense, melancholy and haunted way in which the lovers gaze at each other in *Clerk Saunders* (Ill. 19), the stylization of the scene and its archaic details, the enclosed space and steep perspective, bring home the strangeness of this dream world, and also its underlying anxiety: the Victorians looked back at the Middle Ages through their own romantic preconceptions and obsessions. *Paola and Francesca* (Ill. 20) by Alexander Munro (1825–71), the only piece of true Pre-Raphaelite sculpture, is actually derived from a Rossetti drawing, and shows how the strength of Rossetti's imagination was able to inspire a work of real poetic invention in an otherwise limited and conventional sculptor.[5] The influence of Rossetti can also be seen in the work of Simeon Solomon (1840–1905), a younger admirer. Solomon's early works, like *King David* (Ill. 21), are concerned with Hebraic and Biblical subjects. After a journey to Italy in 1864, where he was profoundly impressed by the paintings of Leonardo, and his followers, Luini and Sodoma, he developed a more sensual and decadent style. Following his conviction in a sordid sex case he became increasingly depraved, and the many chalk drawings of mystical and idealized heads which he produced in his later years tend to be repetitive and debased. Simeon Solomon was a close friend of Swinburne and

[4] "Royal Academy Notes 1859", in *The Works of John Ruskin*, edited by E. Cook and A. Wedderburn, vol. XIV (1904), p. 237.

[5] For a full discussion of this work see "Alexander Munro's Paola and Francesca", by J. Gere, *The Burlington Magazine*, vol. CV (November 1963), pp. 509–10.

16. (below left) *The Stone-Breaker*, 1857, by Henry Wallis
oil on panel 25¾×31 in. (60·3×78·7 cm.)
The City Museum and Art Gallery, Birmingham

17. (below right) *The Travelling Companions*, 1862, by Augustus Egg
oil on canvas 25⅜×30⅛ in. (64·3×76·4 cm.)
The City Museum and Art Gallery, Birmingham

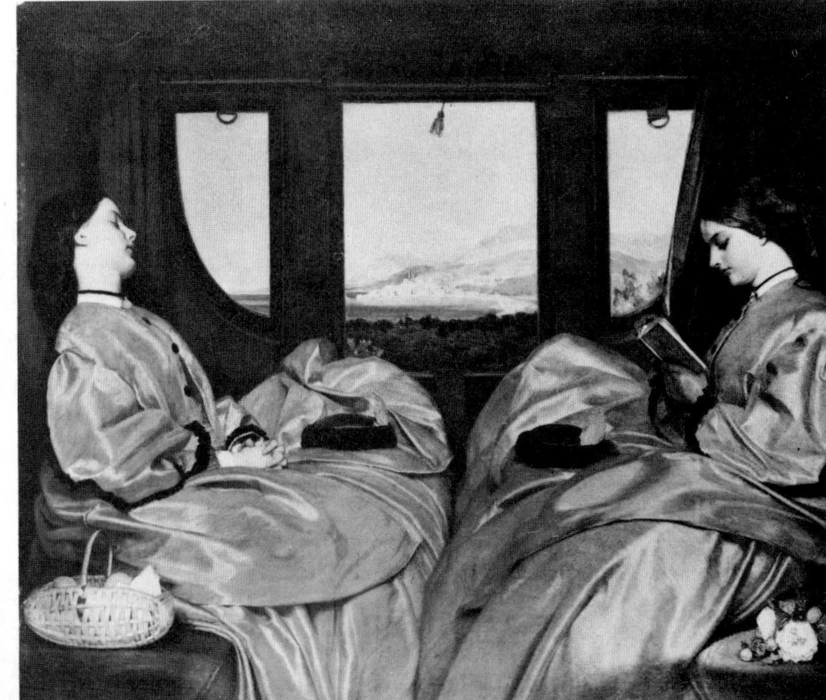

18. *Coast Scene near Dunbar*, 1857, by John Ruskin
watercolour 12½×18½ in. (31·7×46·9 cm.)
The City Museum and Art Gallery, Birmingham

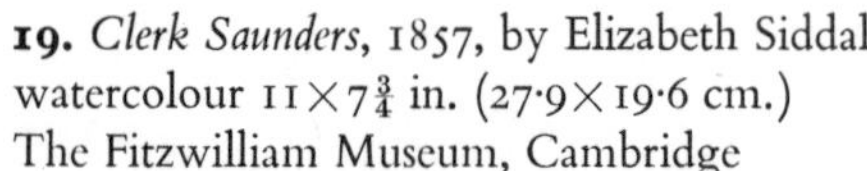

19. *Clerk Saunders*, 1857, by Elizabeth Siddal
watercolour 11×7¾ in. (27·9×19·6 cm.)
The Fitzwilliam Museum, Cambridge

others of Rossetti's circle, and his work is a definite link between the imaginative strain of Pre-Raphaelitism and Aestheticism. A more isolated figure is James Smetham (1821–84), who, like his friend Rossetti, was a passionate admirer of Blake, and whose small, jewelled pictures, which he called idylls, vaguely echo the visionary quality of Blake and his associates. Smetham's *Naboth's Vineyard* (Ill. 22) is precise in its observation of vine leaves and grapes, but is too remote and otherworldly to be profitably compared with the early masterpieces of Pre-Raphaelite art.

Frederick Sandys (1832–1904) on the contrary was much nearer to the original tenets of Pre-Raphaelitism, particularly in his marvellously sensitive, early drawings, and his powerful woodcuts, like his illustration to George Wither's poem, "Life's Journey" (Ill. 23), in Wilmott's "English Sacred Poetry" (1863). The solidity of Sandys's figures, the emotional power of his line, and his haunting observation of natural detail recall the effect of German woodcuts (there is a definite link between Sandys and Dürer), and contrast with the vapid technique of the preceding era. His designs are outstanding even in a period remarkable for its illustrators. Sandys had become friendly with Rossetti as a result of his amusing Pre-Raphaelite satire, *The Nightmare*, published as a zincotype in 1857. He was an intimate of Rossetti's house in Cheyne Walk for several years, and his later subject paintings, like *Morgan-le-Fay* and *Medea* (1864 and 1869 respectively, both in the City Museum and Art Gallery, Birmingham) reflect the latter's influence, though in a rather exaggerated and unconvincing form. Rossetti later accused Sandys of stealing his ideas, and their friendship ended abruptly. Sandys's later *œuvre* is mostly concerned with crayon portraits, which like his earlier oil portraits are evidence of a competent draughtsman and colourist.

Rossetti's imaginative style had its most powerful influence on Edward Burne-Jones (1833–98), but also indirectly stimulated Morris to found his famous firm. Rossetti's poetry directly affected Swinburne, Morris and Wilde, and influenced the whole course of later 19th-century romantic poetry. Burne-Jones is too important to lie within the scope of this essay, and he developed out of a second phase of Pre-Raphaelitism, which had profoundly changed its nature since the founding of

20. (above left) *Paola and Francesca*, 1852, by Alexander Munro
marble height $26\frac{1}{2}$ in. (67·3 cm.)
The City Museum and Art Gallery, Birmingham

21. (above right) *King David*, 1859, by Simeon Solomon
pen and ink $10\frac{3}{8} \times 11$ in. ($26{\cdot}3 \times 27{\cdot}9$ cm.)
The City Museum and Art Gallery, Birmingham

22. (right) *Naboth's Vineyard*, 1856, by James Smetham
oil on board $8\frac{3}{4} \times 6\frac{3}{4}$ in. ($22{\cdot}2 \times 17{\cdot}1$ cm.)
The Tate Gallery, London

the Brotherhood. The idealized world of classical myth and medieval romance through which elegant, though sexless, maidens and heroes wander wistfully is antipathetical to 20th-century taste, but should not obscure the fact that Burne-Jones is a very considerable artist. Nevertheless, even in his own day, his pre-occupations seemed a little remote and unreal, and this is even more true of his followers, most of whom are not worth mentioning. This aspect of Pre-Raphaelitism merged imperceptibly with Aestheticism and Art Nouveau, and continued to exert its influence in provincial centres like Birmingham, where the work of Meteyard, Southall and Gaskin is evidence of a flickering tradition. It was a very different tradition from that of Brown, Windus, Martineau or Brett, which ended eventually in a debased realism. Both traditions at their best produced works of real quality, which were a true expression of 19th-century English romanticism.

The growing interest which the minor Pre-Raphaelites have aroused is reflected in their rising market value. Oil paintings by them tend to be rare, particularly for such one-picture artists as Bowler, Windus, Collins and Stephens, but the discovery of Collinson's *Italian Image Boys* (Ill. 2) suggests that other lost works may come to light. Madox Brown, Arthur Hughes, and Augustus Egg all command high prices, though their less important watercolours and drawings can often be acquired for relatively few dollars. The same is true of Elizabeth Siddal, James Smetham, and Simeon Solomon, whose work is fairly common in the United States (see for instance the Simeon Solomon Exhibition at Durlacher Bros., 1966). Prices for landscapes by Ruskin and Brett, both prolific artists, varies from \$100 to \$1500, and the same is true of Frederic Sandys, whose works differ widely in quality. Burne-Jones has not been included in this essay, but it is worth pointing out that his oils and drawings appear more frequently on the art market than any of the artists mentioned above, and consistently sell for high prices.

23. Finished design for the woodcut *Life's Journey*, 1863, by Frederick Sandys
brush, pen and ink 5¼×4¼ in. (13·3×10·7 cm.)
The City Museum and Art Gallery, Birmingham

BIBLIOGRAPHY

GENERAL

Dictionary of National Biography and Supplements; entries for H. Bowler, J. Brett, F. M. Brown, P. Calderon, C. Collins, J. Collinson, W. Dyce, A. Egg, A. Hughes, R. Martineau, A. Munro, F. Sandys, T. Seddon, J. Smetham, S. Solomon, F. Stephens, W. Windus, T. Woolner.

Bate, H. *The English Pre-Raphaelite Painters: Their Associates and Successors*, 1899.

Pre-Raphaelite Diaries and Letters, 1896, ed. W. M. Rossetti.

Ironside, R., and Gere, T. *Pre-Raphaelite Painters*, 1948.

Fredeman, W. *Pre-Raphaelitism: A Bibliocritical Study*, 1965.

INDIVIDUAL STUDIES

Hueffer, F. M. *Ford Madox Brown: A Record of his Life and Work*, 1896.

Ellis, S. M. "Charles Allston Collins", in *Wilkie Collins, Le Fanu and Others*, 1931, pp. 54–73.

Bodkin, T. "James Collinson", *Apollo*, vol. XXXI (May 1940), pp. 128–33.

Storey, G. A. "Philip Hermogenes Calderon, R.A.", *The Magazine of Art*, vol. XXII (1898), pp. 446–52.

Staley, A. "William Dyce and Outdoor Naturalism", *The Burlington Magazine*, vol. CV (November 1963), pp. 470–76.

Martineau, H. "Echo of a Pre-Raphaelite Painter, R. B. Martineau", *Studio*, vol. CXXXIV (September 1947), pp. 78–79.

Wood, E. *A Consideration of the Art of Frederick Sandys*, 1896.

Letters of James Smetham, with an Introductory Memoir, 1891. Ed. S. Smetham and W. Davies.

Falk, B. "Tragedy of Simeon Solomon: Fall from Glory", in *Five Years Dead*, 1937.

Bennett, M. "William Windus and the Pre-Raphaelite Brotherhood in Liverpool", *Liverpool Bulletin* (Walker Art Gallery Number), vol. VII, no. 3 (1958–59), pp. 19–31.

Woolner, A. *Thomas Woolner R.A., Sculptor and Poet: His Life in Letters*, 1917.

The Early Piano 1780–1850

M. COLT

For well over a hundred and fifty years one of the most sought-after pieces of domestic furniture has surely been the piano. This reached its climax shortly before the last war. Television and popular music brought about a temporary decline, but at present the boredom of both these forms of entertainment has brought about a revival in the keyboard instrument. However, this demand for pianos was satisfied by the grand and upright, and it is only quite recently that the earlier, lesser known square piano has been collected in its own right.

This revival, coupled with the renaissance of the harpsichord, brought about an inquiry into their origins. Considering the short period of time taken for the development of this instrument it is astonishing to see the variations in the design of the piano; an immense amount of thought and ingenuity was put into its manufacture. Even the simplest pianos were made with extreme care, not only for aesthetic purposes but because the instruments were machines and had to function properly.

There were basically three kinds of piano, each having been derived and developed from different sources: first of all the Grand Piano, which is a direct descendant of the harpsichord, then the Square Piano having in form come from the clavichord, and, lastly, the Upright Piano, the antecedents of which are not as obvious as with the other two types. In fact, the upright piano was a more complex development which gained impetus after the demise of the square piano *circa* 1850.

The period we are dealing with was an age of increasing prosperity for the middle classes who could begin to afford more than the basic necessities of life. The richer families were able to own more than one instrument. Contemporary illustrations depict pianos in all sorts of rooms: the 'grand' was usually in the saloon, a 'square' was generally in a boudoir, then there might be an upright grand or a cabinet piano for use as a secondary instrument. The 'cottage' piano came at the end of this period.

Although England has been dubbed an unmusical nation in the 18th century, and it did not have great composers comparable to those of Central Europe music was much appreciated. The wealth of pianos which remains today hardly suggest a non-music-loving people. At this time it had the means to play music, to employ famous musicians and commission distinguished composers for new music. Haydn visited London twice, purchasing several of Broadwood's pianos (Ill. 1); J. C. Bach lived there from 1762 until his death. Mozart visited London as a child in 1764 and although Beethoven did not visit England he was fervently admired and various works including a piano concerto were commissioned from him by Clementi and others. It is interesting to note that Broadwood made over seven thousand squares and over two thousand grands between 1782 and 1802.

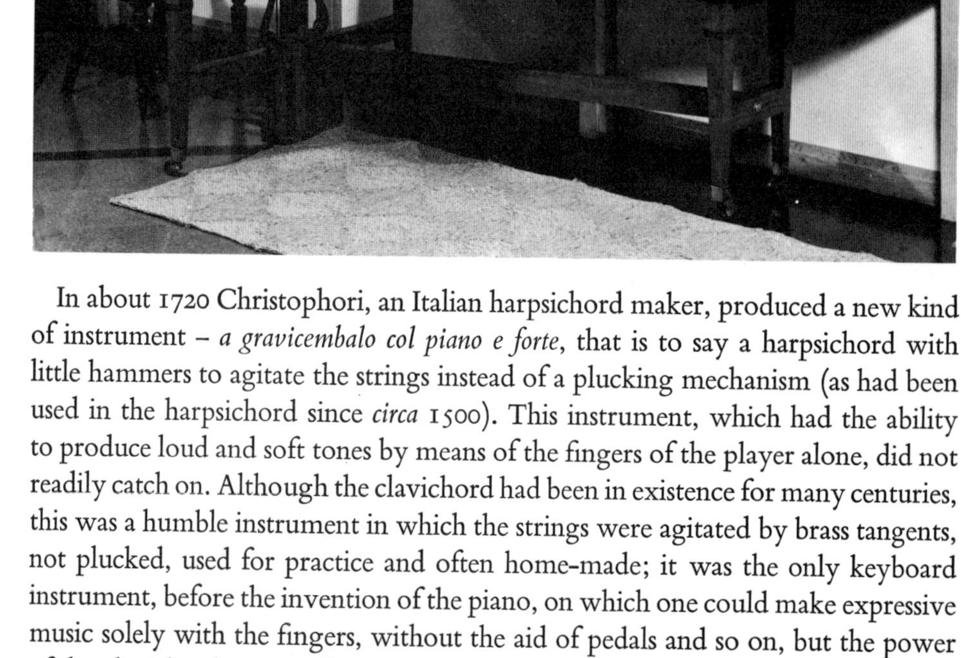

1. Grand pianoforte, 1806, by John Broadwood
five and a half octaves
length 89 in. (226 cm.) width 41 in. (104·1 cm.)
The Colt Clavier Collection, Bethersden, Kent

In about 1720 Christophori, an Italian harpsichord maker, produced a new kind of instrument – *a gravicembalo col piano e forte*, that is to say a harpsichord with little hammers to agitate the strings instead of a plucking mechanism (as had been used in the harpsichord since *circa* 1500). This instrument, which had the ability to produce loud and soft tones by means of the fingers of the player alone, did not readily catch on. Although the clavichord had been in existence for many centuries, this was a humble instrument in which the strings were agitated by brass tangents, not plucked, used for practice and often home-made; it was the only keyboard instrument, before the invention of the piano, on which one could make expressive music solely with the fingers, without the aid of pedals and so on, but the power of the clavichord was, really, insufficient for accompaniment except for a flute or violin, the antique ones being quite loud, compared with modern ones.

There are many theories as to why or how the piano came into existence and what made Christophori build his instruments. Did it emerge in an attempt to make a 'grand' version of the clavichord? – or did he put a keyboard to the dulcimer (in which the strings were struck by small sticks held in the hands, these 'hammers' having each end covered with different materials in order to produce two different kinds of tone)? In spite of all this, the fact remains that the piano was born.

On the Continent, the early classical composers including Bach's sons were seeking a more expressive instrument than the harpsichord, a desire which the piano fulfilled in spite of its many defects. By 1780 the early piano had reached perfection in southern Germany; not to be compared with either the harpsichord or modern piano, it was an ideal instrument in its own right for the interpretation of the music of the period. It had a keyboard of five octaves, FF–f3, a sustaining device and sometimes there was a device for changing the tone colour – remember the dulcimer strings – and some instruments even had a shifting keyboard so that only one string instead of two per note was played on.

2. Action of Broadwood grand pianoforte, 1806
(detail of Illustration 1.)

A fortepiano of this period is shown in illustration 3. Although unsigned it could well be the work of the famous Johann Andreas Stein of Augsburg (1728–92), the friend of Mozart, who was very enthusiastic about Stein's pianos.

Stein learned his craft from J. A. Silbermann, of Strasbourg, and started building organs, harpsichords and fortepianos in Augsburg. His first major work was the organ in the church of the Minorites in Augsburg (1755–57) and soon he had a flourishing business producing many instruments. He most probably built his first pianos in about 1770. His instruments were based on those of Spath & Schmahl, with considerable improvements in design. The earliest surviving Stein piano which is not combined with another instrument is in the Heyer Collection and dated 1773.

This instrument has hollow circular hammers – similar to the rolled parchment ones of Christophori, made from sections of bamboo covered with leather, and used by Stein's eminent pupil Schiedmayer. The compass is five octaves, FF–f3, the natural keys are of ebony and the accidentals of dyed beech covered with bone – not ivory, which was rarely used in early German and Viennese pianos. There is no overhanging lip at the front of the natural keys, which are narrower than nowadays. The keyboard epitomizes elegant simplicity. The case is of cherrywood dyed to simulate mahogany with a double line inlaid on the sides and lid.

Most German and Austrian pianos were made of either walnut or cherrywood, the latter often stained, as exotic woods were rare in Central Europe.

The Viennese action is worked by a 'reflex' movement and is very light and nimble, which makes extremely easy, rapid trills and runs. The English action, descended from Christophori, is heavier and slower, but more direct, and is the forerunner of the modern action. The German Erhardt, who Frenchified his name to Erard when he left Strasbourg for Paris, invented in 1822 the double-repetition form of this action which is virtually the same as a modern action. Broadwood only gave up the older form of the action about 1900.

In this instrument the stringing is bichord and the bridge is in one continuous piece like a harpsichord. The frame is entirely of wood. The dampers are actuated by the *genouillères* (or knee levers). (See colour plate facing p. 252.) The damper rail is ingeniously made so that by raising the left knee, the dampers of the bass notes only are raised, and the right knee the treble.

In this unusually small piano the double-curve bentside and slender legs give an appearance of great lightness and delicacy – compared with an English harpsichord of the same date, the latter appears large and heavy.

The 'desk front' was peculiar to early German and Viennese pianos. It was often usual to add a series of pedals to give a variety of tone effects, although in earlier instruments these tone changes were operated by hand stops, and later there were *genouillères*; these knee levers sometimes persisted till the 1830's in Germany. (See colour plate facing p. 252.) Consequently pianos with as many as five or more pedals do exist. The first sustained the bass note, the second had the same effect on the treble, the third shifted the keyboard to secure *una corda* effects, the fourth inserted felt between the hammers and strings to give a soft tone, and the fifth likewise inserted silk, to give a different tone. Another refinement was to place hard material against the strings to give a 'harpsichord' sound and in the later instruments (after 1820) bells, triangles and drum were included. A 'bassoon' stop put parchment on the strings of the lowest third of the compass.

3. (below left) Viennese fortepiano, *circa* 1785,
by Johann Andreas Stein
five octaves
length 70 in. (177·8 cm.) width 36½ in. (92·7 cm.)
The Colt Clavier Collection, Bethersden, Kent

4. (below right) Viennese fortepiano, *circa* 1820,
by Johann Götting
six octaves
length 92½ in. (234·5 cm.) width 51 in. (129·5 cm.)
The Colt Clavier Collection, Bethersden, Kent

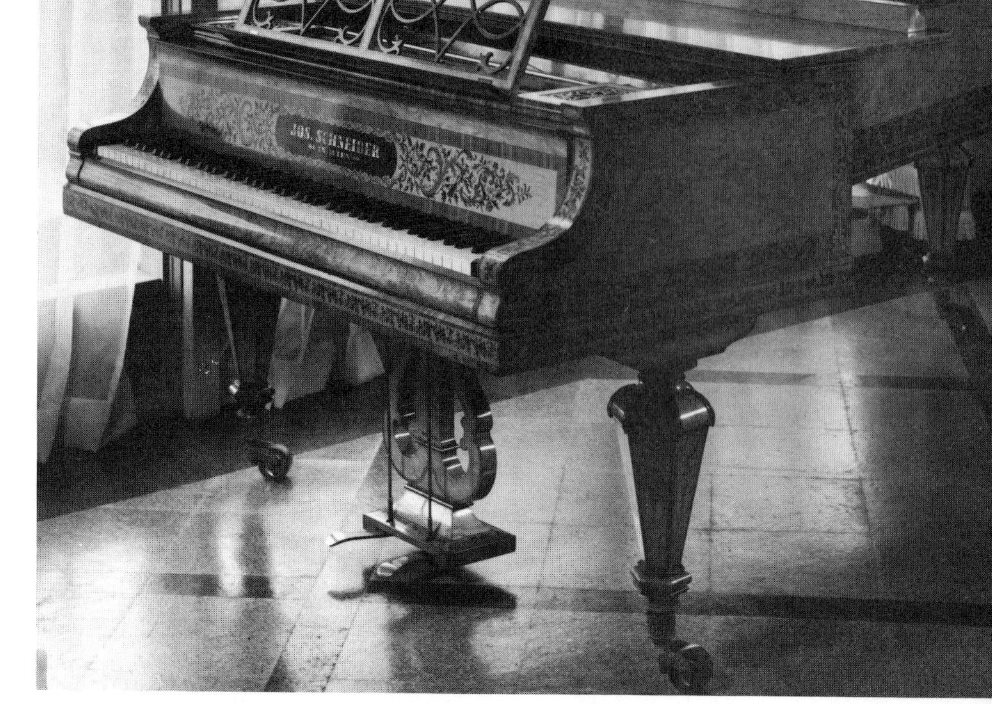

5. Viennese fortepiano, 1851, by Joseph Schneider
seven octaves
length 96 in. (243·8 cm.) width 54 in. (137·1 cm.)
The Colt Clavier Collection, Bethersden, Kent

A fortepiano by Johann Götting, made in Vienna *circa* 1820, is shown in illustration 4. Except that it was not made by Graf of Vienna, the Götting is practically the same as Beethoven's Viennese piano, and its Biedermeier case is typical of the South German school.

There is no iron framing and the instrument has therefore a more solid construction than found in any contemporary English instrument. The case is of cherrywood, the grain being carefully chosen and matched; this golden wood was much used in Central Europe at this time. There is no applied decoration, no moulding and no inlay; such a plain instrument could almost be of modern design. The six and three quarter octave compass was that demanded by the later classical composers of the Viennese school – Schubert, Schumann and Brahms.

Note the great depth of the case between the keybed and the baseboard of the instrument; this is a typically Viennese feature made necessary by the peculiar construction of the action used (Ills 5, 6), since the hammers rest on the keybacks and are not on a rail some inches higher as in English instruments.

Beethoven's Graf piano was quadrichord, an experiment made in an attempt to obtain greater power and help overcome the master's increasing deafness. It was, in fact, less powerful than a trichord piano as thinner strings had to be used, and was, alas, a total failure. It is interesting that Wornum's Imperial Grand, which had great volume, was strung bichord throughout! It should be noted that the hammers on pianos of this period are always leather covered.

6. Action of a Viennese 'Stein', *circa* 1805
the hammer checks obscure view of the hammers which face forward
six octaves
The Colt Clavier Collection, Bethersden, Kent

One sees in the Viennese fortepiano by Joseph Schneider, made in 1851 (Ill. 5), the last traces of the classical grand fortepianos and the first characteristics of the modern grand pianos. The instrument appears to have been exhibited at the Great Exhibition of 1851 – Exhibition Catalogue No. 140. The compass is seven octaves. The internal frame is entirely wooden, but supplemented by three steel braces, and has a wrought-iron hitch pin block. The soundboard is not varnished, a Viennese tradition; English ones were always highly varnished.

Although a 'late' instrument, the hammers have a final covering of thin deerskin leather *over* hard felt. The sound is to most ears 'modern', but it has a transparency lacking in our new instruments.

The case shows supreme workmanship, the basis being American bird's-eye maple, the inlaid banding on every part of the case is a Viennese version of 'Tunbridge Ware' – very fine wood mosaic. This decoration is carried through the legs and pedal lyre even to the vertical edge of the lid. The music rest is beautifully detailed with further inlay and the dampers and frame to which they are hinged are decorated with tulipwood and ivory. There are the usual two pedals.

In England the grand piano developed much later than on the Continent. Only by 1793 had Broadwood ceased to manufacture harpsichords and Kirckman is said to have made them as late as 1809. (Ill. 7.) The earliest English grand pianos of Stodart or Backers looked the same as the harpsichord, but by 1791 the compass was increased to five and a half octaves, and the additional keys in the treble gave a greater curve to the bentside of the instrument, which is even more beautiful than the lesser curve of the harpsichord.

When the Kirckman harpsichord (Ill. 7) was made, Broadwood, his great rival, had ceased manufacture of harpsichords. The similarity of the case work to that of the 1806 Broadwood is striking (Ill. 1); the trestle stand is almost the same, the tapered legs, the panelled effect of the inlay and the cross banding are all similar. This is why many early pianos are mistaken for harpsichords.

The two-manual keyboard and mechanism is typical of the last phase of English harpsichord building, with three strings to each note (2 × 8-foot, 1 × 4-foot, lute stop, buff stop, machine stop and pedal-operated Venetian swell). This was an invention of Tschudi and incorporated as a sort of last effort on the part of the harpsichord builders to compete with the piano in giving dynamic 'expression'. The compass is five octaves.

This classical English pianoforte by Broadwood is dated 1806; it differs only in small details from several others in the author's collection, the earliest of which is dated 1787. The case is in Cuban mahogany. The three centrally placed pedals have an 'embryo lyre' above them. The pedal on the left is to shift the keyboard for the hammers to play on two strings per note and, by lifting a small wooden hand stop in the right-hand key block and depressing this pedal further, the keyboard shifts still more to play on one string per key. This gives an ethereal sound and is the true *una corda*. The central pedal lifts the dampers from middle C downwards in the bass, that on the right upwards from middle C. This pedal system continued until 1825.

The music rest is typical of those of English 18th-century harpsichords and classical pianos, at least to 1832. These have pull-out shelves for candles and the rest itself is adjustable for rake and height.

The compass is five and a half octaves FF–c4 and is trichord throughout. The bridge is not continuous, but divided so that the brass bass strings have their own bridge placed separately from the long bridge which carried the steel strings of the treble. This divided bass bridge was supposed to have been John Broadwood's invention and has two functions: firstly, to obtain the best acoustical effect by placing the bridges on the soundboard advantageously, and secondly to get an even tension for brass and steel strings which differed in tensile strength.

The action is typically English. The bracing system within the instrument is of wood, metal being introduced only in the four arches which cross the gap between wrestplank and counter-wrestplank. The hammers are covered with leather throughout.

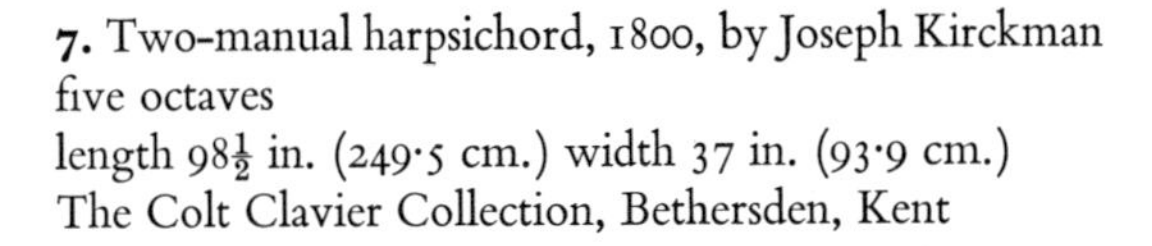

7. Two-manual harpsichord, 1800, by Joseph Kirckman
five octaves
length 98½ in. (249·5 cm.) width 37 in. (93·9 cm.)
The Colt Clavier Collection, Bethersden, Kent

8. Grand pianoforte, *circa* 1819, by John Broadwood
six octaves
length 97$\frac{1}{2}$ in. (247·4 cm.) width 44$\frac{1}{2}$ in. (113 cm.)
The Colt Clavier Collection, Bethersden, Kent

In 1817 Thomas Broadwood sent one of his best pianos (no. 7362) as a gift to Beethoven, in humble appreciation of the great master's genius; this was a six-octave instrument, CC–c4.

A contemporary illustration shows what appear to be two pedals; in fact, there were effectively three pedals. That on the right was divided into two halves so that either the bass or treble dampers could be lifted independently; in fact, exactly the same are found in the 1806 Broadwood described above, but easier to operate in this case.

In all early English grand pianos the damper system is like a set of harpsichord jacks set in a rack and each damper can be removed separately. To prevent these dampers from jumping out of their guides a wooden 'ruler' is placed above them, exactly as in a harpsichord. This model was first produced in 1812, and except in a few rare cases, English grands had been constructed with five octaves until 1790 and five and a half to 1812, after this, the compass was increased to six octaves, simultaneously the fashion changed in preference for turned, screw-in legs, also apparent on square pianos.

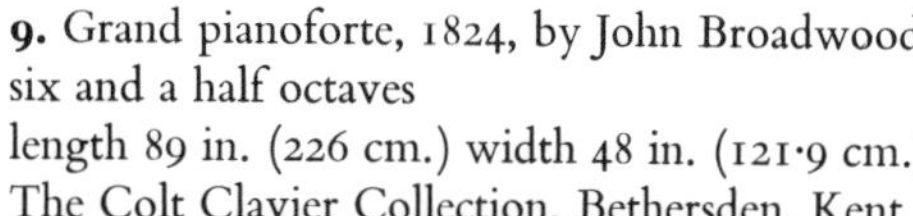

9. Grand pianoforte, 1824, by John Broadwood
six and a half octaves
length 89 in. (226 cm.) width 48 in. (121·9 cm.)
The Colt Clavier Collection, Bethersden, Kent

The 1819 piano illustrated (Ill. 8) is identical to that described as Beethoven's piano, the only difference being that the case is rosewood with brass inlay, whilst Beethoven's is of plain mahogany.

The third Broadwood grand pianoforte illustrated (Ill. 9), numbered 9595 and dated 1824, completes the evolution of the early English grand piano and illustrates the final phase before the advent of a full iron-framed instrument *circa* 1840. The surrounds to the keyboards in the early days were usually of figured sycamore, and a little later of satinwood; generally the edges were cross banded with rosewood or tulipwood. By 1815 the key surrounds were of rosewood with brass inlay. Until the cylinder front became common, the nameboard was separate and secured by two fancy-headed screws, so that removal was easy when making any adjustment to the action.

This piano still retains the elaborate music desk and the *una corda* mechanism. But completely trichord stringing has been abandoned, the eleven lowest bass notes having bichord covered strings, and a metal bracing system is incorporated. This steel frame is 'composite'; that is to say, individual braces are used, three above the soundboard in the treble, the remainder below the soundboard. The symmetry of the plain horizontal strings of the earlier pianos is gradually making way for the ugly, but necessary construction to support the vastly increased tension of the thicker strings. Although the instrument is six and a half octaves, it is no longer than the one of 1806, but the experiment in trying to make a shorter grand piano was not entirely successful as there is lack of resonance in the bass. The tone

10. Square piano, 1787, by John Broadwood
five octaves
length 62 in. (157·4 cm.) width 21 in. (53·3 cm.)
The Colt Clavier Collection, Bethersden, Kent

of the six-octave pianos was full, rich and sombre compared to the earlier five-and-a-half-octave models, which were more silvery and fragile in tone; both being a continuation of the tradition of the sonorous English harpsichord – a tone not so transparent as that of the Germanic instruments. The Viennese instruments were no less sonorous in the bass but with a greater limpidity and clarity of tone, especially in the treble, retaining some of the transparency and brilliance of the Continental harpsichord.

It may be wondered why only two kinds of early piano – the English and Viennese – are usually mentioned; South Germany, and later Austria, developed the early piano before anyone else, and fortunately many examples are with us. England was next to give attention to the fortepiano when instrument builders from Germany brought to this country the skills they had acquired working on pianos based on those of Christophori. It remains a mystery why the development of Christophori's work should have taken place first in Saxony and later England rather than in Italy, where the new instrument was neglected to the extent that we hear of a spinet (in the Heyer Collection) built by Alessandro Riva of Bergamo as late as 1839.

Most books devoted to the history of the piano offer a generalization about English and Viennese pianos on the question of tone and quality. Rimbault states that the tone of Viennese pianos was feeble and that the instrument did not stay in tune as well as the English counterpart, but I find this to be basically untrue.

Amongst refugees from the Seven Years War were numerous piano makers who started the manufacture of (small) square pianos, mainly in London. One of these, Johann Zumpe, became so famous and his instruments so sought after, that his little pianos were offered in exchange for Stradivari violins. As the century wore on, these instruments, whose layout was based on the clavichord, increased in size, compass and tone, but they remained comparatively small and were much used by ladies. They were invariably well made, and were the equivalent of the modern upright piano; the tone was sweet and clear, not particularly sonorous but ideal for the boudoir in consort with several other instruments. We see pictures by Zoffany depicting musical parties using an instrument such as the Broadwood of 1787. (Ill. 10.) This is one of the earliest existing square pianos by this famous maker. The case is of Cuban mahogany with cross banding of satinwood. The piano has only five octaves, with single English action and underdampers; there is no pedal.

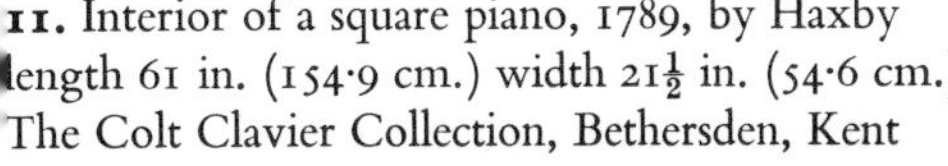

11. Interior of a square piano, 1789, by Haxby
length 61 in. (154·9 cm.) width 21½ in. (54·6 cm.)
The Colt Clavier Collection, Bethersden, Kent

The instrument has a 'French stand' in which a frame with tapered legs and castors fits around the base of the piano case with a music shelf accommodated between the legs. At first these instruments were as small as 4 feet 3 inches long, with a compass of about five octaves, but towards the end of the century the compass was increased in the treble. Late 18th-century music often states 'composed for the harpsichord or pianoforte' with or without 'the additional notes', meaning the extra half octave. This extension was made possible by ingenious cabinet work, the keys passing under the soundboard which had a slot cut to allow the hammers to strike the extra strings, without unduly altering the size of the instruments, as shown in illustration 13. It was only by 1820 that the compass was extended in the bass, which meant increasing the number of strings and enlarging the case to accommodate them and making a much larger and heavier piano. The compass then became six octaves, CC–c4.

The trestle stand was a much simpler affair, and the instrument rested on top of a frame with straight 'Chippendale' legs. These were used for the first square pianos as late as 1796, but when they became elegant and developed five and a half

12. Square piano, 1804, by Erard
five and a half octaves
length 64½ in. (163·8 cm.) width 24 in. (60·9 cm.)
The Colt Clavier Collection, Bethersden, Kent

octaves, they were nearly always put on French stands: the 1806 Broadwood grand (Ill. 1) shows the grand piano version of such a stand. In fact, the name 'French stand' seems a contradiction in terms, since the French used screw-in tapered turned legs for their pianos at least fifteen years before the English and one rarely sees French instruments with 'French stands'. Pianos in this style and with this mechanism were made by John Broadwood from 1784 until 1809.

The interior of a Haxby square piano made in 1789 is shown in illustration 11. Alas, few of this York maker's instruments survive. Those that do show workmanship comparable to those produced in London. The instrument is one of the earliest type using pedals instead of hand stops; they are from the left, buff stop, centre sustaining pedal, and right swell, which lifts the right-hand flap of the lid. The early layout, like a clavichord, is obvious when compared to the later Clementi. Nevertheless Clementi was one of the last of the famous makers to keep the wrest pins on the right.

Illustration 12 shows a mahogany Erard of 1804 from the period of the Consulate, and is the French equivalent of the English 'square'. This action is double, but without escapement, an improvement on the single action, but one which never seemed to take on in England, most probably because the patent for Geib's escapement action expired and his design was adopted generally by 1800 in England. There are four pedals, from left to right, a buff stop, bassoon to the bass notes, sustaining pedal and celeste.

An interesting point about the instrument is that it was in Arnold Dolmetsch's possession in Brussels, where he worked as a student *circa* 1888. The back is also decorated so that the piano can stand in the centre of a room – unlike most English ones, which have a plain back. There is a similar instrument in the refurnished rooms at Malmaison outside Paris.

By 1830 the square piano was losing its aesthetic charm, becoming coarser and heavier and thus losing its *raison d'être*. So by 1851 it was almost obsolete in England, having been ousted by the upright piano which was far more compact and even more sonorous.

Typical of this late period of square pianos is an example by Clementi, of which the interior is shown. (Ill. 13.) This instrument dates from after 1821, since it is fitted with a 'Bridge of Reverberation', invented by Collard, one of Clementi's partners. The adjustable hopper action is visible as are the 'old man's head' dampers. Beyond the bridge is a leather-covered damper rail which damps the unused portion of the strings beyond the main bridge. There is also a secondary bridge so that when this damper rail is raised a sort of 'swell' effect is produced without actually interfering with the main damping.

In France and Germany the classical tradition of design seemed to continue much later than in England. A table piano by Pape dated 1834, although large, is exquisitely made and detailed. (Ill. 14.) The wood used is a combination of burr, elm or mulberry, with classical motifs in the inlay of palisander. It has a compass of six and a half octaves, CC–f4, and a beautiful down-striking action, with trichord stringing. A similar richly ornamented instrument is in Queen Victoria's private sitting-room in Osborne House.

Pape's square pianos witnessed the decline of this type, although the square piano was made in ever-increasing size in America till *circa* 1880, where by 1903 there were still so many in circulation that the Atlantic City Congress of American Piano Manufacturers purchased all the 'square' pianos they could find, erected a huge mountain of them on the heights of Chelsea, and set fire to it. In this holocaust no doubt many instruments of value perished.

Upright harpsichords were being made as early as 1511; but since the action was somewhat complicated by having to pluck the strings horizontally, they were made in small numbers. This form of instrument lingered on and with the advent of the piano it was revived, particularly in Germany, where it was favoured by Friederici, an Austrian of Bozen who went to work in Gera. There was little demand for such instruments at the end of the 18th century as those people who could afford a grand piano were not short of space and those who were, were satisfied with a square. Further the upright grand was ungainly, being sometimes almost 9 feet high; and was naturally liable to tip over. (Ill. 15.)

Such upright grands were made by Clementi, a brilliant composer. He was something of an impresario and also the owner of a fashionable piano and publishing business. He was a prolific maker and many of Clementi's pianos still exist. In 1796 or so the firm of Longman and Broderip, in which Clementi had an interest, went bankrupt, and in 1802 he set up on his own, but seems to have continued the practice of 'buying in' or acquiring instruments from other makers.

To our modern eye the piano shown in illustration 15 has a comic appearance owing to its excessive height of 8 feet 3 inches. Its compass is five and a half octaves, FF–c4. The case is mahogany and the key surround is of satinwood; the piano when closed looks like a tall bureau bookcase. An instrument much like it is in Malmaison.

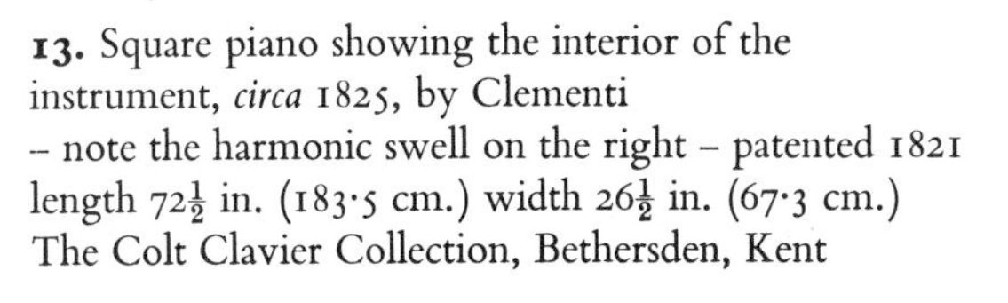

13. Square piano showing the interior of the instrument, *circa* 1825, by Clementi – note the harmonic swell on the right – patented 1821 length 72½ in. (183·5 cm.) width 26½ in. (67·3 cm.) The Colt Clavier Collection, Bethersden, Kent

14. Table piano, 1834, by Pape
about seven octaves
length 73 in. (185·4 cm.) width 33 in. (83·8 cm.)
The Colt Clavier Collection, Bethersden, Kent

15. Upright grand pianoforte, *circa* 1815, by Clementi
five octaves
height 99 in. (246·3 cm.) width 42½ in. (107·9 cm.)
The Colt Clavier Collection, Bethersden, Kent

Nevertheless, after the turn of the 18th century, efforts were made to reduce the extreme height of these instruments by running the strings down to the floor; this was effected by inverting the internal layout and placing the tuning pins at the top of the case, whereas in the Clementi (Ill. 15), *circa* 1815, the tuning pins are immediately above the keys, and the hitch pins are at the top.

This method reduced the height to about 6 feet 6 inches, but since the strike line had to be placed at the top of the case with the wrest pins, another type of action had to be introduced. It was made somewhat noisy and complicated by the use of long wooden stickers between keys and hammers, but did allow for a reduction in height of at least 2 feet.

The appearance of the Henderson cabinet piano made in 1825 is most deceptive (Ill. 16): this richly decorated Regency upright piano in fact contains an automatic mechanism and can be regarded as an early juke box! It has six octaves, FF–f4, and was probably made by Broadwood with the mechanism added by Henderson; behind the nameboard is the signature of one of the Broadwoods' workmen and the date. Here we have the rational development of the Clementi (Ill. 15), for the strings go down to the floor, reducing the height to reasonable proportions. The action is typical of many early uprights with a 'sticker' action: the stickers being similar to those found in organ actions.

There is a second set of small, very hard hammers like those of most street pianos, for use with the barrel mechanism; they are in addition to the hammers worked by the keys, and attack the strings from the rear. The barrel mechanism is wound up like a grandfather clock, with catgut and pulleys and a box with lead weights. There is a lever to lift off the dampers (the mechanical action is without dampers) and a sort of clutch to set the mechanism working.

These economies, however, were not sufficient to bring the instrument within the means of many people and further efforts were made to reduce the height still more and keep the instrument to the same scale as the square. Robert Wornum – the grandfather of the late G. Grey-Wornum, who designed the R.I.B.A. building in London – in conjunction with Wilkinson, produced a masterpiece of charm and ingenuity in 1811 with his cottage pianoforte. It had the usual five and a half octaves, FF–c4, but was only 42 inches high and 48 inches broad, the depth of the main case being only 10 inches and 20 inches, including the keyboard. (Ill. 17.) This instrument could be called the prototype of the modern upright piano.

16. Cabinet piano, 1825, by Henderson: six octaves height 80 in. (203·2 cm.) width 45 in. (114·3 cm.) The Colt Clavier Collection, Bethersden, Kent

17. (below left) Cottage piano, *circa* 1816, by Wilkinson & Wornum: five and a half octaves – one of the first really small Georgian pianos height 42 in. (106·6 cm.) width 48 in. (121·9 cm.) (below right) Instructions for use

This small piano has had much care and attention to detail lavished on it and is one of the first cottage pianos to be expressly designed for the amateur, as will be gathered from the printed instructions under the lid. (Ill. 17.) The case is mahogany with rosewood inlay and cross banding. The key surround is in figured sycamore, and under the keyboard is a secret drawer for music, hidden by the keyboard flap when closed. The back of the instrument is veneered and inlaid, so that the piano can stand in the centre of a room.

An interesting point is that the action is fixed so that by withdrawing a hinge pin it swings forward with the keyboard to facilitate attention to the strings or action. Tuning is simplified by the use of the left-hand pedal which damps one string of each note, making tuning wedges unnecessary. The strings are diagonal to obtain extra length.

It is fascinating to note that the Building Centre now stands on the site of Wornum's premises, and Longman and Broderip, who founded the famous firm that was revived by Clementi in 1802, had their business where Heal's the furnishers now stands in Tottenham Court Road.

Although the piano by Clementi (Ill. 18) appears to be an upright it is in fact a hybrid: technically, it is a square piano placed on its side. It will be seen that below the keyboard, there are only the legs and sustaining pedal. The strings run across the instrument diagonally, and there is an exceedingly ingenious action where the hammers strike the strings towards the soundboard, and the dampers work from behind the strings through the soundboard, the reverse of the typical 'square'.

Very few examples of these pianos exist, no doubt because the cabinet piano (Ills 16, 19) enabled the makers to use longer strings, with a simpler action and dampers without the complications inherent in a square piano placed on its side. The compass is six octaves, FF–f4, and the keyboard is the usual English type with moulded 'boxwood cornice' to the keys.

DIRECTIONS FOR THE NEW PATENT UNIQUE PIANO-FORTE,
MANUFACTURED AND SOLD BY THE PATENTEES,
WILKINSON and WORNUM, No. 315, Oxford Street, and No. 11, Princes Street, Hanover Square, London.
Pianoforte Manufacturers

18. 'Square piano on its side', *circa* 1815, by Clementi
six octaves
height 59 in. (149·8 cm.) width 55 in. (139·7 cm.)
The Colt Clavier Collection, Bethersden, Kent

By 1820 upright grands were no longer made, cabinet pianos having taken their place, but the demise of this type was also soon to come, and by 1850 they were no longer manufactured; the Collard & Collard of 1845 must have been one of the last (Ill. 19) cabinet pianos made. It has an elaborately carved case, cleanly executed. The compass is six and a half octaves, CC–f4, and the action is a 'patent repetition' one – that is to say, a more sophisticated one than that of Henderson.

An odd mixture of styles is combined in one piece of furniture making for an unsatisfactory *chef d'œuvre*. The keyboard surround is inlaid with mother-of-pearl, whilst the legs defy description, probably deriving inspiration from France and the sea. But the wood has been very carefully chosen and the mouldings on the frieze are well carved with classical architectural details. The Grinling Gibbons-style brackets are carved out of the solid. There was even a looking-glass for the pianist to admire herself or alternatively watch the audience.

By 1800 the Viennese had begun to produce the giraffe and *lyraflügel*. A comparatively late instrument (see facing colour plate) made *circa* 1825 by Schleip incorporates both early and late features. At the time of the Empire, Graf produced perhaps the most elaborate and exquisitely detailed instruments in this form, with supports of caryatids, Negroes and Egyptian slaves and with clocks, barometers, etc., on top. In the lofty rooms of the period, these pianos took up little space and were very decorative. Schleip of Berlin was very ingenious and invented a compact action with a mechanical overhead check to the hammers and several features which bear comparison to the upright action developed in England by Wornum, forming the basis of the modern upright piano action. It is a vast improvement upon the English cabinet piano actions which were in use until Wornum's introductions *circa* 1840.

The action is very light, the hammers are leather covered and are provided with

Colour Plate. Lyraflügel, *circa* 1825, by Schleip of Berlin
about six and a half octaves
height 82 in. (208·2 cm.) width 47 in. (119·3 cm.)
The Colt Clavier Collection, Bethersden, Kent

J.C. Schleip
in
Berlin

20. Piano console, 1845, by Pape
nearly seven octaves
height 39 in. (99 cm.) width 54 in. (137·1 cm.)
The Colt Clavier Collection, Bethersden, Kent

cane shanks, very flexible, and unlike any others known to the writer. The piano is strung bichord placed slightly diagonally. There are knee levers to work the tone changes; that on the right is to sustain the tone, that on the left to give *una corda* and the central one operates a 'bassoon' in which parchment is placed in contact with the lower strings.

The compass is six and a half octaves. Although this is what one calls a decorator's piece, it is actually an excellent musical instrument, with a tone like the best Viennese pianos, ideal for classical and early romantic music. It is reputed to have come from Caernarvon Castle.

In most Continental countries the vogue for small upright pianos continued; particularly in Germany, Switzerland and France. Inventive design flourished; small pianos with a compass of five and a half to seven octaves were made, many in the form of a chiffonnier. (Ill. 20.)

Henri Pape was born in Hanover and came to Paris in 1822 to work for Pleyel, who shared with Erard the distinction of being one of the greatest piano builders in France. About 1825 he founded his own piano workshop. Impressed with English cottage pianos, he went even one better and produced in 1839 a compact instrument of nearly seven octaves. (Ill. 20.) It has one of the most sophisticated actions ever made and is beautifully finished. The soundboard is actually the back of the instrument and has been grained to look like the rosewood of the case so that it can be placed free-standing in a room. It predates the modern minipiano by nearly 100 years.

Later it was found that more tone and volume was required, so these little instruments grew, but carried over into the newer versions many of the technical innovations that came about through the desire for miniature upright pianos; the result was that by the last quarter of the 19th century, the upright pianos were competing in popularity with the small boudoir grands.

21. Portable piano, 1783, by Verel
about four octaves
length 39 in. (99 cm.) width 13 in. (33 cm.)
The Colt Clavier Collection, Bethersden, Kent

BIBLIOGRAPHY

Boalch, D. *Makers of the Harpsichord and Clavichord*, London, 1956.

Harding, R. *The Piano-forte...*, Cambridge, 1933.

Hirt, F. J. *Meisterwerke des Klavierbaues...*, Olten, 1955.

Kinsky, G. *Musikhistorisches Museum von Wilhelm Heyer*, vol. 1, Cologne, 1910.

Rimbault, E. F. *The Pianoforte ... with some account of the clavichord, the virginal, the spinet, the harpsichord, etc.*, London, 1860.

Russell, R. *The Harpsichord and Clavichord*, London, 1959.

Some European Collections of Pianos and Other Musical Instruments: Bamberg: The Neupert Collection; Bethersden, Kent: The Colt Clavier Collection; Brussels: Conservatoire Royal de Musique; Copenhagen: Musikhistorisk Museum; Dublin: National Museum; Erlangen: Germanisches Museum (Rück Collection); The Hague: Gemeentemuseum; Leipzig: Stadtgeschichtliches Museum (Heyer Collection); Lisbon: Conservatorio Nacional; Liverpool: Rushworth and Dreaper Collection; London: Fenton House (Benton Fletcher Collection), Hampstead; London: The Victoria and Albert Museum; Milan: Brera; Munich: Deutsches Museum; Paris: Conservatoire National de Musique; Rome: Gorga Collection; Vienna: Kunsthistorisches Museum.

19. (left) Cabinet piano, 1845, by Collard & Collard
six and a half octaves
height 75 in. (190·5 cm.) width 48 in. (121·9 cm.)
The Colt Clavier Collection, Bethersden, Kent

Duelling Pistols

W. KEITH NEAL

The history of the duelling pistol is important as it represents the period in gun-making when the greatest advances were made, particularly in England. It came about as the result of affairs of honour being settled with pistols rather than with swords, and the change-over was due to a large extent to the fact that swords were no longer worn as a part of everyday dress towards the latter part of the 18th century. Another factor was that it was considered a fairer method, as it tended to discourage the bully, who might pick a quarrel with others he knew to be less skilled in fencing. It equalled things up, and had the further advantage of delaying the contest, at least until the seconds had done their best to prevent it. A quarrel in the old days could flare up and be settled on the spur of the moment, during the height of the individual's temper, simply by drawing swords; but with pistol duelling, the process was slower and more dignified, a meeting being arranged at a later date, and the time, place and weapons decided upon formally.

To begin with, the pistols used were the normal holster or saddle pistols such as any gentleman would possess, and these were firearms with side-locks, and barrels from ten to twelve inches in length. Although good enough for self-defence at close quarters, these pistols seldom had the refinements of accurate sights, quick-firing locks or hair triggers. Nor, generally speaking, were they specially fitted to the hand of the man who used them. All these improvements were developed as the result of pistol duelling, and the earliest examples to be found are of English manufacture, where the true duelling pistol was evolved soon after 1760.

The first duelling pistols had long slender barrels, they were fitted well to the hand, so that shooting became instinctive, and the pistol itself formed as it were a prolongation of the arm which held it. By dint of much practice with one pistol a man could be sure of hitting a man-sized target without fail at twenty paces by quick snap-shooting; later on the duelling pistol was made much heavier in the barrel, as the science of slow, deadly accurate target shooting became popular. The heavier barrel prevented flip, and gave the shooter the opportunity of making extremely accurate shooting, such as hitting a wafer at fifteen yards or putting a dozen shots in succession at this distance into a playing card. At first all barrels were smooth bore, and rifled barrels were forbidden by the duelling code as they were considered unfair. In England smooth bores were normally used, although barrels bored with secret rifling, invisible at the muzzle, were produced by several of the leading gunmakers. These appear to have got by the rules, the rifling being so shallow as to be hardly more than a scratch, yet sufficient to have some effect on the ball when the bore was clean and the pistol loaded with a carefully patched ball. This system came in with the heavy barrels of the early 19th century and was undoubtedly influenced by the French and German weapons of the period.

An interesting innovation which came in with the duelling pistol was the wooden case. Until this time pistols were sold either with leather holsters or else in bags of striped cloth made of thick wool or velvet. The cloth bags were known as 'shoddies', being made up from left-over cuttings from the blanket factories making the heavy Hudson Bay pattern bed coverings. This waste product was bought up by women who, working at home, made the pieces into patchwork covers suitable for guns and pistols of all sizes. The wooden case did away with this, and at once became an article of furniture. To begin with, the cases, either of oak or mahogany, had a brass drop handle on the top, Chippendale style, and the edges were chamfered. Inside they were lined with Irish baize and, in the very earliest ones, with pattern paper similar to wall-paper. The fittings were a powder flask, usually of copper, but of hard leather in the earliest examples. Later on the flasks were made with compartments which held bullets, patches and flints beside the powder. There was always a bullet mould and sometimes a patch cutter of steel which stamped out the correct size linen patch to insure a proper gas-tight fit in the bore. A cleaning rod was also included, and in the later examples this often served as a loading rod as well, the end having a brass measure which when filled and placed into the barrel muzzle downwards insured that the exact charge reached the breech with no grains hanging round the sides of the bore. In the very earliest duelling pistol sets a separate brass charger was included in the case. This held the exact charge for which the pistols were regulated to shoot. In addition to these appurtenances there was a turnscrew; this usually had a short flat handle with tapering blade, sometimes with a wide blade on the side as well. Others were made as pairs, the two blades being made to fit into each other, and were combined with a brass pricker for clearing the touch-hole. They were commonly made with reversible blades in case the edge broke, and they were always made of good tempered mainspring steel. So good indeed were these turnscrews that they are frequently missing from the case and in many cases still being used, their handiness and quality being far above anything mass produced today. A supply of bullets and a packet of flints wrapped in brown paper or a tin of caps completed the outfit, although it must be added that in the case of percussion pistols a nipple wrench was also a necessity.

One of the earliest pistols built on duelling lines was made by Griffin of Bond Street, London, and its silver mounts are hallmarked for 1764 in London with the mark of John King. (Ills 1, 2.) The barrel is of Italian origin and signed by the master barrel forger, Lazarino Cominazo. It is octagonal and fluted its entire

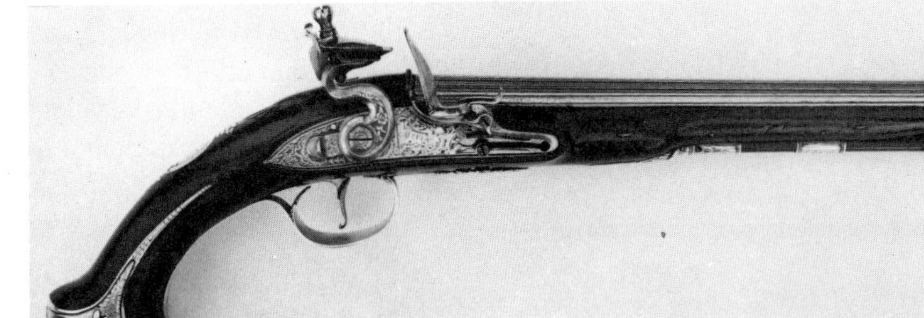

1. Transitional type of the first type of duelling pistol, dated 1764, by Griffin; London length 14¼ in. (38·7 cm.) W. Keith Neal Collection

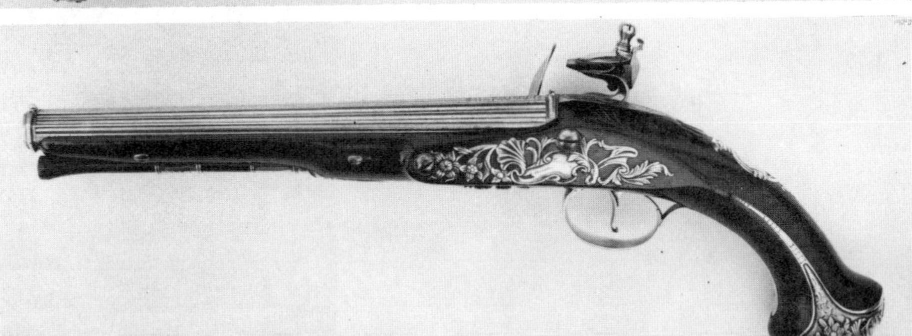

2. Reverse side of Illustration 1, showing silver side plate

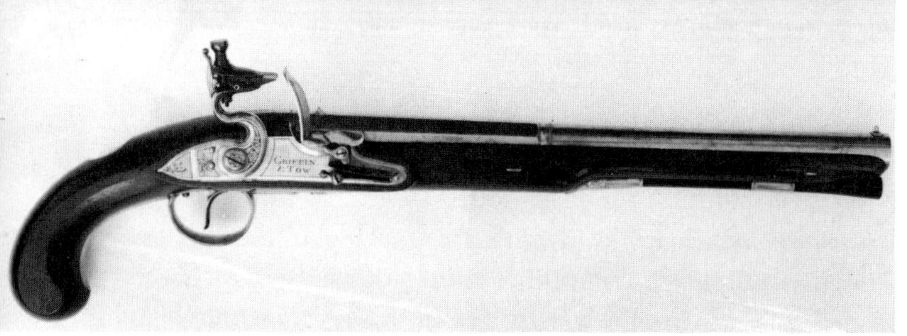

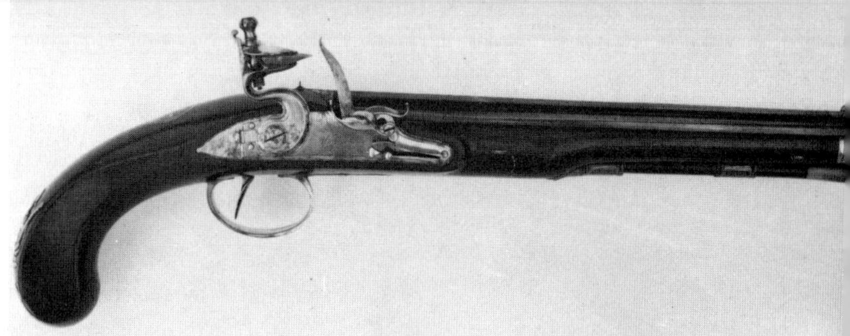

3. (above left) Earliest type of true duelling pistol, *circa* 1773, by Griffin & Tow; London
length 18 in. (45·7 cm.)
W. Keith Neal Collection

4. (above right) Silver-mounted duelling pistol, hall-marked 1774, by Wogdon; London
length 14¾ in. (37·4 cm.)
W. Keith Neal Collection

length and is fitted with both fore-sight and back-sight, which was an essential with all duelling pistols. Fine barrels imported from both Italy and Spain were frequently used for the best quality weapons, it being a legend that their quality was superior to all others. In this there was some truth, not that the workmanship was better, but that the iron ore where these barrels were produced was of finer quality. The ore from the Gardone mines in northern Italy, having a natural content of manganese, was tough and held a very high polish. Strong barrels with less weight were made with it. In the same way, the barrels from Spain used the excellent iron ore from Biscay, and the gunmakers frequently made them from old discarded horseshoe iron; the hammering of the animals' feet on the cobble-stones had rendered such remains of great utility and strength. The bore of this pistol is just over half an inch diameter and the length of the barrel is nine and a quarter inches. The silver escutcheon bears the motto and Crowned Lion of the Royal Family. It may be regarded as an excellent example of the transition period between holster and duelling pistol.

Soon after 1770 Joseph Griffin, who was Master of the Worshipful Company of Gunmakers in 1763–64, took into partnership the gunmaker Tow. The firm from then on became Griffin & Tow, and some of the very finest firearms of the period were made by them. They were quick to take advantage of the new market for finely balanced accurate pistols for duelling, and the pistol shown in illustration 3 is one of a pair of best quality weapons. The barrel is light despite its full twelve inches in length; it is of 'Spanish form', that is to say, the breech end is octagonal, changing to round at a point less than half-way towards the muzzle. It has a well defined front sight and a rear sight with lateral adjustment. The lock has the graceful swan-neck cock and the steel has a friction roller bearing in its base to give the sharpest reaction. The mounts are of steel, lightly engraved, and the finial of the trigger guard is formed as an acorn. On the silver escutcheon are the initials of the King-Harman family for whom these pistols were made. On the barrel are the proof marks of the Gunmakers Company, Griffin's mark 'I.G.' and the Irish registration mark R.764, showing them to have been registered in Roscommon where the family had a seat. The touch-hole is lined with gold. The pistols handle perfectly, the locks have a hair trigger which is adjustable with a small set screw and can be set by pushing the trigger forward. Alternatively they can be fired with the normal trigger pull adjusted to about three pounds. The weight of each pistol is one pound thirteen ounces.

The silver-mounted duelling pistol shown in illustration 4 is by Robert Wogdon of London, who was without doubt the most famous of all the pistol makers.

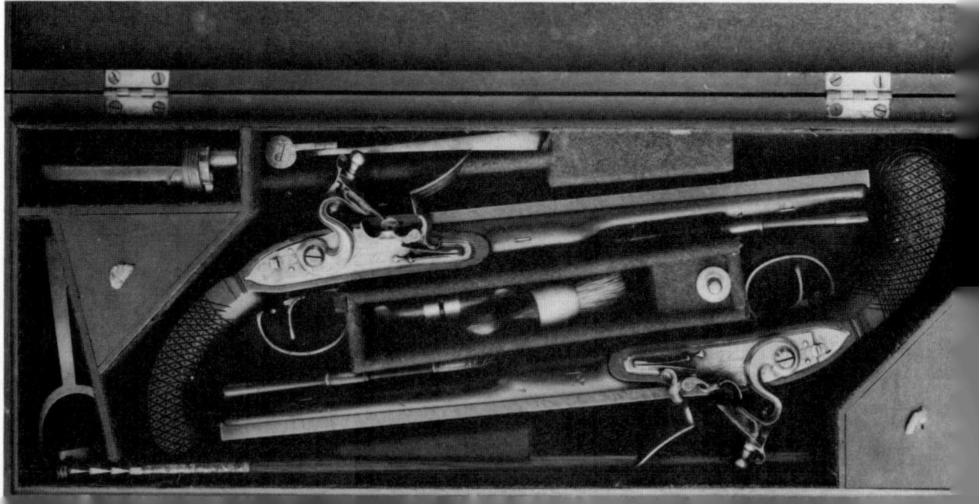

5. A cased set of duelling pistols, *circa* 1780, by Twigg; London
length 15½ in. (39·3 cm.)
W. Keith Neal Collection

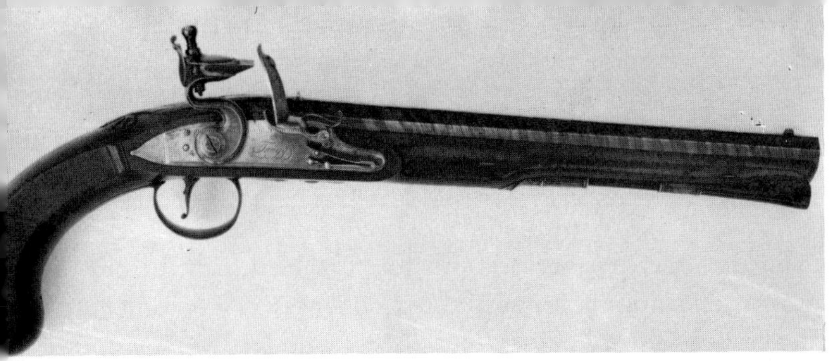

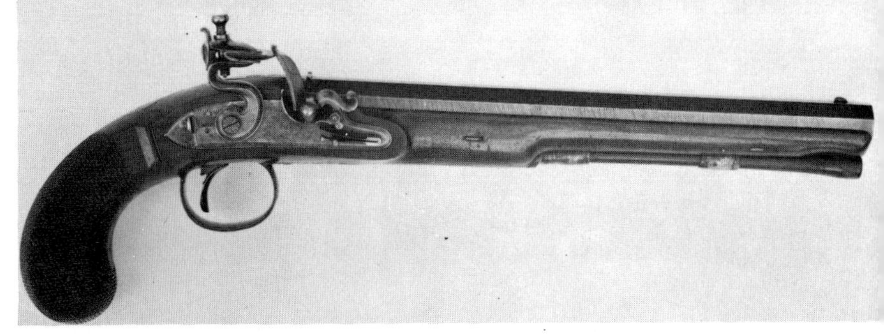

6. (above left) Earliest form of Twigg duelling pistol, *circa* 1770
length 15¼ in. (38·7 cm.)
W. Keith Neal Collection

7. (above right) Early John Manton duelling pistol, dated 1790
length 16½ in. (41·9 cm.)
W. Keith Neal Collection

He specialized in, and made his name by, his skill in making them. His name was a byword, so much so that an affair which had gone beyond the means of settlement by law was known as 'Wogdon's case'. This maker had an enormous output, and all his pistols had a distinctive style. The majority were finished without much decoration but all were superbly made, and deadly. His pistols were specially popular with the Irish, and an anonymous writer signing himself 'An Irish Volunteer' published in 1782 "Stanzas on Duelling inscribed to Wogdon the celebrated pistol maker". It commenced:

"Hail Wogdon! Patron of that leaden death
Which waits alike the bully and the brave;
As well might art recall departed breath,
As any artifice your victims save."

And after many verses referring to famous duels concludes:

"Such milder praise be, Wogdon, still your aim!
Then shall no jury sit upon your life.
Mac-Carthy shall ensure you deathless fame;
The champion thanked by mistress and by wife."

The firm of Wogdon commenced in the Haymarket about the year 1772, and the pistol illustrated is one of his earliest examples; it bears the silver hallmark for 1774 on the mounts. It has a nine-inch barrel with a bore of just under half an inch, which is round in form but has a flat sighting rib running its entire length. The fore-sight is a silver 'spider' and the back-sight placed well back on the breech tang. The silver mounts include a figure of Britannia which forms the butt cap; it also acts as a counterweight to balance the pistol. The pierced butt plate is in the style of the earlier saddle pistols, and an interesting survival. The owner's coat of arms with the motto "Ubi libertas ibi patria" is engraved upon the silver escutcheon. This pair of pistols originally formed part of a garniture comprising duelling pistols, pocket pistols and a carbine with extending butt.

The other most famous maker of this period was John Twigg of Piccadilly. He made his barrels octagonal for the whole length; on the stocks behind the breech was a finely carved shell design, and he was one of the very first gunsmiths to introduce chequering into the stocks. This took the design of a wide diamond pattern with a star in the centre. A pair of his pistols showing this first form of chequering and complete in their original case with accessories is shown in illustration 5. They are signed 'Twigg' on the locks, in script, and again on the barrels in heavy gold letters. These pistols date from *circa* 1780.

Another pistol by Twigg of most graceful proportions is shown in illustration 6. This is one of his earliest examples and dates from *circa* 1770. The barrel is ten inches in length and of stub twist, which shows clearly by the browning. The stock with its flattened side is slender and fits the hand perfectly. The lock is fitted with a special type of pancover which has a detachable base, by which the priming can be kept in place, with the steel thrown back in the safety position. In this way the pistol could be kept fully loaded and primed, but the cock let down rendering it impossible to fire until the lock was cocked and the steel brought into place. In this type of lock the feather spring is divided so that one half of the top arm works on the pancover and the other on the base; this base can be detached from the pancover itself by a small stud in the front of the steel. It was a clever and costly refinement and Twigg was one of the very few makers who fitted it. This pistol weighs only one and a half pounds. Twigg's vintage period dates between 1770 and 1785 and his barrels bear his mark 'I.T.' under a crown, his signature on his duelling pistols was always in script and the finials of the trigger guard have the acorn design. He was one of the greatest of all the English gunmakers and many who were later to become household words learned their trade from him. One of his pupils was John Manton, who rose to be foreman before setting up business on his own in Dover Street in 1780. A typical duelling pistol of John Manton's design is shown in illustration 7. It was made in 1790, its date being established by the original bill of sale still retained in its case. It shows the transition period between the light-barrelled early pistol and the later heavy-barrelled weapon. The flat-sided butt is deeply chequered, and the wood comes right to the muzzle. The barrel, which is octagonal for its entire length, has excellent sights, the back-sight being adjustable laterally. The pan of the lock as well as the touch-hole are lined with gold. The lock has a double bolt which at half cock locks both cock and steel firmly; it is fitted with a hair trigger and a detant, the latter a device to ensure that the sear will not drop into the half cock notch when being fired with the hair trigger. This pistol weighs two pounds. The mounts are of steel, blued and lightly engraved; there is little ornament, but the workmanship is of the very finest.

Another famous maker of duelling pistols was H. W. Mortimer. His style was different from both Manton and Twigg, his stocks being made to curve round towards the butt and his weapons were light and elegant. He frequently carved a rose on the butt end. Such a pistol is shown in illustration 8. It dates also from *circa* 1790.

Although the tendency in England was to produce fine pistols with little decoration there were exceptions, and amongst some of the most beautiful are a pair made by Knubley, who had his shop at Charing Cross, London. (See Ills 9, 10 and colour plate facing p. 265 [below]). The stocks of these pistols are most beautifully inlaid with flowers and foliage in silver and the mounts are of heavy silver deeply cut with figures of Britannia, a Roman warrior, a classical bust, etc. They bear the London hallmark for 1791 and the maker's mark of Moses Brent. The barrels, which retain the classical 'Spanish form', are richly inlaid with gold that is enhanced by the contrast of the fire-blued finish. The locks are also inlaid with gold showing trophies of arms, again with a fire-blued finish. The locks have hair triggers and are finished in the highest quality and, despite the heavy silver mounts and decoration, nothing has been sacrificed for balance and accuracy. These pistols handle as well as it is possible to make them, a combination of beauty and effective gun-making. They were actually used in a duel between an English officer and a French officer in Paris. The Frenchman, who 'called out' the Englishman, was fatally injured in the contest. It was the privilege of the man who was challenged to choose his weapons and the Englishman used his own duelling pistols.

Another highly decorative pair of pistols are shown. (See colour plate facing p. 265 [above].) Like the previous pair, they represent the last word in fine London gun-making. Traditionally made for the Prince Regent, they have individually

8. The classic shaped duelling pistol, *circa* 1790, by H. W. Mortimer; London
length 15½ in. (39·3 cm.)
W. Keith Neal Collection

9. Highly decorated duelling pistols, hallmarked 1791, by Knubley; London
length 15½ in. (39·3 cm.)
W. Keith Neal Collection

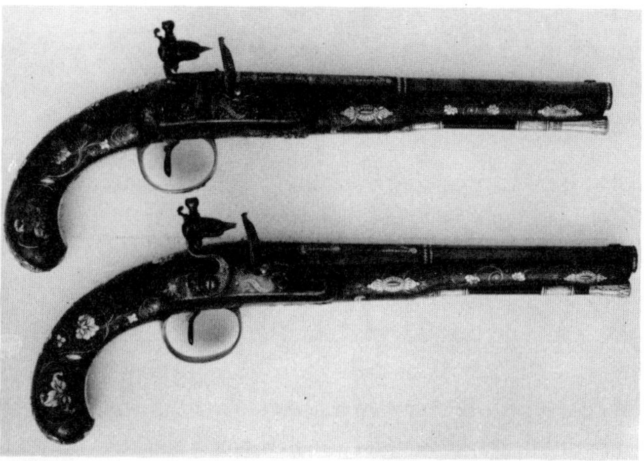

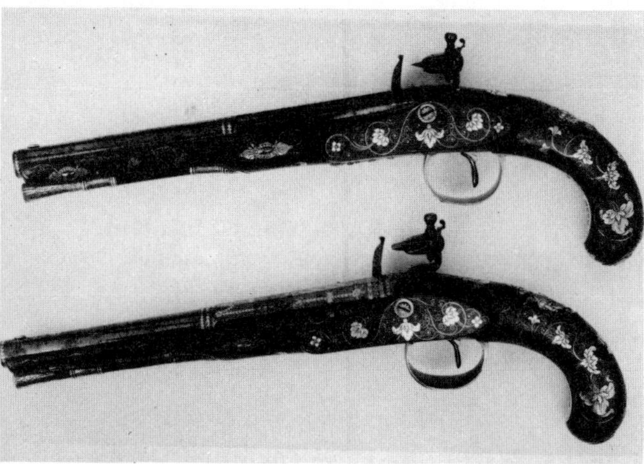

10. Reverse side of Knubley pistols (Ill. 9) with the mounts and inlay of silver and the barrels fire-blued and inlaid with gold

11. (right) Saw-handled duelling pistol, *circa* 1815, by Tatham & Egg; London
length 15½ in. (39·3 cm.)
W. Keith Neal Collection

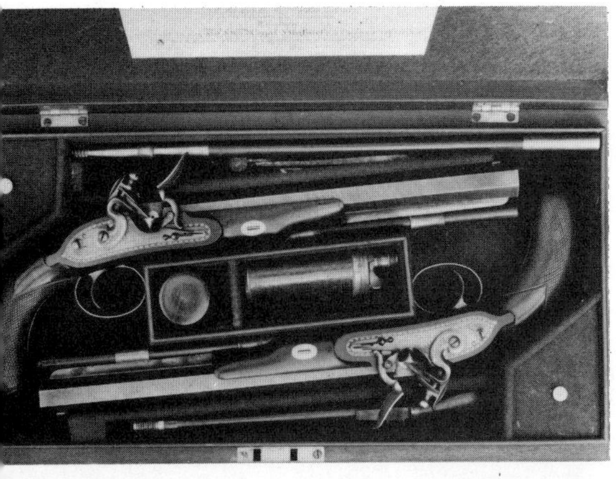

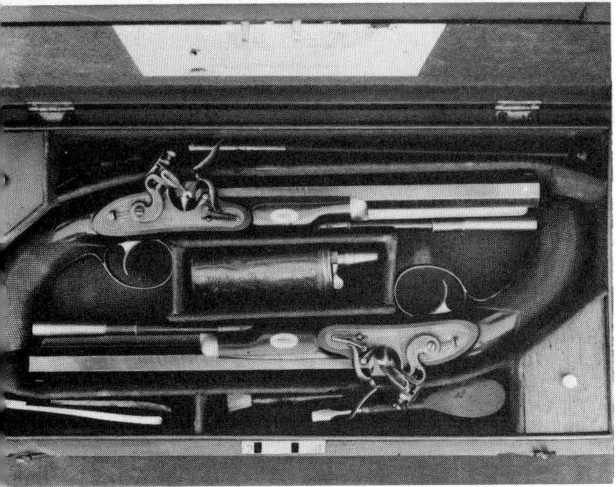

12. A case of Joseph Manton duelling pistols, *circa* 1818, showing his standard pattern
length 15¼ in. (38·7 cm.)
W. Keith Neal Collection

13. A case of James Purdey duelling pistols made in London *circa* 1820
length 16 in. (40·6 cm.)
W. Keith Neal Collection

sculptured silver mounts depicting Andromeda, Medusa and other classical subjects. They are signed by the silversmith Moses Brent and dated for 1800. The locks and barrels are richly inlaid with gold against a fire-blued background showing characteristic trophies of arms, a sunburst, flags, etc., all carried out in the most elegant manner. The weight of each pistol is two and a half pounds, but so well are they balanced that they do not feel unduly heavy in the hand. They are made by Brunn of Charing Cross, London.

Pistols with saw-handled stocks came into fashion early in the 19th century; it was believed that they gave the shooter a more steady grip and they had to be individually fitted to a man's hand. One of the best makers of these was a firm called Tatham and Egg, and a typical pistol made by them is shown in illustration 11. It has a heavy octagon barrel stocked to the muzzle, and in order to give the longest possible sight base, the back-sight is combined with the silver initial plate on the tip of the saw-back. The lock has the graceful spur cock, an innovation which was copied from the French makers, and the pistol can be dated at about the time of Waterloo.

The last development of the flint-lock duelling pistol in England was the heavy barrel target type of weapon which was designed to give super accuracy and was adapted for steady aimed shooting at a mark. It was not suitable or easy to use for snap-shooting on account of its weight. The heavy barrel made the pistol muzzle heavy, and although it gave great steadiness of aim, it destroyed the fine handling qualities so evident in the earlier weapons of the 18th century.

Two typical cases of these pistols are shown. (Ills 12, 13.) The first are by the famous maker Joseph Manton. These pistols are scratch rifled, have his latest quick-firing locks and are accurate enough to hit a penny at twelve yards. The equipment in the mahogany case, which is standard for this date (*circa* 1818), includes a red leather covered combination flask for powder, bullets and patches, a bullet mould, a loading and cleaning rod combined, and a mallet for forcing down the tight-fitting ball. The case has the makers' label in the lid.

The other set is by James Purdey of London and represents the last word in flint-locks, made as late as 1820 and of superb quality throughout. Every part of the lock, stock and barrel shows a finish and workmanship which cannot be surpassed and is in every way equal to the finest guns still produced by hand by this famous firm today.

The Forsyth system using a small charge of loose fulminate powder had been in limited use since its invention in 1808, but few duelling pistols on this method of ignition have survived. One such pistol with a sliding magazine action is shown in illustration 14. It is of the heavy barrel pattern and of excellent quality. The small box-shaped magazine held enough powder for at least a dozen primings and was connected to the hammer by a link. As the hammer fell the false bottom of the magazine left a few grains of the fulminate in the pan which was detonated by the striker.

Following this, and before the percussion cap proper came into use, a paper patch lock pistol was invented. These pistols were fitted with a detachable striker in the head of the hammer, and a supply of these strikers, each with a paper cap fitted into it, was supplied with the pistols. A set of these pistols by Samuel Nock, complete with spare primers, is shown in illustration 15.

The early form of duelling pistol with copper cap ignition is shown in illustration 16. It is also by Samuel Nock and of the highest quality. Of interest is the straight form of stock with the minimum of bend. The purpose of this was an attempt to design a pistol with a heavy target barrel which by the use of this very

14. A Forsyth patent duelling pistol (The magazine fulminate lock superseded the flint-lock soon after 1810 in this form, and was made until it was replaced by the percussion cap system *circa* 1821. This pistol is one of the last to be made on this principle and dates from *circa* 1820)
length 15½ in. (39·3 cm.)
W. Keith Neal Collection

straight stock could be used to some extent for snap-shooting. It should be noted that a back action lock is used; this gave added strength to the stock and came into use soon after 1825.

The final pattern of duelling pistol to be made in England was a very streamlined weapon. It had standard percussion cap ignition and normally no ramrod was attached; it was in fact turning itself into a target pistol. A very fine example of this is shown in illustration 17. It is made by James Purdey and has a seven-inch rifled barrel. The saw handle is constructed of polished horn to fit exactly the owner's hand. The trigger guard has a spur to accommodate the second finger and give greater stability. So perfectly is this weapon designed to fit the hand that one has only to look at the target and bring the weapon up to find the sights correctly aligned. It has an adjustable hair trigger, or can be used with the normal pull-off adjusted to about three pounds. It weighs one pound eleven ounces. This pistol is the culmination of all that was good in the design of the many types of weapons produced before. It is just the right weight; it is equally good for snap-shooting or slow accurate target work and is by far the finest duelling pistol the author has ever handled. It came, however, at a period when duelling in England was almost finished. The law was against it and so was public opinion; to fight a duel was to risk a charge of murder. No longer was it necessary for a gentleman to own and practise with his pistols, and it was left to the die-hard and enthusiast to carry on. This to some extent was done, as pistol shooting as a form of recreation and manly exercise had come to stay, but the demand for the weapons diminished until by 1850 very few indeed were still being made in England.

As England, more than any other country, was responsible for the design and development of the duelling pistol, it is only right to give the greatest prominence to those made there. On the Continent, particularly in France and Belgium, and to a lesser extent in Germany, fine duelling pistols had been made, and the fashion was largely set by the French makers soon after the Revolution. Nicolas Boutet, who was in charge of the manufactory at Versailles during the period of the First Empire, turned out many magnificent sets of pistols. Many of them were ordered by Napoleon for presentation as political gifts or rewards for outstanding service. A typical set of his pistols is shown. (Ill. 18.) The special features are the graceful swamped barrels flaring out at the muzzle, the handle of the stock, which is formed almost at right angles, swelling out to an elaborately carved butt cap, and the long graceful spring which actuates the steel or pancover. These features formed the basic design of Boutet's pistols and his style was copied not only by other makers in France but elsewhere in Europe. The barrels were almost always hair rifled. This consisted of a vast number of grooves, sometimes as many as a hundred, and these, though lightly cut, were enough to give the necessary accuracy. They only functioned in a perfectly clean barrel and the fouling they collected rendered them useless if more than one or two shots were fired. His pistols were the last word in elegance and the gold and silver work was superb. Many of them were works of art rather than practical weapons, and some of the finest do not appear to have ever been fired. Combining as they do fine gunmaking with lavish silver and goldsmith work, they have become great prizes to the collector. The other great French maker was Le Page of Paris. He had

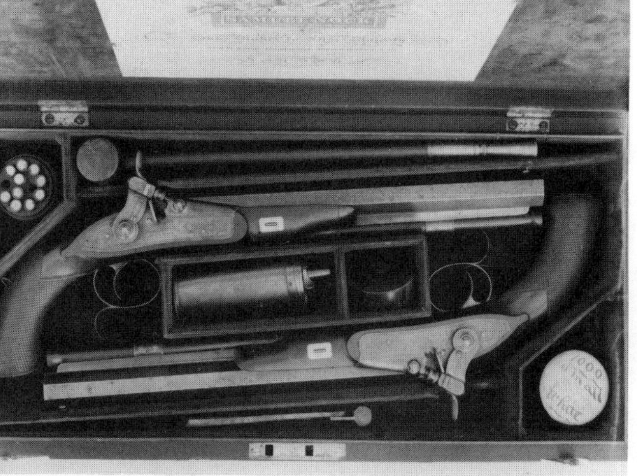

15. A case of early percussion duelling pistols, *circa* 1819, by Samuel Nock; London (They antedate the percussion cap, firing a paper patch in a detachable steel striker)
length 16 in. (40·6 cm.)
W. Keith Neal Collection

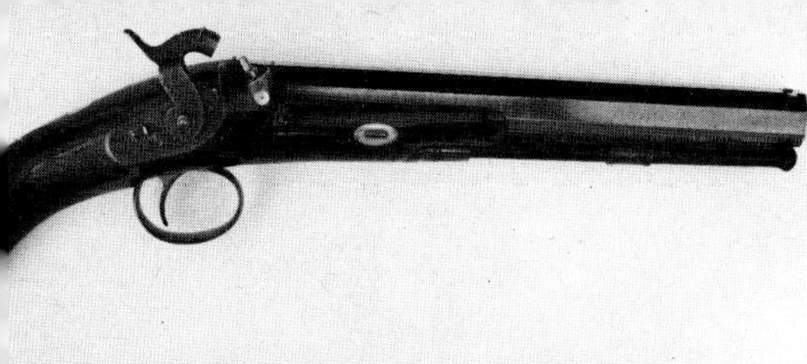

16. (above) Samuel Nock percussion cap duelling pistol with the first form of 'Back action' lock, *circa* 1826 – note the very straight form of stock for snap-shooting
length 16 in. (40·6 cm.)
W. Keith Neal Collection

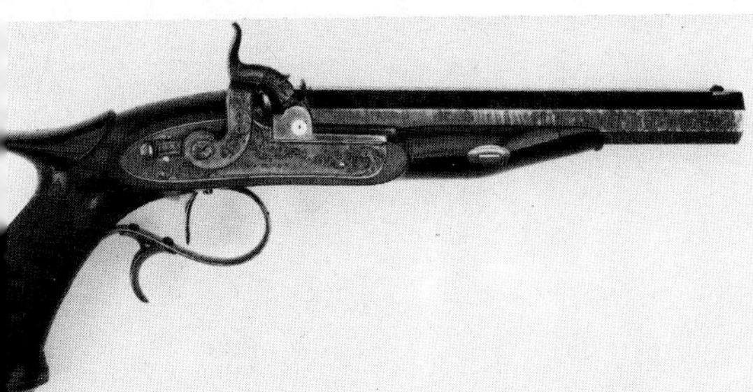

17. (above) Purdey saw-handled rifled pistol made in 1829
length 13¼ in. (33·6 cm.)
W. Keith Neal Collection

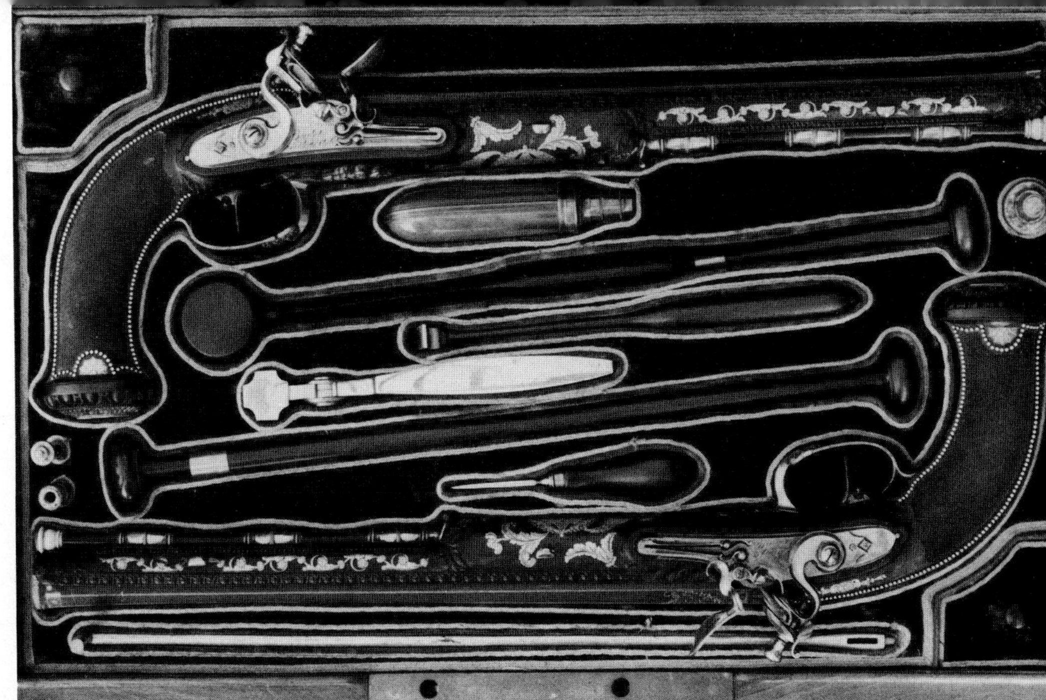

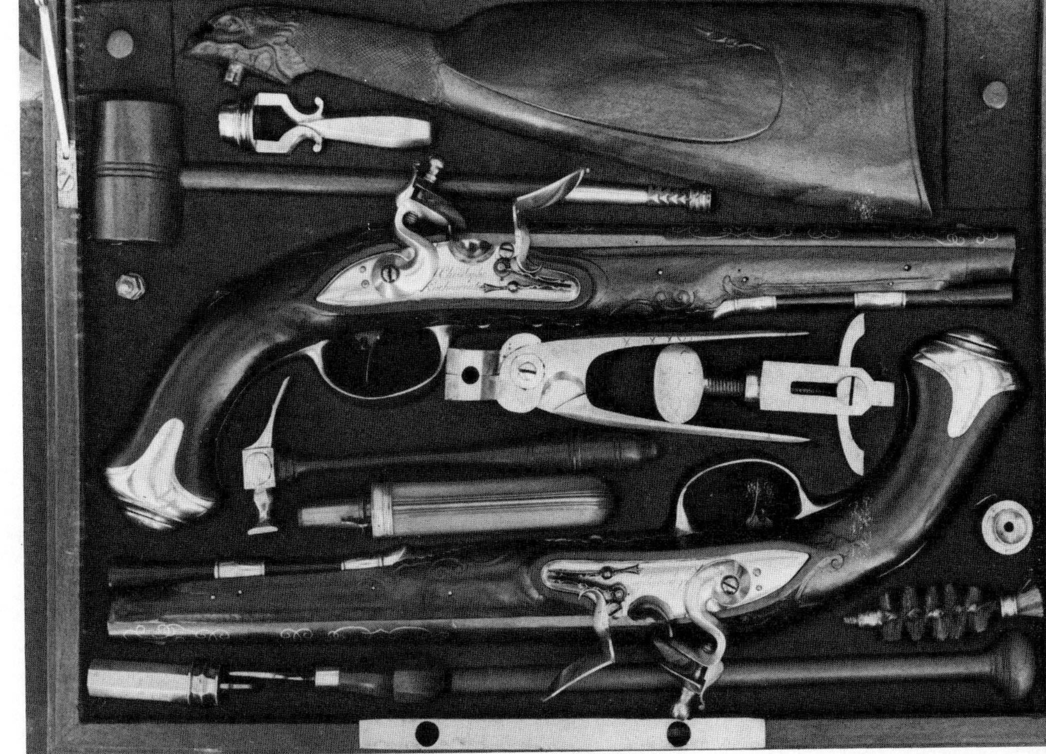

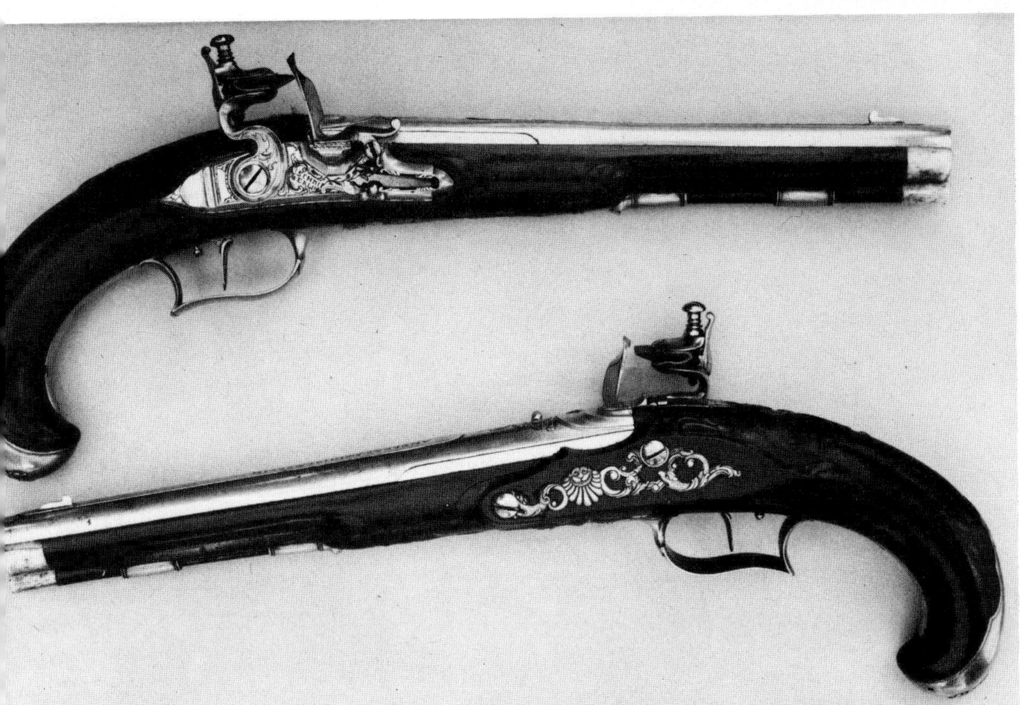

18. (top right) Duelling pistol, *circa* 1805, made by Boutet; Versailles, directeur artiste
length 16½ in. (41·9 cm.)
Formerly W. Keith Neal Collection

19. (above) Duelling pistol, *circa* 1815, made by J. Christophe Kuchenreuter of Regensburg
length 15 in. (38·1 cm.)
Formerly W. Keith Neal Collection

20. (left) Early German duelling pistols, *circa* 1780, by Andreas Schmidt; Berlin
length 15 in. (38·1 cm.)
W. Keith Neal Collection

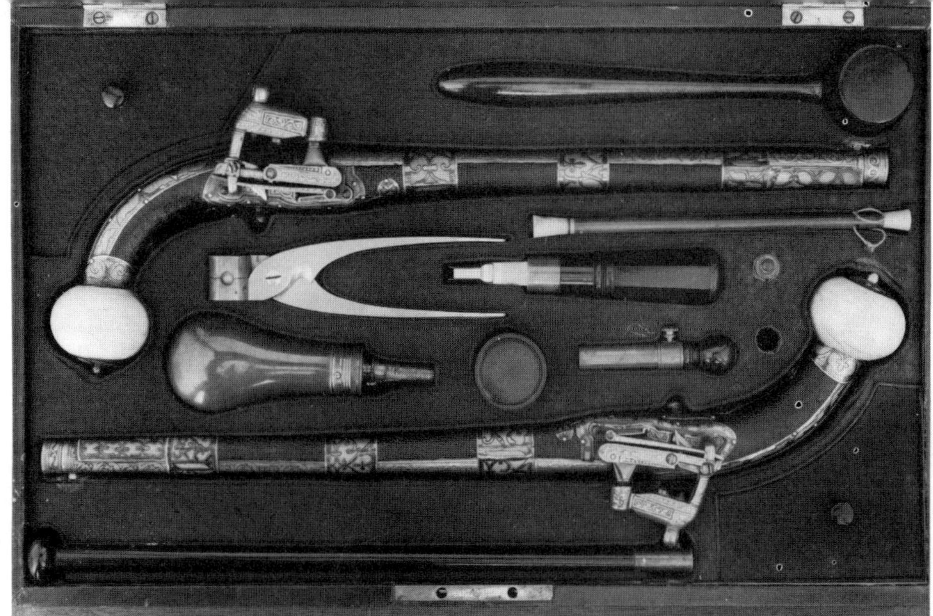

21. Russian duelling pistols of traditional Cossack type, *circa* 1855
length 16½ in. (40·6 cm.)
W. Keith Neal Collection

been making guns from the time of the old régime of Louis XVI. Having survived the Revolution he continued to make the very best firearms, and his pistols, though sometimes elaborate, were much more practical weapons than those of Boutet. It is significant that whereas Napoleon gave away as presents the finest of Boutet's work, the majority of his personal weapons were made by Le Page. A supreme example of the work of this great gunmaker is of a perfectly proportioned pair of pistols made for a child to the order of Napoleon whose Eagle and Cipher they bear, and there is no doubt they were intended for his son the Roi de Rome, on whom was lavished every kind of article, usually a small edition of his father's own possessions. The pistols are eight inches in length and weigh only six ounces, the barrels are hair rifled and have a calibre of 0·36 inch. They are signed in gold on the barrels "Le Page a Paris, Arqbusier de L'Empereur". The Eagle in raised gold is set at the breech and on the locks a bee. Below on the trigger guard is a gold 'N'. The stocks are carved and inlaid with gold showing trophies of arms and classical heads, and the fore-end is carved with a lion's head. They are dated 1814. The case of exotic wood is inlaid with mother-of-pearl, and the accessories are in ivory and tortoiseshell. L'Aiglon was indeed fortunate to be given a pair of pistols such as these.

In Germany the gunmaking family of Kuchenreuter turned out many excellent pairs of duelling pistols, both flint-lock and percussion cap. The stocks were made narrow in the grip and of flattened form and they normally had a metal butt cap. The mounts were usually of brass, sometimes gilded, but occasionally of iron. The barrels were mostly smooth bore and of round section towards the muzzle and they frequently had some silver scroll decoration. Back-sights, often with folding leaves, were always fitted, and the pistols marked 1 and 2 to distinguish them. A typical set signed by J. Christophe Kuchenreuter is shown in illustration 19 and it is particularly well equipped with accessories. A detachable shoulder stock is included, no doubt made for an officer who would wish to use the same pistols for service. The date of these pistols is *circa* 1815. Another pair made by Andreas Schmidt of Berlin and dating from *circa* 1780 show the earlier form. These have nine and a half-inch smooth bore barrels of round form with a flat sighting rib. The mounts are of German silver, decorated with masks. The locks are small and neat, and fitted with hair triggers. They handle well, but lack the smooth oily feeling in the locks of an English weapon.

Other first-class makers in Europe were Lebeda of Prague who enjoyed a very high reputation and produced exceedingly fine percussion pistols. Contriner, Nowotny and Pirko, all of them famous gunmakers of Vienna, turned out many superlative sets of duelling pistols, but the largest production of all was undoubtedly in Paris and Liège, where numerous makers produced duelling pistols from the

Colour Plates. (above) Highly decorated duelling pistols, hallmarked 1815, by Brunn; London (The specially designed silver mounts show classical subjects. These pistols were by tradition made for the Prince Regent)
length 16⅜ in. (41·5 cm.)
(below) Highly decorated duelling pistols, hallmarked 1791, by Knubley; London
length 15½ in. (39·3 cm.)
W. Keith Neal Collection

22. American duelling pistols, *circa* 1798, made in Pennsylvania by J. Lowmaster
length 15½ in. (39·3 cm.)
Formerly W. Keith Neal Collection

plainest type with fluted stocks to the most elaborate, such as those by Gastinne Renette, Devisme, Gauvain and others made for the Paris and London expositions.

The farthest point east to make duelling pistols was in Russia, and excellent pairs bearing the names of armourers in St Petersburg, Moscow and Tula can be found. Some of these were made in the French style influenced by Boutet or Le Page, but pistols of true Russian type were made. Of particular interest is a cased set of pistols, made in the traditional Cossack style with ivory ball butts and miquelet locks, the barrels damascened in gold and the mounts of silver niello work. Pistols of this kind were worn by cavalry officers in the best Russian regiments for dress; many of the later ones were actually made by armourers working in the Kremlin who had been brought there for this purpose from the provinces. The set shown in illustration 21 is very complete. Originally flint-locks, they have been skilfully rebuilt as percussion weapons and are contained in a tooled Russian leather case. The fittings include both cleaning and loading rods and a mallet for driving the bullet, an adjustable powder measure, reversible turnscrew and nipple wrench, cap box, powder flask and bullet mould. Pistols of this type never had a ramrod attached – it was carried separately either in the tunic or the holster – but in this case there is a two-piece folding rod, each end having an ivory head and connected with a strong cord. The two sections being reversed join up with the cord and form a full-length ramrod. These pistols, although built on the lines of a cavalry officer's pistols, are undoubtedly duelling pistols, they have accurate sights, long light smooth bore barrels, and all the equipment necessary in their case.

In America there was little demand for duelling pistols, in most cases where they were needed it was simpler to import them than to make them, as the American gunmaking industry was far more concerned with the making of fine rifles and more essential weapons. In consequence, any duelling pistols of American manufacture, at least before 1800, are extremely rare, and those which do exist and are made in the most characteristic American style come from the neighbourhood of York and Lancaster in Pennsylvania. An interesting pair is shown in illustration 22. They are signed in script on the barrels J. Lowmaster, a maker who is believed to have worked for a time in York, Pennsylvania. They are well made and have good lines, and the mounts are brass with slight decoration. It is curious that one of the pair has been altered to percussion at a later date. Each lock bears the initials of the maker, J.L.

That the Americans could and did occasionally make extremely fine duelling pistols at a rather later date is evident from a presentation pair mounted in gold which were made by Simeon North, of Middletown, Connecticut, in 1820. These were ordered by the State of Connecticut for presentation to Commodore Isaac Hull. The pistols are of the highest quality throughout, but made in the English style. They were deposited in the State Department at Washington, and in 1911 were transferred to the Navy Department, where they may still be seen.

Other makers of duelling pistols in America dating from the first quarter of the 19th century were James Haslett of Baltimore and R. Constable of Philadelphia. Both produced very fine flint-lock pistols in the traditional English style.

A set of duelling pistols today is a collector's item; it represents the combined skill and talent of the metal worker, the wood carver and the engraver, and sometimes the gold and silversmith as well.

They also carry with them a romance, for they were used in good causes as well as bad, and they were bound up with the rules of a society long since past. These and many other factors combine to make the whole subject a most fascinating one, and the ownership and study of the specimens which survive, so rewarding.

Netsuke

W. W. WINKWORTH

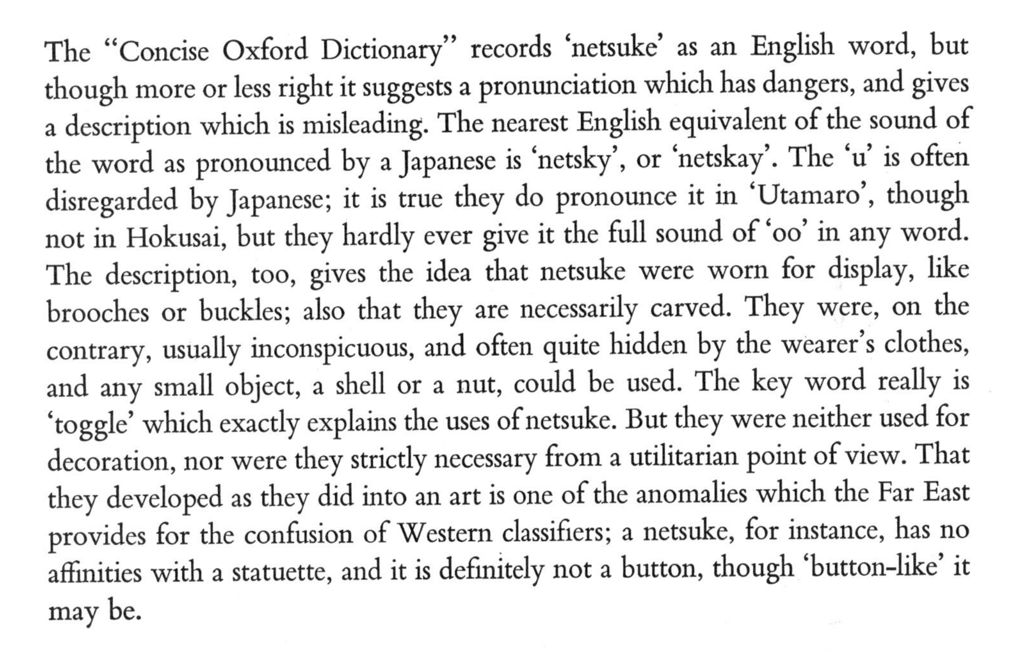

The "Concise Oxford Dictionary" records 'netsuke' as an English word, but though more or less right it suggests a pronunciation which has dangers, and gives a description which is misleading. The nearest English equivalent of the sound of the word as pronounced by a Japanese is 'netsky', or 'netskay'. The 'u' is often disregarded by Japanese; it is true they do pronounce it in 'Utamaro', though not in Hokusai, but they hardly ever give it the full sound of 'oo' in any word. The description, too, gives the idea that netsuke were worn for display, like brooches or buckles; also that they are necessarily carved. They were, on the contrary, usually inconspicuous, and often quite hidden by the wearer's clothes, and any small object, a shell or a nut, could be used. The key word really is 'toggle' which exactly explains the uses of netsuke. But they were neither used for decoration, nor were they strictly necessary from a utilitarian point of view. That they developed as they did into an art is one of the anomalies which the Far East provides for the confusion of Western classifiers; a netsuke, for instance, has no affinities with a statuette, and it is definitely not a button, though 'button-like' it may be.

1. (above) Unique cow signed Ritsu-o; (below) Ho-tri, God of Happiness, unsigned both persimmon wood ('kaki') W. W. Winkworth Collection

NETSUKE

The object resembling a foot-rule, on the left-hand side of the colour plate facing p. 272, is very nearly 24 centimetres ($9\frac{1}{2}$ inches) in length. It is not of course a netsuke, but it was made by a netsuke-carver, who died in 1880, aged sixty-four. It is made of a section of bamboo. Its purpose is to serve as a rest for the hand or wrist of a writer. In general effect, it looks like a hanging scroll or 'picture', either Chinese or Japanese, representing a tree and some bamboo branches growing behind an ornamental water-worn garden rock. In the right-hand upper corner is a poem in Chinese characters, reading downwards, beginning at the extreme top right. This poem is of the formal kind, consisting of four lines, each of five words or Chinese characters; so there are twenty characters in the poem. The last four characters are slightly smaller; they end the inscription, on the left-hand side, except for two square seals, and they give the name of the artist and poet who carved the object and composed the poem. His name, Gyokkin, is not famous either as that of a carver or a man of letters. That, at least, is how I interpret this object, but I am not a scholar in any Far Eastern language.

One of the most useful books on Netsuke is "The Netsuke Handbook of Ueda Reikichi", adapted by Raymond Bushell, and published by Charles Tuttle in Japan. This book gives a reliable account of the subject, and also a list of the names and brief biographies of a large number of the artists whose signatures have been recorded; it runs well into four figures. My friend, the netsuke collector and

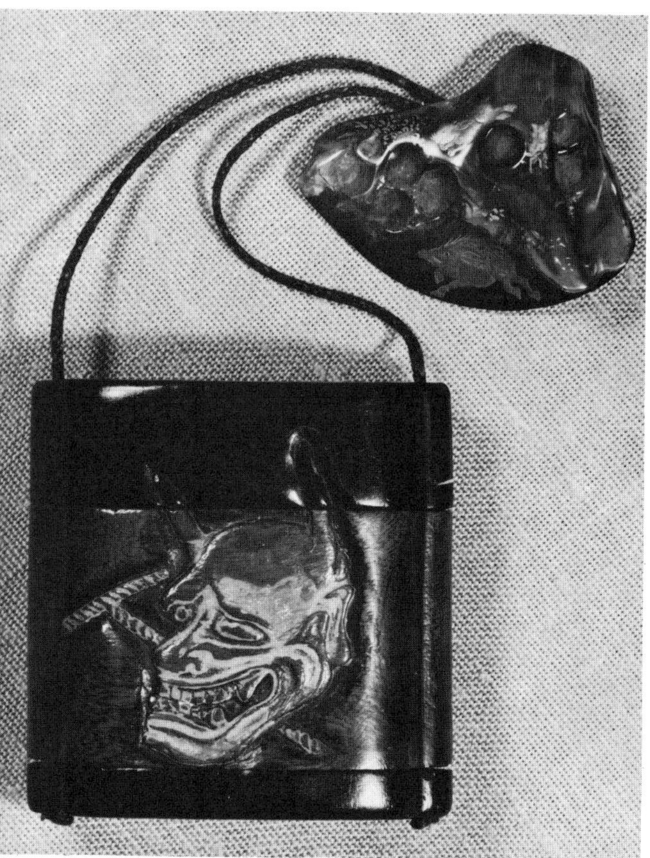

2. Tobacco-box (ton-kotsu) signed Shu-Zan; tortoiseshell netsuke of Mount Fuji with a wild boar in lacquer
W. W. Winkworth Collection

3. Ivory netsuke of a mythical animal – a 'kylin' or Kirin, *circa* 1720
Formerly F. Meinertzhagen Collection

connoisseur Mr Mark Hindson of London, once collaborated with me in drawing up a list of "The Hundred Best Netsuke Carvers". We soon had to extend it to two hundred.

Many of the best netsuke, especially the older ones, are not signed; for instance, the long stagshorn netsuke in the colour plate representing a sort of cucumber or gourd, with a strange creature sitting on its upper end. Netsuke, which are simply toggles, tied to a portable pouch or other object suspended from the girdle and serving to stop the cord from slipping through, can be of almost any size or shape within reason. In many cases, such as that of this long stagshorn netsuke, it is not accurately known how they were worn or would have looked when in use; we can only guess. This one obviously hung down, but exactly how is uncertain.

In the middle of the colour plate is a green-stained ivory representation of a cicada on a bean-pod. This is signed, but Mr Reikichi only notes that the carver, who signed with a single character reading 'Snow', or 'Settsu', may have been a woman. Above it, the circular netsuke of a monkey is also unsigned. The coloured wood netsuke on the bottom right-hand corner is signed Shu-Zan and is by a successor of the famous artist of that name, who is believed never to have signed his pieces; but this point will be discussed later, with reference to the box carved with a mask (Ill. 2), which is also signed Shu-Zan.

Of the objects shown in this colour plate, probably the Green Ivory Cicada is the only one which might be worth over $140. They have been chosen to counteract the impression that netsuke in general are fussy little ivory or wood carvings, all about the same size, valued for the minute detail of the work, or the prettiness of the subject – a sweet little puppy, for instance, or a quaint tiger.

It is true that the record auction price of £900 was paid for a particularly appealing puppy in ivory; it is also true that of the netsuke which have lately fetched over £200, the majority have been animal subjects. It is also true that carvings other than netsuke by netsuke artists, like the ruler-shaped object in the colour plate, or the box (Ill. 2), have never so far fetched over $140 at auctions, with the exception of some lacquer *inro* (medicine boxes) which, although they belong to the sphere of the netsuke, are not necessarily likely to be considered an indispensable part of a netsuke collection. It might therefore seem that the netsuke is a specialized field of collecting, like stamps. This is not so.

The sale-rooms have recently shown that a netsuke can have all the qualities of a first-rate work of art (and some of those of a priceless gem, a diamond or a pearl). A wise Yorkshireman once explained to me what these qualities are. He surprised me, as no doubt he meant to, by not putting Beauty first. It was too common, he said – flowers, eyes, the sky; the first thing was Subject. This was rather a blow, but I had to admit that as far as netsuke are concerned, he was right. The next quality was Colour; again a shock for me, because netsuke, like old silver, cannot exactly be said to be strong in colour, unless the colour of old wood or ivory is to count. The last quality of the three was the cruellest, most cynical of all: 'snob-value'. There is no National Gallery, no Louvre or Hermitage or Prado where netsuke are concerned. This is not only because they have not, despite a few better sale-room prices just lately, so far 'made the grade' or achieved the necessary status and prestige. It is worse than that; they lack size, the one thing needful. "The Diamond as Big as the Ritz" is a startling title for a story. But everyone knows what happens to big diamonds (what happened, let us say, to the Cullinan diamond); they are cut down to smaller, more manageable sizes. A netsuke may be precious but it can never be grand. A two-inch netsuke is a good size; a five-inch one is big; seven or eight inches makes it a gigantic freak.

4. Back view of the Kirin (Ill. 3) showing the absence of the usual cord-holes behind
Formerly F. Meinertzhagen Collection

5. (left) Hanging netsuke with Chinese poem in two lines of seven characters each, stagshorn;
(centre) Ivory netsuke of a 'Finger Citron Fruit', 18th century;
(right) Pipe-case signed by the netsuke carver Ren, showing mandarin ducks
W. W. Winkworth Collection

It must be regretfully admitted, then, that netsuke at present have no prestige, no snob-value, except of course to the chosen few who collect them. They are, in fact, a Cinderella subject. Admirers of Far Eastern art, who are properly aware of the virtues of Ming porcelain, Utamaro prints, or even Chinese snuff-bottles, tend to despise netsuke. It would be unfair to say that they are not properly represented in museums; the truth is, they are not at all well suited for public display. In this respect they are like coins; they need special rooms, like the Coin Room in the British Museum. Like coins, they must be handled and turned over, since top, bottom and each side of a netsuke must be looked at. When I was a member of the British Museum staff, in 1924, I remember seeing a small man peering up through the glass shelf to try to see the bottom of some netsuke, then displayed without curtains, in vitrines which, alas, stood in the full light of the sun. This man, I discovered, was the late Mr Frederick Meinertzhagen. To open the glass case at that time was not easy, but it was of course opened for him, and he then began to tell me many things about netsuke which I never knew before. He and Professor Henri L. Joly were at that time the best authorities on the subject in England. The pioneer, was Albert Brockhaus of Leipzig.

But Meinertzhagen, unlike Joly, was a netsuke specialist; not, however, in any academic sense, since in those days (and the same situation still exists) there were no academic students of netsuke. They were included in the British Museum, not as works of art but as ethnographical specimens, in the now extinct Department of Ceramics and Ethnography, in which I was then an assistant studying Ceramics, which included glass. No one in the Department knew much about netsuke then. I knew that such things existed, because on the mantelpiece of my father's drawing-room there was an ivory cow and calf which I now realize must have been a fine piece by Tomo-tada, a present from my uncle Norman Collie. My father collected English furniture and mezzotint engravings; later under the influence of George Eumorfopoulos and Oscar Raphael he began to collect Chinese ceramics. These were also my own favourite subjects and I had the good luck to be able to study them under the head of my Museum Department, the late Mr R. L. Hobson. I also knew a little about Far Eastern painting from Laurence Binyon's books and from Arthur Waley's "Introduction to the study of Chinese painting" (1923).

The Oriental Ceramic Society was founded about this time in my father's house; but the only member who cared about netsuke except Professor Collie was Oscar Raphael, part of whose collection was bequeathed to the British Museum, where it is now preserved in the Department of Oriental Antiquities.

Before 1914, netsuke had still some prestige. But Oscar Raphael, for instance, and even in his later days Walter Behrens, were naturally inclined towards Chinese art; for at that time fine early examples, far older and historically more remarkable, had already begun to reach England. Beautiful small objects in bronze, jade, and other precious materials of kinds never before seen in the West were imported by Yamanaka's of Bond Street. They continued to sell netsuke, *inro*, prints and other Japanese things too, but they found they could get much higher prices for Chinese works of art, and by 1924 the smaller Japanese objects had become a mere side-line in which they took little interest.

It was in this way that I was able to buy from Yamanaka's the netsuke of a cow in dark kaki wood. (Ill. 1.) I saw it had a signature, but when I showed this to the Japanese shop assistant, although he politely made a show of looking at it, he said it was much too worn to be legible, and anyhow the price was $9.80. But when I later showed it to Mr Meinertzhagen, his attitude was quite different. He at once recognized that the signature was that of Ritsuo. I knew who Ritsuo was,

6. (right) Netsuke in stagshorn based on a Malay Kris handle, 18th century;
(left) copy in ivory by Patrick Woodford
W. W. Winkworth Collection

because a piece of lacquer from his hand was illustrated in the 1911 Encyclopaedia Britannica. This object, a writing-box with a pottery owl on the lid, is still to be seen in the Victoria and Albert Museum, or rather was so, but probably by now is no longer on view, for just as netsuke have little prestige in English museums, lacquer has even less (only Chinese lacquer is in favour at present). I used to wonder why this box was thought so valuable, in 1911; I had never had a piece of Ritsuo's work in my hand, and his subtle effects of colour and texture are impossible to photograph (or were then). Mr Meinertzhagen encouraged me greatly, however, by his obvious excitement, and he told me he had never seen a carved wood netsuke by Ritsuo before, and also that he had no doubt that mine was genuine. His instinct of sportsmanship was, I am sure, what prevented him from offering me what would then have seemed a large price for it; but he did advise me to "hang on to it", which I have done. Neither of us ever saw another.

On the same plate (Ill. 1) is another netsuke representing the Fat God of Happiness, unsigned and made of the same wood and with every appearance of being of the same age. Mr Meinertzhagen found it and (for by that time he had taken to dealing in netsuke) he told me he thought it was certainly contemporary with my cow and might even be also the work of Ritsuo, who since he died in 1747 at an advanced age was probably working around 1700 and before. The cord-holes are very rudimentary and go straight through, always a sign of early work. At the same time, *circa* 1929, he also sold me the Minko Jizo carrying the Hell Witch on his back (illustrated in "The Art of the Netsuke Carver"). Later he wanted to buy both pieces back from me, but though I let him have the Minko, for which he paid me a good price, I kept the other piece which is here illustrated, because it was at that time, *circa* 1935, not worth more than two to six dollars and indeed still would probably pass unnoticed in an auction sale.

Ritsuo's art is still very little known, even in Japan; his paintings are rare and his poetry unpublished. His lacquer is remarkable for its use of coloured pottery inlay and its technical originality. He was never so well supported by rich patrons as Korin, and the fact that he seldom used gold may be connected with this. His friends were, one supposes, literary men, and he specialized in lacquer boxes, *inro* chiefly, imitating old ink-cakes with seal characters in relief. A fine specimen was sold at Sotheby's two years ago for £290. The very few netsuke and sword-guards he made were like his *inro*; it is therefore interesting to find a carved netsuke by him, and if he made one, he must have made others, probably quite modest and probably, like the one here illustrated, in bad condition.

The other great netsuke artist of this early period *circa* 1700 was Yoshimura Shu-Zan. He never signed his netsuke and we can only guess their nature from the descriptions and illustrations in the only Japanese book which discusses these subjects, "Soken Kisho", published at Osaka in 1781. But the *inro* (or tobacco box) illustrated here (Ill. 2) is signed Shu-Zan in *sosho* characters; that is, in a cursive style quite unlike the signatures of other artists who used this name. Moreover, the style is like Yoshimura Shu-Zan's netsuke, since the surface was originally covered with gesso and painted in colours. The wood used is not like the light material known from "Soken Kisho" to have been employed for his netsuke, but that is to be expected; it would have been unpractical. The netsuke, in the shape of Mount Fuji, with a wild boar on it in gold, was attached by me.

Yoshimura Shu-Zan never, as far as is known, used ivory. If he had, the result might have been rather like the Kirin here illustrated. (Ills 3, 4.) This is the netsuke of which Mr Meinertzhagen made a drawing for his book, not one of his best attempts at the difficult art of drawing netsuke; he was entirely self-taught, and

7. (left to right) Whale-tooth; section of walrus tusk; possibly a tiger-tooth; tooth of a marine mammal showing the cord-hole for use as a netsuke
W. W. Winkworth Collection

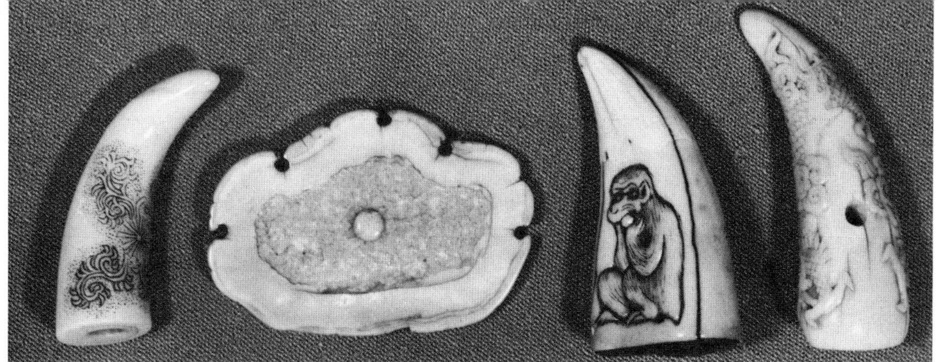

some of his earlier efforts are very crude. The design and large size of this Kirin have resulted, during the last few years, in its being copied in Japan; but the back has never before been shown, and the next forgeries made of it should therefore be better, one hopes. One made a few years ago actually had the signature Minko at the back, an improbable name for an ivory carver. The famous Minko of Tsu practically never used ivory and the forger did not even copy his handwriting correctly, though in other ways he succeeded better; he suggested the clumsy touch of Mr Meinertzhagen's drawing quite well. In the winter before he died, Mr Meinertzhagen wrote and asked me my opinion of this netsuke. I wrote back at length in enthusiastic praise of it. I said it recalled to my mind the paintings of some of the great masters of the Kano school of the late 17th and early 18th century, like Tannyu and Tsune-nobu. Only a month or two before my friend's death, I received a parcel carefully packed in his usual way, the string sealed with his family crest, with a note asking me to accept this favourite netsuke as a present. No other Kirin netsuke is quite like this. One of its peculiarities is that it has no cord-holes through the body; the aperture between the tail and the back must have served for attachment. This hole is roughly finished, and may even have once had a metal ring to carry the heavy leather pouch with a solid metal clasp which was then fashionable, the pipe-holder being also at this date usually leather, not carved ivory or wood. Another feature is the addition of the back legs which are carved in a separate piece, the join being strengthened by a round peg behind the right hind leg. Probably, since this unusually large carving is hollow in the lower part, there was not enough ivory for the hind legs. As netsuke were carved not from solid blocks but from odd pieces, usually triangular, it is easy to see the reason for the use of an extra piece, and other examples have been known to occur, usually of course in the older types; for in later times, when whole tusks were sent to Japan for carving, such expedients became unnecessary.

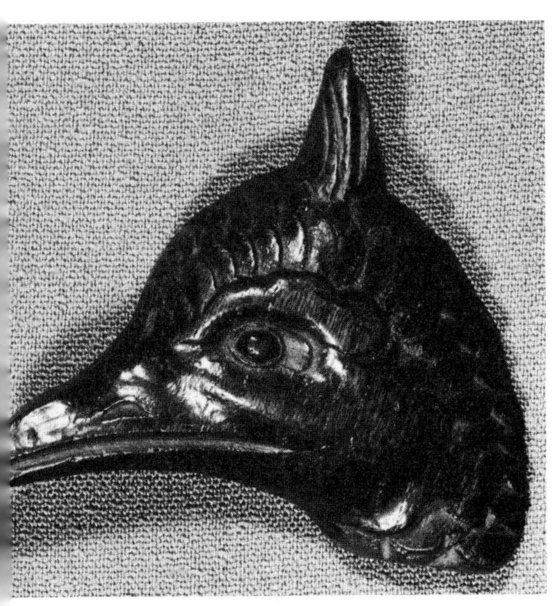

8. Netsuke of a pheasant's head by a screen-carver, paulownia wood
W. W. Winkworth Collection

9. Back of illustration 8 showing large cord-holes for use as a netsuke

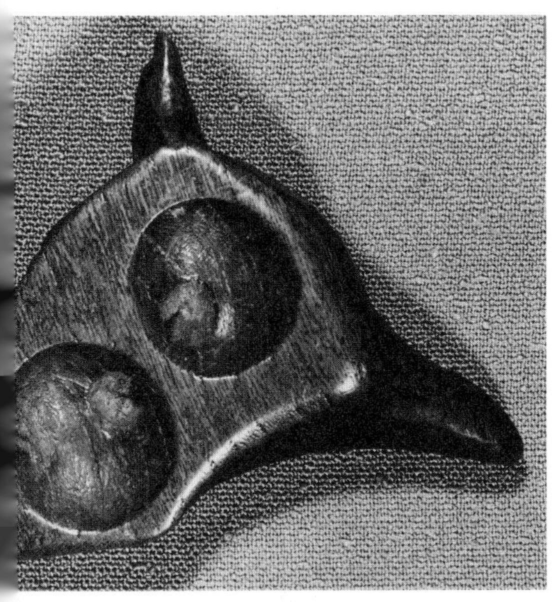

The carved ivory or wood pipe-case (Ill. 5) was a late invention; probably it was introduced by the netsuke artists of the early and middle 19th century. I know of no pipe-case by Minko, but pipe-holders were made by him, and hollow tubular pipe-cases were made by his pupil, or successor, Ikko (Kazu-tora). The example here illustrated is by a slightly later netsuke carver, who used the single seal-character 'Ren' as his signature. The subject represents the Mandarin duck or oshi-dori, the love-bird of the Japanese. I know of no love-bird netsuke by Ren; such a piece would indeed be a collector's prize, for birds are naturally favourite subjects. There is a limited supply; netsuke carvers were not like British bird-artists, who can send an etching of any bird they like yearly to the Royal Academy and be sure of selling several impressions. The netsuke carver's art was conservative; he stuck to certain traditional subjects which had some symbolic meaning. A netsuke was not like a modern Christmas card which need not, nowadays, have any connection with the annual Christian festival, so the collector is always delighted to find some subject which gets away from the regular routine of favourite themes, and in this respect the very few remaining modern carvers of netsuke have an advantage. They can specialize in rare subjects, of which the collector is delighted to have a specimen, even when it is not signed by one of the famous carvers of modern times like Tokoku, Soko, or Masatoshi, whose work was first brought to my notice by

10. (left) Girl wearing an ivory mask;
(right) Magician holding a glass bottle signed by an artist of the 18th century who specialized in glass additions to his netsuke
W. W. Winkworth Collection

11. (left) A netsuke representing, in ivory, a leather purse with its ivory netsuke;
(right) An actual netsuke of the same type, signed by a famous 18th-century carver
W. W. Winkworth Collection

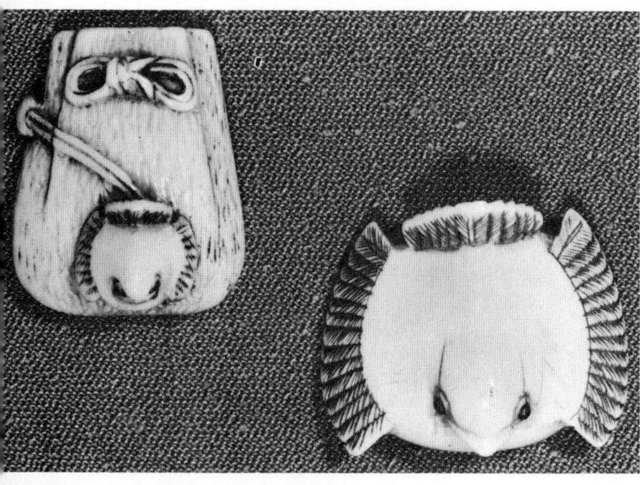

that most perceptive of collectors, Mrs Anne Hull Grundy. It is sad that since the first pioneer efforts of William Simmonds, few modern sculptors have turned their attention to netsuke. It is only in the last five or ten years that forgeries of netsuke have become common. Most of them are feeble attempts to make a piece of commercial ivory look like an antique. They can never re-create the old situation when the solid, more or less flawless tusk was unknown in Japan and the netsuke carvers had to rely on scrappy odds and ends of commercially valueless ivory, full of cracks or with discolorations. These 'defects' were often turned into interesting features by the older carvers, but the modern imitator almost always uses featureless commercial elephant ivory.

I had long possessed a curious netsuke, in stagshorn (Ill. 6, *right*), representing a monstrous creature based on the curious figures used for the ivory or wood handles of the Malay kris, or dagger. These Malay kris-handles are known to have inspired the famous early netsuke carver Yoshimura Shu-Zan, for a copy of one is illustrated in "Soken Kisho" as his work. Another is illustrated in the same book as a specimen of the *to-bori* or foreign carvings treasured as curiosities and used as netsuke. Wishing to possess an ivory example of this rare subject, I commissioned my friend Mr Patrick Woodford to carve a copy of my stagshorn monster (Ill. 6, *left*), for which purpose he used a piece of whale-tooth ivory signing his name with the Japanese characters for 'wood' and 'ford'. He made three copies for me, of which the present example (Ill. 6, *left*) is the best. The others were rather clumsy. What I should like to know is, supposing I had commissioned a modern artist in Japan to do such a copy, or to make an original design for me, signed of course with his name, would it count for customs charges as a work of art not subject to import duty, like a modern picture or sculpture?

The other objects in illustration 5, apart from the pipe-case are, in the centre, a 'Finger Citron' or 'Buddha's Hand' fruit and a long bamboo-leaf with a Chinese poem in cursive script. In the middle of the 19th century, when it was made, Chinese painting and calligraphy enjoyed a special outburst of activity, described by the phrase 'bun-jin-ga', or the 'art of the man of education', the opposite of 'uki-o-ye' or 'popular art'. It is still almost unknown in the West except among a few pioneer art-lovers.

The purpose of the illustration (Ill. 7) showing three horn-shaped netsuke and a flat one, is to show the quality of some of the varieties of ivory used; the flat piece is walrus or 'morse' ivory with a central area of crystalline structure almost impossible to carve. The other three are types of whale or other teeth. The rarest type, the Boar's Tusk netsuke, I have not shown. The pheasant's head (Ill. 8), in wood of wide grain, may have been made by a carver of *ramma*, the decorative panels, often in open work, used as screens between rooms in palaces and temples. At least one netsuke carver, So-shichi, is recorded as having been a carver of these screens. Illustration 9 shows the arrangement of the cord-holes at the back of this object. Illustration 12 shows five wood netsuke; the right-hand one is a tortoise carved by a man who is known to have lived to an advanced age and here states in an inscription on the back that he carved this tortoise at the age of 105!

At the top left is an archer's leather glove; below it is the root of a water-lily, in the Far East an article of food, cut in slices like a cucumber. The other piece is a carving of a pine-cone.

Illustration 13 shows seven mask netsuke of all periods. The beautiful girl in the bottom row is in pottery, and more or less recent; of the three above, two, on the right, are 18th century. The mask is an age-old subject in Japanese art, and examples dating back to the 13th century are not very different in style from those

Colour Plate. Bamboo hand-rest by a literary netsuke-carver, who was also a musician; stagshorn cucumber, a 'hanging netsuke'; green-stained ivory cicada; monkey in a ring, an early netsuke, perhaps about 1740; a painted netsuke of a dancing boy – the hand-rest is about $9\frac{1}{2}$ in. (24 cm.) long. W. W. Winkworth Collection ▶

翠竹兹奇石蒼松留古
柯明窗坐相對試問真
如何
玉琴衜人

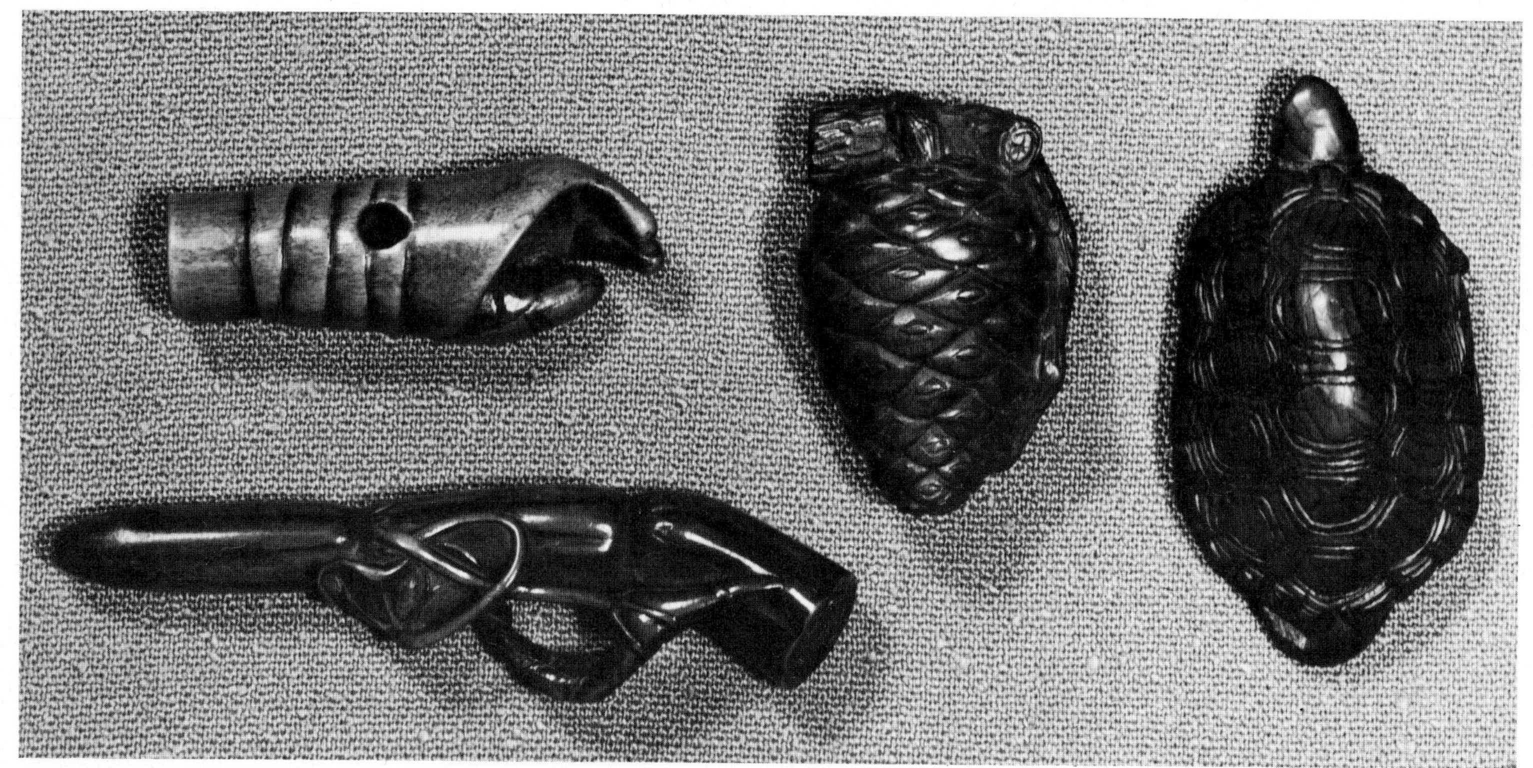

12. (above left to right) Archer's glove; pine-cone; tortoise carved 'at the age of 105'; (below) water-lily root
wood
W. W. Winkworth Collection

13. (below) Netsuke based on actors' masks, all are signed; the second from the left below is in pottery all the rest wood
actual size
W. W. Winkworth Collection

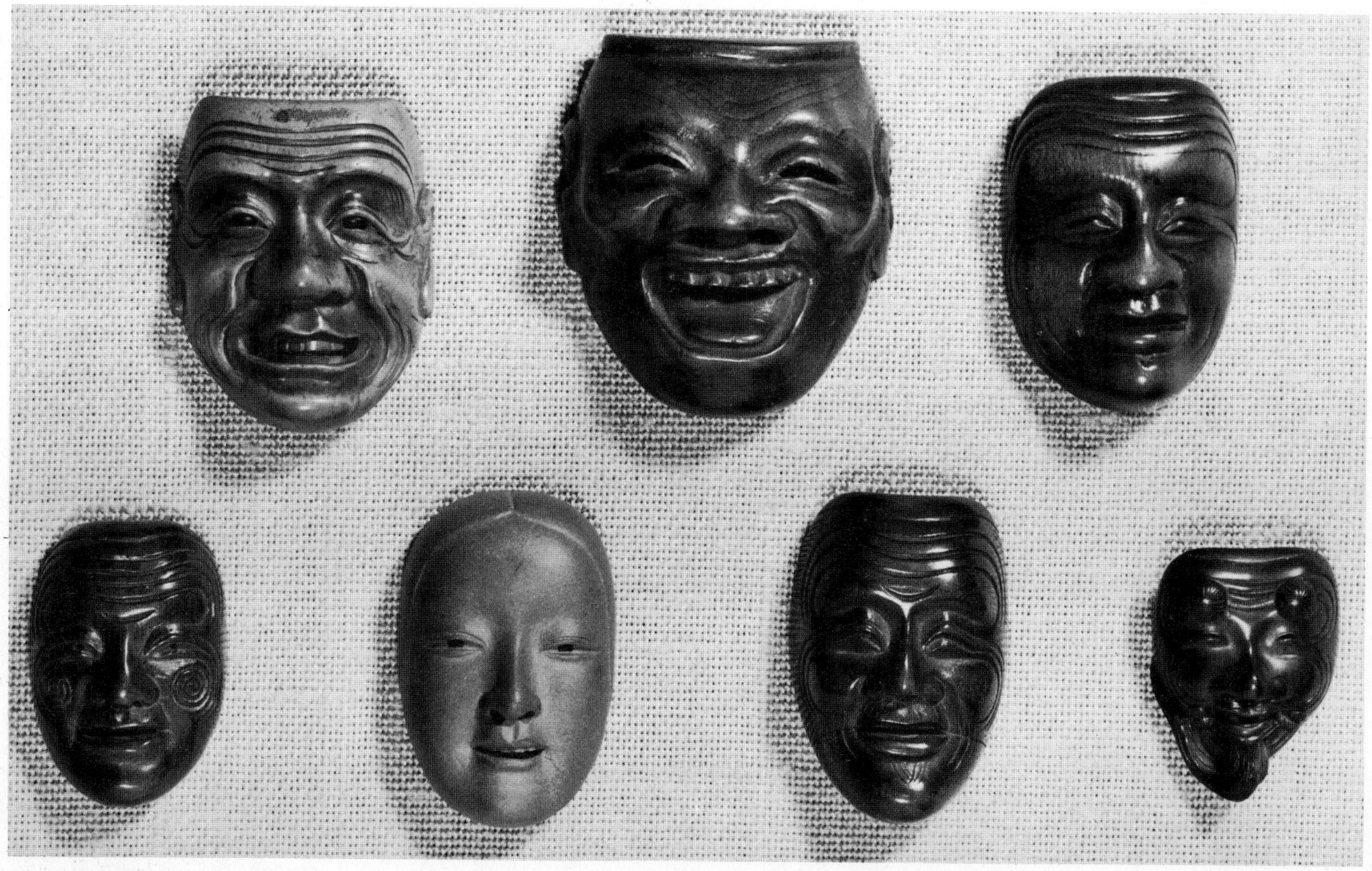

14. (left) The Nine-tailed Fox sniffing the hammer which broke the 'Death Stone'; a fallen notice-board is inscribed 'Sessho seki' ('slaughter stone'); (right) A stylized bird of paulownia wood
W. W. Winkworth Collection

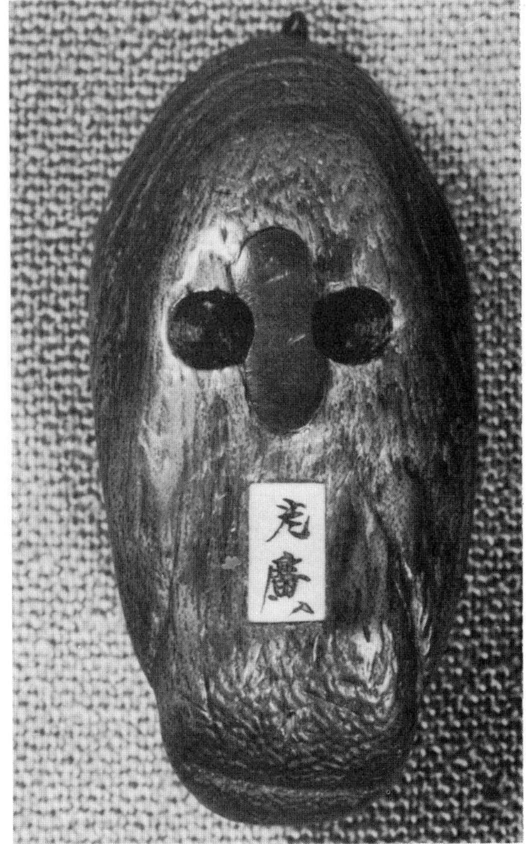

15. The base of the bird shown in illustration 14, showing the ivory label signed Mitsu-hiro, the artist who repaired the piece and thus claimed it as his creation
W. W. Winkworth Collection

16. A crab on a piece of rotten wood, 18th century
actual size
W. W. Winkworth Collection

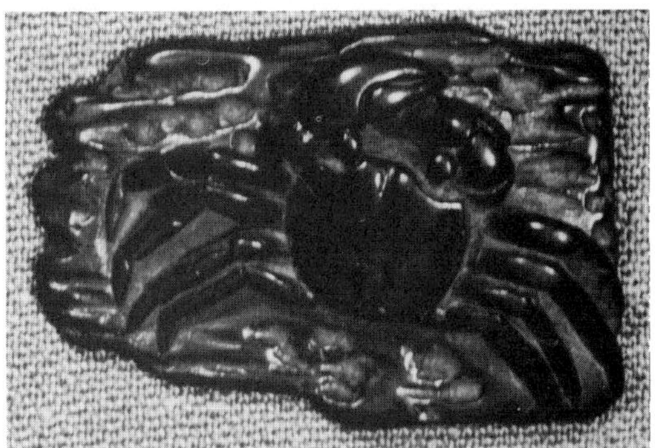

shown here; but we do not yet know which if any of the netsuke masks are older than the 18th century, though some probably are.

Illustration 10 shows a little girl wearing a mask (carved in ivory); the collector will realize that this type of figure with the girl's ivory mask is usually seen in the standing position, as are the larger and more beautiful 17th-century porcelain figures of ladies made by the Kakiemon potters, which, though they are never seen in netsuke form, show the same plastic genius. I only know of one of these in a sitting position (illustrated pl. 63a, in "Japanese Porcelain" by Soame Jenyns, London, 1965); it is in the collection of that great connoisseur, Sir Harry Garner. Ceramic netsuke are of some interest; so far none seem to be known which can certainly be attributed to the great 17th-century potters, like Ninsei; but as he made some quite small objects, as well as his famous large jars and his tea-bowls, there is nothing to prove he never made netsuke. The other figure in illustration 10 is a magician holding a glass bottle. Two other netsuke are known by this artist (Yu-sen), both of which include pieces of glass – which was a rarity in 18th-century Japan, even beads being highly prized. The two ivory netsuke (Ill. 11) show the popularity of the 'stylized sparrow' form. The left-hand example shows a tobacco-bag or purse for money (*kinchaku*) worn hanging from the girdle and supported by a double string with a bead (seen on the left edge), while a toggle in the shape of a stylized sparrow serves as a terminal or 'root-attachment'; the word ne – tsuke literally means just that: *ne*, 'root', *tsuke*, 'attachment'.

Illustration 14 shows, on the right, another kind of stylized bird made of a light wood, the grain of which has been purposely emphasized. A similar bird is illustrated by Mr Raymond Bushell in his adaptation of "The Netsuke Hand-book of Ueda Reikichi"; it is not signed, but my own example is. Illustration 15 shows an ivory panel let into it with the name of a famous ivory carver, Mitsu-hiro. Wood carvings are not absolutely unknown with his signature, but I believe that in this case the bird was not carved by him but acquired and possibly slightly repaired (perhaps, for instance, by adding the piece inlaid between the cord-holes) and then sold to his customers as a sort of *objet trouvé* to which the artist (famous for the extreme delicacy and refinement of his ivory netsuke) has added his beautifully written signature. This adaptation of older pieces was a not uncommon practice.

Illustration 16 shows a crab on a piece of decayed wood – part of a plank, perhaps, washed up by the sea.

Once, when I needed cash, I put this crab into an auction sale hoping that, as a rather uncommon subject, it might fetch say $140. It only fetched $67.20, so I bought it back. Several of the netsuke here illustrated I have bought in London in the last five years for less than $28. During the last three years, I have been forming a collection for a relation of mine, Mr Harry Wight. I have often been able to get interesting things for less than $56; and a masterpiece can often be found for under $140. As it gradually becomes known which netsuke are of the rarest and finest type, the value of masterpieces will inevitably rise. Other Japanese works of art, prints and porcelain especially, are now being eagerly sought by Japanese. This is not true of netsuke. One of their charms is that they can be appreciated by anyone, simply as objects. It is not necessary to have a knowledge of Japan or of Far Eastern art in general in order to enjoy them. Even the signatures of famous artists can be recognized without analysing them or knowing what the characters mean. I knew many signatures by sight long before Meinertzhagen and Hindson taught me to read them correctly. For those who want to know more, there are many books. One of the most useful is "Japanese Art for the Collector" by Newman & Ryerson, published by Bell at a modest price.

English Pictorial Embroidery of the 17th Century

PATRICIA WARDLE

In the Elizabethan period domestic embroidery blossomed into one of the richest and most delightful of the decorative arts in England. The work of professional and amateur alike was then intended to be practical as well as decorative and, although pictorial designs were often used for furnishing embroideries, the embroidered picture as such was virtually unknown.

During the first quarter of the 17th century some Elizabethan types of furnishing embroidery continued to flourish, although the larger pieces of canvas work, i.e. table carpets and bed valances, which had frequently been embellished with pictorial compositions, seem to have fallen from favour. Embroidered linen pillow covers of the characteristic long rectangular shape were still made, however, the latest reference to them so far known being an entry of 1633 in the household accounts of Howard of Naworth.[1] Most 17th-century pillow covers were floral in design, but there are in the Victoria and Albert Museum a set of four from the Abingdon Collection embroidered with stories from Genesis. Each cover (Ill. 1) bears four scenes, under Gothic arches or separated by columns, which Mrs Nancy Cabot has shown to be adapted from illustrations in "Biblicae Historiae" by H. S. Beham, published in Frankfurt in 1537. Details such as the cloud forms, the trees and plants and the coiling stem borders are typical of early 17th-century embroidery, as is the technique of silk stitchery enhanced with silver and gold thread. Much use is made of the decorative filling patterns familiar in blackwork and carried over into crewelwork later in the century.

Bedhangings at this time seem to have been decorated mainly with applied work or with flower and fruit 'slips' embroidered on linen, cut out and sewn on to a richer silk or velvet background, fashions which persisted until the vogue for crewelwork began towards the middle of the century.

Floral designs, often combined with heraldry, were in vogue too for long cushion covers in canvas work, and for the embroidered and Turkeywork chair covers which began to take their place in the second quarter of the century. Among the collection of Elizabethan cushion covers at Hardwick Hall are many with pictorial designs, and a few examples which may be of 17th-century date have survived elsewhere. In the Victoria and Albert Museum is a long cushion cover (Ill. 2), formerly at Saltram in Devon, embroidered with Orpheus charming the animals with his music, which still retains its original green silk lining and fringe. The figures and general composition are adapted from an engraving by Adriaan Collaert (died 1618) after Adam van Noort (1557–1641), but the fruit trees and the large flowers are typical examples of canvas-work 'slips' here incorporated into a pictorial design. Two other versions of the same subject, one in the

[1] Surtees Society, 1878, p. 297.

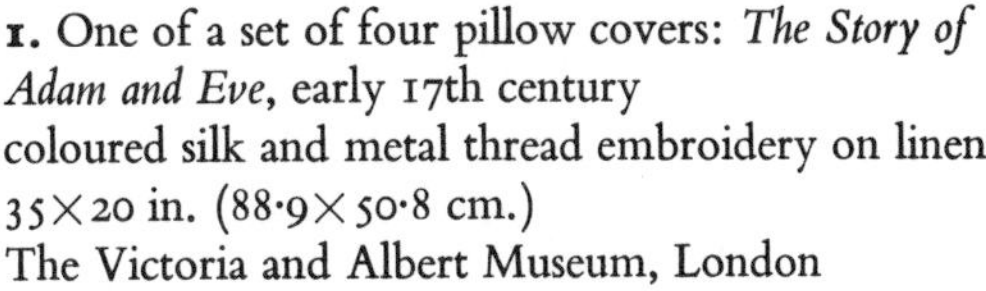

1. One of a set of four pillow covers: *The Story of Adam and Eve*, early 17th century
coloured silk and metal thread embroidery on linen
35×20 in. (88·9×50·8 cm.)
The Victoria and Albert Museum, London

Richmond Collection[2] and one in the Untermyer Collection,[3] may originally have been cushion covers, as may several other panels of similar dimensions in the latter collection which is particularly rich in 17th-century pictorial embroidery.

In the absence of the original make-up it is often difficult to determine whether a given embroidery was intended as a cushion cover or as a picture and perhaps at this period the borderline between the two was indistinct, for the vogue for canvas-work panels intended purely as pictures began in the second quarter of the 17th century. These pictures, usually small in size, are not often dated, but there is an unfinished example in the Victoria and Albert Museum dated 1636. Many of the most constant characteristics of 17th-century canvas-work pictures were inherited from Elizabethan embroidery. The landscape background, with its fantastic country houses on the skyline, large trees and river or pond full of fish, clearly derives from country scenes such as those on the borders of the Bradford table carpet in the Victoria and Albert Museum.[4] Sometimes this landscape dominates the picture as in an unworked panel in the Burrell Collection (Ill. 3), where characters in the story of Balaam are relegated to a corner of the composition otherwise peopled with the shepherd, huntsman and fisherman so often found in Elizabethan design.

In a group of pictures notable for minuteness of detail in both drawing and

[2] *The Connoisseur*, vol. XCVI, 1937, p. 147, no. VII.

[3] Hackenbroch, Y. *English and other Needlework, Tapestries and Textiles in the Irwin Untermyer Collection*, London, 1960, fig. 37.

[4] Nevinson, J. L. "Catalogue of English Domestic Embroidery of the 16th & 17th Centuries." Victoria and Albert Museum, 1938, pl. III.

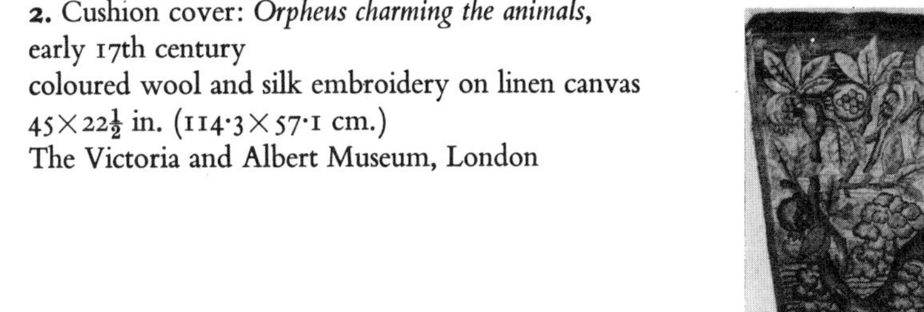

2. Cushion cover: *Orpheus charming the animals*, early 17th century
coloured wool and silk embroidery on linen canvas
45×22½ in. (114·3×57·1 cm.)
The Victoria and Albert Museum, London

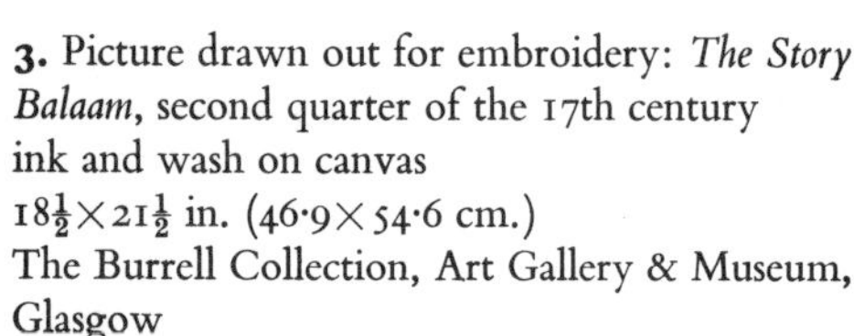

3. Picture drawn out for embroidery: *The Story of Balaam*, second quarter of the 17th century
ink and wash on canvas
18½×21½ in. (46·9×54·6 cm.)
The Burrell Collection, Art Gallery & Museum, Glasgow

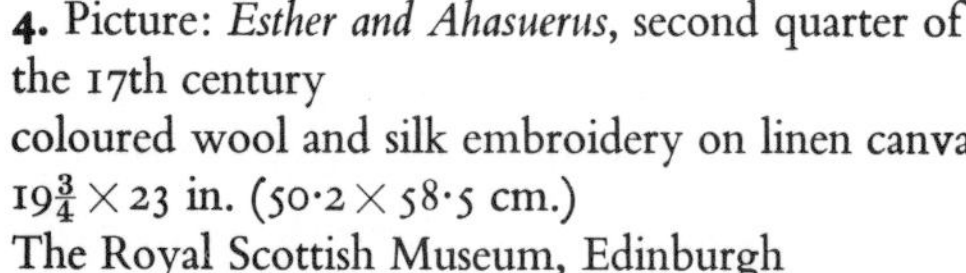

4. Picture: *Esther and Ahasuerus*, second quarter of the 17th century
coloured wool and silk embroidery on linen canvas
19¾×23 in. (50·2×58·5 cm.)
The Royal Scottish Museum, Edinburgh

execution, however, the story element predominates. A typical example is a representation of Esther and Ahasuerus in the Royal Scottish Museum (Ill. 4), notable for the neat rendering of patterned carpet, floor and architectural background. Meticulous designs of this sort may perhaps be earlier in date than the more common examples in which episodes in the story are combined in a landscape setting with large trees, flowers, birds, insects and animals of which the favourite four, occurring again and again, are the lion, leopard, unicorn and spotted stag. All these features appear in a large picture of the story of Abraham in the Victoria and Albert Museum (Ill. 5) and another of very similar design in the Untermyer Collection.[5] The scene of Abraham entertaining his angelic guests is given prominence in both designs, while other parts of the story are shown on a smaller scale elsewhere in the picture. Other features which constantly recur are curtained pavilions with domed tops, fountains and flower-covered arbours, all of which have antecedents in Elizabethan embroidery, particularly in the group of bed valances in which personages in courtly dress are depicted in the setting of a formal garden. The garden subject is occasionally found in 17th-century work too. In the Untermyer Collection[6] there is a fine picture of a musical party in a garden dating from about the middle of the century.

Designs originally made for canvas work, however, proved readily adaptable to other techniques. About the middle of the 17th century there began a fashion for embroidering pictures on small panels of a thick white satin which usually has green threads woven into the selvage. Coloured silk embroidery in long and short, satin and split stitches was often used to render the subjects in a form of needle-painting with flat neat stitchery and careful shading of colours. Even more popular, however, was the raised work technique commonly known as stumpwork, which involved the creation of a three-dimensional effect. The bodies of figures were padded, their hands and faces either padded or rendered by small wooden forms, while clothes, petals of flowers, curtains of pavilions and other suitable features were carried out in areas of detached button-hole filling stitches (in the manner of needlepoint lace) worked separately and partially attached to the ground material, or in separate pieces of embroidered silk. Additional details

[5] Hackenbroch, Y. *op. cit.*, fig. 73.
[6] *Ibid.*, fig. 81.

5. Picture: *The Story of Abraham*, middle of the 17th century
coloured wool and silk embroidery on linen canvas
43×22 in. (109·2×55·8 cm.)
The Victoria and Albert Museum, London

were rendered in darned silk pile, in metal strip bound round with coloured silks, in beads, pieces of mica or in many varieties of metal purl (painted coiled wire). While raised figures in needlework were made in many parts of Europe, and particularly in Germany, from the late 15th century, it does not seem necessary to look so far afield for the origins of stumpwork, which seems to be a development of the raised flowers, either padded or worked in detached button-holing, commonly found in Elizabethan and early 17th-century embroidery. In the 17th century the technique seems to have been referred to as embossed or raised work and the origin of the term 'stumpwork' is unknown. The earliest use of it so far discovered is the phrase "embroidery on the stamp", which occurs in "A New and Complete Dictionary of Arts and Sciences", published in London in 1754–55.

The favourite subjects for pictures in all techniques were taken from the Old Testament. A typical example in the Victoria and Albert Museum, signed MY and dated 1656, features the story of David and Bathsheba. (Ill. 6.) Prominence is given to Bathsheba bathing, a scene allowing for the introduction of an arbour and a fountain. Typical features are the sun, moon and clouds at the top and the small patch of grass allotted to each figure or scene as a base. This piece may be compared with an almost identical design in tent stitch on canvas, signed SC and dated 1661, in the Ashmolean Museum. (Ill. 7.) Solomon and the Queen of Sheba, Joseph and Potiphar's Wife, David and Abigail and Susanna and the Elders were other popular themes. Stories from the New Testament are of rare occurrence by comparison. Often the characters are dressed in 17th-century costume. Figures of kings and queens were popular too as well as female figures representing the Elements, Seasons, Five Senses or various virtues. Classical scenes, like those in Elizabethan embroidery, were usually inspired by Ovid's "Metamorphoses"; an example is *Alpheus and Arethusa* in the Victoria and Albert Museum[7] adapted from an engraving by Crispin van der Passe. The elaborate oval framework in this picture is often used to surround scenes or half-length portraits of women.

The design of most of these pictures suggests a childish taste and this is borne out by documentary evidence and by occasional inscriptions on the embroideries themselves. In the Victoria and Albert Museum, for example, is a picture signed Martha Hollis, AE 10, 1660 (see colour plate facing p. 285), while a spirited rendering of *The Overwhelming of Pharaoh's Hosts in the Red Sea*, in the Lady Lever Art Gallery, Port Sunlight (Ill. 9) is associated with Damaris Pearce who died at the age of twenty in 1679. A eulogy preserved with the picture remarks that such skill with the needle is "scarce credible of one so young".[8] Many pictures are, however,

[7] Nevinson, J. L. "English Domestic Embroidery Patterns of the 16th & 17th Centuries", *Walpole Society*, vol. XXVIII, 1939–40, pl. V.

[8] Macquoid, T. *Needlework in the Lady Lever Art Gallery Collections*, London, 1928, p. 134. Catalogue of the Leverhulme Collection, vol. III.

6. Picture: *David and Bathsheba*, signed MY, dated 1656
silk, metal thread and metal purl embroidery and stumpwork on white satin
21×17 in. (53·3×43·1 cm.)
The Victoria and Albert Museum, London

embroidered in a much more clumsy fashion by girls of far less skill. Documentary evidence shows that most wealthy households engaged special teachers to train their daughters in needlework, but by no means all the pupils excelled at it. Nevertheless, however crude the 17th-century embroideries, they are exceeded in this respect by modern copies of stumpwork pictures which turn up from time to time. Whether or not deliberately intended as fakes, they are unlikely to deceive the experienced eye, in spite of the 17th-century dates they often bear, as they usually incorporate pieces of 19th-century silk brocades and machine-made lace.

Though most of the pictures were probably the work of children, the drawing of the designs, usually carried out in ink and wash in an accomplished manner, and the existence of so many almost identical scenes, suggests a common source and the work of a professional draughtsman. Scattered references from the 16th century onwards testify that many needlewomen, then as now, relied on the hands of others to draw their embroidery designs for them, and it seems highly probable that the satin or canvas panels could be bought with the designs ready drawn, perhaps adapted from a stock set of patterns to suit the requirements of the individual customer. No evidence has so far come to light as to whence the supplies came in the 17th century, but there are plenty of trade-cards and advertisements put out by haberdashers and milliners in the 18th century which mention pattern drawing as among the services offered. Occasionally a piece is found which seems to have been drawn by the youthful worker herself. Such a picture, of extreme naïvety and childish drawing, is that of *Susanna and the Elders* in the Untermyer Collection.[9]

Although the creators of the designs remain elusive, the sources of inspiration are now well known. By far the most popular Biblical scenes were the engravings in Gerard de Jode's "Thesaurus Sacrarum Historiae Veteris Testamenti", published in Antwerp in 1585.[10] The episodes in the stories of Abraham (Ill. 5) and of David and Bathsheba (Ills 6, 7, 8) were adapted from these illustrations. Other favourite scenes from the same source were Susanna and the Elders and Eliezer and Rebekah. Frontispieces of contemporary editions of the Bible also furnished ideas for embroidery designs.[11] Flowers, birds and animals seem to have been adapted, though by no means closely copied, from contemporary herbals and bestiaries, as well as books intended more specifically for embroiderers such as Richard Shorleyker's "A schole-house for the needle" of 1624, J. Boler's "The Needle's Excellency" of 1634 and publications of the 1660's and 1670's issued by P. Stent and J. Overton.[12] Boler's book has by way of introduction a long poem by John Taylor, the Water-poet, in which the favourite motifs of the day are neatly listed:

> "Flowers, Plants and Fishes; Beasts, Birds, Flyes and Bees,
> Hills, Dales, Plaines, Pastures, Skies, Seas, Rivers, Trees."

Political subjects, no doubt lacking in appeal to the young, are rarely found. There is in the Victoria and Albert Museum a panel embellished with a symbolic design connected with King Charles the Martyr, adapted from the frontispiece of "Eikon Basilike", published in 1649, with a figure of the young Prince of Wales with emblems symbolic of his future reign.[13] In the Lady Lever Art Gallery, Port Sunlight, there is a canvas-work picture with a design commemorating two memorable defeats for Popery, the failure of the Spanish Armada and of the Gunpowder Plot.[14] The design, copied from an engraving published in 1621, appealed to the embroideress, Dame Dorothy Selby, so much that she had it inscribed on her tombstone (she died in 1641). In a quite separate category are the

[9] Hackenbroch, Y. *op. cit.*, fig. 45.

[10] Graves Cabot, N. "Pattern Sources of Scriptural Subjects in Tudor and Stuart Embroideries", Bulletin of the Needle and Bobbin Club, New York, vol. XXX, no. 3, 1948.

[11] Hackenbroch, Y. *op. cit.*, Introduction.

[12] Nevinson, J. L. "Peter Stent and John Overton, Publishers of Embroidery Designs", *Apollo*, vol. XXI, 1936, p. 279.

[13] Nevinson, J. L. *Walpole Society*, *op. cit.*, pl. VII.

[14] *ibid.*, pl. VI.

7. (below left) Picture: *David and Bathsheba*, signed SC and dated 1661
coloured wool and silk embroidery on linen canvas
14×18 in. (35·5×45·7 cm.)
The Ashmolean Museum, Oxford

8. (below right) Engraving of *Bathsheba bathing* from Gerard de Jode, *Thesaurus Sacrarum Historiae Veteris Testamenti*, Antwerp, 1585

embroidered miniatures of Charles I of which a considerable number are known.[15] These seem to be professional work and their date is a matter for conjecture.

Pictorial panels in all techniques were sometimes made up into small cushions and, much more frequently, used to cover wooden boxes in which the owners kept their trinkets and knick-knacks. These boxes may be rectangular with flat tops, or more elaborate with tall lids with sloping sides, drawers inside and doors or falling flaps in front. They usually stand on four ball feet and may be finished off with metal handles and locks. The pictorial panels usually show a series of connected episodes such as scenes in the life of Joseph or Jacob, the edges of which may be finished off with braid or more strongly bound with lacquer, painted wood or tortoiseshell. The inside of the doors may be decorated with stiff formal flowers in laid work of coloured silks and occasionally the box is further embellished with an elaborate three-dimensional miniature garden. (Ill. 10.) Usually the interior of the box, which may be fitted with ink or scent bottles, is lined with pink or blue silk edged with silver braid, while in the lid there may be a mirror or perhaps a print or a piece of marbled paper. Occasionally large cabinets of the period are found embellished, usually on the inside only, with embroidery. The making of a small cabinet seems to have been a regular task allotted to a young worker when she had finished her samplers and perfected all the needlework skills involved. The work of one child, Martha Edlin (see colour plate facing p. 285), handed down to her descendants, gives an unusually complete record. In 1668, at the age of eight, she had completed her first sampler; in the following year her whitework sampler was finished. Her casket, embellished with figures of the Seven Virtues, Music and the Four Elements, bears the date 1671 while her final effort was a beadwork jewel-box finished in 1673. In the casket are still preserved small needlework trifles and a charming silver toy tea service which was no doubt given her as a reward for industry.

11. Mirror frame: *Charity, Jael and Sisera*, signed A.P. and dated 1672
coloured silk and metal purl embroidery and stumpwork on white satin with a tortoiseshell frame
23×28 in. (58·4×71·1 cm.)
The Metropolitan Museum of Art, New York
(Gift of Mrs Thomas J. Watson, 1939)

Mirror frames too were decorated with embroidery, usually with a figure on each of the four sides and the usual decorative elements, flowers, animals, birds and insects, disposed around the rest of the framework. (Ill. 11.) Beadwork mirror frames of similar design also occur and sometimes boxes were covered with beadwork or pictures worked wholly in beads sewn to the satin ground. More ambitious are the baskets of beads strung on wire, which often incorporate a pictorial scene in the base, with elaborate flowers decorating the sides. (Ill. 12.)

Embroidered book-covers were extremely popular in the first half of the 17th century. They were often embellished with elaborate designs such as that of Adam and Eve in the Garden of Eden on a Book of Common Prayer and a Bible of 1607 in the Untermyer Collection,[16] or of the stories of Abraham and Jonah on a tent-stitch cover for a Bible of 1613 in the Victoria and Albert Museum.[17] It was common at this period for small prayerbooks, Bibles and copies of metrical versions of the Psalms to be bound together and the covers are frequently worked with single Old Testament figures or figures symbolizing the Virtues. (Ill. 13.)

Seventeenth-century pictorial embroideries have survived in such numbers because they were treasured by the families of the girls who made them and because they were also valued for their naïve charm. It might be expected that many of the features of pictorial embroidery would appear on the sampler, the other school exercise, but they are not so often found as might be supposed. Some of the 'spot' motif samplers worked on linen grounds occasionally include typical

[15] Nevinson, J. L. "Victoria & Albert Museum Catalogue", pl. XXXII and p. 46.
[16] Hackenbroch, Y. *op. cit.*, fig. 53.
[17] Nevinson, J. L. "Victoria & Albert Museum Catalogue", pl. XXXIV and p. 50.

9. Picture: *The Overwhelming of Pharaoh's Hosts in the Red Sea*, attributed to Damaris Pearce, about 1675
coloured silk and metal thread embroidery and stumpwork on white satin
13×22 in. (33×55·8 cm.)
The Lady Lever Art Gallery, Port Sunlight

10. Cabinet: *The Story of Abraham and Isaac*, signed SV, third quarter of the 17th century
coloured silk and metal thread embroidery with stumpwork and laid work on white satin
12×5×9 in. (30·4×12·7×22·8 cm.)
The Victoria and Albert Museum, London

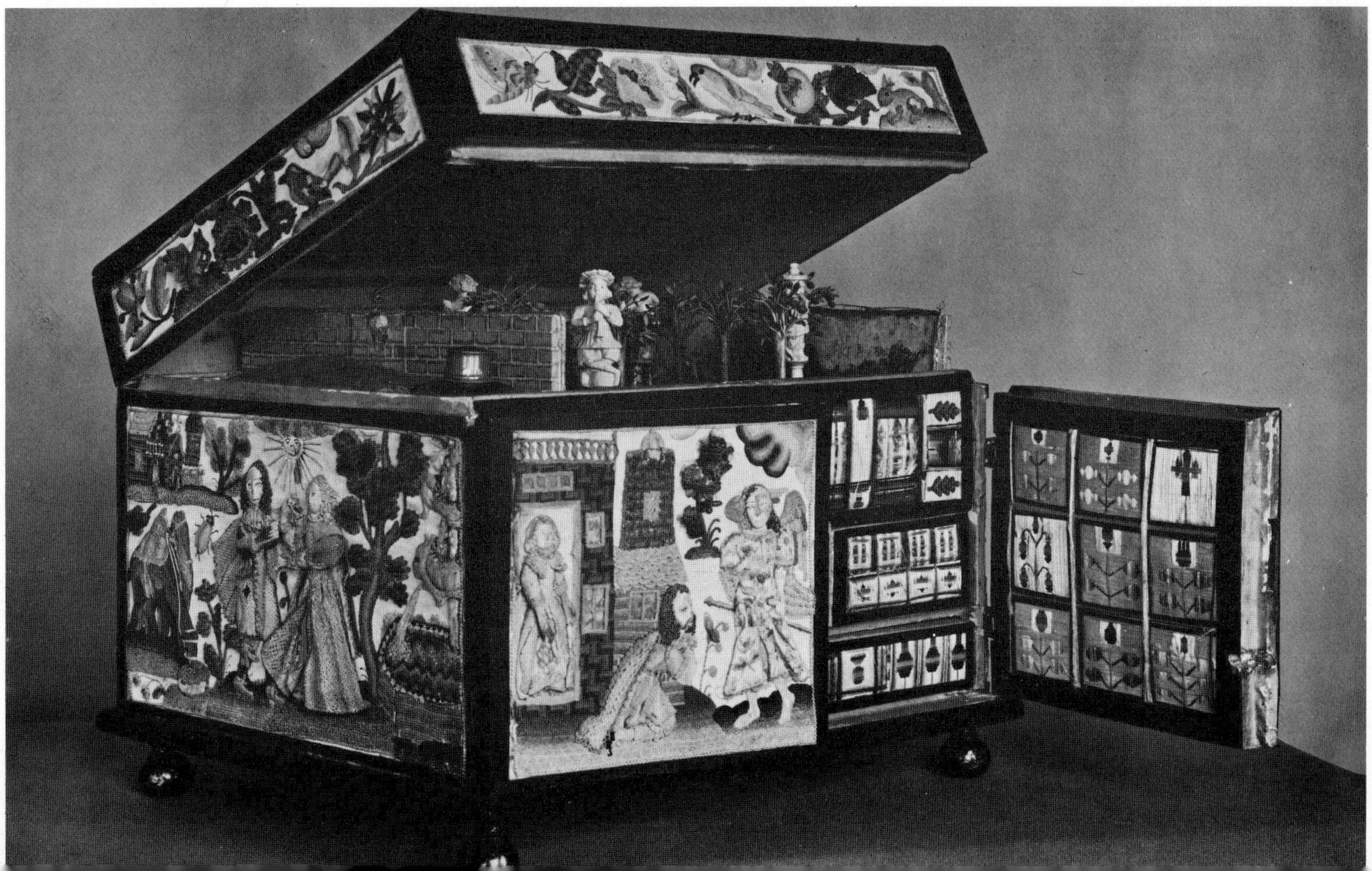

Æ 10
Martha
1660
Hollis

12. Basket: *A King and Queen*, third quarter of the 17th century
beadwork and stumpwork on white satin and wire
27×32×7 in. (68·5×81·2×17·7 cm.)
The Metropolitan Museum of Art, New York
(Gift of Mrs Thomas J. Watson, 1939)

13. Binding for a Book of Common Prayer of 1639 and a Bible with Metrical Psalms of 1640: *Peace and Plenty*, about 1640
coloured silk and metal thread embroidery on white satin
7½×5 in. (19×13 cm.)
The Bodleian Library, Oxford

animal or flower motifs, while the long narrow samplers, familiar throughout the century, sometimes bear figures like those in the pictorial work, and occasional flowers worked in detached button-holing. In general, however, the sampler consisted of a series of geometrical floral patterns worked in a variety of techniques which bore little relation to contemporary types of embroidery. Childish work seems in fact to have had little effect on the more serious embroidery of the period.

Remarkably little trace of these youthful efforts is to be seen in the other main group of 17th-century embroidery to have survived, the hangings worked in crewel wools on a linen and cotton twill weave ground. In the Richmond Collection[18] there is an unusual example of a picture of *Isaac and Rebekah* in this technique, but the hangings usually show only an occasional lion or leopard on the grassy mounds at the base of the tree designs. An exception to this rule are the bed-hangings in the Victoria and Albert Museum, signed by Abigail Pett and probably dating from the third quarter of the century. (Ill. 14.) These incorporate familiar motifs such as a fishpond and hunting scene as well as small animals amongst the exotic trees and birds. The rather naïve drawing and the presence of these elements suggest that the design was drawn by Abigail herself. A curtain at Colonial Williamsburg in which pavilions with striped curtains and crudely drawn figures appear amongst the exotic leafy stems and a cushion cover of 1659 in the Victoria and Albert Museum with a naïve design of figures and stylized flowers may also be examples of amateur designs.

The craze for stumpwork was short-lived, for it seems to have died out in the 1680's. A late example is a picture of *The Judgment of Solomon* in the Victoria and Albert Museum, dated 1686. The other two techniques, canvas work and flat silk embroidery, continued to flourish into the following century, however, although design underwent a considerable change. Portraits of royal personages became popular and Biblical subjects were superseded by pastoral themes, although some elements, such as the inclusion of outsize flowers in the design, lingered on. At the very end of the 17th century pictorial canvas work began to come into fashion again for upholstery. It enjoyed a great vogue in the first half of the 18th century, classical and pastoral subjects or scenes from plays being the most popular. Very few surviving examples can be assigned a date in the 17th century, but there is a set of tall-backed chairs in the Untermyer Collection[19] equipped with slip covers with pictorial designs which may belong to the last decades of the century.

Completely different in character from any of the pieces already discussed is a series of pictures preserved until 1922 at Corby Castle, Carlisle. The pictures, of subjects from the life of the Virgin and the childhood of Christ, were commissioned by William Howard, Lord Stafford (1611–80) from the most famous professional embroiderer of the day, Edmund Harrison. One of the best preserved of the series, *The Visitation*, is now in the Royal Scottish Museum. (Ill. 15.) The sophisticated design and the skilled technique, which includes the use of the method of couching gold thread with coloured silks (*or nué*) perfected by Flemish embroiderers of the 15th century, are quite unlike any other English work of the period. This picture, a companion piece and a larger example, the *Adoration of the Shepherds* in the Victoria and Albert Museum, the *Betrothal of the Virgin* in the Fitzwilliam Museum, Cambridge, bear the date 1637 inscribed on the back. Edmund Harrison, a prominent member of the Broderers' Company, held the office of Embroiderer under both Charles I and II. Documentary evidence shows that he was responsible for embroidering liveries and masque costumes, but this

[18] "The Connoisseur", vol. xcv, 1935, p. 321, no. X.
[19] Hackenbroch, Y. *op. cit.*, figs. 120–22.

Colour Plates. (above) Picture, signed Martha Hollis, AE 10, 1660
coloured silk and metal thread and purl embroidery on white satin 20×25 in. (50·8×63·5 cm.)
◀ The Victoria and Albert Museum, London
(below) Samplers, cabinet and jewel-box embroidered by Martha Edlin between 1668 and 1673
height of jewel-box 12 in. (30·5 cm.). Mrs Gillian Lewis and the Victoria and Albert Museum, London

14. Detail of one of a set of bed-hangings, signed by Abigail Pett, third quarter of the 17th century
crewel embroidery on cotton and linen twill
75×88 in. (190·5×223·5 cm.)
The Victoria and Albert Museum, London

set of pictures is the only work known to be by him which has survived. They are, in fact, the only professional embroideries which can be attributed to a known English master of the craft.

It is tempting to suggest that a set of embroideries commissioned by a member of the Sandys family, one of which is dated 1633,[20] came from Harrison's workshop. The set, made for the Chapel of the Holy Ghost at Basingstoke, includes a fine rendering of the Last Supper on a purple velvet ground, which is still in the possession of the descendants of the family. This was intended for hanging above the altar, an area often embellished with a painting of the same subject, as church inventories of the Laudian period testify. Although there was a revival of ecclesiastical embroidery under Laud, pictorial work is not very common. It is more usual to find rich silk or velvet cushions or hangings decorated with gold and silver fringes, with perhaps the monogram of Christ or some other symbol as the sole embroidered decoration. In Winchester College, however, is preserved an altar cushion embellished with a rendering of the Last Supper in raised work, within an elaborate oval framework adorned with scallop shells and cherub's heads, favourite design motifs of the period *circa* 1636–37 from which the cushion dates. In the corners appear the four evangelists beneath domed canopies. Another representation of the Last Supper occurs on an altar dossal preserved in the church of Weston Favell in Northamptonshire. (Ill. 16.) The scene is set off by a background of long white beads, a technique occasionally found in embroidered hangings of the late 17th and early 18th centuries. It is said to have been worked by Jane, the wife of Sir John Holman, Bart., and is dated 1698.

[20] Wardle, P. "A Laudian Embroidery", Bulletin of the Victoria and Albert Museum, vol. I, no. I, p. 26.

15. Picture: *The Visitation*, embroidered by Edmund Harrison, about 1637
coloured silk and metal thread embroidery on linen
24×23¼ in. (60·9×59 cm.)
The Royal Scottish Museum, Edinburgh

16. Altar dossal: *The Last Supper*, said to have been made by Jane, the wife of Sir John Holman, Bart., dated 1698
coloured wool, silk and metal thread embroidery and beadwork on linen
38×48 in. (96·6×122 cm.)
Weston Favell Church, Northamptonshire

English Enamels in the 18th Century

BERNARD WATNEY

1. Birmingham snuff-box inscribed in Russian 'God save Elizabeth I, Empress of all the Russians', other inscription commemorates the battle of Kunersdorf, 12 August 1759, fought between Frederick the Great and a combined Austrian and Russian army under Saltnikof
$3\frac{1}{4} \times 2\frac{1}{2} \times 1\frac{1}{4}$ in. (8·2×6·3×3·1 cm.)
Eric Benton Collection

In Europe the art of enamelling[1] was not an innovation of the 18th century; it had already been widely exploited for hundreds of years, certainly from the third century A.D. As witness of this, splendid things still survive which were made by jewellers and goldsmiths from the Dark Ages onwards in the enamelling techniques known as *cloisonné* and *champlevé*. Towards the end of the 15th century a somewhat different technique, that of painting in coloured enamels on a ground of plain enamel, was developed in France, at Limoges, to be modified elsewhere for miniatures and watches, and then given increased scope during the 18th century with the widespread fashion for snuff-boxes, *bonbonnières* and the like. England, in particular, had important centres of production in London, Birmingham, Liverpool and South Staffordshire, from whence enamels were exported to the Continent and even as far afield as Russia. (Ill. 1.) Base metals were now used almost exclusively and sheets of copper were cut, stamped or worked into shape, then covered with a layer of opaque white or coloured enamel and fired, giving a bonded, vitreous coating on all surfaces. These blanks could be painted, gilded or transfer printed in the same manner as porcelain and then refired, before being fitted in silver or gilt-metal mounts. Transfer printing, which was an English invention, provided a method of mass-produced decoration. It was introduced during the mid-18th century into an already established enamel manufacture producing painted miniatures and objects of vertu. None the less, transfer-printed decoration could not have quite the same prestige as fine-quality painted work. "I shall send you a trifling snuff-box, only as a sample of the new manufacture at Battersea, which is done with copper plates." This revealing sentence was written by Horace Walpole in a letter dated 18 September 1755.

In the past, students of 18th-century enamels have generally regarded the Battersea factory, on the south bank of the Thames, 1753–56, as having introduced transfer printing and also as having been the first English concern to produce any quantity of painted enamels. Recent research shows that neither of these two suppositions is likely to be correct,[2] as in the first place the method of transfer printing on enamels seems to have been discovered in Birmingham, and secondly, while Battersea undoubtedly manufactured the finest printed wares, there is no evidence to show that painted designs were done there. We must, however, be wary of ascribing all early painted enamels to the provinces and the following advertisement in the "London Daily Advertiser", 20 March 1747, suggests that some of the early painted snuff-boxes were, in fact, decorated in London: "To be sold by auction . . . at Geare's Public Sale-Warehouse in Threadneedle Street

[1] That is, fusing coloured glass on to precious or base metals.

[2] Watney, B. and Charleston, R. *Trans. English Ceramic Circle*, vol. 6, part 2, 1966.

2. Three Battersea wine labels with rare inscriptions, about 1755
coloured transfer prints width $2\frac{7}{8}$ in. (7·3 cm.)
Eric Benton Collection

behind the Royal Exchange. . . . Likewise the effects of an Enameller deceas'd, consisting of watches, rings, and snuff boxes, painted and blank plates, some colours, etc." Mr Toppin has recorded the names of at least ten enamellers from among a much larger number working in London between 1709 and 1757.[3] A few of these such as George Michael Moser, "Chaser and Painter in enamel colours", were doubtless responsible for manufacturing entire articles; many more, however, are likely to have decorated enamel blanks that had been made by someone else. Such a one was James Goddard: "the branch of enamelling professed by this Artist is painting in Enamel History, Figures and Flowers, on watch cases, *Etwees* etc". This latter group had its counterpart in the independent "enamellers on china ware" who lived in the metropolis, among whom were James Giles and William Duesbury. In fact, some artists decorated both materials, as "painters brought up in the snuff-box way" could easily adapt themselves to painting on china and vice versa. In this respect an interesting study could be made of the painting on enamel lids of Chelsea porcelain snuff-boxes to discover if the style of decoration is ever the same on both box and lid.

It is a difficult enough exercise to attempt to single out the individual decorators of porcelain where the painting is unsigned, although the object itself can be identified as, say, Worcester or Bow; but with enamels there is greater anonymity as the blanks have no known factory characteristics. There is little doubt, however, that Birmingham was the main centre for the manufacture of enamel blanks and gilt mounting frames, providing a ready source of supply for London enamellers, including the Battersea transfer-printing establishment. For some years before 1753, the date when the Battersea factory was founded, there was a far greater number of enamel decorators in Birmingham and the neighbouring South Staffordshire towns than in London[4] and this number increased rapidly during the third quarter of the 18th century. It was to Birmingham that the Irish engraver John Brooks came with his novel idea of transfer printing enamels and ceramics. On 10 September 1751 he made his first unsuccessful application for patent rights:[5] the

> "humble petition of John Brooks of Birmingham in the county of Warwick, engraver. Showeth that the petitioner has by great study application and expense found out a method of printing, impressing, and reversing upon enamel and china from engraved, etched and mezzotinto plates, and from cuttings on wood and mettle, impressions of History, Portraits, Landskips, Foliages, Coats of Arms, Cyphers, Letters, Decorations, and other Devices. That the said art and method is entirely new and of his own invention and for as much as it will be for the service of the public. . . ."

Brooks did not stay long in Birmingham for we know that in 1753 he helped to found the Battersea factory, the partnership being given in the Rate Books as "Messrs Janssen, Delamain and Brooks". While at Battersea, Brooks made two further unsuccessful petitions for a patent which were dated 25 January 1754 and April 1755 respectively. In both, he describes himself as "John Brooks of York Place in the parish of Battersea in the county of Surrey, engraver". The first York Place petition shows that he was claiming to print on glass as well as enamel and china, and he makes special mention of transfer printing on stone and earthenware.

[3] Toppin, A. J. *Trans. English Porcelain Circle*, no. 4, 1932, pp. 67–68.
[4] *Ibid.*
[5] Watney and Charleston, *loc. cit.*

3. Crucifix, possibly Battersea, about 1755
coloured transfer print length $2\frac{13}{16}$ (7·1 cm.)
width $1\frac{11}{16}$ in. (4·6 cm.)
Mavis Bimson Collection

4. Battersea snuff-box, printed in brown with *Infants* as *Commerce, Arts, and Sciences* on the sides, about 1755
$3\times2\frac{1}{4}\times1\frac{1}{4}$ in. (7·6×5·7×3·1 cm.)
Geoffrey Godden Collection

5. Coloured transfer print of Maria Gunning, about 1753; probably Birmingham
$3\frac{3}{8}\times2\frac{3}{4}$ in. (8·5×6·9 cm.)
Egan Mew Collection, Wolverhampton Museum

The second York Place petition adds delf to the list of wares that he could print upon and makes special mention of printing china ware.

The Battersea factory came to an end in 1756, after existing less than three years, with the bankruptcy first of Janssen "of London, Merchant", and then Brooks "of Battersea in the County of Surrey Engraver" on 12 and 27 January respectively. Some idea of the output of this short-lived factory may be obtained from two advertisements which appeared in the "London Daily Advertiser". The first of these, dated 28 February 1756, is the announcement of the sale of the contents of Janssen's house in St Paul's Churchyard:

> "Also a quantity of beautiful enamels, colour'd and uncolour'd, of the new manufactory carried on at York House at Battersea, and never yet exhibited to public view, consisting of Snuff-boxes of all sizes of great variety of Patterns, of square & oval pictures of the Royal Family, History & other pleasing subjects, very proper ornaments for Cabinets of the Curious, Bottle Tickets with Chains for all sorts of Liquor (Ill. 2), and of different Subjects, Watch-cases, Toothpick-cases, Coat & Sleeve Buttons, Crosses (Ill. 3), and other Curiosities, mostly mounted in metal, double gilt."

The second advertisement appeared from 31 May until 9 June 1756 and concerns the sale at York Place of

> "The Housho'd Furniture and entire Stock, of Stephen Theodore Janssen, Esq; consisting of a great Variety of beautiful enamelled Pictures, Snuff-Boxes (Ill. 4), Watch Cases, Bottle-Tickets, &c. great Variety of the like Enamels not completely finished, great Variety of Black [a misspelling for blank] Enamels of various Sizes, Copper-Frames for mounting of the unfinished Enamels, with all the Utensils, &c. belonging to the Manufactory; as also a great Number of Copper Plates beautifully engraved by the best Hands, some hundred Dozens of Stone Plates and Dutch Tiles, painted and plain, with many other Particulars, which will be specified in the printed Catalogue. . . ."

It was common 18th-century practice for factories to have a stock of goods from other concerns to fill gaps in their output or to replenish depleted stock. For example, Caughley blue-and-white and undecorated porcelain was stocked by Chamberlain's Worcester factory and Worcester was sometimes decorated at Derby. Furthermore, Matthew Boulton, having no enamelling shop himself, at any rate in 1782, had a small stock of decorated enamels at Soho, in Staffordshire, which had been made elsewhere. In this respect the sales of bankrupt stock from Battersea reveal an odd assortment of goods, but confining our attention to the enamels, while it is fairly certain that the enamel blanks and mounting frames were made in Birmingham, there is an added possibility that some of the decorated examples, such as tooth-pick cases and buttons, also came from Birmingham, the great centre for buttons and toys. It is significant that some Birmingham, but no Battersea, examples of these objects are known.

There is ample evidence to show that both the unfinished stock and the engraved copper plates from the York House factory were used later, especially at Birmingham. Battersea enamels, as we know them, are printed in attractive pale colours, and sometimes in gold, showing great brilliance of line. Any overpainting is in fine translucent colour to enhance, rather than hide, the engraved line. The prints, mostly attributed to Ravenet, have at times an almost Titianesque quality depicting classical, mythological (see colour plate facing p. 292) and allegorical designs as well as portraits and religious subjects. However, as a result of the bankruptcy,

6. Coloured transfer print of George III as Prince of Wales, about 1753; Battersea: length 5¼ in. (13·3 cm.) Sir William and Lady Mullens, *ex* Ionides Collection

7. Two Birmingham plaques with coloured transfer prints showing *Le Jeu des Quatre-Coins* after Lancret and *The Fishing Party*, about 1753. Ionides Collection

some Battersea enamels appear to have been overpainted in bold colours at a later date; Battersea printed box tops were fitted to non-Battersea bases and vice versa, and typical Battersea mounts and shaped enamel blanks were used elsewhere. Apart from the occurrence of actual reprints, re-engravings of Battersea originals were popular on later enamels, but few of them were of high quality. Thus we must inevitably have reservations in accepting prints as Battersea which have been taken from indifferently inked, worn, or re-engraved plates especially where harsh colours have been used, such as plum-pink, deep red-brown or inky-black. Furthermore, enamels enriched with coloured grounds and raised white or gilt scrollwork post-date Battersea and belong properly to later in the 18th century.

The enamels produced by Brooks in his pre-Battersea, or Birmingham period, are probably represented by the pair of very large portraits of the Gunning sisters in the Victoria and Albert Museum which have required considerable overpainting *en camaïeu* to strengthen the printed outlines. In contrast, a smaller pair of Gunning plaques often shows evidence of increased mastery over the transfer-printing process, and many of these examples can be ascribed to Battersea with some confidence. However, the only known pair of coloured plaques of these fashionable Irish beauties is not quite up to the Battersea standard. (Ill. 5.) Probably one of the earliest Battersea enamels is the portrait of George III as a young prince (Ill. 6); this is also considerably overpainted but the engraved line has been transferred more successfully. The same design occurs as a fine impression on paper, signed "Ravenet sculp", published first in 1749 and then in 1751. As a matter of interest, traces of Ravenet's signature can be found on the majority of enamel plaques bearing the portrait of the Duke of Cumberland, whether printed in gold or other colours.[6]

We must now turn our attention to a much larger group of printed enamels which take their main inspiration from the French school of Watteau, Boucher and Lancret, but even the most accomplished examples rarely attain the high standard of Battersea work. (See colour plate facing p. 292.) This group appears to have been in existence before Battersea was founded and to have continued long afterwards, into the late 18th century. Battersea designs were soon assimilated, for the decoration of snuff-boxes, both by direct use of original plates and by re-engravings of such themes as *Infants as Arts and Sciences* and the numerous cherubic variants on Battersea labels. This transfer-printed group has close connections with some painted enamels which, as we shall see later, have a number of typical Birmingham features. (See colour plate facing p. 292.) The earliest printed specimens show the same lack of clarity in the outlines as those which we consider to have been done by Brooks at Birmingham, and once more there is evidence that considerable overpainting was required to reveal the design. These enamels are principally associated with the names of Robert Hancock and Louis Boitard, whose designs are also well known on early Bow and Worcester porcelain.

The relationship of Hancock to enamels has been hopelessly confused since the initial observation by R. W. Binns in 1865 that an enamel 'watch-back' in the Worcester Works Museum with a print of *The Tea Party* is signed "R.H.f.". Binns suggested that this was a Battersea enamel, and so it seemed to follow as a natural corollary that Hancock must have worked at Battersea. The scholarly and logical Bernard Rackham, keeper at the Victoria and Albert Museum, was the first to contest this line of argument, but he lacked the vital evidence of transfer printing

[6] Bimson, M., Dept. of Research Laboratory, British Museum, has recently discovered Ravenet's initials in the margin of a plaque depicting *Perseus and Andromeda*.

8. (below) Two Birmingham snuff-boxes with painted decoration, about 1753
Egan Mew Collection, Wolverhampton Museum

9. (right) Two Birmingham snuff-boxes with engine-turned, copper bases, one faintly printed and painted over in brown monochrome showing *Two Lovers in a Cornfield*, the other a painted scene after Wouwerman, 1753–6
diameter 2⅜ in. (6 cm.) height 1⅛ in. (2·8 cm.)
Eric Benton Collection

in Birmingham which would have suggested an alternative source for early enamels. Egan Mew and Gerald Mander, who both possessed a collector's knowledge and love of the subject, almost stumbled on to the truth, that the group associated with Hancock was separate from Battersea; in fact, Mander must surely have done so had he not died, in 1961, before he was able to marshal the scattered items of information among his jottings. He knew, for example, that John Taylor, an already long-established button maker and snuff-box maker, was transfer printing on enamels in Birmingham at least as early as 1766:

> "At Mr. Taylor's we met again and he made and ennamel'd a landscape on the top of a box before us which he afterwards gave me as a curiosity from my having seen it done. The method of doing it is this: a stamping instrument managed only by one woman first impresses the picture on paper, which paper is then laid even upon a piece of white enamel and rubbed hard with a knife, or instrument like it, till it is marked upon the box. Then there is spread over it with a brush some metallic colour reduced to a fine powder which adheres to the moist part and, by putting it afterwards into an oven for a few minutes, the whole is completed by fixing the colour."[7]

Eleven years before this, in 1755, another visitor wrote: "We saw the manufactory of Mr. Taylor, the most considerable maker of gilt-metal buttons, and enamelled snuff boxes."[8] In 1781 W. Hutton, the Birmingham historian, stated that "to this uncommon genius" we owe "the numerous race of enamels".

The earliest mention of transfer printing at Birmingham, apart from John Brooks's important petition of 1751, is an advertisement in the "Liverpool Advertiser", 11 February 1757, concerning the proposed publication of a pamphlet by Thomas Lawrensen which would contain a description of "the new and curious art of printing or rather reprinting, from copper plates, upon porclane, enammel and earthenware, as lately practised at Chelsea, Birmingham etc".

A study of printed enamels, especially dated examples, and comparison with similar transfers on early Bow and Worcester porcelain gives convincing evidence of a direct continuation in the Boitard–Hancock group of enamels from the early 1750's into the 1770's. Furthermore, a comparison between this group and Birmingham painted enamels helps to establish their origin, especially where both painted and printed decoration are found side by side on the same piece. (Ill. 7.) An advertisement of 16 September 1751, in "Aris's Birmingham Gazette", underlines the fact that enamelling was already a widespread trade in the Midlands by the time that transfer printing was introduced:

> "Abraham Seeman, Enamelling Painter, at Mrs. Weston's in Freeman St. Birmingham, makes and sells all sorts of enamelling colours, especially the Rose

[7] Edmond George Petty, Baron Fitzmaurice. *The Life of William, Earl of Shelburne*. London, 1875–76, vol. 1, pp. 400–1, description by Lady Shelburne.

[8] Lloyd, S. *The Lloyds of Birmingham with some account of the Founding of Lloyds Bank*. Birmingham, 3rd ed., 1909.

10. Birmingham snuff-box with coloured transfer print showing *Peeping Tom*, derived from *Pensent-ils au raison* by Boucher, about 1756
width 4 in. (10·1 cm.) height 1½ in. (3·8 cm.)
The Victoria and Albert Museum, London

11. Birmingham snuff-box with coloured transfer print showing seated lovers on the lid and flowers on the sides, inscribed inside 'Sarh Walton 1755'
2×2½ in. (5×6·3 cm.)
The Victoria and Albert Museum, London

Colour Plates. (above left) Birmingham snuff-box with coloured transfer prints including *Autumn*, after Watteau, on the lid, about 1756
3×2¼ in. (7·6×5·7 cm.)
Courtesy Sotheby & Co., London
(above right) Birmingham snuff-box showing elaborate filigree work on a blue enamel ground and painted decoration, about 1754
3×2⅜ in. (7·6×5·8 cm.)
Courtesy Sotheby & Co., London
(below left) Battersea plaque with coloured transfer print of *Danae and the Shower of Gold*, about 1754
4×3¼ in. (10·1×8·2 cm.)
Sir William and Lady Mullens Collection
(below right) Battersea plaque with coloured transfer print of *Venus and the Triton*, about 1754
4×3¼ in. (10·1×8·2 cm.)
Sir William and Lady Mullens Collection

Colours, likewise all sorts for China Painters. N.B. Most of the eminent Painters of Birmingham, Wednesbury and Bilston have made use of the above colours to their satisfaction."

Mander was to some extent aware of this when he catalogued the Egan Mew Collection at Wolverhampton and separated a group of painted enamels which he ascribed to Birmingham, although he gave them too late a date, probably because he considered that the majority were made at Soho by Matthew Boulton. His main contribution, nevertheless, was to show that typical Birmingham work included enamel buttons and enamel snuff-boxes with mother-of-pearl, pressed horn, japanned, copper-gilt or Sheffield plate bases. He also noted a style of painted decoration which he ascribed to an unknown Birmingham artist depicting "a type of delicately coloured moss rose, butterfly and bee design" (Ill. 8), and he drew attention to the copper-gilt mounts, often elaborately chased "in the manner of the Soho works". It is strange that Mander got this far without seeming to notice that some printed enamels also had Sheffield plate or turned, copper-gilt bases (Ill. 9), and that painted insects and flower sprays on the sides and bases of boxes with printed lids (Ills 8, 10, 11) could be matched with the painted decoration amongst his Birmingham group. Indeed this latter connection is shown to advantage on the finest pieces, the beautifully made caskets with French figure scenes. These scenes can be either printed or painted, and in both cases the closely similar styles of floral side painting suggest a single factory of origin. (Ills 12, 13, 14, 15.)

The name Battersea has been used for so long as a generic term for practically all high-quality English enamels that it came as a shock to many when Rackham proposed, in 1924, that most of the best painted work on enamels in the Schreiber Collection was done in Staffordshire and not at Battersea. We can now go further than Rackham, with the suggestion that some of the earliest and finest examples were made in Birmingham.[9] As well as those painted with moss roses and insects, as described by Mander, there is a somewhat later group of the late 1750's and early 1760's, which calls for special mention and of which it would still be possible to form a most handsome collection. They are superbly made, and finished with the finest quality mounts which, on snuff-boxes, are sometimes fitted with a filigree, or rope twist thumb-piece. A scent bottle, Schreiber No. 407, displays the typical flower painting of this group, in the Meissen or Chelsea style, as well as an apple-green ground, which is also found on a circular snuff-box. (Ill. 16.) A bright mustard-yellow was sometimes used as an alternative ground colour, especially on boxes with slightly fluted surfaces. (Ill. 17.) The particular style of flower painting associated with this group is uncommon as a side decoration for printed enamels, although an unusually early example is illustrated by Hughes.[10]

The faint, powdery appearance of the outlines in the early printed work, ascribed to Birmingham, is an effect that might well be expected from first attempts at printing by the process described in Lady Shelburne's journal. This process differs from the usual method in which the copper plate is inked with enamel colour, the design printed on paper and then transferred on to enamel. Egan Mew, when discussing a plaque depicting *The Free British Fishery Society*,[11] founded by royal charter 25 October 1750, noted that it was "very different from and very inferior to, the general run of Battersea production. . . ". Mew discovered that the vice-president of this society had been Alderman Stephen Theodore Janssen and he

[9] Watney and Charleston. *Trans. E.C.C.*, vol. 6, part 2, 1966.
[10] Hughes, T. and B. *English Painted Enamels*. London, 1951, pl. 12*a*.
[11] Catalogue of the Schreiber Collection, vol. 3, "Enamels and Glass". London, 1924, pl. 32, no. 64.

12. Birmingham painted casket, about 1754
length $7\frac{1}{4}$ in. (18·4 cm.)
ex Ionides Collection

13. Birmingham casket with coloured transfer prints and flower painting about 1754
$8\frac{1}{2}\times5\frac{1}{2}\times3\frac{1}{4}$ in. (21·5×13·9×8·2 cm.)
Sir William and Lady Mullens Collection

14. Birmingham casket showing typical japanned and gilt-metal work, about 1754
ex Ionides Collection

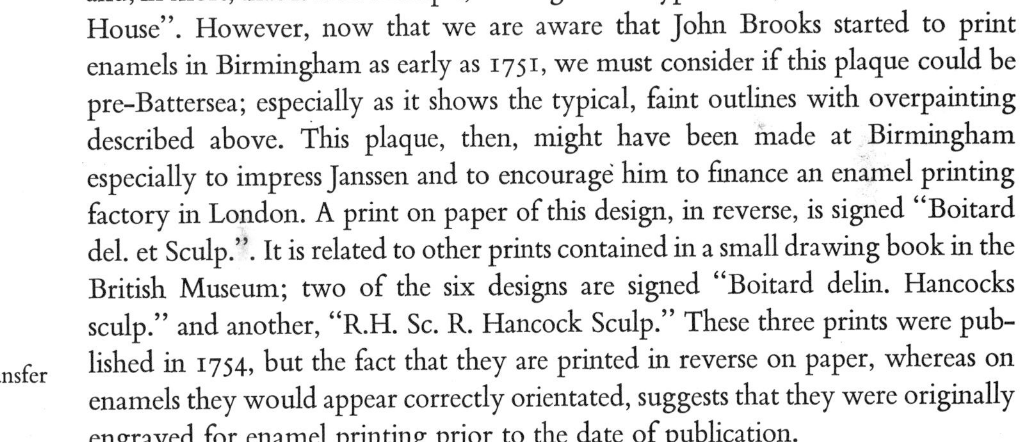

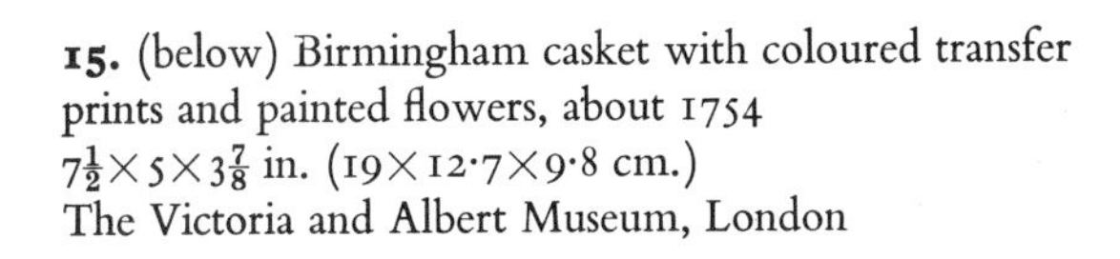

15. (below) Birmingham casket with coloured transfer prints and painted flowers, about 1754
$7\frac{1}{2} \times 5 \times 3\frac{7}{8}$ in. ($19 \times 12{\cdot}7 \times 9{\cdot}8$ cm.)
The Victoria and Albert Museum, London

concluded that, "it seems pretty certain that the plaque was produced in 1752–3, and, in short, that it is an example, although not a typical one, of the work at York House". However, now that we are aware that John Brooks started to print enamels in Birmingham as early as 1751, we must consider if this plaque could be pre-Battersea; especially as it shows the typical, faint outlines with overpainting described above. This plaque, then, might have been made at Birmingham especially to impress Janssen and to encourage him to finance an enamel printing factory in London. A print on paper of this design, in reverse, is signed "Boitard del. et Sculp.". It is related to other prints contained in a small drawing book in the British Museum; two of the six designs are signed "Boitard delin. Hancocks sculp." and another, "R.H. Sc. R. Hancock Sculp." These three prints were published in 1754, but the fact that they are printed in reverse on paper, whereas on enamels they would appear correctly orientated, suggests that they were originally engraved for enamel printing prior to the date of publication.

Designs of the Boitard–Hancock group on early enamel plaques are considerably retouched and often have a pair of swans painted in the foreground. (Ill. 7.) These finely detailed designs would appear to date from between 1751 and 1754 and from then onwards the transfer prints tend to be progressively bolder and the overpainting is less elaborate. The earliest known dated box, inscribed "Sarh Walton, 1755" (Ill. 11), is decorated with an overpainted print of *Seated Lovers* and has painted 'Birmingham' flowers on the sides. Another documentary printed piece is a beaker-cup in the Birmingham Museum, inscribed "L.S. 1756". (Ill. 18.)

The same technique of printing, sometimes from the same copper plates, appears to have been used not only on early enamels but also on Worcester porcelain dating from about 1754, the so-called 'smoky primitives'. In a year or two, however, there had been an improvement in technique giving greater clarity of outline as shown by comparing prints, such as the Hancock signed *Tea Party*, on both enamels and Bow and Worcester porcelain. This design always appears to be

16. Birmingham snuff-box with painted decoration on an apple-green ground, about 1760
diameter $2\frac{1}{4}$ in. (5·7 cm.)
Courtesy Sotheby & Co., London

17. Birmingham snuff-box with painted decoration on a yellow ground, about 1760
$2\frac{3}{8} \times 1\frac{3}{4}$ in. (6×4·4 cm.)
Courtesy Sotheby & Co., London

18. Birmingham beaker-cup with coloured transfer of *The Embrace Observed* and *A Woman with a basket of Flowers*, inscribed 'L.S. 1756'
height 2 in. (5 cm.)
The City Museum and Art Gallery, Birmingham

signed "R.H.f." on enamels even when used in the late 1760's framed by a blue ground with raised white enamel scrolls. It does not seem to have been used on enamels much earlier than 1756 and belongs to a group of patterns which are found in association on snuff-boxes; these include *The King of Prussia*, popular during the Seven Years War, 1756–63, and re-engravings of *Infants* as *Arts, Science and Commerce*, after Battersea and thus probably post-1756. The porcelain bearing this *Tea Party* print also dates from about 1756 and there is an impression on paper which is not reversed, published 24 November 1756.

The more we study this printed group the less is the need to suppose that Hancock was at Battersea and at Bow before going to Worcester *circa* 1756. Hancock would have completed his term of apprenticeship to a Birmingham engraver in 1753 or thereabouts and there now seems to be every indication that after this he remained in Birmingham until he went to Worcester. His engraved copper plates were first used in Birmingham, possibly by John Taylor, for decorating enamels and porcelain.

The story has yet to be written of the part played by the South Staffordshire towns of Wednesbury and Bilston in the early and later production of enamels, but we may find that, in a number of instances, there were small factories each specializing in one part of enamel manufacture. Snuff-boxes in the form of fruit and animal or bird heads are usually considered to be of Bilston manufacture as well as ornate enamels with coloured grounds, and inscribed patch-boxes with steel or glass mirrors set into the lids. Gerald Mander catalogued two small boxes and box tops at the Wolverhampton Museum, as characteristic of Wednesbury, the decoration being in white enamel on an intense blue ground.

Finally, mention must be made of Liverpool, where it is likely that a group of enamels were made with portraits derived from engravings in *Bell's British Theatre* and *Bell's Shakespeare*. There are the large portrait plaques of *Pitt* and *The King of Prussia*, the latter signed "J. Sadler, Liverp: Enaml:". Then there is *The Concert Party* which was brought forward as typical of Hancock's style, in an attempt to prove that he worked at Battersea. In fact, it is taken from a copper plate engraved by James Basire for the frontispiece of *The Muse's Delight*, a music book printed, published and sold by John Sadler of Liverpool in 1754.

BIBLIOGRAPHY

Rackham, B. *Catalogue of the Schreiber Collection*, vol. 3, *Enamels and Glass*. London, 1924.

Mew, E. *Battersea Enamels*. London, 1926.

Toppin, A. J. "Notes on Janssen and the Artists of the Battersea factory", *Trans. English Porcelain Circle*, no. 4, 1932.

Hughes, H. W. "Authorship of some designs on Porcelain and Enamel", *Trans. English Ceramic Circle*, vol. I, no. 3, 1935.

Cook, C. *The Life and Work of Robert Hancock*. London, 1948.

Hughes T. and B. *English Painted Enamels*. London, 1951.

Cook, C. "James Gwin and his designs on Battersea Enamels", *Apollo*, vol. LV, March 1952.

Cook, C. "John Brooks and his engravings on Battersea Enamels", *Apollo*, vol. LV, May 1952.

Cook, C. "Louis P. Boitard and his designs on Battersea Enamels", *Apollo*, vol. LVII, March 1953.

Cook, C. "New Light on Battersea Wares", *The Antique Collector*, vol. 24, June 1953.

Cook, C. "Simon François Ravenet and his engravings on Battersea Enamels", *Trans. E.C.C.*, vol. 3, part 4, 1955.

Cook, C. *Supplement to the Life and Work of Robert Hancock*. London, 1955.

Hackenbroch, Y. *Chelsea and other English Porcelain, Pottery and Enamel in the Irwin Untermyer Collection*. London, 1957.

Watney, B., and Charleston, R. Four papers, "Petitions for Patents concerning Porcelain, Glass and Enamels with special reference to Birmingham 'The Great Toyshop of Europe'", *Trans. E.C.C.*, vol. 6, part 2, 1966.

Reed Instruments

EDWARD O. POGSON

Since the Stone Age, and possibly earlier, man has made noises on pipes. The earliest pipes known were those made out of animal bone. The first sophisticated reed instrument to appear on the scene was the Greek *aulos*. Representations of this instrument being played appear on Greek pottery and in some forms of the instrument the player is shown as having his cheeks bound with a leather device known as a *phorbeia*. The lips would have no control of the reed; the performer would use his mouth cavity like the bag of a bagpipe, and a continuous supply of wind power could be maintained by the use of the trick of breathing through the nose and exhaling through the mouth (a difficult enough accomplishment I can assure you) while the *phorbeia* helped to keep the wind bag operational. The range of the instrument was stated to be two and a half octaves. The *aulos* was a shawm and the progenitor of all our modern woodwind. It was not exclusive to Greece – the Egyptians, the Hittites, the Jews and others all knew and used this instrument – and it must have come to Europe and the Middle and Near East perhaps from China, where there was an advanced civilization when the British were still disporting themselves in woad. The Romans imported the *aulos* into their Empire – together with the rest of Greek culture – where it was known as the tibia.

With the coming of the Dark Ages a curtain descends and the next we hear of the shawm is that, in *circa* 1200, it reappeared in Southern Europe and established itself as the mainstay of the then wind band. It was eventually made in five or six sizes from the soprano pitched in about D to the great double quint bass which required two men to operate it.

With the coming of the oboe – *circa* 1675 – it disappeared almost overnight; but not quite – it lived on in north-eastern Spain, where it flourishes to this very day. All over northern Spain a form of shawm called the *dulzina* is played, but the direct descendants of the ancient and medieval shawms are the *tiple* and *tenora* which are played in the *coblas* (bands) which accompany the Sardana dance. The Sardana was a kind of harvest thanksgiving dance and was accompanied by three or four musicians – usually a bagpipe, one or two treble shawms (tiples) and the pipe and tabor (another medieval hangover which I will describe when we come to flutes) – or indeed anything that was handy.

About the middle of the 19th century – at the time that valves were applied to brass instruments – one José Ventura of Figureas ('Pep de Figureas') re-vamped the Sardana Cobla, and this became standard all over Catalonia.

The cobla performs, in the open air of course, on a two-tiered trestle – the brass at the back slightly higher than the shawms, pipe and tabor and string bass on the front. Apart from the tabor there are no drums. The combination consists of two trumpets in B♭ or C, valve trombone, also in B♭ or C, and two fiscornes. The

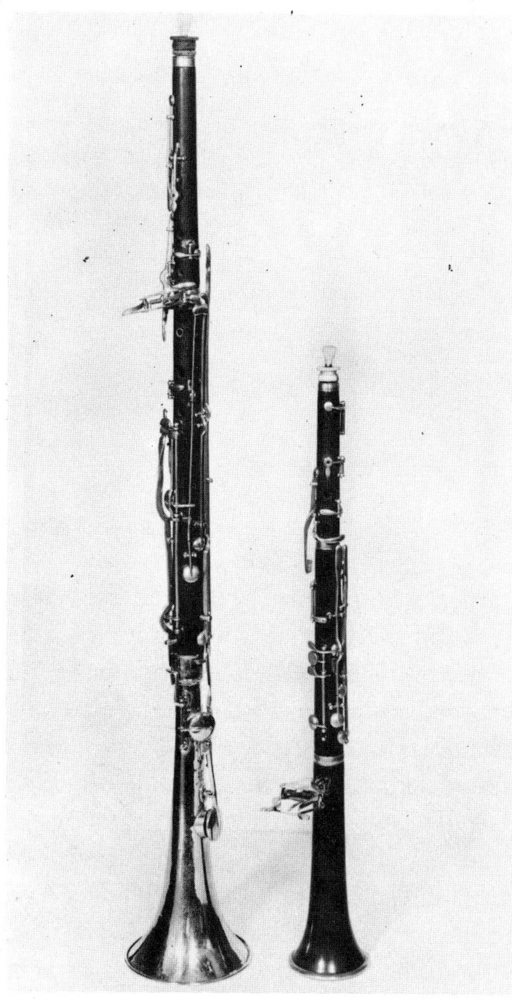

1. (left) Tenora, anonymous
(right) Tiple by Pill, St Felieu de Pallarols
both early 20th century
34 in. (86·3 cm.) and 22½ in. (57·1 cm.)
E. O. Pogson Collection

fiscorne is a bass flügel-horn with rotary valves and is of Czech manufacture (Kohlert). It is held straight out like a vast bugle.

The front line reads, from left to right, pipe (in Catalan *fluviol*) and tabor, two treble shawms (tiples) and two tenor shawms (tenoras) and bass – often a three-stringer played with a Dragonetti bow. The tiples are pitched in F – one fourth above the oboe, and the tenoras in B♭ like the clarinet, and each has a distinctive role to play. The tenoras play the soulful and romantic passages in a rubato style with much vibrato, while the tiples play with a cheeky staccato approach. The musicians play from parts, and well-orchestrated parts they are, and the procedure is this. The cobla being assembled, the fluviol player plays quite a long solo introductory preamble and, having thus delivered himself he strikes the tabor with a loud whack and the music strikes up. The effect is incredible – for sheer electric sizzling brilliance there is no comparable sound and it is distinctive beyond belief. The Sardana procedure is thus: the cobla assembles at about 10.30–11 at night when the populace are out promenading or sitting in the open-air cafés. You can hear the shawms preluding a quarter of a mile off. This tuning up is a signal for the dancers to take their places. The dance, which to the uninitiated looks easy, is in reality very complicated and the best performers are the elderly men, for some odd reason, and you will get the polite 'death eye' if you try to join in and do not know it.

Each Sardana lasts about twenty minutes, and two are played before the orchestral gentlemen retire for refreshment. When they reappear after some twenty minutes they deliver themselves of another two and, as an encore, a half Sardana.

The whole proceedings last about two and a half hours.

We do not know for certain how the ancient and medieval shawms were sounded, but of the Catalan shawms there is no doubt. The sounding apparatus consists of a pirouette (in Catalan *tudel*) which is like a wooden trumpet mouthpiece with a staple passing through it and to which the reed is firmly affixed – the end of the staple being on a level or just below the rim of the pirouette. The reed is broad and short and is double – being made of two blades of *Arundo donax* – a giant grass that grows all round the Mediterranean shore. The best cane for this purpose comes from the Var valley around Fréjus in southern France; but good enough cane abounds in Spain.

The reed is pushed firmly on the staple and can be controlled by the lips while the lips are pushed up against the pirouette. This gives the shawmist greater control of the reed, and enables him to play for long periods without fatigue. José Ventura, incidentally, played first tenora in his new-deal cobla.

The keywork on these instruments underwent constant improvement as time went on. The keys shown in illustration 1 are typical early 20th-century – quite simple. Nowadays the instruments are fitted with Boehm-type keywork and are thoroughly up to date.

One curious anomaly – most of the coblas play in the Brillante pitch – like our late Victorian sharp pitch, and this of course makes the bright sound still brighter. Other coblas play in the A440 pitch – our modern pitch. The most difficult thing about shawm playing is holding the note steady. Owing to the wide short reed and the big and rapidly widening bore, the notes 'fly' very easily, and it is the good shawmist's job to hold them steady.

These instruments are made of the wood of the jujube tree and it is of warm reddish brown colour. The range of the tiple is about two and a half octaves, written low A to top E; and the tenora three octaves: low F (on extensions) to top G or thereabouts.

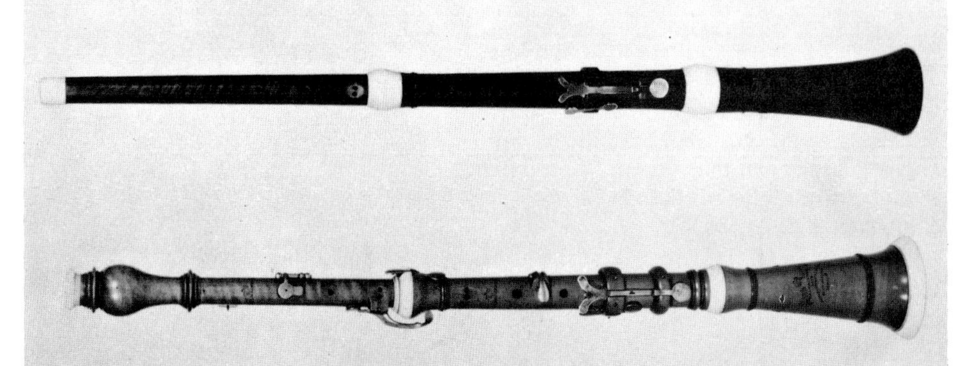

2. (above) Oboe, *circa* 1780, by Millhouse-Newark
stained boxwood, ivory and two silver keys
23 in. (58·4 cm.)
(below) Oboe, *circa* 1730, by Dalmaine; London
boxwood with seven keys
23 in. (58·4 cm.)
E. O. Pogson Collection

If, in the summer, you are in the Costa Brava and you see a notice up with the legend "Hoy Noche Sardanas", wait until the evening and you will hear a sound that our medieval forebears knew so well, and which has nearly been lost.

OBOES

The oboes are direct descendants of the shawms. The oboe itself came to England via France where it was evolved. Charles II imported eight players for his private band, and it quickly established itself to be a great favourite. The instrument was a far more refined machine than its predecessor – the bore was narrower, the tone holes smaller and the double reed much longer and narrower than the shawm shape, and the cane blades which formed it were bound together direct on to the staple, which was corked at the non-blowing end. This reed which was pushed into the top of the tube was controlled entirely by the lips – there was no pirouette.

The early instruments (Ill. 2), made mostly in boxwood with ivory mounts, sometimes stained to a deep shade of brown, were furnished with three keys – one for low C and the other two for E♭ – one either side of the instrument. The reason for this was that some players held the oboe left hand over right and some right over left; thus the right hand lower would play the E♭ with the right hand and vice versa for the left. The unwanted hole would then be sealed up and the instrument would become two-keyed. There was no 'speaker' or octave key. The note holes for F and G were made by boring two small holes thus ●● and that part of the body slightly flattened. In this way if one of the holes only was uncovered, the notes F♯ and G♯ could be obtained. With this simple mechanism two full chromatic octaves were available (except low C♯) – the second octave readily overblowing by lip pressure. The oboe, having a conical bore, overblew in octaves of course.

The keywork remained thus for about 100 years, and oboes of the late 17th century looked much the same as those of the late 18th century. One of the reasons for the oboe's success was its great suitability for indoor playing, as the tone was gentle and had a vast dynamic range. During this first 100 years the oboe appeared in other sizes. There was the oboe d'amore, pitched in A, and the cor anglais pitched in F. The oboe d'amore, which is possibly the orchestra's most aristocratic sound, was a great favourite of Johann Sebastian Bach, who wrote extensively for it. The cor anglais, which was neither a horn nor English, was first constructed in an angled form thus < or in a semicircular form thus C. I have handled quite a few of them, and when they play, they play well. I wonder if 'anglais' was originally 'anglé'? Much later, in the late 19th century, came the bass oboe (sometimes called the baritone) pitched in C – one octave below the normal oboe. The oboe d'amore, cor anglais and bass oboe all had elongated staples to take the reed and make the playing position more comfortable, and bulbous pear-shaped bells. This shape was claimed to give the instruments their distinctive tone. It does not do this, but curiously enough a number of notes in the upper register around G, A and B can be tuned by scraping the top inside of the bell where it begins to flare. There was one other oboe: the oboe di caccia – the hunting oboe – which was pitched in F like the cor anglais, but had a flared bell like a clarinet. It is said that this was played before the Master before and after the Hunt. I must say

3. (left to right) Oboe, 1930, by Lorré; Paris
24 in. (60·9 cm.)
Oboe d'amore, 1935, by Louis; London
25½ in. (64·7 cm.)
Cor anglais, 1930, by Lorré; Paris
31½ in. (80 cm.)
Bass oboe, 1935, Cabart; Paris
41½ in. (105·4 cm.)
E. O. Pogson Collection

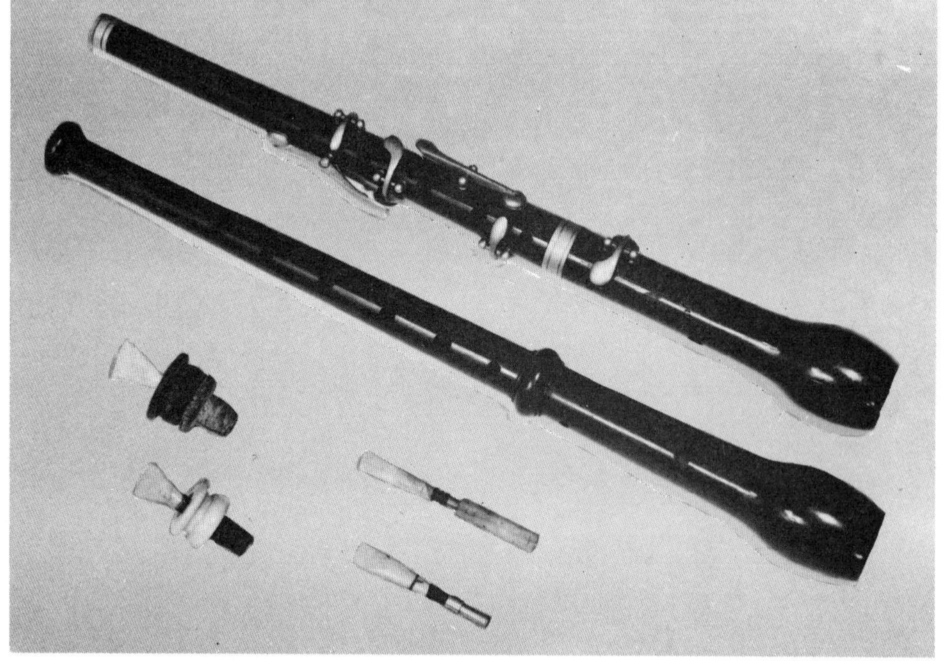

4. (above) Keyless and keyed musettes, anonymous, late 19th century, cocus wood 7 in. (17·7 cm.)
(below) Tenora reed and pirouette, Tiple reed on pirouette; Cor anglais and oboe reeds
E. O. Pogson Collection

that I find the idea of this procedure faintly ludicrous, and I can hardly think of an instrument more unsuitable for the job. The keywork gradually developed to its present-day complexity. From the late 17th to the late 18th centuries it looked like the Millhouse two-keyed instrument, and by *circa* 1830 like the seven-keyed Dalmaine, which still retains the old F–F♯ fingerings. (Ill. 2.) Today the family consists of the oboe, oboe d'amore, cor anglais and the bass oboe. (Ill. 3.)

The French made an attempt to popularize oboes in E and D for military band use – but it was abortive; also musettes, which were originally played like a bagpipe, but were later played with an oboe-type reed, were sold as musical toys with and without keywork – but they passed into limbo. (Ill. 4.)

5. (below left) Heckelphone, 1930, by Wm Heckel of Beibrich-am-Rhein
maple 53 in. (134·6 cm.) with crook
E. O. Pogson Collection

6. (below right) Bassoon, *circa* 1830, by Savary; Paris
maple 50½ in. (128·2 cm.) extreme height 97½ in. (247 cm.)
E. O. Pogson Collection

THE HECKELPHONE

The Heckelphone is the German version of the bass oboe (Ill. 5), although in conception and design all the two instruments have in common is their key and pitch.

The heckelphone was invented and made by Wilhelm Heckel of Beibrich-am-Rhein in the early years of the present century – *circa* 1904. Like the bass oboe it is pitched in C – one octave below the normal oboe – and is furnished like the lower oboes with a staple, in this case big enough to be termed a crook, on which is mounted the reed. This is a double reed and can take two forms, one similar to a big cor anglais reed or the other like a smallish bassoon reed. Most players prefer the latter as it allows greater latitude of embouchure, and is a good deal safer in the lowest register. The sound is powerful and sonorous, and with the bassoon-type reed can be played for extended periods without fatigue.

The instrument is made of maple, and the keywork of nickel silver is massive and efficient in a Teutonic way. Strauss used the heckelphone in "Electra" and "Salome", where it can be heard to advantage.

I have seen Heckel's catalogue in which he advertises heckelphones of different sizes – the family once again. I have only met the normal heckelphone in C, and I have yet to encounter any reed player who has come across any other. Perhaps they were 'pipe dreams', or maybe some are lurking to be discovered. The range of the heckelphone is from A (low) to top G or even higher, i.e. three chromatic octaves.

BASSOONS

The bassoon, like the heckelphone, is made of maple. (Ill. 6.) Its ancestors were the shawms and the pommers and its function to be the bass of the reed ensemble. The whole family going from bottom up consisted of the contra (one octave below

7. (top to bottom) Clarinet in C, *circa* 1790, by Goulding & Dalmaine; London
boxwood and ivory with five keys 23½ in. (59·6 cm.)
Clarinet in C, 1830, probably Belgian
boxwood with transitional keywork 23 in. (58·4 cm.)
Clarinet in B♭, 1850, Buffet; Paris, Boehm system
boxwood 27 in. (68·5 cm.)
Clarinet in B♭, 1930, Selmer; Paris
African blackwood 27 in. (68·5 cm.)
E. O. Pogson Collection

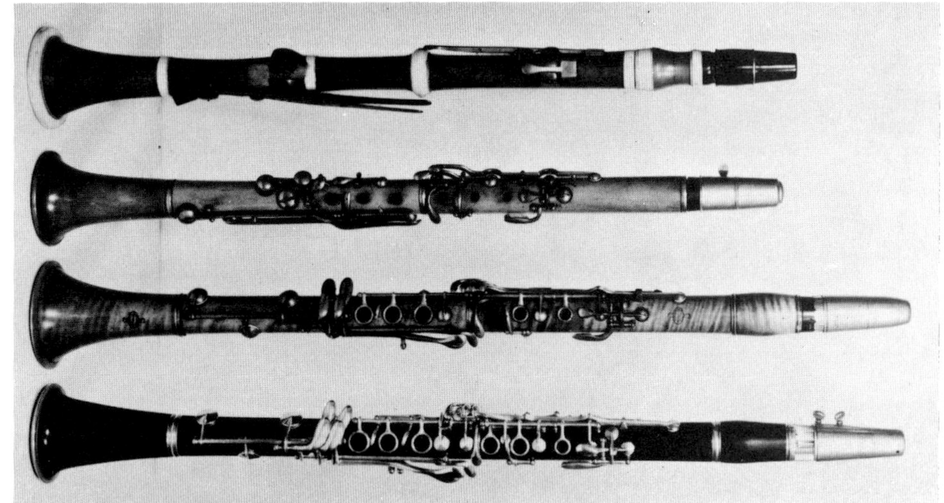

8. (left) Sub-contra clarinet in E♭, 1930, Selmer; Paris
cocus wood 50 in. (127 cm.)
extreme length 84 in. (213·3 cm.)
(right) Bass clarinet in B♭ down to E♮ only, Selmer; Paris
African blackwood 35 in. (88·9 cm.)
extreme length 56 in. (142·2 cm.)
E. O. Pogson Collection

the normal bassoon), the bassoon, the tenoroon, the altoon and what Alan Cooper was pleased to call the oon – actually it was called the octave bassoon. Only the normal and the contra have survived. The bassoon has an immense range from bottom B♭ upwards, nearly four octaves; it depends considerably on the ear and adaptability of the player. You can play a scale with the reed – a broad double one in one position; turn it round and you will probably play another.

All instruments of the reed variety are a glorious approximation; only the lowest note (all holes closed) is fixed in pitch. All the rest, to a greater or lesser degree, have to be jockeyed into position by the player, and the bassoonist, more than any other reed player except the shawmist, has this problem as a way of life.

CLARINETS

The clarinet was a German invention by J. C. Denner (1635–1707) and a latecomer on the reed scene. The principle of the cylinder bore and single reed overblowing twelfths was known but it did not emerge as a serious instrument until Mozart's time. (Ill. 7.)

The family was numerous. There was the high A♭, so small that you needed a long-fingered dwarf to play it, high E♭, D, C, B♭, A, in G when it was known as the clarinet d'amore. Then came the alto in E♭, and the alternative with extensions in F – the basset horn, the bass (one octave below the normal B♭), the sub-contra in E♭ and the contra in B♭ (one octave below the bass). (Ill. 8.) Brian Manton Myatt describes the bass clarinet as 'the voice of God'.

The clarinet is the most difficult of the woodwind instruments to play. Tone, articulation, pitch – all are difficult, but it has one great feature: it can emerge in its lowest notes from *ppp* to *fff* and back again to inaudibility in perfect safety – a feat none of the others can do. It is used extensively in military bands where its one drawback is lack of volume out of doors.

First examples were in boxwood with two keys, the speaker and A. As time went on more keys were added as composers and players got more ambitious. These early examples were very difficult to play: the fingers had to span enormous distances and if the open holes were not completely covered, it was easy to produce a succession of squawks.

While early flutes and oboes had silver keys, clarinets seem mostly to have had brass keys. From two keys there was a gradual evolution to the full Boehm system of today and finality seems almost to be reached.

Clarinets have been made in boxwood (with ivory mounts), grenadilla, cocus and African blackwood, plated brass and ebonite – the last two for use in the heat of the tropics. Philip Bate has the only known specimen in ivory – it is sad, but it won't play!

9. Tabor and stick $2\frac{1}{2} \times 4\frac{1}{2}$ in. (6·3 × 11·4 cm.)
(right) Fluviol (Catalan one-handed pipe), anonymous ebony and ivory with three keys 9 in. (22·8 cm.)
E. O. Pogson Collection

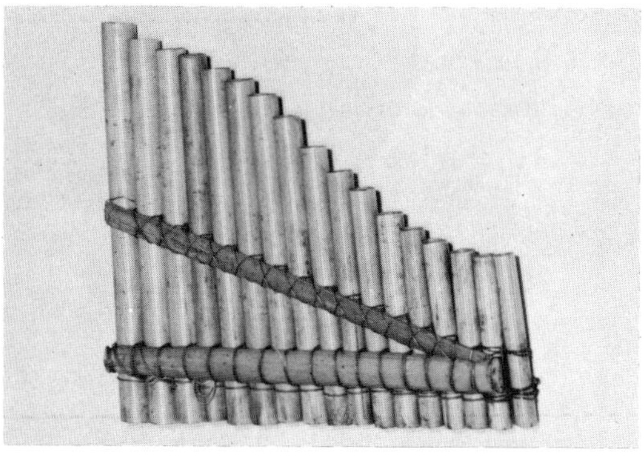

10. Panpipes or Syrinx – two octaves and one note in E major
E. O. Pogson Collection

FLUTES

Flutes can properly be classed as reed instruments. They are played with an air reed. In the case of the transverse flute the air reed is split on the side of the embouchure hole opposite the lips from which a flat stream of air is emitted. This sets the column of air vibrating in the flute tube, and a note is thus formed. Recorders are also flutes – but fipple flutes. The fipple is the arrangement in the mouthpiece which artificially splits the air reed. The great difference is that with the transverse flute the tone has a great dynamic range, while the recorder has very little; this is also true of flageolets and the like. It is possible to find an early piccolo with both fipple and normal heads and the difference of tone the same tube will produce is quite startling. The Catalan fluviol (Ill. 9) is a one-hand fipple flute played with the left hand only. It is furnished with three keys and is the exception to the rule as its sound is powerful. The tabor was played at the same time by the same player with his right hand.

Flutes have been made in many sizes: piccolos in C and for military use in E♭ and D♭, the normal flute in C, the alto flute in G, and the bass flute in C. Flutes have been made in all kinds of materials. The very early examples of the Stone Age were pierced animal bone. The Panpipes or Syrinx was made of a series of one-note reed flutes, each stopped at the bottom end and bound together. The example has two diatonic octaves and one note in the key of E major. (Ill. 10.)

Flutes have been constructed in boxwood, ivory, cocus, grenadilla, African blackwood, glass, porcelain, ebonite and perspex, also in plated brass, stainless steel, silver, gold and platinum.

The first flutes had no keys. Then one for E♭ was added, then more keys until today's Boehm system has been reached. The flute had small open holes and a conical bore, the narrowest end at the bottom at the onset. Some of the turning of the ivory instruments was exquisite and the silver mounts very beautiful. This also applies to the boxwood instruments. These early instruments had a sweet but small tone. There came the inevitable demand for more volume and experiments were made by Nicholson, an eminent player of the early 19th century, with larger holes. (Ill. 11.) This was not the answer, and today's flute with cylinder bore and large tone holes actuated by keywork gradually came into being, the combined work and ideas of many men. The range of the flute is three chromatic octaves.

SAXOPHONES

The saxophone is the rare case of an instrument invented by one man, Adolph Antoine Joseph Sax (1814–94), which has remained almost static in conception to this day. Sax produced the instrument *circa* 1835, and it is thought that he visualized it as a link between the woodwind and brass in military bands. The consort again appeared. There were six sizes – the sopranino, alto and baritone in E♭ and the soprano, tenor and bass in B♭. The sopranino and soprano were straight, and the rest doubled back for ease of handling. The soprano was also made in the curved shape. He also constructed instruments in C and F for orchestral use, but the only two to emerge were the C tenor (the C melody) and the C soprano. I have seen and tried an F alto: a small batch were imported from America in the 1930's. As time passed detail improvements were effected. The double speaker key was made one automatic key. (Ill. 12.) The range was extended down from B♮ to B♭. Recently Messrs Selmer produced a baritone down to low A, but even this was not new as in the 1920's Messrs Boosey made a C tenor down to A for Bert Ralton, the then bandleader at the Savoy Hotel.

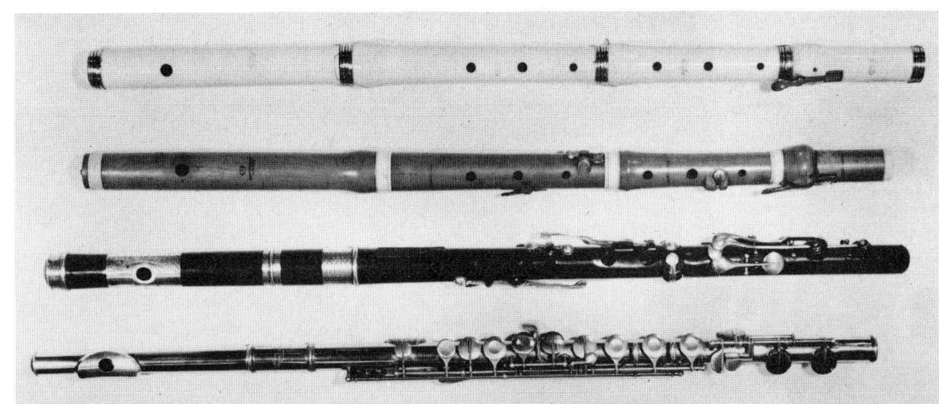

11. (top to bottom) Flute, in C, *circa* 1735, by Stainsby Jr
ivory with silver mounts and one silver key
24½ in. (62·2 cm.)
Flute, late 18th century, by Bambridge; London
boxwood with four keys 24 in. (60·9 cm.)
Nicholson flute, 1830, made by Prowse; London
cocus wood with silver keys 26 in. (66 cm.)
Flute, 1935, by Rudall Carte
stainless steel 26 in. (66 cm.)
E. O. Pogson Collection

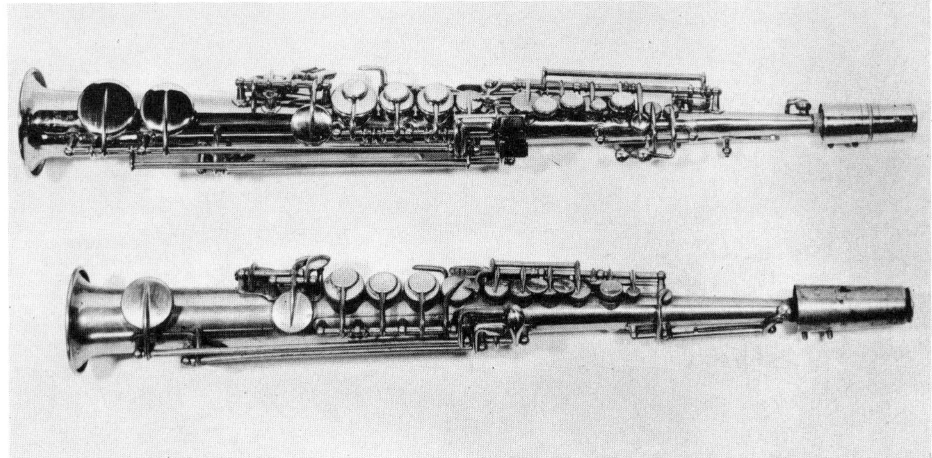

12. (above) Modern sopranino saxophone in E♭, 1930, by Beucher; (American) automatic octave keys and down to B♭
20 in. (50·8 cm.)
(below) Early sopranino saxophone, with two simple octave keys and descending to B♮ only, *circa* 1860, by Buffet; Paris
18 in. (45·7 cm.)
E. O. Pogson Collection

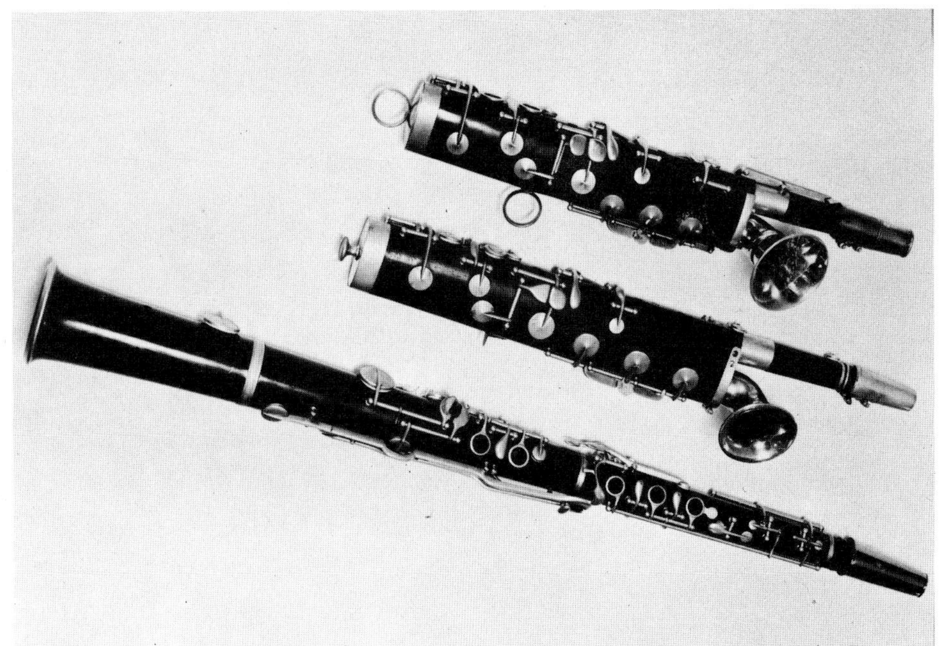
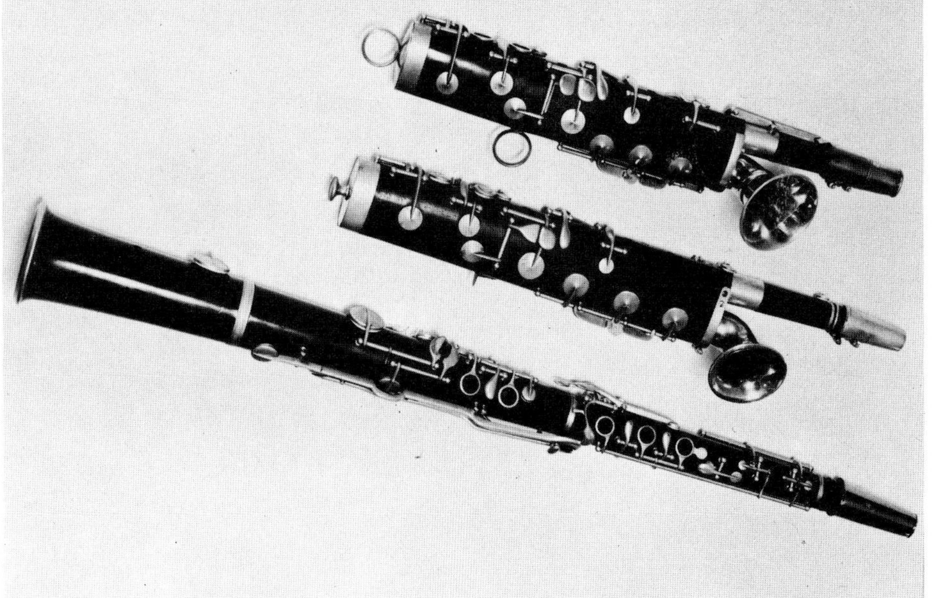

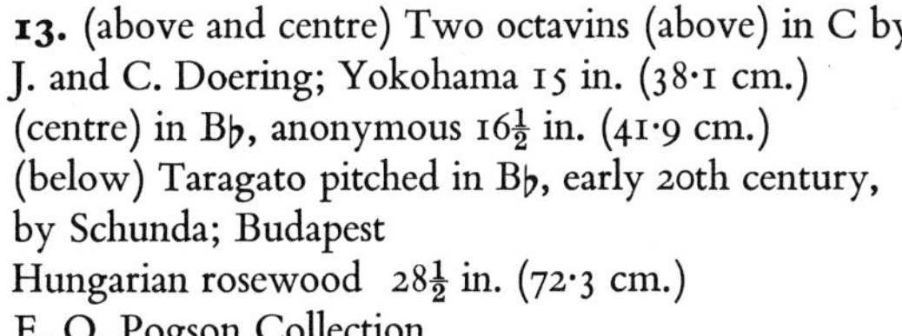

13. (above and centre) Two octavins (above) in C by J. and C. Doering; Yokohama 15 in. (38·1 cm.)
(centre) in B♭, anonymous 16½ in. (41·9 cm.)
(below) Taragato pitched in B♭, early 20th century, by Schunda; Budapest
Hungarian rosewood 28½ in. (72·3 cm.)
E. O. Pogson Collection

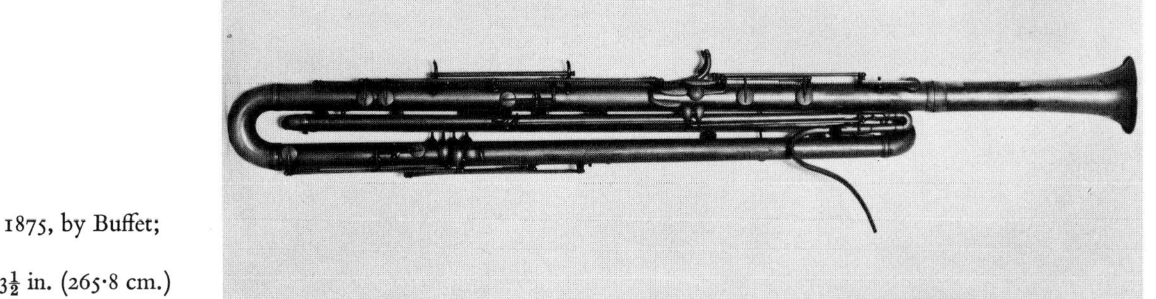

14. Baritone sarrusophone in F, *circa* 1875, by Buffet; Paris
51 in. (129·5 cm.) extreme length 183½ in. (265·8 cm.)
E. O. Pogson Collection

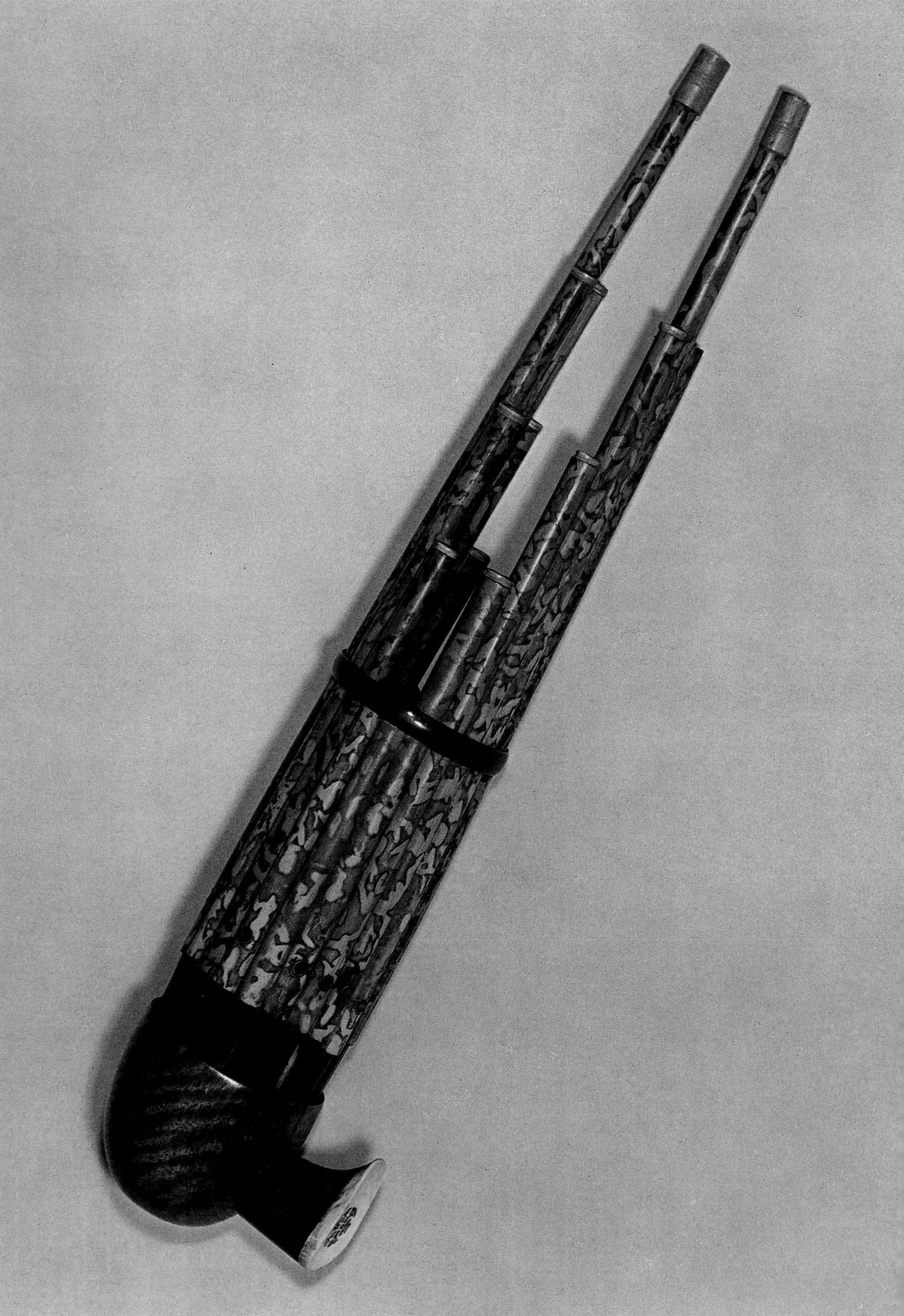

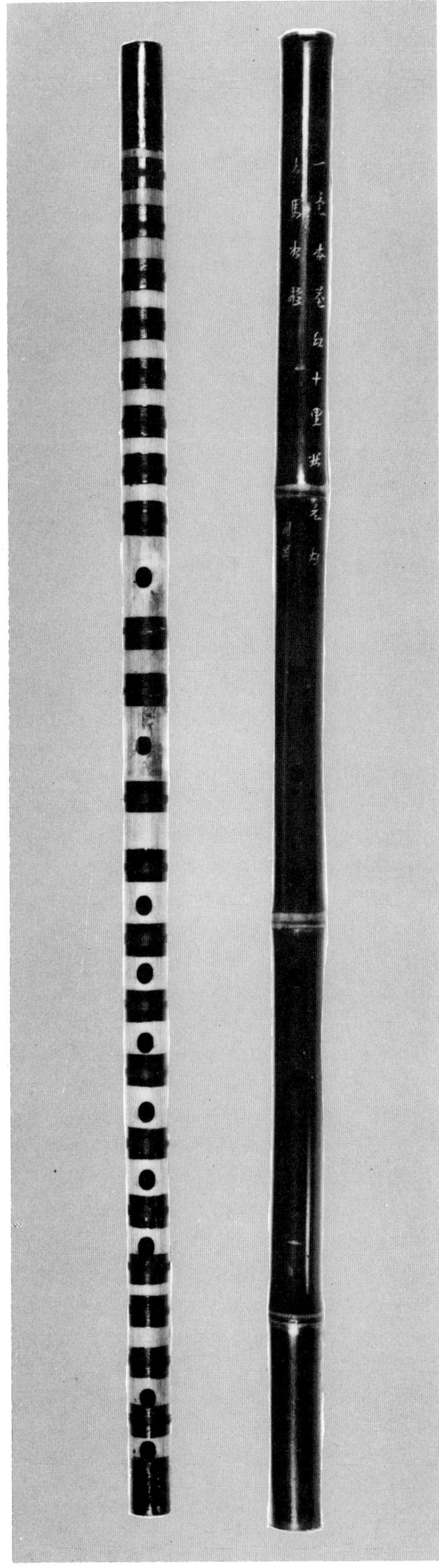

15. (left) Ti-tsú 24 in. (60·9 cm.)
(right) Hsiao 24 in. (60·9 cm.)
E. O. Pogson Collection

The saxophone has been slow to make inroads into the orchestra, but a few composers – Bizet and Ravel for example – have used it. The Marcel Mule Quartet have shown us how beautiful and lyrical the sound can be, as has Michael Krein in England. Early virtuosi were Rudy Wiedoft and Sigurd Rascher, while the jazz scene has produced some astonishing performers.

The range of the saxophone is two and a half octaves, but the alto and tenor can be made to produce a further chromatic octave above the range by cross-fingering.

There have been several reed instruments that have not caught on. The taragato was originally a Hungarian shawm. (Ill. 13.) It was played with a double reed, but it was re-launched *circa* 1900 with a single reed mouthpiece in what was an attempt to create a Hungarian national instrument. Its shawm origins can be seen in the pierced bell. It is virtually a wooden soprano sax with Barret action keywork and made by Schunda of Budapest. The octavin is another soprano-sax-pitched instrument, this time doubled back on itself like a bassoon but with a much smaller bore than the taragato. I have an example in B♭ and one in C. (Ill. 13.)

In 1856 Bandmaster Sarrus patented the sarrusophone. It was a conical brass tube instrument made in no less than nine sizes and played with a double reed. It was intended, no doubt, to be played out of doors, but the sound was coarse and the instrument never became popular. (Ill. 14.)

ORIENTAL INSTRUMENTS

This is a vast field and I can only describe the instruments that I have collected and made to work. The Chinese have had flutes and shawms for thousands of years. They are mostly simple in construction but beautifully made. There is the *hsiao*, made of brown bamboo with several unique features. It is blown through an embouchure hole cut in the end, and is held straight out like an oboe or clarinet. It has five holes in front and one behind, and the holes at the end are for tassels or so forth – the characters on the head are two lines of poetry. (Ill. 15.)

The common Chinese flute, the *ti-tsú* (Ill. 15) is made of bamboo or similar material. It is usually bound at 1-inch intervals along its length and ornamented with tassels through holes at the bottom end provided for that purpose. It has the conventional six finger holes and embouchure hole and another between them that is covered with a thin membrane like goldbeater's skin. This produces a Kazoo-like effect. Calling the lowest note D, a two-octave diatonic scale is provided, but the F♯ is more like F♮ than F♯.

THE SHENG

The most curious and ancient of Chinese instruments is the *sheng* (colour plate opposite). It is made in two sizes of which that illustrated is the smaller. It is of great antiquity, and is supposed to represent a sitting bird with its wings folded up. It is a mouth organ, not blown but sucked. This is reputed to be desperately hard on the lungs, and I can believe it. Most of the pipes (some are dummies) are pierced, and at the bottom of each pierced pipe is a copper reed, and these are inserted in the bowl-like base. The holes must be closed for the notes to sound. The player holds it slantwise over his right shoulder. The sheng, which employs the 'free reed' principle to sound, was the forerunner of the harmonium, the concertina, the accordion and the mouth organ.

Colour Plate. The Sheng, an ancient Chinese instrument
12 in. (30·5 cm.)
E. O. Pogson Collection

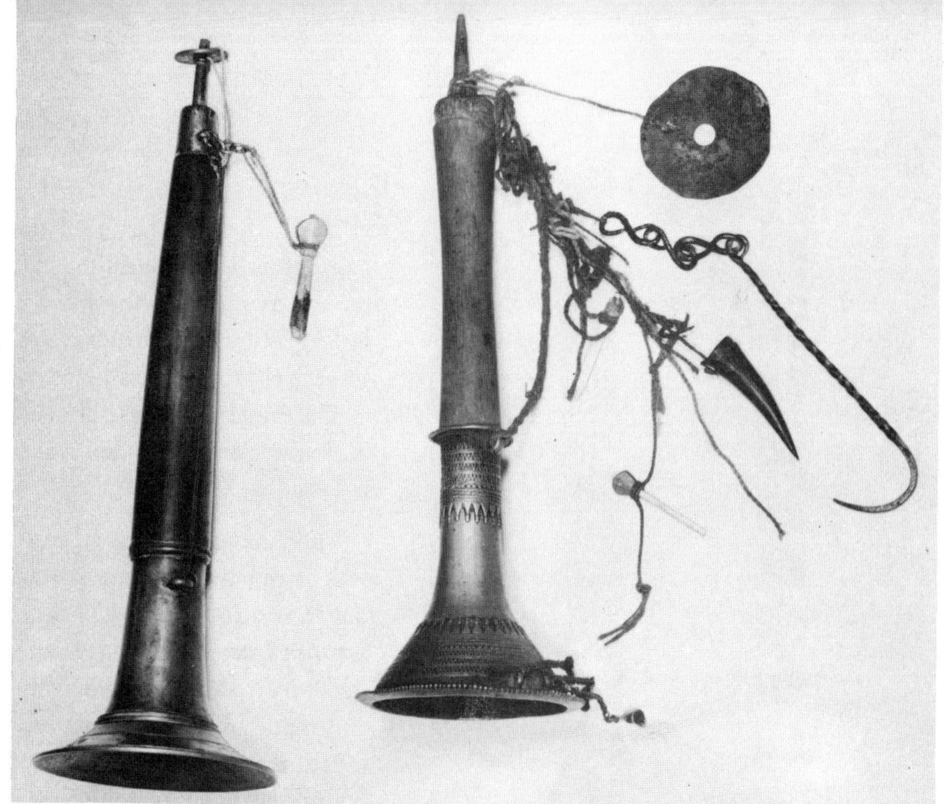

16. (top left) Ceylon version of the 'Indian Clarinet'
(top right) A shawm or 'Indian Clarinet'
10½ in. (26·6 cm.)
E. O. Pogson Collection

17. (bottom left) Three ocarinas in C and E♭ with tuning slides and in G without
(centre) 'Hot Fountain Pen', 1935, by Lewin Mold; London
ebonite and plastic 10¼ in. (26 cm.)
(bottom right) A Swanee whistle or lotus flute, 1925, anonymous; London
10½ in. (26·6 cm.)
E. O. Pogson Collection

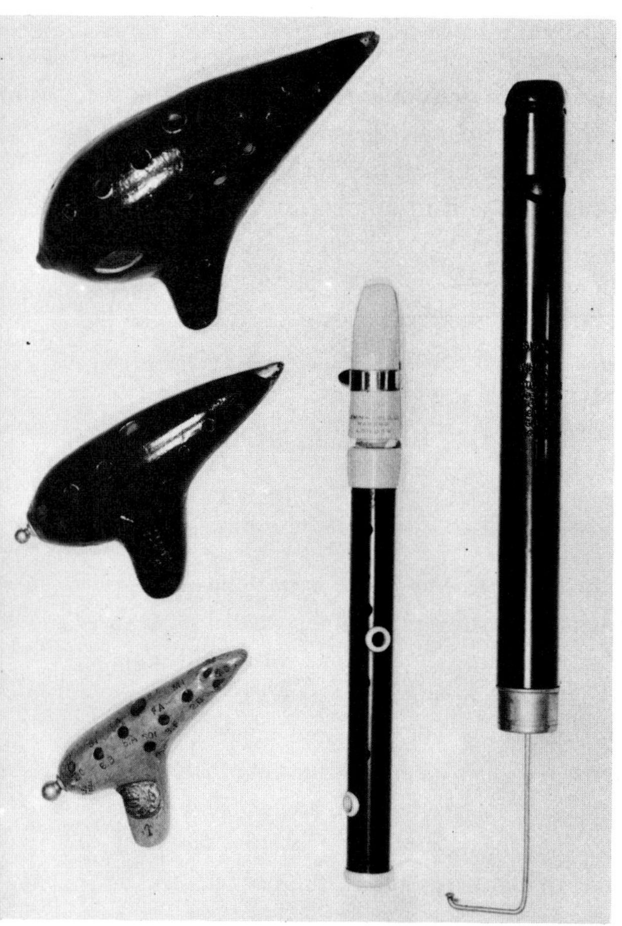

INDIAN

The label attached to this instrument (Ill. 16) says 'Indian Clarinet', Madras Presidency, Ganjam District. It is not a clarinet; it is a shawm and a curious mixture of crudity and sophistication. The bell is a fine and complicated brass casting with three small chains with tassels depending from the rim. The body is roughly finished bamboo with seven finger holes and there is a conical brass staple at the top, attached to this by bits of string it is the shawmist's *multum in parvo* do-it-yourself kit. There is a hook to hang the instrument on the clothing when not in use – the pirouette – a roughly cut disc of sheet iron, two reeds of durra (maize grass) with wooden pegs to keep them open and prevent damage, and a small animal horn which is a mandrel for making reeds. This shawm plays seven notes.

CEYLON

This is a similar shawm to the previous example; the pirouette is a pierced Ceylonese one cent piece dated 1870, and the two instruments are essentially the same. (Ill. 16.) Both are played with the reed wholly in the mouth with no lip contact in the ancient manner.

MUSICAL TOYS

Ever since the first shepherd boy took a corn stalk and flattened one end to make a double reed and blew down it to produce a note, there must have been musical toys. He would have found out how to bore some holes in it and thus would be able to play tunes. The ubiquitous toy is the whistle, the 'penny whistle' which nowadays will cost you about 50 cents. It is, of course, a fipple flute. It requires no upkeep, and sometimes you can find one with an astonishing range. I have a Near Eastern example in bamboo which will give most of three diatonic octaves in the unlikely key of B.

Then there are ocarinas. (Ill. 17.) The ocarina was rediscovered in Italy in the mid-19th century; the idea was originally Chinese. Their ocarina was like a truncated triangle but the essence was the same. The best ocarinas (and they can vary from very good to unplayable) were in earthenware and made by Fehn of Vienna and Mezzetti of Paris. Some even have a tuning slide. At a somewhat earlier date Bainbridge of London was making single, double and even treble pipe

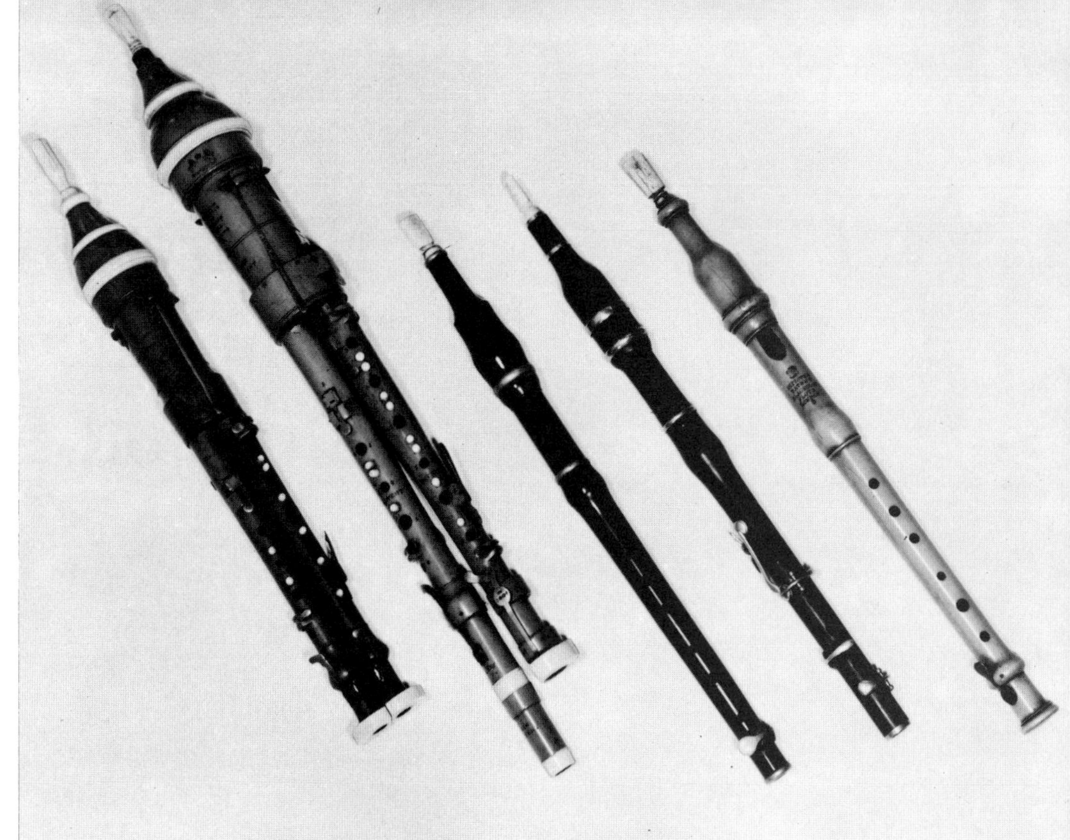

18. A selection of single and double flageolets, early 19th century, by Bainbridge; London
E. O. Pogson Collection

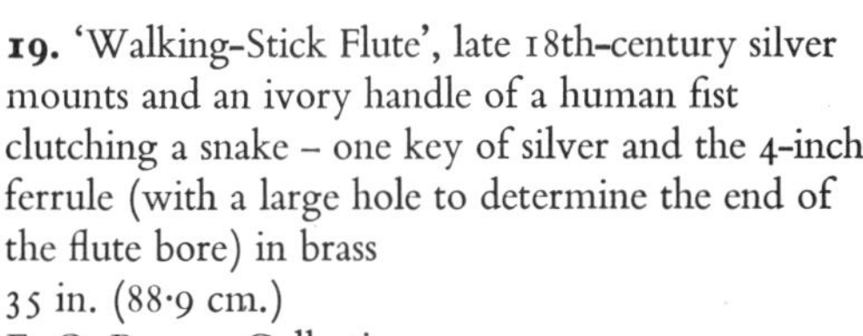

19. 'Walking-Stick Flute', late 18th-century silver mounts and an ivory handle of a human fist clutching a snake – one key of silver and the 4-inch ferrule (with a large hole to determine the end of the flute bore) in brass
35 in. (88·9 cm.)
E. O. Pogson Collection

flageolets. (Ill. 18.) These were drawing-room dilettante instruments beautifully made of boxwood, ivory and silver keywork, and with a singular feebleness of sound. These, again, were fipple flutes.

The Swanee whistle (Ill. 17) was an infinitely variable fipple flute – a tube with a slide which must have provided accompaniments for more comic gags than any other instrument.

In the 1920's there was a curious little instrument called a 'Hot Fountain Pen'. (Ill. 17.) This was a small clarinet with single reed and cylinder bore and no keys. This could only play its fundamental scale, but Adrian Rollini, the famous bass sax player of the period, used it with telling effect.

A more elegant toy was the 'Walking Stick Flute'. (Ill. 19.) This was indeed a walking-stick, bored out and furnished with embouchure hole, six finger holes and one key – for E as a general rule. The end of the flute was fitted with a long four- or five-inch metal ferrule with large holes therein which determined the end of the flute and prevented damage.

Every reed instrument is worth preserving if only as evidence of man's ingenuity. The late 17th century and onwards had makers whose works were delightful examples of the turners' and silversmiths' craft. Silver-mounted ivory flutes are elegant, especially those of makers like Stainsby Jnr, and this applies to all boxwood instruments. But every instrument has an appeal of some sort – sometimes the solution or part solution of a playing problem. There must be thousands of these instruments still lying about forgotten in attics, cellars and glory holes, for many thousands were made. Happy hunting, collectors!

BIBLIOGRAPHY

The Galpin Society Journals.
Baines, A. *Woodwind Instruments and their History* (2nd ed.), 1962.
Rockstro, R. S. *The Flute* (2nd ed.), 1932.
Bate, P. A. T. *The Oboe*, 1956.
Rendall, F. G. *The Clarinet*, 1954.
Languill, L. *The Bassoon*, 1948.

Bronzes by French 'Animalier' Sculptors of the 19th and 20th Centuries

ANDREW CIECHANOWIECKI

The animal form has never been neglected in French art, either in painting or in sculpture: the impressive 17th-century bronze dog by Barthélémy le Prieur; the later Flemish influence which resulted in the painted work of Desportes or Oudry, to name but two; the horses of Coustou; and, even as late as 1827, the pointer sculpted by F. G. Giraud, and Theodore Gechter's horses – all these testify to a strong and always present, if sometimes dormant, tradition. The 19th century was to raise the *animalier* art, hitherto considered an inferior one, to unexpected heights, and was to witness the creation of a whole school of animal sculptors of international fame. The year 1831 – and its Salon where Delacroix, Barye, Brascassat and Alfred de Dreux exhibited side by side – can be considered a historical date in the annals of French animal art, which, inspired by romantic trends, was now to take on a striking new form. It is in Romanticism, in its all-powerful urge to break with the classical precept of the adulation of the human body, academically treated by generations of artists bred in the various schools, that we must seek the answer to this sudden and new interest in animals, both wild and, later, domestic. What could be a more insolent way of defying academicism than for an artist to turn his back on the human form and devote his attention to animals? This attitude coupled with a return to nature and a romantic interest in exotic beasts, so stimulating to the imagination, is certainly the main reason for the appearance and further development of a powerful school of *animalier* sculptors. In one particular way they were all to be true to Romanticism and break away from the traditions of animal art as known in France before: in the feeling that the animal must be shown free, at liberty, and often even as Liberty's symbol. Oudry's beasts were painted as captives. Barye, who also knew them only in the terrible conditions of a primitive zoo, the new Paris Jardin des Plantes, studying them there with love and patience, was to show them against a dreamy dark background, his own paradise landscape, a compound of Barbizon and of an imaginary desert. But they are invariably free, as free as those horses of Mêne, an early work dated 1831, now in the Petit Palais, which are given the meaningful title *Chevaux en Liberté*. Liberty, a tenet of Romanticism, is probably the strongest underlying trend to be found in all the *animaliers*.

1. Cheval Turc, *circa* 1850, by Antoine Louis Barye
bronze height 15½ in. (39·3 cm.)
Private Collection, London

It is Antoine Louis Barye's (1795–1875) undisputed achievement to have set the stage, by his talent and personality, for an understanding of animal sculpture in France. His talent was so genuine, his personality so powerful, that he imposed himself and the ideas he stood for without much opposition. The Salons of 1831, 1833 and 1850 are milestones of his triumphant career which owed all to merit and nothing to artistic 'lifemanship'. The world of his models is nearly always a world of powerful, fierce wild beasts – they haunt him like an obsession through-

2. Galloping horse, by Christophe Fratin
bronze $6\frac{1}{2} \times 12$ in. (16·5×30·4 cm.)
Private Collection, London

out all his life. Their dynamic strength, taut muscles, proudness and cruelty, grandeur and intensity, bring out all that was romantic in his soul. But his animals are never portraits: they are 'Barye' lions, tigers or jaguars. If we compare his early plaquettes, their design hard and brittle, strongly showing the goldsmith's hand, with the Lion and Serpent of 1832 and the Seated Lion of 1847 (see colour plate facing p. 312), we see the process of simplification, of dropping all that was still superfluous, of striving towards a fuller synthesis of the animal depicted. Bonnat's words, "Barye had known the instincts of the animal and rendered them with a power equal to that of Balzac in his passionate researches into the depths of the human heart", are nearer to the truth than many other statements on the artist. In his impassioned striving to show the essence of an animal, Barye on the one hand transgresses the limits of Romanticism, becoming a realist whose truth, the artistic truth he aims at, is based on a synthesis of elements found in patient anatomic studies, but at the same time he remains a classicist, owing perhaps more to Bosio, his master, than is generally acknowledged. This classicism is not only evident *circa* 1846 when in his figures Barye reaches out for Greek canons of beauty, but coupled with an interest in the newly discovered art of Assyria and Egypt, it underlies the whole of his work. That striving for harmony, for a synthetic, artistically true but beautiful animal – what is it if not an expression of classicism? He remains nevertheless always a Romantic at heart, loving and idealizing his animals, giving them heroic proportions, larger than life, and endowing them with 'superhuman' qualities. A Romantic in his choice of subjects, in his spiritual make-up, but a sculptor whose form goes from the severe simplifications of the perennial, and always modern, classical ideal of beauty, to the artistic truth of a great realist – that is how Barye appears to us today.

Following Barye and taking advantage of his success, which was the result as much of his great talent as of a public demand created by him and which had to be filled, a whole group of animal sculptors came to the fore in Paris in the second and third quarter of the century. They are too numerous to be listed here; many were only skilful imitators, but some must be mentioned and their work discussed.

Among them, Christophe Fratin (1800–64), a pupil of Géricault, is certainly the most interesting. His art is wholly Romantic, both in spirit as well as in form. His subjects, unlike Barye's, are more tame: stags, horses, cattle – but shown usually in movement, dynamic and powerful. Even when not moving, a romantic wind sweeps through their manes and tousles their coats. His is a typically pictorial type of sculpture: complicated and clever in composition, rich in texture and finish, truer to a romantic conception of the animal shown than to nature which he studied, like all his contemporaries, with such care. Fratin's surfaces translate into a sculptural idiom the thick *impastos* of Romantic painting, so dear to his master Géricault, giving the same feeling of spontaneous, free and easy creation; they are so natural in their freshness and softness, when compared with the studied elegance or contrived arabesque of some compositions. In this last characteristic, as well as in his humorous bronzes, Fratin strikes the baroque note – never far at any time from the Romantics.

A different individuality emerges from the *œuvre* of Pierre Jules Mêne (1810–79), a decade younger than Fratin and fifteen years Barye's junior. This difference in age brings him not only out of the reach of Classicism but nearly out of that of Romanticism: only in a few of his earlier works, like the Jaguar and dead gazelle, 1841, can Barye's or Fratin's romantic influence be felt. A realistic approach to his subject, rational, well studied and true, was to be the keynote of his production. Truth, realistic truth based on solid, anatomical studies, is the aim of Mêne's work.

3. Greyhound and King Charles Spaniel, *circa* 1848, by Pierre Jules Mêne
bronze height $6\frac{1}{2}$ in. (16·5 cm.)
Private Collection, London

4. Jockey on horseback, *circa* 1860, by Pierre Jules Mêne
bronze height 17 in. (43·1 cm.)
Courtesy Mallett at Bourdon House Ltd, London

Like his contempory Daguerre in his daguerreotypes, he tries to recapture a fleeting movement, slow or fast, an expression, a mood, an individual character, not a type. His animals, and amongst them his numerous dogs, are always individual portraits, they are *this* or *that* dog, horse or goat; in fact, most of them have names and are known to have existed. Realism blends more and more with naturalism in a passionate attempt to reproduce animal life as it really is, with photographic exactitude. Nevertheless this never leads to prosaic or pedestrian vulgarization. Mêne is too competent and too clever an artist to become boring, and the literary anecdote does not find its way into his sculpture, which remains a moving document, a sculptural *tour de force* of composition, sense of anatomy and movement, coupled with a faultless technique. His is not a great art – he is neither the great sculptor *per se* as Barye, nor the great sculptor-painter as Fratin – but his art, consummate and unobtrusive, is genuine and true.

An interesting factor in the evolution of Mêne's work is the appearance *circa* 1855 of a strong Landseer influence. It can be explained by the painter's popularity in France, where he exhibited and received the Great Gold Medal at the Universal Exhibition of 1855, but more so, by the admiration he aroused in Rosa Bonheur, a close friend of Mêne and his trusted adviser. After her journey to England and Scotland she became a devoted admirer of Landseer, and his influence, as well as that of the Scottish landscape, can be found in her own work.[1] It is possible therefore that she provides the link, otherwise difficult to find, between the eminent Victorian and Mêne, who never went to England. Be it as it may, his group After the hunt in Scotland, 1861, is directly connected with Landseer, while some of his pointers sculpted at the same time have that 'human' type of face which is characteristic of Landseer's always anecdotal work. Fortunately this element of sentimentality which creeps into Mêne's sculpture is not unduly important and can be discounted in the general valuation of his art, as can be the larger human figures in bronze which he made towards the end of his life.

Among the many types of animals sculpted by the earlier *animaliers*, the bird was nearly completely forgotten. It was to become the province of Jules Moigniez (1835–94). Imitative in his other work, his dogs following Mêne slavishly but competently and his horses romantic in the tradition of Fratin, he developed a highly individual, unmistakable style in the handling of birds, in particular of waterfowl. Realistic in his approach, with a clever, almost baroque composition of his groups, Moigniez appears as the last among the great 19th-century *animaliers* to offer a new, undiscovered world to his public, a world of which he became a masterful interpreter.

It is much more difficult to establish today the true value of Emmanuel Frémiet (1824–1910). One of the most popular artists of his period, he wanted his fame to rest on his monumental compositions (now with few exceptions forgotten), and not on his public appeal as an *animalier*. He stressed the point forcibly, saying "I have not studied specially to be an *animalier*, I am professor of drawing at the Jardin des Plantes, that is all. Rude taught me sculpture and I have only adapted my art to what pleased me, to the vagaries of my fantasy." And it is in these expressions of the artist's fantasy that lies his merit. His cats and dogs sculpted with intelligence, ironical humour and understanding live their own life. True to nature, they have something to say – they are not only portraits but actors on a stage. Charming and whimsical, they show that the great master was at his best

5. Pair of gulls and a crab, *circa* 1870, by Jules Moigniez
bronze height 10¼ in. (26 cm.)
Private Collection, London

[1] Rosa Bonheur wrote in a letter, after having met Landseer (1856): "He is the greatest painter of animals and I believe that he will remain the greatest of his kind. . . . His work is full of poetic grandeur and rare intelligence."

6. Napoleon III mounted on Philippe, *circa* 1855, by Emmanuel Frémiet
bronze height 14½ in. (36·8 cm.)
Private Collection, London

when 'off duty'. But one aspect of Frémiet's more monumental production must here be stressed: his horses in equestrian monuments. In these, the historian doubled the *animalier*. Whereas all Barye's horses can be brought down to one common denominator, to the heroic *demi-sang*, a fitting mount for his heroes, Frémiet's horses are always individuals, historically as appropriate as all the other elements of costume and armour which he so painstakingly studied. The intellectual in the historian, the naturalist in the *animalier*, combine to produce wonderful evocations of a past age, lacking nevertheless the sweeping grandeur of great art.

Rosa Bonheur (1822–99), who, like so many of her contemporaries, both painted and sculpted, is again a painterly sculptor. Her figures, with carefully studied surfaces, pictorially differentiating between shorn and unshorn fleece, have much more of the freshness and appeal of well-studied nature, presented in a straightforward, honest way, than many of her paintings.

Among the lesser *animaliers* the name of Auguste Cain (1821–94) should not be forgotten. Son-in-law of Mêne and very popular in his time, he is a striking example of the influence his greater predecessors had on him and lesser artists like Isidore Bonheur (1827–1901) – Rosa's brother – Paul Delabrierre (1829–1912), or Henri Jacquemart (1824–96). They do not achieve a profile, an individuality of their own. In lions Barye is the model, even if Cain sometimes equals him in pathos and power; in birds Moigniez is slavishly if intelligently copied; in dogs Mêne is the forerunner. The later *animaliers*, popular and prized, are the best proof, if any was needed, of the part played by Barye, Fratin, Mêne and Moigniez in creating a genre, in shaping all of its numerous possibilities, so that lesser, not so original talents could only produce variations on a theme already set.

7. Dog stretching, *circa* 1870, by Emmanuel Frémiet
bronze height $2\frac{3}{4}$ in. (6·9 cm.)
Private Collection, London

One of the most striking characteristics of 19th-century art, above all among the *animaliers*, is the strong interdependence of painting and sculpture. It is underlined by their apprenticeships: Barye, pupil of Gros, Fratin of Géricault, Delabrierre of Delestre, Rosa Bonheur of her father Raymond and of Cogniet, Jacquemart of Delaroche, and Gardet of Millet. But also in everyday life the contacts were close: it was Barye who brought Delacroix in touch with the world of wild beasts and it is the same Delacroix who painted, but thirty years later than its prototype, a lion nearly identical with Barye's Lion and Serpent; Barye's friendship with the Barbizon school, from which he borrowed landscape backgrounds; Rosa Bonheur and Brascassat, influencing Mêne's work, who found models of his horses in those of Horace Vernet, whom he fervently admired and whose works he collected; the great influence of Landseer on Mêne, already mentioned, and earlier that of Géricault, both on Barye and Fratin; Mêne, influencing Troyon – these contacts appear continually and their pattern is well worth studying. Certainly it was not always painting influencing sculpture. Often the opposite is true, showing how new and sometimes even revolutionary was the art of the *animaliers* in a field which seldom leads in artistic evolution. This may be partly due to the fact that versatility was dear to the heart of the Romantics, and that most of the earlier *animaliers* were both painters and sculptors at the same time. This brought them nearer to the Renaissance ideal of the artist, which in their period became again the goal to achieve.

This conscious return to the Renaissance can also be read into another phenomenon common to all the *animaliers*: the scientific study of the subject of their art. Never since the time when the artists of the Quattrocento were passionately studying the human anatomy was such a stress put on scientific truth. Géricault himself set the example here with his splendid *écorché* horse, to be followed in the same field by Fratin. Barye drew innumerable skeletons, minutely measuring dead animals and building his models from the bone, through muscles and sinews up to the skin. Mêne, spending hours covering pages of his notebooks at the Jardin des Plantes; Frémiet, as a young man making drawings of comparative anatomy and remaining throughout his life a scientist at heart, pedantic in his care for detail; Rosa Bonheur studying a goat that she kept at home – all testify to something more than mere artistic exactitude. It is the spirit of the 19th century, closer to that of the Renaissance than is often thought, rational, materialistic, believing the human mind to be omnipotent, mistrusting inspiration, and seeing the only way to an ultimate artistic goal in a positive scientific approach to everything.

There is also another common trait with the Renaissance artists which is shared by most of the *animaliers*. This, the technological interest in their art, is partly the result of their upbringing (several of them were either sons of metal-workers or worked in their youth for them), but is also inherent in the philosophy of the 19th century, akin to that of the Renaissance, with its admiration for the great technical discoveries and new processes put into the hands of an affranchised man. The technical quality of their work means more to the *animaliers* than to most previous

8. Grazing ewe (shorn), *circa* 1845, by Rosa Bonheur
bronze height 6 in. (15·2 cm.)
Courtesy Mallett at Bourdon House Ltd, London

Colour Plate. Seated lion, 1847, by Antoine Louis Barye
bronze height 7 in. (17·7 cm.)
Peter Claas Collection, London

9. (above) Tigress bringing a dead peacock to her cubs, 1873, by Auguste Cain
bronze height $16\frac{1}{2}$ in. (41·9 cm.)
Sir Joshua Rowley Bart. Collection

10. (below) Buffalo attacked by a mountain lion, by Georges Gardet
bronze height 9 in. (22·8 cm.)
Courtesy Bernard Black Gallery, New York

11. Tiger, by Rembrandt Bugatti bronze height 16½ in. (41·9 cm.) Private Collection, Paris

generations. Barye edits his bronzes himself, lovingly working on the patination which in his hands achieves a wonderful gamut of green, greenish black or brown hues, and carefully finishes the after-work so that his bronzes are a revelation not only in modelling but also in execution. The same can be said about Mêne, whose after-work is always masterly, of Fratin and also of Moigniez, who, in accord with the baroque tendencies of his art, experiments successfully with the brown, golden and reddish tones of patination, so popular with the artists of the 17th century. These discoveries were copied by the lesser *animaliers* in a similar way to the model themselves: lions always had Barye's green patination, birds the lustrous brown one, so dear to Moigniez.

The *animaliers*, together with other 19th-century artists, have, on the other hand, one great advantage over previous generations – the appearance of a new social and economic force in the artistic world, the industrialist bronze-makers, editors of their work. They had already started to be so numerous in Paris at the beginning of the 19th century, that in 1818 they could organize themselves into a *Réunion des Fabricants de Bronze*. But the decisive date is 1839 when A. Collas invented his *appareil réducteur*, a mathematically correct reducing apparatus which could reduce any piece of sculpture to a needed size. In the words of one of the men who most profited by it, namely the great founder, F. Barbédienne, this discovery "did for sculpture what Gutenberg had long before done for the written thought". It made possible exact 'editions' of pieces of sculpture by 'editors', the great founders like Barbédienne or the brothers Susse (the word *éditeur* being used for the first time in 1839 in connection with the founder Debraux d'Englure). These come in as intermediaries between the artist and the public, helping the first by contracts signed with him and trying to educate the latter by producing for its benefit works of art in a size that could be placed in a normal bourgeois apartment. Although something similar had been done by Sèvres in biscuit figures of the 18th century, this novelty caught on quickly with the public, and a whole industry was created practically overnight, having its apogee between 1840 and 1865. The great national and international exhibitions, another achievement of the century, displayed the products of this new art and thus helped to spread the fashion for them. The *bronze d'art*, a typical French production to start with, helps us, as Metman rightly says, "to judge, understand and love French society of the 19th century". Owing to the personalities and good taste of some of the great founders, to mention only Barbédienne or Susse, the best works of the past, as well as those of contemporary artists, became known, popular and sought after. In this one case at least, technological achievements helped to spread those of the arts.

But the same process put demands on the artists which did not always have the best results. They also produced (and edited) numerous ornamental bronzes like candelabra, clocks, caskets and vases which, notwithstanding fascinating decorative detail, as a whole are lamentably bad. Barye, Mêne, Cain, Moigniez are among those artists who unsuccessfully tried to create for the bronze-makers objects which would combine utilitarian and artistic qualities.

The genuine merit of the work of the *animaliers*, coupled with the technological processes of their reproduction and the publicity offered by the Great Exhibitions, made their art known and extremely popular in France and abroad. Barye, notwithstanding some small setbacks, was very popular and highly thought of in his own country, and found in American collectors, like W. T. Walters of Baltimore, who ordered a full set of all his works, or Cyrus J. Lawrence, the prototype of many other patrons and admirers in the United States. Strangely enough his popularity never spread seriously to England. Even the Press does not mention his work exhibited at the Great Exhibitions. His monumental, synthetic style did not appeal to the Victorians, who must also have been shocked by the apparent cruelty of so many of his fighting scenes. Fratin, on the other hand, equally popular in France, found rich and influential patrons in England, where he came several times during the fourth decade of the century. One of his patrons was the sixth Viscount Powerscourt (1815–44). The high opinion in which Fratin was held in England is best illustrated by the citation for his medal at the Great Exhibition of 1851, in which he is called "the most celebrated sculptor of animals at the present day". Mêne's popularity was equally great and not only were his works exported in large quantities to England and exhibited there at various exhibitions, where they received high prizes "for the perfection in modelling the figures of animals and for the truth and beauty of his representations" (1862), but also some of his models were copied in England. These copies in metal (bronze and cast iron), made by Coalbrookdale Foundry and in biscuit ('Parian body') by Copeland, testify to the place in English affections taken by the Frenchman's work. Frémiet, the only artist of this group to be elected to the Royal Academy, was equally well known and popular, and Moigniez's birds also found their way to England in large quantities.

12. Goats, by Rembrandt Bugatti
bronze height 7½ in. (19 cm.)
Private Collection, Strasbourg

It is in fact most peculiar that England, which had had such a long and splendid tradition of animal art in painting, and visibly such an interest and need of animal sculpture that she imported so many pieces by French *animaliers* (in spite of her distrust of French sculpture, considered by the Victorians on the whole to be immoral), never produced a similar school of her own. The only English *animalier* – if one discounts the few earlier pieces by Joseph Gott (1785–1860) – John Macallan Swan (1847–1910), is late in date and a pupil of the Frenchman, Frémiet.

Germany also, whilst importing many bronzes by French *animaliers*, produced only one interesting sculptor in this field: August Gaul (1869–1921), whose nobly static animals are a throwback to Neo-classicism.

In France, on the other hand, although animal sculpture slowly went out of fashion in the early 1900's, this genre still produced in our century three outstanding artists: Georges Gardet, Rembrandt Bugatti and François Pompon, who successfully kept up the great tradition of an art spanning the whole of the 19th century.

Georges Gardet (1863–1939), acclaimed as the greatest *animalier* of his period, was the most conservative and traditional among the three artists named. Creator of powerful and monumental forms, full of vitality and dynamism (Panther and Python, 1887, Bison and Tiger, 1900), he nevertheless never broke out of the magic circle of formal canons laid down in the previous period. The critic who praised Gardet as "a worthy successor of Barye and Mêne" unbeknown to himself put a finger on the weakest point of the artist who could equal a master of the past but

13. Cock, 1913, by François Pompon
bronze height 9⅞ in. (25 cm.)
Musée d'Art Moderne, Paris

14. Goose, 1908, by François Pompon
bronze height 6⅛ in. (15 cm.)
Musée d'Art Moderne, Paris

was unable to represent the animal form in terms of a more contemporary sculptural idiom.

This was to be achieved by the Milanese born and bred Rembrandt Bugatti (1885–1916). Interested in animals as a subject since the age of twelve, it was in Paris, where he came to work in 1900, that he seriously took up, as the first foreigner, that very French art which is *animalier* sculpture. And it is perhaps this foreignness which enabled him to break away from the tradition of Barye and his school. Strongly influenced by the impressionist sculpture of Paul Trubetzkoy, Bugatti created a new style which a German critic so appropriately called *Augenblickskulptur*. His animals – and there is a wide range of them, including elephants, tigers, lions, jaguars, panthers, bisons, hyenas, wolves, dogs, horses, stags, goats, camels, giraffes, pelicans, flamingoes – were as carefully studied as those of Barye, also in lengthy sittings in the same Jardin des Plantes. But his purpose was different. Instead of striving to produce a type, Bugatti's aim was to capture movement, that fleeting movement of jumping, running, playing or feeding. Sometimes the various movements of several animals are brought together in one composition and cleverly contrasted. A painterly surface, shimmering in the light, creates an added impression of movement, of transition and life. This unusual sculpture, so in keeping with the aesthetic ideas of the period, soon made the young Italian famous, especially after a small exhibition held in 1907. But Bugatti did not stop at these achievements. On the one hand he successfully applied himself to the human figure, even on a monumental scale, on the other in his *animalier* sculpture, in which he always chose small dimensions, he experimented with stylization of the form. While still concerned with movement, his line becomes more graphic and his forms more and more simplified. Had it not been for a premature death by his own hand, Bugatti would probably have evolved towards Cubism, a foretaste of which can be found in the works dating from the last, busiest and most interesting years of his all too short life. This fascinating evolution from Impressionism towards Cubism places him among the pace-setters in sculpture of the first quarter of our century.

Light, that obsession of the Impressionists, and its interdependence with the shape and colour of the animal form, was to become the field of experimentation of the last great *animalier* François Pompon (1855–1933). Although older than Gardet and Bugatti, the vagaries of a tragic life brought him success and fame only in old age. Working as a pointer for Mercié, Falguière and finally for Rodin, it is in the latter's studio that he matured and found his own artistic fulfilment. His animals and birds, so lovingly sculpted, are constructed like a Cézanne landscape, shedding all that is superfluous. Light, the lyrical softness of its reflection in polished surfaces; light achieving an effect of colour in the transposed planes and reliefs of his famous White Bear, 1922; light serving to balance the various shapes, to eliminate unnecessary detail – that is the keynote of Pompon's highly original art. Whereas all his predecessors saw movement as the sole creator of form, Pompon builds his stylized, Egyptian-influenced bodies and their movement by letting light be the architect. Made famous overnight by his contributions to the Salon d'Automne of 1922, it is in the last and artistically fully mature decade of his life that Pompon produced a notable series of splendid works, in which he achieved a rare glyptic power and monumentality in spite of exiguous sizes.

If – summing up – we want to look at the art of the animal sculptors against the background of French sculpture generally, we will see that after the giants, after Rude, Carpeaux, Dalou, Rodin, Maillol and Bourdelle, the art of the *animaliers* can take an honourable place, or even more. Intentionally dropping the human figure and using it only as an accessory to the animal, they avoided the pitfalls of sentimentality, literary anecdote and fussy composition, from which even the greatest are not always free, particularly in the 19th century. In their evolution from the Romantic conceptions of Barye, tempered by his classical restraint, through the realism of Mêne and Frémiet's intellectual naturalism, to the Impressionism of Bugatti and his and Pompon's experiments in the idiom of the day, they always achieved a high level of genuine, original and honest art, and in some of their best work real greatness.

SHORT BIOGRAPHIES

BARYE, Antoine Louis (1795–1875)
Son of a goldsmith, he worked for the engraver Fourier and later became a pupil of the sculptor F. J. Bosio and of A. Gros. He studied also at the Ecole des Beaux-Arts. After leaving that school, he modelled animals for the goldsmith Fauconnier, and exhibited for the first time at the Salon of 1827. His great success came in 1831 with the Tiger devouring a gavial; universal acceptance in 1833 with the Lion and Serpent. In spite of small setbacks, his position was always secure; he obtained many prizes and medals, and also the customary distinctions such as the Cross of the Legion of Honour and membership of the Academy of Fine Arts (1868). He was also from 1854 professor of drawing at the Museum of Natural History. He received many commissions from the State, both during the reign of Louis-Philippe and under the Second Empire. Very popular in France and in the United States, he found many patrons in that country (W. T. Walters, Cyrus Lawrence). His production in sculpture, both monumental and small bronzes, in paintings, watercolours and lithographs, is very considerable.

His early sculptures were cast by J. H. Gonon and Debraux d'Englure, but later Barye, an expert in the handling of metal, edited his bronzes himself. In 1838 he took a commercial licence and established himself as a *bronzier*, publishing his first catalogue in 1847. Becoming bankrupt, he had to give up his models to Emile Martin, who edited them on his own account from 1848 to 1857, when Barye redeemed his works and started a foundry of his own with a considerable output. His last catalogue shows 230 models, mostly groups, but also *bronzes d'ameublement*. At his death in 1875, F. Barbédienne[2] purchased 80 per cent of the available models and started re-editing them with two different types of signature. Other models were re-edited by Susse Frères.[3]

FRATIN, Christophe (1800–64)
Son of a taxidermist, he was a pupil of the sculptor C. A. Pioche and of J. L. A. T. Géricault. He exhibited regularly at the Salon (1831–63) and achieved great popularity in France, England and in the United States. He received several medals and prizes at various exhibitions and was commissioned by the State to do some larger pieces of animal sculpture

[2] Ferdinand Barbédienne (1810–92) is one of the most important founders of the 19th century. In collaboration with A. Collas, the inventor of the process of scale reduction, he opened his factory in 1838. He exported about 15 per cent of his large production, which amounted to more than 1,000 pieces annually. His foundry, the largest and most important in the world, employed up to 300 workmen. Highly thought of by his contemporaries, Barbédienne won, amongst other prizes, three great medals 'for excellence' at the Great Exhibition in London, 1862, and the 'grand prix' in Paris, 1889. During his lifetime he published over 1,200 models, from antique to contemporary artists; the latter he generously encouraged. Barbédienne, a business genius, was a man of great personal taste and was certainly the ideal editor of bronzes, who did much to propagate art and 'le goût du beau'. He started casting some of Barye's models as early as 1853 and in 1875 he bought, after the artist's death, about 80 per cent of the models which Barye had edited himself. Re-editing them, Barbédienne signed his casts, in the first years after Barye's death, with his own monogram (F. B.), later with his full name. These casts vary in quality, depending on the period of execution.

[3] The firm of Susse are amongst the most important bronze founders and editors of the 19th century. Started by Jean Victor Susse (1806–60) and J. B. Amédée Susse (1808–80), it remained in the hands of their descendants until 1926, when it was reorganized as a limited company. After some years of editing in plaster the Susse brothers held the first Exhibition of their work in 1839, and in 1840 they organized a large atelier of *bronzes d'art*. Their output was very considerable and 50 per cent of it was exported. Together with Barbédienne they did much to popularize the small 19th-century bronze.

(at Metz, Paris, Compiègne and elsewhere). He worked in bronze, terracotta and plaster.

His early work was edited in plaster by Susse Frères (1834); later, Fratin cast his bronzes at his own expense in the workshop of E. Quesnel,[4] and towards the end of his life some of them were edited by A. Daubré.[5] Fratin organized three sales of his work (1857, of terracottas only); the last one, with a catalogue enthusiastically prefaced by Jules Janin, was held in 1859.

MÊNE, Pierre Jules (1810–79)

Son of a metal turner, he learned casting from his father. Self-taught, at a later date he received some tuition from the sculptor R. Compaire. Already known for his biscuit models and small bronzes, he exhibited for the first time at the Salon of 1833 and in the same year started his own foundry. He was a regular contributor to the Salon until the year of his death. Extremely popular with the public and the critics, he received numerous medals, including a 1st Class medal conferred twice, and the Cross of the Legion of Honour in 1861. His popularity was also very great in England, where he showed at the Great Exhibitions of 1851 and 1862. Without attaining the reputation of Barye, he was certainly one of the most popular artists of his time. He did not curry favour with the Government and only one of his works was purchased by the State. Mêne's house in Paris, which he shared with his son-in-law Cain, was an important artistic centre.

Mêne usually edited his work himself, taking great care with the modelling and delicate after-work. For a short time, *circa* 1849, some models were cast by Dufailly fils.[6] After Mêne's death many of his models were cast by Cain, to pass, towards the end of the century, into the hands of Susse Frères, together with the latter's own models. Susse printed two undated catalogues which show 217 models by Mêne, edited by them. Some models must also have passed into the hands of F. Barbédienne, probably directly after Mêne's death. Both the Susse and Barbédienne casts are signed by the founder.

In England some of his models were copied both in bronze and in cast iron, with a bronze finish, by Coalbrookdale Company.[7] The first ones are usually inscribed, the latter not. There also exist some bronzes either made by the artist for the London art dealers Ackermann's or copied by them from his models. They are appropriately inscribed. Mêne's models were also copied in 'Parian Body' by Copeland *circa* 1860. The Nymphenburg porcelain factory also reproduced some of his work.

FRÉMIET, Emmanuel (1824–1910)

Son of an artist, he studied under the painter Werner and afterwards became a pupil of F. Rude. At the beginning of his career he concentrated exclusively on animals, which he exhibited at the Salon between 1843 and 1855. Later his field widened, but he still returned very often to animal subjects (1860–80). He remained a regular contributor to the Salon until 1908. Enjoying the patronage of the Imperial Court and of later Governments, he became the most popular and most highly esteemed artist of his period, who did not want to be thought of only as an *animalier*, but stressed his more recent compositions and figures. Loaded with honours, he received all the medals and distinctions possible; he succeeded Barye as Professor at the Museum in 1875, was President of the Academy of Fine Arts and Grand Officer of the Legion of Honour. He was elected an A.R.A. in 1904. His *œuvre* includes many equestrian monuments, the famous Fontaine de l'Observatoire, many other full-size pieces of sculpture commissioned by the State, small bronze statuettes and even medals.

Frémiet seems to have edited many of his works himself, both in a bronze and in a plaster version, publishing a catalogue of them in *circa*

[4] E. Quesnel (active 1811–47), a relatively small firm of Paris founders, cast many Fratin models, both large and small, *circa* 1835. They were cast at the artist's expense and not edited by the founder.

[5] Alfred Daubré (died 1885) was established as *bronzier d'art* at 48 Boulevard de Strasbourg from 1855. He edited some of Fratin's later work.

[6] Possibly son of the sculptor François Dufailly (died 1809).

[7] Coalbrookdale Company, with works situated near Madeley Market in Shropshire, was started towards the end of the 17th century. In 1707 the foundry was bought by a Bristol manufacturer named Darby, whose son built, in 1779, the first cast-iron bridge in England, over the Severn. In the middle of the 19th century, the foundry, managed by Mr Crookes, achieved a great reputation not only for its technical products but also for its art works cast in iron and bronze. Coalbrookdale commissioned artists like Carrier-Belleuse and J. Bell to model for them. It is not known if the Mêne models cast by Coalbrookdale were commissioned, or merely copied from the existing ones. The casts in bronze are usually inscribed with the foundry's name, but those in iron are not; possibly as they were not for sale but only for exhibition, to prove the excellence of iron casting, rivalling bronzes. Similar examples were shown at the Great Exhibition of 1862.

1860. Later some of the models were bought and edited by F. Barbédienne, who signed his casts.

BONHEUR, Marie Rosalie, called Rosa (1822–99)
Daughter and pupil of the painter Raymond Bonheur, and sister of the animal sculptor Isidore (1827–1901), she also studied under Léon Cogniet. To start with, her interests centred on sculpture, examples of which she exhibited alongside pictures at the Salon between 1842 and 1848, but later the *génie de couleur* prevailed, and she seldom sculpted again. Famous from 1848, when she received a gold medal, she enjoyed a popularity not often found by living artists. This popularity in France, England and the United States did not wane, although her best works are covered by the decade 1850–60. She was the recipient of many French and foreign medals and distinctions, being in some cases the first woman ever to receive them.

Her bronzes are rare. They were all edited by her brother-in-law Hippolyte Peyrol, who in 1852 married the artist's sister Juliette (1830–91). Peyrol successfully exhibited some of his work at the Great Exhibition in London, 1862. He also edited bronzes by Isidore Bonheur.

CAIN, Auguste Nicolas (1821–94)
Son of a butcher, he worked as an apprentice to the trade before becoming an artist. Pupil of the sculptor A. Guionnet and later of F. Rude, he was also strongly influenced by P. J. Mêne, whose daughter he married in 1852. He worked together with his father-in-law and, thanks to the latter's contacts, received numerous important Government commissions (Tuileries, Louvre, Trocadéro, Chantilly, the Hôtel de Ville, Paris), both under the Second Empire and the Republic. He was the recipient of many prizes and medals in France and abroad, including the Officer's Cross of the Legion of Honour. Very popular with the public in France and England, as well as with the critics, he exhibited regularly at the Paris Salon (from 1846).

Cain's large output of smaller bronzes, statuettes and *bronzes d'ameublement* was edited by the artist who, living together with P. J. Mêne, shared his foundry and continued to run it after the latter's death. For larger sculpture, as for instance in the case of the monument to the Duke of Brunswick in Geneva (1878), the casting was done by F. Barbédienne. It would seem that towards the end of the century Cain himself sold his models to Susse Frères, together with Mêne's models. Susse published two undated catalogues which give 110 and 120 models by Cain respectively, of which 56 were *bronzes d'ameublement*, the rest statuettes, all of animal subjects. Cain also made some portrait plaquettes.

GARDET, Georges (1863–1939)
Son of the sculptor Joseph Gardet, he studied under the painter Millet and the sculptor Frémiet, soon revealing an outstanding talent. His first great success came at the Salon of 1887 when he exhibited his Panther and Python (Parc de Montsouris). He received many commissions from the State and at the Great Exhibition of 1900 was awarded the Grand Prix for his monumental sculpture (groups of lions and tigers now at Vaux-le-Vicomte, and, together with Dalou, the lions flanking the Pont Alexandre III). He was the recipient of many medals, including the Cross of the Legion of Honour.

He seems to have edited most of his bronzes himself, but some models were edited by Barbédienne and Susse.

BUGATTI, Rembrandt (1885–1916)
Son of Carlo, the well-known interior designer and furniture-maker and brother of the motoring pioneer, he studied desultorily at the Academy of Fine Arts in Milan. But his real school was in fact his father's workshop, where he learnt the technical excellence of the latter's profession. As a boy of twelve, he started modelling animals. Leaving Milan, he went through Turin and Venice to Antwerp and finally to Paris, where he was to settle (1900). In the last two towns he had ample opportunity to study animals in their Jardins des Plantes. He also came under the influence of the Russian-born Paul Trubetzkoy who lived in Italy. He exhibited for the first time in Paris at the Salon of 1904, but his great success came as a result of a small exhibition (twenty models), held in the atelier of Bugatti's protector and friend, the founder A. A. Hébrard in 1907. He continued to exhibit regularly at the Salon, receiving several medals and awards, including the Cross of the Legion of Honour, until his tragically premature suicidal death in 1916.

All Bugatti's bronzes were edited by the founder A. A. Hébrard.[8]

POMPON, François (1855–1933)
Son of a poor Burgundian handworker, he studied at the Ecole des Beaux-Arts at Dijon,

[8] A. A. Hébrard was the owner of one of the most important foundries in Paris. He edited the works of Degas and Dalou and also did much to encourage younger artists. His bronzes are technically excellent and were usually edited in limited series. The firm no longer exists.

moving later to Paris, where for years he was to struggle with dire poverty. He worked as a pointer for Mercié, Falguière and finally for Rodin, in whose atelier he stayed for fifteen years. It is there that he acquired a high degree of artistic culture and was encouraged to pursue his own artistic line.

Pompon started by sculpting portraits but from 1888 he turned towards the animal form, which was to bring him fame. In 1908 Rodin said "You will be a great artist" – but recognition by the public came late, only at the Salon d'Automne of 1922. From that moment onwards he was the object of innumerable articles, books and pamphlets, and received several distinctions, including the Cross of the Legion of Honour. He was also commissioned to do a large piece of sculpture for the City of Paris.

In his will he left all his works (300) to the State. They are now at Dijon.

Pompon's bronzes were edited by the founder A. A. Hébrard.

BIBLIOGRAPHY

Many of the artists discussed in this essay have never been the subject of any serious study, and information about them can best be found in articles in the contemporary art Press listed in the biographical dictionaries by Thieme-Becker or the more specialized Lami. See also:

Alexandre, A. *Les Artistes célèbres: A. L. Barye*, Paris, 1889.
Ballu, R. *l'Oeuvre de Barye*, Paris, 1890.
Biez, J. de. *E. Frémiet*, Paris, 1910.
Catalogue of the Exhibition: "Barye, sculptures, peintures, aquarelles". Paris, Musée du Louvre, 1956–57 (with bibliography).
Courrières, E. de. *F. Pompon*, Paris, 1926.
Faure-Frémiet, P. *Frémiet.* Paris, 1934.
Klumpke, A. *Rosa Bonheur, sa vie, son œuvre.* Paris, 1908.
Lami, S. *Dictionnaire des sculpteurs de l'Ecole Française au XIX*[e] *siècle*, vols. 1–4, Paris, 1914.
Rey, R. *F. Pompon*, Paris, 1928.
Sacchetti, R. *Rembrandt Bugatti sculpteur, Carlo Bugatti et son art*, Paris, 1907.
Saunier, C. *Barye*, Paris, 1925.

Sundials;
an Introduction to Scientific Instruments

P. G. COOLE

A complete survey of the field of scientific instruments could hardly be compressed into a single volume let alone a short article; there is not even an exact definition of what constitutes a scientific instrument. In the second half of the 19th century, when the volumes of classified abridgments of patents were being compiled, Class 76 was entitled "Abridgments of Specifications relating to Optical, Mathematical, and Other Philosophical Instruments; including Nautical, Astronomical, and Meteorological Instruments". This would seem to be fairly all-embracing, but the preface shows that a certain amount of specialization had been considered, most of it logical, if at times surprising. Specula or reflectors for scientific purposes are included, but not mirrors or looking-glasses, and reflectors for lighthouses "will be found in the series relating to 'Lamps, Candlesticks &c'"; lenses are within the scope of the work unless they are for magic lanterns or apparatus for producing scenic effects and apparitions.

A brief glance through the index shows that the enjoyment to be derived from the use of technical jargon is no new idea. There are sympiesometers, a "suspensor applicable to maritime purposes", cosmometers, thaumatropes for which one is referred to Phenakistoscopes, "Mnemonics, optically assisted by chromatic charts" and helypsometers. A Horometer is found not to tell the time but to solve problems in trigonometry, and an Antimeter is for measuring angles, not disapproval. However, the purpose of most of the instruments was and still is measurement.

Today certain types of instruments have come under the aegis of various specialists. Gone are the days when a man could, and did, collect astrolabes for decorative purposes in the same way that lesser mortals collect horse-brasses. Now they are subjects for serious and scholarly research. For many years astrolabes have constituted a dangerous field for the amateur as there are many fakes and reproductions and some of these are sufficiently old to puzzle the experts. Optical, surveying and navigational instruments have also tended to become specialist studies. However, the academicians are facing competition from the interior decorator when it comes to obtaining specimens.

The use of scientific instruments for decorative purposes is no new thing. Some of the early instruments are ornamented to the point where the possibility of their practical use becomes highly problematical and it is more than likely that they were designed to be presents for princes, and intellectual status symbols, to be looked at rather than used.

The collector of scientific instruments has an advantage over his colleague in the art world: he is able to base his opinions on fact rather than fancy. However decorative an instrument may be, it must be capable of fulfilling the function for which it was intended within, or greater than, the degree of accuracy expected

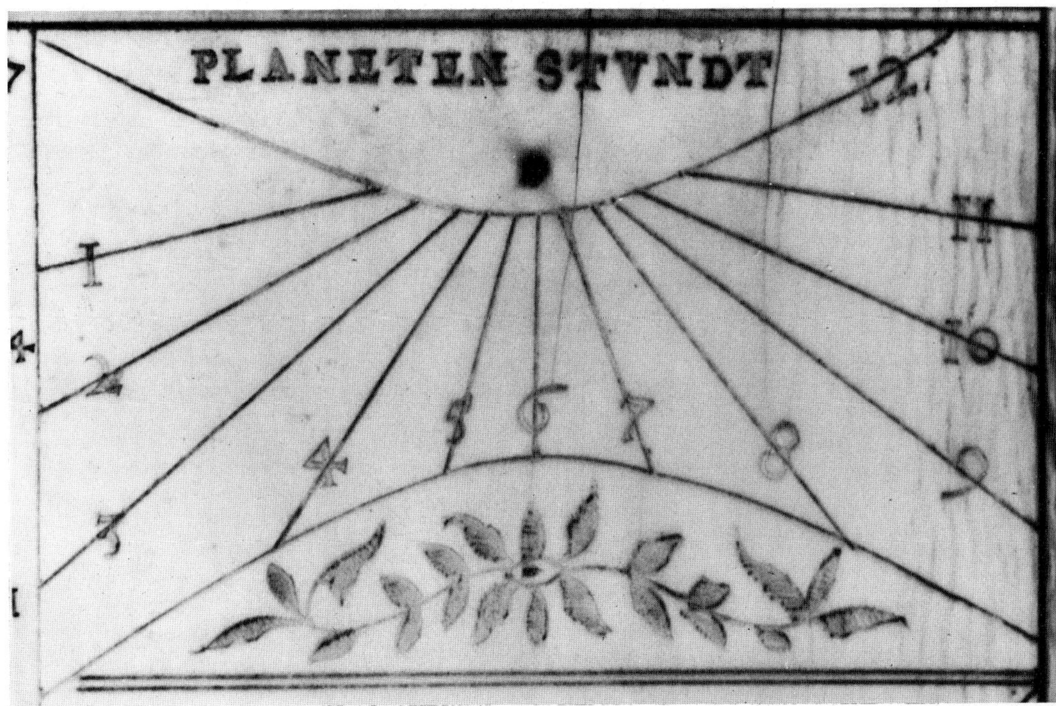

1. (above right) Detail from an ivory diptych dial, 1607, by Paulus Reinman of Nuremberg
The British Museum, London

2. (above left) Top of an astronomical compendium, *circa* 1595, probably German
$3\frac{3}{8} \times 3\frac{1}{2}$ in. (8·6 × 8·8 cm.). The British Museum, London

3. (left) Equatorial dial showing the plumb-bob for levelling the instrument and the quadrant for setting the latitude, *circa* 1760, by L. T. Müller of Augsburg
octagonal $2\frac{5}{8}$ in. (6·8 cm.) wide. The British Museum, London

4. (below right) Analemnatic dial, *circa* 1700, by Thomas Tuttell of London – the lower dial acts as a sun compass to orient the dial $4 \times 3\frac{1}{8}$ in. (10 × 8 cm.). The British Museum, London

5. (below left) Pocket dial, *circa* 1700, by Nicholas Bion of Paris – the gnomon is adjustable for latitude and is engraved with a scale of degrees, the bird's beak acts as the index
$3 \times 2\frac{1}{2}$ in. (7·4 × 6·4 cm.). The British Museum, London

6. Ivory diptych dial with vertical and horizontal dial for the string gnomon, *circa* 1700; Nuremberg – on the lower leaf is a pin gnomon dial for the hours *ab ortus* and *ab occasus*
The British Museum, London

7. *Viatorium*, 1587, by Ulrich Schneip of Munich – the dial plate may be tilted and the scale of latitudes is set below the levelling bob, the tip of which acts as an index
$2\frac{1}{8} \times 1\frac{1}{2}$ in. (5·5 × 3·7 cm.)
The British Museum, London

Colour Plate. An astronomical compendium, showing the complexity attained by some makers; dated 1596, by Johann Antonius Lindin of Heilbronn
5 × 3 in. (12·8 × 7·8 cm.)
(above left) Ring or 'Poke' dial, dated 1575, by Humphrey Cole of London – it is designed for use between the latitudes 50° and 56° – the hour lines can be seen on the inside surface
diameter $2\frac{7}{8}$ in. (7·3 cm.)
(above right) A dial in the form of a star, dated 1550, by an unidentified maker 'H.F.' – it can be adjusted for use between 30 and 55 degrees – the time is indicated in the shadows cast by the ends of the rays on to the scales engraved on the edges
diameter $1\frac{7}{8}$ in. (4·6 cm.)
The British Museum, London

at a particular period. The price to be paid for this advantage is a certain amount of study; obviously the purpose of the instrument must be correctly identified before its merit can be assessed. This and the discovery that there is often more than one way to obtain the same solution are among the particular delights experienced by the collector.

Possibly the easiest approach to the entire field of scientific instruments is through the study of non-mechanical time indicators. This is not just a complicated alternative name for sundials; the positions and movements of heavenly bodies other than the sun are used. The basic theory and practice is comparatively simple, involving no advanced astronomy, but it does require some knowledge of the varying time systems which were still in use in Europe in the 16th and 17th centuries. This knowledge combined with a little imagination will solve most of the basic problems of identifying the various types of dials and their uses.

Although it is possible, to some extent, to find the time by reference to any heavenly body, it is the sun, moon or the constellations of the Great or Little Bears which are most commonly used. Of these, the sun is the easiest, especially as our time system is based on the apparent motion of the sun. During the day the passage of time can be referred to the sun's height (altitude), its bearing (azimuth), or a combination of the two; all sundials depend on these facts to indicate the hour and may be classified according to the information they use. There are, however, two additional factors to be taken into consideration: the latitude of the observer and the annual variation of the sun's altitude (declination). Some method of compensation for these variables is usually built into the dial.

If a rod is placed upright in the ground the shadow of its tip will move west to east during the day and noon will be indicated when the shadow crosses a line (the meridian) drawn due north and south through the bottom end of the rod. If twelve[1] more lines are added radiating from the bottom of the rod at equal angles the shadow will indicate the twelve hours of the day, but the length of these hours will vary with the length of the day. This is an archaic method of time reckoning, but was still being incorporated in sundials of the 17th century, being called the Planetary Hours,[2] and were numbered either 1–12 or VI–XII–VI. They can be recognized by the equally radiating lines and the straight noon line numbered 6 or XII according to the count being used. (Ill. 1.) Even if this type of dial was not incorporated a converter was sometimes included. (Ill. 2.) The design is based on that of an astrolabe, the curved lines for the unequal hours are laid out inside a circle numbered 1–12, 1–12; to the centre is pivoted an eccentric circle, divided for the signs of the zodiac and an index. In use the index is placed to agree with the hour shown on a standard type of dial and the sign in which the sun is; the planetary hour may then be read off at the point where the index and eccentric meet.[3]

The failure of this type of dial to indicate what may be called ordinary hours arises through the shadow being received on a flat surface while the sun moves in a circular path. If the rod is placed in the centre of a circular plate or ring which is divided into twenty-four equal parts the shadow will show 'equal hours' throughout the year, provided the circle is tilted at an angle equal to the latitude of the observer. In this position the surface of the circle will be parallel to the equator, and thus this type is known as an equatorial dial. (Ill. 3.) It is usually possible

[1] Thirteen lines are needed as the series is actually 0–12, although the first is not numbered.

[2] They are also known as the Unequal Hours. This is a confusing term as they were equal to each other in any day but unequal from day to day throughout the year.

[3] The eccentric is used to compensate for the declination which affects the length of the day.

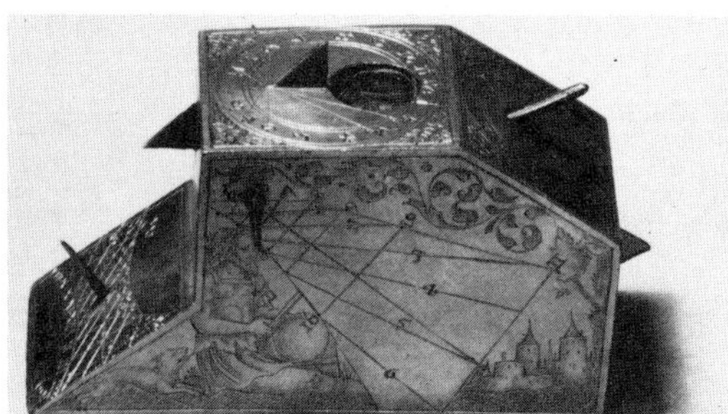

8. Block dial with seven separate hour scales on the various faces, dated 1577, by Simon Schmidlkoffer the Younger (of Munster?)
$2\frac{1}{4} \times \frac{7}{8}$ in. (5·6 × 2·3 cm.)
The British Museum, London

to vary the angle of inclination so that the instrument can be used at various latitudes.

If the divisions on the equatorial ring are projected on to a plane surface and the rod becomes the edge of a triangular 'gnomon' we have the more familiar type of sundial seen in gardens and on buildings, but also used in portable instruments. (Ills 4 (upper part) and 5.) The rod form was retained in the string gnomons found on most folding tablet or diptych dials. (Ills 6, 7.) Because the hour lines are obtained by projection the angles between them are not successively equal, although the noon line still runs north and south. It is possible to project the hour lines on to any surface and this was done to produce the so-called block dials (Ill. 8) and also the vertical dials incorporated in the diptych. (Ill. 6.)

As it is necessary that the noon line shall lie due north and south a magnetic compass was incorporated in the portable dials. However, the reference line for the compass needle will be found not to agree with the noon line on the dial, but to be offset to the east or west according to the age of the instrument. This offset was intended to compensate for the difference between true and magnetic north which is known as the variation,[4] and as this difference varies both annually and from place to place on the earth's surface some of the compasses were fitted with an adjustable variation index. Some dials will be found with two variation lines, one partly erased; this extra line was added later to 'modernize' the instrument and permit its continued use, and was a correction for the annual variation.

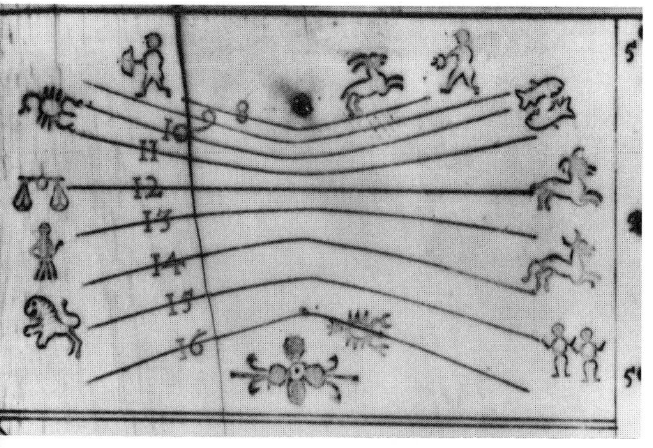

9. Another dial from the ivory diptych by Paulus Reinman (see illustration 1)

The most common form of plane dial is set out on a horizontal surface and designed for a particular latitude; if it is transported in a northerly or southerly direction it will lose its accuracy. To some extent this can be compensated by inclining the dial so that the edge of the gnomon is still parallel to the earth's axis. (Ill. 7.) However, it was more common to provide a means of altering the angle of the gnomon and adding extra hour scales for different latitudes. (Ill. 5.) In the diptych dials the inclination of the string gnomon was varied by threading the upper end through different holes.

So far we have been dealing with dials converting the solar bearing into time. The influence of declination has been eliminated in the design or, as in the case of the planetary hours, incorporated in the time-measuring system, but its existence has been noted. (Ill. 2, footnote 3.) Declination will cause the shadow cast by the tip of the rod or pin gnomon to move along different paths during the course of the year; these paths can be plotted to produce the declination lines as shown in illustration 9. The lines are referred to the signs of the zodiac, which is the usual practice. The numbers on the left show the hours of daylight, and the series could be inverted to give the hours of darkness; naturally the total of the two numbers on any line is always twenty-four.

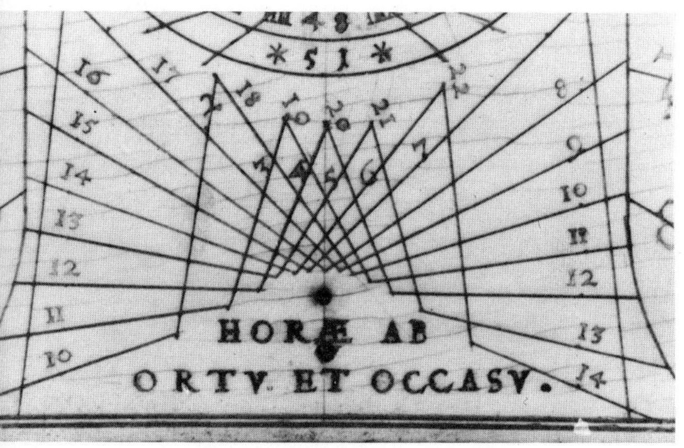

10. Detail from an ivory diptych dial, dated 1607, by Hans Troschel of Nuremberg
The British Museum, London

It is obvious that as the length of the day varies so will the times of the sun's rising and setting, and three systems were used with counts starting from one or both of these times; we will return later to the one using both, and deal first with the *horae ab ortus* and the *horae ab occasus.* (Ill. 10.) Both systems count twenty-four equal hours and, as a sundial is normally only used by day, neither of the counts shown will be complete, the *horae ab ortus* will start on the left from one and continue far enough to record the hours in the longest day, and the set for the *horae ab occasus* will terminate with twenty-four on the right, the count having started on the left with the number of hours since sunset. In practice the numerals

[4] The modern term variation is used instead of declination to avoid confusion with solar declination. However, the older word may be found on some instruments. The variation shown on old dials must be corrected if the dial is being used today.

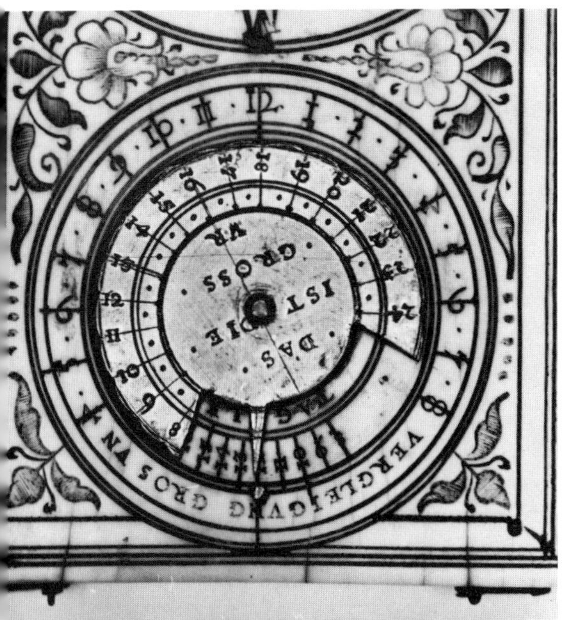

11. Detail from an ivory diptych dial, *circa* 1600, (by Hans Ducher?); Nuremberg
The British Museum

1 and 24 rarely appear on dials owing to the extreme length of the shadow cast by the sun when it is at a low angle. As the length of the day increases, the starting-point for the *horae ab ortus* will have a retrograde movement and at the same time the length of the shadow cast by the gnomon will decrease, therefore the lines on the dial will have to be inclined to the right; the reverse will apply for the *horae ab occasus*. These lines, together with declination lines, are also found on plane dials and use the shadow cast by the tip of a notch in the inclined edge of the gnomon or a small bar fitted crosswise in a similar position.

The *horae ab ortus*, sometimes incorrectly called the Babylonian hours, were used mainly in the Nuremberg area and, not unnaturally, are known as the Nuremberg Hours. These constitute the third system referred to earlier as the count does not continue past sunset and so up to twenty-four, but a new count is started which continues until sunrise so that the total of both counts will be twenty-four.

The use of the *horae ab occasus* was much more widespread and was known by a variety of names, the two most common being the Italian Hours and the Bohemian Hours, although they were often called more simply 'Welsch Uhr' (foreign time); to add to the confusion the term 'Gross Uhr' was applied as well, this being opposed to the 'Klein Uhr', which is the same as the modern count with two sets of twelve equal hours starting from midday or midnight.

There is one big disadvantage to both the *ab ortus* and *ab occasus* systems; the time of midday will alter as the datum varies and by the same amount; in addition, and this was probably more important, the time of the sun's rising or setting would vary by approximately twice, according to which system was being used. That these systems were indeed being used and were not just curiosities is proved by the existence of dials fitted with converters. Illustration 11 shows a converter for the 'Gross Uhr' and 'Klein Uhr', the series of numbers for the index representing the number of hours of daylight; this could be found by consulting the declination dial (Ill. 9); with the pointer set correctly the two systems could be compared and the conversion made. Illustration 12 shows a similar converter for the *horae ab ortus*, in this case probably the Nuremberg Hours. When comparing the two illustrations it must be remembered that the twelve-hour system is on the fixed part of the first, but the movable part of the second. Both have been set at approximately the equinox, and so a twelve-hour day, and it can be seen that noon would equal either 18 or 6, depending on which system is being used. The errors arise partly from bad setting and partly from poor construction, but this may have been deliberate as there is some doubt as to when the count actually started, at the time of true sunset or at the end of twilight; the latter is more likely and was certainly the case in Florence where the sun always set at half-past twenty-three.

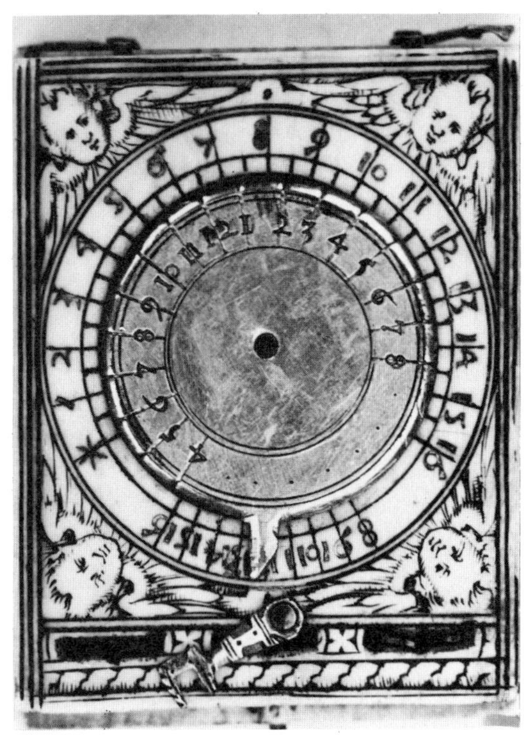

12. Lid of an ivory diptych dial, *circa* 1600, possibly by Paulus Reinman of Nuremberg
The British Museum, London

Before leaving the various time systems it should be noted that the familiar twelve-hour count may also be called the *horae ab meridies*, which is reasonable, or 'Deutsch Uhr', which is somewhat vague when you consider that there was no united Germany in the 16th and 17th centuries. However, 'Deutschland' can be found included in the latitude tables for 48°, together with Burgundy, Brittany, Switzerland, Hungary, Austria and others, so that it was probably roughly equivalent to the old 'Alamannia'. The latitude tables referred to can be found on the ivory diptych dial made in Nuremberg by the Ducher or Tucher family at the end of the 16th and beginning of the 17th centuries.

To obviate the necessity for orienting the dial and the attendant problems of magnetic variation one can ascertain the time from the sun's altitude alone, but here the effect of declination must be taken into account; luckily this is a constant,

13. Quadrant made for Richard II, 1399; English length of side 3½ in. (9 cm.)
The British Museum, London

14. Ivory pillar dial, *circa* 1700, probably French height 3⅝ in. (9·3 cm.)
The British Museum, London

15. Chalice dial made for Bartholomew, Abbot of Aldersbach, dated 1554
height 5⅜ in. (13·8 cm.)
The British Museum, London

seasonable variable occasioned by the inclination of the earth's axis to the plane of its orbit. All that is needed is some form of instrument, with sights, capable of measuring the angle of elevation, and a conversion table; the latter could be dispensed with by reproducing it graphically on the instrument so that the time could be obtained by a direct reading. The easiest instrument to convert is the quadrant (Ill. 13) which, as its name implies, consists of a quarter of a circle with a scale of degrees on the curved edge and sights on one of the straight edges; a plumb-bob is suspended from a hole near the apex, and the cord is used as an index for the scale of degrees; a small bead fitted to the cord can be moved to provide the declination co-ordinate and act as the index for the hour lines laid out on the surface of the quadrant.[5] The pattern of the lines will vary according to the particular time to be measured and the way in which the declination scale is divided, and may be straight lines, regular arcs or irregular curves.

The pillar or cylinder dial (Ill. 14) is a more popular form of altitude instrument. The circumference is divided by date rather than by sign and the hour lines are more or less spiral. The top is removable and fitted with a folding gnomon of the correct length. In use the top is rotated until the gnomon lies over the appropriate vertical line, then the dial is turned until the gnomon points towards the sun and the end of the shadow will indicate the time. As with the plane dial the pattern of lines on the cylinder can be projected on to any surface to produce other forms; they can even be turned inside out as in the chalice dial. (Ill. 15.) Some of these chalice dials have two sets of hour lines so that they can be used when filled with water; the second set of lines will correct the refraction error caused by the light passing through the liquid. In either case the dial is placed on a horizontal surface and turned until the shadow falls on the vertical line corresponding to the season. As an alternative the hour scales were engraved on the inside of a broad ring which was provided with a suspension loop, the scales were on one side and opposite them the ring was pierced with a hole through which the sun could shine to indicate the hour.

Probably the best known of the altitude dials is the universal ring. Basically it is similar to the equatorial dial (Ill. 3) but instead of being hinged to a base-plate the equatorial ring is pivoted inside another ring so that it can fold flat; stops are fitted to ensure that the two rings lie at a right angle to each other when the dial is in use (Ill. 16); the gnomon is replaced by a declination bar with a slide containing a hole, the latitude scale is engraved on the outer ring and is used in conjunction with the index on the suspension. To use the universal ring, first set the correct latitude and declination; on these dials the declination is often shown in terms of signs, days and degrees.[6] The dial is then held up by its ring and turned until the sunlight passing through the hole in the slide falls on a line scribed inside the equatorial ring. This dial has two disadvantages: it cannot be correctly used at the equinoxes or near midday as one or both of the rings will interrupt the sun's rays.

With any altitude dial there are always two possible readings as the angles for any two hours equally apart from noon must be the same and although it may be easy to decide between 10 a.m. and 2 p.m., it is more difficult when it comes to readings taken between 11.30 a.m. and 12.30 p.m.

The apparent movement of the sun from east to west is used by the magnetic

[5] It is easiest to hold the quadrant upright and move it until the sun shines through both holes, when the time can be read. An actual sight can be taken if the sun is partially obscured and the risk of blinding lessened.

[6] With instruments made before the calendar was changed from Julian to Gregorian, ten days must be subtracted for the date used to set the declination.

16. Universal ring dial, *circa* 1750, French or English
The British Museum, London

17. (above) Portable wooden equatorial dial, *circa* 1700, French
$4\frac{5}{8} \times 4\frac{1}{4}$ in. (11·8 × 10·6 cm.)
The British Museum, London

18. (below) Dieppe dial, *circa* 1700, by Charles Bloud
$2\frac{7}{8} \times 2\frac{1}{2}$ in. (7·3 × 6·6 cm.)
The British Museum, London

azimuth dial (Ill. 17) to measure the passage of time. The curved hour lines, similar to those on the lower part of illustration 2, are crossed by a series of concentric circles which represent the declination lines. If the dial is laid flat and the figure XII turned away from the sun the time will be shown by the north end of the needle against the appropriate declination line, although correction should be made for variation. With the magnetic azimuth dial it is sometimes possible to get some idea of the time when the sunlight is too weak to cast an effective shadow. This idea may have occurred to Charles Bloud of Dieppe when he produced his version of the diptych dial. (Ill. 18.) An equatorial dial is set out on the lid and provided with a removable pin gnomon, the correct inclination for latitude is produced by setting the point of a strut, pivoted in a slot in the right-hand edge of the base against the scale on the underside of the lid. Obviously this dial could only be used during the summer and autumn when the sun is above the equator, but this is also the time when it is most likely to be unobscured. For the rest of the year Bloud fitted a magnetic azimuth dial. His design differs from that of illustration 17; there are no declination lines and the hours are set out on part of an ellipse whose ends are joined by an ornamental scroll; this is mounted so that it can move along two slots cut along the north–south line of the compass. The end of one of the pegs securing the hour scale engages an eccentric groove cut in the underside of a disc, with a calendar scale, rotating in a recess in the base; as this disc is turned the hour scale will move north and south to compensate for the declination so that the time can be read directly from the needle. It is possible that this type owes something to the hour converter shown in illustration 2 which, in turn, was derived from the astrolabe.

The Bloud type of azimuth dial should not be confused with the analemna seen on the lower part of illustration 4, which is an ancestor of the sun compass. Although broadly speaking the constructional methods for both are the same, the analemnatic dial uses the shadow cast by a stile or vertical gnomon to indicate the time; the stile is adjusted for declination instead of the hour scale as in the Bloud dial. On the dial by Thomas Tuttell (Ill. 4) the lower dial acts as a sun compass to orient the upper dial. After setting the declination the instrument is turned until the same time is indicated by both dials, when the alignment will be correct. However, unless the dial is comparatively large and particularly well made this method of orientation is not particularly accurate, although the error is probably less than that arising from incorrect compensation for variation.

In addition to correction for variation another factor must be taken into consideration when reading a sundial, the difference between True and Mean Solar Time known as the Equation of Time.[7] As the efficiency of mechanical time-keeping improved, it was found that the apparent daily movement of the sun was not as regular as had been popularly assumed and the clock would only agree with the sundial four times in the year; at other times the difference could be as much as a quarter of an hour either way. As far as the man in the street was concerned this difference did not matter, but it was important to the man who wanted to keep his watch or clock right, and for this reason many of the larger dials made from the end of the 17th century onwards have an 'equation table' engraved on them showing the amount to be added or subtracted to give mean time.[8] This difference is often forgotten by people consulting sundials and they attribute the apparent error to bad workmanship on the part of the dial maker.

[7] This difference is caused by the fact that the earth's orbit is elliptical, with the sun at one focus, so the linear speed of the earth will vary throughout the year.

[8] An equation table is included in *Whitaker's Almanack*.

New Guinea Sculpture

ANTHONY FORGE

New Guinea is a huge island, only exceeded in size by Greenland; the interior is everywhere difficult, being mainly either mountains or swamps. The coasts are only safely navigable even by large canoes at certain seasons of the year, and only the major river systems provide any possibility of easy communication. The population, probably between two and three million, lives in small villages each of which was, before the Europeans arrived, a political and war-making unit, usually in a state of permanent hostility with some of its neighbours. These units were rarely more than 1,000 strong and usually much less. Apart from a very few cases no form of kingship or chieftainship has been reported; the affairs of the villages were managed by agreement of all the adult males, a democratic but somewhat time-consuming system of government. Given these circumstances, it is easy to understand the enormous proliferation of cultures and societies within the island. Over 1,000 separate languages and dialects have been identified, and even within these groups one can frequently find quite substantial changes in customs and art styles between villages only a few miles apart and speaking the same language. A tribe in New Guinea is not a single political and cultural unit of the sort found in Africa, but is primarily a linguistic unit sharing similar social structure and culture, often with considerable variation within its borders, and shading gradually into neighbouring tribes without any clear change of custom or style.

It is therefore obvious that one of the most common and fruitful foci of art production in all societies except our own, the royal Court with its demand for fine works to express its state, and the resources to reward full-time craftsmen, must be totally absent from New Guinea. In fact, there are no professional artists, every man is primarily a garden cultivator, the largest part of his productive effort goes into growing yams or taro, or sweet potato in the Highlands, and it is on these activities that his claim to the respect of his fellows principally rests. Before European contact steel was unknown, tools were of polished stone, shell or bone, with awls and chisels of bone and animal teeth and knives of bamboo; fire was also used for such jobs as hollowing out canoes and drums, while sand or sandstone were available as abrasives, with certain snake and lizard skins and even rough leaves for finer polishing. With this unpromising equipment, and as an essentially non-professional activity, New Guinea artists have nevertheless produced works of great sophistication and refinement which place the island among the great art-producing areas of the world.

The diversity of language and culture is faithfully reflected in the styles of New Guinea art – there are at least ten major stylistic areas in the island[1] and more in the

[1] See Linton and Wingert, *Arts of the South Seas*, New York, 1946, and the more recent account by Bühler in Bühler, Barrow and Mountford, *Oceania and Australia. The Art of the South Seas*, London, 1961.

1. Housepost in a ceremonial house of Kanganaman village, Iatmul tribe, Middle Sepik area about 180 in. (457·2 cm.) shown

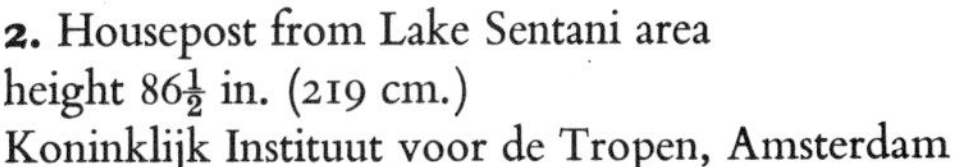

2. Housepost from Lake Sentani area height 86½ in. (219 cm.) Koninklijk Instituut voor de Tropen, Amsterdam

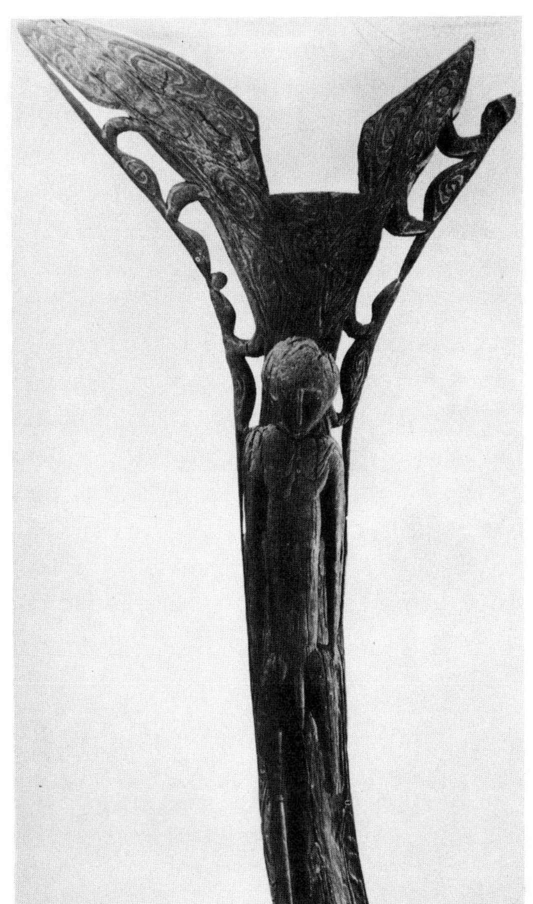

rest of Melanesia, from which New Guinea can hardly be separated on artistic grounds. Within each of these major areas are many tribes creating their own distinctive works, drawing on stylistic elements common to the whole area, but adapting them to the style and genius of the particular culture. There have been many speculations about the origins of certain stylistic features found in parts of New Guinea – Indian, South-east Asian and Indonesian origins have been vigorously advanced – but apart from a few coastal areas of West New Guinea, where recent Indonesian influence is obvious and historically attested, they remain essentially speculations and often contradictory ones at that.[2] Whatever its origins, whether the stylistic basis of New Guinea art is wholly imported or wholly indigenous, there is no doubt at all that the traditional art as seen and collected in the 19th and 20th centuries is totally indigenous in treatment. Wherever the motifs originated, they have been welded into a coherent style by each tribe, the style persists and has value for them because it forms part of their life, and particularly their ritual life, and its forms are charged with meaning by their own symbol system, having reference to their society and environment.

Art in New Guinea is universal – there is no culture without some form of artistic expression, but the materials exploited and the types produced vary. The large population of the Central Highlands, living in valleys from 5,000 to 7,000 feet above sea-level, with mountain peaks up to 15,000, falls into two main groups separated from each other by the peoples of the Telefomin area and the Star mountains. In neither the Eastern nor the Western Highlands is figure carving or much painting on objects found. Wigs and head-dresses are the main form of artistic expression; the latter are often huge, made principally from feathers, particularly from birds of paradise; they are impressive and when worn with full regalia by men in rituals the ensemble with the painted face and decorated body is certainly a work of art, even if it does not fall into any of the main categories recognized in our society. Sculpture, apart from low-relief panels with abstract designs from Telefomin, is absent from the contemporary cultures of the whole of the Highlands area. Remarkable polished stone human and animal forms, mainly made as pestles, have been found, but are apparently the sole remains of an archaic culture.

It is in the Lowlands of New Guinea, along the great river systems and on the islands off the coast, that the richness and diversity of the art is to be found. Sculpture cannot really be distinguished from architecture on the one hand and painting and decorative art on the other. Large works, particularly figure carvings, are frequently found as posts or other structural parts of the men's ceremonial houses that form the basis for ritual and political organization in most of the lowland areas. (Ills 1, 2.) These ceremonial houses are the centre of artistic activity in the village; their architectural forms are various but they are usually much larger and more magnificent versions of the dwelling houses. Their exteriors are often decorated with paintings, carvings and decorative thatch and matting, and face on to a piazza where village ceremonial and dances take place. Entrance to the house is restricted to adult, initiated males who are responsible for the preparation and performance of the ceremonial on which the health and prosperity of the community is believed to depend. Ceremonial is performed to maintain the benevolence of spirits but also to express the pride of the performers in their skill and their prowess in war, as gardeners, as lovers, and in general their prestige as a village and as individuals. Although offerings are made to spirits, and invocations

[2] Bühler, *op. cit.*, and Schmitz, C. A. *Historische Probleme in Nordost-Neuguinea, Huon Halbinsel.* Wiesbaden, 1960.

3. Loin cloth of bark cloth painted in black and brown, Lake Sentani area
length 51 in. (129·5 cm.)
Rijksmuseum voor Volkenkunde, Leiden

are sung, these often seem secondary to the more secular concerns of competitive display of magnificence and ostentation in carving, painting and decoration of everything, especially the performers. This is not to say that there is no aesthetic consideration involved, for although size and dazzling painting are vital criteria of excellence in New Guinea eyes, beauty of form and harmonious relationship between forms are highly valued. The success of a figure or painting is in fact related to its ability to satisfy aesthetic canons which appear to be universal, although the indigenous languages have no words for such matters, tending to use only a vocabulary of size, brightness and magnificence, and concepts such as magical potency of the completed work.

Sculpture in New Guinea has then two main functions. Firstly, to represent spirits and by representing them open up a means of communication, and in some senses a means of exercising some sort of control over the spirits through manipulations of their images. The idea of a God with completely free will seems to be unknown in New Guinea. Secondly, sculpture, and art in general, expresses the prestige of the village and the pride of the clans that make up the village, in opposition to other villages and other clans. This essential competitiveness reaches down to the level of the individual, where personal ornaments and decorations and the workmanship and beauty of household utensils and tools express the prestige of the owner.

It is in the sacred art of the ceremonial house that the basic forms of any particular art style are to be found. Typically the most sacred carvings are of spirits in anthropomorphic form; frequently the carvings incorporate birds or other animals, usually totemic, serving to indicate the clan which owns the figure and claims the spirit as its own. The spirit may not be represented by only one form, but may be immanent in several different artistic forms, one as a carving in the round, another as a mask, a different form again in painting on the flat, and so on. One of these forms will be considered the most sacred, but all are prototypes for the forms used in decorative and other non-sacred art. The art of any one tribe then is based on the exploitation of a comparatively few sacred forms, whose refinement and persistence are sanctioned by the values of the culture expressed in the religion. There are some exceptions, such as the remarkable and exciting bark cloth paintings of Lake Sentani (Ill. 3), whose spiky and violent forms have no apparent relationship to the monumental, almost serene, forms of Sentani sculpture. (Ill. 2.)

The most sacred anthropomorphic figures are usually of hardwood and are often, in New Guinea terms, old; some may even be more than 100 years. (Ill. 4.) The less sacred forms may utilize a wide variety of materials – basketry (Ill. 5), turtle shell (Ill. 6), bark cloth over a cane frame (Ill. 7), pottery (Ill. 8) and combinations of these. The collection of sacra belonging to a clan of Torembi village in the Middle Sepik illustrates the variety. (Ill. 9.) A pair of masks with

4. Figure of clan spirit, Yuat River, Middle Sepik area, 19th century
height 96½ in. (244·5 cm.)
Museum für Völkerkunde und Schweizerisches Museum, Basel

Colour Plate. *Hohao* 'Ancestor' board, western Elema, Gulf of Papua, collected before 1890
height 55½ in. (140·9 cm.)
The National Museum of Ireland, Dublin

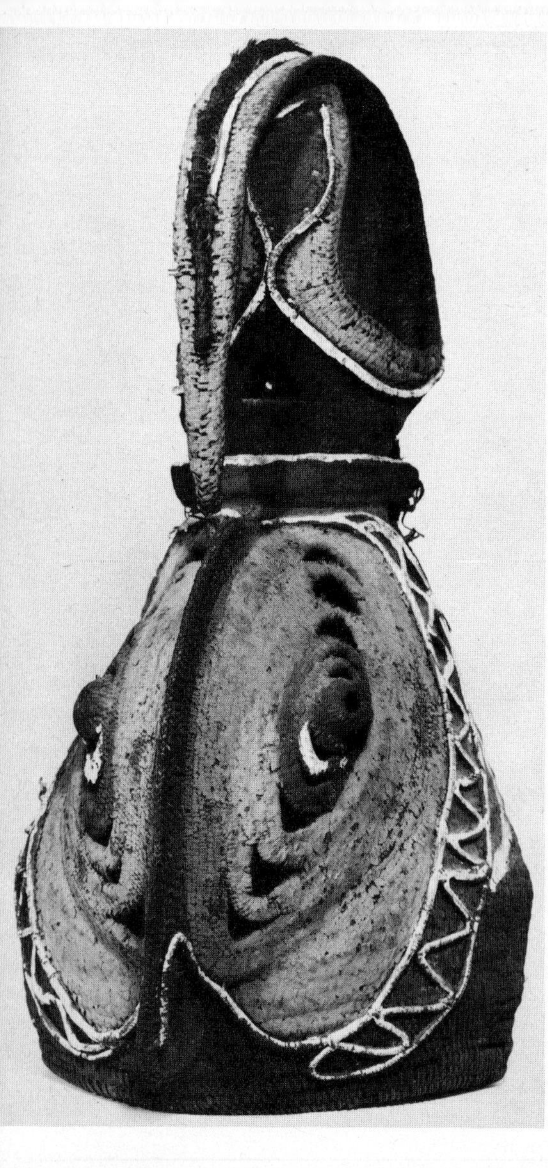

5. (left) Helmet mask of coil basketry surmounted by a highly stylized cockatoo beak, Abelam tribe, Sepik district
height 23 in. (58·4 cm.)
Private Collection, London

7. (right) Mask of bark cloth on a cane frame, Orokolo village, Elema, Gulf of Papua
height 47¼ in. (120 cm.)
The Blackwood Collection, The Pitt-Rivers Museum, Oxford

6. (below) Mask in the form of a fish made from turtle shell plates sewn together, Mabuiag Island, Torres Strait, collected in 1885
length 49¼ in. (125 cm.)
The British Museum, London

8. A pottery gable finial for a ceremonial house, with a female figure with a fish eagle perched on her shoulders, Yentchan village, Iatmul, Middle Sepik area, 19th century
height 21 in. (53·3 cm.)
Private Collection, London

wooden faces on a basketry frame flank a female half-figure also of basketry but with a portrait head modelled in a mixture of clay, oil and lime on an actual skull. The skull of a pig dedicated to the spirits concerned, and a fresh fringe of decorative fibre, show the respect with which such pieces are treated. The addition of leaves, tassels, feathers and other decorations to a completed work is common and sometimes reaches such a scale that the carving itself is scarcely visible. Flute heads from the Yuat River are of very striking form (Ill. 10); however, when used in ceremony they were so covered with shell valuables that only the eyes, nose and mouth were discernible.[3]

This passion for decoration, which may obscure the form of major figures, often transforms mundane objects into works of art. Objects carried and used by men, such as lime spatulae (Ill. 15) and containers, bowls and spoons, and the huge bowls used for serving food on ceremonial occasions in the Admiralty Islands (Ill. 11), show the combination of the desire for splendour and display successfully disciplined to produce a fine sculptural style. Hand drums of hour-glass shape are another type that attract the greatest skill in their treatment. The example from the Tami area (Ill. 12) shows the typical stylization of the human face from this area as used in figures and masks, but here perfectly adapted to the functional shape of the drum; the snake again is a motif frequent in major figures,[4] here used with bands of conventional decoration to produce a totality of great quality. The canoe prow boards from the Massim area, at the south-east end of the island (Ill. 13) show the way in which what is basically decoration is used freely and imaginatively to produce a work of art in the highest sense of the term; such boards also show the very common New Guinea manner of treating a motif – in this case the curved beak and eye of the frigate bird which is used in varying sizes and positions, some single, some interlaced into scrolls – so that apart from the two human figures almost all the prow board is composed of this single motif.

The desire for a decorated surface would seem universal in New Guinea art; major figures often have patterns engraved or painted on their flatter surfaces (e.g. the legs of Ill. 4). In some cases pattern may become dominant even in major figures as, for instance, in the magnificent openwork boards of the Tschuosh. (Ill. 14.) Although their actual purpose is uncertain, they were certainly highly regarded and formed a part of the clan sacra.[5] The main body is composed of scrolls and flowing forms engraved in relief on both sides and pierced at every available opportunity. The scrolls in the example shown are formed from fish eagles with curled, interlocking tails; in other examples only the hooked beak and

[3] Illustrated in Mead, M., "Tamberans and Tumbuans in New Guinea" in *Natural History*, vol. XXXIV, no. 3. New York, 1934.

[4] Cf. pl. 43 in Bodrogi, T., *Oceanic Art*, Budapest, 1959.

[5] There is a very interesting discussion of these boards in Newton, D., *Malu*, New York, 1963.

9. Sacred masks of a clan of Torembi village, Tschuosh tribe, Middle Sepik area, 19th century
height of wooden mask about 24 in. (60·9 cm.)

10. Head of a sacred flute, Yuat River, Middle Sepik area
height $20\frac{1}{2}$ in. (52 cm.)
Private Collection, Basel (On deposit at the Museum für Völkerkunde und Schweizerisches Museum, Basel)

the head of the fish eagle are shown, but the interlocking scroll form is maintained. The body is surmounted by a head, said to be of the sago beetle, very flatly treated with a massive protruding nose; at the bottom is a row of spikes, joined to the body by a series of highly stylized birds' heads; on the spikes would be hung magical bundles or possibly some form of offering. Although closely related to the decorated utilitarian hooks very common in the whole of New Guinea, the Tschuosh boards are so designed that any mundane use of the spikes for hanging up net bags or other large containers is impossible. They provide an unusual example of the development and elaboration of a utilitarian form to provide a sacred one. As far as these things can be determined it seems that all the fine versions of these boards were made before contact with Europeans and therefore with neolithic equipment; as such they are remarkable technical feats as well as beautiful objects.

The desire for pattern draws in not only bird and animal motifs but very frequently employs stylized human figures. Carvings of the human form, seated, and with arms bent so that elbow and knee touch, are found throughout Oceania. They are of two main types: the first with the arms and legs in front of the body and the hands resting on the sides of the head (Ill. 15); the second with the arms and legs splayed out sideways so that they form a zigzag. It is this latter form that is very commonly used as an element in designs and patterns. The interpretation of such highly stylized forms is beset with dangers and often must be speculative not only for the ethnographer but sometimes also to the artists who produced them. The designs as such are traditional and ancestral, their value partly derived from the fact that they were used by the ancestors and are therefore associated with them and their supernatural powers. Further, such stylized motifs are not merely representations of one thing; a form may be human arms, or legs, or a bat, and the interpretation may vary not only with context but also with the interpreter. In general, it seems that such motifs are several different things at the same time; thus a human form may be made up of forms that are themselves each bats. (Ill. 16.)

Shields, either of large, upright shape designed to be used by spearmen, or the shorter type with arrangements to sling them so that both hands can be left free to use a bow and arrows, are very common throughout the island. Although strictly functional in a society where warfare and raiding were everyday affairs and important avenues to prestige, they are invariably decorated, often with designs of great beauty and complexity. Carved in low relief and brightly painted, they seem to have been designed to impress the enemy when two sides met in open combat. (With their bright colours they would have been worse than useless in ambush, one of the most favoured and deadly forms of New Guinea fighting.) All the shield designs that have so far been studied, even the most abstract, seem to be anthropomorphic representations, and in some cases they can be definitely identified as clan spirits or other supernaturals. It seems, therefore, that the shields not only protected the warrior physically but also invoked supernatural aid both for defence and directly to attack the enemy. Edmund Leach, in an analysis of the painted shields of the Trobriand Islands, has suggested that the designs, apparently devoid of the remotest human reference, are in fact representations of the dreaded flying witches of the area, and as such their function was very probably, through supernatural means, directly to harm the enemy.[6]

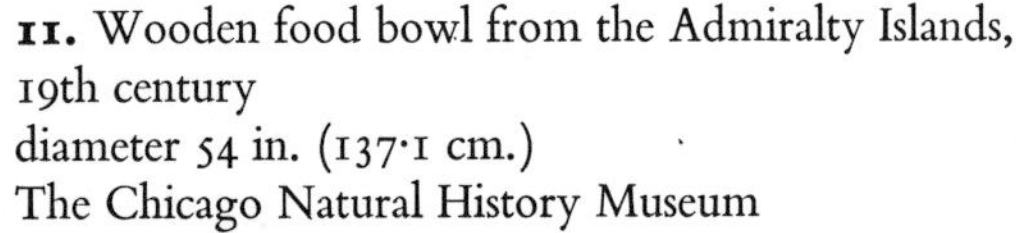

11. Wooden food bowl from the Admiralty Islands, 19th century
diameter 54 in. (137·1 cm.)
The Chicago Natural History Museum

Such conventionalizations of the human form occur in cultures that lack any 'naturalistic' anthropomorphic carving as such – for instance, many of the small

[6] Leach, E. R. "A Trobriand Medusa?" *Man*, vol. LIV, p. 158. London, 1954.

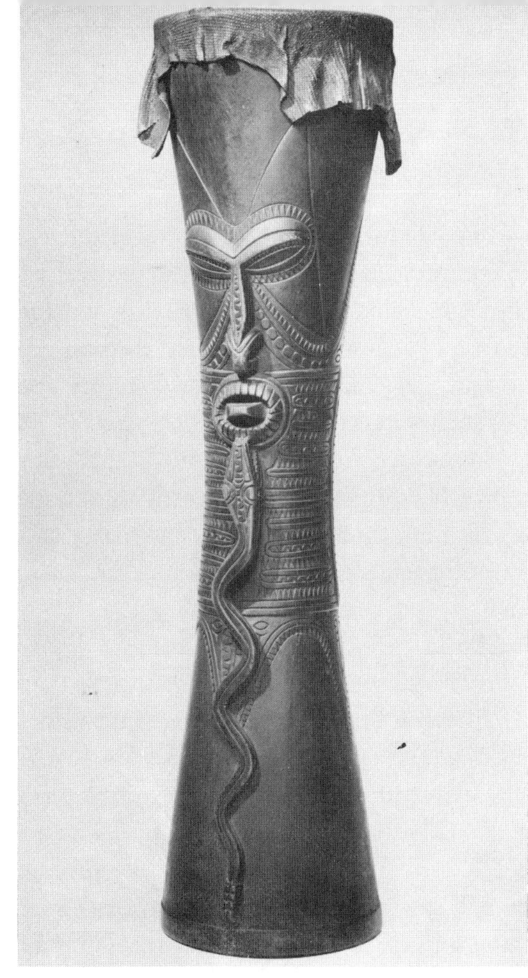

groups of the Upper Sepik – but are not restricted to them. Great freedom is taken with the human form in all the Lowland cultures. The colour plate and illustration 17 are both ancestral boards (*Hohao*) from the Western Elema peoples of the Gulf of Papua; they were both produced for the same purpose and the craftsmanship in both is of the highest standard; both were undoubtedly equally valid and effective to the carvers and their public. The simplified 'naturalism' of one (see colour plate facing p. 332) is perhaps more limited in its reference to other forms of Elema ceremonial art, compared to the highly stylized version (Ill. 17) which is composed of forms that are found in other types of carving, in masks (Ill. 7), and in the everyday objects whose decoration is a sign of high status.

This multiple reference is perhaps the outstanding feature of symbolism in New Guinea art. It makes any iconography of the sort familiar from art historians' studies of civilized cultures virtually impossible, but helps to explain how New Guinea artists, although consciously trying to produce works that are validated by ancestral practice, can still preserve a considerable freedom to vary and innovate within the limits of the style of their culture. By combining and recombining elements of design, each element itself sanctioned by ancestral usage, gradual stylistic change can take place. Such slow change and development of styles is undoubtedly the main way in which the numerous sophisticated styles of the island have evolved, but such evolution has rarely taken place in isolation. Borrowings from neighbouring groups seem to have been frequent; such borrowings were sometimes motivated by novelty value, but even so have resulted in imitations or reinterpretations of the foreign object being produced and being incorporated into the local style. Trade in art works of all sorts including minor sacred objects has been reported from all over the island; this trade sometimes was large and extensive, as in the voyages that in various stages linked together the whole south coast of Papua, from the Torres Straits to the Massim area at the south-east end of the island.[7] Nor was novelty the only reason for borrowing. An Abelam village, in the Sepik District in which I have lived, abandoned the ancestral style of façade painting when it built a new ceremonial house, and adopted the style used by a group some ten miles to the west. The reason for this change was not the superior aesthetic qualities of the new style – indeed as the artists were unused to it the result was very poor – but because the area from which the style came grew longer yams than those they grew themselves. Among the Abelam there is a yam cult involving competitive growing and exchanging of yams, and the length of the yams a man can grow is the main index of his prestige. The change of style was intended to tap superior supernatural power, and by so doing directly to improve the quality of the long yams which formed one of the main foci of the Abelams' interests and values.

Art in New Guinea is inherently powerful in some rather ill-defined supernatural way; representations of spirits or ancestors are not merely idols, physical foci of cults directed towards obtaining their benevolence, but are a means of reaching the supernatural and influencing its actions in a positive way. Through carving and painting man becomes a partner with the supernatural, able to use its

[7] Mead, M., *op. cit.*, and Seligman, C. G. *The Melanesians of British New Guinea*. Cambridge, 1910.

12. (above left) Hand drum with lizard skin tympanum, Tami area, Huon Gulf
height 24 in. (60·9 cm.)
The University Museum of Archaeology and Ethnology, Cambridge

13. (above right) Prow board from a canoe, Massim area, south-east Papua
length 28 in. (71·1 cm.)
The British Museum, London

14. Sacred hook in the form of a pierced panel, Gaigo Revwi (Gaikarobi) village, Tschuosh tribe, Middle Sepik area
height 60 in. (152·4 cm.)
The University Museum of Archaeology and Ethnology, Cambridge

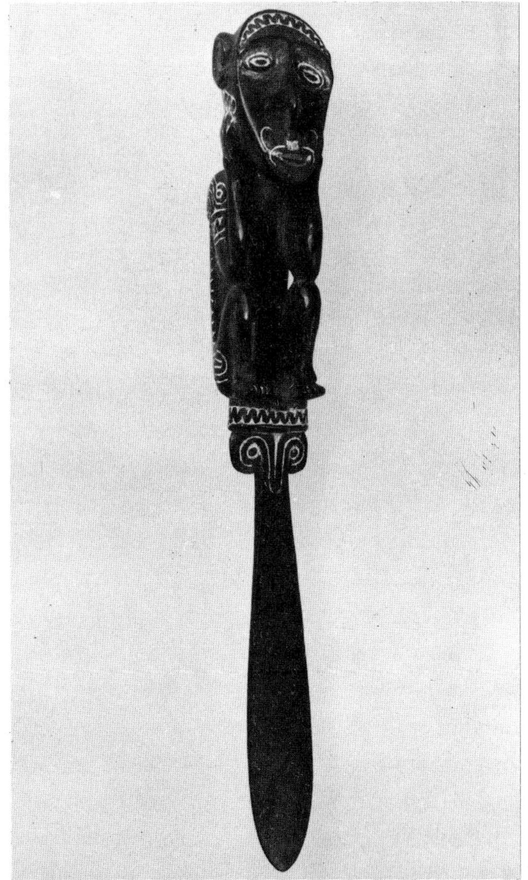

15. (above) Handle of a lime spatula, Massim area, south-east Papua
overall length $10\frac{1}{2}$ in. (26·6 cm.)
The British Museum, London

16. (below left) Shield, Asmat area, south-west New Guinea
height 55 in. (139·7 cm.)
Courtesy Gallery 43, London

17. (below right) *Hohao* plaque, western Elema, Gulf of Papua
height $33\frac{1}{2}$ in. (85 cm.)
The Buffalo Museum of Science, Buffalo, New York

power to further his interests. This does not detract from the aesthetic element – pleasing works and beautiful works are considered more satisfactory and therefore more effective than less aesthetically successful works. When the Abelam village mentioned above found that the next season's yams were no better the explanation was simple: the artists had executed the designs badly, they were therefore not powerful. It is true that the emphasis in such statements is on the 'correctness' of the designs, and that 'correctness' is not explicitly connected with beauty, but collection of judgements on what is good and 'correct' from both artists and non-artists leaves no doubt that 'correctness' implies those qualities of symmetry and balance, harmonious relationship between forms, effective use of colour, etc., that form the basis of all aesthetic judgement.

The various cults provide a stimulus for art production, and a context highly charged with emotion which gives to the various forms a symbolic value that they preserve in other contexts. These cults express and reinforce the paramount values of the society. In addition to spirits linked to the clans, cults of the dead are common and ancestors and folk heroes are frequently represented (see colour plate facing p. 332, Ills 1, 17), while masks are usually manifestations of the spirits themselves or of minor spirits associated with the main clan spirits. (Ills 5, 7, 9.) Specific dead are also commemorated in some cultures, not only in the form of trophy skulls often decorated and adorned and found in many of the head-hunting societies, but sometimes, as on the Middle Sepik, in beautifully worked portraits modelled on the actual skull of the deceased ancestor. (Ill. 9.) It may well be that this close link with religion, which served as a spur to the elaboration and refinement of the art of many New Guinea cultures, explains also the speed with which the art disintegrates when faced with intensive European contact. It is not that the artists are converted to Christianity, but rather that the traditional systems of explanation are unable to cope with European technology and that the small and relatively isolated worlds in which the art developed are opened up. There have been a few attempts to integrate the aeroplane, the jeep and cash, the new symbols and values, into the traditional forms of cult and art, but these new things are too much from outside and their creation is not only not understood but unimaginable, and the attempts have all failed.

Whatever the future of New Guinea art it undoubtedly has a glorious past. A survey as brief as this can give no more than a taste of the variety of objects and forms to be found in the island. Produced by a neolithic technology and exploiting every conceivable material they could find, the New Guinea artists expressed their desire to control the supernatural, display their pride in themselves and satisfy their aesthetic needs in a manner that produced a multitude of objects of great beauty and vigour, that can be appreciated far outside the small and simple societies in which they were produced.

BIBLIOGRAPHY

Bodrogi, T. *Oceanic Art.* Budapest, 1959.

Bühler, A., Barrow, T. and Mountford, C. P. *Oceania and Australia. The Art of the South Seas.* London, 1961.

Firth, R. *Art and Life in New Guinea.* London, 1936.

Guiart, J. *The Arts of the South Pacific.* London, Paris, 1963.

Kooijman, S. *The Art of Lake Sentani.* New York, 1959.

Linton, R., and Wingert, P. S. *Arts of the South Seas.* New York, 1946.

Newton, D. *Art Styles of the Papuan Gulf.* New York, 1961.

Chinese Export Porcelain

MICHEL BEURDELEY

1. (above left) Dutchman: "Very fine barbarian who has removed his hat and carries his cane and sword. He travels for 7 months, arrives in the summer or autumn, and goes home in winter." – painted by a Chinese pupil of the Jesuit priest Fr. Castiglione (detail), mid-18th century
Mottahadeh Collection, New York

2. (above right) In the same series as illustration 1: "English woman, she uses snuff to drive away bad smells" (detail) Mottahadeh Collection, New York

3. Medal of the French East India Company, 1668

Any porcelain that came from the Far East was known in Europe over several centuries as 'East India Company Porcelain' or more simply as 'India porcelain'. For instance, Don Carlos, the son of Charles V, the Holy Roman Emperor, ordered an inventory of his possessions in which figures "Una porcelana grande de la Yndia". Neither 17th- nor 18th-, nor indeed 19th-century collectors and specialists were able to distinguish between Chinese and Japanese porcelain. Gabriel Saint-Aubin made accurate drawings of pieces for auction sale catalogues in the 18th century, which prove how profoundly ignorant were his contemporaries. And indeed buyers in those days do not seem to have attached particular value to the origin of the objects they bought. In 1738, one of the directors of the French East India Company wrote to his agent in Canton: "Send me all you can find whether it be Chinese or Japanese." Only a century ago, the scholarly Jacquemart wrote his key work, "The History of Porcelain" and expatiated poetically about Japanese 'famille rose' (an exclusively Chinese style) and Chinese chrysanthemum–peony motifs (an undoubted Japanese prerogative!). Perhaps the Europeans had some excuse for their ignorance, for the Chinese author of a reputed work on porcelain was able to write, at the beginning of the 20th century:

> "The Westerners place on their tables, long, oval K'ang-hsi dishes. The colours are pretty, the brush strokes sure and clean. These dishes were produced, in particular, by religious teachers at the beginning of the reign. In the centre of the dish there is a medallion surmounted with the King's crown. On the side, a lion and a two-winged dog. The date, which follows the solar calendar, is written out in old Latin. . . ."

The use of the word India to designate oriental porcelain has continued until present times owing to a confusion, so often observed in history, between the producer and the merchant who delivers the wares. 'Coromandel' lacquer screens, for instance, come from northern China, but were *shipped* to Europe from the Coromandel coast of India. "China Export Porcelain" or "China Trade Porcelain" comes nearer to describing the subject of this article than the French "Porcelaine de la Compagnie des Indes" (East India Company Porcelain) and has happily replaced the totally inaccurate "Oriental Lowestoft"; but only the Dutch "Porcelain Made to Order" (or "Bespoke Porcelain") really fits the case. The Chinese porcelain which we are going to talk about was based on the shapes and designs of European pottery, porcelain, silver and pewter. The Chinese artist copied or adapted the themes found in prints of the period, which were particularly concerned with scenes from mythology, the Bible, love and gallantry, the sea, hunting and even politics and the Masonic mysteries. Apart from these subjects special mention should be made of religious and armorial designs.

4. Rectangular 'blue and white' bottle with the arms of the Vilas-Boas family, early 17th century, Wan-li period: height 12¼ in. (31·1 cm.)
The British Museum, London

5. Group in polychrome porcelain showing portraits said to be of Admiral Duff and his wife, Ch'ien-lung period: height 7½ in. (19 cm.)
Formerly Jacques Couque Collection, Paris

FIRST EUROPEAN CONTACTS WITH CHINA

It was on 15 August 1517, the Feast of the Virgin Mary's Assumption, that the Portuguese, those frontiersmen of the sea, landed at Tamao on the coast of China. Fernão Pires de Andrade, the 'capitão', soon obtained the good will of the local population, and sailed up the Pearl River to anchor off Canton. He unfortunately left his brother Simão behind, who behaved atrociously to his Chinese neighbours, and thereafter the 'foreign devils' were feared and treated with contempt.

Nevertheless, the local merchants understood that there was profit to be drawn from more or less clandestine trade with the 'foreign devils', and they had the backing of the Viceroy at Canton. Thus the Portuguese were tolerated so long as they remained on the desert islands at the mouth of the river, and here they set up temporary markets from July to November.

Later, the Fukien authorities asked the Portuguese to help them in subduing the pirates who infested the mouth of the river, and in return were granted leave to settle on the small island of Macao, where they held their first fair in 1558.

Soon temporary straw huts gave way to solid buildings "straight and close like the teeth of a comb" as the author of the "Annals of the Ming Dynasty" wrote.

In 1560 there were 900 Portuguese in Macao, as well as numbers of Malays and Indians. A town council was set up. A few years later the town had three hospitals, three churches and five monasteries. But expansion and prosperity were soon threatened, for as early as 1600 the Dutch tried to capture Macao.

Sixteenth-century 'blue and white' porcelain, often bearing Portuguese inscriptions, is in some sort the ancestor of Chinese export porcelain. A small porringer, adapting a design in silver and dated 1541, is usually considered the oldest of such wares. It can be seen at Beja, in Portugal. Strictly speaking, however, a ewer bearing an armillary sphere should be given pride of place. For the sphere is the emblem of King Manuel of Portugal (1469–1521), although the underside of the ewer bears the 'Hsüan-Tê' mark (1426–35), dating it a hundred years before the Portuguese anchored off Cathay! – but it may well be counterfeit.

There is an exceptionally rare bottle in the Victoria and Albert Museum, one of four or five scattered about the world. The inscription states that it was made for a certain Jorge Alvarez in 1552, and it was in that year that Saint Francis Xavier, the great missionary of the East, died in the hut of a certain Jorge Alvarez. Such pieces are of course extremely rare, and are seldom within the reach of the ordinary collector; a 'blue and white' with Portuguese inscriptions, for instance, fetched about $4880 in 1961 at Sotheby's.

The 15th century was Portuguese, as far as China was concerned. But as early as 1604, the 'Freebooters' as the Dutch themselves liked to be known, seized a Lusitanian ship, the *Catarina*, and sold its cargo of porcelain in Amsterdam at great profit. This 'carrack' porcelain, late Ming in style and called after the Dutch ships that brought it to Europe, shows no sign of European influence. Both in shape and decoration it is entirely Chinese. Except for the square vase decorated with a coat of arms in the British Museum (Ill. 4), none of this porcelain could be properly described as being especially manufactured for the West.

In 1619, the Dutch established Batavia. In 1622, Cornelis de Reyers once again attacked Macao, but was driven off after bloody fighting. The Dutch then went to Formosa and bought porcelain from the Chinese engaged in the coastal trade. It is at this time, about 1635, that we can begin to speak of 'Made to order' or 'Bespoke' china. The Europeans sent wooden models for the Chinese potters to copy. This is the so-called 'transition' period, when the shapes were European, but the 'blue and white' decoration remained in the Chinese tradition. Dating from this period,

6. Jug copied from Delft-ware showing a corpulent person seated on a barrel, Ch'ien-lung period height 13¾ in. (35 cm.)
Formerly Yves Mallié Collection, Paris

7. 'Famille verte' tureen of the K'ang-hsi period length 15 in. (38 cm.)
Comte de Mahuhet Collection, Paris

8. Jug with *grisaille* decoration of the portrait of George Washington, early 19th century
height 10⅝ in. (27 cm.)
The Metropolitan Museum of Art, New York

however, there are large vases, with handles and high pedestals, that are copies of Nevers pottery.

The fall of the Ming Dynasty in 1644, the partial destruction of Ching-tê-Chên and the wars with England and France brought about the decline of Dutch power and trade. From 1660 onwards, Chinese exports suffered a period of eclipse, from which the Japanese porcelain manufacturers profited. A Dutch establishment on the small island of Deshima, opposite Nagasaki, was for two centuries the only link between Japan and the West.

By the end of the 17th century, the monopoly of Far Eastern porcelain, held until then by the Dutch, passed into the hands of the English.

In 1699 an English ship, the *Macclesfield*, received permission to enter the port of Canton, whence it set sail again with a small cargo of china and tea. From then on, the English established themselves in Canton and set up the first godowns and dwelling-houses overlooking the port, within the limits prescribed by the Chinese authorities. The fashion for Chinese porcelain developed and with it the trade increased, reaching a climax in the 18th century. (Ill. 7.) Henceforth, as Defoe asserted, there was no elegant home without its Chinese vases. In 1735, the vessels *Grafton* and *Harrison* carried 240,000 pieces of porcelain. The number of pieces exported to England throughout the 18th century is estimated at twenty-five to thirty million.

Soon the Danes and Swedes began to take part in this fruitful trade: between 1750 and 1775 alone, Sweden imported approximately eleven million pieces of china. In 1760, three ships "on the India run" brought back to Denmark 307,318 teacups and 149,337 coffee-cups. France made only sporadic attempts to enter the Eastern trade until Law set up the "Compagnie des Indes" in 1719, but thereafter took a substantial share. In 1723, the cargoes of the clippers *Vierges de Grace* and *Danae* comprised 349,972 items, of which only 348 came from Japan.

Imports continued at the same rate throughout the greater part of the 18th century, but in the reign of Louis XVI, porcelain produced at Vincennes and Sèvres competed with Chinese imports. Finally in the latter part of the century, the newly created United States of America joined the European trade. (Ill. 8.) The boats set sail from New York, Boston, Philadelphia and Salem, loaded with 'ginseng', a medicinal root very much appreciated in China, following the traditional route round the Cape of Good Hope. From 1786 to 1799, one ship-owner alone sent forty-five vessels to the Far East. In 1788 another sea route was opened up by the *Columbia*; it weathered Cape Horn and sailed up the Pacific coast-line to what is now British Columbia, where a cargo of furs was loaded. It called at Hawaii on its way to Canton. From 1800 onwards, about thirty ships were engaged in regular trading between China and the United States. They made massive profits from the sale of their return journey cargo which consisted of tea, silks, nankeen, lacquer-ware, spices, ivory, porcelain and, of course, the famous jars of stone ginger. About 1795 the China trade was bringing more profit to the United States than to any other country.

CANTON

In the 18th century, Canton was the only Chinese port open to Europeans. At first trade was done in temporary stalls and booths but soon took on such proportions that the whole character of the settlement was changed. Towards the end of the century thirteen factories faced the Pearl River. The exteriors of these European buildings were in strange contrast to their interiors, which were entirely Chinese. Relations between the Chinese and the Europeans, a "vicious and depraved

9. *Grisaille* decoration on a punch bowl showing European 'factories' at Canton, along the Pearl River, Ch'ien-lung period
diameter 14¼ in. (36·1 cm.)
The British Museum, London

10. Box enamelled in coral in the shape of a carp, early Ch'ien-lung period
Private Collection, Lisbon

11. Terrine in the form of a goose with decoration 'au naturel', Ch'ien-lung period
height 14¼ in. (36 cm.)
Formerly C. T. Loo Collection, Paris

race" were governed by the most rigorous rules. The Europeans were strictly isolated and forbidden to leave the area allotted to them. A few hundred yards back from the factories stood the buildings used by the 'Hong Merchants' who alone were entitled to trade with the foreigners. Segregation was so strict that the only link between the two communities was that of money making. European traders, after spending several years on the banks of the Pearl River, knew no more of Canton than when they first arrived. (Ill. 9.)

The 'Hong Merchants' forwarded foreign orders for porcelain to Ching-tê-Chên. But, for Europeans only passing through Canton, there were a hundred or so small workshops which could carry out designs to order on white, undecorated porcelain sent from Ching-tê-Chên for the purpose. This local craft, entirely concerned with export, was naturally held in contempt by the educated Chinese. Nevertheless, quite apart from the attraction conferred by age, the artlessness of these pieces gives them a spontaneous charm which is far from negligible.

FORMS AND SHAPES

PORCELAIN AND POTTERY

As we have seen, pottery models were sent to China as early as the beginning of the 18th century to be copied by the local potters, with the aim of meeting the taste of European customers. Naturally enough, Dutch and particularly Delft ware influenced the Chinese craftsmen. Indeed, by the middle of the 17th century such exchanges were so frequent that it is sometimes difficult to tell whether China copied Holland or vice versa. Are carp-shaped boxes of Flemish or Chinese origin? (Ill. 10.) This fish, it should be remembered, is one of the most ancient symbols of the Celestial Empire. Little cows with flowery garlands are undoubtedly copied from Delft, whilst Delft parrots clearly ape their cousins in biscuit of the K'ang-hsi period. Are the large goose terrines copies of Rato? (Ill. 11.) The question has not yet been finally resolved.

At the end of the 17th century the French potteries at Nevers, Lille, Rouen, and a little later at Montpellier and Moustiers, were furnishing numerous models of tankards, pitchers, goblets, water-coolers, vases with handles on high pedestals, posy-holders, and square flagons which they themselves had copied from Italy.

At the beginning of the 18th century table ware by various manufacturers, hors d'œuvre dishes with handles, spice boxes and sugar casters were also copied in Chinese porcelain. One of the most curious of such pieces is a flat tureen with scalloped edges (Ill. 12) in the Pierre Vandermeersch Collection, Paris; the handle of the lid is in the form of a coiled snake. It is an exact copy of a tureen made at Rouen at the end of the 17th century. The Chinese tried to imitate the famous blue and red Rouen enamels. But since they possessed neither the same ingredients nor the same clay, they only achieved an adaptation, but with quite happy results.

Models sent out from England were scrupulously copied. (Ill. 13.) Battersea comfit and patch boxes, Worcester punch bowls and beer mugs, Staffordshire openwork plates, Wedgwood pipe-clay tureens, Battersea or Bow lidded boxes shaped like quails or partridge. The Bow Pottery became so impregnated with sinophilia that all its wares were stamped "Made at New-Canton 1750"!

The first pottery at Meissen in Saxony sent various models: tobacco jars, small multi-lobed cups with the monogram of Augustus Rex in blue on a yellow ground, Chinese statuettes, fruit baskets standing on pedestals in the shape of tree-trunks, dogs lying down or sitting up, the famous pug-dogs enamelled in naturalistic colours. (Ill. 14.) All these were copied with such exactness that only the expert eye can perceive the origin of manufacture. (See colour plate facing p. 345.)

12. (above right) Imitation Rouen faïence tureen
Pierre Vandermeersch Collection, Paris

13. (right centre) Tureen in the form of a boar's head, whose shape is inspired by similar examples in cream ware
length 15 in. (38 cm.)
Formerly C. T. Loo Collection, Paris

14. (top left) Coral porcelain dog slightly different from the famous pugs from Meissen
height $7\frac{1}{4}$ in. (18·5 cm.)
Formerly C. T. Loo Collection, Paris

15. (above) Saucer in imitation Sèvres porcelain with enamel decoration after Cotteau, about 1790
diameter $5\frac{3}{8}$ in. (13·6 cm.)
The British Museum, London

16. (below) Vase in the form of an urn copied from an example of Swedish porcelain from Marienberg, 1775
The Metropolitan Museum of Art, New York

17. (below) Wine-cooler for bottles, in 'Famille verte' enamels, early 18th century
diameter $21\frac{3}{4}$ in. (55 cm.)
Formerly Serge Blazy Collection, Paris

Colour Plate I. (above) Bowl after William Hogarth, *The Gates of Calais; or The Roast Beef of Old England* diameter 16 in. (40·5 cm.) Delplace Collection, Brussels

18. Small flower-pot holder, after an original model in silver, early 18th century
Medeiros e Almeida Collection, Lisbon

19. 'Famille verte' jug after a model in silver plate, early 18th century
height $10\frac{1}{4}$ in. (26 cm.)
Formerly Yves Mallié Collection, Paris

20. 'Famille verte' dish with the armorial bearings of England, K'ang-hsi period
The British Museum, London

Colour Plate II. (below) Dancing group after a Meissen model
height $5\frac{3}{8}$ in. (13·6 cm.)
The Victoria and Albert Museum, London

France, in its turn, sent its earliest soft paste models to be copied and then Sèvres followed with vases, 'gros-bleu' cups with polychrome enamels in light relief, such as those immortalized by Cotteau. The little saucer reproduced opposite is an excellent example. (Ill. 15.)

From Sweden came flower-pot holders, and urns (Ill. 16) which were so successful that the Chinese continued to make them for fifty years and sent them to all their markets in Europe and to the United States.

This seems to be the right place to advise the reader and collector to exercise the greatest caution in the matter of dating and identifying pieces. No matter how rare a piece might be, the Chinese potter would continue to reproduce it, stocking up 'white' examples, that is to say in an un-enamelled state. For example, I once happened on a cooling bowl (monteith) in Palermo decorated with magnificent 'famille rose' enamels, and it so happened that a few years before a similar bowl had passed through my hands, but this one was decorated in 'famille verte' enamels! (Ill. 17.)

SILVER AND PEWTER WARE

Pottery and porcelain were not the only models used by potters of the Celestial Empire; they were also provided with silver and pewter articles and with goldsmiths' drawings from Europe to copy. A number of eight-sided 'famille verte' dishes with gadrooned borders are imitations of French silver dishes of the Régence period. The 'famille rose' or 'famille verte' knife-handles copy silver knives known as 'à crosse'.

England in the 18th century, having supplanted Holland in the Far Eastern market, despatched to its representatives in Canton candle-sticks, teapots, coffee-pots, sugar casters, sauce boats, tureens and covered meat dishes, oil-jars, trays, bowls and glassware, all of which are faithfully reproduced in porcelain. Still in 'famille verte', small ribbed coolers with handles (Ill. 18) and helmet-shaped goblets are copies of silver-plated articles. (Ill. 19.) The art of working in precious metals is very different to that of ceramics and yet we find details, such as pinning for example, faithfully reproduced though they are quite unnecessary in pottery.

A less noble substance, but widely used in the 17th and 18th centuries in Europe – pewter – cannot be passed over. Tankards, bowls with handles, goblets, wall cisterns with their basins, pots for everyday use, all were reproduced with great precision in polychrome porcelain and even in 'blanc-de-Chine'.

DECORATION – INFLUENCES

ARMORIAL BEARINGS

Table services of export china ware decorated with coats of arms deserve special study, for they can tell us a great deal. For instance, when the arms of husband and wife appear together and taking into account other factors, it is possible to date a service to within a very few years. (In general two years elapsed between the placing of an order and delivery.) As an example let us take the service made for Charles O'Brien, a peer of Ireland, Lieutenant-General of the King of France's Armies, awarded the Order of the Sanctus Spiritus on 1 January 1746 and promoted Marshal of France in 1757. Since his arms showed the collar of the Sanctus Spiritus but not the Marshal's baton, it is easy to deduce that the service was ordered between 1746 and 1757.

There are many other criteria which help to date such services. At the end of the 17th and beginning of the 18th centuries, during the reign of the great emperor K'ang-hsi (1662–1722) armorial bearings occupied the whole of the centre of the dish, whilst the border was decorated in Chinese style. The 'famille

21. Dish decorated with the Imperial arms of Russia
diameter 13 in. (33 cm.)
Formerly Pierre Blazy Collection, Paris

22. Dish with the Hohenzollern family armorial bearings carrying the proud device 'Gott mit Uns'
length 18⅜ in. (46·6 cm.)
The British Museum, London

23. Bottle decorated after a design by Cornelius Pronck entitled *A Visit to the Doctor's*
height 11 in. (28 cm.)
Formerly C. T. Loo Collection, Paris

verte' dish in the British Museum, reproduced opposite, is typical of this period. In the centre are the arms of England and the word 'Engelandt', which suggests that this dish reached Europe aboard a Dutch ship, rather than in one on His Majesty's Service. (Ill. 20.) The wide rim is divided into twelve sections, decorated alternately with a flower vase and Chinese young women.

Round about 1730–46, the coat of arms still took up a considerable space, but the floral 'famille rose' border remained Chinese. As the century advanced, however, the armorial bearings diminished in size and towards the end were replaced by a monogram. A return to Antiquity was then, of course, the fashion and the rim was decorated with a blue band spangled with golden stars or a sepia band entwined with ribbons.

The Ching-tê-Chên craftsmen scrupulously copied the designs that were sent to them. Indeed they were over-faithful, which sometimes produced surprising results. For instance a plate bearing the arms of the Andros family in Guernsey is also decorated with the words 'green', 'blue' and 'red', used by the artist in Europe to indicate the colouring required by his sketch; the Chinese artist no doubt thought they enhanced the effect!

The great ones of the earth everywhere owned armorial table services. Peter the Great, Emperor of Russia, ordered a set of pharmaceutical jars decorated with the two-headed eagle; an order, by the way, prompted by the low price of Chinese wares rather than from any aesthetic motive. Catherine the Great owned a table service decorated with the arms of Russia (Ill. 21), which was so exact a replica of that at Gatschina, the Imperial summer residence, that the identification marks (numbers in red and Cyrillic lettering, incomprehensible to the Chinese) are indistinguishable. Little remains of the Spanish Royal Family's china ware, but the British Museum owns a 'blue and white' flask that belonged to Philip II, and the Escorial has a Philip V pitcher decorated with polychrome armorial bearings. There are two large fluted vases in an English collection which bear the arms of the French Regent and elsewhere there are a few pieces with the Royal Arms of France. But once again let me warn you to be cautious, there are far more imitations about than genuine articles. For instance there are a number of entirely genuine pieces, made in China from Chinese clay but which have been overlaid with Dutch decoration; this is not too bad . . . but there are also Japanese copies (which can be recognized by the raised mark found on the foot) and copies made in France by the firm of Samson in the 19th century.

The British Museum possesses a dish with the arms of the Hohenzollerns; under a sumptuously decorated tent, two rural deities support the royal coat of arms of the Prussian family with the proud device 'Gott mit Uns'. (Ill. 22.) The Swedish East India Company offered King Gustavus III a service for his castle at Gripsholm. Queen Juliana-Maria of Denmark, wife of Frederick V, had a service made with her name inscribed on the wide golden border.

Great cities followed the royal example. One sometimes finds the coat of arms of Amsterdam or that of The Hague, recognizable thanks to the stork's long beak. Church dignitaries ordered large sets; that belonging to José de Castro, Bishop of Oporto, Patriarch of Lisbon, was composed of five hundred pieces.

SKETCHES AND MODELS

The various East India Companies did not confine themselves to sending out samples to be copied, whether ceramic or in precious metals. For their customers were insistent that wares should suit their taste. An agent of the French company received an imperative order, "Cease making dragons, send us flowers." Some of

24. Punch-bowl decorated with a mythological scene in polychrome enamel
diameter 15 in. (38·1 cm.)
Formerly Sparks Collection, London

25. *Moses saved from the waters*, an unexpected subject painted by Chinese artists on a plate
diameter 8½ in. (21·6 cm.)
The Victoria and Albert Museum, London

26. Plate decorated in polychrome enamel with the scene *Jesus in the midst of the Elders*
The Victoria and Albert Museum, London

the best European artists made sketches or models for plates, vases, soup tureens etc. to be carried out in China. But this obvious and comparatively simple procedure does not seem to have been widely followed; few of these sketches and models have survived. Sketches for a table service designed by Christian Precht in 1736, and intended for Count Axel Sparre, have been found amongst the archives of Maltesharm Castle in Sweden. The set is conceived as a whole but there are variations from piece to piece. The dishes are divided diagonally, each half decorated by totally different arabesques and scrolls.

Cornelius Pronck (1691–1759) made several sketches for the great Dutch East India Company, whose motto 'Concordiae resparvae crescunt' can be found on small sherbet-cups. One of the best-known sketches, *Lady with a Parasol*, which was adapted from a 17th-century Chinese porcelain, was often used during the K'ang-hsi period in iron-red enamel and later in 'famille rose' Ch'ien-lung enamels. Another sketch attributed to Pronck, *A Visit to the Doctor's*, also appears on a number of pieces. (Ill. 23.) Finally another design, *Cluster of ostrich feathers on a chequered background* is often attributed to Pronck, though there is no documentary evidence to support the claim.

THEMES TAKEN FROM PRINTS AND ENGRAVINGS

The main source used by Chinese potters was, however, European prints and engravings. In 1698 the French ship *Amphitrite* arrived in Canton with a large number of engravings by Poussin, Le Sueur and Mignard. This was during the reign of K'ang-hsi and most of the themes were reproduced in 'blue and white' porcelain. In the following reign, Ch'ien-lung, 'grisaille' scenes appear, almost indistinguishable from the original hatchings of the engraving and carried out in Chinese ink. In a letter dated 25 January 1722, Father Entrecolles, a Jesuit missionary wrote: "We tried to paint some vases with the finest black Chinese ink, but we were not successful."

The scenes and subjects which the Chinese artists preferred fall into a number of categories such as: mythological, Biblical, love and gallantry, marine, hunting and sporting, political and masonic. To these can be added themes from the folklore of each country concerned. Let us take a glance at each of these main headings.

MYTHOLOGY

Such themes are usually found on dishes and plates and much more rarely on articles such as vases, pots, jars and so on. (Ill. 24.) The design is outlined either in blue, purple-violet or Chinese black. Some of the pieces are enamelled in 'famille rose' such as the *Judgement of Paris*, of which there are several examples. The slightly slant-eyed young shepherd is shown admiring the voluptuous forms of the goddesses Hera, Aphrodite and Pallas Athene, as each claims the prize for beauty. This pagan scene may well have surprised the artists of Cathay who had not been bred to depict nudity. One of the most successful pieces, which imitates the tones of the engraving perfectly is *Achilles being dipped in the Styx* which according to tradition was based on a Le Sueur engraving. This dish has one unusual feature: there is a polychrome shield on the reverse side.

BIBLICAL THEMES

The Chinese treated Biblical subjects whose meaning, it must be said, was totally alien to them, with just the same enthusiasm. It would be very interesting to find the original which served as a model for the grisaille cup *Moses saved from the waters* in the Victoria and Albert Museum (Ill. 25): Pharaoh's daughter (wearing a small crown) and her three handmaidens, accompanied by a little

27. A Dutch ship on a smallish dish with a Chinese rim, probably by a Cantonese artist
diameter 10⅝ in. (27 cm.)
Private Collection, Paris

28. Cup representing whale fishers in the Arctic after Adriaen van Salm
height 19¼ in. (4·9 cm.)
The Rijksmuseum, Amsterdam

29. 'Blue and white' bottle with the symbols of the Passion, early 17th century
height 15⅜ in. (38·9 cm.)
The British Museum, London

greyhound, are depicted against a landscape of pure fantasy, which is difficult to reconcile with the Nile valley.

A polychrome plate, formerly from the collection of Basil Ionides (now in the British Museum) is equally interesting; the theme of the decoration apparently being *Jesus in the midst of the Elders*. (Ill. 26.) The floral border is in a purely Chinese manner. Also in the British Museum is a dish representing *The Triumph of Mordecai*. Although the subject may appear to be inspired by an engraving by Beauvarlet, the treatment is an imitation of Italian majolica.

SCENES OF LOVE AND GALLANTRY

We all know that the Chinese always excelled in such themes. Their erotic paintings are often masterpieces. Characters such as 'le voyeur' or Peeping Tom of La Fontaine's "Tales" are a commonplace of Chinese literature. In the 18th century French artists such as Boucher, Pater, Watteau, Joullin and Moreau le Jeune were the most highly prized by the Chinese. This does not mean that the work of others was not warmly welcomed: the Dutch artist Picard, whose touch recalls the contemporary French mannerisms, for instance. In this connection there is a curious plate with a design taken from a woodcut by A. Bloemaert (born in Haarlem in 1634); the Chinese artist no doubt found the Dutch landscape somewhat monotonous so he added a range of mountains for good value.

THE SEA AND SHIPS

Travellers by sea, breaking their voyage at Canton, gave their orders directly to the merchants; it is thus not surprising that maritime subjects should have been so much in vogue especially from the second half of the 18th century onwards. (Ill. 27.) Even the poorest sailor could bring back a bowl depicting the 'Departure' or 'Return' of the Sailor, or the 'Portrait' of the ship he was sailing in, as a souvenir. Some shipbuilding families, in St-Malo particularly, still have some such specimens which have a sentimental value.

These ship 'portraits' though made to a specific order were stereotypes. For example: a dish in the Guimet Museum, dated 1765, shows the ship *Vryburg* captained by Jacob Ryzick. A similar dish in the British Museum shows the same ship captained by Christ. Schooneman; the date is different. The perspective effect, which enables both the stern and the prow of the ship to be depicted in the same design, is especially noteworthy: (this anomaly is also to be found in European earthenware of the same period).

All these articles arrived 'white' from Ching-tê-Chên to be decorated on the spot in the workshops of Canton. A French traveller's account (1797) provides an insight into this procedure:

> "We were driven by curiosity every day to visit the different merchants in Canton. Usually we went to the workshops of the decorators, and painters of porcelain. The biscuit-ware is painted and then covered with glaze. If one wants articles painted with a design brought from Europe, it has to be sent to 'Kin Tet Chin' but then it is not ready until the following year. Travellers who cannot wait this long, buy the pieces of porcelain in the white in Canton, and have them painted there and then in their presence. In this case the painting is done on top of the glaze, and the two are fused by firing."

Shipbuilders and all the administrators of the Far Eastern trading companies had whole dinner services made with their coats of arms. On the ship plying between Macao and Lisbon, the ship's dinner service was of Chinese manufacture.

In France, the Count of Maurepas, Secretary of State to the Admiralty, had a

30. Bottle decorated *en grisaille* with a portrait of Calvin
The Victoria and Albert Museum, London

31. Punch-bowl showing a fox-hunt in full cry, late 18th century
diameter 13¾ in. (35 cm.)
Formerly Count de Bondy Collection, Paris

32. Medallion from a punch-bowl showing a horse-race, late 18th century
Henry Francis du Pont Winterthur Museum, Delaware

dinner service showing a galley. The Abbé Terray, the syndic to the French East India Company, and the Duke of Penthièvre, High Admiral of France, both ordered special services.

Apart from these services which, in spite of their interest, are ordinary table ware, several pieces exist with semi-maritime subjects. There is for example a polychrome plate, the design of which shows a Dutch vessel lying at anchor in a bay under a table-topped peak, which puzzled collectors a long time. It is in fact Table Bay, discovered in 1503 by Antonio de Saldanha, and is where Cape Town stands today.

No less interesting is a cup known as the "Whale Hunt" in the Rijksmuseum in Amsterdam. (Ill. 28.) Sailors in frail open boats on a very rough sea are harpooning enormous whales, whilst another sailor in the foreground is shooting at a polar bear, watched benevolently by a seagull perched on a rock. Near by are ships flying Batavian flags. These scenes are inspired by the grisailles of Adriaen van Salm, an artist who lived in the middle of the 17th century. The artlessness of this drawing is far removed, it must be admitted, from the minute precision of the Dutch painter, but it seems likely that the Chinese artist never saw the original and had to rely on Delft plates reproducing the same motif.

RELIGIOUS THEMES

First of all, let us dismiss the legend according to which pieces with religious themes are known as 'jesuit porcelain'; there is no basis for such an appellation. Let us recall briefly the exploits of those remarkable priests who went to the Court of the Emperor of China. Father Matteo Ricci, a famous Italian Jesuit, spent twenty years before gaining admittance to the Palace of Wan-li. He used his extraordinary gifts as mathematician and astronomer, and his skill in making astrolabes and clocks, to win over the Emperor.

Until K'ang-hsi came to the throne (1662) there were few Jesuits in China. Though they were treated as no more than Imperial civil servants, they had been allowed to build a church within the walls of Peking. They played a more important part in the artistic field. Father Castiglione, with the assistance of Father Attiret, a well-known painter, founded a school of painting connected with the Ching-tê-Chên workshops. This school had a marked influence on objects intended for the Imperial Palace. Later, however, rivalries caused by the arrival of Franciscans and Dominicans and conflicts over ancestor worship led to the dissolution of the order in 1773, a great disaster for Christianity in China.

In fact, pieces of porcelain depicting religious subjects are rare up to the 18th century. A bottle in the British Museum on which the symbols of the Passion are shown in blue on a white ground dates from the last years of the reign of Wan-li, which is exceptional. (Ill. 29.) After the partial destruction of the Ching-tê-Chên works, following dynastic disputes, all that we possess are a few bowls, bottles and plates, bearing religious insignia and dating from the end of the 17th century. The square basin with floral 'famille verte' decoration surrounding the monogram of the Society of Jesus, on display in the Museum of Antique Art in Lisbon, is one of the first polychrome pieces known to us.

In the 18th century, many more themes were used and executed in either Chinese ink, red *camaïeu* or polychrome enamels: *The Birth of Jesus*, *The Baptism of Christ*, *The Crucifixion*, *The Resurrection* and *The Ascension*. It is strange to note that this spate of production coincides with the reigns of Yung-cheng and Ch'ien-lung, emperors who were relentlessly anti-Christian, the Jesuits being merely tolerated at that time. It is obvious that the Chinese ceramic artists considered the execution

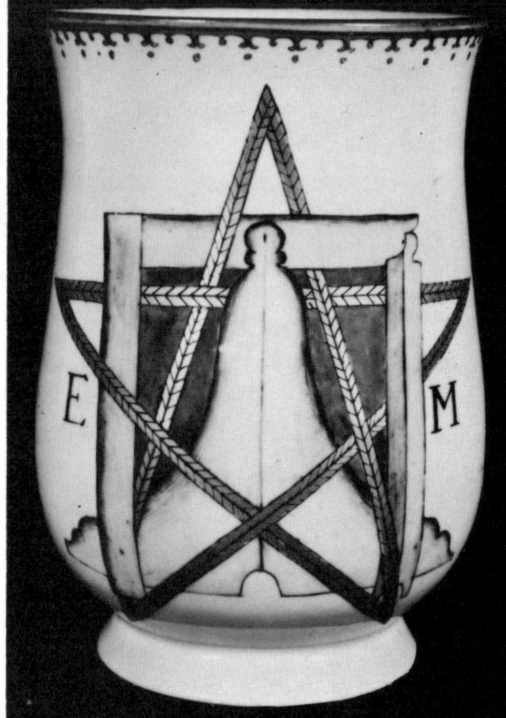

33. Mug with Masonic emblems and initials E.M., mid-18th century
height 6¼ in. (15·9 cm.)
The British Museum, London

34. 'Blue and white' plate showing a house being wrecked during a revolt in Rotterdam in 1690
diameter 7⅞ in. (20 cm.)
The British Museum, London

35. Small bowl with a saucer depicting a curious birth which took place in the Netherlands in 1647
Nijstad Collection, The Hague

of commissions by pious families or congregations merely as lucrative work. Apart from a majority of articles especially related to the Catholic religion, some exist with the portraits of the great reformers, Luther and Calvin. (Ill. 30.) The British Museum even has in its possession two rare dishes, one showing a synagogue, and the other a figure of John of Leyden, the Anabaptist leader.

MISCELLANEOUS THEMES

Sporting subjects constitute another favourite theme which flourished particularly in the second part of the 18th century, and the first years of the 19th century. A certain number of punch bowls show fox-hunting scenes (Ill. 31) or the incidents of horse races. (Ill. 32.) (We should not forget that the famous Epsom Derby was founded in 1782.)

It seems that during the same period (the end of the 18th century, and the first years of the 19th century) a certain number of masonic emblems (Ill. 33), such as suns in glory, planets, crescent moons, Solomon's seals, squares and compasses, were very much the rage in England and in the United States. Other themes were drawn from contemporary history, perpetuating the more colourful aspects of events. And here again, the Chinese were impartial and without malice. For instance two pitchers were produced, one bearing the portrait of the Duke of Cumberland, the victor of Culloden, and the other that of the Young Pretender, Bonnie Prince Charlie, who was defeated.

One bowl of exceptionally high quality in the Delplace Collection in Brussels is decorated with a copy of one of Hogarth's works now in the Tate Gallery: *The Gates of Calais; or The Roast Beef of Old England.* (See colour plate facing p. 345.) It recalls a trip to the Continent which Hogarth made in 1748, when he was subjected to "warlike display, pompous parading of religion, and much ado about nothing". Hogarth's anger had been aroused, for he had made a sketch of the drawbridge at Calais and was arrested and expelled from France.

Finally certain pieces commemorate isolated incidents which do not fit into any category. They were made to the order of individual customers who wished to perpetuate some strange event of importance to themselves. Such pieces were usually made for the Dutch market. For instance one depicts the pillaging of a certain Jacob van Zuyle's home at Nyevelt, Rotterdam in 1690. (Ill. 34.) This worthy had ordered the execution of a prisoner. Another shows a stirring childbirth scene; a bull has tossed a young woman high into the sky and the child appears floating in mid-air. (Ill. 35.) When the child grew to man's estate, he felt that such an unusual entry into the world was worth commemorating and ordered a set of china depicting the scene.

Chinese export porcelain was long considered a minor art. But the distinction between 'major' and 'minor' arts which we have inherited from Renaissance Italy implies a scale in values. We do not share this attitude. Shang ritual bronzes, Byzantine mosaics, medieval stained glass, were in their time major arts, just as was the weaving of the nomad tribes of Asia. Any rigorous classification is inevitably arbitrary. The cultivated Chinese, for instance, consider painting and calligraphy as noble arts and sculpture as a craft.

The artists of the Celestial Empire viewed with a fresh and somewhat astonished eye the artistic products of the West, when they were set to copy from or seek inspiration in paintings, prints or precious metalwork. Their vision is not the same as ours, and it is in this that lies the charm of Chinese export porcelain. It was no doubt a hybrid art, but it is full of fantasy and the Chinese were able to demonstrate their undoubted superiority in the art of firing earth and clay.

Ancient Peruvian Gold

ADRIAN DIGBY

Paradoxically the Inca period, about which we know more than about any other in Peruvian archaeological history, is the one from which fewest golden relics have survived. The "Gold of the Indies" was for the most part melted down, either by the *Conquistadors* themselves or by European monarchs and bankers. Britain was as guilty of this iconoclasm as the Spaniards. During the 19th century, for example, vast quantities of gold were looted from graves in Costa Rica and melted down under the auspices of the Bank of England. In Peru, *huaqueros* or treasure hunters armed with a long probing rod wandered about pushing their rods into the sand seeking for ancient graves. Once they encountered an obstacle they dug recklessly in search of the gold and pottery they hoped to find, taking no account of stratification or other data useful to archaeologists. As often as not they melted the gold down. Otherwise they sold it with the pottery vessels as curios to passing travellers.

It is only recently that the artistic qualities of the Peruvian goldsmiths' work have been fully recognized. Within living memory the British Museum used to pay the bullion value plus ten per cent for Peruvian gold – simply to prevent it from being melted down. Today collectors are ready to pay many times that value, and the demand has inspired forgers to make replicas, often so accurate that experts are deceived. Other forgers, more imaginative perhaps but less gifted, produce incredible monstrosities which the beginner would recognize as forgeries.

If Inca gold specimens are rare, the gold of earlier periods, preserved in the ground until discovered either by the archaeologist or the *huaquero*, has survived in substantial quantities. Today the stringent antiquities laws of the Peruvian government make it almost impossible to take ancient gold or other antiquities out of the country legitimately, and most specimens in the great museums of Europe or in private collections are the souvenirs of travellers, obtained from *huaqueros* in the old days, but undoubtedly a fairly flourishing business in smuggling antiquities adds specimens, which should legally remain in Peru, to the number of specimens outside their country of origin, and were it possible to prove that they came out after the enactment of the Peruvian laws governing the export of antiquities, the Peruvian government would have a very strong case for insisting on their return.

1. Chavin sheet gold ornament in the form of a puma
The Textile Museum, Washington, D.C.

Most national museums of archaeology have examples of Peruvian gold, and there are a few famous private collections. In Peru the most outstanding among the private collections are those of Señor Mujica Gallo, and Señor Rafael Larco Hoyle. In North America the Robert Woods Bliss Collection is outstanding. In Europe there is no collection which can rival these, but many interesting specimens can be seen in museums.

The history of gold-working, which was the beginning of metallurgy in the

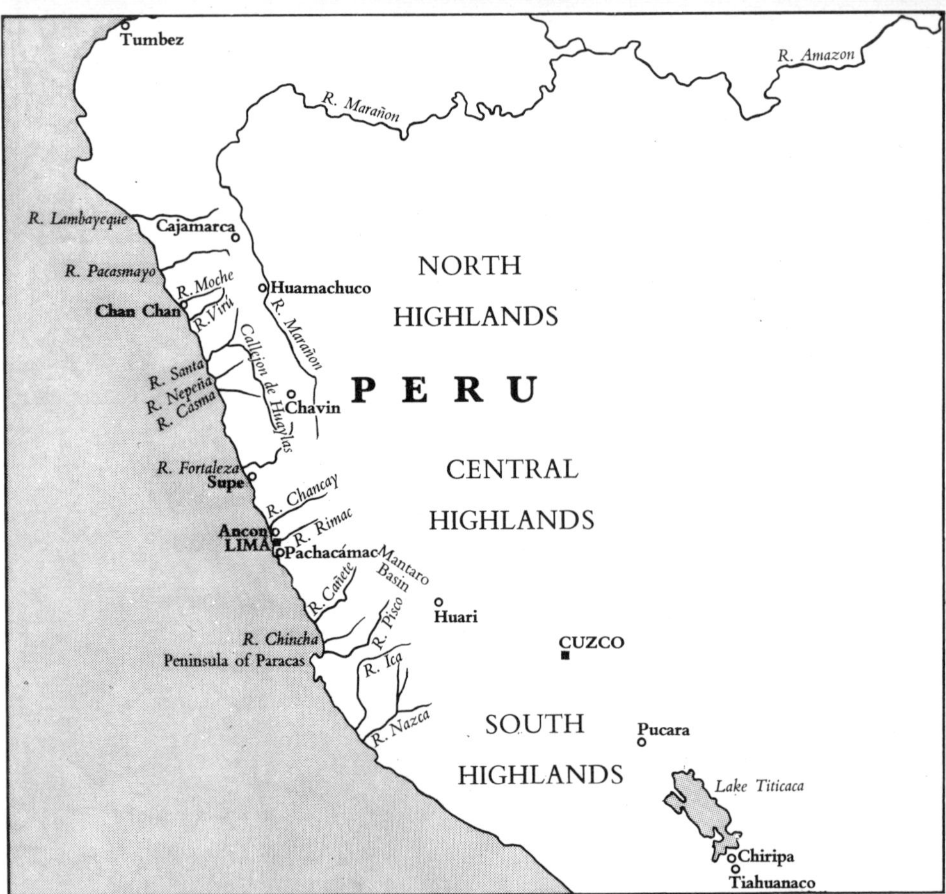

Map of Ancient Peru

2. Chavin gold headband from Lambayeque
diameter 6¾ in. (17·1 cm.)
The Museum of the American Indian, New York

3. Pectoral ornament, Chavin style,
earlier than A.D. 950
The Cleveland Museum of Art, Ohio

New World, is a long one. The earliest gold-workers, so far as we know, were the people of the Chavin culture which takes its name from the narrow valley of Chavin de Huantar in the northern Andes. The site is a religious one, consisting of a temple building and various rectangular enclosures. The works are on such a scale that archaeologists do not believe they could have been built by the limited population the valley would support. They therefore believe that the site was a centre for pilgrims, who came to worship, to contribute labour to the building of the temple, and then to return home with ideas of Chavin art styles implanted in their minds. The theory is supported by the fact that traces of art from other parts of Peru dating from this period 1500 B.C. to 400 B.C. all show a close affinity with Chavin. They worshipped a feline god, probably the puma, who is either represented naturally, or as a man with ferocious teeth, and sometimes also with snakes, which may well represent lightning issuing from his head.

Stone-working is the medium of expression *par excellence* at Chavin, but pottery and gold-working were also practised. The only technique they knew of working gold was to hammer it flat, and then to emboss it by laying it on some yielding substance like skin, and to hammer out a design with a thin pointed tool. We can easily imagine how gold-working came about. Nuggets of natural gold would be found in the dry beds of streams in summer. We can visualize people hammering these attractive lumps to detach flakes, the only technique they knew. But the soft gold would merely dent instead of flaking. Repeated hammering would flatten it. But it must have hardened the gold too. Some genius must have thought of annealing it, that is to say softening it by heating. How this occurred we shall never know. Perhaps they knew that food was softened by cooking and tried roasting it. Perhaps they thought this new substance they had found had some affinity with fire. This is idle speculation. All we know for certain is that they must have devised some means of annealing, otherwise they could not have beaten the gold into the thin plates which they used for making headbands, crowns, ear ornaments and pectoral ornaments to sew on their *ponchos*. Nearly always the subject chosen was some variant of the puma god.

A very charming example of the latter in a fairly naturalistic form is a little embossed plate (Ill. 1) which belongs to the Textile Museum in Washington. The

Colour Plate. Gold necklace, Chimu culture and
a gold llama, Inca period
necklace length 25 in. (63·5 cm.), llama 2½ in. (6·3 cm.)
The British Museum, London

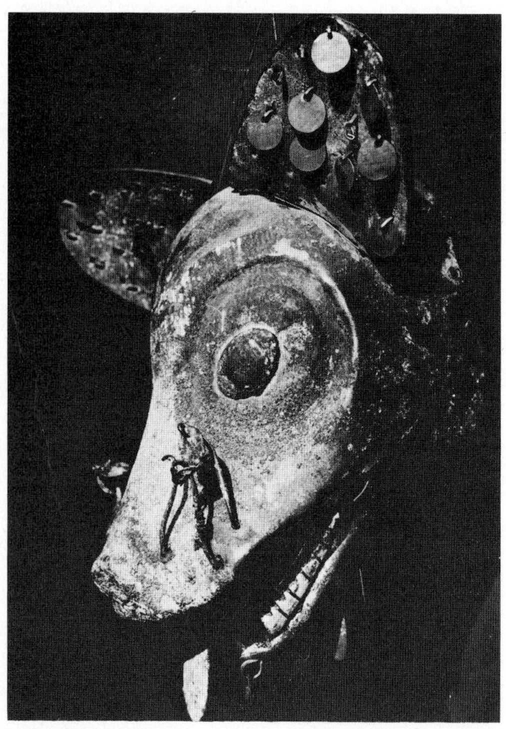

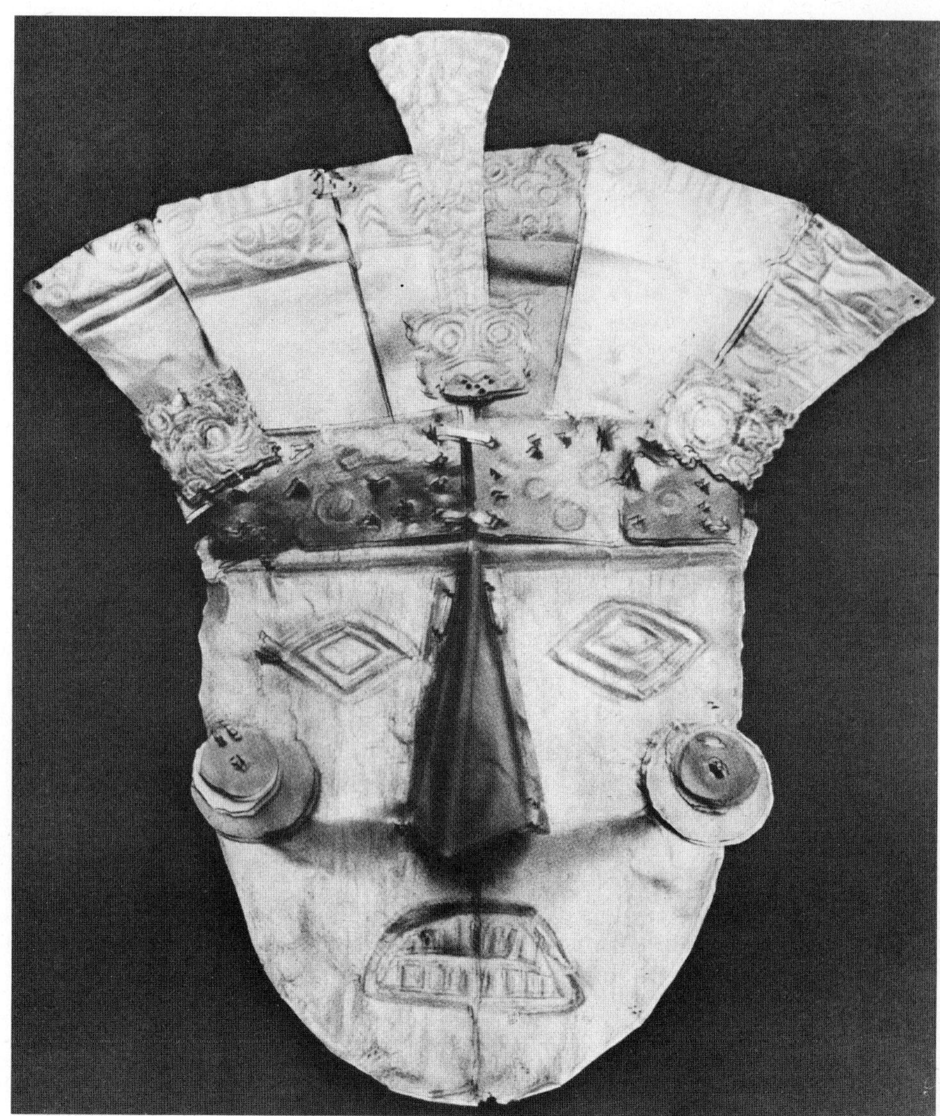

4. (right) Funeral mask, Nasca, 7th or 8th century
height 12⅝ in. (32 cm.)
The Mujica Gallo Collection, Lima

5. (below right) Mouth mask, Nasca
width 5¼ in. (13·3 cm.)
The British Museum, London

6. (above left) Fox's head, Moché civilization
length 6 in. (15·2 cm.)
Linden-Museum, Stuttgart

7. (below left) Deity (container for coca), Proto-Chimu or Mochica, between the 4th and 8th centuries
height 24¾ in. (62·5 cm.)
The Mujica Gallo Collection, Lima

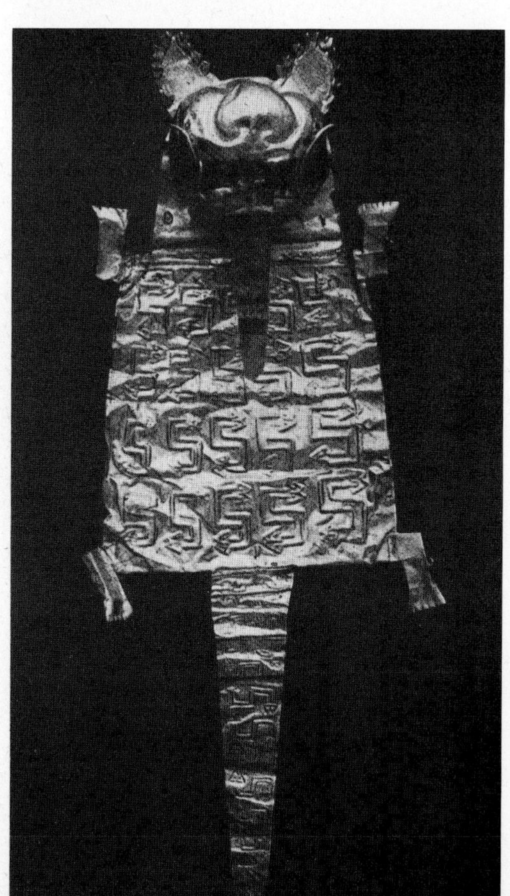

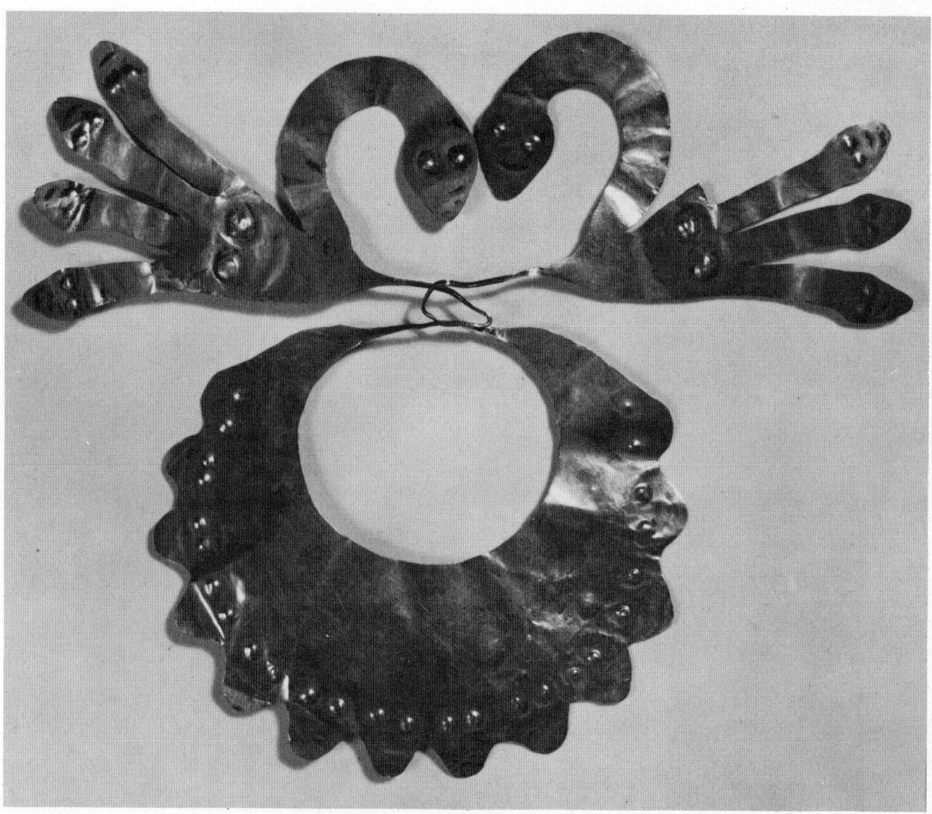

8. Stirrup-spout vessel, attributed to Chavin culture
The American Museum of Natural History, New York

9. Whistling vase, late coastal Tiahuanaco culture
height, excluding plumes 8½ in. (21·4 cm.)
Dumbarton Oaks, Washington, D.C.

head is characterized by the long and overlapping canine teeth which are such an important feature of the iconography of this god, and the tail ends in another head of similar but smaller form. This reduplication is a quite common phenomenon in Peruvian art. A very similar head forms a kind of buckle on a headband found at Lambayeque and now in the Museum of the American Indian in New York. (Ill. 2.) Two features are interesting in this circlet, the deep and rather heavy, almost sculptural treatment of the head, which is reminiscent in form of the stone-working which was the major art of the Chavin people, and the restraint of the artist who left the rest of the band unembellished. As a final example of the art of Chavin in gold there is a very fine pectoral ornament in the form of a mask of the jaguar god, with the projecting fangs and the snakes mentioned earlier. (Ill. 3.)

The religious unity which was such a characteristic of the Chavin period seems to have broken down *circa* 400 B.C. for this is followed by a period of technical innovations in all fields, carried out on a regional basis. Irrigation systems were developed, and different building materials were tried. Pottery was fired in an oxidizing furnace to produce a red ware in place of the black previously used, and there were great developments in textile design. In the art of metal-working alloys began to be used, which implies a knowledge of the art of smelting. While new inventions began locally they soon spread to neighbouring areas. Art in this period seems to have been subordinated to technical improvements. In only two places were there any outstanding artistic achievements: Salinar in the North, where modelled pottery carried on some of the traditional shapes of the Cupisnique culture, a derivative of Chavin, and Paracas in the South, where wonderful textiles in beautiful colours reproduced to some extent the iconography of the older universal religion. This process continued for a period of about four hundred years. Some authorities believe it was longer. In the early years of the Christian era the techniques of the 'experimental' period we have been considering reached their ultimate development, and the craftsmen produced art of the highest order. The five centuries which were the Golden Age of Peru are named the Master Craftsman Period. Two great civilizations, with different techniques and different schools of art, were to dominate the period. In the North, the people of Moché in the Chicama valley became the heirs of the Salinamar and Chavin cultures. In the South the Nasca culture grew out of the neighbouring Paracas cultures, and so also indirectly inherited the Chavin tradition. The great difference between Moché and Nasca, between North and South, is most clearly shown in the pottery. That of the former was beautifully modelled in the round, but limited to two colours, red and cream. In the Nasca pottery, relief and sculptural qualities were almost unknown, but they painted their vessels in brilliant colours with designs inspired by the textiles of Paracas. This difference is noticeable too in the gold- and metal-working of the two areas.

While the Mochica were adapting advanced metal techniques, casting, soldering, smelting and alloying their metals, Nasca goldsmiths kept the simple hammering and embossing of gold and silver. Their wares included masks both for the living and the dead, figures of men and gods and animals, bracelets, greaves and various pendants. All were beaten flat to obtain the greatest display from the smallest quantity of gold. The masks for the living and the dead can be distinguished by the presence or absence of orbits. The masks for the dead, or funerary masks, were really false faces to be placed at the top of a bundle of textiles in which the body of the deceased, with knees drawn up into the chest, and arms folded, was wrapped. A fine example of this type of mask (Ill. 4) probably dates from the end of the Nasca period, between the 7th and 8th centuries A.D. It also shows the technical

10. A pair of ear spools, Chimu culture
diameter $3\frac{1}{2}$ in. (8·8 cm.)
The Museum of Primitive Art, New York

11. Crown, Chimu, 12th or 13th century
height $7\frac{7}{8}$ in. (20 cm.)
The Mujica Gallo Collection, Lima

limitations of the Nasca people. It is made of a number of thin plates hammered out and embossed. The nose, which if it were made integrally with the rest of the plate, would have had to be hammered over a former and repeatedly annealed, simply consists of a triangular piece of metal bent and sewn on to the rest of the face with a flat ribbon of gold about one-sixteenth of an inch thick, as also are the embossed plates which form the head-dress. Closely related to the facial masks were curious ornaments sometimes known as mouth masks. (Ill. 5.) In essence they are very large nose ornaments, suspended from a perforation in the septum of the nose. The aperture for the mouth is surrounded by a scalloped and embossed plate, and projecting like whiskers are a series of snakes, two of which curve upwards and inwards as if to frame the eyes. This is clearly a survival of the snakes' heads we have seen as an appendage of the puma god of Chavin, but the ornament lacks the sculptural qualities of the earlier work.

In the same tradition of thin highly embossed sheets are curious zoomorphic ornaments, examples of which can be seen in the collections both of the late Robert Woods Bliss and of Señor Mujica Gallo. They have been variously interpreted as birds, or moths. The latter interpretation seems more plausible, for how else could the twin spiral appendages be interpreted except as moths' antennae? Their use is unknown. It has been suggested that they were dance wands, held by the thin stem at the base, but they might equally be used as ornaments to be fixed in a head-dress. The British Museum has a very fine example of a wristlet, made of a simple sheet embossed with rows of puma or some other kind of feline ornaments and bent round into a penannular shape.

In strong contrast to the simple embossed plates of Nasca, the Mochica tradition, which covered valleys of Peru, displayed far greater technical skill, and far greater artistic ability. We have suggested that the use of heat to anneal the metal may have been known in Chavin times. It is certain that the Mochica were able to cast gold and other metals and to solder them. Whether these developments took place locally, or whether they were introduced from the valleys of Colombia where fine castings by the *cire perdue* or lost wax process were made is uncertain.

Whether the Mochica influenced the Chibcha, or were influenced by them, or whether both styles of figurine were evolved independently is uncertain. In the realm of animal art, perhaps the finest specimen ever made is a head of a fox (Ill. 6) about six inches high, which was found in the Pyramid of the Moon, Moche, and which is now in the Linden-Museum, Stuttgart. In this remarkable work there is a mixture of gold, silver and copper and the teeth are represented by a shell overlay. But it is perhaps significant that these techniques are only known in the north of Peru at this time. But whatever the origin of the new techniques they widened the possibilities of the goldsmiths enormously, and they were able to achieve sculptural effects in sheet metal which were quite beyond the ability of their southern contemporaries.

But perhaps the most interesting class of objects made possible by the new techniques were little figures of birds and animals, usually not more than an inch high and half an inch across, which were worn as ear-rings or used as mounts for pins or spatulas. In the Gallo Collection there are quite a number of these objects. A spatula is surmounted by a monkey with a condor on its back, for example. Much of the gold plate must have been hammered and soldered by goldsmiths, but the plaited crest on the condor's head was cast by the *cire perdue* process.

It is probable that these little pendant ear-rings were worn by women, for the ornaments worn by the men, which we can see on almost every Mochica vase, if we need a reference, were large mushroom-shaped objects usually about

12. Double-spouted vase, Chimu culture
height $9\frac{7}{8}$ in. (25 cm.)
The Mujica Gallo Collection, Lima

13. Two beakers with turquoise inlay, Chimu culture, 12th or 13th century
heights $7\frac{1}{4}$ in. (19 cm.) and $8\frac{5}{8}$ in. (22 cm.)
The Mujica Gallo Collection, Lima

14. Gold beaker, Chimu culture
height $7\frac{5}{8}$ in. (20 cm.)
The British Museum, London

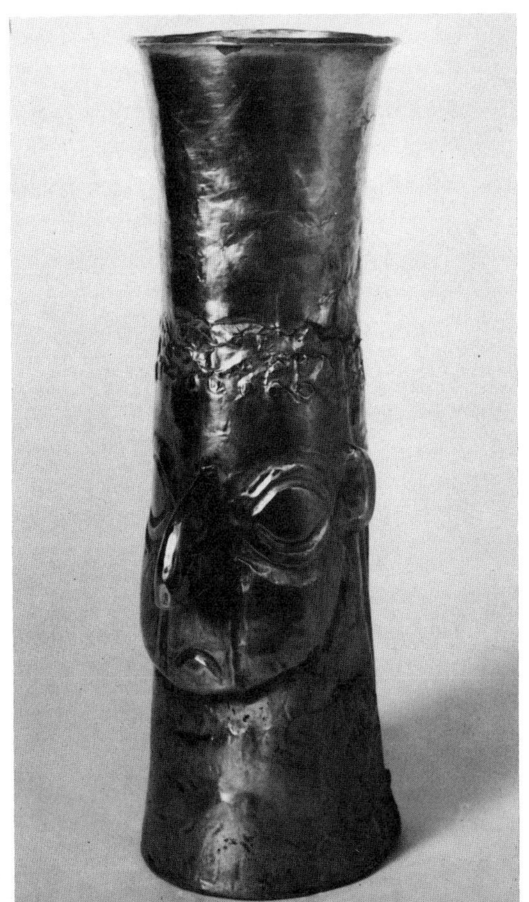

three inches across the face, and sometimes more, and the stem perhaps a half or three-quarters of an inch in diameter. These were sometimes inlaid with stones and shells to form a picture, or supported pendent tassels of gold strip cut to represent snakes. These almost universal reptiles share the place of honour with the puma in almost all early Peruvian art.

But we must not think of gold as being limited to small personal ornaments and animal representations in Mochica times. Almost every article of clothing of the well-to-do might either be made in gold or adorned with it as well as many everyday objects.

Head-dresses were set with gold plates. If we study the pottery we find that they were made in many forms, varying from simple turbans to animal skins and helmets, some with enormous axe-like projections. The turbans were bound with ribbons, sometimes no doubt of gold. At any rate gold ribbons about three-quarters of an inch wide and suitable for such a purpose have been found. More elaborate were the embossed gold plates which they used to attach to their head-gear. In Señor Rafael Larco Hoyle's collection there are two such plates, both about ten and a half inches in diameter. In each the central feature is a deeply embossed face, a jaguar head on one, and a lion face on the other. Both have a large axe-shaped crest of sheet metal in the form of an axe blade, and the area on each side of the face of both pieces is cut away to emphasize two zoomorphic figures, birds in one, alligators in the other, which flank the face. The emphasis is still on beating out the sheet to paper thinness to make the greatest display from the limited quantity of material, but two new technical ideas go to the making of these objects. A wooden matrix, or possibly one of stone, must have been used behind the faces which are raised into relatively high relief; and the use of the cut-out, or negative space, to emphasize the outline of the subsidiary figures.

Necklaces, either single strings of gold beads or various combinations of beads and precious stones, were made in an almost infinite variety of sizes and shapes of beads. As in the earlier Chavin period metal plaques were sewn on to clothing, and the extreme form of this can be seen in a woven woollen *poncho* completely covered with overlapping rectangular pieces of gold, arranged like tiles on a roof, and strictly comparable to the so-called lizard mail of the 11th century in Europe.

Mochica goldsmiths did not limit themselves to objects of clothing and personal ornament. They made drinking bowls and other utilitarian objects of the precious metal. Some of their weapons, such as throwing sticks, were covered with thin gold foil. Tweezers for removing surplus hair from the face were also made of gold or silver – sometimes plain almost circular discs joined by a narrow bent stripe of metal, sometimes complicated contrivances in which the eyes of the double-headed snake are inlaid with shell and the figure of the man was also inlaid.

From this wealth of gold, and from the scenes figured on the pottery, we can deduce that the Mochica were a rich and warlike people with a hierarchical society. No doubt it was theocratic to a large degree and in this case we would expect the most spectacular goldwork to be devoted to religious objects. Indeed this seems to be the case, for by far the most spectacular and interesting piece of gold ever discovered is a replica in gold of a puma skin (Ill. 7), which no doubt represents the same feline god which dominated the art of Chavin. There is a head in high relief, from the open jaws of which protrudes a long tongue. The body and tail, flattened as if they were a skin, extend to make the total length of the effigy 62·5 centimetres or just about two feet. The whole of the body, which is formed like a pouch, is embossed with the design of double-headed serpents. It is believed to have been used for the offering of coca.

15. Tumi, Chimu culture
The Mujica Gallo Collection, Lima

The double-headed snake motif was developed further and frequently appears as an interlocking design on painted pottery. This gives very strong grounds for believing that the famous gold stirrup-spouted vessel (Ill. 8) in the American Museum of Natural History may in fact belong to the Mochica culture in the Master Craftsman Period. It is sometimes attributed to the Chavin horizon on account of the shape of the stirrup spout, but the interlocking pattern of the snakes is surely later, and it seems unlikely that the people of the Chavin horizon would have had the technical skill to make the vessel.

But the material prosperity and even the warlike activities of the Mochica were no guarantee of political survival, and after a period of about five hundred years the Mochica were to come under the domination of the people of Tiahuanaco on the shores of Lake Titicaca in the Bolivian Highlands.

From some time after A.D. 500 to *circa* A.D. 900, the culture and the art-forms of the mountaineers from this site seem to have dominated the whole of Peru. It was not the first time that the Highlands had imposed their culture on the coast, and, as we shall see, it was not the last. Tiahuanaco, like Chavin, was a religious centre, but we do not know whether the domination of Tiahuanaco was religious or whether it was accomplished by force of arms. The style of Nasca was completely subordinated to Tiahuanaco. The Mochica only survived in the extreme North, in the valleys of Lambayeque and Picera.

The Tiahuanaco style is best known from pottery and textiles, with sterner shapes in the pottery, with naturalistic heads, both human and the jaguar, and conventionalized geometric patterns in the textiles. The most characteristic vessel shape introduced from Tiahuanaco was a beaker, flat at the base and with flaring sides. Gold beakers were made at this time, and became a legacy which the principal succeeding cultures copied.

A number of very large funerary masks have been found on the northernmost point of the Peruvian coast, which some authorities attribute to this, others to the next period, and they will be described below. The contribution to gold-working does not seem to have been very great in this Tiahuanaco period, but there is one remarkable vessel which must be mentioned. It is a whistling vase. (Ill. 9.) That is to say there are two chambers joined by a pipe. The rear chamber is an ordinary beaker, the front one a hollow human figure with a whistle concealed in the head. As water flowed from the rear chamber through the pipe into the front one, air was expelled through the whistle. The device was not new, for examples were made in pottery in the Mochica period, but the inspiration to undertake this most ambitious and complicated piece of metal-working clearly belongs to Tiahuanaco, as can be seen by the characteristic flaring beaker which forms the rear chamber and the typical Tiahuanaco features of the man who forms the front chamber.

Some time in the 11th or 12th century the influence of Tiahuanaco was thrown off, and once more individual states established themselves on the coast. The period which followed was one of large, well-organized communities living in cities built of *adobe* bricks. Some of these cities grew to enormous size. The capital of the Chimu, known as Chan Chan, was more than six miles in extent. Archaeologists generally call the whole period that of the City Builders. There were, of course, numerous separate communities but the Chimu were by far the most important. They dominated the whole of the northern area. In many respects the Chimu were reminiscent of the Mochica, for the same shapes and artistic emblems were used. But one great change had taken place. Concentrations of large numbers of people led to what might almost be called mass-production methods. Stereotyped designs appeared in the textiles and the pots were made with moulds. There was an

16. Representative Inca pottery, between 14th and 16th centuries
amphora 3⅞ in. (9·8 cm.) maximum diameter
vessels' height 1½ in. (3·9 cm.)
University Museum, Cuzco

17. Gold female figure, Inca, between 14th and 16th centuries
height 8⅞ in. (22·6 cm.)
University Museum, Cuzco

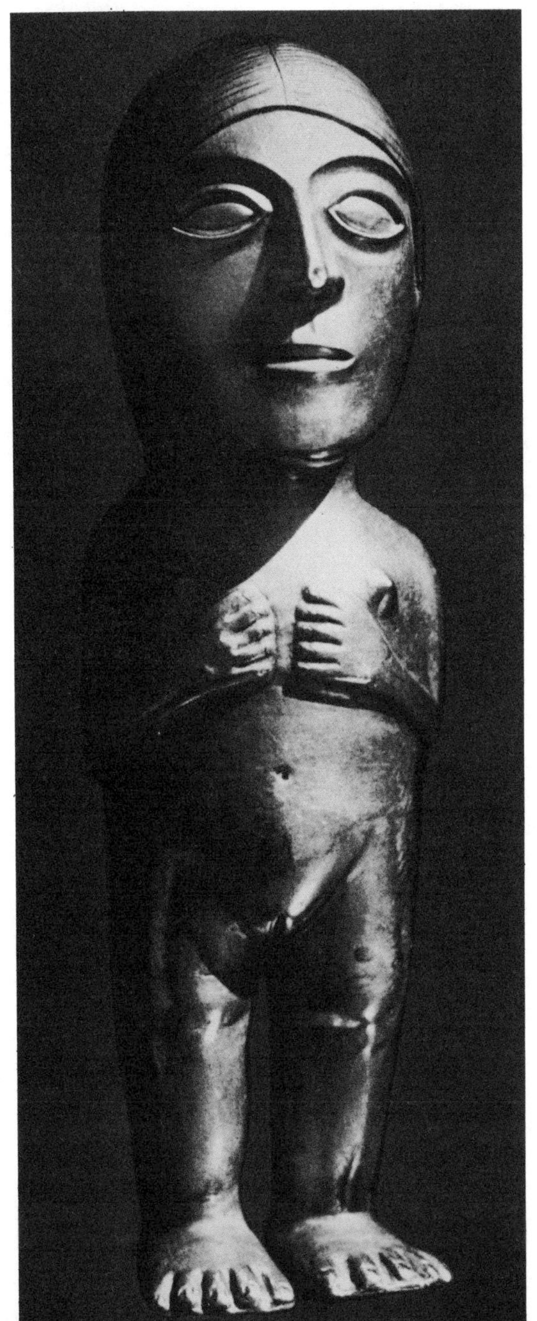

inevitable lowering of standards. The masterpieces of the Mochica were replaced by similar articles of high technical quality, but without the feeling that the Master Craftsmen gave to individual pieces. This tendency did not reach so far in the art of gold-working because it was not practical to introduce embossing machinery into the working of gold and perforce the working had to be done by hand, but the same spirit seemed to be at work. More or less standard designs, whether of men or conventional patterns, seem to have been repeated *ad nauseam*. The gold is beaten if anything thinner than in earlier periods and much of the jewelry looks tawdry, for all the world like the penny toys of tin which one could buy before the First World War. But the goldsmiths were more skilled technically than ever. Much of their energy was misapplied. A replica in gold of a double-spouted Chimu vessel (Ill. 12) is the most remarkable example of misplaced ingenuity that could be found. The whole is built up of thin pieces of gold carefully soldered together, but the elaborate castellated bridge between the spouts, with its thin edges of metal and its triangles cut in the sides, is tawdry in the extreme.

In the same vein they made great cylindrical crowns (Ill. 11) similarly embossed, and many of the ear spools had the same rather tinselly appearance. Others, it must be admitted, were of beautiful workmanship and avoided the tawdry appearance of much of the Tenniveso. Here there may be mentioned the beautiful pair of ear spools in the Museum of Primitive Art in New York. (Ill. 10.)

The Chimu goldsmiths were on occasions capable of magnificent work. Among their finest productions must be counted beakers of two types, those with an effigy head in sharp relief and those of Tiahuanaco shape, of comparatively thick sheet embossed with elaborate geometric and zoomorphic designs, and inlaid with turquoise, which can only have been used for ritual purposes or rulers' feasts. Such a beaker is that shown in illustration 13, which belongs today to Señor Mujica Gallo.

The effigy beakers are represented by a specimen in the British Museum (Ill. 14), and in a sense require even more skilful treatment than the flaring beakers because of the difficulty of beating out the long projecting nose. Both types of beaker are hammered out from discs of gold, with constant annealing, and very careful hammering on wooden formers. If a beaker of the effigy type is examined it will be found to have a relatively thick rim, but the wall of the vessel becomes thinner as it works down and in places has the thickness almost of a piece of tinfoil.

There is an almost infinite variety of objects of personal ornament made in this period: bracelets, gorgets, head ornaments and necklaces. The beads themselves vary from very small spherical objects to representations of natural objects such as sharks' vertebrae, or miniature masks like those in the colour plate facing p. 352. Collars, breast-plates and head ornaments are all of thin sheets of gold and embossed with designs representing men or animals. Lastly funerary masks for mummy packs reached an enormous size, measuring almost two feet across. Traces of pigment, either red or green, show that they were painted. This in itself is interesting in so far as it shows that the Chimu were prepared to use the precious gold not only for its decorative value, but merely as a background material for a painted effigy.

Also of ritual significance were ceremonial knives with a semi-lunar blade, and surmounted by figures of men or animals carefully and elaborately worked and richly inlaid with turquoise. (Ill. 15.)

In the 13th century the Incas, an expanding and warlike tribe, clashed with the growing Chimu state and incorporated it in the Inca empire which stretched ultimately from Ecuador to Chile.

We have a wealth of information about the Incas and their gold. It was for ever

18. Silver llama with gold and cinnabar inlay
The American Museum of Natural History, New York

19. Gold plaque in the shape of a *tumi*, Inca period, between 14th and 16th centuries
height 7¾ in. (19·5 cm.)
University Museum, Cuzco

foremost in the minds of the Conquistadors, and material sent home to Spain for King Philip II was recorded with all the meticulousness of accountants. Pizarro's venture was to some extent a commercial one and gold occupied a large part of the Conquistadors' reports.

They had come to a land where gold was plentiful by any standards. It had been of almost sacred importance to the Incas, for ever since Manoc Capac arrayed himself in a golden costume and displayed himself glistening in the sunshine from a mountain top, claiming his kinship with the sun, gold became a perquisite with the Inca and his family. For two hundred years or so conquering Inca armies had been returning laden with gold from defeated cities. The produce of the mines driven into the hill-sides, or of surface pits, was transported by right to the Inca, and there were inspectors at the mines to see that none of it was withheld. Skilled craftsmen from all over the empire were transported to Cuzco to work for the Incas. It is not surprising, therefore, that we hear that the famous sun disc was "of solid gold and shaped like a cartwheel". An effigy of the sun-god was made of the finest gold and as big as a man. It is said that cracks between building stones were filled with gold like cement between bricks, and that the whole of the inside walls of one temple were covered with a curtain of gold plate. There are stories too of artificial gardens laid out with plants and trees of gold and silver. With all these accounts before us and with our knowledge of the rapacity of the Conquistadors we can understand the pathetic story of the captive Inca, Atahuallpa, offering to ransom himself by filling his prison to a height of eight feet with solid gold. We can also understand why so little of this gorgeous booty has survived. Indeed the known pieces of Inca gold extant today include a few replicas in gold of typical pottery vessels (Ill. 16), the beaker, and the aryballus, and an occasional chisel or other implement and little figures of men and women and llamas, which were used as votive effigies. Almost always these figures were made from thin plate hammered to shape and soldered together. Very small figures were cast solid. There is quality of restraint and soberness about the art of the Inca period in strong contrast to the variety of the Master Craftsman period and flamboyance of the City Builders, which is absent in the Inca gold that we can still see today. Perhaps the most important is the figure of a woman now in the University Museum at Cuzco. (Ill. 17.) This figure is 22·6 centimetres (almost nine inches) high, but similar figures of the same general type made in either gold or silver have been found as small as about an inch and a half high. The llamas, similar to that in the colour plate facing p. 352, are made up of small sections and soldered or brazed together. They are among the most attractive of all the Peruvian antiquities which have survived to us. But the British Museum specimen is far surpassed by a little silver llama (Ill. 18) wearing a blanket or saddlecloth of gold inlay and cinnabar, in the American Museum of Natural History in New York.

Of crowns and jewelry practically nothing remains. A repoussé plaque, in the shape of a *tumi* or knife in the University Museum in Cuzco (Ill. 19), is barely distinguishable from several pieces of Chimu work save by the emblem of the sun.

Such trivia are the surviving witnesses to the wealth of Inca gold. Gone are the great jars weighing anything from 20 to 58 pounds given to the king of Spain. Gone too are the full-size effigy of the sun-god and the disc "shaped like a cartwheel", and almost gone are traces of the gold and silver artificial gardens. A few minute fragments of the gold vegetation can be seen in private collections, but they hardly even suggest the appearance of the Inca garden.

It is perhaps an irony of history that the gold of the Chimu has survived while that of their conquerors has vanished almost without trace.

Early Ballooning Prints

COLONEL R. L. PRESTON

Throughout the ages pictures have depicted historical events. The early history of ballooning is recorded in about 500 prints. Many of these prints were hand-coloured and the decorative effect of ballooning prints has such charm as to cause much demand and therefore to make them rare and valuable, at the same time producing many reproductions of little value on modern paper. There were two types of balloons: the hot-air balloon invented by Joseph and Etienne Montgolfier in 1782 known as a 'Montgolfier', and the hydrogen, invented in 1783 by Professor Charles.

The hot-air balloon was suspended between two masts and inflated by hot air from a fire on a platform, with another fire in a brazier in the balloon to provide hot air during flight. The hydrogen balloon was inflated by an apparatus in which sulphuric acid was passed over iron filings to make gas and the balloon was controlled by dropping ballast or valving the gas. Later came coal gas and helium.

There are many portrait prints of Joseph Michel Montgolfier (1740–1810) and Etienne Jacques Montgolfier (1745–88), the two brothers, paper manufacturers, who lived at Annonay, Lyons, and who had the idea for a hot-air balloon after watching stray ash floating into the air from a fire. They constructed a 74-foot-high balloon in the garden of M. Reveillon, another paper manufacturer, and on 19 September 1783 a wicker cage, with a sheep, a cock and a duck in it, was suspended below the balloon; the fire was lit and the first free unmanned ascent was made from Versailles. The flight lasted eight minutes.

There are about a dozen prints of this event. (Ill. 1.)

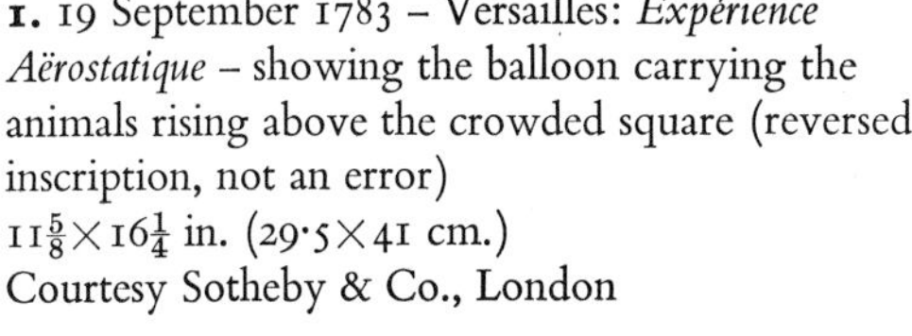

1. 19 September 1783 – Versailles: *Expérience Aërostatique* – showing the balloon carrying the animals rising above the crowded square (reversed inscription, not an error)
$11\frac{5}{8}\times16\frac{1}{4}$ in. (29·5×41 cm.)
Courtesy Sotheby & Co., London

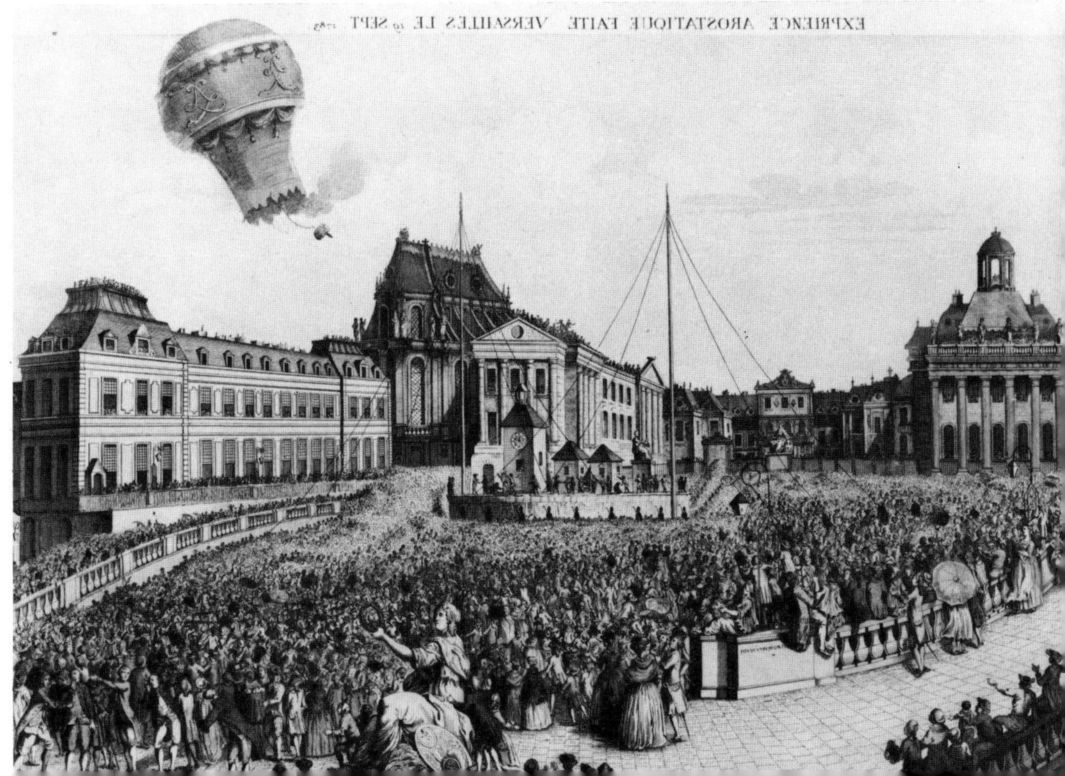

2. (above left) 21 November 1783 – La Muette, Paris
12×9½ in. (30·5×24 cm.)
Courtesy Sotheby & Co., London

3. (below left) 21 November 1783 – Paris: *Expérience Aërostatique de M. Montgolfier au Châtu. de la Muette, le 21 9bre, 1783*, published *A Paris chez Esnauts et Rapilly*
10⅜×7¼ in. (26·3×18·5 cm.)
Courtesy Sotheby & Co., London

4. (above right) 19 January 1784 – Lyons: *Premier Expérience, de la Machine Aërostatique nommée le Flesselle . . .* and *Départ de la Machine Aërostatique*, etching after Cogell, by St Aubin
approximately 13¼×9⅛ in. (33·7×46·5 cm.)
Courtesy Sotheby & Co., London

5. (below right) 27 August 1783 – Gonesse: General Alarm of the Inhabitants of Gonesse, occasioned by the Fall of the Air Balloon of Mr Montgolfier, published Decr 1st, 1783 by John Wallis at his Map Warehouse Ludgate Street
9¼×11¾ in. (23·5×28·8 cm.)
Courtesy Sotheby & Co., London

J. F. Pilâtre de Rozier (1756–85), who was the world's first pilot, made the first ascent in Montgolfier's balloon from Versailles on 21 November 1783. The flight lasted twenty-five minutes. There are many beautiful prints of this event – both of the ascent and the landing. (Ills. 2, 3.) During 1784 a number of flights were made in the Montgolfier-type balloons; a specially beautiful balloon was 'le Flesselle' which flew from Lyons on 19 January 1784. (Ill. 4.) About the same time as Montgolfier, Jacques Alexandre César Charles (1746–1823), helped by two mechanics (the brothers Robert), designed and made the first hydrogen balloon. On 27 August 1783, Charles's first unmanned balloon rose from the Champ de Mars and flew to Gonesse, about 10 miles from Paris. The inhabitants at Gonesse, believing it to be something from another world, shot at it and attacked it with pitchforks. There are numerous prints of this event, some of which describe the balloon as a Montgolfier, which is incorrect as it was a 'Charles' hydrogen balloon. (Ill. 5.) There are many fake copies of these prints. On 1 December 1783, Charles, accompanied by the elder of the Robert brothers, took off from the Tuileries and after being in the air for two hours descended at Nesle, about 27 miles from Paris. Here Charles re-ascended alone and rose to the height of 9,000 feet, and landed safely, but was so frightened he never made another flight. There are many prints showing this historic event. (Ills 6, 7.)

6. (right) 1 December 1783 – Tuileries Gardens, Paris: *Expérience Célébre faites à Paris*, published *se vend à Paris chez le Noir Md Fournisseux du Cabinet des Estampes, Demeurant au Louvre*
$13\frac{3}{4} \times 10$ in. (35×25·5 cm.)
Courtesy Sotheby & Co., London

8. (far right) 7 January 1785 – Dover: The Channel Crossing
$11\frac{1}{4} \times 6\frac{7}{8}$ in. (28·5×17·5 cm.)
Courtesy Sotheby & Co., London

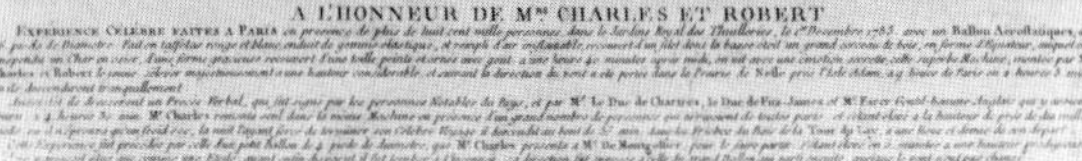

7. (right) 1 December 1783 – Nesle: *Globe Aërostatique*, after Desrais, by Denis, published *A Paris chez Jacques Chereau*
$8\frac{7}{8} \times 12\frac{3}{4}$ in. (22·6×32·2 cm.)
Courtesy Sotheby & Co., London

TO THE RIGHT HONOURABLE LORD GRENVILLE,

CHANCELLOR OF THE UNIVERSITY OF OXFORD. &c. &c. &c.

This PLATE representing the ASCENT of M^r. SADLER, the celebrated BRITISH AERONAUT, at OXFORD. at the COMMEMORATION, July 7. 1810., Is most respectfully dedicated by his Lordship's most obedient humble Servant.

Colour Plate. 7 July 1810 – Oxford: This plate, representing the Ascent of Mr Sadler, the celebrated British Aeronaut, at Oxford at the Commemoration. Coloured aquatint, after E. M. Jones, by Havell, published 29 April, 1811, by E. M. Jones
$13\frac{5}{8} \times 8\frac{7}{8}$ in. ($34{\cdot}5 \times 22{\cdot}5$ cm.)
The Royal Aeronautical Society, London

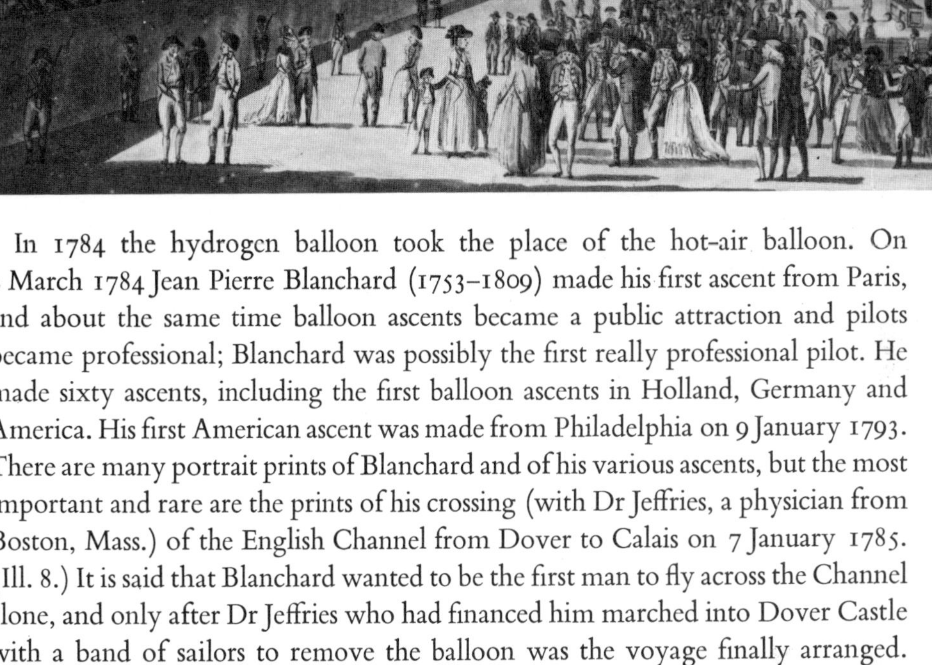

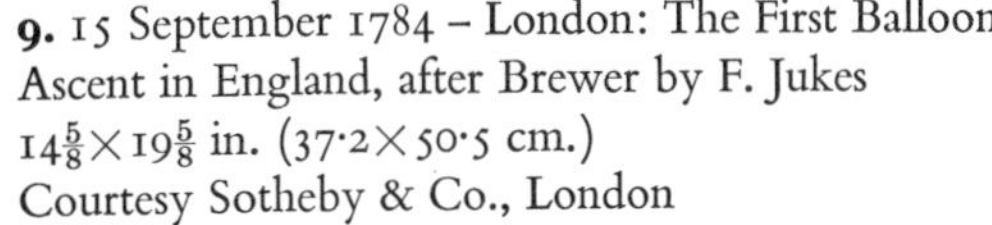

9. 15 September 1784 – London: The First Balloon Ascent in England, after Brewer by F. Jukes
$14\frac{5}{8} \times 19\frac{5}{8}$ in. ($37{\cdot}2 \times 50{\cdot}5$ cm.)
Courtesy Sotheby & Co., London

10. (below left) 13 May 1785 – London: An exact Representation of Mr Lunardi's New Balloon, printed and sold by Carington Bowles
$13\frac{1}{4} \times 9\frac{7}{8}$ in. ($33{\cdot}5 \times 25{\cdot}2$ cm.)
Courtesy Sotheby & Co., London

11. (below centre) 29 June 1785 – London: V. Lunardi Esq., Mrs Sage, G. Biggin Esq., *The Three Favorite Aerial Travellers*, printed in sepia after H. Rigaud, by F. Bartolozzi
$13 \times 9\frac{5}{8}$ in. ($33 \times 24{\cdot}5$ cm.)
Courtesy Sotheby & Co., London

12. (below right) 1 October 1812 – Dublin: Part of the balloon in which Mr Sadler ascended from Dublin Oct. 1st, 1812, coloured aquatint by R. Havell
$13\frac{1}{4} \times 9\frac{1}{8}$ in. ($33{\cdot}5 \times 23$ cm.)
Courtesy Sotheby & Co., London

In 1784 the hydrogen balloon took the place of the hot-air balloon. On 2 March 1784 Jean Pierre Blanchard (1753–1809) made his first ascent from Paris, and about the same time balloon ascents became a public attraction and pilots became professional; Blanchard was possibly the first really professional pilot. He made sixty ascents, including the first balloon ascents in Holland, Germany and America. His first American ascent was made from Philadelphia on 9 January 1793. There are many portrait prints of Blanchard and of his various ascents, but the most important and rare are the prints of his crossing (with Dr Jeffries, a physician from Boston, Mass.) of the English Channel from Dover to Calais on 7 January 1785. (Ill. 8.) It is said that Blanchard wanted to be the first man to fly across the Channel alone, and only after Dr Jeffries who had financed him marched into Dover Castle with a band of sailors to remove the balloon was the voyage finally arranged. Blanchard, up till 1814, gave balloon and parachute demonstrations, often with his wife, who was killed when her balloon caught fire during a firework display from her balloon in Paris.

The first balloon ascent in England was made by Vincent Lunardi (1759–1806),

13. 12 May 1785 – Ireland: The Preservation of Sir Richd. McGuire, on the 12 May, 1785, mezzotint, after J. J. Barralet, by Willm. Ward
17¾×23½ in. (45×60 cm.)
Courtesy Sotheby & Co., London

a Neapolitan secretary to the Neapolitan Ambassador in London. On 15 September 1784 he made the first ascent from the parade ground of the Honourable Artillery Company at Moorfields, London and landed at Ware in Hertfordshire. (Ill. 9.) He made twelve ascents in England and left in 1787 for the Continent where he made several ascents. He died in poverty in Lisbon on 31 July 1806. There are many portraits of Lunardi but most of them are out of books. One of his balloons was covered with the Union Jack. (Ill. 10.) It is interesting to note here that frequently prints of balloon flights were made before the flight actually took place. There is a print of Lunardi, Mrs Sage and Mr Biggin making a flight. This flight, with three people, never took place, as their weight was such that the balloon failed to rise and there were only two people in the actual flight. (Ill. 11.)

The first English-born aeronaut was James Sadler of Oxford (1751–1826). He made his first flight from Oxford on 4 October 1784. There is a fine print of an ascent from Oxford (see colour plate facing p. 365) and several of an ascent from Dublin on 1 October 1812 (Ill. 12).

The first Irish aeronaut, born at Wicklow, was Richard Crosbie (1755–1800) who made a short flight from Dublin on 19 January 1785, but he was a heavy man, and on 12 May 1785 his place in his balloon was taken by Richard McGuire (1754–93), who jumped into the balloon basket on seeing that the balloon would not rise. The balloon ascended and he flew out to sea where he was rescued by Lord Henry Fitzgerald. On McGuire's return to Dublin he was received by the

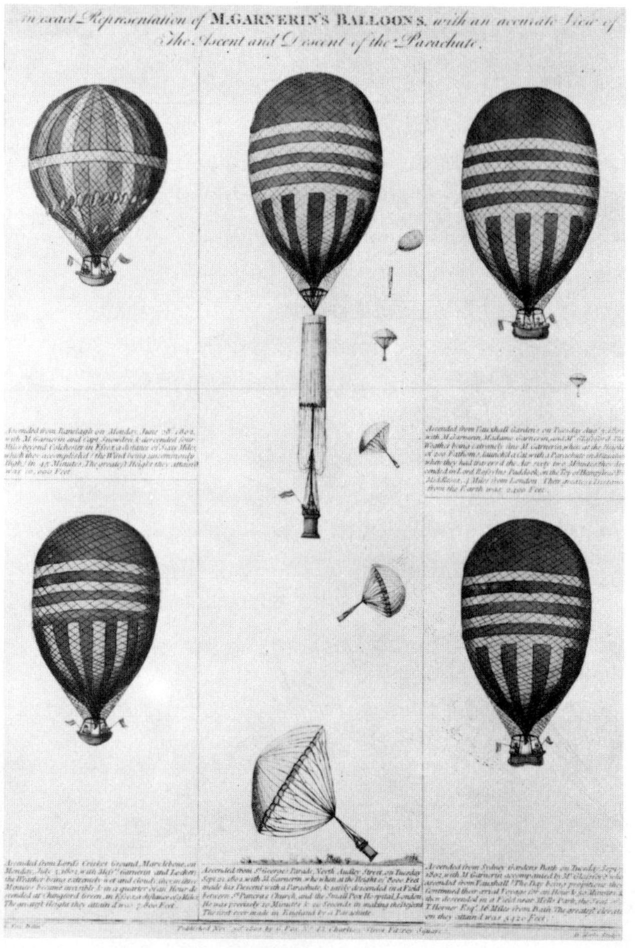

14. 1802 – London: An exact Representation of M. Garnerin's Balloons with an accurate View of The Ascent and Descent of the Parachute, coloured aquatint, after G. Fox, by H. Merke
14×9⅞ in. (35·5×25 cm.)
Courtesy Sotheby & Co., London

15. (right) 3 December 1804 – Paris: *Fête du Sacre et Couronnment de leurs Majestés Impériales*, after Le Cœur, by Marchand, with aquatinting by Gautier
11⅞×17⅜ in. (30·2×44 cm.)
Courtesy Sotheby & Co., London

16. (above left) 9 September 1836 – London: The Vauxhall Royal Balloon, coloured lithograph, after Black, by F. Alvey: $10\frac{1}{2}\times 8\frac{3}{8}$ in. ($26{\cdot}7\times 21{\cdot}3$ cm.)
Courtesy Sotheby & Co., London

17. (above right) 1 August 1831 – London: The New London Bridge, as it appeared when opened in presence of Their Majesties, on the 1st August, 1831, coloured aquatint, published by R. H. Laurie
$10\frac{1}{4}\times 16\frac{7}{8}$ in. ($26{\cdot}2\times 42{\cdot}7$ cm.)
Courtesy Sotheby & Co., London

18. (below left) 24 July 1837 – London and Lee: The only Authentic Sketch of the Ascent of the Vauxhall Balloon with Mr Cocking's Parachute, coloured lithograph, published by W. Spooner
$14\times 9\frac{1}{2}$ in. ($35{\cdot}5\times 24$ cm.)

19. (below right) 26 June 1794 – The Battle of Fleurus showing General Jourdan giving to his generals the information obtained by his captive balloon: $7\frac{7}{8}\times 12$ in. ($20\times 30{\cdot}5$ cm.)
Courtesy Sotheby & Co., London

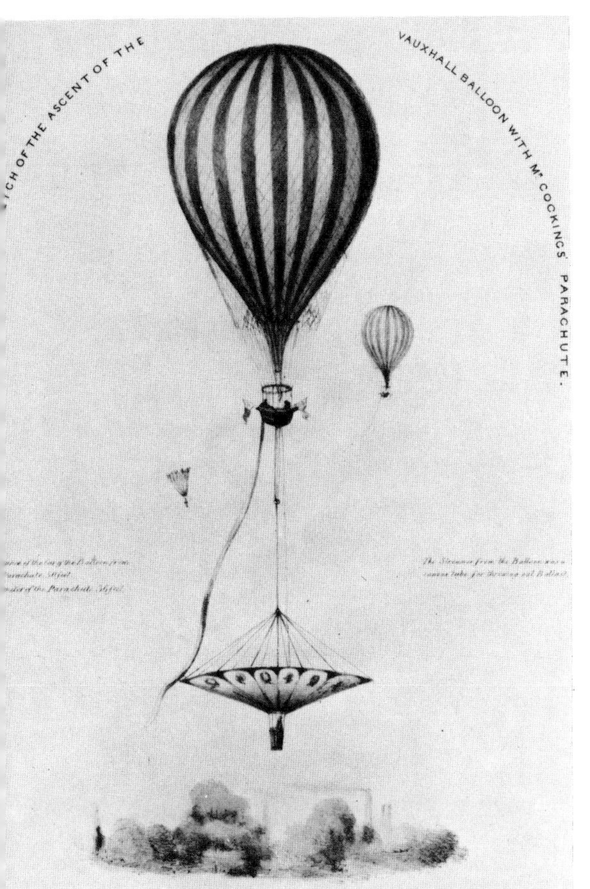

Duke of Rutland, the Lord-Lieutenant, who immediately knighted him for his pluck and spirit, thus Sir Richard McGuire became the first knight of the air. (Ill. 13.)

On 22 October 1797 from Parc Monceau, Paris, André Jacques Garnerin (1769–1825) became the first man to descend from a balloon by means of a parachute. He also made the first parachute descent in England. His wife Jeanne Geneviève (1779–1847) was the first professional woman parachutist. (Ill. 14.) At Napoleon's Coronation on 3 December 1804, Monsieur Garnerin organized an aeronautical display at the Place de la Concorde, Paris. One of the events was the ascent of a huge balloon from the Square of Notre-Dame. This unmanned balloon ascended, covered with a huge gilt inscription and a crown. It is rumoured that the next day the balloon was seen low over Rome. It hit the ground and rose again; but left the decorative crown on Nero's tomb before falling into Lake Bracciano. The obvious resemblance between the two dictators did not please the superstitious Napoleon, who promptly lost all interest in balloons. (Ill. 15.) There are a number of prints of Garnerin's ascents and descents with his parachutes.

Charles Green (1785–1870) was another famous balloonist who made 526 balloon ascents; there are many prints of his Vauxhall Royal balloon (Ill. 16) and of his flight from London to Weilburg, in Nassau, Germany, of 480 miles in eighteen hours.

There were two professional aeronauts between 1823 and 1853 named George and Margaret Graham, and there are some charming prints of their flights, especially the ones of the opening of London Bridge on 1 August 1831. (Ill. 17.)

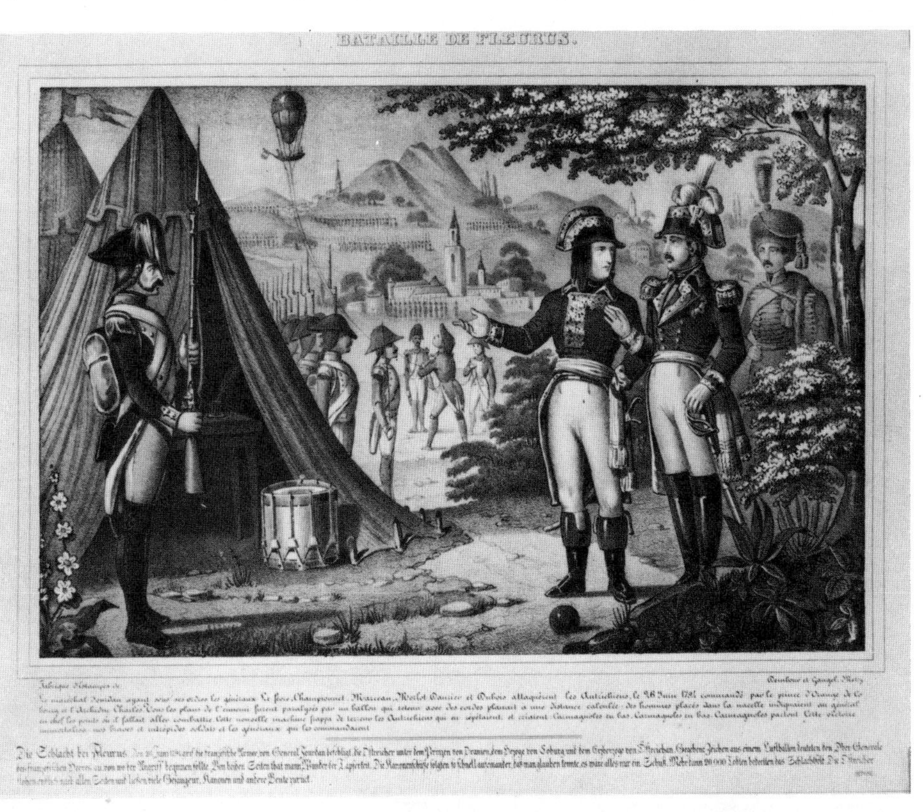

20. 1783 – London: Mr Martyn's Design for an Aerostatic Globe, aquatint, published Octr 2 1784 by T. Martyn: $13\frac{1}{2} \times 10\frac{5}{8}$ in. (34·2×27 cm.) Courtesy Sotheby & Co., London

21. (below left) 1784 – Paris: *Vaisseau Royal Aérien* $10\frac{5}{8} \times 7\frac{7}{8}$ in. (27×20 cm.) Courtesy Sotheby & Co., London

22. (below right) The Year 2000: The Century of Invention, showing the world in the year 2000, motor-cars crowd the street, buildings including Eton College Chapel are on wheels, men with wings and guns fly, there are balloons with sails, and in the centre the army is mechanized: $15\frac{1}{8} \times 19\frac{7}{8}$ in. (38·3×50·5 cm.). Courtesy Sotheby & Co., London

On 24 July 1837 Robert Cocking (1777–1837) decided to demonstrate his full-size cone parachute from a balloon. (Ill. 18.) When over Lee Green at an altitude of 5,000 feet he was released. His parachute crumpled up in the air and Cocking was killed. This accident is illustrated in about half a dozen prints. Military ballooning was started by Nicolas Jacques Conte and Captain Courtelle in 1794 and was used for reconnaissance purposes at the Battle of Fleurus (26 June 1794), at the Battle of Ourthe and the Siege of Mainz (1796–97). There are several prints of balloons being used in the Battle of Fleurus. (Ill. 19.)

There were many prints of balloon designs and projects, though many of them have been extracted from books. (Ills 20, 21.) Caricatures of ballooning (Ill. 22) form several sets of prints. There are several of Abbé Moilan and the engraver Janinet who attempted an unsuccessful ascent in Paris on 11 July 1784. One balloon caught fire and the public were so annoyed that it caused a riot. In the caricature of the event Moilan is portrayed as a cat and Janinet as a donkey.

In addition to prints mentioned in this article, there are also prints concerning flights or events of the following: Paolo Andreani (1763–1823), Aimé Argand (died 1803), Jacob Degen (1756–1846), James Decker (active 1785), Elisa Garnerin (1791–1854), Nicholas François Gay-Lussac (1778–1850), Count Francesco Zambeccari (1752–1812); and later 19th-century prints such as those of: Professor P. Cornillot (active 1825), Henry Giffard (1825–82), James Glaisher (1809–1903), Fanny Godard (active 1825), John Hampton (active 1838–51), William Samuel Henson (1805–88), J. W. Hoare (active 1837–39), Mr Livingston (*circa* 1819–22), Comte de Lennox (active 1834–37), Charles Paternoster (active *circa* 1854), Samuel John Pauly (active *circa* 1816), Dr Potain (1765–1838), John Sadler (active *circa* 1814). They are well worth collecting and some are very rare.

The auction prices of ballooning prints vary between \$2.80 and \$350, but owing to the shortage and demand they are increasing in value.

Undoubtedly the finest collection of ballooning prints is the private collection of Monsieur Charles Dollfus of Paris, but the collector may see excellent collections by appointment at The Patent Office, Southampton Buildings, Chancery Lane, London, W.C.2; the Hodgson-Cuthbert Collection at the Royal Aeronautical Society, 4 Hamilton Place, London, W.1; the collection at l'Aéro Club de France, 6 Rue Galilé, Paris XVIe; and the Landaus Collection at The Institute of Aeronautical Sciences of New York.

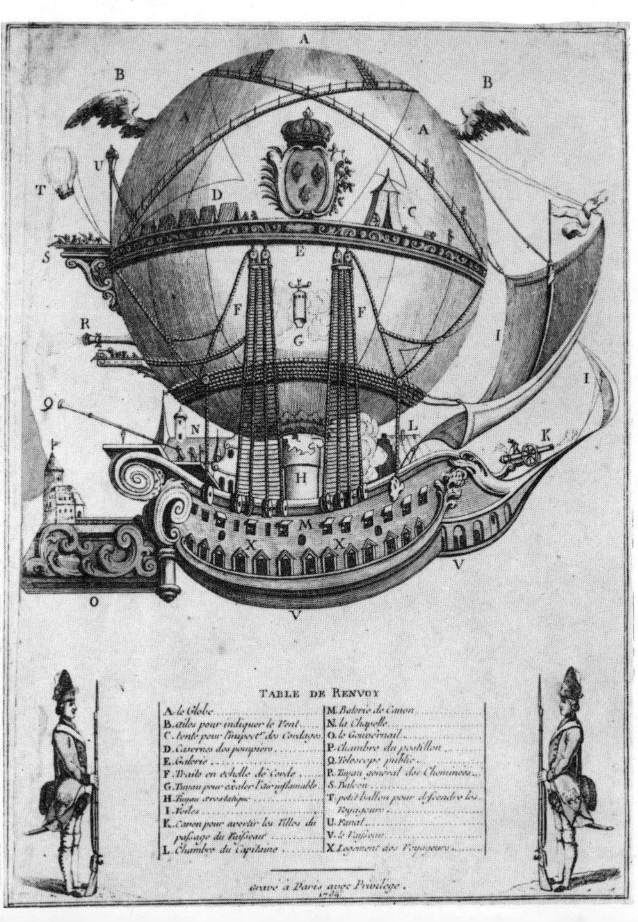

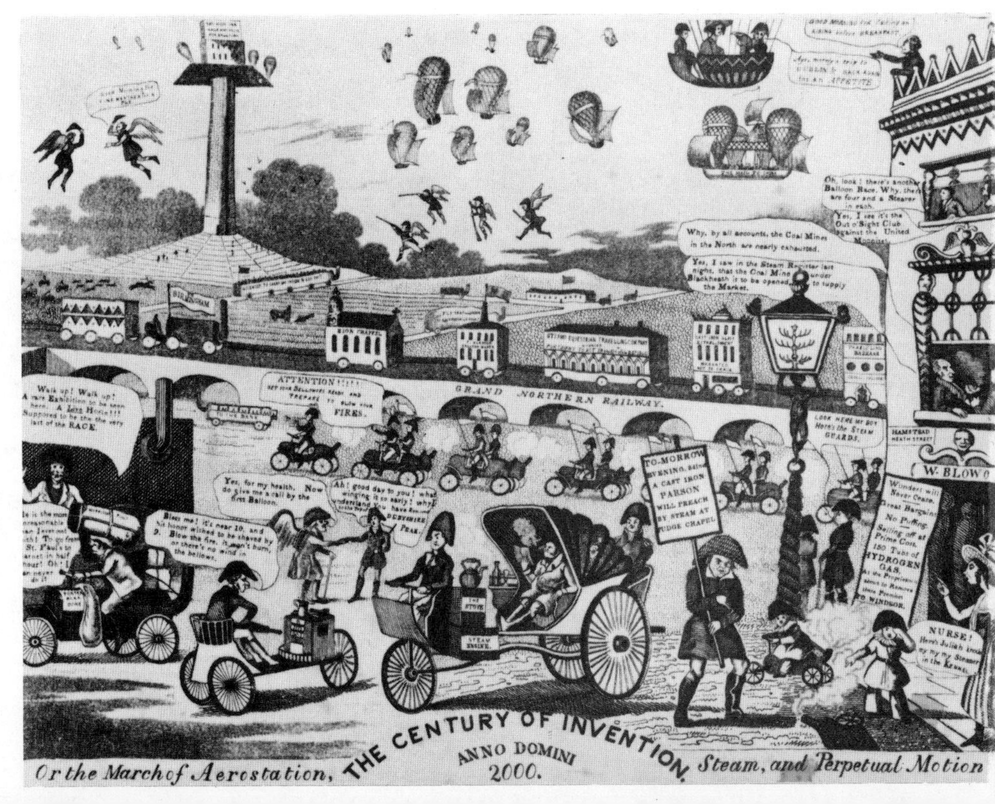